INTERNATIONAL ORGANIZATION AND GLOBAL GOVERNANCE

INTERNATIONAL ORGANIZATION AND GLOBAL GOVERNANCE

A Reader

SECOND EDITION

Friedrich Kratochwil
European University Institute

Edward D. Mansfield
University of Pennsylvania

PEARSON
Longman

New York • San Francisco • Boston
London • Toronto • Sydney • Tokyo • Singapore • Madrid
Mexico City • Munich • Paris • Cape Town • Hong Kong • Montreal

Executive Editor: Eric Stano
Acquisitions Editor: Edward Costello
Senior Marketing Manager: Elizabeth Fogarty
Production Manager: Stacey Kulig
Project Coordination, Text Design, and Electronic Page Makeup: Pre-Press Company
Cover Design Manager: Wendy Ann Fredericks
Cover Designer: Joseph DePinho
Cover Art: © ImageZoo/Images.Com
Senior Manufacturing Buyer: Dennis J. Para
Printer and Binder: R. R. Donnelley and Sons
Cover Printer: Phoenix Color Corporation

For permission to use copyrighted material, grateful acknowledgment is made to the copyright holders on page 444, which are hereby made part of this copyright page.

Library of Congress Cataloging-in-Publication Data

International organization and global governance : a reader / [edited by] Friedrich Kratochwil, Edward D. Mansfield.-- 2nd ed.
    p. cm.
    Originally published: International organization. New York: HarperCollins College Publishers, ©1994.
    Includes bibliographical organization.
    1. International organization. 2. International agencies. 3. International relations.
I. Kratochwil, Friedrich V. II. Mansfield, Edward D., 1962-
JZ1318 .I57 2005
341.2--dc22   205018113

Please visit our Web site at http://www.ablongman.com

ISBN 0-321-34917-2

3 4 5 6 7 8 9 10 — DOC — 08

CONTENTS

INTRODUCTION

Regimes, Institutions, and Governance in the International System

FRIEDRICH KRATOCHWIL and EDWARD D. MANSFIELD

INTERNATIONAL ORGANIZATION: SUBFIELD OR APPROACH TO THE STUDY OF WORLD POLITICS?

Over the last few decades, the study of international organization has evolved in important ways. Earlier research on this topic focused on analyzing particular international organizations, their structures, and their programs. The number of these organizations and the range of issues-areas that they cover have increased dramatically over the last half-century, ranging from international public unions—such as the World Postal Union—to the whole array of functional organizations assembled under the auspices of the United Nations, to the various non-governmental organizations (NGOs), such as Amnesty International or Médecins sans Frontieres (Doctors without Borders). An understanding of these organizations remains crucial to the study of international organization.

Of late, however, scholars have displayed an increasing amount of interest in understanding how international politics is organized and governed—issues that extend well beyond the subfield's traditional focus on transnational interest groups, international bureaucracies, and formal intergovernmental exchanges. This interest has stemmed at least partly from the proliferation of less formal mechanisms for organizing global affairs, including networks of activists that are addressing issues such as the environment and human rights, and participants in new "public-private" partnerships of delivering aid and providing public services. Similarly, global conferences addressing the environment (for example, those held in Rio de Janeiro and Kyoto) or human rights draw attention to specific problems, often resulting in "protocols" that chart the future course for policies or comprehensive new codifications (such the Law of the Sea, UNCLOS III). These developments suggest that the web of interactions between governments and subnational groups is much richer than many traditional perspectives on international politics acknowledge.

The purpose of this volume is to present a variety of seminal studies that address the organization of international politics, how international affairs are governed, and how variations in international forms influence international relations—

as well as some of the most important contemporary scholarship on these issues. The following articles examine the field of international organization from a variety of different theoretical viewpoints and cover a broad range of crucially important aspects of international affairs, including international economic relations, international security, the global environment, and international law. Together, they offer a rich and wide-ranging perspective on international organization.

Understanding how international politics is *organized* entails more than just being familiar with the structure and the functions of different organizations or how these organizations influence the international policy process. Such an understanding also involves addressing how heightened international transactions of various kinds in recent decades have eroded the "hard shell" of nation-states, increasing their sensitivity and vulnerability to events and actions taking place beyond their borders. Equally important are the changing boundaries between the public and the private spheres in international affairs, especially the growing role that nonstate actors have come to play. These actors have played this role as partners in implementing policies with states (for example, by delivering relief services in peacekeeping operations or foreign aid projects) and by directly sharing power in regulatory regimes (for example, in the area of banking supervision, where the increasing divergence between the law and the territorial state has led to new forms of public-private cooperation).

While it is quite common to interpret these changes as shifting power from the state to the market and other extra-state actors, many scholars of international organization argue that this characterization is misleading. States have responded to these developments by extending their jurisdiction—for example, expanding the "extraterritorial" application of revenue codes and criminal law. They also have forged global governmental networks to increase their reach and effectiveness.

In this sense, governance in the international system has undergone a series of interesting and important changes. Many scholars of international organization maintain that governments are less able to rule in the way we traditionally think of this term; that is, as a sovereign who is situated at the apex of power and who can utilize the advantages of hierarchy. Much governing occurs through rule-making in complex transnational negotiating and policy implementation networks. Furthermore, these scholars argue that, as in the case of the European Union, new forms of governance can evolve even if they are not stepping-stones to a new and different kind of state or remaining elements of a confederacy. Not only has power been transferred to Brussels; power has also been dispersed to sub-national political units (such as regions), so that the old vocabulary of a "federal state" or a "confederation" is simply inadequate to describe current conditions. Rather, what has emerged, in the view of these scholars, is a multilevel governance structure in which power is shared in new and complex ways.

By addressing these issues, the study of international organization poses a stark challenge to realist and neorealist theories of international relations analysis. These theories, which have been especially influential, posit that the international system is "anarchic," that states are functionally similar units who behave as unitary, rational actors, and that patterns of international relations are shaped primarily by the distribution of power among the leading states in the global system. Theories of international organization have challenged realist theories of various grounds.

First, they have argued that realists exaggerate the extent to which governance within countries is hierarchical and guided by governments with sovereign authority that supersedes the law. Checks and balances, the limitation of government by natural rights and constitutional means, as well as the "sharing" of power all suggest, in the view of many scholars of international organization, that the distinction between domestic hierarchy and international anarchy is overdrawn.

Equally, these observers maintain that identifying social order with a central government and its enforcement capacities is misleading. Even states that had centralized the means of violence, such as the Soviet Union and its allies, could not prevent their disintegration. Moreover, the governments of "failed states" throughout Africa and central Asia have been unable to effectively govern their domestic affairs. There seems to be a much more contingent relationship between hierarchy and order than many traditional theories of international relations acknowledge.

Second, scholars of international organization have challenged the characterization of the international arena as anarchic. Traditional theories of international relations refer to the global system as anarchic because it lacks a government and central decision-making institutions. But anarchy also refers to the Hobbesian state of nature stemming from the absence of norms and common understandings that makes life, in Thomas Hobbes's famous words, "nasty, brutish, and short." While the first meaning of the term presupposes the existence of common rules and norms (since some neorealist theories are based on the paradigm of a competitive market, with the assignment of property rights, contract law, and dispute settlement procedures that are necessary for the market to function), the second meaning implies the absence of social order. Based on the second meaning, however, various scholars of international organization question how many of the factors emphasized by realists—such as alliances or the balance of power—could function. How, these scholars ask, would actors in the international system even know which units are entitled to be sovereign?

Consequently, the study of international organization has both a critical and a constructive function for theory-building in the field of international relations. Its critical function consists of examining the fundamental assumptions on which theories of international relations rest. Its constructive function lies in the development of a framework for systematically analyzing world politics. To that end, scholarship on international organization—taken as a collective singular—focuses on issues of organizing rather than on specific organizations and their output. It addresses how actors in the international system are constituted, how they attain (and lose) their status, and what characterizes the practices by which they interact. Over the last two decades, it has therefore become increasingly common to distinguish between *institutions*—defined as settled practices circumscribed by constitutive and regulative rules—and formal *organizations* that are palpable entities characterized by formal bureaucratic hierarchies and that are capable of issuing directives and administering programs and activities.

Much of this volume focuses on the role played by international institutions. Traditional realist and neorealist theories of international relations attach little importance to such institutions, viewing them as having little independent effect on global outcomes. These theories maintain that shifts in the distribution of capabilities are the driving forces underlying the international system. Scholars of international organization have criticized this view, emphasizing that institutions have a substantial effect on international relations. Moreover, these scholars argue that international institutions shape the strategic context in which power is exercised in ways that realists do not appreciate, such as by helping actors to interpret each other's actions and responses in strategic settings. Was an opponent's action a challenge intended to upset the status quo or an attempt to defend legitimate interest? Was the observed behavior opportunistic risk-taking or the result of a defensive strategy that requires an assurance rather than a threat to diffuse the conflict?

International institutions can help answer these questions by enhancing the transparency of a state's behavior, clarifying issues, establishing benchmarks for legitimacy, and facilitating the flow of information that is needed to resolve problems faced by parties to the institution. Various articles in this book therefore address issues of legitimization, transparency, and what has been referred to as the "epistemic function" of international institutions.

FROM REGIMES TO GLOBAL GOVERNANCE

Authoritative decision making in an issue-area rarely rests within the domain of a single international organization, even if its mandate has been defined in "functional" terms. As the literature on international regimes has suggested, functioning regimes consist of an assembly of formal organizations, norms, and principles in a given issue-area. The practices of international regimes and global governance are therefore quite complex.

So, too, are the influences on international regimes. One influence that has received considerable attention is the relative power position of the leading state in the international system. Whether a "hegemon" exists, however, is hardly the sole influence of this sort. A key reason why scholars of international organization began studying regimes in the late 1970s and early 1980s was their suspicion that international cooperation—particularly on economic matters—might be jeopardized by the erosion of United States hegemony and the ascendancy of Japan, Germany, or other powers whose interests were at odds with the rules and norms reflecting U.S. preferences. But as subsequent research showed, a hegemon's decline (if, in fact, U.S. hegemony had actually declined, an issue that was hotly debated) does not necessarily mean the end of cooperative regimes as long as a small group of powers benefits from the arrangement and is willing to support and sustain it. Thus, the global order based on multilateral institutions proved surprisingly resilient during the second half of the twentieth century, in stark contrast to the period between World War I and World War II. This stability was all the more apparent when, in the aftermath of the Soviet empire's collapse, Eastern European states as well as Russia itself aimed to enter the multilateral institutions that had formerly been made up of the "free world."

Furthermore, regime theorists emphasized, the changes that do occur in the global system stem from far more than the rise and decline of hegemons. For example, policy makers sometimes experience "cognitive" revolutions—such as viewing the world's oceans as an integrated whole, rather than as a territorial sea, a high sea, and a continental shelf, with each having a different international regime. This new and holistic approach contributed to the comprehensive UNCLOS III treaty codifying the Law of the Sea.

Equally, policies that fail can stimulate regime change. More specifically, the evaluation of programs that do not achieve their stated goals can prompt policy change, add new features to the issue-area covered by the regime, and introduce new actors in both the planning and the implementation stage. This is most evident in the case of international regimes that aim to promote development. For example, many of the policy failures of the World Bank have generated opposition in the developing world. Addressing this opposition sometimes involved reaching the local grass roots, particularly if these policy failures attracted the attention of trans-national activist networks. To this end, including new voices in the developmental dialogue can be helpful, as exemplified by the World Bank's establishment of the World Bank-NGO Working Group in 1987. Similarly, when the UN expanded its peacekeeping operations to include peacemaking missions involving a much broader scope of activities, a close collaboration involving national governments, the UN, and NGOs became necessary.

Finally, various observers have argued that many of the problems associated with globalization are the result of unintended policy consequences. This argument has raised the prominence of regulatory issues in international affairs. *Good governance*—both in the private sector and the public sphere—became the watchword. Even the UN jumped on the bandwagon. By 1987, the World Bank had pioneered this approach by declaring underdevelopment to be an issue of governance. Since then, various international organizations (for example, the World Trade Organization, the International Monetary Fund, and the UN itself) have played a substantial role in shaping policies designed to promote development.

Heightened accountability and transparency of state institutions was supposed to promote peace and prosperity by making them conform to democratic criteria and by using highly interventionist methods to increase surveillance and benchmarking of these institutions. These new means were indirect and continuous, rather than direct and episodic, and relied on surveillance and capillary control rather than direct intervention or punishment. The legitimacy for such measures stems largely from the technical know-how and expertise that professionals in international organizations have acquired in handling these situations, rather than from the consent of the population or the international community acting through their representatives.

Sometimes, however, such efforts falter. In East Timor, for example, UN-led efforts to build democratic and participatory structures were not only at odds with Indonesia's interests, they also created conflicts since local political institutions were based on traditional notions of legitimacy rather than Western notions of human rights, individual freedom, and interest representation. In general, then, it remains to be seen whether these sorts of measures will be sufficient to bring about meaningful change.

ORGANIZATION OF THE BOOK

This reader addresses the issues that we have raised in this introductory essay. Chapters 1 and 7 examine how scholars have studied international relations in an organizational context. Chapter 1 takes up the issue of anarchy in the international system, providing a number of critiques of realist perspectives on this issue. Chapter 2 addresses how international institutions can facilitate cooperation in the global arena. Chapter 3 focuses on the variations in organizational forms across international regimes and how those variations affect international outcomes. Chapter 4 analyzes the roles played by specific international organizations, especially their roles in creating norms and determining what behavior is legitimate. Chapter 5 examines the epistemic function played by international institutions that promotes the flow of information and expertise in various issue-areas. Chapter 6 takes up the process of economic integration and the role that international institutions have played in fostering integration. Chapter 7 addresses the transformation of international politics from a number of influential perspectives in the field of international organization.

ACKNOWLEDGMENTS

In the process of publishing this volume, we have accumulated various debts that we are pleased to acknowledge. We are grateful to Edward Costello, the Political Science editor at Pearson Longman, for encouraging us to undertake this project, and to Joshua Duennebier for guiding the book through the production process. We also appreciate the many useful comments and suggestions made by various anonymous reviewers that did much to improve the book. For financial and research support, we would like to thank the European University Institute and the Christopher H. Browne Center for International Politics at the University of Pennsylvania. We are particularly grateful to the members of our families, Petra Hoelscher and Charlotte, Katherine, and Liv Mansfield. This book is dedicated to them.

CHAPTER 1

The Presumption of Anarchy

This chapter addresses the claim made by various scholars of international relations that the international system is anarchic, in the sense that the system lacks a supraordinate governing body with the authority to enforce agreements between countries, settle interstate disputes, and the like. That countries operate in an anarchic global environment is a chief tenet of realism and neorealism, theories that invoke the "Hobbesian" state of nature as a justification for this assessment.[1] In the absence of a sovereign to enforce laws, Thomas Hobbes argued that cooperation is impossible. Contracts, in his view, were central to enforcing cooperation; without a sovereign (or a Leviathan, as he put it), contracts were "mere words." Since without out a sovereign individuals in society could not be counted on to fulfill their obligations, no exchange could take place. For realists, therefore, interstate conflict is to be expected and cooperation between states is puzzling.

A number of interesting perspectives exist on this puzzle. Various sociologists, for example, have pointed out that conflict actually stimulates certain forms of cooperation, such as banding together in the face of a common enemy. This, in turn, can foster a sense of community and common identity among the cooperating parties. Furthermore, many scholars of international relations have argued that international institutions and regimes can promote interstate cooperation, although there is considerable disagreement among these researchers about why institutions and regimes have this effect. Later chapters of this book include a variety of perspectives on the ways that international institutions stimulate cooperation in the global system.

Consistent with realist views, Hobbes believed that fear was the most decisive emotion that can be appealed to in founding a society. However, he also realized that founding a society was part of a larger political project. He was well aware, for

---

[1] In addition to emphasizing that the international system is anarchic, these theories argue that states are functionally similar units that behave as unitary, rational actors and that international relations are shaped primarily by the distribution of power among the leading states in the system.

example, that the fear of eternal damnation might be stronger than the fear of punishment by the sovereign. Thus, eliminating such transcendental considerations from public life was seen as one of the most important preconditions for the establishment of a functioning secular order. Equally, Hobbes believed that the state of nature among sovereign rulers is not as bad as that between individual people (since states can ameliorate the security dilemma and create islands of trust in which commerce and science can develop), an argument to which most realists have paid scant attention.

This discussion raises several issues. First, to what extent does the existence of transnational societies promote trust and facilitate boundary-transcending exchanges, even in the absence of a global sovereign with the ability to enforce international agreements? Second, how were individual members of society, such as merchants, able to develop practices that facilitated international trade? Third, is it really the case that fear can be counted on in order to overcome problems of collective action in the international system? Finally, even without assuming that one can change people's self-interested nature, is it impossible to set ambition against ambition so that a stable structure emerges from these checks and balances? Here the republican tradition from Machiavelli to Botero and the founders of the United States has offered several suggestions. Even Immanuel Kant thought that a clever constitutional design could enable a republic of "devils" to attain considerable stability. But his grand design, by which people can make law their "master," depends on being able to extend law to the international arena. It also hinges on limitations on resorting to force that have to be guaranteed by domestic structures rather than by a world government guided by some super-Leviathan, thereby helping to resolve the problem of how liberty can be preserved while the destructive forces of anarchy are checked.

These issues have roots in the field of political theory, but they bear heavily on international relations as well. The articles in this chapter address them and analyze how the anarchy problématique informs our understanding of international politics. Helen Milner critiques the alleged logic of anarchy. She examines the equivocal use of this term by some of the leading realists and neorealists and argues that they have created a false dichotomy between the anarchic character of the international system and the hierarchical character of domestic settings. Stressing issues of legitimacy (rather than simply those of structures and the arrangements that underlie the distinction between hierarchy and anarchy) and focusing on the nature of interdependent decision-making in the international arena, she argues that the problem of international cooperation is more one of realist theory than one of political practice.

Alexander Wendt addresses the anarchy problématique by showing the importance of the interacting parties' historical experiences. In his view, neither the structure of the international system nor the actors that exist in that system is a given; rather they *form through interactions*. Global structures are outgrowths of historical encounters among actors and they enable as well as constrain actors. Thus, the historical experience of actors might lead them to view each other as threats, leading to the type of situation that realists emphasize. However, they might be indifferent to each other, creating the basis for a liberal international order. They also might identify positively with one another (as occurred in Western Europe after World War II), laying the basis for a cooperative security system. Wendt argues that significantly different patterns of politics can emerge in an anarchic environment, depending on whether the actors are driven by myopic notions of self-interest, recognize the legitimate interests of others, or identify with other actors.

Friedrich Kratochwil and John Ruggie survey the study of international organization. They maintain that international organization (taken in its generic singular) is an approach to the study of world politics rather than just a subfield of international relations. They then attempt to place research on international regimes in a historical and analytical context. Furthermore, Kratochwil and Ruggie analyze how political practice contributes to the evolution of international systems. In this context, the contrafactual validity of norms and the availability of pleadings (excuses, inapplicability, exemptions, etc.) are particularly important for understanding the effectiveness and stability of regimes. However, they argue that these points are neglected or obscured by the standard methods of a positivist science, which tries to explain phenomena in terms of an observational language instead of acknowledging that the human world is "made" by actors and characterized by their intersubjective understandings. These understandings, in turn, should enter into any account and assessment of compliance with regime norms.

The Assumption of Anarchy in International Relations Theory: A Critique

HELEN MILNER

In much current theorizing, anarchy has once again been declared to be the fundamental assumption about international politics. Over the last decade, numerous scholars, especially those in the neo-realist tradition, have posited anarchy as the single most important characteristic underlying international relations. This article explores implications of such an assumption. In doing so, it reopens older debates about the nature of international politics. First, I examine various concepts of "anarchy" employed in the international relations literature. Second, I probe the sharp dichotomy between domestic and international politics that is associated with this assumption. As others have, I question the validity and utility of such a dichotomy. Finally, this article suggests that a more fruitful way to understand the international system is one that combines anarchy and interdependence.

. . .

CONCEPTS OF ANARCHY

Anarchy has been accorded a central role in international politics, especially in recent theoretical writings. Robert Art and Robert Jervis, for instance, assert that "anarchy is the fundamental fact of international relations."[2] For them, any understanding of international politics must flow from an understanding of this fact. Robert Gilpin defines the fundamental nature of international politics as "a recurring struggle for wealth and power among independent actors in a state of anarchy."[3] For Kenneth Waltz, anarchy is the first element of structure in the international system.[4] It is for him the structural feature from which all other consequences derive. Recent studies of international cooperation have also started from the assumption that the international system is anarchic. Robert Axelrod defines his central question as being "under what conditions will cooperation

---

Anarchy is one of the most vague and ambiguous words in language. George Cornewall Lewis[1]

I would like to thank David Baldwin, James Caporaso, Alexander George, Joanne Gowa, Stephan Haggard, Ted Hopf, Robert Jervis, Robert Keohane, Fritz Kratochwil, Kathleen McNamara, Henry Nau, Susan Peterson, Kamal Shehadi, and Jack Snyder for their helpful comments.

emerge in a world of egoists without central authority?"[5] He believes anarchy is especially relevant to international politics since "today nations interact without central authority."[6] The condition of anarchy provides the baseline for his game-theoretic analysis. As he concludes,

> Today, the most important problems facing humanity are in the area of international relations, where independent, egoistic nations face each other in a state of near anarchy. Many of the problems take the form of an iterated Prisoner's Dilemma.[7]

Other scholars have used this analogy between anarchy and the Prisoners' Dilemma as well. In *After Hegemony,* Robert Keohane begins his effort to explain international cooperation by assuming that anarchy is the fundamental fact about international politics. He describes the initial international environment as one peopled by egoistic, anomic states, pursuing their self-interests in a self-help system without any centralized authority. He shows that even in this environment, which resembles single-play Prisoners' Dilemma, states can find cooperation to be in their narrow self-interest.[8]

This view of anarchy as the central condition of international politics is also apparent in the explanation of cooperation that emerges in Kenneth Oye's edited volume, *Cooperation Under Anarchy.* As the title suggests, this volume's fundamental premise about international politics is that it is anarchic. The first sentence of the volume asserts that "Nations dwell in perpetual anarchy, for no central authority imposes limits on the pursuit of sovereign interests."[9] Moreover, the authors view their central question as being "what circumstances favor the emergence of cooperation under anarchy" and see the structure of the international system as resembling a Prisoners' Dilemma. Assuming anarchy to be primary, they then proceed to diagnose what factors make cooperation possible in such an environment. For all of these authors then—although less so for Keohane—anarchy is taken to be the central background condition of international politics. All their analyses flow from this assumption. But what do these authors mean by anarchy?

Anarchy has at least two meanings. The first meaning that anarchy carries is a lack of order. It implies chaos or disorder. The *Oxford English Dictionary,* for instance, lists political disorder as its primary definition. Such lack of order is often associated with the existence of a state of war. It is thus linked to the Hobbesian analogy of politics in the absence of a sovereign, which realists use as a model of international politics. As Hedley Bull describes the realist view,

> The Hobbesian tradition describes international relations as a state of war of all against all, an arena of struggle in which each state is pitted against every other. International relations, on the Hobbesian view, represent pure conflict between states and resemble a game that is wholly distributive or zero-sum. . . . The particular international activity that, on the Hobbesian view, is most typical of international activity as a whole . . . is war itself.[10]

In this view then, the international system is a chaotic arena of war of all against all.

But are chaos, lack of order, and constant threat of war what scholars mean by the anarchic nature of the system? It does not seem to be. Persistent elements of order in international politics have been noted by many. International order, defined in a strong sense as "a pattern of activity that sustains the elementary or primary goals of a society of states, or international society"[11] is not lacking in international relations. Such order implies the existence of a common framework of rules and institutions guiding international practices, and some such framework has existed among states at many times.[12] For Hedley Bull, order in the form of "international society has always been present in the modern international system because at no stage can it be said that the conception of the common interests of states, of common rules accepted and common institutions worked by them, has ceased to exert an influence."[13]

Others as well have noted the elements of order and society that mark international politics. Much of the recent literature on international regimes makes this point. Regimes serve to constrain and guide states' behaviour according to common norms and rules, thereby making possible patterned, or orderly, behaviour. Indeed, the authors of *Cooperation Under Anarchy* seek to explain such order. While initially seeing international politics in the Hobbesian image of a system marked by persistent war and lacking limits on states' behaviour, they eventually note that

> an international society—albeit a fragmented one—exists. . . . To say that world politics is anarchic does not imply that it entirely lacks organization. Relationships among actors may be carefully structured in some issue-areas, even though they remain loose in others.[14]

In this strong sense of a set of patterned behaviour promoting various goals or norms, order is not what the international system lacks.

In a weaker sense, order is also apparent. Discovery of the orderly features of world politics amidst its seeming chaos is perhaps the central achievement of neo-realists. For example, Gilpin points out that "the relationships among states have a high degree of order and that although the international system is one of anarchy (i.e., absence of formal governmental authority), the system does exercise an element of control over the behavior of states."[15] Waltz also finds order in the regularized patterns of state behaviour that he observes. The timeless and recurrent formation of balances of power constitutes such a pattern. . . .

Recurrent balancing by states suggests the order lurking in the seeming chaos of international politics. While states themselves may not realize it, like firms in a perfect market, their behaviour is being constrained into an orderly outcome. Again, the behaviour of states is being influenced to produce unintended order. In this case, however, states' behaviour is not guided by their norms or goals, but rather by structures beyond their control. In this weaker sense, then, as well, lack of order does not seem to be the distinguishing feature associated with the system's anarchy. Thus although anarchy may refer to a lack of order in international politics, such a conception is not what most IR scholars mean by it.

The second definition of anarchy is the lack of government. It is the first meaning of anarchy given in the *Oxford English Dictionary* and is common among political scientists. Among the many uses Waltz makes of anarchy, the notion of an absence of government is central.[16] In the *Cooperation Under Anarchy* volume, anarchy is also defined as a "lack of common government."[17] . . . This meaning of anarchy then relates to the lack of something, this time to a common government or authority.

But what exactly is lacking? What is meant by government or authority? Many discussions in international politics fail to define government and/or authority or define them in very different ways. They tend also to use government and authority interchangeably. But the two are distinct concepts. Waltz, for instance, associates anarchy with lack of government, which deals with the means used to organize how and when force can be employed. Government, for him, has a Weberian cast to it; it implies a monopoly on the legitimate use of force:

> The difference between national and international politics lies not in the use of force but in the different modes of organization for doing something about it. A government, ruling by some standard of legitimacy, arrogates to itself the right to use force. . . . A government has no monopoly on the use of force, as is all too evident. An effective government, however, has a monopoly on the *legitimate* use of force, and legitimate means here that the public agents are organized to prevent and to counter the private use of force.[18]

For others, government denotes something different. It is less associated with force than with the existence of institutions and laws to maintain order. Lack of government means the absence of laws, a legislature to write them, a judiciary to enforce them, and an executive to administer them. For example, Martin Wight notes,

> Anarchy is the characteristic that distinguishes international politics from ordinary politics. The study of international politics presupposes absence of a system of government, as the study of domestic politics presupposes the existence of one. . . . But it is roughly the case that, while in domestic politics the struggle for power is governed and circumscribed by the framework of law and institutions, in international politics law and institutions are governed and circumscribed by the struggle for power.[19]

Others suggest that it is a particular function of government that the international system lacks. For the authors of "Cooperation Under Anarchy," anarchy means the absence of a central authority to enforce states' adherence to promises or agreements.[20] The means for hierarchical rule enforcement are missing. The emphasis in this volume is on institutions and authority, rather than force, as central to governance. Different definitions of government are thus used in the literature.

These three notions of government offer different visions of what is lacking in international politics. Which of these best fits standard notions of government? The definition of government as a monopoly over the legitimate use of force has three problems. The first involves the issue of monopoly. How much of a monopoly of force must a government have to exist? Most governments do not possess an absolute monopoly over the legitimate use of force. For instance, the US government does not; citizens have the right to self-defence and they have the constitutional right to bear arms. When the right to use force legitimately (under certain circumstances) is diffused to 240 million people, can a government in Waltz's terms be said to exist?. . . As Hobbes states emphatically, "A covenant not to defend myself from force by force is always void."[21] The right to self-defence through the legitimate use of force weakens any monopoly over legitimate coercion possessed by a government. A *monopoly* over the use of force then is probably not the distinguishing feature of a government.[22]

Perhaps the defining feature of government in this definition is the legitimacy of using force. This, though, raises the issue of what legitimacy means and how it is determined. A sense of legitimacy allows a government to use force without prompting the resistance of (or use of force by) society. Lack of such a sense is conducive to civil war. But does not the issue of the legitimacy of force arise internationally as well? The use of force in international politics is not always considered illegitimate; some uses seem legitimate to a majority of states. Even Morgenthau notes the range of legitimate and illegitimate uses of force in international politics:

> legitimate power, that is power whose exercise is morally or legally justified, must be distinguished from illegitimate power. . . . The distinction is not only philosophically valid but also relevant for the conduct of foreign policy. Legitimate power, which can invoke a moral or legal justification for its exercise, is likely to be more effective than equivalent illegitimate power, which cannot be justified. That is to say, legitimate power has a better chance to influence the will of its objects than equivalent illegitimate power. Power exercised in self-defense or in the name of the United Nations has a better chance to succeed than equivalent power exercised by an "aggressor" nation or in violation of international law. Political ideologies . . . serve the purpose of endowing foreign policies with the appearance of legitimacy.[23]

The use of force internationally then can be legitimate—or more or less legitimate—just as can its use domestically. This conception of what international politics lacks—a monopoly on the legitimate use of force—is not as clear as it seems, since governments lack such monopolies and since the legitimacy issue arises in international as well as domestic politics.

Third, this conception of government reveals a narrow notion of politics. It reduces both international and domestic politics to the use of force. Government ultimately depends on the threat of force, as does international politics.[24] This is implicit in the Weberian definition of government. As Weber himself notes, "the threat of force, and in the case of need its actual use, is the method which is specific to political organization and is always the last resort when others have failed."[25] It is difficult in terms of this definition to see much distinction between international and domestic politics.

Other notions of government stress the existence of institutions and laws that maintain order. Government is based on more than coercion; it rests on institutionalised practices and well-accepted norms. Governments legislate, adjudicate, resolve Prisoners' Dilemmas, and provide public goods, for example—all of which require more than mere coercion to accomplish. This broader institutional definition conforms more to standard notions of government than does the conception linked to force. The *Encyclopedia of the Social Sciences* defines government as a system of social control which has "acquired a definite institutional organization and operate[s] by means of legal mandates enforced by definite penalties."[26] . . . Government in this standard definition centres on three notions: institutions, law, and legitimacy.

Institutions are valued in this definition not for themselves but for the functions they perform and the way in which they perform them. Governing institutions provide social order through their legal institutions and sense of legitimacy. But, as noted earlier, the provision of order is not unique to government. Order exists in the international system; it is simply provided through different means. David Easton makes this point:

The fact that policies recognized as authoritative for the whole society must exist does not imply or assume that a central governmental organization is required in order to make decisions and effectuate them. Institutional devices for making and executing policy may take an infinite variety of forms. The clarity and precision with which the statuses and roles of legislators and administrators are defined will depend upon the level of development of a particular society. Societies could be placed on a continuum with regard to the degree of definition of such roles. . . .[27]

The provision of order may not require formal institutions or laws. But supposedly the manner in which order is provided is what distinguishes the two areas. Within the state, law and hierarchy prevail; within the international system, power without legitimate authority dominates. Anarchy is equated with lawlessness.

But international governing institutions and a body of international laws do exist. It seems not to be their existence that matters, but their capacity for commanding obedience. This capacity depends much on their perceived legitimacy, as it does for domestic institutions. These institutions will have little influence internationally or domestically if they lack legitimacy. It is an actor's belief that an institution's commands or a law are binding or valid that gives them much of their force. As Weber recognized, an order that is seen as legitimate is far more likely to be obeyed than one that appeals only to self-interest or habit. But custom, personal advantage, purely affectual or ideal motives of solidarity, do not form a sufficiently reliable basis for a given domination. In addition, there is normally a further element, the belief in legitimacy.[28]

Legitimacy then appears to be the linchpin upon which conceptions of government rest. It, more than institutions or laws, is what distinguishes domestic and international politics. Lack of legitimacy seems in the end to be what many IR scholars have in mind when they talk about anarchy. Anarchy as a lack of government is for them transformed into a discussion of lack of authority, or legitimacy. Both Waltz and the *Cooperation Under Anarchy* authors end up here. But government and authority should not be conflated. Not all governments have *de facto* authority over their subjects. Authority is often tied to the notion of legitimacy; it implies a belief in the validity or bindingness of an order.[29] It is not just laws or governing institutions that international politics may lack, but most importantly a sense of legitimacy.

But does the absence of authority provide a firm basis for the distinction between domestic and international politics? May not some domestic systems lack centralized authority and legitimacy, while certain international systems—e.g., the Concert of Europe[30]—enjoy high levels of legitimacy? Can and should we draw a rigid dichotomy between the two on the basis of anarchy defined this way?

ANARCHY AND THE DICHOTOMY BETWEEN DOMESTIC AND INTERNATIONAL POLITICS

The renewed focus on anarchy in international politics has led to the creation of a sharp distinction between domestic and international politics. Politics internationally is seen as characterized primarily by anarchy, while domestically centralized authority prevails. One of the most explicit statements of this position is in

Waltz's *Theory of International Politics.* His powerful articulation of this dichotomy is interesting to examine closely since it is the clearest logical statement of the consequences of the anarchy assumption.

Waltz makes three separate claims about the distinction between the two areas. First, anarchy as a lack of central authority implies that international politics is a decentralized competition among sovereign equals. . . . A second distinction flows from the assumption of anarchy. As a lack of centralized control over force, anarchy implies that world politics is a self-help system reliant primarily on force. This also distinguishes international from national politics. . . . Finally, international politics is seen as the only true "politics":

> National politics is the realm of authority, of administration, and of law. International politics is the realm of power, of struggle, and of accommodation. The international realm is preeminently a political one. The national realm is variously described as being hierarchic, vertical, centralized, heterogeneous, directed, and contrived; and international realm, as being anarchic, horizontal, decentralized, homogeneous, undirected, and mutually adaptive.[31]

A very sharp distinction is drawn between the two political arenas on a number of different grounds, all of which flow from the assumption of anarchy. While some societies may possess elements of both ordering principles—anarchy and hierarchy, the conclusion of many is that such a rigid dichotomy is empirically feasible and theoretically useful.[32] In this section the utility of such a distinction is examined. Is it empirically and heuristically helpful? To answer this question, it is important to examine Waltz's three distinctions because they represent the logical outcome of adopting the assumption of anarchy as the basis of international politics. While his views are the most explicit and perhaps extreme statement of this dichotomy, they do reflect the implicit understanding of neo-realist theory in general.

The first line of demarcation between domestic and international politics is the claim that centralization prevails in the former and decentralization in the latter. What is meant by centralization or its opposite? Centralization seems related to hierarchy. As Waltz notes, "The units—institutions and agencies—stand *vis-à-vis* each other in relations of super- and subordination."[33] Apparently, it refers to the number of, and relationship among, recognized centres of authority in a system. Domestic politics has fewer, more well-defined centres that are hierarchically ordered, while in international politics many centres exist and they are not so ordered. . . .

Such a view of domestic politics is hard to maintain. Who is the highest authority in the US? The people, the states, the Constitution, the executive, the Supreme Court, or even Congress. *De jure,* the Constitution is; but, *de facto,* it depends upon the issue. There is no single hierarchy of authority, as in some ideal military organization. Authority for deciding different issues rests with different groups in society. Authority is not highly concentrated; it is diffused. This was the intention of the writers of the Constitution, who wanted a system where power was not concentrated but rather dispersed. It was dispersed not only functionally through a structure of countervailing 'checks and balances', but also geographically through federalism.[34]

Moreover, this decentralization is not unique to the US. One of the main concerns in comparative politics has been to locate the centres of authority in different nations and relate their different degrees of political centralization and decentralization along some continuum. Authority in some states may be fairly centralized, while in others it is highly decentralized, as in the debate over "strong" and "weak" states.[35] But the central point is that states exhibit a very broad range of values along this continuum, and not all of them—or perhaps even the majority—may be more centralized than the international system.

A second issue is to what extent the international system is decentralized. The point made above that the concentration of authority in any system is best gauged along a continuum, and not a dichotomy, is relevant. Where along the continuum does the international system fit? The answer to this depends on two factors: what issue we are discussing (e.g., fishing rights, the use of nuclear weapons, or control of the seas) and what time period we have in mind. The first factor raises the issue of the fungibility of power. Curiously, Waltz assumes it is highly fungible: force dominates and a hierarchy of power exists internationally—i.e., "great powers" are identifiable. This view centralizes power much more than does assuming it is infungible. The issue of change over time is also important. The international system may evince different levels of centralization and decentralization—e.g., the nineteenth-century Concert of Europe versus the post–World War II system.[36]

To deal with these issues, Waltz has to relinquish his more legalistic notion of the international system as one of sovereign equals. At times, he indeed does this. In discussing anarchy, he posits that all states are equal and thus that authority internationally is highly decentralized. But when talking of the distribution of capabilities he recognizes that states are not equal and that only a few great powers count. In this latter discussion, he implies that capabilities are highly centralized in the international system. . . .

The issue of the centralization of power internationally touches on another distinction between domestic and international politics. . . . The argument is that states are sovereign, implying that they are functionally equal and hence not interdependent. They are duplicates, who do not need one another. Domestically, the units within states are differentiated, each filling some niche in the chain of command. For many domestic systems, this is not accurate. For instance, in federal systems each state is functionally equal and no generally agreed upon chain of command between the states and the national government exists. On some issues at some times, states have the final say; on others, the central government.

On the other hand, there is the question of whether all nation-states are functionally equivalent. If states are all "like units," why only examine the great powers? Waltz realizes this is a problem. He admits that "internationally, like units sometimes perform different tasks." Moreover, "the likelihood of their doing so, varies with their capabilities."[37] Thus he acknowledges that states with different capabilities perform different functions; hence, they are not all "like" units. . . .

It is difficult to assume both that all states are equal (principles 1 and 2) *and* that all states are not equal as a result of the distribution of their capabilities (principle 3). Waltz might claim that they are equal in function but not in capabilities; however, as he himself states, one's capabilities shape one's functions. The point is, as others have noted before, the distribution of resources internationally creates a division of labour among states; differentiation and hierarchy exist and provide governing mechanisms for states, just as they do for individuals within states. Most importantly, the distinction among different international systems and within nation-states over the degree of centralization of authority as well as over the degree of differentiation among their units is variable and should be viewed along a continuum, rather than as a dichotomy.[38]

A second means of separating domestic and international politics is to differentiate the role and importance of force in the two arenas. For Waltz, domestically force is less important as a means of control and is used to serve justice; internationally, force is widespread and serves no higher goal than to help the state using it. But is the importance of force so different in the two realms? As noted before for theorists like Waltz, Carr, and Weber, the threat of the use of force—in effect, deterrence—is ultimately the means of social control domestically. Threats of sanctions are the state's means of enforcement, as they are internationally. When norms and institutions fail to maintain social control, states internally and externally resort to threats of force. It may be that norms and institutions are more prevalent forms of control domestically than internationally. But this depends on the state in question. In some countries, belief in the legitimacy of government and institutions, being widespread and well-developed, might suffice to maintain control. However, the fact that more civil wars have been fought in this century than international ones and that since 1945 more have died in the former should make one pause when declaiming about the relative use of force in the two realms.[39]

Since at times the frequency of violence domestically is acknowledged, perhaps the point is that force is legitimate and serves justice domestically and not internationally.[40] Again, this depends upon the perceived legitimacy of the government and the particular instance of use. Have the majority of people in the Soviet Union, Poland, Ethiopia, South Africa, Iran, or the Philippines—to name just a few—felt that the state's use of force serves justice (all of the time? some of the time?)? Whether force serves justice domestically is an issue to be studied, not a given to be assumed. On the other hand, is it never the case that force serves justice internationally? Is it always, or most of the time, "for the sake of [the state's] own protection and advantage"? States have been known to intervene forcefully for larger purposes. The fight against Germany in World War II by the US, for example, helped serve justice regardless of whether America's own protection was a factor. The distinction between international and domestic politics on this issue does not appear as clear as is claimed.

A third dichotomy between the two arenas asserts that power and politics operate internationally. Domestically, authority, administration, and law prevail; internationally, it is power, struggle, and accommodation. For some, the latter alone is politics. This distinction is the hardest to maintain. Disputes among political parties, local and national officials, the executive and the legislature, different geographic regions, different races, capital and labor, industry and finance, organized and unorganized groups, etc. over who gets how much and when occur constantly within the nation. Morgenthau recognizes this:

The essence of international politics is identical with its domestic counterpart. Both domestic and international politics are a struggle for power, modified only by the different conditions under which this struggle takes place in the domestic and in the international spheres. . . .[41]

Similarly, Inis Claude holds that international order is maintained by a balance of power among opposing forces, just as it is domestically. In attacking the notion that governments maintain peace through some monopoly of force, Claude returns to Morgenthau to make his point:

Morgenthau's espousal of the concept of the state's 'monopoly of organized violence' is contradicted by his general conception of politics: "Domestic and international politics are but two different manifestations of the same phenomenon: the struggle for power." In his terms, "The balance of power . . . is indeed a perennial element of all pluralistic societies."[42]

For him, as for Morgenthau, societies are pluralistic, and thus the role of government is "the delicate task of promoting and presiding over a constantly shifting equilibrium."[43] Politics domestically and internationally is about balancing power. To assume that a state has a monopoly of power and that this is "the key to the effectiveness of [it] as an order-keeping institution may lead to an exaggerated notion of the degree to which actual states can and do rely upon coercion."[44] Unlike Morgenthau and other realists, Claude sees factors other than coercion— such as, norms and institutions—as being more important both domestically and internationally to the maintenance of order, but like them he views the balance of power as fundamental to the two realms. Unlike Waltz, all of these authors find relations within nations and among them to be political and to be based on similar political processes.

Overall, the sharp distinctions between the two realms are difficult to maintain empirically. More importantly, any dichotomous treatment of domestic and international politics may have heuristic disadvantages.[45] Two heuristic problems exist with the radical separation of international and domestic politics. First, the isolation of international politics as a realm of anarchy with nothing in common with other types of politics is a step backward conceptually. Throughout the 1950s and 1960s, political scientists worked to incorporate international relations into the main body of political science literature. They strove to end the prevailing conception of international relations as a *sui generis* field of study and to apply methods of analysis to it from other branches of political science, mainly domestic politics. . . .[46]

The problem with reverting back to a situation where international politics is seen as unique is that one is less likely to use the hypotheses, concepts, and questions about politics developed elsewhere. International politics must then reinvent the wheel, not being able to draw on other political science scholarship. The radical dichotomy between international and domestic politics seems to represent a conceptual and theoretical step backwards.

A second and related heuristic problem is the tendency implicit in this separation of the two fields to view all states as being the same. Waltz, for one, wants us to conceive of states as like units and to avoid looking within them at their internal arrangements. His is a systemic level theory. But the issue is whether it is possible and/or fruitful to abstract from all of domestic politics. All states are not the same; and their internal characteristics, including their goals and capabilities, affect international politics importantly, as Waltz is forced to admit. This is reflected in the tension between his ordering principles, the first two of which give primacy to structural pressures while the third makes certain agents key. Using systemic theory, he wants to "tell us about the forces the units are subject to," but he also notes that "in international politics, as in any self-help system, the units of greatest capability set the scene of action for others as well as for themselves."[47] The units do matter.

Moreover, the differences among states—even the strongest—are not trivial and may be useful to conceptualize for understanding international relations better. Developing continuums along which all politics—domestic and international—are understable can be fruitful. Some, such as Roger Masters, Ernest Gellner, and Chadwick Alger have compared international politics with primitive political systems and developing countries and have produced interesting insights about the international system from this comparison.[48] Using hypotheses and concepts from comparative politics can enrich international relations theory, while limiting this cross-fertilization is likely to hurt the field. As argued, politics in the two arenas are similar. William T. R. Fox stated long ago that

> Putting "power" rather than "the state" at the center of political science makes it easier to view international relations as one of the political sciences. So conceived, it is possible for some scholars to move effortlessly along the seamless web which connects world politics and the politics of such less inclusive units as the state or the locality, and to emphasize the political process, group behaviour, communications studies, conflict resolution, and decision-making.[49]

The argument here concurs with those who would add to this focus on power a concern with norms and institutions, which also may play similar roles in the domestic and international arenas. Conceptions unifying, and not separating, these two arenas are heuristically fruitful.

THE ASSUMPTION OF INTERDEPENDENCE

The current tendency to over-emphasize the centrality of anarchy to world politics may not be the most useful way to conceptualize international politics. As other scholars have pointed out, such reductionism overlooks another central fact about international politics, namely the interdependence of the actors. This section explores the notion of interdependence, suggests why it is also a key *structural* feature of the international system, and notes some of its implications for world politics. Other scholars have made some of these points before, but in this time when anarchy reigns supreme in the discipline a reminder of the importance of other aspects of the international system can be valuable.

What do we mean by interdependence? There are two related notions of interdependence. First, the notion of "strategic interdependence" implies, as Schelling puts it, a situation in which "the ability of one participant to gain his ends is dependent to an important degree on the choices or decisions that the other participant will make."[50] In this situation, an actor cannot get what s/he wants without the cooperation of other actors. This notion fits the conventional definition of the term, which refers to a situation in which the actors face mutual costs from ending their relationship.[51] . . .

Interdependence is *not* the opposite of anarchy as we have defined it—i.e., an absence of central authority. The two concepts represent different aspects of the international system. As with anarchy, the definition of interdependence says nothing about the degree of order, the likelihood of war, the inherency of conflicting interests, or the primary means used to achieve one's goals in the international system. Links between these latter variables and either anarchy or interdependence are empirical, *not* conceptual, statements. Anarchy and interdependence do not conflict on these dimensions, as is often supposed, since neither concept says anything about them a priori. The two concepts are not opposite ends of some single continuum. The extent of hierarchical authority relations—i.e., of anarchy—does not necessarily affect the degree of interdependence present. Two coequal actors can be in a situation of strategic interdependence—i.e., can be unable to attain their goals without the cooperation of the other—just as easily as can two actors in a hierarchical relationship. *A priori* one cannot determine the extent of their interdependence from the degree of hierarchy/anarchy present in their relationship, and vice versa. The two concepts are logically independent.[52]

This definition of interdependence also does *not* imply either that the actors' interests are in harmony or that power relations are unimportant. The assumption that interdependence implies harmony or cooperation is widespread.[53] In part this is a consequence of the links between international trade theory and interdependence. An interdependent situation is seen as one where an extensive division of labour exists so that each party performs a different role and thus has complementary interests. Everyone gains from such a situation; it is a positive-sum game. But, as Schelling, among others, has pointed out, interdependent situations are really mixed-motive games. Both conflicting and harmonious interests are evident. Each gains from continuing the relationship, but the distribution of these gains involves struggle. Harmony is not the result of interdependence; rather, a mix of conflict and cooperation is. *A priori* it is impossible to tell which will prevail.

. . .

Reasons why interdependence is a central feature of the international system are connected with its implications for the system. Empirically, the international system has structural features that imply interdependence is important; moreover, viewing the system as interdependent may generate useful theoretical insights. Two important points can be made. First, interdependence means that the actors are linked. While states remain sovereign, their actions and attainment of their goals are conditioned by other actors' behaviour and their expectations and perceptions about this. In a situation of strategic interdependence, one's best choice depends on the choice others make. Thus the game is about anticipating others' behaviour.

One's expectations and perceptions of their behaviour shape one's own choices. Scholars using game theoretic models of international politics recognize this. For instance, authors in "Cooperation Under Anarchy" use the image of an iterated Prisoners' Dilemma to explore international interactions, but they tend not to note that this implies that strategic interdependence is as fundamental to the actors as is anarchy.

Much of international relations involves this type of strategic game. One's best choice of how to spend one's resources—e.g., on guns or on butter—depends on one's expectations about how others are spending theirs. This understanding of international politics leads to a focus on states' expectations about and perceptions of others, as seen in Robert Jervis' works.[54] Structural imperatives—such as changes in some objective distribution of capabilities—are not the sole guide to behaviour. Furthermore, this strategic focus leads to an interest in factors that shape expectations and perceptions—factors like past behaviour patterns, institutions, and cognitive processes. Finally, emphasizing interdependence draws attention to issues involving communication and information. In situations of strategic interdependence, the more one knows about the true preferences of other actors, *ceteris paribus,* the better off one may be. The gathering of reliable information and the reduction of costs associated with this then become key problems for states. . . . If, on the other hand, some set of objective structural factors shapes states' behaviour, then issues of communication and information exchange among states are relatively unimportant. Viewing the international system as a web of interdependencies necessitates a focus on the linkages among actors; it directs attention to their perceptions and knowledge of each other and their communications.

Second, if the international system is viewed as characterized by structural interdependence, then the mechanisms of the system look different from those in the neo-realist model. For this model, the anarchic international system is like a perfect market. Many similar actors coact in such a way that some equilibrium results. Communication, concern about other actors' likely behaviour, institutionalized practices, none of these matter. The structure of the system, through some invisible hand, selects behaviour appropriate for the states. This metaphor can be misleading for international politics. As Waltz's third ordering principle argues, at any time only a few states count—the great powers. The number of important actors, or the number of important actors each state interacts with, in international politics is small. The metaphor that is more relevant, then, is *not* a perfectly competitive market but an oligopolistic or monopolistic one.[55] These markets are defined as having only a few large actors. Such markets are characterized by extensive interdependence; how each firm maximizes its profits depends on the choices (about price and quantity produced) other firms make. The behaviour of others then shapes the best strategy for each, as is true for states in the international system.

A second interesting feature of these markets is that they tend to be unstable. They bring forth a mixture of conflictual and cooperative behaviour. Periods marked by stable collusive monopoly pricing where all are enriched tend to be followed by bitter competitive price wars where some may be ruined. Such unstable, mixed behaviour seems more characteristic of international politics than does the steady-state equilibrium of a perfectly competitive market. In these oligopolistic markets, periods of cooperation depend upon the establishment of various means of tacit communication as well as of norms and institutionalized practices that elicit cooperative behaviour by signalling and/or constraining the behaviour of others.[56] On the other hand, periods of price warfare are usually the result of attempts to manipulate the relationship in order to redistribute the gains from it. Fights over cheating and ultimately who gets how much are commonplace. The mechanisms by which cooperation is established and the reasons that conflict occurs in these markets appear very similar to those in international politics.

In addition, these markets feature a subtle balancing mechanism. No firm wants to let any other gain so much it can become dominant and drive the others out of business; relative gains matter. Survival dictates that the attempts of any one to dominate be met by cooperative behaviour on the part of others to prevent this. Balancing behaviour is thus engendered, much as in international politics. These imperfect markets, which are characterized by strategic interdependence, may then function more like the international system than do perfect markets. Furthermore, the study of these types of markets is likely to contribute to out understanding of international relations.

A final point about imperfect markets is that they produce indeterminate outcomes as well as unstable ones. They are rarely single-exit situations; a unique solution is not structurally given.[57] Instead, outcomes depend upon the interaction of different actors, each making different assumptions about the others' likely behaviour. Some range of outcomes is, however, possible to identify; it lies between the outcomes predicted by perfect markets and monopoly. This indeterminacy may be frustrating, but it too may more adequately represent politics. Focusing on actors' interdependence can alleviate the strong structural determinism associated with metaphors using perfect markets. Politics seems ultimately to be about choice—choice in the presence of uncertainty, incomplete information, and guesses about the intentions of other actors. Seeing the international system as one characterized by strategic interdependence among sovereign states and thus modelled on these imperfect or oligopolistic markets can provide many empirically and heuristically useful ways of looking at international politics.

. . .

NOTES

1. George Cornewall Lewis, *Remarks on the Use and Abuse of Some Political Terms,* Facsimile of 1832 text (Columbia, 1970), p. 226.
2. Robert Art and Robert Jervis (eds.), *International Politics,* 2nd edition (Boston, 1986), p. 7.
3. Robert Gilpin, *War and Change in World Politics* (Cambridge, 1981), p. 7.
4. Kenneth Waltz, *Theory of International Politics* (Reading, Mass., 1979), p. 88.
5. Robert Axelrod, *The Evolution of Cooperation* (NY, 1984), p. 3.
6. Axelrod, *Evolution,* p. 4.
7. Axelrod, *Evolution,* p. 190.
8. Robert Keohane, *After Hegemony: Cooperation and Discord in the World Political Economy* (Princeton, 1984), chs. 5, 6 esp. pp. 73, 85, 88. He later relaxes this restrictive assump-

tion, citing various forms of interdependence which may mitigate this anarchy. See ch. 7, esp. pp. 122–23.

9. 'Cooperation Under Anarchy,' *World Politics,* 38 (Oct. 1985), p. 1.
10. Hedley Bull, *The Anarchical Society* (NY, 1977), pp. 24–25.
11. Bull, *Anarchical Society*, p. 8.
12. Bull, *Anarchical Society*, pp. 15–16 and ch. 2.
13. Bull, *Anarchical Society*, p. 42.
14. Oye, 'Cooperation Under Anarchy', p. 226.
15. Gilpin, *War and Change,* p. 28.
16. Waltz, *Theory,* p. 102.
17. See Axelrod and Keohane in Oye, 'Cooperation Under Anarchy', p. 226.
18. Waltz, *Theory,* pp. 103–4.
19. Martin Wight, *Power Politics* (NY, 1978), p. 102.
20. Oye, 'Cooperation Under Anarchy', pp. 1–2.
21. Thomas Hobbes, *Leviathan* (Indianapolis, 1958), ch. 14, p. 117.
22. Robert Dahl deals with this issue of monopoly by adding a new dimension to the definition of monopoly. He sees government as having a monopoly over the regulation of what constitutes the legitimate use of force. See his *Modern Political Analysis,* 4th edition (Englewood Cliffs, NJ, 1984), p. 17.
23. Hans Morgenthau, *Politics Among Nations,* 6th edition (NY, 1985), p. 34.
24. Waltz, *Theory,* p. 88.
25. Max Weber, *Economy and Society,* ed. Guenther Roth and Claus Wittich (Berkeley, 1978), I, p. 54. Weber, unlike Waltz, emphasizes elsewhere institutions and legitimacy as well as force to explain politics.
26. *Encyclopedia of the Social Sciences,* p. 13. The *Dictionary of Political Science,* ed. Joseph Dunner (NY, 1964), p. 217, provides a similar definition: 'government is the agency which reflects the organization of the statal (politically organized) group. It normally consists of an executive branch, a legislative branch, and a judicial branch.'
27. David Easton, *The Political System* (NY, 1965), pp. 137–8.
28. Weber, *Economy and Society,* I, p. 231; see also I, p. 31.
29. See, for example, Eckstein, 'Authority Patterns'; Easton, *Political System,* pp. 132–33.
30. See Robert Jervis, 'Security Regimes', *International Organization,* 36 (Spring 1982), pp. 357–78 for a discussion of the legitimate order formed under this system.
31. Waltz, *Theory,* p. 113.
32. Waltz, *Theory,* pp. 115–16.
33. Waltz, *Theory,* p. 81.
34. Waltz recognizes this: see *Theory,* pp. 81–82. But it never influences his very sharp distinction between the ordering of domestic and international politics.
35. See, for example, Peter Katzenstein (ed.), *Between Power and Plenty* (Ithaca, 1978).
36. Waltz does note the differences in systems in terms of the number of great powers, or poles. He suggests the consequences of this are different levels of stability in the system. Ruggie also sees differences in systems over time. But his focus is on the divide between the medieval and the modern (post-seventeenth century) systems. See John Gerard Ruggie, 'Continuity and Transformation in the World Polity: Towards a Neorealist Synthesis', *World Politics* 35 (Jan. 1983), pp. 261–85.
37. Waltz, *Theory,* p. 47.
38. Waltz admits that anarchy and hierarchy are ideal types. But he rejects their use as a continuum, preferring for theoretical simplicity to see them as dichotomies. See

Theory, p. 115. Moreover, he simply posits that the an anarchic ideal is associated with international politics more than it is with domestic politics.

39. Melvin Small and J. D. Singer (eds.), *Explaining War* (Beverly Hills, 1979), pp. 63, 65, 68–69.
40. Waltz, *Theory,* p. 103.
41. Morgenthau, *Politics Among Nations,* pp. 39–40.
42. Inis Claude, *Power and International Relations* (NY, 1962), p. 231.
43. Claude, *Power and IR,* p. 231.
44. Claude, *Power and IR,* p. 234.
45. For Waltz this is the ultimate test of an assumption, see Waltz, *Theory,* p. 96.
46. See, for example, Herbert Spiro, *World Politics: The Global System* (Homewood, II., 1966), esp. ch. 1.
47. Waltz, *Theory,* p. 72.
48. Roger Masters, 'World Politics as a Primitive Political System', *World Politics,* 16 (July 1964), pp. 595–619; Ernest Gellner, 'How to Live in Anarchy', The *Listener,* 3 April, 1958, pp. 579–83; Chadwick Alger, 'Comparison of Intranational and International Politics', *APSR,* 62 (June 1963), pp. 406–19.
49. W. T. R. Fox, *The American Study of International Relations* (Columbia. SC., 1968), p. 20.
50. Thomas Schelling, *Strategy of Conflict* (Cambridge, Mass., 1960), p. 5.
51. See David Baldwin, 'Interdependence and Power: A Conceptual Analysis'. *International Organization,* 34 (Aut. 1980), pp. 471–506. This conception of interdependence does not include the notion of sensitivity, as employed by Robert Keohane and Joseph Nye in *Power and Interdependence* (Boston, 1977). The notion of vulnerability is the most well-accepted definition.
52. Waltz is confusing on this point. He sees the two as opposed but linked; however, he cannot decide which way the linkage runs. Anarchy for him implies equality, sameness, and hence independence of actors, on the one hand. On the other, he claims interdependence is highest when states are equal. If this is true, then anarchy may well be characterized by very high levels of interdependence, since all states are equal.
53. See Edward Hallett Carr, *The Twenty Years' Crisis, 1919–1939* (NY, 1939). Also see the discussion of neoliberal institutionalism in Joseph Grieco, 'Anarchy and the Limits of Cooperation', *International Organization,* 42 no. 33 (Summer 1988), pp. 485–508.
54. Robert Jervis, *The Logic of Images in International Relations* (Princeton, 1970), and *Perception and Misperception in International Politics* (Princeton, 1976).
55. A metaphor Waltz resorts to later, see *Theory,* pp. 129–36.
56. The rules of thumb that Schelling discusses in *Strategy of Conflict* are one type of tacit communication.
57. Solutions in oligopolistic markets are possible to identify if one assumes away strategic interdependence. For instance, Cournot-Nash and Stacklebreg equilibria are identifiable if one holds constant the other's behaviour in price or quantity decisions.

Anarchy Is What States Make of It: The Social Construction of Power Politics

ALEXANDER WENDT

...Does the absence of centralized political authority force states to play competitive power politics? Can international regimes overcome this logic, and under what conditions? What in anarchy is given and immutable, and what is amenable to change?

The debate between "neorealists" and "neoliberals" has been based on a shared commitment to "rationalism."[1] Like all social theories, rational choice directs us to ask some questions and not others, treating the identities and interests of agents as exogenously given and focusing on how the behavior of agents generates outcomes. As such, rationalism offers a fundamentally behavioral conception of both process and institutions: they change behavior but not identities and interests. In addition to this way of framing research problems, neorealists and neoliberals share generally similar assumptions about agents: states are the dominant actors in the system, and they define security in "self-interested" terms. Neorealists and neoliberals may disagree about the extent to which states are motivated by relative versus absolute gains, but both groups take the self-interested state as the starting point for theory.

This starting point makes substantive sense for neorealists, since they believe anarchies are necessarily "self-help" systems, systems in which both central authority and collective security are absent. The self-help corollary to anarchy does enormous work in neorealism, generating the inherently competitive dynamics of the security dilemma and collective action problem. Self-help is not seen as an "institution" and as such occupies a privileged explanatory role vis-à-vis process, setting the terms for, and unaffected by, interaction. Since states failing to conform to the logic of self-help will be driven from the system, only simple learning or behavioral adaptation is possible; the complex learning involved in redefinitions of identity and interest is not.[2] Questions about identity- and interest-formation are therefore not important to students of international relations. A rationalist problématique, which reduces process to dynamics of behavioral interaction among exogenously constituted actors, defines the scope of systemic theory.

By adopting such reasoning, liberals concede to neorealists the causal powers of anarchic structure, but they gain the rhetorically powerful argument that process can generate cooperative behavior, even in an exogenously given, self-help system. Some liberals may believe that anarchy does, in fact, constitute states with self-interested identities exogenous to practice. . . .

Yet some liberals want more. When Joseph Nye speaks of "complex learning," or Robert Jervis of "changing conceptions of self and interest," or Robert Keohane of "sociological" conceptions of interest, each is asserting an important role for transformations of identity and interest in the liberal research program and, by extension, a potentially much stronger conception of process and institutions in world politics.[3] "Strong" liberals should be troubled by the dichotomous privileging of structure over process, since transformations of identity and interest through process are transformations of structure. Rationalism has little to offer such an argument, which is in part why, in an important article, Friedrich Kratochwil and John Ruggie argued that its individualist ontology contradicted the intersubjectivist epistemology necessary for regime theory to realize its full promise. . . .[4]

The irony is that social theories which seek to explain identities and interests do exist. Keohane has called them "reflectivist";[5] because I want to emphasize their focus on the social construction of subjectivity and minimize their image problem, following Nicholas Onuf I will call them "constructivist." . . .[6] Constructivism's potential contribution to a strong liberalism has been obscured, however, by recent epistemological debates between modernists and postmodernists, in which Science disciplines Dissent for not defining a conventional research program, and Dissent celebrates its liberation from Science.[7] Real issues animate this debate, which also divides constructivists. With respect to the substance of international relations, however, both modern and postmodern constructivists are interested in how knowledgeable practices constitute subjects, which is not far from the strong liberal interest in how institutions transform interests. They share a cognitive, intersubjective conception of process in which identities and interests are endogenous to interaction, rather than a rationalist-behavioral one in which they are exogenous.

My objective in this article is to build a bridge between these two traditions (and, by extension, between the realist-liberal and rationalist-reflectivist debates) by developing a constructivist argument, drawn from structurationist and symbolic interactionist sociology, on behalf of the liberal claim that international institutions can transform state identities and interests. . . .

My strategy for building this bridge will be to argue against the neorealist claim that self-help is given by anarchic structure exogenously to process. . . . I argue that self-help and power politics do not follow either logically or causally from anarchy and that if today we find ourselves in a self-help world, this is due to process, not structure. There is no "logic" of anarchy apart from the practices that create and instantiate one structure of identities and interests rather than another; structure has no existence or causal powers apart from process. Self-help and power politics are institutions, not essential features of anarchy. *Anarchy is what states make of it.* . . .

ANARCHY AND POWER POLITICS

Classical realists such as Thomas Hobbes, Reinhold Niebuhr, and Hans Morgenthau attributed egoism and power politics primarily to human nature, whereas structural realists or neorealists emphasize anarchy. The difference stems in part from different interpretations of anarchy's causal powers. Kenneth Waltz's work is important for both. In *Man, the State, and War,* he defines anarchy as a condition of possibility for or "permissive" cause of war, arguing that "wars occur because there is nothing to prevent them."[8] It is the human nature or domestic politics of predator states, however, that provide the initial impetus or "efficient" cause of conflict which forces other states to respond in kind.[9] Waltz is not entirely consistent about this, since he slips without justification from the permissive causal claim that in anarchy war is always possible to the active causal claim that "war may at any moment occur."[10] But despite Waltz's concluding call for third-image theory, the efficient causes that initialize anarchic systems are from the first and second images. This is reversed in Waltz's *Theory of International Politics,* in which first- and second-image theories are spurned as "reductionist," and the logic of anarchy seems by itself to constitute self-help and power politics as necessary features of world politics.[11]

This is unfortunate, since whatever one may think of first- and second-image theories, they have the virtue of implying that practices determine the character of anarchy. In the permissive view, only if human or domestic factors cause A to attack B will B have to defend itself. Anarchies may contain dynamics that lead to competitive power politics, but they also may not, and we can argue about when particular structures of identity and interest will emerge. In neorealism, however, the role of practice in shaping the character of anarchy is substantially reduced, and so there is less about which to argue: self-help and competitive power politics are simply given exogenously by the structure of the state system. . . .

Anarchy, Self-help, and Intersubjective Knowledge

Waltz defines political structure on three dimensions: ordering principles (in this case, anarchy), principles of differentiation (which here drop out), and the distribution of capabilities.[12] By itself, this definition predicts little about state behavior. It does not predict whether two states will be friends or foes, will recognize each other's sovereignty, will have dynastic ties, will be revisionist or status quo powers, and so on. . . . Put more generally, without assumptions about the structure of identities and interests in the system, Waltz's definition of structure cannot predict the content or dynamics of anarchy. Self-help is one such intersubjective structure and, as such, does the decisive explanatory work in the theory. The question is whether self-help is a logical or contingent feature of anarchy. In this section, I develop the concept of a "structure of identity and interest" and show that no particular one follows logically from anarchy.

A fundamental principle of constructivist social theory is that people act toward objects, including other actors, on the basis of the meanings that the objects have for them. States act differently toward enemies than they do toward friends because enemies are threatening and friends are not. Anarchy and the distribution of power are insufficient to tell us which is which. U.S. military power has a different significance for Canada than for Cuba, despite their similar "structural" positions, just as British missiles have a different significance for the United States than do Soviet missiles. The distribution of power may always affect states' calculations, but how it does so depends on the intersubjective understandings and expectations, on the "distribution of knowledge," that constitute their conceptions of self and other. . . . It is collective meanings that constitute the structures which organize our actions.

Actors acquire identities—relatively stable, role-specific understandings and expectations about self—by participating in such collective meanings.[13] Identities are inherently relational: "Identity, with its appropriate attachments of psychological reality, is always identity within a specific, socially constructed world," Peter Berger argues. . . .[14]

Identities are the basis of interests. Actors do not have a "portfolio" of interests that they carry around independent of social context; instead, they define their interests in the process of defining situations. . . .[15] Sometimes situations are unprecedented in our experience, and in these cases we have to construct their meaning, and thus our interests, by analogy or invent them de novo. . . . This seems to be happening today in the United States and the former Soviet Union: without the cold war's mutual attributions of threat and hostility to define their identities, these states seem unsure of what their "interests" should be.

An institution is a relatively stable set or "structure" of identities and interests. Such structures are often codified in formal rules and norms, but these have motivational force only in virtue of actors' socialization to and participation in collective knowledge. Institutions are fundamentally cognitive entities that do not exist apart from actors' ideas about how the world works.[16] This does not mean that institutions are not real or objective, that they are "nothing but" beliefs. As collective knowledge, they are experienced as having an existence "over and above the individuals who happen to embody them at the moment."[17] In this way, institutions come to confront individuals as more or less coercive social facts, but they are still a function of what actors collectively "know." Identities and such collective cognitions do not exist apart from each other; they are "mutually constitutive." . . . .[18]

Self-help is an institution, one of various structures of identity and interest that may exist under anarchy. Processes of identity-formation under anarchy are concerned first and foremost with preservation or "security" of the self. Concepts of security therefore differ in the extent to which and the manner in which the self is identified cognitively with the other, and, I want to suggest, it is upon this cognitive variation that the meaning of anarchy and the distribution of power depends. Let me illustrate with a standard continuum of security systems.

At one end is the "competitive" security system, in which states identify negatively with each other's security so that ego's gain is seen as alter's loss. Negative identification under anarchy constitutes systems of "realist" power politics: risk averse actors that infer intentions from capabilities and worry about relative gains and losses. At the limit—in the Hobbesian war of all against all—collective action is nearly impossible in such a system because each actor must constantly fear being stabbed in the back.

In the middle is the "individualistic" security system, in which states are indifferent to the relationship between their own and others' security. This constitutes "neoliberal" systems: states are still self-regarding about their security but are concerned primarily with absolute gains rather than relative gains. One's position in the distribution of power is less important, and collective action is more possible (though still subject to free riding because states continue to be "egoists").

Competitive and individualistic systems are both "self-help" forms of anarchy in the sense that states do not positively identify the security of self with that of others but instead treat security as the individual responsibility of each. Given the lack of a positive cognitive identification on the basis of which to build security regimes, power politics within such systems will necessarily consist of efforts to manipulate others to satisfy self-regarding interests.

This contrasts with the "cooperative" security system, in which states identify positively with one another so that the security of each is perceived as the responsibility of all. This is not self-help in any interesting sense, since the "self" in terms of which interests are defined is the community; national interests are international interests. In practice, of course, the extent to which states' identification with the community varies, from the limited form found in "concerts" to the full-blown form seen in "collective security" arrangements. Depending on how well developed the collective self is, it will produce security practices that are in varying degrees altruistic or prosocial. This makes collective action less dependent on the presence of active threats and less prone to free riding.[19] Moreover, it restructures efforts to advance one's objectives, or "power politics," in terms of shared norms rather than relative power.[20]

On this view, the tendency in international relations scholarship to view power and institutions as two opposing explanations of foreign policy is therefore misleading, since anarchy and the distribution of power only have meaning for state action in virtue of the understandings and expectations that constitute institutional identities and interests. . . .

Because states do not have conceptions of self and other, and thus security interests, apart from or prior to interaction, we assume too much about the state of nature if we concur with Waltz that, in virtue of anarchy, "international political systems, like economic markets, are formed by the coaction of self-regarding units."[21] We also assume too much if we argue that, in virtue of anarchy, states in the state of nature necessarily face a "stag hunt" or "security dilemma."[22] These claims presuppose a history of interaction in which actors have acquired "selfish" identities and interests; before interaction (and still in abstraction from first- and second-image factors) they would have no experience upon which to base such definitions of self and other. To assume otherwise is to attribute to states in the state of nature qualities that they can only possess in society.[23] Self-help is an institution, not a constitutive feature of anarchy. . . .

Anarchy and the Social Construction of Power Politics

If self-help is not a constitutive feature of anarchy, it must emerge causally from processes in which anarchy plays only a permissive role. This reflects a second principle of constructivism: that the meanings in terms of which action is organized arise out of interaction. This being said, however, the situation facing states as they encounter one another for the first time may be such that only self-regarding conceptions of identity can survive; if so, even if these conceptions are socially constructed, neorealists may be right in holding identities and interests constant and thus in privileging one particular meaning of anarchic structure over process. In this case, rationalists would be right to argue for a weak, behavioral conception of the difference that institutions make, and realists would be right to argue that any international institutions which are created will be inherently unstable, since without the power to transform identities and interests they will be "continuing objects of choice" by exogenously constituted actors constrained only by the transaction costs of behavioral change.[24] Even in a permissive causal role, in other words, anarchy may decisively restrict interaction and therefore restrict viable forms of systemic theory. I address these causal issues first by showing how self-regarding ideas about security might develop and then by examining the conditions under which a key efficient cause—predation—may dispose states in this direction rather than others. . . .

Consider two actors—ego and alter—encountering each other for the first time. Each wants to survive and has certain material capabilities, but neither actor has biological or domestic imperatives for power, glory, or conquest (still bracketed), and there is no history of security or insecurity between the two. What should they do? Realists would probably argue that each should act on the basis of worst-case assumptions about the other's intentions, justifying such an attitude as prudent in view of the possibility of death from making a mistake. Such a possibility always exists, even in civil society; however, society would be impossible if people made decisions purely on the basis of worst-case possibilities. Instead, most decisions are and should be made on the basis of probabilities, and these are produced by interaction, by what actors *do*.

In the beginning is ego's gesture, which may consist, for example, of an advance, a retreat, a brandishing of arms, a laying down of arms, or an attack.[25] For ego, this gesture represents the basis on which it is prepared to respond to alter. This basis is unknown to alter, however, and so it must make an inference or "attribution" about ego's intentions and, in particular, given that this is anarchy, about whether ego is a threat.[26] The content of this inference will largely depend on two considerations. The first is the gesture's and ego's physical qualities, which are in part contrived by ego and which include the direction of movement, noise, numbers, and immediate consequences of the gesture. The second consideration concerns what alter would intend by such qualities were it to make such a gesture itself. Alter may make an attributional "error" in its inference about ego's intent, but there is also no reason for it to assume a priori—before the gesture—that ego is threatening, since it is only through a process of signaling and interpreting that the costs and probabilities of being wrong can be determined. Social threats are constructed, not natural. . . .

It is through reciprocal interaction, in other words, that we create and instantiate the relatively enduring social structures in terms of which we define our identities and interests. . . .

The simple overall model of identity and interest-formation . . . applies to competitive institutions no less than to cooperative ones. Self-help security systems evolve from cycles of interaction in which each party acts in ways that the other feels are threatening to the self, creating expectations that the other is not to be trusted. Competitive or egoistic identities are caused by such insecurity; if the other is threatening, the self is forced to "mirror" such behavior in its conception of the self's relationship to that other.[27] Being treated as an object for the gratification of others precludes the positive identification with others necessary for collective security; conversely, being treated by others in ways that are empathic with respect to the security of the self permits such identification.[28]

Competitive systems of interaction are prone to security "dilemmas," in which the efforts of actors to enhance their security unilaterally threatens the security of the others, perpetuating distrust and alienation. The forms of identity and interest that constitute such dilemmas, however, are themselves ongoing effects of, not exogenous to, the interaction; identities are produced in and through "situated activity." . . .[29] We do not *begin* our relationship with the aliens in a security dilemma; security dilemmas are not given by anarchy or nature. Of course, once institutionalized such a dilemma may be hard to change (I return to this below), but the point remains: identities and interests are constituted by collective meanings that are always in process. . . .

Predator States and Anarchy as Permissive Cause

The mirror theory of identity-formation is a crude account of how the process of creating identities and interests might work, but it does not tell us why a system of states—such as, arguably, our own—would have ended up with self-regarding and not collective identities. In this section, I examine an efficient cause, predation, which, in conjunction with anarchy as a permissive cause, may generate a self-help system. In so doing, however, I show the key role that the structure of identities and interests plays in mediating anarchy's explanatory role.

The predator argument is straightforward and compelling. For whatever reasons—biology, domestic politics, or systemic victimization—some states may become predisposed toward aggression. The aggressive behavior of these predators or "bad apples" forces other states to engage in competitive power politics, to meet fire with fire, since failure to do so may degrade or destroy them. One predator will best a hundred pacifists because anarchy provides no guarantees. . . .

In an anarchy of two, if ego is predatory, alter must either define its security in self-help terms or pay the price. This follows directly from the above argument, in which conceptions of self mirror treatment by the other. In an anarchy of many, however, the effect of predation also depends on the level of collective identity already attained in the system. If predation occurs right after the first encounter in the state of nature, it will force others with whom it comes in contact to defend themselves, first individually and then collectively *if* they come to perceive a common threat. The emergence of such a defensive alliance will be seriously inhibited if the structure of identities and interests has already evolved into a Hobbesian world of maximum insecurity, since potential allies will strongly distrust each other and face intense collective action problems; such insecure allies are also more likely to fall out amongst themselves once the predator is removed. If collective security identity is high, however, the emergence of a predator may do much less damage. If the predator attacks any member of the collective, the latter will come to the victim's defense on the principle of "all for one, one for all," even if the predator is not presently a threat to other members of the collective. If the predator is not strong enough to withstand the collective, it will be defeated and collective security will obtain. But if it is strong enough, the logic of the two-actor case (now predator and collective) will activate, and balance-of-power politics will reestablish itself.

The timing of the emergence of predation relative to the history of identity-formation in the community is therefore crucial to anarchy's explanatory role as a permissive cause. Predation will always lead victims to defend themselves, but whether defense will be collective or not depends on the history of interaction within the potential collective as much as on the ambitions of the predator. . . . "Mature" anarchies are less likely than "immature" ones to be reduced by predation to a Hobbesian condition, and maturity, which is a proxy for structures of identity and interest, is a function of process. . . .

The role of predation in generating a self-help system, then, is consistent with a systematic focus on process. Even if the source of predation is entirely exogenous to the system, it is what states *do* that determines the quality of their interactions under anarchy. In this respect, it is not surprising that it is classical realists rather than structural realists who emphasize this sort of argument. The former's emphasis on unit-level causes of power politics leads more easily to a permissive view of anarchy's explanatory role (and therefore to a processual view of international relations) than does the latter's emphasis on anarchy as a "structural cause"; neorealists do not need predation because the system is given as self-help.

This raises anew the question of exactly how much and what kind of role human nature and domestic politics play in world politics. The greater and more destructive this role, the more significant predation will be, and the less amenable anarchy will be to formation of collective identities. Classical realists, of course, assumed that human nature was possessed by an inherent lust for power or glory. My argument suggests that assumptions such as this were made for a reason: an unchanging Hobbesian man provides the powerful efficient cause necessary for a relentless pessimism about world politics that anarchic structure alone, or even structure plus intermittent predation, cannot supply. One can be skeptical of such an essentialist assumption, as I am, but it does produce determinate results at the expense of systemic theory. A concern with systemic process over structure suggests that perhaps it is time to revisit the debate over the relative importance of first-, second-, and third-image theories of state identity-formation. . . .

INSTITUTIONAL TRANSFORMATIONS OF POWER POLITICS

Let us assume that processes of identity- and interest-formation have created a world in which states do not recognize rights to territory or existence—a war of all against all. In this world, anarchy has a "realist" meaning for state action: be insecure and concerned with relative power. Anarchy has this meaning only in virtue of collective, insecurity-producing practices, but if those practices are relatively stable, they do constitute a system that may resist change. . . .

In the remainder of this article, I examine three institutional transformations of identity and security interest through which states might escape a Hobbesian world of their own making. In so doing, I seek to clarify what it means to say that "institutions transform identities and interests," emphasizing that the key to such transformations is relatively stable practice.

Sovereignty, Recognition, and Security

In a Hobbesian state of nature, states are individuated by the domestic processes that constitute them as states and by their material capacity to deter threats from other states. In this world, even if free momentarily from the predations of others, state security does not have any basis in social recognition—in intersubjective understandings or norms that a state has a right to its existence, territory, and subjects. Security is a matter of national power, nothing more.

The principle of sovereignty transforms this situation by providing a social basis for the individuality and security of states. Sovereignty is an institution, and so it exists only in virtue of certain intersubjective understandings and expectations; there is no sovereignty without an other. These understandings and expectations not only constitute a particular kind of state—the "sovereign" state—but also constitute a particular form of community, since identities are relational. The essence of this community is a mutual recognition of one another's right to exercise exclusive political authority within territorial limits. These reciprocal "permissions" constitute a spatially rather than functionally differentiated world—a world in which fields of practice constitute and are organized around "domestic" and "international" spaces rather than around the performance of particular activities. . . .

Sovereignty norms are now so taken for granted, so natural, that it is easy to overlook the extent to which they are both presupposed by an ongoing artifact of practice. When states tax "their" "citizens" and not others, when they "protect" their markets against foreign "imports," when they kill thousands of Iraqis in one kind of war and then refuse to "intervene" to kill even one person in another kind, a "civil" war, and when they fight a global war against a regime that sought to destroy the institution of sovereignty and then give Germany back to the Germans, they are acting against the background of, and thereby reproducing, shared norms about what it means to be a sovereign state.

If states stopped acting on those norms, their identity as "sovereigns" (if not necessarily as "states") would disappear. The sovereign state is an ongoing accomplishment of practice, not a once-and-for-all creation of norms that somehow exist apart from practice. . . .[30] Thus, saying that "the institution of sovereignty transforms identities" is shorthand for saying that "regular practices produce mutually constituting sovereign identities (agents) and their associated institutional norms (structures)." Practice is the core of constructivist resolutions of the agent-structure problem. . . .

This may tell us something about how institutions of sovereign states are reproduced through social interaction, but it does not tell us why such a structure of identity and interest would arise in the first place. Two conditions would seem necessary for this to happen: (1) the density and regularity of interactions must be sufficiently high and (2) actors must be dissatisfied with preexisting forms of identity and interaction. Given these conditions, a norm of mutual recognition is relatively undemanding in terms of social trust, having the form of an assurance game in which a player will acknowledge the sovereignty of the others as long as they will in turn acknowledge that player's own sovereignty. Articulating international legal principles such as those embodied in the Peace of Augsburg (1555) and the Peace of Westphalia (1648) may also help by establishing explicit criteria for determining violations of the nascent social consensus. . . .[31] But whether such a consensus holds depends on what states do. If they treat each other as if they were sovereign, then over time they will institutionalize that mode of subjectivity; if they do not, then that mode will not become the norm.

Practices of sovereignty will transform understandings of security and power politics in at least three ways. First, states will come to define their (and our) security in terms of preserving their "property rights" over particular territories. We now see this as natural, but the preservation of territorial frontiers is not, in fact, equivalent to the survival of the state or its people. Indeed, some states would probably be more secure if they would relinquish certain territories—the "Soviet Union" of some minority republics, "Yugoslavia" of Croatia and Slovenia, Israel of the West Bank, and so on. The fact that sovereignty practices have historically been oriented toward producing distinct territorial spaces, in other words, affects states' conceptualization of what they must "secure" to function in that identity, a process that may help account for the "hardening" of territorial boundaries over the centuries.

Second, to the extent that states successfully internalize sovereignty norms, they will be more respectful toward the territorial rights of others. This restraint is *not* primarily because of the costs of violating sovereignty norms, although when violators do get punished (as in the Gulf War) it reminds everyone of what these costs can be, but because part of what it means to be a "sovereign" state is that one does not violate the territorial rights of others without "just cause." A clear example of such an institutional effect, convincingly argued by David Strang, is the markedly different treatment that weak states receive within and outside communities of mutual recognition. . . .[32] What keeps the United States from conquering the Bahamas, or Nigeria from seizing Togo, or Australia from occupying Vanuatu? Clearly, power is not the issue, and in these cases even the cost of sanctions would probably be negligible. One might argue that great powers simply have no "interest" in these conquests, and this might be so, but this lack of interest can only be understood in terms of their recognition of weak states' sovereignty. I have no interest in exploiting my friends, not because of the relative costs and benefits of such action but because they are my friends. The absence of recognition, in turn, helps explain the Western states' practices of territorial conquest, enslavement, and genocide against Native American and African peoples. It is in *that* world that only power matters, not the world of today.

Finally, to the extent that their ongoing socialization teaches states that their sovereignty depends on recognition by other states, they can afford to rely more on the institutional fabric of international society and less on individual national means—especially military power—to protect their security. The intersubjective understandings embodied in the institution of sovereignty, in other words, may redefine the meaning of others' power for the security of the self. In policy terms, this means that states can be less worried about short-term survival and relative power and can thus shift their resources accordingly. Ironically, it is the great powers, the states with the greatest national means, that may have the hardest time learning this lesson; small powers do not have the luxury of relying on national means and may therefore learn faster that collective recognition is a cornerstone of security. . . .

Cooperation Among Egoists and Transformations of Identity

. . . In the traditional game-theoretic analysis of cooperation, even an iterated one, the structure of the game—of identities and interests—is exogenous to interaction and, as such, does not change. A "black box" is put around identity- and interest-formation, and analysis focuses instead on the relationship between expectations and behavior. The norms that evolve from interaction are treated as rules and behavioral regularities which are external to the actors and which resist change because of the transaction costs of creating new ones. The game-theoretic analysis of cooperation among egoists is at base behavioral.

A constructivist analysis of cooperation, in contrast, would concentrate on how the expectations produced by behavior affect identities and interests. The process of creating institutions is one of internalizing new understandings of self and other, of acquiring new role identities, not just of creating external constraints on the behavior of exogenously constituted actors. Even if not intended as such, in other words, the process by which egoists learn to cooperate is at the same time a process of reconstructing their interests in terms of shared commitments to social norms. Over time, this will tend to transform a positive interdependence of *outcomes* into a positive interdependence of *utilities* or collective interest organized around the norms in question. These norms will resist change because they are tied to actors' commitments to their identities and interests, not merely because of transaction costs. A constructivist analysis of "the cooperation problem," in other words, is at base cognitive rather than behavioral, since it treats the intersubjective knowledge that defines the structure of identities and interests, of the "game," as endogenous to and instantiated by interaction itself.

The debate over the future of collective security in Western Europe may illustrate the significance of this difference. A weak liberal or rationalist analysis would assume that the European states' "portfolio" of interests has not fundamentally changed and that the emergence of new factors, such as the collapse of the Soviet threat and the rise of Germany, would alter their cost-benefit ratios for pursuing current arrangements, thereby causing existing institutions to break down. The European states formed collaborative institutions for good, exogenously constituted egoistic reasons, and the same reasons may lead them to reject those institutions; the game of European power politics has not changed. A strong liberal or constructivist analysis of this problem would suggest that four decades of cooperation may have transformed a positive interdependence of outcomes into a collective "European identity" in terms of which states increasingly define their "self" interests.[33] Even if egoistic reasons were its starting point, the process of cooperating tends to redefine those reasons by reconstituting identities and interests in terms of new intersubjective understandings and commitments. . . . Through participation in new forms of social knowledge, in other words, the European states of 1990 might no longer be the states of 1950.

Critical Strategic Theory and Collective Security

The transformation of identity and interest through an "evolution of cooperation" faces two important constraints. The first is that the process is incremental and slow. Actors' objectives in such a process are typically to realize joint gains within what they take to be a relatively stable context, and they are therefore unlikely to engage in substantial reflection about how to change the parameters of that context (including the structure of identities and interests) and unlikely to pursue policies specifically designed to bring about such changes. . . .

A second, more fundamental, constraint is that the evolution of cooperation story presupposes that actors do not identify negatively with one another. Actors must be concerned primarily with absolute gains; to the extent that antipathy and distrust lead them to define their security in relativistic terms, it will be hard to accept the vulnerabilities that attend cooperation. This is important because it is precisely the "central balance" in the state system that seems to be so often afflicted with such competitive thinking, and realists can therefore argue that the possibility of cooperation within one "pole" (for example, the West) is parasitic on the dominance of competition between poles (the East–West conflict). Relations between the poles may be amenable to some positive reciprocity in areas such as arms control, but the atmosphere of distrust leaves little room for such cooperation and its transformative consequences.[34] The conditions of negative identification that make an "evolution of cooperation" most needed work precisely against such a logic.

This seemingly intractable situation may nevertheless be amenable to quite a different logic of transformation, one driven more by self-conscious efforts to change structures of identity and interest than by unintended consequences. Such voluntarism may seem to contradict the spirit of constructivism, since would-be revolutionaries are presumably themselves effects of socialization to structures of identity and interest. How can they think about changing that to which they owe their identity? The possibility lies in the distinction between the social determination of the self and the personal determination of choice, between what Mead called the "me" and the "I."[35] The "me" is that part of subjectivity which is defined in terms of others; the character and behavioral expectations of a person's role identity as "professor," or of the United States as "leader of the alliance," for example, are socially constituted. Roles are not played in mechanical fashion according to precise scripts, however, but are "taken" and adapted in idiosyncratic ways by each actor. Even in the most constrained situations, role performance involves a choice by the actor. The "I" is the part of subjectivity in which this appropriation and reaction to roles and its corresponding existential freedom lie.

The fact that roles are "taken" means that, in principle, actors always have a capacity for "character planning"—for engaging in critical self-reflection and choices designed to bring about changes in their lives. But when or under what conditions can this creative capacity be exercised? Clearly, much of the time it cannot: if actors were constantly reinventing their identities, social order would be impossible, and the relative stability of identities and interests in the real world is indicative of our propensity for habitual rather than creative action. The exceptional, conscious choosing to transform or transcend roles has at least two preconditions. First, there must be a reason to think of oneself in novel terms. This would most likely stem from the presence of new social situations that cannot be managed in terms of preexisting self-conceptions. Second, the expected costs of intentional role change—the sanctions imposed by others with whom one interacted in previous roles—cannot be greater than its rewards.

When these conditions are present, actors can engage in self-reflection and practice specifically designed to transform their identities and interests and thus to "change the games" in which they are embedded. Such "critical" strategic theory and practice has not received the attention it merits from students of world politics (another legacy of exogenously given interests perhaps), particularly given that one of the most important phenomena in contemporary world politics, Mikhail Gorbachev's policy of "New Thinking," is arguably precisely that.[36] Let me therefore use this policy as an example of how states might transform a competitive security system into a cooperative one, dividing the transformative process into four stages.

The first stage in intentional transformation is the breakdown of consensus about identity commitments. In the Soviet case, identity commitments centered on the Leninist theory of imperialism, with its belief that relations between capitalist and socialist states are inherently conflictual, and on the alliance patterns that this belief engendered. In the 1980s, the consensus within the Soviet Union over the Leninist theory broke down for a variety of reasons, principal among which seem to have been the state's inability to meet the economic-technological-military challenge from the West, the government's decline of political legitimacy at home, and the reassurance from the West that it did not intend to invade the Soviet Union, a reassurance that reduced the external costs of role change. These factors paved the way for a radical leadership transition and for a subsequent "unfreezing of conflict schemas" concerning relations with the West.[37]

The breakdown of consensus makes possible a second stage of critical examination of old ideas about self and other and, by extension, of the structures of interaction by which the ideas have been sustained. In periods of relatively stable role identities, ideas and structures may become reified and thus treated as things that exist independently of social action. If so, the second stage is one of denaturalization, of identifying the practices that reproduce seemingly inevitable ideas about self and other; to that extent, it is a form of "critical" rather than "problem-solving" theory. The result of such a critique should be an identification of new "possible selves" and aspirations. New Thinking embodies such critical theorizing. . . .

Such rethinking paves the way for a third stage of new practice. In most cases, it is not enough to rethink one's own ideas about self and other, since old identities have been sustained by systems of interaction with *other* actors, the practices of which remain a social fact for the transformative agent. In order to change the self, then, it is often necessary to change the identities and interests of the others that help sustain those systems of interaction. The vehicle for inducing such change is one's own practice and, in particular, the practice of "altercasting"—a technique of interactor control in which ego uses tactics of self-presentation and stage management in an attempt to frame alter's definitions of social situations in ways that create the role which ego desires alter to play.[38] In effect, in altercasting ego tries to induce alter to take on a new identity (and thereby enlist alter in ego's effort to change itself) by treating alter *as if* it already had that identity. . . .

Yet by themselves such practices cannot transform a competitive security system, since if they are not reciprocated by alter, they will expose ego to a "sucker" payoff and quickly wither on the vine. In order for critical strategic practice to transform competitive identities, it must be "rewarded" by alter, which will encourage more such practice by ego, and so on. Over time, this will institutionalize a positive rather than a negative identification between the security of self and other and will thereby provide a firm intersubjective basis for what were initially tentative commitments to new identities and interests. . . .

NOTES

1. See Robert Keohane, "International Institutions: Two Approaches," *International Studies Quarterly* 32 (December 1988), pp. 379–96.
2. On neorealist conceptions of learning, see Philip Tetlock, "Learning in U.S. and Soviet Foreign Policy," in George Breslauer and Philip Tetlock, eds., *Learning in U.S. and Soviet Foreign Policy* (Boulder, CO: Westview Press, 1991), pp. 24–27. On the difference between behavioral and cognitive learning, see ibid., pp. 20–61; Joseph Nye, "Nuclear Learning and U.S.–Soviet Security Regimes," *International Organization* 41 (Summer 1987), pp. 371–402; and Ernst Haas, *When Knowledge Is Power* (Berkeley: University of California Press, 1990), pp. 17–49.
3. See Nye, "Nuclear Learning and U.S.–Soviet Security Regimes"; Robert Jervis, "Realism, Game Theory, and Cooperation," *World Politics* 40 (April 1988), pp. 340–44; and Robert Keohane, "International Liberalism Reconsidered," in John Dunn, ed., *The Economic Limits to Modern Politics* (Cambridge: Cambridge University Press, 1990), p. 183.
4. Friedrich Kratochwil and John Ruggie, "International Organization: A State of the Art on an Art of the State," *International Organization* 40 (Autumn 1986), pp. 753–75.
5. Keohane, "International Institutions."
6. See Nicholas Onuf, *World of Our Making* (Columbia: University of South Carolina Press, 1989).
7. On Science, see Keohane, "International Institutions"; and Robert Keohane, "International Relations Theory: Contributions of a Feminist Standpoint," *Millennium* 18 (Summer 1989), pp. 245–53. On Dissent, see R. B. J. Walker, "History and Structure in the Theory of International Relations," *Millennium* 18 (Summer 1989), pp. 163–83; and Richard Ashley and R. B. J. Walker, "Reading Dissidence/Writing the Discipline: Crisis and the Question of Sovereignty in International Studies," *International Studies Quarterly* 34 (September 1990), pp. 367–416. For an excellent critical assessment of these debates,

see Yosef Lapid, "The Third Debate: On the Prospects of International Theory in a Post-Positivist Era," *International Studies Quarterly* 33 (September 1989), pp. 235–54.

8. Kenneth Waltz, *Man, the State, and War* (New York: Columbia University Press, 1959), p. 232.

9. Ibid., pp. 169–70.

10. Ibid., p. 232. This point is made by Hidemi Suganami in "Bringing Order to the Causes of War Debates," *Millennium* 19 (Spring 1990), p. 34, fn. 11.

11. Kenneth Waltz, *Theory of International Politics* (Boston: Addison-Wesley, 1979).

12. Waltz, *Theory of International Politics,* pp. 79–101.

13. For an excellent short statement of how collective meanings constitute identities, see Peter Berger, "Identity as a Problem in the Sociology of Knowledge," *European Journal of Sociology,* vol. 7, no. 1, 1966, pp. 32–40. See also David Morgan and Michael Schwalbe, "Mind and Self in Society: Linking Social Structure and Social Cognition," *Social Psychology Quarterly* 53 (June 1990), pp. 148–64. In my discussion, I draw on the following interactionist texts: George Herbert Mead, *Mind, Self, and Society* (Chicago: University of Chicago Press, 1934); Peter Berger and Thomas Luckmann, *The Social Construction of Reality* (New York: Anchor Books, 1966); Sheldon Stryker, *Symbolic Interactionism: A Social Structural Version* (Menlo Park, CA: Benjamin/Cummings, 1980); R. S. Perinbanayagam, *Signifying Acts: Structure and Meaning in Everyday Life* (Carbondale: Southern Illinois University Press, 1985); John Hewitt, *Self and Society: A Symbolic Interactionist Social Psychology* (Boston: Allyn & Bacon, 1988); and Jonathan Turner, *A Theory of Social Interaction* (Stanford, CA: Stanford University Press, 1988). Despite some differences, much the same points are made by structurationists such as Bhaskar and Giddens. See Roy Bhaskar, *The Possibility of Naturalism* (Atlantic Highlands, NJ: Humanities Press, 1979); and Anthony Giddens, *Central Problems in Social Theory* (Berkeley: University of California Press, 1979).

14. Berger, "Identity as a Problem in Sociology of Knowledge," p. 111.

15. On the "portfolio" conception of interests, see Barry Hindess, *Political Choice and Social Structure* (Aldershot, UK: Edward Elgar, 1989), pp. 2–3. The "definition of the situation" is a central concept in interactionist theory.

16. In neo-Durkheimian parlance, institutions are "social representations." See Serge Moscovici, "The Phenomenon of Social Representations," in Rob Farr and Serge Moscovici, eds., *Social Representations* (Cambridge: Cambridge University Press, 1984), pp. 3–69. See also Barry Barnes, *The Nature of Power* (Urbana: University of Illinois Press, 1988). Note that this is a considerably more socialized cognitivism than that found in much of the recent scholarship on the role of "ideas" in world politics, which tends to treat ideas as commodities that are held by individuals and intervene between the distribution of power and outcomes. For a form of cognitivism closer to my own, see Emanuel Adler, "Cognitive Evolution: A Dynamic namic Approach for the Study of International Relations and Their Progress," in Emanuel Adler and Beverly Crawford, eds., *Progress in Postwar International Relations* (New York: Columbia University Press, 1991), pp. 43–88.

17. Berger and Luckmann, *The Social Construction of Reality,* p. 58.

18. See Giddens, *Central Problems in Social Theory;* and Alexander Wendt and Raymond Duvall, "Institutions and International Order," in Ernst-Otto Czempiel and James Rosenau, eds., *Global Changes and Theoretical Challenges* (Lexington, MA: Lexington Books, 1989), pp. 51–74.

19. On the role of collective identity in reducing collective action problems, see Bruce Fireman and William Gamson, "Utilitarian Logic in the Resource Mobilization Perspective," in Mayer Zald and John McCarthy, eds., *The Dynamics of Social Movements*

(Cambridge, MA: Winthrop, 1979), pp. 8–44; Robyn Dawes et al., "Cooperation for the Benefit of Us—Not Me, or My Conscience," in Jane Mansbridge, ed., *Beyond Self-Interest* (Chicago: University of Chicago Press, 1990), pp. 97–110; and Craig Calhoun, "The Problem of Identity in Collective Action," in Joan Huber, ed., *Macro-Micro Linkages in Sociology* (Beverly Hills, CA: Sage, 1991), pp. 51–75.

20. See Thomas Risse-Kappen, "Are Democratic Alliances Special?" unpublished manuscript, Yale University, New Haven, CT, 1991. This line of argument could be expanded usefully in feminist terms. For a useful overview of the relational nature of feminist conceptions of self, see Paula England and Barbara Stanek Kilbourne, "Feminist Critiques of the Separative Model of Self: Implications for Rational Choice Theory," *Rationality and Society* 2 (April 1990), pp. 156–71. On feminist conceptualizations of power, see Ann Tickner, "Hans Morgenthau's Principles of Political Realism: A Feminist Reformulation," *Millennium* 17 (Winter 1988), pp. 429–40; and Thomas Wartenberg, "The Concept of Power in Feminist Theory," *Praxis International* 8 (October 1988), pp. 301–16.

21. Waltz, *Theory of International Politics*, p. 91.

22. See Waltz, *Man, the State, and War*; and Robert Jervis, "Cooperation Under the Security Dilemma," *World Politics* 30 (January 1978), pp. 167–214.

23. My argument here parallels Rousseau's critique of Hobbes. For an excellent critique of realist appropriations of Rousseau, see Michael Williams, "Rousseau, realism, and Realpolitik," *Millennium* 18 (Summer 1989), pp. 188–204. Williams argues that far from being a fundamental starting point in the state of nature, for Rousseau the stag hunt represented a stage in man's fall. On p. 190, Williams cites Rousseau's description of man prior to leaving the state of nature: "Man only knows himself; he does not see his own well-being to be identified with or contrary to that of anyone else; he neither hates anything nor loves anything; but limited to no more than physical instinct, he is no one, he is an animal." For another critique of Hobbes on the state of nature that parallels my constructivist reading of anarchy, see Charles Landesman, "Reflections on Hobbes: Anarchy and Human Nature," in Peter Caws, ed., *The Causes of Quarrel* (Boston: Beacon, 1989), pp. 139–48.

24. See Robert Grafstein, "Rational Choice: Theory and Institutions," in Kristen Monroe, ed., *The Economic Approach to Politics* (New York: Harper Collins, 1991), pp. 263–64. A good example of the promise and limits of transaction cost approaches to institutional analysis is offered by Robert Keohane in his *After Hegemony* (Princeton, NJ: Princeton University Press, 1984).

25. Mead's analysis of gestures remains definitive. See Mead's *Mind, Self, and Society*. See also the discussion of the role of signaling in the "mechanics of interaction" in Turner's *A Theory of Social Interaction*, pp. 74–79 and 92–115.

26. . . . On attributional processes in international relations, see Shawn Rosenberg and Gary Wolfsfeld, "International Conflict and the Problem of Attribution," *Journal of Conflict Resolution* 21 (March 1977), pp. 75–103.

27. The following articles by Noel Kaplowitz have made an important contribution to such thinking in international relations: "Psychopolitical Dimensions of International Relations: The Reciprocal Effects of Conflict Strategies," *International Studies Quarterly* 28 (December 1984), pp. 373–406; and "National Self-Images, Perception of Enemies, and Conflict Strategies: Psychopolitical Dimensions of International Relations," *Political Psychology* 11 (March 1990), pp. 39–82.

28. These arguments are common in theories of narcissism and altruism. See Heinz Kohut, *Self-Psychology and the Humanities* (New York: Norton, 1985); and Martin Hoffmann, "Empathy, Its Limitations, and Its Role in a Comprehensive Moral Theory," in William

Kurtines and Jacob Gewirtz, eds., *Morality, Moral Behavior, and Moral Development* (New York: Wiley, 1984), pp. 283–302.

29. See C. Norman Alexander and Mary Glenn Wiley, "Situated Activity and Identity Formation," in Morris Rosenberg and Ralph Turner, eds., *Social Psychology: Sociological Perspectives* (New York: Basic Books, 1981), pp. 269–89.

30. See Richard Ashley, "Untying the Sovereign State: A Double Reading of the Anarchy Problematique," *Millennium* 17 (Summer 1988), pp. 227–62. . . .

31. See William Coplin, "International Law and Assumptions About the State System," *World Politics* 17 (July 1965), pp. 615–34.

32. David Strang, "Anomaly and Commonplace in European Expansion: Realist and Institutional Accounts," *International Organization* 45 (Spring 1991), pp. 143–62.

33. On "European identity," see Barry Buzan et al., eds., *The European Security Order Recast* (London: Pinter, 1990), pp. 45–63.

34. On the difficulties of creating cooperative security regimes given competitive interests, see Robert Jervis, "Security Regimes," in Stephen D. Krasner, ed., *International Regimes* (Ithaca, NY: Cornell University Press, 1983), pp. 173–94; and Charles Lipson, "International Cooperation in Economic and Security Affairs," *World Politics* 37 (October 1984), pp. 1–23.

35. See Mead, *Mind, Self, and Society.* For useful discussions of this distinction and its implications for notions of creativity in social systems, see George Cronk, *The Philosophical Anthropology of George Herbert Mead* (New York: Peter Lang, 1987), pp. 36–40; and Judith Howard, "From Changing Selves Toward Changing Society," in Judith Howard and Peter Callero, eds., *The Self-Society Dynamic* (Cambridge: Cambridge University Press, 1991).

36. For useful overviews of New Thinking, see Mikhail Gorbachev, *Perestroika: New Thinking for Our Country and the World* (New York: Harper & Row, 1987); Vendulka Kubalkova and Albert Cruickshank, *Thinking New About Soviet "New Thinking"* (Berkeley: Institute of International Studies, 1989); and Allen Lynch, *Gorbachev's International Outlook: Intellectual Origins and Political Consequences* (New York: Institute for East–West Security Studies, 1989). It is not clear to what extent New Thinking is a conscious policy as opposed to an ad hoc policy. The intense theoretical and policy debate within the Soviet Union over New Thinking and the frequently stated idea of taking away the Western "excuse" for fearing the Soviet Union both suggest the former, but I will remain agnostic here and simply assume that it can be fruitfully interpreted "as if" it had the form that I describe.

37. See Daniel Bar-Tal et al., "Conflict Termination: An Epistemological Analysis of International Cases," *Political Psychology* 10 (June 1989), pp. 233–55. For an unrelated but interesting illustration of how changing cognitions in turn make possible organizational change, see Jean Bartunek, "Changing Interpretive Schemes and Organizational Restructuring: The Example of a Religious Order," *Administrative Science Quarterly* 29 (September 1984), pp. 355–72.

38. See Goffman, *The Presentation of Self in Everyday Life;* Eugene Weinstein and Paul Deutschberger, "Some Dimensions of Altercasting," *Sociometry* 26 (December 1963), pp. 454–66; and Walter Earle, "International Relations and the Psychology of Control: Alternative Control Strategies and Their Consequences," *Political Psychology* 7 (June 1986), pp. 369–75.

International Organization: A State of the Art on an Art of the State

FRIEDRICH KRATOCHWIL and JOHN GERARD RUGGIE

International organization as a field of study has had its ups and downs. . . . In the interwar period, the fate of the field reflected the fate of the world it studied: a creative burst of work on "international government" after 1919, followed by a period of more cautious reassessment approaching the 1930s, and a gradual decline into irrelevance if not obscurity thereafter. . . . The fate of theory and the fate of practice were never all that closely linked after World War II. Indeed, it is possible to argue, with only slight exaggeration, that in recent years they have become inversely related: the academic study of international organization is more interesting, vibrant, and even compelling than ever before, whereas the world of actual international organizations has deteriorated in efficacy and performance. Today, international organization as a field of study is an area where the action is; few would so characterize international organizations as a field of practice.

Our purpose in this article is to try to figure out how and why the doctors can be thriving when the patient is moribund. To anticipate the answer without, we hope, unduly straining the metaphor, the reason is that the leading doctors have become biochemists and have stopped treating and in most cases even seeing patients. . . .

What we are suggesting, to pose the issue more directly, is that students of international organization have shifted their focus systematically away from international institutions, toward broader forms of international institutionalized behavior. We further contend that this shift does not represent a haphazard sequence of theoretical or topical "fads" but is rooted in a "core concern" or a set of puzzles which gives coherence and identity to this field of study.[1] The substantive core around which the various theoretical approaches have clustered is the problem of international governance. And the observable shifts in analytical foci can be understood as "progressive problem shifts," in the sense of Imre Lakatos's criterion for the heuristic fruitfulness of a research program.[2] This evolution has brought the field to its current focus on the concept of international regimes. To fully realize its potential, the research program must now seek to resolve some serious anomalies in the regime approach and to link up the informal ordering devices of international regimes with the formal institutional mechanisms of international organizations.

In the first section of this article, we present a review of the literature in order to trace its evolution. This review draws heavily on articles published in *International Organization*, the leading journal in the field since its first appearance in 1947, and a source that not only reflects but in considerable measure is also responsible for the evolution of the field. The second section critiques the currently prevalent epistemological practices in regime analysis and points toward lines of inquiry which might enhance the productive potential of the concept as an analytical tool. Finally, we briefly suggest a means of systematically linking up regimes and formal organizations in a manner that is already implicit in the literature.

PROGRESSIVE ANALYTICAL SHIFTS

As a field of study, international organization has always concerned itself with the same phenomenon: in the words of a 1931 text, it is an attempt to describe and explain "how the modern Society of Nations governs itself."[3] In that text, the essence of government was assumed to comprise the coordination of group activities so as to conduct the public business, and the particular feature distinguishing international government was taken to lie in the necessity that it be consistent with national sovereignty. . . .

However, there have been identifiable shifts in how the phenomenon of international governance has been conceived, especially since World War II—so much so that the field is often described as being in permanent search of its own "dependent variable." Our reading of the literature reveals four major analytical foci, which we would place in roughly the following logical—and more or less chronological—order.

Formal Institutions

The first is a formal institutional focus. Within it, the assumption was made or the premise was implicit that (1) international governance is whatever international organizations do; and (2) the formal attributes of international organizations, such as their charters, voting procedures, committee structures, and the like, account for what they do. To the extent that the actual operation of institutions was explored, the frame of reference was their constitutional mandate, and the purpose of the exercise was to discover how closely it was approximated.[4]

Institutional Processes

The second analytical focus concerns the actual decision-making processes within international organizations. The assumption was gradually abandoned that the formal arrangements of international organizations explain what they do. This perspective originally emerged in the attempt to come to grips with the increasingly obvious discrepancies between constitutional designs and organizational practices. . . .

Over time, this perspective became more generalized, to explore overall patterns of influence shaping organizational outcomes.[5] The sources of influence which have been investigated include the power and prestige of individual states, the formation and functioning of the group system, organizational leadership positions, and bureaucratic politics. The outcomes that analysts have sought to explain have ranged from specific resolutions, programs, and budgets, to broader voting alignment and the general orientation of one or more international institutions.

Organizational Role

In this third perspective, another assumption of the formal institutionalist approach was abandoned, namely, that international governance *is* whatever international organizations *do*. Instead, the focus shifted to the actual and potential roles of international organizations in a more broadly conceived process of international governance.[6] This perspective in turn subsumes three distinct clusters.

In the first cluster, the emphasis was on the roles of international organizations in the resolution of substantive international problems. Preventive diplomacy and peace-keeping were two such roles in the area of peace and security,[7] nuclear safeguarding by the International Atomic Energy Agency (IAEA) was another.[8] Facilitating decolonization received a good deal of attention in the political realm,[9] providing multilateral development assistance in the economic realm.[10] The potential role of international organizations in restructuring North-South relations preoccupied a substantial number of scholars throughout the 1970s,[11] as did the possible contributions of international organizations to managing the so-called global commons. . . .[12]

The second cluster of the organizational-role perspective shifted the focus away from the solution of substantive problems per se, toward certain long-term institutional consequences of the failure to solve substantive problems through the available institutional means. This, of course, was the integrationist focus, particularly the neofunctionalist variety.[13] It was fueled by the fact that the jurisdictional scope of both the state and existing international organizations was increasingly outstripped by the functional scope of international problems. And it sought to explore the extent to which institutional adaptations to this fact might be conducive to the emergence of political forms "beyond the nation state. . . ."[14]

The third cluster within the organizational-role perspective began with a critique of the transformational expectations of integration theory and then shifted the focus onto a more general concern with how international institutions "reflect and to some extent magnify or modify" the characteristic features of the international system.[15] Here, international organizations have been viewed as potential dispensers of collective legitimacy,[16] vehicles in the international politics of agenda formation,[17] forums for the creation of transgovernmental coalitions as well as instruments of transgovernmental policy coordination,[18] and as means through which the global dominance structure is enhanced or can possibly come to be undermined.[19]

The theme that unifies all works of this genre is that the process of global governance is not coterminous with the activities of international organizations but that these organizations do play some role in that broader process. The objective was to identify their role.

International Regimes

The current preoccupation in the field is with the phenomenon of international regimes. Regimes are broadly defined as governing arrangements constructed by states to coordinate their expectations and organize aspects of international behavior in various issue-areas. They thus comprise a normative element, state practice, and organizational roles. . . . The focus on regimes was a direct response both to the intellectual odyssey that we have just traced as well as to certain developments in the world of international relations from the 1970s on.

When the presumed identity between international organizations and international governance was explicitly rejected, the precise roles of organizations *in* international governance became a central concern. But, apart from the focus on integration, no overarching conception was developed *of* international governance itself. And the integrationists themselves soon abandoned their early notions, ending up with a formulation of integration that did little more than recapitulate the condition of interdependence which was assumed to trigger integration in the first place.[20] Thus, for a time the field of international organization lacked any systematic conception of its traditional analytical core: international governance. The introduction of the concept of regimes reflected an attempt to fill this void. International regimes were thought to express both the parameters and the perimeters of international governance.[21]

The impact of international affairs during the 1970s and beyond came in the form of an anomaly for which no ready-made explanation was at hand. Important changes occurred in the international system, associated with the relative decline of U.S. hegemony: the achievement of nuclear parity by the Soviet Union; the economic resurgence of Europe and Japan; the success of OPEC together with the severe international economic dislocations that followed it. Specific agreements that had been negotiated after World War II were violated, and institutional arrangements, in money and trade above all, came under enormous strain. Yet—and here is the anomaly—governments on the whole did not respond to the difficulties confronting them in beggar-thy-neighbor terms. Neither systemic factors nor formal institutions alone apparently could account for this outcome. One way to resolve the anomaly was to question the extent to which U.S. hegemony in point of fact had eroded.[22] Another, and by no means entirely incompatible, route was via the concept of international regimes. The argument was advanced that regimes continued in some measure to constrain and condition the behavior of states toward one another, despite systemic change and institutional erosion. In this light, international regimes were seen to enjoy a degree of relative autonomy, though of an unknown duration.[23]

In sum, in order to resolve both disciplinary and real-world puzzles, the process of international governance has come to be associated with the concept of international regimes, occupying an ontological space somewhere between the level of formal institutions on the one hand and systemic factors on the other. Hence, the notion that the concern with international regimes is but another academic fad from which the field has suffered throughout the postwar period itself betrays a misunderstanding of the considerable intellectual continuity that has brought the field to the present point. . . .[24]

Conflict and Cooperation

These shifts in analytical foci have been accompanied by an analytical shift of a very different sort, perhaps most clearly expressed in the premises of recent methodological approaches. Take the rational-choice approach as one instance.[25]

It raises the promise and offers the possibility that two strands of thinking about international relations which have been distinct if not oppositional in the past may become unified. Typically, the opposition has been expressed in the conflict/cooperation dichotomy. . . . Moreover, it has been inferred from this premise that these two realms of international life require (from the vantage point of conflict studies) or make possible (from the vantage point of cooperation studies) two very different modes of analysis. Realism and to a lesser extent Marxism have tended to dominate the former strand, and liberalism in its many guises— Ricardian trade theory, Wilsonian idealism, functionalism, and interdependence imperatives—the latter.

What we find in the recent literature inspired by the rational-choice perspective, on the contrary, is the claim that *both* conflict *and* cooperation can be explained by a *single* logical apparatus.[26] Moreover, the differences between the two branches now are understood to reflect situational determinants not structural determinants. . . . Interestingly, developments in some neo-Marxist approaches have proceeded on precisely analogous lines, insofar as the traditional opposites, unity and rivalry, have been collapsed within a single "world system" framework. . . . Approaches informed by hermeneutics and language philosophy are reaching much the same conclusions as well.[27] And in each case, the concept of regimes is found to be a useful focal point for analysis.

In summary, that branch of the study of international relations which calls itself international organization is lively and productive. It is once again focusing squarely on the phenomenon of international governance, and it is pursuing its object of study in innovative ways that are bringing it closer to the theoretical core of more general international relations work. These are no mean accomplishments. And they are not diminished by the fact that serious problems remain to be resolved.

PROBLEMS IN THE PRACTICE OF REGIME ANALYSIS

One of the major criticisms made of the regimes concept is its "wooliness" and "imprecision."[28] The point is well taken. There is no agreement in the literature even on such basic issues as boundary conditions: Where does one regime end and another begin? What is the threshold between nonregime and regime? Embedding regimes in "meta-regimes," or "nesting" one within another, typifies the problem; it does not resolve it. . . .[29]

The only cure for wooliness and imprecision is, of course, to make the concept of regimes less so. Definitions can still be refined, but only up to a point. Two fundamental impediments stand in the way. One is absolute: ultimately, there exists no external Archimedian point from which regimes can be viewed as they "truly" are. This is so because regimes are conceptual creations not concrete entities. As with any analytical construction in the human sciences, the concept of regimes will reflect commonsense understandings, actor preferences, and the particular purposes for which analyses are undertaken. Ultimately, therefore, the concept of regimes, like the concept of "power," or "state," or "revolution," will remain a "contestable concept."[30]

Well short of this absolute impediment stands another. It is not insuperable, but a great deal of work will have to be done in order to overcome it. The problem is this: the practice of regime analysis is wracked by epistemological anomalies—anomalies that more often than not go unnoticed in the literature. These anomalies debilitate any endeavor to achieve clarity and precision in the concept of regimes and to enhance its productive capacity as an analytical tool. In the paragraphs that follow, we flag three related epistemological problem areas. . . .

Ontology Versus Epistemology

International regimes are commonly defined as social institutions around which expectations converge in international issue-areas. The emphasis on convergent expectations as the constitutive basis of regimes gives regimes an inescapable intersubjective quality. It follows that we *know* regimes by their principled and shared understandings of desirable and acceptable forms of social behavior. Hence, the ontology of regimes rests upon a strong element of intersubjectivity.

Now, consider the fact that the prevailing epistemological position in regime analysis is almost entirely positivistic in orientation. Before it does anything else, positivism posits a radical separation of subject and object. It then focuses on the "objective" forces that move actors in their social interactions. Finally, intersubjective meaning, where it is considered at all, is inferred from behavior.

Here, then, we have the most debilitating problem of all: epistemology fundamentally contradicts ontology! Small wonder that so much disagreement exists on what should be fairly straightforward empirical questions: Did Bretton Woods "collapse" in 1971–73, or was the change "norm governed"? Are recent trade restraints indicative of dangerous protectionism or not? . . .

In many such puzzling instances, actor *behavior* has failed adequately to convey intersubjective *meaning*. And intersubjective meaning, in turn, seems to have had considerable influence on actor behavior. It is precisely this factor that limits the practical utility of the otherwise fascinating insights into the collaborative potential of rational egoists which are derived from laboratory or game-theoretic situations.[31] To put the problem in its simplest terms: in the simulated world, actors cannot communicate *and* engage in behavior; they are condemned to communicate *through* behavior. In the real world, the situation of course differs fundamentally. Here, the very essence of international regimes is expressed in cases such as that of France in 1968, asking for "sympathy and understanding" from its trading partners, as France invoked emergency measures against imports after the May disturbances of that year—and getting both from GATT (General Agreement on Tariffs and Trade) even though *no* objective basis existed in fact or in GATT law for doing so. But a positivist epistemology simply cannot accommodate itself to so intersubjective an ontology. Hence, the case is treated in the literature as illustrating cynicism, complicity, and the erosion of respect for the GATT regime.[32]

The contradiction between ontology and epistemology has elicited surprisingly little concern in the regimes literature. Once it is realized just how problematical the contradiction is, however, what options exist to deal with it? One possibility would be to try to deny it somehow. Theodore Abel's classic neopositivist response to the challenge posed by Weber's concept of *Verstehen* might ʒ as a model: the concept aids in "the context discovery," Abel contended, but mately it is not a method relevant to "the context of validation." Hence it poses no challenge.[33] This response may have been viable a generation ago, but it no longer is. Interpretive epistemologies . . . are simply too well developed today to be easily dismissed by charges of subjectivism[34]—or . . . of idealism.

A second possibility would be to try to formulate a rendition of the intersubjective ontology which is compatible with positivist epistemology. In view of the influence currently enjoyed in international relations theory by analogies and metaphors drawn from microeconomics, one plausible means of executing this maneuver would be to follow the economists down the road of "revealed preferences"—that consumption behavior, for example, reveals true consumer preferences. If our epistemology does not enable us to uncover meaning, the analogous reasoning would hold, then let us look for "revealed meaning," that is, for "objective" surrogates. It should suffice to point out that this is a solution by displacement: it displaces the problem into the realm of assumption—namely that "objective" surrogates can capture "intersubjective" reality—which of course is not uncharacteristic of the manner in which economists handle difficult problems.

That leaves us with the third and only viable option, of opening up the positivist epistemology to more interpretive strains, more closely attuned to the reality of regimes. . . .

Norms in Explanation

There is a closely related problem having to do with models of explanation. The standard positivist model works with an initial condition plus a covering law, on the basis of which it hypothesizes or predicts an occurrence. Even a single counterfactual occurrence may be taken to refute the covering law.[35] (A probabilistic formulation would, of course, appropriately modify the criteria for refutation, but it would not alter the basic structure of the explanation.)

Now consider the fact that what distinguishes international regimes from other international phenomena—from strategic interaction, let us say—is a specifically normative element.[36] Indeed, one of the four analytical components of the concept of regimes is specified to be norms—"standards of behavior defined in terms of rights and obligations." And it has become customary to maintain that change in the normative structure of regimes produces change *of,* as opposed merely to *within,* regimes.[37]

The positivist model of explanation is not easily applied to cases in which norms, so defined, are a significant element in the phenomena to be explained. . . . Two problems in particular need to be raised.[38]

First, unlike the initial conditions in positivist explanations, norms can be thought of only with great difficulty as "causing" occurrences. Norms may "guide" behavior, they may "inspire" behavior, they may "rationalize" or "justify" behavior, they may express "mutual expectations" about behavior, or they may be ignored. But they do not effect cause in the sense that a bullet through the heart causes death or an uncontrolled surge in the money supply causes price inflation.

Hence, where norms are involved, the first component of the positivist model of explanation is problematical.

The second is even more so. For norms are counterfactually valid. No single counterfactual occurrence refutes a norm. Not even many such occurrences necessarily do. Does driving while under the influence of alcohol refute the law (norm) against drunk driving? Does it when half the population is implicated? To be sure, the law (norm) is *violated* thereby. But whether or not violations also invalidate or refute a law (norm) will depend upon a host of other factors, not the least of which is how the community assesses the violation and responds to it. What is true of drunk driving is equally true of the norms of nondiscrimination in international trade, free and stable currency exchanges, and adequate compensation for expropriated foreign property. . . .

Let it be understood that we are not advocating a coup whereby the reign of positivist explanation is replaced by explanatory anarchy. But we would insist that, just as epistemology has to match ontology, so too does the explanatory model have to be compatible with the basic nature of the particular scientific enterprise at hand. The impact of norms within international regimes is not a passive process, which can be ascertained analogously to that of Newtonian laws governing the collision of two bodies. Hence, the common practice of treating norms as "variables"—be they independent, dependent, intervening, or otherwise—should be severely curtailed. So too should be the preoccupation with the "violation" of norms as the beginning, middle, and end of the compliance story. Precisely because state behavior within regimes *is* interpreted by other states, the rationales and justifications for behavior which are proffered, together with pleas for understanding or admissions of guilt, as well as the responsiveness to such reasoning on the part of other states, all are absolutely critical component parts of any explanation involving the efficacy of norms. Indeed, such communicative dynamics may tell us far more about how robust a regime is than overt behavior alone. And only where noncompliance is widespread, persistent, and unexcused—that is, presumably, in limiting cases—will an explanatory model that rests on overt behavior alone suffice.[39]

To be sure, communicative dynamics may be influenced by such extracontextual factors as state power, but that is no warrant for ignoring them. On the contrary, it suggests a potentially important relationship to be explored.[40] Similarly, the fact that verbal behavior may lend itself to manipulation suggests only that it be treated as judiciously as any other piece of scientific evidence.

The Hierarchy of Analytical Components

The concept of international regimes is said to be a composite of four analytical component parts: principles ("beliefs of fact, causation, and rectitude"), norms ("standards of behavior defined in terms of rights and obligations"), rules ("specific prescriptions and proscriptions for action"), and decision-making procedures ("prevailing practices for making and implementing collective choice").[41] At first blush, the four fit together neatly in the specific case that was uppermost in everyone's mind when this conception was initially hammered out: the GATT-based trade regime.[42] The principle that liberalized trade is good for global welfare and international peace was readily translated by states into such norms as nondiscrimination, which in turn suggested the most-favored-nation rule, all of which led to negotiated tariff reductions based on reciprocal concessions. But matters were complicated right from the start by the fact that GATT contained not one but at least *two* such "scripts," and that the second stood in stark contrast to the first. The second ran from the responsibility of governments to stabilize their domestic economies on through the norm of safeguarding the balance of payments and, under certain circumstances, domestic producers, to rules defining specific GATT safeguarding provisions, and finally to establishing mechanisms of multilateral surveillance over their operations.[43] Different governments of course weighted these two scripts differently, but over time they seem not to have been unduly perturbed by the need to live with the ambiguity of their juxtaposition. Ambiguity, however, *is* more troublesome for analysts, *even when* it is a deliberate creation of policy makers.[44] And therein lies another epistemological tale.

The notion still prevails in the regimes literature that the four analytical components are related instrumentally and that the greater the coherence among them is, the stronger the regime will be.[45] There is an a priori attractiveness to this notion, in the sense that our collective research program would be eased considerably were it to obtain. But reality is not so obliging. Let us take up first the instrumentalist idea.

A basic epistemological problem with instrumentalism is its presumption that it is always possible to separate goals (presumably expressed in principles and norms) from means (presumably expressed in rules and procedures), and to order them in a superordinate-subordinate relationship. But this relationship need not hold. As R. S. Summers has aptly remarked: "However true this might be of constructing houses or other artifacts, it is not always so in law. In law when available means limit and in part define the goal, the means and the goal thus defined are to that extent inseparable." . . .[46] Thus, notions such as reciprocity in the trade regime are *neither* its ends *nor* its means: in a quintessential way, they *are* the regime—they *are* the principled and shared understandings that the regime comprises.

The idea that the four regime components should also be coherent, and that coherence indicates regime strength, is even more profoundly problematical. The basic epistemological problem with this notion is its presumption that, once the machinery is in place, actors merely remain programmed by it. But this is clearly not so. Actors not only reproduce normative structures, they also change them by their very practice, as underlying conditions change, as new constraints or possibilities emerge, or as new claimants make their presence felt. Lawyers call this "interstitial lawmaking,"[47] and sociologists, the process of "structuration."[48] Only under extremely unusual circumstances could we imagine parallel and simultaneous changes having taken place in each of the four component parts of regimes such that they remained coherent—assuming that they were so at the outset. In any case the robustness of international regimes has little to do with how coherent they remain—how coherent is the very robust U.S. Constitution?—but depends on the extent to which evolving and even diverging practices of actors express principled reasoning and shared understandings.

We have now reached the same conclusion through three different routes: the conventional epistemological approaches in regime studies do not and cannot suffice. . . .

REGIMES AND ORGANIZATIONS

The progressive shift in the literature toward the study of international regimes has been guided by an abiding concern with the structures and processes of international governance. Despite remaining problems with this framework of analysis, the most serious of which were flagged in the previous section, a great deal has been accomplished in a relatively short span of time. Along the way, however, . . . international institutions of a formal kind have been left behind. This fact is of academic interest because of the ever-present danger of theory getting out of touch with practice. But it is also of more than academic interest. The Secretary General of the United Nations, to cite but one serious practical instance, has lamented that the malfunctioning of that institution seriously inhibits interstate collaboration in the peace and security field. . . .[49] In order for the research program of international regimes *both* to contribute to ongoing policy concerns *and* better reflect the complex and sometimes ambiguous policy realm, it is necessary to link up regimes in some fashion with the formal mechanisms through which real-world actors operate. In point of fact, the outlines of such linkages are already implicit in the regime approach. Our purpose in this final section is no more than to underscore the specific dimensions that are highlighted by an interpretive epistemology.

There has been a great deal of interest in the regimes literature recently in what can be described as the "organizational-design" approach. The key issue underlying this approach is to discern what range of international policy problems can best be handled by different kinds of institutional arrangements, such as simple norms of coordination, the reallocation of international property rights, or authoritative control through formal organizations. For example, an international fishing authority would probably be less appropriate and less able to avoid the early exhaustion of fisheries' stock than would be the ascription of exclusive property rights to states. Where problems of liability enter the picture, however, as in ship-based pollution, authoritative procedures for settling disputes would become necessary. The work of Oliver Williamson and William Ouchi is very suggestive here, demonstrating the relative efficacy of the institutionalization of behavior through "hierarchies" versus through transaction-based informal means. . . .[50]

For its part, an interpretive epistemology would emphasize three additional dimensions of the organizational-design issue. The intersubjective basis of international regimes suggests that *transparency* of actor behavior and expectations within regimes is one of their core requirements. And, as has been shown in such diverse issue-areas as international trade, investment, nuclear nonproliferation, and human rights, international organizations can be particularly effective instruments by which to create such transparency. . . .[51]

The second is *legitimation*. A regime can be perfectly rationally designed but erode because its legitimacy is undermined.[52] Or a regime that is a logical nonstarter can be the object of endless negotiations because a significant constituency views its aims to be legitimate.[53] If a regime enjoys both it is described as being "stable" or "hegemonic." The important point to note is that international organizations, because of their trappings of universality, are the major venue within which the global legitimation struggle over international regimes is carried out today. . . .

The third dimension we would describe as *epistemic*. Stephen Toulmin has posed the issue well: "The problem of human understanding is a twofold one. Man knows, and he is also conscious that he knows. We acquire, possess, and make use of our knowledge; but at the same time, we are aware of our own activities as knowers."[54] In the international arena, neither the processes whereby knowledge becomes more extensive nor the means whereby reflection on knowledge deepens are passive or automatic. They are intensely political. And for better or for worse, international organizations have maneuvered themselves into the position of being the vehicle through which both types of knowledge enter onto the international agenda. . . .[55]

In short, the institutional-design approach, complemented by a concern with transparency creation, the legitimation struggle, and epistemic politics, can push the heuristic fruitfulness of the regime research program "forward" yet another step, linking it "back" to the study of international organizations.

CONCLUSION

In this article, we set out to present a "state of the art" of the field of international organization circa 1985. Our conclusions can be restated very quickly. In the first section, we tried to dispel the notion that the field has been floundering from one "dependent variable" to another, as academic fashions have dictated. On the contrary, the analytical shifts have been progressive and cumulative and have been guided by an overriding concern with what has always preoccupied students of international organization: how the modern society of nations governs itself.

In the second section we pointed out, however, that the currently ascendant regimes approach is internally inconsistent in a manner that has deleterious effects. The reason for its inconsistency is the tension between its ontological posture and its prevailing epistemological practices. In contrast to the epistemological ideal of positivism, which insists on a separation of "object" and "subject," we proposed a more interpretive approach that would open up regime analysis to the communicative rather than merely the referential functions of norms in social interactions. Thus, what constitutes a breach of an obligation undertaken within a regime is not simply an "objective description" of a fact but an intersubjective appraisal. . . .

Finally, in our third section, we identified some linkages between the analytical construct of international regimes and the concrete entities of international organizations. Students of international organization have already assimilated from the organizational design school the lesson that the provision of routine and predictable policy frameworks is not synonymous with the construction of formal hierarchies. An interpretive epistemology would suggest further that international organizations can contribute to the effectiveness of informal ordering mechanisms, such as regimes, by their ability to enhance (or diminish) intersubjective expectations and normatively stabilized meanings, which are the very bases of regimes. International organizations do so, we pointed out, through the modalities of transparency creation, focusing the legitimation struggle, and devising future regime agendas via epistemic politics. Thus reinvigorated, the study of formal organizations may yet come to reinvigorate the practice of formal organizations.

NOTES

1. Thomas Kuhn uses the notion "sets of puzzles" in his discussion of preludes to paradigms; see Kuhn, *The Structure of Scientific Revolutions* (Chicago: University of Chicago Press, 1962), and *The Essential Tension* (Chicago: University of Chicago Press, 1977).

2. The criterion of the fruitfulness of a research program, and issues connected with progressive versus degenerate problem shifts, were introduced by Imre Lakatos, "Falsification and the Methodology of Scientific Research Programmes," in Lakatos and Alan Musgrave, eds., *Criticisms and the Growth of Knowledge* (Cambridge: Cambridge University Press, 1970).

3. Edmund C. Mower, *International Government* (Boston: Heath, 1931).

4. A distinguished contribution to this literature is Leland M. Goodrich and Anne P. Simons, *The United Nations and the Maintenance of International Peace and Security* (Washington, DC: Brookings, 1955). See also Klaus Knorr, "The Bretton Woods Institutions in Transition," *International Organization* [hereafter cited as *IO*] 2 (February 1948); Walter R. Sharp, "The Institutional Framework for Technical Assistance," *IO* 7 (August 1953); and Henri Rolin, "The International Court of Justice and Domestic Jurisdiction," *IO* 8 (February 1954).

5. The most comprehensive work in this genre remains Robert W. Cox and Harold K. Jacobson, eds., *The Anatomy of Influence: Decision Making in International Organization* (New Haven: Yale University Press, 1973).

6. Inis L. Claude's landmark text, *Swords into Plowshares* (New York: Random House, 1959), both signaled and contributed to this shift.

7. Lincoln P. Bloomfield, ed., *International Force—A Symposium, IO* 17 (Spring 1973); James M. Boyd, "Cyprus: Episode in Peacekeeping," *IO* 20 (Winter 1966); Robert O. Matthews, "The Suez Canal Dispute: A Case Study in Peaceful Settlement," *IO* 21 (Winter 1967); Yashpal Tandon, "Consensus and Authority behind UN Peacekeeping Operations," *IO* 21 (Spring 1967); David P. Forsythe, "United Nations Intervention in Conflict Situations Revisited: A Framework for Analysis," *IO* 23 (Winter 1969); John Gerard Ruggie, "Contingencies, Constraints, and Collective Security: Perspectives on UN Involvement in International Disputes," *IO* 28 (Summer 1974); and Ernst B. Haas, "Regime Decay: Conflict Management and International Organization, 1945–1981," *IO* 37 (Spring 1983).

8. Robert E. Pendley and Lawrence Scheinman, "International Safeguarding as Institutionalized Collective Behavior," in John Gerard Ruggie and Ernst B. Haas, eds., special issue on international responses to technology, *IO* 29 (Summer 1975); and Joseph S. Nye, "Maintaining a Non-Proliferation Regime," in George H. Quester, ed., special issue on nuclear nonproliferation, *IO* 35 (Winter 1981).

9. Ernst B. Haas, "The Attempt to Terminate Colonization: Acceptance of the UN Trusteeship System," *IO* 7 (February 1953); John Fletcher-Cooke, "Some Reflections

on the International Trusteeship System," *IO* 13 (Summer 1959); Harold K. Jacobson, "The United Nations and Colonialism: A Tentative Appraisal," *IO* 16 (Winter 1962); and David A. Kay, "The Politics of Decolonization: The New Nations and the United Nations Political Process," *IO* 21 (Autumn 1967).

10. Richard N. Gardner and Max F. Millikan, eds., special issue on international agencies and economic development, *IO* 22 (Winter 1968).

11. Among many other sources, see Branislav Gosovic and John Gerard Ruggie, "On the Creation of a New International Economic Order: Issue Linkage and the Seventh Special Session of the UN General Assembly," *IO* 30 (Spring 1976).

12. David A. Kay and Eugene B. Skolnikoff, eds., special issue on international institutions and the environmental crisis, *IO* 26 (Spring 1972); Ruggie and Haas, eds., special issue, *IO* 29 (Summer 1975); and Per Magnus Wijkman, "Managing the Global Commons," *IO* 36 (Summer 1982).

13. Various approaches to the study of integration were summarized and assessed in Leon N. Lindberg and Stuart A. Scheingold, eds., special issue on regional integration, *IO* 24 (Autumn 1970).

14. Ernst B. Haas, *Beyond the Nation State: Functionalism and International Organization* (Stanford: Stanford University Press, 1964).

15. The phrase is Stanley Hoffmann's in "International Organization and the International System," *IO* 24 (Summer 1970). A similar position was advanced earlier by Oran R. Young, "The United Nations and the International System," *IO* 22 (Autumn 1968).

16. Inis L. Claude, Jr., "Collective Legitimization as a Political Function of the United Nations," *IO* 20 (Summer 1966); cf. Jerome Slater, "The Limits of Legitimization in International Organizations: The Organization of American States and the Dominican Crisis," *IO* 23 (Winter 1969).

17. A representative sampling would include Kay and Skolnikoff, eds., special issue, *IO* 26 (Spring 1972); Robert Russell, "Transgovernmental Interaction in the International Monetary System, 1960–1972," *IO* 27 (Autumn 1973); Thomas Weiss and Robert Jordan, "Bureaucratic Politics and the World Food Conference," *World Politics* 28 (April 1976); Raymond F. Hopkins, "The International Role of 'Domestic' Bureaucracy," *IO* 30 (Summer 1976); and John Gerard Ruggie, "On the Problem of 'The Global Problematique': What Roles for International Organizations?" *Alternatives* 5 (January 1980).

18. The major analytical piece initiating this genre was Robert O. Keohane and Joseph S. Nye, "Transgovernmental Relations and International Organizations," *World Politics* 27 (October 1974); cf. their earlier edited work on transnational relations and world politics, *IO* 25 (Summer 1971).

19. Robert Cox's recent work has been at the forefront of exploring this aspect of international organization: "Labor and Hegemony," *IO* 31 (Summer 1977); "The Crisis of World Order and the Problem of International Organization in the 1980's," *International Journal* 35 (Spring 1980); and "Gramsci, Hegemony and International Relations: An Essay in Method," *Millennium: Journal of International Studies* 12 (Summer 1983).

20. Robert O. Keohane and Joseph S. Nye, "International Interdependence and Integration," in Fred I. Greenstein and Nelson W. Polsby, eds., *Handbook of Political Science,* vol. 8 (Reading, MA: Addison-Wesley, 1975). The point is also implicit in Ernst Haas's self-criticism, "Turbulent Fields and the Theory of Regional Integration," *IO* 30 (Spring 1976).

21. John Gerard Ruggie, "International Responses to Technology: Concepts and Trends," *IO* 29 (Summer 1975).

22. This is the tack taken by Susan Strange, "Still an Extraordinary Power: America's Role in a Global Monetary System," in Raymond E. Lombra and William E. Witte, eds.,

Political Economy of International and Domestic Monetary Relations (Ames: Iowa State University Press, 1982); and Bruce Russett, "The Mysterious Case of Vanishing Hegemony: Or, Is Mark Twain Really Dead?" *IO* 39 (Spring 1985).

23. See Stephen D. Krasner, "Introduction," in Stephen D. Krasner, ed., *International Regimes* (Ithaca, NY: Cornell University Press, 1983); and Robert O. Keohane, *After Hegemony* (Princeton: Princeton University Press, 1984), for discussions of this thesis.

24. The fad-fettish is argued by Susan Strange, "Cave! Hic Dragones: A Critique of Regime Analysis," in Krasner, ed., *International Regimes.*

25. The public-choice approach to the study of international organization began with the use of public goods theory in the early 1970s, went on to explore the theory of property rights later in the decade, and has come to focus on game theory and microeconomic theories of market failure to explain patterns of international governance. See, respectively, Bruce M. Russett and John D. Sullivan, "Collective Goods and International Organizations," *IO* 25 (Autumn 1971), and John Gerard Ruggie, "Collective Goods and Future International Collaboration," *American Political Science Review* 66 (September 1972); John A. C. Conybeare, "International Organization and the Theory of Property Rights," *IO* 34 (Summer 1980); and Keohane, *After Hegemony.* A useful review of the relevant literature may be found in Bruno S. Frey, "The Public Choice View of International Political Economy," *IO* 38 (Winter 1984).

26. In the context of rational-choice theory generally, the argument was first articulated by John Harsanyi, "Rational Choice Models of Political Behavior vs. Functionalist and Conformist Theories," *World Politics* 21 (July 1969). In the international relations literature, it is implicit in Robert Jervis, "Cooperation under the Security Dilemma," *World Politics* 30 (January 1978), and explicit in Robert Axelrod, "The Emergence of Cooperation among Egoists," *American Political Science Review* 75 (June 1981), as well as in Keohane, *After Hegemony.*

27. Richard K. Ashley, "The Poverty of Neorealism," *IO* 38 (Spring 1984), and Friedrich Kratochwil, "Errors Have Their Advantage," *IO* 38 (Spring 1984).

28. See Susan Strange, in Krasner, ed., *International Regimes.*

29. This route is taken by Vinod K. Aggarwal, *Liberal Protectionism: The International Politics of Organized Textile Trade* (Berkeley: University of California Press, 1985).

30. On "contestable concepts," see William Connally, *The Terms of Political Discourse,* 2d ed. (Princeton: Princeton University Press, 1983).

31. Most notable among such works is Robert Axelrod's *Evolution of Cooperation* (New York: Basic, 1984), and Axelrod, "Modeling the Evolution of Norms" (Paper delivered at the annual meeting of the American Political Science Association, New Orleans, 29 August–1 September 1985). For an attempt to incorporate progressively more "reflective" logical procedures into sequential Prisoner's Dilemma situations and to expose them to more realistic data sets, see Hayward R. Alker, James Bennett, and Dwain Mefford, "Generalized Precedent Logics for Resolving Insecurity Dilemmas," *International Interactions* 7, no. 2 (1980), and Hayward Alker and Akihiro Tanaka, "Resolution Possibilities in 'Historical' Prisoners' Dilemmas" (Paper delivered at the annual meeting of the International Studies Association, Philadelphia, 18 March 1981).

32. This case, and the more general problem of interpretation which it reflects, are discussed by John Gerard Ruggie, "International Regimes, Transactions, and Change: Embedded Liberalism in the Postwar Economic Order," in Krasner, ed., *International Regimes.*

33. Theodore F. Abel, "The Operation Called *Verstehen,*" *American Journal of Sociology* 54 (November 1948).

34. For a good selection of readings that begins with Weber, includes the neopositivist response, the Wittgensteinian school, phenomenology, and ethnomethodology, and

ends with hermeneutics and critical theory, see Fred R. Dallmayr and Thomas A. McCarthy, *Understanding and Social Inquiry* (Notre Dame: University of Notre Dame Press, 1977).

35. On the importance of the logical form of *modus tollens* in the hypothetical deductive explanation scheme, see Karl Popper, *The Logic of Scientific Discovery* (New York: Harper & Row, 1968), chaps. 3 and 4.

36. One of the distinctive characteristics of strategic interaction is that ultimately it rests upon a *unilateral* calculation of verbal and nonverbal cues: "A's expectation of B will include an estimation of B's expectations of A. This process of replication, it must be noted, is not an interaction between two states, but rather a process in which decision-makers in one state work out the consequences of their beliefs about the world; a world they believe to include decision-makers in other states, also working out the consequences of their beliefs. The expectations which are so formed are the expectations of one state, but they refer to other states." Paul Keal, *Unspoken Rules and Superpower Dominance* (London: Macmillan, 1984), p. 31.

37. See Krasner, "Introduction," *International Regimes.*

38. Some of these and related issues are discussed more extensively in Kratochwil, "The Force of Prescriptions," *IO* 38 (Autumn 1984).

39. Account should also be taken of that fact that different types of norms—implicit versus explicit, constraining versus enabling, and so on—function differently in social relations. Consult Edna Ullman-Margalit, *The Emergence of Norms* (Oxford: Clarendon, 1977), and H. L. A. Hart, *The Concept of Law* (Oxford: Oxford University Press, 1961). Moreover, compliance too is a variegated and complex phenomenon, as discussed by Oran R. Young, *Compliance and Public Authority* (Baltimore: Johns Hopkins University Press, 1979).

40. It is well established that the so-called hegemonic stability thesis, for example, leaves a good deal about regimes still to be accounted for. See the original formulation and test by Robert O. Keohane, "Theory of Hegemonic Stability and Changes in International Economic Regimes," in Ole Holsti et al., eds., *Change in the International System* (Boulder: Westview, 1980); and, most recently, Duncan Snidal, "The Limits of Hegemonic Stability Theory," *IO* 39 (Autumn 1985).

41. Krasner, "Introduction," *International Regimes,* p. 2.

42. These issues were discussed at length at the October 1980 UCLA conference in preparation for the regimes book edited by Krasner.

43. The interplay between these two scripts forms the basis of Ruggie's interpretation of the postwar trade and monetary regimes presented in "Embedded Liberalism."

44. The proclivity of international relations theorists to resolve ambiguity and contradiction in images of international order, and the schema on the basis of which they do so, are explored by John Gerard Ruggie, "Changing Frameworks of International Collective Behavior: On the Complementarity of Contradictory Tendencies," in Nazli Choucri and Thomas Robinson, eds., *Forecasting in International Relations* (San Francisco: Freeman, 1978).

45. Cf. Haas, "Regime Decay."

46. R. S. Summers, "Naive Instrumentalism and the Law," in P. S. Hacker and J. Raz, eds., *Law, Morality, and Society* (Oxford: Clarendon, 1977).

47. This is simply another name for the role of precedent in legal interpretation and development.

48. Anthony Giddens, *A Contemporary Critique of Historical Materialism* (Berkeley: University of California Press, 1981), p. 19: "According to the theory of structuration, all social action consists of social practices, situated in time-space, and organized in a skilled and knowledgeable fashion by human agents. But such knowledgeability is always

'bounded' by unacknowledged conditions of action on the one side, and unintended consequences of action on the other. . . . By the duality of structure I mean that the structured properties of social systems are simultaneously the *medium and outcome of social acts.*"

49. United Nations, *Report of the Secretary-General on the Work of the Organization, 1982* (A/37/1).

50. Oliver Williamson, *Markets and Hierarchies* (New York: Free, 1975), and William Ouchi and Oliver Williamson, "The Markets and Hierarchies Program of Research: Origins, Implications, Prospects," in William Joyce and Andrew van de Ven, eds., *Organization Design* (New York: Wiley, 1981). From the legal literature, see Cuido Calabresi and Douglas Melamed, "Property Rules, Liability Rules, and Inalienability: One View of the Cathedral," *Harvard Law Review* 85 (April 1972); Philip Heyemann, "The Problem of Coordination: Bargaining with Rules," *Harvard Law Review* 86 (March 1973); and Susan Rose-Ackerman, "Inalienability and the Theory of Property Rights," *Columbia Law Review* 85 (June 1985).

51. The GATT multilateral surveillance mechanisms are, of course, its chief institutional means of establishing intersubjectively acceptable interpretations of what actors are up to. For a treatment of investment which highlights this dimension, see Charles Lipson, *Standing Guard: Protecting Foreign Capital in the Nineteenth and Twentieth Centuries* (Berkeley: University of California Press, 1985); for nonproliferation, see Nye, "Maintaining a Nonproliferation Regime," and for human rights, John Gerard Ruggie, "Human Rights and the Future International Community," *Daedalus* 112 (Fall 1983). The impact of intergovernmental information systems is analyzed by Ernst B. Haas and John Gerard Ruggie, "What Message in the Medium of Information Systems?" *International Studies Quarterly* 26 (June 1982).

52. Puchala and Hopkins, "International Regimes," in Krasner, ed., *International Regimes,* discuss the decline of colonialism in terms that include this dimension.

53. The New International Economic Order is a prime example.

54. Stephen Toulmin, *Human Understanding* (Princeton: Princeton University Press, 1972), p. 1.

55. Ruggie analyzes this process in "On the Problem of 'The Global Problematique.'"

CHAPTER 2

International Institutions and the Practice of Cooperation

This chapter addresses the issue of international collaboration. It lays out some of the key theoretical perspectives on this topic and then analyzes collaboration within the European system and the international system. From the standpoint of practical politics, the historical experiences of World War I, the interwar period, and the multilateral order that emerged after World War II have had a particularly important influence on existing international regimes. But increasing interdependencies between countries and the process of globalization placed strains on various regimes. It is useful to examine how the organizational framework put in place over the past half century has responded to these challenges and whether these responses are adequate.

The case for regimes can be made from various theoretical perspectives. In general, regime theorists argue that international interactions depend on the expectations of actors, and that the norms and rules of a regime help to shape and stabilize expectations. Thus, even from the standpoint of realist theories, which tend to place little emphasis on international institutions, regimes can serve a useful function. A politically powerful state, for example, is likely to prefer the establishment of rules and norms that inform weaker countries about what it views as permissible conduct—and that promote such conduct—over having to monitor the behavior of these countries and intervene whenever its interests are at stake. Of course, this does not mean that the rules and norms serve the interests of weaker states. Indeed, it is quite likely that these rules will reflect the preferences of the most powerful countries. Nevertheless, it is through the existence of such rules that an "economy" of force is achieved. Instead of *ex post* punishment, international order can be facilitated through the *ex ante* structuring of actors' expectations.

From the liberal perspective, however, focusing primarily on the coercive function of norms is too limiting. For liberals, the realization of joint gains is facilitated by the existence of rules that also lower the costs of international transactions. Unlike realists, who emphasize the factors determining whether regimes will be supplied, liberals focus on the demand for regimes, irrespective of whether a hegemon exists and enforces them. One influential insight that emerges from research by liberals is that because a small group of states can often benefit from the adoption of certain rules and norms, they might be willing to establish and maintain international regimes, even in the absence of a hegemon. As such, liberal theory shifts attention from enforcement of rules and norms to the identification of joint gains that a regime could help to generate.

Furthermore, as liberals like David Hume have pointed out, not all situations in international affairs resemble Prisoners' Dilemmas. Many situations resemble games of coordination, in which the interests of actors do not diverge, but actors still need rules to determine exactly how to solve their coordination problem. Thus, nobody will much care whether cars drive on the left or on the right side of the road, but they care a great deal about the need for some rules of the road to stabilize behavior.

Cognitivists and constructivists also have studied international collaboration. Cognitivists and constructivists agree that the objects of the social world are not simply given; instead they are created through the experiences and understandings of actors. But these schools of thought do not necessarily share the same methodological orientation. Constructivist accounts emphasize "understanding" as opposed to "explanation" (as in positivist accounts, like those of liberals and realists). In terms of international regimes, they focus on the question of how issue-areas are defined, on the role that knowledge plays in such a construction, and on how learning feeds back into the design of international regimes.

The articles in this chapter elaborate on these themes. Robert Keohane's article focuses on the differences between two approaches to international institutions. One is "rationalist." This approach emphasizes instrumental reasoning characteristic of the Hobbesian and liberal paradigms, where goals are determined by tastes or preferences that are taken as given. Institutions promote cooperation, in the view of this school of thought, by affecting how states calculate the costs and benefits associated with taking particular actions. The other approach is "reflective." In a more sociological vein, it stresses the intersubjective character of our understandings—whether individuals and decision makers have similar understandings of events and actions in international affairs. These understandings, in turn, provide the basis for international cooperation by establishing both constitutive rules (those that enable actions to take place by establishing what is legal or permissible) and regulative rules (those that constrain the behavior of actors by prohibiting certain actions).

Stephen Krasner's seminal article initiated the debate over international regimes and is written from a realist perspective. In it, he advances a widely used definition of regimes. Namely, regimes are a "set of implicit or explicit principles, norms, rules, and decision-making procedures around which actors' expectations converge" (p. 73). For Krasner, a key question is why the multilateral institutions that were undergirded by U.S. hegemony in the post–World War II era continued to perform quite well as American power waned in the 1970s. He is also concerned with how to conceptualize the influence of regimes on behavior within a positivist framework. Krasner argues that regimes are intervening variables that mediate between the underlying power structure and the choices of states. But he allows for a more autonomous role of norms (in the form of drawing a contrast between rules and principles) when distinguishing between change *within* regimes and changes *of* regimes.

Ernst Haas's article addresses how issues emerge on the international landscape. Haas focuses less on the rational design of institutions than on the dynamics of negotiation and learning that lead to the formation of an international regime. Two factors are particularly important in studying these dynamics: the cognitive style of decision makers and the way in which issue linkage occurs. Furthermore, since regimes link facts and values, questions of how "consensual knowledge" evolve are crucial. For Haas, knowledge is not simply a means to help actors achieve their preferences. Knowledge also has a social and political dimension that involves changing the preferences of actors. To that extent, whether institutions are successful and effective depends in large measure on whether they are able to control or transform their environment.

Friedrich Kratochwil's article addresses the historical dimension of organizational activity in the international arena. He focuses on two episodes of the constitutional engineering of international institutions. The first took place after World War I; the other took place after World War II. He shows that the "Versailles" design of international institutions was seriously flawed because it could not address the changing nature of state goals after World War I. Equally, it was seriously flawed by the contradictory economic and security policies that the victorious powers adopted via defeated Germany. The second episode was much more successful because it inhibited states from taking unilateral measures that would undermine the multilateral order and because it helped to resolve long-standing security problems between Germany and France by increasing their political and economic integration.

Another key feature of this episode has been the transformative changes brought about by globalization. These changes, Kratochwil argues, were driven less by the design of states than by various ad hoc adjustments that created new relationships among social groups, domestic institutions, and international regimes and organizations. Although these transformative changes have often been interpreted as the victory of the market over the state, Kratochwil maintains that such an interpretation is too superficial. While the state has lost some of its policy autonomy, its demise is not in the offing and the trust in market-based solutions has waned as crises and scandals have demonstrated that serious problems of governance need to be addressed in the emerging global order.

International Institutions: Two Approaches

ROBERT O. KEOHANE

...To understand the conditions under which international cooperation can take place, it is necessary to understand how international institutions operate and the conditions under which they come into being. This is not to say that international institutions always facilitate cooperation on a global basis: on the contrary, a variety of international institutions, including most obviously military alliances, are designed as means for prevailing in military and political conflict. Conversely, instances of cooperation can take place with only minimal institutional structures to support them. But all efforts at international cooperation take place within an institutional context of some kind, which may or may not facilitate cooperative endeavors. To understand cooperation and discord better, we need to investigate the sources and nature of international institutions, and how institutional change takes place.

"Cooperation" is a contested term. As I use it, it is sharply distinguished from both harmony and discord. When harmony prevails, actors' policies *automatically* facilitate the attainment of others' goals. When there is discord, actors' policies hinder the realization of others' goals, and are not adjusted to make them more compatible. In both harmony and discord, neither actor has an incentive to change his or her behavior. Cooperation, however, "requires that the actions of separate individuals or organizations—which are not in pre-existent harmony—be brought into conformity with one another through a process of policy coordination" (Keohane, 1984:51). This means that when cooperation takes place, each party changes his or her behavior *contingent* on changes in the other's behavior. We can evaluate the impact of cooperation by measuring the difference between the actual outcome and the situation that would have obtained in the absence of coordination: that is, the myopic self-enforcing equilibrium of the game. Genuine cooperation improves the rewards of both players.

International cooperation does not necessarily depend on altruism, idealism, personal honor, common purposes, internalized norms, or a shared belief in a set of values embedded in a culture. At various times and places any of these features of human motivation may indeed play an important role in processes of international cooperation; but cooperation can be understood without reference to any of them. This is not surprising, since international cooperation is not necessarily benign from an ethical standpoint. Rich countries can devise joint actions to extract resources from poor ones, predatory governments can form aggressive alliances, and privileged industries can induce their governments to protect them against competition from more efficient producers abroad. The analysis of international cooperation should not be confused with its celebration. As Hedley Bull said about order, "while order in world politics is something valuable, . . . it should not be taken to be a commanding value, and to show that a particular institution or course of action is conductive of order is not to have established a presumption that that institution is desirable or that that course of action should be carried out" (Bull, 1977:98).

Cooperation is in a dialectical relationship with discord, and they must be understood together. Thus to understand cooperation, one must also understand the frequent absence of, or failure of, cooperation, so incessantly stressed by realist writers. But our awareness of cooperation's fragility does not require us to accept dogmatic forms of realism, which see international relations as inherently doomed to persistent zero-sum conflict and warfare. . . .

Realist and neorealist theories are avowedly rationalistic, accepting what Herbert Simon has referred to as a "substantive" conception of rationality, characterizing "behavior that can be adjudged objectively to be optimally adapted to the situation" (Simon, 1985:294). But adopting the assumption of substantive rationality does not commit the analyst to gloomy deterministic conclusions about the inevitability of warfare. On the contrary, rationalistic theory can be used to explore the conditions under which cooperation takes place, and it seeks to explain why international institutions are constructed by states (Axelrod, 1984; Keohane, 1984; Oye, 1986).

That rationalistic theory can lead to many different conclusions in international relations reflects a wider indeterminacy of the rationality principle as such. As Simon has argued, the principle of substantive rationality generates hypotheses about actual human behavior only when it is combined with auxiliary assumptions about the structure of utility functions and the formation of expectations. Furthermore, rationality is always contextual, so a great deal depends on the situation posited at the beginning of the analysis. Considerable variation in outcomes is therefore consistent with the assumption of substantive rationality. When limitations on the cognitive capacities of decision-makers are also taken into account—as in the concept of bounded rationality—the range of possible variation expands even further.

. . . Traditionally counterposed to rationalistic theory is the sociological approach to the study of institutions, which stresses the role of impersonal social forces as well as the impact of cultural practices, norms, and values that are not derived from calculations of interests (Barry, 1970; Gilpin, 1981). Yet the sociological approach has recently been in some disarray, at least in international relations: its adherents have neither the coherence nor the self-confidence of the rationalists. Rather than try in this essay to discuss this diffuse set of views about international relations, I will focus on the work of several scholars with a distinctive and similar point of view who have recently directly challenged the predominant rationalistic analysis of international politics. These authors, of whom the best-known include Hayward Alker, Richard Ashley, Friedrich Kratochwil, and John Ruggie, emphasize the importance of the "intersubjective meanings" of international institutional activity (Kratochwil and Ruggie, 1986:765). In their view, understanding how people think about institutional norms and rules, and the discourse they engage in, is as important in evaluating the significance of these norms as measuring the behavior that changes in response to their invocation.

These writers emphasize that individuals, local organizations, and even states develop within the context of more encompassing institutions. Institutions do not merely reflect the preferences and power of the units constituting them; the institutions themselves shape those preferences and that power. Institutions are therefore *constitutive* of actors as well as vice versa. It is therefore not sufficient in this view to treat the preferences of individuals as given exogenously: they are affected by institutional arrangements, by prevailing norms, and by historically contingent discourse among people seeking to pursue their purposes and solve their self-defined problems.

In order to emphasize the importance of this perspective, and to focus a dialogue with rationalistic theory, I will treat the writers on world politics who have stressed these themes as members of a school of thought. . . . I have . . . coined a phrase for these writers, calling them "reflective," since all of them emphasize the importance of human reflection for the nature of institutions and ultimately for the character of world politics.

My chief argument in this essay is that students of international institutions should direct their attention to the relative merits of two approaches, the rationalistic and the reflective. Until we understand the strengths and weaknesses of each, we will be unable to design research strategies that are sufficiently multifaceted to encompass our subject-matter, and our empirical work will suffer accordingly.

The next section of this essay will define what I mean by "institutions," and introduce some distinctions that I hope will help us to understand international institutions better. Defining institutions entails drawing a distinction between specific institutions and the underlying practices within which they are embedded, of which the most fundamental in world politics are those associated with the concept of sovereignty. I will then attempt to evaluate the strengths and weaknesses of the rationalistic approach, taking into account the criticism put forward by scholars who emphasize how actors are constituted by institutions and how subjective self-awareness of actors, and the ideas at their disposal, shape their activities. . . .

INTERNATIONAL INSTITUTIONS: DEFINITIONS AND DISTINCTIONS

"Institution" is an even fuzzier concept than cooperation. Institutions are often discussed without being defined at all, or after having been defined only casually. Yet it sometimes seems, as a sociologist lamented half a century ago, that "the only idea common to all usages of the term 'institution' is that of some sort of establishment of relative permanence of a distinctly social sort" (Hughes, 1936:180, quoted in Zucker, 1977:726). In the international relations literature, this vagueness persists. We speak of the United Nations and the World Bank (part of the "United Nations System"), IBM and Exxon, as institutions; but we also consider "the international monetary regime" and "the international trade regime" to be institutions. Hedley Bull refers to "the balance of power, international law, the diplomatic mechanism, the managerial system of the great powers, and war" as "the institutions of international society" (Bull, 1977:74).[1] John Ruggie discusses "the institutional framework of sovereignty" (Ruggie, 1986:147), and Stephen Krasner writes about "the particular institutional structures of sovereignty" (Krasner, 1987:11).

It may help in sorting out some of these troubling confusions to point out that "institution" may refer to a *general pattern or categorization* of activity or to a *particular* human-constructed arrangement, formally or informally organized. Examples of institutions as general patterns include Bull's "institutions of international society," as well as such varied patterns of behavior as marriage and religion, sovereign statehood, diplomacy, and neutrality. Sometimes norms such as that of reciprocity, which can apply to a variety of situations, are referred to as institutions. When we speak of patterns or categorizations of activity as institutions, the particular instances are often not regarded themselves as institutions: we do not speak of the marriage of the Duke and Duchess of Windsor, international negotiations over the status of the Panama Canal, or the neutrality of Sweden in World War II as institutions. What these general patterns of activity have in common with specific institutions is that they both meet the criteria for a broad definition of institutions: both involve persistent and connected sets of rules (formal or informal) that prescribe behavioral roles, constrain activity, and shape expectations.

Specific institutions, such as the French state, the Roman Catholic church, the international nonproliferation regime, or the General Agreement on Tariffs and Trade, are discrete entities, identifiable in space and time. Specific institutions may be exemplars of general patterns of activity—the United Nations exemplifies multilateral diplomacy; the French state, sovereign statehood; the Roman Catholic church, organized religion. But unlike general patterns of activity, specific institutions have unique life-histories, which depend on the decisions of particular individuals.

General patterns of "institutionalized" activity are more heterogeneous. Some of these institutions are only sets of entities, with each member of the set being an institution. Bull's institution of international law, for instance, can be seen as including a variety of institutions codified in legal form. In this sense, all formal international regimes are parts of international law, as are formal bilateral treaties and conventions. Likewise, the institution of religion includes a variety of quite different specific institutions, including the Roman Catholic church, Islam, and Congregationalism. Other general patterns of activity can be seen as norms that are applicable to a wide variety of situations, such as the norm of reciprocity (Keohane, 1986b).

It is difficult to work analytically with the broad ordinary-language definition of institutions with which I have started, since it includes such a variety of different entities and activities. In the rest of this essay, therefore, I will focus on institutions that can be identified as related complexes of rules and norms, identifiable in space and time. This conception of the scope of my analytical enterprise deliberately omits institutions that are merely categories of activity, as well as general norms that can be attached to any of a number of rule-complexes. It allows me to focus on *specific institutions* and on *practices*. As explained below, it is the mark of a practice that the behavior of those engaged in it can be corrected by an appeal to its own rules. This means that practices are deeply embedded—highly institutionalized in the sociological sense of being taken for granted by participants as social facts that are not to be challenged although their implications for behavior can be explicated.

Specific institutions can be defined in terms of their rules. Douglass North (1987:6) defines institutions as "rules, enforcement characteristics of rules, and norms of behavior that structure repeated human interaction." Institutions can be seen as "frozen decisions," or "history encoded into rules" (March and Olson, 1984:741). These rules may be informal or implicit rather than codified: in fact, some very strong institutions, such as the British constitution, rely principally on unwritten rules. To be institutionalized in the sense in which I will use the term, the rules must be durable, and must prescribe behavioral roles for actors, besides constraining activity and shaping expectations. That is, institutions differentiate among actors according to the roles that they are expected to perform, and institutions can be identified by asking whether patterns of behavior are indeed differentiated by role. When we ask whether X is an institution, we ask whether we can identify persistent sets of rules that constrain activity, shape expectations, and prescribe roles. In international relations, some of these institutions are formal organizations, with prescribed hierarchies and the capacity for purposive action. Others, such as the international regimes for money and trade, are complexes of rules and organizations, the core elements of which have been negotiated and explicitly agreed upon by states.[2]

This definition of specific institutions incorporates what John Rawls has called the "summary view" of rules, in which "rules are pictured as summaries of past decisions," which allow the observer to predict future behavior (Rawls, 1955:19). Rules such as these can be changed by participants on utilitarian grounds without engaging in self-contradictory behavior. This definition is useful as far as it goes, but it does not capture what Rawls calls "the practice conception" of rules. A practice in the sense used by Rawls is analogous to a game such as baseball or chess: "It is the mark of a practice that being taught how to engage in it involves being instructed in the rules that define it, and that appeal is made to those rules to correct the behavior of those engaged in it. Those engaged in a practice recognize the rules as defining it" (Rawls, 1955:24). Were the rules of a practice to change, so would the fundamental nature of the activity in question.

Someone engaged in a practice has to explain her action by showing that it is in accord with the practice. Otherwise, the behavior itself is self-contradictory. As Oran Young points out, "It just does not make sense for a chess player to refuse to accept the concept of checkmate, for a speaker of English to assert that it makes no difference whether subjects and predicates agree, or for an actor in the existing international society to disregard the rules regarding the nationality of citizens." In international relations, the "menu of available practices" is limited: "a 'new' state, for example, has little choice but to join the basic institutional arrangements of the states system" (1986:120).

The concept of a practice is particularly applicable to certain general patterns of activity such as sovereignty and multilateral diplomacy. Their rules, many of which are not codified, define what it means to be sovereign or to engage in multilateral diplomacy.[3] Like the rules of chess and the grammar of the English language, respect for state sovereignty and multilateral diplomacy are taken for granted by most of those who participate in them. When fundamental practices are violated, as in the seizure of the American Embassy in Teheran in 1979, disapproval is virtually universal. . . .

Rawls' distinction helps us to see the specific institutions of world politics, with their challengeable rules, as embedded in more fundamental practices. Just as the actors in world politics are constrained by existing institutions, so are institutions, and prospects for institutional change, constrained by the practices taken for granted by their members. For each set of entities that we investigate, we can identify institutionalized constraints at a more fundamental and enduring level.

Consider, for instance, the practice of sovereign statehood, which has been fundamental to world politics for over three hundred years. At its core is the principle of sovereignty: that the state "is subject to no other state and has full and exclusive powers within its jurisdiction without prejudice to the limits set by applicable law" (*Wimbledon* case, Permanent Court of International Justice, series A, no. 1, 1923; cited in Hoffmann, 1987:172–73). Sovereignty is thus a relatively precise legal concept: a question of law, not of fact, of authority, not sheer power. As a legal concept, the principle of sovereignty should not be confused with the empirical claim that a given state in fact makes its decisions autonomously. . . .

Sovereign statehood is a practice in Rawls' sense because it contains a set of rules that define it and that can be used to correct states' behavior. These rules are fundamental to the conduct of modern international relations. Extraterritorial jurisdiction for embassies is such a central rule, implied by the modern conception of sovereignty; immunity from ordinary criminal prosecution for a state's accredited diplomats is a corollary of this principle. More generally, as Martin Wight has argued, the norm of reciprocity is implied by that of sovereignty, and respect for reciprocity is therefore part of the practice of sovereign statehood: "It would be impossible to have a society of sovereign states unless each state, while claiming sovereignty for itself, recognized that every other state had the right to claim and enjoy its own sovereignty as well. This reciprocity was inherent in the Western conception of sovereignty" (Wight, 1977:135).

Treating sovereign statehood as a practice does not imply that the process of recognizing entities as sovereign is automatic: on the contrary, states follow political convenience as well as law in deciding which entities to regard as sovereign. But once an entity has been generally accepted by states as sovereign, certain rights and responsibilities are entailed. Furthermore, acceptance of the principle of sovereignty creates well-defined roles. Only sovereign states or entities such as international organizations created by states can make treaties and enforce them on subjects within their jurisdictions, declare and wage wars recognized by international law, and join international organizations that are part of the United Nations System.

. . . I have begun with a broad definition of institutions as persistent and connected sets of rules that prescribe behavioral roles, constrain activity, and shape expectations. I have focused my attention, however, on specific institutions and practices. Specific institutions can be defined in the first instance in terms of rules;

but we must recognize that specific institutions are embedded in practices. In modern world politics, the most important practice is that of sovereignty. To understand institutions and institutional change in world politics, it is necessary to understand not only how specific institutions are formulated, change, and die, but how their evolution is affected by the practice of sovereignty.

THE RATIONALISTIC STUDY OF INTERNATIONAL INSTITUTIONS

Rationalistic research on international institutions focuses almost entirely on specific institutions. It emphasizes international regimes and formal international organizations. Since this research program is rooted in exchange theory, it assumes scarcity and competition as well as rationality on the part of the actors. It therefore begins with the premise that if there were no potential gains from agreements to be captured in world politics—that is, if no agreements among actors could be mutually beneficial—there would be no need for specific international institutions. But there are evidently considerable benefits to be secured from mutual agreement—as evidenced for millennia by trade agreements, rules of war, and peace treaties, and for the last century by international organizations. Conversely, if cooperation were easy—that is, if all mutually beneficial bargains could be made without cost—there would be no need for institutions to facilitate cooperation. Yet such an assumption would be equally as false as the assumption that no potential gains from agreements exist. It is the combination of the potential *value* of agreements and the *difficulty* of making them that renders international regimes significant. In order to cooperate in world politics on more than a sporadic basis, human beings have to use institutions.

Rationalistic theories of institutions view institutions as affecting patterns of costs. Specifically, institutions reduce certain forms of uncertainty and alter transaction costs: that is, the "costs of specifying and enforcing the contracts that underlie exchange" (North, 1984:256). Even in the absence of hierarchical authority, institutions provide information (through monitoring) and stabilize expectations. They may also make decentralized enforcement feasible, for example by creating conditions under which reciprocity can operate (North, 1981; Williamson, 1981, 1985; Keohane, 1984; Moe, 1987). At any point in time, transaction costs are to a substantial degree the result of the institutional context. Dynamically, the relationship between these institutionally affected transaction costs and the formation of new institutions will, according to the theory, be curvilinear. If transaction costs are negligible, it will not be necessary to create new institutions to facilitate mutually beneficial exchange; if transaction costs are extremely high, it will not be feasible to build institutions—which may even be unimaginable.

In world politics, sovereignty and state autonomy mean that transaction costs are never negligible, since it is always difficult to communicate, to monitor performance, and especially to enforce compliance with rules. Therefore, according to this theory, one should expect international institutions to appear whenever the costs of communication, monitoring, and enforcement are relatively low compared to the benefits to be derived from political exchange. Institutions should persist as long as, but only so long as, their members have incentives to maintain them. But the effects of these institutions will not be politically neutral: they can be expected to confer advantages on those to whom their rules grant access and a share in political authority; and insofar as the transaction costs of making agreements outside of an established institution are high, governments disadvantaged within an institution will find themselves at a disadvantage in the issue area as a whole. More generally, the rules of any institution will reflect the relative power positions of its actual and potential members, which constrain the feasible bargaining space and affect transaction costs.[4]

These transaction-cost arguments have been applied in qualitative terms to international relations. As anticipated by the theory, effective international regimes include arrangements to share information and to monitor compliance, according to standards established by the regime; and they adapt to shifts in capabilities among their members (Finlayson and Zacher, 1983; Keohane, 1984: chapter 10; Aggarwal, 1985; Lipson, 1986; Haggard and Simmons, 1987). Furthermore, the access rules of different international regimes affect the success of governments in the related issue areas (Krasner, 1985:123). As a general descriptive model, therefore, this approach seems to do quite well: international regimes work as we expect them to.

However, the rationalistic theory has not been used to explain why international institutions exist in some issue areas rather than in others. Nor has this theory been employed systematically to account for the creation or demise of such institutions. Yet the theory implies hypotheses about these questions: hypotheses that could be submitted to systematic, even quantitative, examination. For instance, this theory predicts that the incidence of specific international institutions should be related to the ratio of benefits anticipated from exchange to the transaction costs of establishing the institutions necessary to facilitate the negotiation, monitoring, and enforcement costs of agreements specifying the terms of exchange. It also predicts that in the absence of anticipated gains from agreements, specific institutions will not be created, and that most specific institutions in world politics will in fact perform the function of reducing transaction costs. Since the theory acknowledges the significance of sunk costs in perpetuating extant institutions, and since its advocates recognize that organizational processes modify the pure dictates of rationality (Keohane, 1984: chapter 7), its predictions about the demise of specific institutions are less clear.

The rationalistic theory could also help us develop a theory of compliance or noncompliance with commitments.[5] For international regimes to be effective, their injunctions must be obeyed; yet sovereignty precludes hierarchical enforcement. The game-theoretic literature suggests that reputation may provide a strong incentive for compliance (Kreps and Wilson, 1982). But we do not know how strong the reputational basis for enforcement of agreements is in world politics, since we have not done the necessary empirical work. What Oliver Williamson calls "opportunism" is still possible: reputations can be differentiated among partners and violations of agreements can often be concealed. Historically, it is not entirely clear to what extent governments that renege on their commitments are in fact punished for such actions. Indeed, governments that have defaulted on their debts have, it appears, not been punished via higher interest rates in subsequent periods for their defections (Eichengreen, 1987; Lindert and Morton, 1987).

Rationalistic theory can often help us understand the direction of change in world politics, if not always its precise extent or the form that it takes. For instance, there are good reasons to believe that a diffusion of power away from a hegemonic state, which sponsored extant international regimes, will create pressures on these regimes and weaken their rules—even though it is dubious that hegemony is either a necessary or a sufficient condition for the maintenance of a pattern of order in international relations (Keohane, 1984). . . .

Yet even on its own terms, rationalistic theory encounters some inherent limitations. The so-called Folk Theorem of game theory states that for a class of games that includes 2 × 2 repeated Prisoners' Dilemma, there are many feasible equilibria above the maximum points of both players (Kreps, 1984:16). We cannot predict which one will emerge without knowing more about the structure of a situation—that is, about the prior institutional context in which the situation is embedded. This means that the conclusions of formal models of cooperation are often highly dependent on the assumptions with which the investigations begin—that they are context-dependent. To be sure, once we understand the context, it may be possible to model strategies used by players to devise equilibrium-inducing institutions (Shepsle, 1986). The literatures on bureaucratic politics and agency theory complicate matters further by suggesting that the organizational "actor" will not necessarily act as "its" interests specify, if people within it have different interests (Moe, 1984; Arrow, 1985). Thus even on its own terms rationalistic theory seems to leave open the issue of what kinds of institutions will develop, to whose benefit, and how effective they will be.

Even within the confines of the rationalistic research program, therefore, formal theory alone is unlikely to yield answers to our explanatory puzzles. Rationalistic theory is good at posing questions and suggesting lines of inquiry, but it does not furnish us with answers. . . .[6]

Rationalistic theory also needs to extend its vision back into history. To do so in a sophisticated way entails a departure from the equilibrium models emphasized by neoclassical economic theory. It requires intellectual contortions to view the evolution of institutions over time as the product of a deterministic equilibrium logic in which rational adaptation to the environment plays the key role. Institutional development is affected by particular leaders and by exogenous shocks—chance events from the perspective of a systemic theory. Theories of "path-dependence" in economics demonstrate that under specified conditions, accumulated random variations can lead an institution into a state that could not have been predicted in advance (David, 1985; Arthur, Ermoliev and Kaniovski, 1987; see also March and Olson, 1984:745). From a technological standpoint, path-dependence occurs under conditions of increasing rather than decreasing returns—resulting for instance from positive externalities that give established networks advantages over their competitors, from learning effects, and from the convergence of expectations around an established standard. Examples include the development of the typewriter keyboard, competition between different railroad gauges or between Betamax and VHS types of video recorders, and between gasoline and steam-powered cars. Viewed from a more strictly institutional perspective, path-dependence can be a result of sunk costs. Arthur Stinchcombe (1968:120–21) points out that if "sunk costs make a traditional pattern of action cheaper, and if new patterns are not enough more profitable to justify throwing away the resource, the sunk costs tend to preserve a pattern of action from one year to the next."

Surely the General Agreement of Tariffs and Trade (GATT), the International Monetary Fund (IMF), and the United Nations are not optimally efficient, and they would not be invented in their present forms today; but they persist. In some cases, this may be a matter of sunk costs making it rational to continue involvement with an old institution. Sometimes the increasing returns pointed to by path-dependence theorists may account for this persistence. Or considerations of power and status may be more important than the functions performed by the institutions. . . .

REFLECTIVE APPROACHES

Scholars imbued with a sociological perspective on institutions emphasize that institutions are often not created consciously by human beings but rather emerge slowly through a less deliberative process, and that they are frequently taken for granted by the people who are affected by them. In this view the assumption of utility maximization often does not tell us much about the origins of institutions; and it also does not take us very far in understanding the variations in institutional arrangements in different cultures and political systems. Ronald Dore, for instance, suggests that Oliver Williamson's attempt to construct "timeless generalizations" perhaps "merely reflects the tendency of American economists to write as if all the world were America. Or perhaps [Williamson] does not have much evidence about America either, and just assumes that 'Man' is a hard-nosed short-run profit maximizer suspicious of everyone he deals with" (Dore, 1983:469).

Values, norms and practices vary across cultures, and such variations will affect the efficacy of institutional arrangements. This point can be put into the language of rationalistic theory: institutions that are consistent with culturally accepted practices are likely to entail lower transaction costs than those that conflict with those practices. But such a statement merely begs the question of where the practices, or the preferences that they reflect, came from in the first place. The most ambitious form of rationalistic theory, which takes fundamental preferences as uniform and constant, is contradicted by cultural variation if preferences are meaningfully operationalized. The more modest form of this theory, which treats variations in preferences as exogenous, thereby avoids seeking to explain them.

Similar problems arise with explanations of changes in institutions over time. Rationalistic theories of specific institutions can be applied historically, as we have seen. Each set of institutions to be explained is viewed within an institutional as well as material context: prior institutions create incentives and constraints that affect the emergence or evolution of later ones. Change is then explained by changes in opportunity costs at the margin, as a result of environmental changes.

Such an approach has been highly revealing, as the literature on institutional change in economics demonstrates (North, 1981). However, these rationalistic theories of specific institutions have to be contextualized before they are empirically useful: that is, they must be put into a prior framework of institutions and practices. Only with this prior knowledge of the situation at one point in time to guide us, can we use this theory effectively to improve our knowledge of what is likely to happen next. We can then work our way back through the various levels of analysis—explaining actor behavior by reference to institutional constraints and opportunities, explaining specific institutions by reference to prior institutions, explaining those institutions by reference to fundamental practices. Up to a point, rationalistic theory can pursue its analysis backwards in time; and it can only gain by becoming more historically sensitive. But as Field (1981) pointed out and as North (1981) has recognized in the field of economic history, at some point one must embed the analysis in institutions that are not plausibly viewed as the product of human calculation and bargaining. And ultimately, the analysis has to come to grips with the structures of social interaction that "constitute or empower those agents in the first place" (Wendt, 1987:369).

International institutions are not created *de novo* any more than are economic institutions. On the contrary, they emerge from prior institutionalized contexts, the most fundamental of which cannot be explained as if they were contracts among rational individuals maximizing some utility function. These fundamental practices seem to reflect historically distinctive combinations of material circumstances, social patterns of thought, and individual initiative—combinations which reflect "conjunctures" rather than deterministic outcomes (Hirschman, 1970), and which are themselves shaped over time by path-dependent processes. Rationalistic theory can help to illuminate these practices, but it cannot stand alone. Despite the ambitions of some of its enthusiasts, it has little prospect of becoming a comprehensive deductive explanation of international institutions.

Quite apart from this limitation, the writers whom I have labeled "reflective" have emphasized that rationalistic theories of institutions contain no *endogenous* dynamic. Individual and social reflection leading to changes in preferences or in views of causality—what Hayward Alker refers to as *historicity* (Alker, 1986) and what Ernst Haas discusses under the rubric of *learning* (Haas, 1987)—is ignored. That is, preferences are assumed to be fixed. But this assumption of fixed preferences seems to preclude understanding of some major changes in human institutions. For example, as Douglass North points out, "the demise of slavery, one of the landmarks in the history of freedom, is simply not explicable in an interest group model" (North, 1987:12). Nor, in the view of Robert Cox, is American hegemony explicable simply in power terms: on the contrary, it implies a "coherent conjunction or fit between a configuration of material power, a prevalent collective image of world order (including certain norms) and a set of institutions which administer the order with a certain semblance of universality" (Cox, 1986:223).

From this perspective, rationalistic theories seem only to deal with one dimension of a multidimensional reality: they are incomplete, since they ignore changes taking place in consciousness. They do not enable us to understand how interests change as a result of changes in belief systems. They obscure rather than illuminate the sources of states' policy preferences. The result, according to Richard Ashley, has been a fundamentally unhistorical approach to world politics, which has reified contemporary political arrangements by denying "history as process" and "the historical significance of practice" (Ashley, 1986:290; see also Alker, 1986; Kratochwil, 1986).

Some analysts in the reflective camp have sought to correct this lack of attention to historicity and learning. In analyzing Prisoner's Dilemma, Alker (1985) emphasizes not merely the structure of payoff matrices but the sequential patterns of learning taking place between actors over the course of a sequence of games. And Ruggie (1986) has argued that only by understanding how individuals think about their world can we understand changes in how the world is organized—for instance, the shift from medieval to modern international politics. Socially influenced patterns of learning are crucial, as Karl Deutsch and Ernst Haas—the teachers, respectively, of Alker and Ruggie—have always emphasized.

Reflective critics of the rationalistic research program have emphasized the inadequacies of rationalism in analyzing the fundamental practice of sovereign statehood, which has been instituted not by agreement but as a result of the elaboration over time of the principle of sovereignty. Sovereignty seems to be *prior* to the kinds of calculations on which rationalistic theory focuses: governments' strategies assume the principle of sovereignty, and the practice of sovereign statehood, as givens. Indeed, according to some critics of rationalistic thinking, sovereignty is of even more far-reaching significance, since it defines the very nature of the actors in world politics. Ruggie conceptualizes sovereignty as a "form of legitimation" that "differentiates units in terms of juridically mutually exclusive and morally self-entailed domains." Like private property rights, it divides space in terms of exclusive rights, and establishes patterns of social relationships among the resulting "possessive individualists," whose character as agents is fundamentally shaped by sovereignty itself (Ruggie, 1986: 144–47). . . .

The criticisms of rationalistic theory, both from within the framework of its assumptions and outside of them, are extensive and telling. The assumption of equilibrium is often misleading, and can lead to mechanical or contorted analysis. Rationalistic theory accounts better for shifts in the strength of institutions than in the values that they serve to promote. Cultural variations create anomalies for the theory. It does not take into account the impact of social processes of reflection or learning on the preferences of individuals or on the organizations that they direct. Finally, rationalistic theory has had little to say about the origins and evolution of practices, and it has often overlooked the impact of such practices as sovereignty on the specific institutions that it studies.[7]

Yet the critics have by no means demolished the rationalistic research program on institutions, although taking their argument seriously requires us to doubt the legitimacy of rationalism's intellectual hegemony. To show that rationalistic theory cannot account for changes in preferences because it has omitted important potential explanatory factors is important, but it is not devastating, since no social science theory is complete. Limiting the number of variables that a theory considers can increase both its explanatory content and its capacity to concentrate the scholarly mind. Indeed, the rationalistic program is heuristically so powerful precisely because it does not easily accept accounts based on post hoc observation of values or ideology: regarding states as rational actors with specified utility functions forces the analyst to look below the surface for interests that provide incentives to behave in apparently anomalous ways. In quite a short time, research stimulated by rationalistic theory has posed new questions and proposed new hypotheses about why governments create and join international regimes, and the conditions under which these institutions wax or wane. A research program with such a record of accomplishment, and a considerable number of interesting but still untested hypotheses about reasons for persistence, change, and compliance, cannot be readily dismissed.

Indeed, the greatest weakness of the reflective school lies not in deficiencies in their critical arguments but in the lack of a clear reflective research program that could be employed by students of world politics. Waltzian neorealism has such a research program; so does neoliberal institutionalism, which has focused on the evolution and impact of international regimes. Until the reflective scholars or others sympathetic to their arguments have delineated such a research program and shown in particular studies that it can illuminate important issues in world politics, they will remain on the margins of the field, largely invisible to the preponderance of empirical researchers, most of whom explicitly or implicitly accept one or another version of rationalistic premises. Such invisibility would be a shame, since the reflective perspective has much to contribute.

As formulated to date, both rationalistic and what I have called reflective approaches share a common blind spot: neither pays sufficient attention to domestic politics. It is all too obvious that domestic politics is neglected by much game-theoretic strategic analysis and by structural explanations of international regime change. However, this deficiency is not inherent in the nature of rationalistic analysis: it is quite possible to use game theory heuristically to analyze the "two-level games" linking domestic and international politics, as Robert Putnam (1988) has done. At one level reflective theory questions, in its discussion of sovereignty, the existence of a clear boundary between domestic and international politics. But at another level it critiques the reification of the state in neorealist theory and contemporary practice, and should therefore be driven to an analysis of how such reification has taken place historically and how it is reproduced within the confines of the domestic-international dichotomy. Such an analysis could lead to a fruitful reexamination of shifts in preferences that emerge from complex interactions between the operation of international institutions and the processes of domestic politics. Both Kenneth Waltz's "second image"—the impact of domestic politics on international relations—and Peter Gourevitch's "second image reversed" need to be taken account of, in their different ways, by the rationalist and reflective approaches (Waltz, 1959; Gourevitch, 1978). . . .[8]

NOTES

1. Bull also declares that "states themselves are the principal institutions of the society of states" (1977:71), which implies that he subscribed to the view, discussed below, that the international institution of sovereignty is prior to the state.

2. *International regimes* are specific institutions involving states and/or transnational actors, which apply to particular issues in international relations. This is similar to the definition given by Krasner (1983), but makes it clearer that regimes are institutions, taking advantage of the definition of institutions given above. *Formal international organizations* are purposive institutions with explicit rules, specific assignments of roles to individuals and groups, and the capacity for action. Unlike international regimes, international organizations can engage in goal-directed activities such as raising and spending money, promulgating policies, and making discretionary choices.

3. These practices have evolved over the course of decades or centuries and can therefore be considered in Young's terminology to be *spontaneous* orders: "the product of the action of many men but . . . not the result of human design" (Young, 1983:98, quoting Hayek, 1973:37).

4. The assertion that hegemony is necessary for institutionalized cooperation, and the less extreme view that hegemony facilitates cooperation, can both be interpreted within this framework as declaring transaction costs to be lower when a hegemon exists than when power resources are more fragmented.

5. For a pioneering exploration of these issues, see Young (1979).

6. The theoretical indeterminacy of rationalistic theory suggests that in international relations, as in the economics of institutions, "theory is now outstripping empirical research to an excessive extent" (Matthews, 1986:917).

7. This does not mean, however, that rationalistic theory is incapable of contributing to our understanding of the evolution of practices. As Wendt argues, "there is no a priori reason why we cannot extend the logic of [rationalistic] analysis to the analysis of generative structures" (Wendt, 1987:368). In notes to the author, Barry Weingast has illustrated this point by sketching a functional, transaction-cost argument for the existence of sovereignty, as a set of relatively unambiguous conventions, known to all players and not revisable ex post, which facilitate coordination and signaling.

8. Recently major work has been done on links between domestic and international politics, by scholars trained in comparative politics. Unlike the critics of rationalistic theory discussed above, however, these writers emphasize international structure, material interests, and state organization as well as the role of ideas and social patterns of learning. Also unlike the critics of rationalist international relations theory, these writers have engaged in extensive and detailed empirical research. See Zysman (1983), Katzenstein (1985), Gourevitch (1986), and Alt (1987).

BIBLIOGRAPHY

Aggarwal, V. K. (1985) *Liberal Protectionism: The International Politics of Organized Textile Trade.* Berkeley: University of California Press.

Alker, H. R. Jr. (1985) From Quantity to Quality: A New Research Program on Resolving Sequential Prisoner's Dilemmas. Paper delivered at the August meeting of the American Political Science Association.

Alker, H. R. Jr. (1986) The Presumption of Anarchy in World Politics. Draft manuscript, Department of Political Science, M.I.T., August.

Alt, J. A. (1987) Crude Politics: Oil and the Political Economy of Unemployment in Britain and Norway, 1970–85. *British Journal of Political Science* 17:149–99.

Arrow, K. J. (1985) The Economics of Agency. In *Principals and Agents: The Structure of Business,* edited by J. W. Pratt and R. J. Zeckhauser, pp. 37–51. Boston: Harvard Business School Press.

Arthur, W. B., Y. M. Ermoliev and Y. M. Kaniovski. (1987) Path-Dependent Processes and the Emergence of Macro-Structure. *European Journal of Operational Research* 30:294–303.

Ashley, R. K. (1986) The Poverty of Neorealism. In *Neorealism and Its Critics*, edited by R. O. Keohane, New York: Columbia University Press.

Axelrod, R. (1984) *The Evolution of Cooperation*. New York: Basic Books.

Barry, B. (1970) *Sociologists, Economists and Democracy.* London: Macmillan.

Bull, H. (1977) *The Anarchical Society*. New York: Columbia University Press.

Cox, R. W. (1986) Social Forces, States and World Orders: Beyond International Relations Theory. In *Neorealism and Its Critics*, edited by R. O. Keohane, pp. 204–55. New York: Columbia University Press.

David, P. A. (1985) Clio and the Economics of QWERTY. *American Economic Review Proceedings* 75:332–37.

Dore, R. (1983) Goodwill and the Spirit of Market Capitalism. *British Journal of Sociology* 34:459–82.

Eichengreen, B. (1987) Till Debt Do Us Part: The U.S. Capital Market and Foreign Lending, 1920–1955. Cambridge: NBER Working Paper no. 2394 (October).

Field, A. J. (1981) The Problem with Neoclassical Institutional Economics: A Critique with Special Reference to the North/Thomas model of pre-1500 Europe. *Explorations in Economic History* 18:174–98.

Finlayson, J. A. and M. W. Zacher (1983) The GATT and the Regulation of Trade Barriers: Regime Dynamics and Functions. In *International Regimes*, edited by S. D. Krasner, pp. 273–315. Ithaca: Cornell University Press.

Gilpin, R. (1981) *War and Change in World Politics.* New York: Cambridge University Press.

Gourevitch, P. A. (1978) The Second Image Reversed: International Sources of Domestic Politics. *International Organization* 32:881–912.

Gourevitch. P. A. (1986) *Politics in Hard Times.* Ithaca: Cornell University Press.

Haas, E. B. (1987) Adaptation and Learning in International Organizations. Manuscript. Berkeley: Institute of International Studies.

Haggard, S. and B. A. Simmons. (1987) Theories of International Regimes. *International Organization* 41:491–517.

Hayek, F. A. (1973) *Rules and Order.* Vol. 1 of *Law, Legislation and Liberty.* Chicago: University of Chicago Press.

Hirschman, A. D. (1970) The Search for Paradigms as a Hindrance to Understanding. *World Politics* 22(3):329–43.

Hughes, E. C. (1936) The Ecological Aspect of Institutions. *American Sociological Review* 1:180–89.

Katzenstein, P. J. (1985) *Small States in World Markets.* Ithaca: Cornell University Press.

Keohane, R. O. (1984) *After Hegemony: Cooperation and Discord in the World Political Economy.* Princeton: Princeton University Press.

Keohane, R. O., ed. (1986a) *Neorealism and Its Critics.* New York: Columbia University Press.

Keohane, R. O. (1986b) Reciprocity in International Relations. *International Organization* 40:1–27.

Krasner, S. D., ed. (1983) *International Regimes.* Ithaca: Cornell University Press.

Krasner, S. D. (1985) *Structural Conflict: The Third World against Global Liberalism.* Berkeley: University of California Press.

Krasner, S. D. (1987) Sovereignty: An Institutional Perspective. Manuscript. Stanford, CA: Center for Advanced Study in the Behavioral Sciences, October.

Kratochwil, F. (1986) Of Systems, Boundaries and Territoriality: An Inquiry into the Formation of the State System. *World Politics* 39:27–52.

Kratochwil, F. and J. G. Ruggie. (1986) International Organization: A State of the Art on an Art of the State. *International Organization* 40:753–76.

Kreps, D. M. (1984) Corporate Culture and Economic Theory. Manuscript. Stanford, CA: Graduate School of Business, Stanford University.

Kreps, D. and R. Wilson (1982) Reputation and Imperfect Information. *Journal of Economic Theory* 27:253–79.

Lindert, P. H. and P. J. Morton (1987) How Sovereign Debt Has Worked. University of California, Davis, Institute of Governmental Affairs, Research Program in Applied Macroeconomics and Macro Policy, Working Paper series no. 45, August.

Lipson, C. (1986) Bankers' Dilemmas: Private Cooperation in Rescheduling Sovereign Debts. In *Cooperation under Anarchy*, edited by K. Oye, pp. 200–25. Princeton: Princeton University Press.

March, J. and J. Olson (1984) The New Institutionalism: Organizational Factors in Political Life. *American Political Science Review* 79:734–49.

Matthews, R. C. O. (1986) The Economics of Institutions and the Sources of Growth. *Economic Journal* 96:903–18.

Moe, T. M. (1984) The New Economics of Organization. *American Journal of Political Science* 28:739–77.

Moe, T. M. (1987) Interests, Institutions and Positive Theory: The Politics of the NLRB. *Studies in American Political Development* 2:236–99.

North, D. C. (1981) *Structure and Change in Economic History.* New York: W. W. Norton.

North, D. C. (1984) Government and the Cost of Exchange in History. *Journal of Economic History* 44:255–64.

North, D. C. (1987) Institutions and Economic Growth: An Historical Introduction. Paper prepared for the Conference on Knowledge and Institutional Change sponsored by the University of Minnesota, Minneapolis, November.

Oye, K. A., ed. (1986) *Cooperation under Anarchy.* Princeton: Princeton University Press.

Putnam, R. D. (1988) Diplomacy and Domestic Politics: The Logic of Two-Level Games. *International Organization* 42:427–60.

Rawls, J. (1955) Two Concepts of Rules. *Philosophical Review* 64:3–32.

Ruggie, J. G. (1986) Continuity and Transformation in the World Polity: Toward a Neorealist Synthesis. In *Neorealism and Its Critics*, edited by R. O. Keohane, pp. 131–57. New York: Columbia University Press.

Schepsle, K. (1986) Institutional Equilibrium and Equilibrium Institutions. In *Political Science: The Science of Politics*, edited by H. F. Weisberg, pp. 51–81. New York: Agathon Press.

Simon, H. A. (1985) Human Nature in Politics: The Dialogue of Psychology with Political Science. *American Political Science Review* 79:293–304.

Stinchcombe, A. L. (1968) *Constructing Social Theories.* New York: Harcourt, Brace and World.

Waltz, K. N. (1959) *Man, the State and War.* New York: Columbia University Press.

Wendt, A. E. (1987) The Agent-Structure Problem in International Relations Theory. *International Organization* 41:335–70.

Wight, M. (1977) *Systems of States*, edited with an introduction by H. Bull. Leicester: Leicester University Press.

Williamson, O. E. (1981) The Modern Corporation: Origins, Evolution, Attributes. *Journal of Economic Literature* 19:1537–68.

Williamson, O. E. (1985) *The Economic Institutions of Capitalism.* New York: Free Press.

Young, O. R. (1979) *Compliance and Public Authority*. Washington: Resources for the Future.

Young, O. R. (1983) Regime Dynamics: The Rise and Fall of International Regimes. In *International Regimes*, edited by S. D. Krasner, pp. 93–114. Ithaca: Cornell University Press.

Young, O. R. (1986) International Regimes: Toward a New Theory of Institutions. *World Politics* 39:104–22.

Zucker, L. G. (1977) The Role of Institutionalization in Cultural Persistence. *American Sociological Review* 42:726–43.

Zysman, J. (1983) *Governments, Markets and Growth*. Ithaca: Cornell University Press.

Structural Causes and Regime Consequences: Regimes as Intervening Variables

STEPHEN D. KRASNER

DEFINING REGIMES AND REGIME CHANGE

Regimes can be defined as sets of implicit or explicit principles, norms, rules, and decision-making procedures around which actors' expectations converge in a given area of international relations. Principles are beliefs of fact, causation, and rectitude. Norms are standards of behavior defined in terms of rights and obligations. Rules are specific prescriptions or proscriptions for action. Decision-making procedures are prevailing practices for making and implementing collective choice.

This usage is consistent with other recent formulations. Keohane and Nye, for instance, define regimes as "sets of governing arrangements" that include "networks of rules, norms, and procedures that regularize behavior and control its effects."[1] Haas argues that a regime encompasses a mutually coherent set of procedures, rules, and norms.[2] Hedley Bull, using a somewhat different terminology, refers to the importance of rules and institutions in international society where rules refer to "general imperative principles which require or authorize prescribed classes of persons or groups to behave in prescribed ways."[3] Institutions for Bull help to secure adherence to rules by formulating, communicating, administering, enforcing, interpreting, legitimating, and adapting them.

Regimes must be understood as something more than temporary arrangements that change with every shift in power or interests. Keohane notes that a basic analytic distinction must be made between regimes and agreements. Agreements are *ad hoc*, often "one-shot," arrangements. The purpose of regimes is to facilitate agreements. Similarly, Jervis argues that the concept of regimes "implies not only norms and expectations that facilitate cooperation, but a form of cooperation that is more than the following of short-run self-interest."[4] For instance, he contends that the restraints that have applied in Korea and other limited wars should not be considered a regime. These rules, such as "do not bomb sanctuaries," were based purely on short-term calculations of interest. As interest and power changed, behavior changed. Waltz's conception of the balance of power, in which states are driven by systemic pressures to repetitive balancing behavior, is not a regime; Kaplan's conception, in which equilibrium requires commitment to rules that constrain immediate, short-term power maximization (especially not destroying an essential actor), is a regime.[5]

Similarly, regime-governed behavior must not be based solely on short-term calculations of interest. Since regimes encompass principles and norms, the utility function that is being maximized must embody some sense of general obligation. One such principle, reciprocity, is emphasized in Jervis's analysis of security regimes. When states accept reciprocity they will sacrifice short-term interests with the expectation that other actors will reciprocate in the future, even if they are not under a specific obligation to do so. . . . It is the infusion of behavior with principles and norms that distinguishes regime-governed activity in the international system from more conventional activity, guided exclusively by narrow calculations of interest.

A fundamental distinction must be made between principles and norms on the one hand, and rules and procedures on the other. Principles and norms provide the basic defining characteristics of a regime. There may be many rules and decision-making procedures that are consistent with the same principles and norms. *Changes in rules and decision-making procedures are changes within regimes,* provided that principles and norms are unaltered. . . .

Changes in principles and norms are changes of the regime itself. When norms and principles are abandoned, there is either a change to a new regime or a disappearance of regimes from a given issue-area. For instance, Ruggie contends that the distinction between orthodox and embedded liberalism involves differences over norms and principles. Orthodox liberalism endorses increasing the scope of the market. Embedded liberalism prescribes state action to contain domestic social and economic dislocations generated by markets. Orthodox and embedded liberalism define different regimes. The change from orthodox liberal principles and norms before World War II to embedded liberal principles and norms after World War II was, in Ruggie's terms, a "revolutionary" change.

Fundamental political arguments are more concerned with norms and principles than with rules and procedures. Changes in the latter may be interpreted in different ways. For instance, in the area of international trade, recent revisions in the Articles of Agreement of the General Agreement on Tariffs and Trade (GATT) provide for special and differential treatment for less developed countries (LDCs). All industrialized countries have instituted generalized systems of preferences for LDCs. Such rules violate one of the basic norms of the liberal postwar order, the most-favored-nation treatment of all parties. However, the industrialized nations have treated these alterations in the rules as temporary departures necessitated by the peculiar circumstances of poorer areas. At American insistence the concept of graduation was formally introduced into the GATT Articles after the Tokyo Round. Graduation holds that as countries become more developed they will accept rules consistent with liberal principles. Hence, Northern representatives have chosen to interpret special and differential treatment of developing countries as a change within the regime.

Speakers for the Third World, on the other hand, have argued that the basic norms of the international economic order should be redistribution and equity, not nondiscrimination and efficiency. They see the changes in rules as changes of the regime because they identify these changes with basic changes in principle. There is a fundamental difference between viewing changes in rules as indications of change within the regime and viewing these changes as indications of change between regimes. The difference hinges on assessments of whether principles and norms have changed as well. Such assessments are never easy because they cannot be based on objective behavioral observations. . . .

Finally, it is necessary to distinguish the weakening of a regime from changes within or between regimes. *If the principles, norms, rules, and decision-making procedures of a regime become less coherent, or if actual practice is increasingly inconsistent with principles, norms, rules, and procedures, then a regime has weakened.* Special and differential treatment for developing countries is an indication that the liberal regime has weakened, even if it has not been replaced by something else. . . .

In sum, change within a regime involves alterations of rules and decision-making procedures, but not of norms or principles; change of a regime involves alteration of norms and principles; and weakening of a regime involves incoherence among the components of the regime or inconsistency between the regime and related behavior.

DO REGIMES MATTER?

It would take some courage, perhaps more courage than this editor possesses, to answer this question in the negative. This project began with a simple causal schematic. It assumed that regimes could be conceived of as intervening variables standing between basic causal variables (most prominently, power and interests) and outcomes and behavior. The first attempt to analyze regimes thus assumed the following set of causal relationships (see Figure 1).

Regimes do not arise of their own accord. They are not regarded as ends in themselves. Once in place they do affect related behavior and outcomes. They are not merely epiphenomenal.

The independent impact of regimes is a central analytic issue. The second causal arrow implies that regimes do matter. However, there is no general agreement on this point, and three basic orientations can be distinguished. The conventional structural views the regime concept as useless, if not misleading. Modified structural suggests that regimes may matter, but only under fairly restrictive conditions. And Grotian sees regimes as much more pervasive, as inherent attributes of any complex, persistent pattern of human behavior.

. . . Susan Strange represents the first orientation. She has grave reservations about the value of the notion of regimes. Strange argues that the concept is pernicious because it obfuscates and obscures the interests and power relationships that are the proximate, not just the ultimate, cause of behavior in the international system. "All those international arrangements dignified by the label regime are only too easily upset when either the balance of bargaining power or the perception of

Basic casual variables ———→ Regimes ———→ Related behavior and outcomes

FIGURE 1

national interest (or both together) change among those states who negotiate them."[6] Regimes, if they can be said to exist at all, have little or no impact. They are merely epiphenomenal. The underlying causal schematic is one that sees a direct connection between changes in basic causal factors (whether economic or political) and changes in behavior and outcomes. Regimes are excluded completely, or their impact on outcomes and related behavior is regarded as trivial.

Strange's position is consistent with prevailing intellectual orientations for analyzing social phenomena. These structural orientations conceptualize a world of rational self-seeking actors. The actors may be individuals, or firms, or groups, or classes, or states. They function in a system or environment that is defined by their own interests, power, and interaction. These orientations are resistant to the contention that principles, norms, rules, and decision-making procedures have a significant impact on outcomes and behavior. . . .

The second orientation to regimes, modified structural, is most clearly reflected [by] Keohane[7] and Stein.[8] Both of these authors start from a conventional structural realist perspective, a world of sovereign states seeking to maximize their interest and power. . . .

In a world of sovereign states the basic function of regimes is to coordinate state behavior to achieve desired outcomes in particular issue-areas.[9] Such coordination is attractive under several circumstances. Stein and Keohane posit that regimes can have an impact when Pareto-optimal outcomes could not be achieved through uncoordinated individual calculations of self-interest. The prisoners' dilemma is the classic game-theoretic example. Stein also argues that regimes may have an autonomous effect on outcomes when purely autonomous behavior could lead to disastrous results for both parties. The game of chicken is the game-theoretic analog. Haas and others . . . suggest that regimes may have significant impact in a highly complex world in which *ad hoc*, individualistic calculations of interest could not possibly provide the necessary level of coordination.[10] If, as many have argued, there is a general movement toward a world of complex interdependence, then the number of areas in which regimes can matter is growing.

However, regimes cannot be relevant for zero-sum situations in which states act to maximize the difference between their utilities and those of others. Jervis points to the paucity of regimes in the security area, which more closely approximates zero-sum games than do most economic issue-areas. Pure power motivations preclude regimes. Thus, the second orientation, modified structuralism, sees regimes emerging and having a significant impact, but only under restrictive conditions. It suggests that the first cut should be amended as in Figure 2. . . .

While the modified structural approach does not view the perfect market as a regime, because action there is based purely upon individual calculation without regard to the behavior of others, the third orientation does regard the market

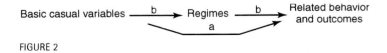

FIGURE 2

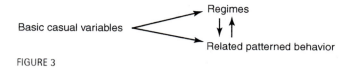

FIGURE 3

as a regime. Patterns of behavior that persist over extended periods are infused with normative significance. A market cannot be sustained by calculations of self-interest alone. It must be, in Ruggie's terms, *embedded* in a broader social environment that nurtures and sustains the conditions necessary for its functioning. Even the balance of power, regarded by conventional structural realist analysts as a purely conflictual situation, can be treated as a regime.[11] The causal schema suggested by a Grotian orientation either closely parallels the first cut shown in Figure 1, or can be depicted as in Figure 3. Patterned behavior reflecting calculations of interest tends to lead to the creation of regimes, and regimes reinforce patterned behavior.

The Grotian tradition . . . offers a counter to structural realism of either the conventional or the modified form. It rejects the assumption that the international system is composed of sovereign states limited only by the balance of power. . . . States are rarified abstractions. Elites have transnational as well as national ties. Sovereignty is a behavioral variable, not an analytic assumption. The ability of states to control movements across their borders and to maintain dominance over all aspects of the international system is limited. Security and state survival are not the only objectives. Force does not occupy a singularly important place in international politics. Elites act within a communications net, embodying rules, norms, and principles, which transcends national boundaries. . . .

Regimes are much more easily encompassed by a Grotian worldview. But, as the arguments made by Jervis, Keohane, Stein, Lipson, and Cohen indicate, the concept is not precluded by a realist perspective. The issue is not so much whether one accepts the possibility of principles, norms, rules, and decision-making procedures affecting outcomes and behavior, as what one's basic assumption is about the normal state of international affairs. Adherents of a Grotian perspective accept regimes as a pervasive and significant phenomenon in the international system. Adherents of a structural realist orientation see regimes as a phenomenon whose presence cannot be assumed and whose existence requires careful explanation. The two "standard cases" are fundamentally different, and it is the definition of the standard case that identifies the basic theoretical orientation. . . .

In sum, conventional structural arguments do not take regimes seriously: if basic causal variables change, regimes will also change. Regimes have no independent impact on behavior. Modified structural arguments, represented here by a number of adherents of a realist approach to international relations, see regimes as mattering only when independent decision making leads to undesired outcomes. Finally, Grotian perspectives accept regimes as a fundamental part of all patterned human interaction, including behavior in the international system.

EXPLANATIONS FOR REGIME DEVELOPMENT

For those authors who see regimes as something more than epiphenomena, the second major issue posed by a schematic that sees regimes as intervening variables between basic causal factors and related outcomes and behavior becomes relevant. What is the relationship between basic causal factors and regimes? What are the conditions that lead to regime creation, persistence, and dissipation? Here regimes are treated as the dependent variable.

A wide variety of basic causal variables have been offered to explain the development of regimes. The most prominent in this volume are egoistic self-interest, political power, norms and principles, habit and custom, and knowledge. The last two are seen as supplementary, augmenting more basic forces related to interest, power, and values.

1. Egoistic Self-interest

The prevailing explanation for the existence of international regimes is egoistic self-interest. By egoistic self-interest I refer to the desire to maximize one's own utility function where that function does not include the utility of another party. The egoist is concerned with the behavior of others only insofar as that behavior can affect the egoist's utility. All contractarian political theories from Hobbes to Rawls are based on egoistic self-interest. In contrast, pure power seekers are interested in maximizing the difference between their power capabilities and those of their opponent. . . .

Stein[12] elaborates two circumstances under which unconstrained individual choice provides incentives for cooperation. The first occurs when such choice leads to Pareto-suboptimal outcomes: prisoner's dilemma and the provision of collective goods are well-known examples. Stein refers to this as the dilemma of common interests. Its resolution requires "collaboration," the active construction of a regime that guides individual decision making. Unconstrained individual decision making may also be eschewed when it would lead to mutually undesired outcomes and where the choice of one actor is contingent on the choice made by the other: the game of chicken is a prominent example. Stein refers to this as the dilemma of common aversions; it can be resolved through "coordination." Coordination need not be formalized or institutionalized. So long as everyone agrees to drive on the right side of the road, little more is needed. (Stein's concept of collaboration conforms with the definition of regimes used here. It is not so clear that coordination involves regimes. Coordination may only require the construction of rules. If these rules are not informed by any proximate principles or norms, they will not conform to the definition of regimes set forth earlier.)

While Stein employs a game-theoretic orientation, Keohane utilizes insights from microeconomic theories of market failure to examine dilemmas of common interests. He is primarily concerned with the demand for regimes, the conditions under which *ad hoc* agreements fail to provide Pareto-optimal outcomes. He maintains that "Regimes can make agreement easier if they provide frameworks for establishing legal liability (even if these are not perfect); improve the quantity and quality of information available to actors; or reduce other transactions costs, such as costs of organization or of making side-payments."[13] These benefits provided by regimes are likely to outweigh the costs of regime formation and maintenance when there is asymmetric information, moral hazard, potential dishonesty, or high issue density. In addition, the costs of forming regimes will be lower when there is a high level of formal and informal communication among states, a condition more likely to be found in open political systems operating under conditions of complex interdependence.

Egoistic self-interest is also regarded as an important determinant of regimes by several other authors. Young argues that there are three paths to regime formation: spontaneous, in which regimes emerge from the converging expectations of many individual actions; negotiated, in which regimes are formed by explicit agreements; and imposed, in which regimes are initially forced upon actors by external imposition. The first two are based on egoistic calculations. . . .

2. Political Power

The second major basic causal variable used to explain regime development is political power. Two different orientations toward power can be distinguished. The first is cosmopolitan and instrumental: power is used to secure optimal outcomes for the system as a whole. In game-theoretic terms power is used to promote joint maximization. It is power in the service of the common good. The second approach is particularistic and potentially consummatory. Power is used to enhance the values of specific actors within the system. . . . In game-theoretic terms power is used to maximize individual payoffs. It is power in the service of particular interests.

a. Power in the Service of the Common Good

The first position is represented by a long tradition in classical and neoclassical economics associated with the provision of public goods. The hidden hand was Adam Smith's most compelling construct: the good of all from the selfishness of each; there could be no more powerful defense of egoism. But Smith recognized that it was necessary for the state to provide certain collective goods. These included defense, the maintenance of order, minimum levels of welfare, public works, the protection of infant industries, and standards for commodities.[14] Economists have pointed to the importance of the state for establishing property rights and enforcing contracts; that is, creating conditions that prevent predatory as opposed to market behavior. The state must create institutions that equate public and private rates of return.[15] Keynesian analysis gives the state a prominent role in managing macroeconomic variables. For all of these arguments the purpose of state action is to further general societal interests.

The contemporary economist who has become most clearly associated with arguments emphasizing the instrumental role of power for cosmopolitan interests in the international system is Charles Kindleberger. In *The World in Depression,* Kindleberger argues that the depression of the 1930s could have been prevented by effective state leadership. An effective leader would have acted as a lender of last resort and provided a market for surplus commodities. In the interwar period the United States was able but unwilling to assume these burdens, and Great Britain was willing but unable. The result was economic chaos. In a more recent statement Kindleberger has listed the following functions that states perform for the international trading system:

1. Protecting economic actors from force.
2. Cushioning the undesirable effects of an open system by, for instance, providing adjustment assistance for import-competing industries.
3. Establishing standards for products. In the absence of such standards inordinate energy may be wasted finding information about products.
4. Providing a national currency that can be used as an international reserve and transactions currency.
5. Constructing public works such as docks and domestic transportation systems.
6. Compensating for market imperfections by, for instance, becoming a lender of last resort when private financial institutions become so cautious that their conservatism could destroy global liquidity.[16]

Despite its emphasis on political action, Kindleberger's perspective is still profoundly liberal. . . . A market economy will maximize the utility of society as a whole. Political power is put at the service of the common good.

b. Power in the Service of Particular Interests

The articles in this volume are less oriented toward cosmopolitan ends; rather, they focus on power as an instrument that can be used to enhance the utility of particular actors, usually states. A game-theoretic analogy makes it easier to distinguish between two important variants of the viewpoint of power in the service of particular interests. The first assumes that pay-offs are fixed and that an actor's choice of strategy is autonomously determined solely by these pay-offs. The second assumes that power can be used to alter pay-offs and influence actor strategy.

The first approach closely follows the analysis that applies when purely cosmopolitan objectives are at stake, except that political power is used to maximize individual, not joint, pay-offs. Under certain configurations of interest, there is an incentive to create regimes and the provision of these regimes is a function of the distribution of power. . . . Hegemons provide these goods not because they are interested in the well-being of the system as a whole, but because regimes enhance their own national values.

. . . The theory of hegemonic leadership suggests that under conditions of declining hegemony there will be a weakening of regimes. Without leadership, principles, norms, rules, and decision-making procedures cannot easily be upheld. No one actor will be willing to provide the collective goods needed to make the regime work smoothly and effectively. Stein's analysis, on the other hand, suggests that as hegemony declines there will be greater incentives for collaboration because collective goods are no longer being provided by the hegemon. The international system more closely resembles an oligopoly than a perfect market. . . .

For Stein, interests alone can effectively sustain order. Hegemonic decline can lead to stronger regimes.

The second line of argument associated with power in the service of specific interests investigates the possibility that powerful actors may be able to alter the pay-offs that confront other actors or influence the strategies they choose. . . .

In this context Oran Young develops the notion of imposed regimes. Dominant actors may explicitly use a combination of sanctions and incentives to compel other actors to act in conformity with a particular set of principles, norms, rules, and decision-making procedures. Alternatively, dominant actors may secure de facto compliance by manipulating opportunity sets so that weaker actors are compelled to behave in a desired way. . . .

When a hegemonic state acts to influence the strategy of other actors the regime is held hostage to the persistence of the existing distribution of power in the international system. If the hegemon's relative capabilities decline, the regime will collapse. Young argues that imposed orders are likely to disintegrate when there are major shifts in underlying power capabilities. . . .

3. Norms and Principles

To this point in the discussion, norms and principles have been treated as endogenous: they are the critical defining characteristics of any given regime. However, norms and principles that influence the regime in a particular issue-area but are not directly related to that issue-area can also be regarded as explanations for the creation, persistence, and dissipation of regimes. The most famous example of such a formulation is Max Weber's *Protestant Ethic and the Spirit of Capitalism*. Weber argues that the rise of capitalism is intimately associated with the evolution of a Calvinist religious doctrine that fosters hard work while enjoining profligacy and uses worldly success as an indication of predestined fate. . . .[17] Such values are critical constraints on self-interested calculations that would too often lead to untrustworthy and dishonest behavior.[18]

Financing by various pariah groups around the world offers a clear example of the way in which noneconomic norms have facilitated market activity. For instance, bills of exchange were devised by Jewish bankers during the late Middle Ages to avoid violence and extortion from the nobility: safer to carry a piece of paper than to carry specie. However, the piece of paper had to be honored by the recipient. This implied a high level of trust and such trust was enhanced by conventions: established practices were reinforced by the exclusionary nature of the group, which facilitated surveillance and the application of sanctions. The importance of conventions for the use of bills of exchange is reflected in the fact that they were frequently used in the Mediterranean basin in the 16th century but they were not used at the interface with the non-Mediterranean world in Syria where, according to Braudel, "two mutually suspicious worlds met face to face. . . . "

. . . John Ruggie's highly original analysis of the postwar economic regime argues that it was founded upon principles of embedded rather than orthodox liberalism. The domestic lesson of the 1930s was that societies could not tolerate the consequences of an untrammeled market. This set of diffuse values, which permeated the capitalist world, was extended from the domestic to the international sphere in the Bretton Woods agreements.

This discussion suggests that there is a hierarchy of regimes. Diffuse principles and norms, such as hard work as a service to God, condition behavior in specific issue-areas. In international relations, the most important diffuse principle is sovereignty. . . .

4. Usage and Custom

The last two sets of causal variables affecting regime development are usage and custom, and knowledge. . . . Usage and custom, and knowledge are not treated in this volume as exogenous variables capable of generating a regime on their own. Rather, they supplement and reinforce pressures associated with egoistic self-interest, political power, and diffuse values.

Usage refers to regular patterns of behavior based on actual practice; custom, to long-standing practice. . . .[19] Patterned behavior accompanied by shared expectations is likely to become infused with normative significance: actions based purely on instrumental calculations can come to be regarded as rule-like or principled behavior. They assume legitimacy. A great deal of western commercial law, in fact, developed out of custom and usage initially generated by self-interest. Practices that began as *ad hoc* private arrangements later became the basis for official commercial law. . . .[20]

5. Knowledge

The final variable used to explain the development of regimes is knowledge. Like usage and custom, knowledge is usually treated as an intervening, not an exogenous, variable. In an earlier study Ernst Haas . . . defined knowledge as "the sum of technical information and of theories about that information which commands sufficient consensus at a given time among interested actors to serve as a guide to public policy designed to achieve some social goal. . . ."[21] Knowledge creates a basis for cooperation by illuminating complex interconnections that were not previously understood. Knowledge can not only enhance the prospects for convergent state behavior, it can also transcend "prevailing lines of ideological cleavage. . . ."[22]

For knowledge to have an independent impact in the international system, it must be widely accepted by policy makers. Stein points out that rules concerning health, such as quarantine regulations, were radically altered by new scientific knowledge such as the discovery of the microbe that causes cholera, the transmission of yellow fever by mosquitoes, and the use of preventive vaccines. Prior to developments such as these, national health regulations were primarily determined by political concerns. After these discoveries, however, national behavior was determined by an international regime, or at least a set of rules, dictated by accepted scientific knowledge. . . .[23]

New knowledge can provide the basis for . . . evolutionary change, which usually involves altering rules and procedures within the context of a given set of principles and norms. In contrast, revolutionary change, which generates new principles and norms, is associated with shifts in power. As an example of evolutionary change, . . . the fixed exchange rate system agreed to at Bretton Woods was based upon understandings derived from the interwar experience and then-current knowledge about domestic monetary institutions and structures. States were extremely sensitive to competitive devaluation and were not confident that domestic monetary policy could provide insulation from external disturbances. It was much easier to accept a floating exchange rate regime in the 1970s because the knowledge and related institutional capacity for controlling monetary aggregates had substantially increased. . . .

CONCLUSION

In approaching the two basic questions that guided this exercise—the impact of regimes on related behavior and outcomes, and the relationship between basic causal variables and regimes—the essays in this volume reflect two different orientations to international relations. The Grotian perspective, which informs the essays of Hopkins and Puchala and of Young, sees regimes as a pervasive facet of social interaction. It is catholic in its description of the underlying causes of regimes. Interests, power, diffuse norms, customs, and knowledge may all play a role in regime formation. These causal factors may be manifest through the behavior of individuals, particular bureaucracies, and international organizations, as well as states.

The structural realist orientation . . . is more circumspect. The exemplar or standard case for the realist perspective does not include international regimes. Regimes arise only under restrictive conditions characterized by the failure of individual decision making to secure desired outcomes. The basic causal variables that lead to the creation of regimes are power and interest. The basic actors are states.

. . . A more serious departure from structural reasoning occurs when regimes are seen as autonomous variables independently affecting not only related behavior and outcomes, but also the basic causal variables that led to their creation in the first place. . . .

NOTES

1. Robert O. Keohane and Joseph S. Nye, *Power and Interdependence* (Boston: Little, Brown, 1977), p. 19.
2. Ernst Haas, "Technological Self-Reliance for Latin America: the OAS Contribution," *International Organization* 34, 4 (Autumn 1980), p. 553.
3. Hedley Bull, *The Anarchical Society: A Study of Order in World Politics* (New York: Columbia University Press, 1977), p. 54.
4. Robert Jervis, "Security Regimes," in Stephen D. Krasner, ed., *International Regimes* (Ithaca, NY: Cornell University Press, 1983), p. 357.
5. Kenneth Waltz, *Theory of International Relations* (Reading, MA: Addison-Wesley, 1979); Morton Kaplan, *Systems and Process in International Politics* (New York: Wiley, 1957), p. 23; Kaplan, *Towards Professionalism in International Theory* (New York: Free Press, 1979), pp. 66–69, 73.
6. Susan Strange, "*Cave! hic dragones*: A Critique of Regime Analysis," in Stephen D. Krasner, ed., *International Regimes* (Ithaca, NY: Cornell University Press, 1983).
7. Robert O. Keohane, "The Demand for International Regimes," in Krasner, ed., *International Regimes*, op. cit.

8. Arthur A. Stein, "Coordination and Collaboration: Regimes in an Anarchic World," in Krasner, *International Regimes,* op. cit.

9. Vinod K. Aggarwal emphasizes this point. See his "Hanging by a Thread: International Regime Change in the Textile/Apparel System, 1950–1979," Ph.D. diss., Stanford University, 1981, chap. 1.

10. Ernst B. Haas, "Words Can Hurt You; or, Who Said What to Whom About Regimes," in Krasner, *International Regimes,* op. cit.

11. Bull, *The Anarchical Society,* chap. 5.

12. Stein, "Coordination and Collaboration," op. cit.

13. Keohane, "The Demand for International Regimes," op. cit., p. 338.

14. There is a lively debate over precisely how much of a role Smith accords to the state. Some (see, for instance, Albert Hirschman, *The Passions and the Interests* [Princeton: Princeton University Press, 1977], pp. 103–104) maintain that Smith wanted to limit the folly of government by having it do as little as possible. Others (see, for instance, Colin Holmes, "Laissez-faire in Theory and Practice: Britain 1800–1875," *Journal of European Economic History* 5, 3 [1976], p. 673; and Carlos Diaz-Alejandro, "Delinking North and South: Unshackled or Unhinged," in Albert Fishlow et al., *Rich and Poor Nations in the World Economy* [New York: McGraw-Hill, 1978], pp. 124–25) have taken the intermediate position endorsed here. Others see Smith trying to establish conditions for a moral society that must be based on individual choice, for which a materialistically oriented, egoistically maintained economic system is only instrumental. See, for instance, Leonard Billet, "The Just Economy: The Moral Basis of the Wealth of Nations," *Review of Social Economy* 34 (December 1974).

15. Jack Hirschleifer, "Economics from a Biological Viewpoint," *Journal of Law and Economics* 20 (April 1977); Weber, *Economy and Society,* pp. 336–37; Douglass C. North and Robert Paul Thomas, *The Rise of the Western World: A New Economic History* (Cambridge: Cambridge University Press, 1973), chap. 1.

16. Charles P. Kindleberger, "Government and International Trade," *Princeton Essays in International Finance* (International Finance Section, Princeton University, July 1978). Adam Smith was less enamoured with leadership. He felt that reasonable intercourse could only take place in the international system if there was a balance of power. Without such a balance the strong would dominate and exploit the weak. See Diaz-Alejandro, "Delinking North and South," p. 92.

17. For a recent discussion see David Laitin, "Religion, Political Culture, and the Weberian Tradition," *World Politics* 30, 4 (July 1978), especially pp. 568–69. For another discussion of noneconomic values in the rise of capitalism see Hirschman, *The Passions and the Interests.*

18. Fred Hirsch, *The Social Limits to Growth* (Cambridge: Harvard University Press, 1976), chap. 11. See also Michael Walzer. "The Future of Intellectuals and the Rise of the New Class," *New York Review of Books* 27 (20 March 1980).

19. Max Weber, *Economy and Society* (Berkeley: University of California Press, 1977), p. 29.

20. Leon E. Trakman, "The Evolution of the Law Merchant: Our Commercial Heritage," Part I, *Journal of Maritime Law and Commerce* 12, 1 (October 1980) and Part II, ibid., 12, 2 (January 1981); Harold Berman and Colin Kaufman, "The Law of International Commercial Transactions *(Lex Mercatoria),*" *Harvard International Law Journal* 19, 1 (Winter 1978).

21. Ernst Haas, "Why Collaborate? Issue-Linkage and International Regimes," *World Politics* 32, 3 (April 1980), pp. 367–68.

22. Ibid., p. 368.

23. Stein, "Coordination and Collaboration," op. cit.

Why Collaborate? Issue-Linkage and International Regimes

ERNST B. HAAS

I. WHY STUDY REGIMES?

This essay is yet another attempt to specify the particular mode of international collaboration we call a "regime." . . .

. . . Under what conditions do convergences of interest arise that call for the creation of regimes? How can there be international collaboration despite the persistence of conflict and of differentials in the power of actors?

Institutionalized collaboration can be explored in terms of the interaction between changing knowledge and changing social goals. It seems axiomatic that parties in conflict will, under conditions of changing understanding of their desires and of the constraints under which they must act, seek to define an area of joint gains. The definition of joint gains must be based on the goals of the actors *and* on the calculations ("knowledge") that influence the choice of goals. What, then, about the social power of certain groups and the hegemonic position of strong states in world politics?

If it were possible to predict the outcome of international negotiations by projecting the power of the parties, our question would be answered. If social classes and governments never changed their minds about individual and joint gains, there would be no question. But under conditions of complex interdependence, no such projection is possible. The existence of an unstable hierarchy of issues on the international agenda means that minds are being changed all the time. Hence we focus on changing knowledge and changing goals. . . .

We will begin by exploring relationships between types of interdependence, issues, and the need for collaboration. Next, we will inquire how issues become "linked" into packages called "issue areas." By examining the role of changing knowledge and social goals in defining the content of such packages, four patterns of cognition for choosing regimes are developed. Finally, we will look into the type of organizational arrangements that correspond to various types of regimes. . . .

II. INTERDEPENDENCE, ISSUES, AND ISSUE-AREAS

Negotiations may be controversial or smooth, laden with conflict or free of it. As long as the parties agree on the benefits to be derived from collaboration, conflict does not arise. During the 19th century, for instance, it was taken for granted by all concerned that British investment in Argentine beef production and electric utilities was beneficial for both Britain and Argentina. Negotiating the capital and technology transfers considered appropriate then did not pose a problem. No *issue*, no controversy arose until Britain sought to intervene, diplomatically or militarily, to protect the British investment against Argentine efforts to change the understanding under which it had been introduced earlier. Collaboration becomes conflictual only when the parties begin to disagree on the distribution of benefits to be derived. . . .

Interdependence

. . . If Britain considers herself relatively insensitive to a change, we say that Argentina is *more vulnerable* than Britain. Sensitivity is measured by the perceived effects of interrupting a pattern of interdependence. Vulnerability is measured by the opportunity costs incurred by making alternative arrangements for collaboration when the initial arrangement breaks down. Unequal sensitivity and vulnerability amount to *asymmetrical interdependence:* Britain is less dependent on Argentina than Argentina is on Britain. . . . The construction of international arrangements regulating interdependence—which we call regimes—under conditions of complex interdependence depends on how the asymmetries are perceived by the participants. Their definition of the issues requiring regulation is a function of the perceived costs of asymmetrical interdependence. Calculations of sensitivity and vulnerability therefore inform the discussion of remedial measures.

Any two countries may collaborate on a number of topics at the same time. There is not necessarily a connection between these topics in the minds of the actors. Some may become controversial issues while others remain free of conflict. . . .

Our first step must be to clarify what is meant by "issue" and by "linking issues." The discussion of linkages will enable us to specify what we mean by "issue-area." We will then be able to discuss how knowledge may or may not be used in the establishment of linkages, and how issue-areas differ from each other.

Issues and Issue-Areas

Issues are separate items that appear on the agenda of negotiators. In the [Law of the Sea] (LOS) negotiations, some of the issues are concerned with the width of the territorial sea and the national economic zone, who can mine the deep sea for manganese nodules and under what conditions, who can draw up rules for fisheries conservation, and whether marine pollution should be controlled by national or multilateral means. The issues in international monetary collaboration include the size and type of reserve assets held by the International Monetary Fund, the conditions under which members can draw on them, and the proportion to be used for maintaining international liquidity, protecting the balance-of-payments positions of certain members, and compensating other members for losses incurred because of foreign trade vicissitudes. The agenda also includes, of course, the question of whether there should be fixed, flexible, or floating exchange rates. In what sense are these issues connected with each other?

It is possible to think of monetary management as being made up of separate issues. Central banks will negotiate to increase liquidity, shore up each other's currencies, and fix the rate of exchange between currencies either by manipulating the currency market or through administrative regulation. In negotiating a conflict, each issue can be handled separately. Monetary management was largely handled this way prior to the Bretton Woods Agreement. Efforts were made to deal with monetary issues as packages only when it was generally recognized that the resolution of *each* of these issues had an effect on the overall economic health of the participants. Degrees of currency fluctuation were no longer considered in terms of the short-term balance of payments alone but also in conjunction with overall rates of growth, inflation, and deflation. Previously separate monetary issues had been converted by the actors themselves into an *issue-area,* a recognized cluster of concerns involving interdependence not only among the parties but among the issues themselves. . . . We can speak, since 1944, of the existence of an internationally recognized monetary issue-area. . . .

Things are more complicated in ocean management because no consensus on knowledge has emerged to give coherence to the consensus on goals. The ocean matters to governments because their citizens use it to fish, sail ships, extract oil, fight wars, and conduct research; they also now recognize that the oceans help determine the weather and that it may not be a good idea to use them as the world's garbage dump. Each of these activities has given rise to conflicts among countries. Governments have sought to resolve them by means of bilateral treaties and multilateral conventions establishing basic ground rules for behavior. But until very recently, each issue was approached separately. . . .

In 1967 a new doctrine was announced: the oceans were to be considered "the common heritage of mankind," and the totality of their resources a means for redistributing income and welfare among all countries. To achieve this, it was no longer possible to consider issues separately since each issue was thought to contribute to increased equality among states. More importantly, effects of interdependence *among* issues were now recognized: changing marine technology could result in over-fishing, unacceptable pollution, greater ship disasters; and the mining of deep-sea minerals could depress the price of the same minerals mined on land. As a result, the Law of the Sea Conference was convened by the United Nations to resolve the cluster of issues by means of a single treaty. Ocean matters became, for the first time, a tentatively recognized issue-area. But, as we shall see, there is a considerable distance between the cognitive event of issue-area recognition and the institutional event of regime construction: the inter-issue Law of the Sea negotiations . . . dragged on for a decade.

There are important differences between the construction of regimes for money and for the oceans. Knowledge relevant to ocean management is far less consensual than the macroeconomic professional consensus that existed between 1950 and 1970. Although oceanographers, fisheries specialists, and mining engineers accumulated a great deal of technical information during these decades, neither they nor government officials have succeeded in *integrating* this information into a strategy for realizing the common heritage of mankind. Global welfare is indeed recognized as an overriding social goal; but there is no consensus on *how* the management of specific resources can be aggregated into attaining it in the form of joint gains. . . .

State power is a vital mediating agent in the absence of consensual knowledge. Those who claim the knowledge and the ability to act can negotiate for private goods they are able to control. When they want others to be barred from the benefits of fisheries conservation and prevented from polluting the shoreline, they create exclusive national zones; when they want to exploit a high-sea resource, they invoke the principle of open access. Nobody has the power to impose a global regime, but many have the power to impose private spheres; and a few have the capability to monopolize deep-ocean mining.

The LOS negotiations (like the parallel effort to construct the NIEO [New International Economic Order]) constituted a case of "premature" issue-packaging. The package was the result of a negotiating strategy adopted by the weak— first in UNCTAD and later in all international economic forums. In addition, the character of the resources to be subjected to a regime may explain the difference in outcomes. Ocean-related resources constitute a very heterogeneous group of concerns, united only by the fact that they are situated on or under the water. Money, on the other hand, is a universal medium on which all economic activity depends; for better or for worse, the management of money responds to some widely accepted theories. The management of ocean resources does not. . . .

Knowledge

Knowledge has emerged in our argument as a basic ingredient for exploring the development of issue-areas. A further explication of this notion is essential if I am to avoid being labelled a technocratic determinist. I do *not* mean that knowledge is a synonym for the discoveries of natural science, the opposite of ideology, the sole basis for establishing objective truth, superior to politics, or a substance that makes experts wise and politicians clowns.

Knowledge is the sum of technical information and of theories about that information which commands sufficient consensus at a given time among interested actors to serve as a guide to public policy designed to achieve some social goal. Knowledge incorporates scientific notions relating to the social goal. Such notions are rarely free from ideological elements. Nor are they necessarily free from the self-interest of their proponents. . . . None of this matters for our purposes. As long as these activities are accepted as a basis for public policy by groups and individuals professing varying political ideologies, we consider such notions as consensual. Knowledge is the professionally mediated body of theory and information that transcends prevailing lines of ideological cleavage.

Internationally, then, the sharing of a fund of knowledge among governments otherwise in opposition to each other is a form of cognitive convergence. When Soviet and American engineers agree on the properties of strategic weapons, and economists on the determinants of the business cycle and how to model it (and there is evidence that such agreement has occurred), certain ideological differences are being bridged by converging modes of thought. The same happens when pollutants are identified, measured, and related to the quality of life, or when the trade-offs among various sources of energy are assessed. . . .

But *who is* knowledgeable—the technical expert, the businessman, the politician, the peasant? Another way to put this question is to ask at what point knowledge is consensual. The monetary theory underlying the Bretton Woods regime existed in the professional literature before 1945; an effort to put it to work internationally was made in 1933. The management doctrine underlying the LOS negotiations had been developed by Arvid Pardo before 1967. Neoclassical economic development doctrine was challenged before 1974. What matters is not when a given view was first developed, but when it attains general acceptance as a guide to public policy. It is normal that technical specialists originate a particular body of knowledge and claim relevance for it. Knowledge becomes salient to regime construction only after it has seeped into the consciousness of policy makers and other influential groups and individuals.[1] In 1945, Keynesian economics was widely accepted by economists and labor leaders, had made important inroads into the U.S. bureaucracy, but was still being resisted by the business community; a few years later, some key business groups made their peace with it. Pardo's approach to ocean management has not been accepted by specialists or governments. The "basic human needs" doctrine has officially taken the place of older development views without completely pre-empting them; it is not yet consensual, but it has its adherents. A claim to knowledge becomes consensual whenever it succeeds in dominating the policy-making process—and that implies acceptance by all major actors involved in that process. In the NIEO negotiations, no such consensus exists. The *dependencia* doctrine is the property of the poor; it is *their* way of organizing the appropriate knowledge, but not the lore on which the rich rely. It is therefore not knowledge in the sense in which the term is used here.

Knowledge constitutes only one dimension of our exploration into issue-areas and issue-linkages. Regimes are constructed by states through the medium of multilateral negotiation. The linking of issues that remained separate in earlier periods can be interpreted as a kind of learning. But learning is but another word for reinterpreting one's interests. Interests may—but need not—change with more consensual knowledge. We now inquire into negotiations and learning as an aspect of issue-linkage that takes into account the varying interests and goals of the parties.

Knowledge, Linkages, and Issue-Areas

Issue-specific negotiations usually deal with topics on which there is an accepted body of knowledge. Economists in general agree on the effects that exchange rate systems have on the benefits derived from trade; fisheries specialists subscribe to the principle of the "maximum sustainable yield." . . . This means that in issue-specific negotiations on these topics there is a high degree of certainty about the efficacy of the *immediate* solution; benefits can be calculated fairly reliably as long as the existing base of knowledge remains unchanged. All other things being equal, the narrower the scope of issues to be negotiated, the higher the degree of certainty about efficient solutions. However, when we assume a dynamic situation of rapidly changing knowledge, the pattern is reversed. Experts can no longer be sure that accepted solutions will bring certain benefits. They will be tempted to expand the scope of topics as they suspect that knowledge in cognate fields has something to tell them about the efficacy of broader types of solutions. For instance, fisheries specialists concerned only with optimal harvesting of a fixed stock may begin to think about artificially manipulating the size of the stock when (1) the means for doing this become known, and (2) fish stocks are considered as a constituent of overall dietary calculations. Under such conditions, inter-issue negotiations offer a greater hope of efficient solutions even though the knowledge base is itself changing and far from conclusive. Greater certainty is a hope, not a scientific given.

Why link issues? Since changes in knowledge and social goals do not necessarily go together we have no warrant for arguing that all economic regimes relying on scientific and technological information *must* owe their origin to this confluence. Nor are we entitled to argue that issues *will* be linked simply because we live under conditions of complex interdependence. Successful negotiations for institutionalizing international collaboration depend on the congruence of interests as much as on changes in consensual knowledge. It follows that issue-linkage will not succeed if the states with a strong stake in the existing distribution of benefits, and the capability to control it, prefer to keep things as they are. The United States and the Soviet Union, for example, saw no reason to link the issues of peaceful nuclear energy and the proliferation of nuclear weapons as long as each was able to control the process of technological diffusion. The desire to construct the non-proliferation regime arose only when the process seemed to pass out of their control. Issue-specific negotiations tend to favor the coalition of states who have long had an interest in the issue and who dominate the resource. Issue-linkage, on the other hand, is favored by those who want "in": a regime that links issues will come into existence only if the "outs" somehow manage to persuade the "ins."

There are three ways of persuasion. (1) One can link issues by introducing into the agenda of multilateral negotiations items that are not connected by any intellectual coherence at all; we call this "tactical linkage." The objective is simply to obtain additional bargaining leverage, to extract a *quid pro quo* not obtainable if the discussion remains confined to a single issue. (2) Issue-linkage may also be attempted, however, to maintain the cohesion of one's coalition. The coalition is held together by a commitment to some overriding social goal, even though the partners disagree with respect to the knowledge necessary to attain it. . . . We call this behavior pattern "fragmented linkage." (3) Issue-linkage may also proceed on the basis of cognitive developments based on consensual knowledge linked to an agreed social goal. This is the pattern of greatest interest to the construction of regimes; we call it "substantive linkage."

Power is present as a mediating agent in all three modes. The credibility of a tactical linkage depends on the "linkee's" perception of the linker's ability and willingness to withhold collaboration if the linkage is refused. In fragmented linkage situations, the potential defectors from the coalition must be held in line by means of side-payments or promises, and the opposing coalition must be effectively threatened. Even in situations of substantive linkage, knowledge is rarely so consensual as to eliminate the role of threat and reward as a way of persuading the weaker negotiating partners. But the use of power is always limited by the perception of complex interdependence that motivates the parties to negotiate in the first place.

Tactical issue-linkage is a negotiating ploy that eschews reliance on intellectual coherence among the issues linked. . . . Deep-sea nodule mining can be regulated without also worrying about the right of passage through straits. Yet these issues were in fact linked because the victims of asymmetrical interdependence wished to link them and had enough leverage to succeed. Tactical linkage is a cheap way to increase pay-offs because it expands the agenda of possible benefits to be derived. . . . What is called "package dealing" and "linkage politics" in journalistic accounts of foreign policy conforms to this pattern; so does the legislative practice of log-rolling. Tactical issue-linkage, then, is simply a way of maximizing the separate gains of the parties, even though the outcome of the negotiations may be an agreement that establishes a new regime.

Fragmented linkages are best illustrated by the NIEO negotiations, which constitute an attempt to realize some joint gains, even though it is far from clear how the gains will be distributed.[2] Uncertainty over distribution *is* a reason for issue-linkage. If the linkers are uncertain about the interdependence effects of the issues, it is safer to link, in the interest of gaining maximum concessions and holding their coalition together—even in disregard of knowledge that may suggest that linking is unwise substantively and unacceptable to the opposition politically. Thus we find in the NIEO that every outstanding economic grievance of the South is linked to an overarching argument for global redistribution of resources, ranging from such immediate matters as aid and debt relief to the long-range considerations of technology transfer, commodity price stability, and nonreciprocal tariff treatment. The intellectual justification for the package was worked out by the UNCTAD economists in a series of studies that were widely challenged by economists in the developed countries. Professional knowledge is far from consensual. . . . In general, the entire package *is* related to the global redistribution of resources. There is some coherence from the point of view of the coalition attempting the linkage; but if there is none for the opposing party, we still lack a base of consensual knowledge.

Hence it is the principle of substantive linkage that is of greatest interest to us. We are concerned with explaining how negotiators link issues into packages in deference to some intellectual strategy or evolving awareness of causal understanding. . . .

This proposition must not be overstated: substantive knowledge *alone* cannot legitimate a holistic package of issues. The legitimation depends on the acceptance of a new understanding on the part of key political actors. Governments—even when exposed to novel insights about energy, growth, pollution, or food—cannot be expected to stop considering their policies within the perspective of what passes for the national interest. Substantive issue-linkage depends on learning that the national interest can be redefined or broadened, and that international collaboration is *required* for the realization of national goals. *Knowledge can legitimate collaborative behavior only when the possibility of joint gains from the collaboration exists and is recognized.*

All modes are "rational" in the sense that the actors show concern over cause and effect, and the relationship between ends and means, in seeking to attain a specific goal. But the types of rationality differ. . . .

Substantive issue-linkages lend themselves to holistic prescriptions of salvation. Many holists consider them to be the most conscious of complex systems of cause and effect, most sensitive to many ends and purposes, and most attuned to scan the full range of the means available for solving "the problem." Hence, they consider only this mode "rational" in the common use of the term, and issue-packages agreed upon by any process less rational as just another case of sub-optimizing. This view is not helpful if we wish to understand how regimes come into being; substantive issue-linkage can be effected by cognitive means short of the holistic extreme.

We now apply these propositions about issue-areas and issue-linkage to the way actors order their goals and apply knowledge in the construction of regimes. Issue-linkage refers to negotiating behavior. Our next concern is with the negotiators' structure of perceptions.

III. KNOWLEDGE AND GOALS: HOW TO ORDER THEM TO CHOOSE REGIMES

Knowledge and Goals in Overcoming Dependency

The actors whose cognition is of interest are thinking beings: they do not normally act randomly. . . . Actors can be expected to utilize whatever knowledge is available to help them in the calculation of advantage, whether they do so efficiently or not.

The regimes of concern here all have to do with wealth, welfare, and economic equality among nations. All the goals that matter to the actors are articulated in the global debate about the New International Order. That debate encompasses the conflict over goals associated with an open international economy and the Bretton Woods regime on the one hand, and the revolt of the Third World against that regime on the other. It pits the "liberal" ideology of the wealthy North against the antidependency ideology of the South. Asymmetrical, complex interdependence, as perceived by the underdeveloped countries, provides the basis for the confrontation; the shared goal of the South is to overcome dependency. That goal contains several different development strategies which provide the occasion for the introduction of knowledge.

Import-substituting industrialization is one of the strategies. Its proponents are concerned with raising aggregate national income; they expect the benefits accruing to a few successful enterprises to trickle down into the rest of the society eventually. . . .

Others propose the strategy of economic and technological self-determination. They associate dependency with the structure of capitalism and its global division of labor. The factors causing dependency are thought to include education, the media, the habits of the "center" classes in the "periphery" and their unholy alliances with the elites of the North, as well as the behavior of foreign investors. . . . No single goal can be attained without paying attention to a wide variety of economic, scientific, and social policies now considered relevant. Hence, goals "expand" and "become interconnected."

Redefining Goals

Changes in goals and in knowledge are crucial to our argument. But in the real world neither one changes all the time. We summarize the two processes under discussion without assuming covariation. The goals of governments, in modern times, change because new groups, parties, opinions, and demands enter the national political arena rapidly and in large numbers, reflecting the process of accelerating social mobilization. . . . But this expansion of goals may occur *without* a coherent intellectual understanding of causes and effects, and *without* a complete mastery of the means considered necessary and sufficient to attain the ends. . . .

Similarly, knowledge about causes and effects, means and ends may expand rapidly and command an increasing consensus among the experts who generate it. Consensual knowledge may or may not infect the politicians. . . .

The hallmark of complex interdependence is uncertainty: there are too many goals, all competing for attention; there is no agreement on the best means for attaining them; the understanding of causes is subject to ideological disputation, not consensus; what is a cause to one actor is an effect to another. In short, *goals cannot be ordered into a hierarchy of importance or salience equally acceptable to all.* International collaboration, the effort to regulate asymmetrical interdependence, is an attempt to reduce uncertainty when a multiplicity of values are at stake and the simplest strategy for reducing uncertainty—autarky—is not practicable. Linking issues is fallible man's way of marshaling what knowledge he has in order to attain his goals. Constructing issue-areas by way of substantive linkages implies some ordering. . . .

We can now come back to our discussion of how linkages among issues are negotiated. Issue-specific negotiations do not involve these kinds of uncertainties and coping mechanisms because I do not associate them with complex interdependence. They do not refer to situations in which the need for a new regime is felt, though they are commonly used for adapting and maintaining existing institutional arrangements. We may therefore disregard issue-specific negotiations. In tactical linkage negotiations, knowledge is either not consensual or irrelevant; therefore it cannot inform the negotiations in a systematic fashion. . . .

Linking issues on the basis of fragmented or complete substantive awareness of applicable knowledge is our real concern: actors espousing an "expanding" set of goals seem doomed to relying on what is known or knowable about the physical and social world. . . . They therefore share a commitment to consensual knowledge, whether on a partial or a more complete basis. . . .

Goals considered by politicians are:

Beliefs of experts about knowledge become:		Specific, static	Innterconnected, expanding
	More consensual	Pragmatic	Rational
	Not more consensual	Eclectic	Skeptic

FIGURE 1

Four Cognitive Styles

Goals and knowledge may be combined. Figure 1 suggests schematically how issue-areas develop from separate issues. Each cell captures a particular cognitive style, a particular convergence of ways of thinking about knowledge and action. One may think of the units in the cells as individuals or decision-making teams such as delegations to conferences. . . .

The distinction between static-specific and interconnected-expanding goals has been explained. A clarification about "consensual" knowledge is now needed. What matters is not that substantive knowledge about soil chemistry, ocean currents, or the biology of fish stocks is changing, but that there be a constant and active evolution of ideas about how scientific knowledge can and should be related to politics and policy making. Not merely information, but the management of *knowledge for action* is the vital consideration for the growth of issue-areas. . . . "More consensual" knowledge includes efforts to pick and choose, from among scientific disciplines and endeavors, those items that can be combined in a comprehensive effort to achieve the social or political goals of concern to us. The two modes opt for different principles of organization. They also use different ideologies to justify one procedure or the other.

The Rational Mode

In the rational mode, there is covariation between changes in knowledge and changes in goals. Experts increasingly agree on the management of knowledge for action; politicians accept their consensus as they make it part of their striving to attain more ambitious goals. The combination implies an acceptance of synoptic planning as the appropriate administrative technique. . . . The rational mode presupposes inspiration by a comprehensive doctrine which is the source of the planners' optimism. . . . Rationalists consider themselves masters of technique and substance, means and ends, causes and effects.

Of course, an ordering of goals is achieved by such means—however temporarily. *This ordering depends on the acceptance of the goals and the knowledge by all important actors,* or the exclusion from decision making of any actors who do not share the faith. Has such a situation ever existed in the history of international collaboration? One can think of experts who advocated doctrines of this kind and failed to convince all of the key actors of their vision: such was Arvid Pardo's fate

in the Law of the Sea negotiations, Robert Triffin's in the reform of the international monetary system, and Lord Orr's in the field of food.

In the heyday of the Northern economic boom after World War II. Keynesian
macroeconomics came close to providing such a consensus. . . .

We now know that the consensus was temporary. The goals of many of the
actors changed; the NIEO reflects the change. Consensual economics disinte-
grated into "left" and "right" Keynesianism, neoconservativism and neo-Marxism.
Each school has its own way of linking issues, or of not linking them. The rational
mode has not demonstrated its staying power—whether the knowledge comes
from economics, oceanography, or nuclear engineering.

The Eclectic Mode

Eclecticism is the logical obverse of rationalism. Knowledge is not used in decision
making so as to arrive at a more integrated understanding among sectors and disciplines. Fisheries experts, geophysicists, petroleum engineers, and naval architects
go their separate professional ways; they make little effort to reinterpret their specialized knowledge under the conceptual roof of "managing the common heritage
of mankind." Politicians and administrators also make no concerted effort to
change the social objectives to which they are committed. They continue to conserve fish stocks instead of planning to meet nutritional needs; they encourage the
construction of supertankers, issue leases for ocean mining, exclude foreign pol-
luters from straits and harbors—all without integrating these objectives into an
ordered set of priorities for the oceans.

"Eclectics" comprise the large number of actors who are content to continue
doing what they have always done. They believe neither in salvation by way of
more consensual knowledge about techniques nor in the possibility of fashioning
more integrated and ambitious goals. . . . Such actors may engage in package-
dealing when they encounter one another in international negotiations; but the
deals feature the *tactical* linking of issues.

Whether or not conceptual integration takes place is a matter judged by the
outside observer on his own terms. The participants, unmindful of the distinctions
made by us, may well consider their activities as constructing issue-areas in line
with the best scientific knowledge available to them. The key is the mode of decision making they adopt; eclecticism prevails if no attempt is made to transcend disjointed incrementalism. The participants do not use methods of synoptic
assessment; they do not construct formal models of the oceans including *all* activities of concern; they do not attempt to make a joint simulation of cost-benefit
alternatives covering fishing, mining, shipping, and pollution control (and hence,
there is no real appreciation of trade-offs). Politicians package issues in line with
coalitional and bargaining dynamics, rather than in terms of agreement on integrated objectives to be attained. . . .

The Skeptic Mode

What if goals entertained by politicians do become broader, more interconnected,
and more consensual, but the accompanying knowledge remains or becomes fragmented? The effort to order issues along a hierarchy of priorities is made, but there

is no adequate, accepted body of knowledge informing the order. The ordering is merely rhetorical: one set of negotiators is committed to one line of analysis with its source of certainty while another set professes quite a different approach. Agreement among actors on the hierarchy is not likely to be long-lived. . . .

"Skeptics," therefore, are either impatient or unconcerned with knowledge. They do not believe in, or are unwilling to wait for, the arrival of consensus among the experts. . . . Synoptic planning and analytic techniques coexist with disjointed incrementalism in making decisions. . . . The larger goals are approached through hit-or-miss programs and single-shot solutions that are not consistently justified in terms of some overarching logic or method.

The Pragmatic Mode   But what if there is an increasing body of consensual knowledge among experts, which is not fully matched among politicians with an expanding set of social goals recognizing intellectual interconnections? The situation prevails when publics and policy makers become aware of unwanted and unanticipated consequences of industrialism while also wanting its benefits. Goals do change in recognition of more consensual knowledge, but not all actors agree on how the goals ought to be ordered. Pragmatists attempt to use the analytical techniques associated with what Lindblom calls "strategic planning." They do seek to contrive substantive linkages on the basis of such efforts at integrating knowledge. But pragmatic experts can never be sure to find an understanding and sympathetic audience among all of their political masters.

While rationalists strive for the aggregating of goals into issue-areas, pragmatists tend to experiment with combining two or three issues; they may consent to decompose them into separate issues once they are convinced that the aggregation is conceptually faulty or politically ineffective. Pragmatists would prefer to link issues substantively at all times, but will settle for partial substantive linkage when they must. . . . As single goals change and coalitions among actors shift, so does the order of priorities among goals. Improved knowledge may help in the ordering; but knowledge, too, is rarely final and uncontested. Pragmatists must work on the border of relative and temporary certainty and of occasionally ordered social goals. Hence, they must settle for stop-and-go tactics—attempts at grasping larger wholes, followed by periods of retrenchment. . . .

IV. COGNITIVE PROCESSES, CHANGE, AND REGIMES

My purpose is to suggest an ideal-typical definition of regimes, to inquire how, in our era, international collaboration can flourish in a setting of conflict, how islands of order can form in an ocean of disorder. Different modes of cognition can suggest how men redefine their interests to attempt the realization of joint gains in some fields while continuing to play the zero-sum game in others. Negotiation on the basis of substantive linkages does not guarantee successful regimes. Cooperation on an informal basis can certainly take place in the absence of full-fledged regimes. . . .

Hypotheses of Change

. . . The four hypotheses that follow make claims about cognitive styles, issue-linkage, the prominence of state power in the linkage, and the capacity of any resulting regime to survive. We assume that the cognitive style informing the negotiations characterizes all the important parties: all are rationalists, skeptics, eclectics, or pragmatists. The more complex situation of mixtures of prevalent styles will be taken up when we discuss "learning through negotiation."

1. If the negotiating conference is characterized by *eclecticism,* issues will be linked exclusively in a tactical manner. The credibility of the linkage is largely a function of the will and the ability of key parties to impose it, including the manipulation of technical information. It is unlikely that a regime will emerge; if it does, it will not outlive the first important technological innovation.

2. If the negotiating conference is dominated by the *rational mode,* substantive issue-linkage on the basis of agreed doctrines will prevail. Power differentials among states are not important as mediating instruments. The resulting regime will be as stable as the doctrinal consensus on which it rests.

3. If the negotiators are *skeptics,* fragmented issue-linkage will prevail, and the will and capability of powerful states can be expected to remain important as instrumentalities for rewarding coalition partners and paying off opponents. The resulting regime will be weak and unstable.

4. If the negotiators are *pragmatists,* they will first attempt substantive issue-linkage and withdraw to fragmented linkage when this becomes politic. State power is a factor in reaching an agreement, but not an essential one. The resulting regime, though including fewer issues than had been hoped, will nevertheless be fairly stable. It will also be capable of being adapted and adjusted so as to include additional issues later.

Regime stability implies several things. The norms, rules, and procedures that make up the regime will not be challenged by the members so as to throw the existence of the arrangement into doubt. The rights of the parties will be generally respected and obligations will be carried out. Challenges will take the form of conduct specified by the regime's procedures. . . .

Structural Explanation of Change

Students of international regimes are in disagreement as to whether changes in the rules of collaborative games among nations are best explained in "structural" or in "cognitive" terms. While my explanation is cognitive, the burden of this section is to suggest that the differences can be reconciled with the help of the notion of the "national interest," albeit not a platonic ideal interest, but interest perceived by actors and identified by analysts.

In the structural explanation, we seek to identify deep-seated patterns or conditions in the international system and to ask whether these have or have not changed. We can then explain new institutional patterns in terms of such changes. The differential in power, influence, and stratification among states is the condition of greatest interest to the structuralist. He sees the world in terms of changing balances between "weak" (or new, or underdeveloped) states and "hegemonic" (or strong, industrialized, and—potentially or actually—militarily dominant) states. International regimes flourish when hegemonic states define them, operate them, and pay for them; they decline when hegemons change their minds. Naturally, the rules of a regime are tailored to the national interests of the hegemons. The law of the sea was dictated by those who owned big navies, merchant marines, and fishing fleets before 1967; monetary order was maintained by the economically most powerful: Britain before 1914, the United States between 1945 and 1971. When the relative power position of the hegemon eroded—for whatever reasons—the regime had to change. Structuralists do not worry about differences in *how* the national interest may be understood by various groups, bureaucracies, and individuals within a state. The strength of the state is taken as the key ingredient of the explanation, and the balance of power among states as the predictor of specific regimes.

This approach can be applied to our way of explaining regime construction. It explains fully the situation in which no new consensual knowledge enters the negotiating process. Interests are considered fixed. When a given state lacks the capability to make its interests prevail and new actors challenge its former primacy, the game changes. One may then say that international collaborative arrangements that reflect *static* knowledge of cause-and-effect patterns and *settled* views about the relationship of means to ends *are* a reflection of established stratification patterns. Since there are no influential ideas challenging the prevailing technical wisdom of how to manage money or fish stocks, choice is effectively constrained by prevalent schedules of opportunity costs. When the distribution of power and influence among states changes—as it surely has since 1960—national interests that had previously lacked the opportunity to be heard, now become very audible indeed. But since these "weak" states lack the ability to challenge the prevailing technical knowledge they must seek a better deal on the basis of the negotiating processes we have identified with tactical and fragmented linkages. The weak must rely on their numerical strength and their ability to forge coalitions by granting or withholding benefits desired by the "strong." More voices mean more interests, more demands, and more complex negotiations; they are made more complicated still if, at the same time, changes within the hegemonic states undermine their ability to take a clear position. Expressed in terms of the cognitive modes presented above, the structural explanation of change is consistent with the skeptical and the eclectic types of process. The absence of new knowledge in the model forces reliance on less-than-substantive ways of linking issues. . . .

Cognitive Explanation of Change

In the pragmatic and rational modes of negotiating, emphasis is put on the use of increasingly consensual new knowledge in making more ambitious policies. An explicit additional variable is introduced to explain change—a variable that accentuates new ways in which actors think. Since actors can be expected to make use of whatever help they can get in reducing their uncertainty about how to attain their increasingly complex and ambitious objectives, this knowledge will be put to use through cognitive means. . . . The addition of new knowledge is . . . associated with new communications channels, think tanks, international research institutes, and efforts to model "world systems" at national and international, public and private institutions. Substantive issue-linkage then prevails, though it may be mixed with fragmented linkage. State power remains in the picture to the extent that the pure rationalist style does not prevail.

Learning Through Negotiation

To students of international organizations condemned to follow the debates of United Nations bodies, it may seem odd to associate these discussions with the idea of learning. In fact, the iteration of familiar patterns of behavior suggests the analogy of the anthill rather than that of the academy. . . . [But] insects cannot transcend stereotyped behavior without genetic change, [yet] people can by drawing on experience. One kind of experience consists of making use of information that becomes available. Another kind integrates various bodies of information to construct theories and other intellectual aids. Such processes can be experienced by individuals, groups, organizations, and even states. . . . Learning, in the context of regime construction, is the cumulative recognition of knowledge necessary for realizing joint gains; learning must be Pareto-optimal. We know that learning has taken place when the actors adopt new rules of behavior that make use of new information and knowledge, or adopt ways for the search for such knowledge. . . .

Actors who seek to use new knowledge to link issues substantively cannot be said to act contrary to their national interests. There is no need to assume the sudden victory of dispassionate wisdom over selfish interest. But why assume the contrary—that actors will continue to cut off their noses to spite their faces when it is within their power to enjoy both wisdom and self-interest? New knowledge, then, is used to redefine the content of the national interest. Awareness of newly understood causes of unwanted effects usually results in the adoption of different, and more effective, means to attain one's ends. . . . If we adopt this perceptual notion of the national interest, we must discard the idea of "structurally necessary" regimes; nothing is *absolutely* necessary. Necessity is a function of perception, of knowledge; it is time-bound. . . .

How can we conceptualize the process of learning to use new knowledge in the redefinition of national interests? Obviously, the impulse may come from many sources in domestic political systems and may be diffused through many international agencies, public and private. The knowledge, however, does not become politically relevant until it shows up as an ingredient in the formulation of national demands for altering the existing pattern of interdependence. The empirical locus for the next encounter is the process of negotiating new regimes.

Hence, learning is a form of persuasion, and persuasion implies an initial disagreement among the parties, which is gradually resolved or settled by compromise. Learning through negotiation is more likely to take place in a setting in which *no single* cognitive style characterizes the negotiators, but where pragmatists encounter skeptics or eclectics. Learning is associated with mixed cognitive settings rather than with the pure types hypothesized above. The knowledge is unevenly diffused and not completely consensual; there is conflict over goals; power is perceived to be asymmetrically distributed, though not concentrated in one country for purposes of all issues and sectors of concern. In the negotiations that ensue for resolving conflicts over clashing national interests so as to find a zone of joint gains, learning takes place if and when the bargaining positions of the parties begin to *converge* on the basis of consensual knowledge tied to consensual goals (or interests), and when the *concessions* that are exchanged by the parties are perceived as instrumental toward the realization of the joint gains.

. . . *Learning as conceptualized above occurs only when pragmatists and rationalists have the edge over their eclectic and skeptic colleagues. . . .*

But what if the pragmatists and rationalists are not successful? If no convergence occurs on any dimension, there will be no regime. The LOS is again our example, and it demonstrates the prevalence of a process that is just as much part of the creation and diffusion of new knowledge as the forging of substantive issue-linkages. New information may actually sensitize negotiators to possible future gains that are best realized without a regime. New knowledge on fisheries conservation, pollution control, and off-shore mining had the effect of making several Third-World governments determined to reap these advantages for themselves alone, to the exclusion of others. Their example was soon followed by all countries that espoused the formula of a 200-mile economic zone. . . .

The mixture of cognitive styles leads us to a second set of hypotheses about regime construction.

1. If the negotiations are dominated by a conflict between rationalists and pragmatists, the solution will still feature the use of substantive issue-linkage dominated by consensual knowledge. There is no clear case that illustrates this pattern, though approximations to it are found in the U.N. Environmental Program. A relatively stable regime will result.

2. If the negotiations are dominated by a conflict between eclectics and pragmatists and the new information is unpersuasive with respect to joint gains, any issue-linkage will be purely tactical. That case is illustrated by the LOS negotiations. If there is a regime, it will be unstable.

3. If the negotiations are dominated by conflict between skeptics and eclectics, fragmented issue-linkage will dominate, and various partial regimes will be built. None will be stable because the controversy over goals to be achieved continues even if knowledge does not become more consensual. The NIEO is in this situation now.

4. If the negotiations are dominated by conflict between skeptics and pragmatists, the possibility exists that fragmented issue-linkage will yield to substantive linkages, though these may well be temporary and dependent on the next turn of the screw of knowledge. Regimes will be more stable than in case 3 and less stable than in case 1 because this hypothesis incorporates the notion of learning-by-negotiation; skeptics respect new knowledge though they do not wish to wait for it. The food regime comes close to presenting a current example.

V. REGIMES AND ORGANIZATIONS

. . . Historically, regimes have been created for regulating single issues rather than issue-areas. Hence, lawyers speak of regimes for fishing, allocation of radio frequencies, pure food and drugs, money, or foreign investment. Norms, rules, and procedures—centralized in international organizations or left to the decentralized network of national officials—have existed for many years. Such arrangements are not of interest here. The term "regime" as used here is reserved to the situation in which rapid changes in scientific knowledge and political expectations combine to produce the types of visions represented in the contemporary debate about the global economic order.

Regimes are norms, procedures, and rules agreed to in order to regulate an issue-area. Norms tell us *why* states collaborate; rules tell us *what,* substantively speaking, the collaboration is about; procedures answer the question of *how* the collaboration is to be carried out. Procedures, therefore, involve the choice of whether specific administrative arrangements should be set up to regulate the issue-area. Administration involves organization. . . .

Norms

Why would states wish to collaborate with respect to managing and regulating the process of improving their technological positions? The purposes of those who demand a regime—and hence the norms underlying collective action—can be summarized as the *acquisition of a capability* to act in a specific domain, either nationally or collectively. This includes creating the ability to make decisions, to analyze a situation, to set up new relationships, as well as to fashion physical goods, and perfect, adjust, or change decision making norms or manufacturing facilities or habits of action so as to better exploit something already in place.

Procedures

Whatever the strength of the norm, the next question must be: *How* shall the norm be implemented? I distinguish between four procedural modes. (1) A *common framework* seeks to affect national behavior through exchanges of information and common rules of reporting and record-keeping. In the language of organization theory, the division of labor sought here is confined to "pooling" separate capabilities without re-arranging them in the search for a common product. (2) A *joint facility* is a more ambitious and demanding way of pooling capabilities by seeking to harmonize and standardize the behavior of the participants through the imposition of common routines. The actors agree to a loose division of labor, not merely by keeping each other informed but by changing routinized ways of doing things so as to meet an agreed standard. (3) A *common policy* is more demanding still. It calls for the ordering and scheduling of national behavior in such a way that the participants agree to adjust their action to the planned needs of the collectivity by re-arranging prior patterns—a type of division of labor called "sequencing" in organization theory. (4) A *single policy* substitutes a centralized set of plans and objectives for the national ones. Since in doing so it absorbs the pre-existing commitments of the national actors, the resulting pattern of interaction (and the division of labor among the parts) is far more complex than in the other instrumentalities: the interaction is "reciprocal."

The pooling of instrumentalities of action through a common framework calls for very simple coordinating bodies. Interbureaucratic committees of high civil servants suffice. When a joint facility is to be operated, however, a research staff may be necessary to devise the appropriate standards and norms; the staff need be no more than a working party of independent experts, convened when necessary. But it often develops into an international secretariat, which then comes to service the interbureaucratic committee. These institutions are sufficient for setting out common ground rules for national action. Sequencing is more ambitious, since priorities for action must be established. Some parts of the whole must act before others; some kinds of previously legitimate action will become illicit. Creation of a common policy thus demands a capacity to make joint commitments; that is the task of councils of ministers and summit conferences, aided by lower-level committees of national civil servants and rudimentary international staffs. It must be understood, however, that these lower-level bodies are incapable of making commitments without the agreement of their superiors. A single policy, and the relationships of reciprocity it implies, calls for a full-fledged "government," whether in the federal tradition or in some other approximation. In short, there is no need for a formal organization if the actors opt merely for a common framework; but there is need for a very elaborate organization if a single policy is deemed necessary.[3]

Types of Regimes

When the norm is accepted with roughly equal fervor among all participants in a regime, the varieties of rules and procedures give us the types presented in Figure 2.

The five possible regimes are labelled in conformity with what organization theory has to say about the character of the activities: pooling/aiding, standardizing/scheduling, forecasting, targeting, and planning. (1) Actors proceeding within a common framework engage essentially in collecting and exchanging information. Their pooling of information is supplemented with technical assistance from the better- to the poorer-endowed countries when existing capabilities are unevenly distributed among the members. (2) If they wish to do more than share information, they must choose a joint facility. If they so choose, information is not only pooled, but new information requested and the substantive area of concern is subjected to standardized monitoring procedures. The standardization of information processing amounts to "shaping" the information into accepted bodies of knowledge used in making policies. If capabilities are unevenly distributed, the richer are expected to aid the poorer by allocating a disproportionate share of common resources to them. Allocation implies that joint action is "scheduled"; there has to be some understanding on who is to give whom how much before the activity can be carried out effectively.

Procedures	Rules		
	Share information	Increase knowledge	Channel/foreclose action
Common framework	Yes (1)	No	No
Joint facility	Yes	Yes (2)	No
Common policy	Yes	Yes (3)	Yes (4)
Single policy	Yes	Yes	Yes (5)

FIGURE 2

A common policy also requires the sharing of information and the increasing of knowledge. In addition, it carries with it understandings that each actor will seek to attain a desirable outcome by a certain time. The outcome is decided collectively, but each participant remains in charge of implementing the decision. (3) One way of accomplishing this involves forecasting without setting targets for achievement. The collective forecasting of the future is an exercise in increasing knowledge, but the forecasts need not call for action. (4) If action is desired, the results of the forecasts are translated into targets for each of the participants. Targeting without forecasting and the sharing of information is not conceivable. (5) Finally, a single policy for a set of states presupposes all of the above, plus commitment to a firm plan of action which is implemented by the central organization. . . .

How to Choose Regimes

In choosing among the possibilities, a decision maker must weigh a number of factors. What is his cognitive stance? What is the stance of the opposing coalition? How should evolving knowledge be incorporated into his political strategy or ideology? What is the norm? . . .

These questions can be combined in one overarching concern: what is the appropriate membership for a regime? The choice is between centralization and de-centralization. One can think in terms of a uniform and global regime, with procedures placed under the guardianship of a single organization, as opposed to the coexistence of several regionally diverse regimes, with a diffuse set of rules binding different types of states to different obligations, and a congeries of overlapping organizations. Moreover, diverse regional regimes can also coexist within global arrangements. Everything still depends on the norm selected and the cognitive stance associated with it.

The committed rationalist must opt for a planning regime: he depends on increasingly consensual knowledge—obtained by way of pooling, standardizing, and allocating informational resources—to attain his social and economic goals. Targeting, forecasting, and planning presuppose the success of increasing and managing knowledge. The skeptic, though depending on whatever knowledge is currently at hand, wants to attain his complexly linked social goals without waiting for an increased consensus on knowledge. His choice would then be a standardizing-scheduling regime. The pragmatist will swing back and forth between the forecasting and targeting regimes, attempting at first to choose as the rationalist would, but compelled to fall back on the less powerful regimes if he is unable to arrive at a satisfactory method of connecting the issues calling for collaboration. For the eclectic, only a pooling-aiding regime is appropriate.

In terms of the more familiar organizational dynamics, we must conclude that the rationalist will seek institutional solutions that are centralized in a single organization integrating all activities thought germane to the issue-area. His desire for institutional coherence suggests no other solution. Skeptics and pragmatists, however, are compelled to sacrifice institutional coherence to less precise arrangements. Skeptics may well prefer to forgo the creation of formal organizations altogether, as may eclectics. When confronted with the possibility that a no-organization regime will fail to attain the objectives suggested by its norm, the skeptic and the pragmatist will agree to hit-or-miss institutional tinkering that may take a multi-organizational and multi-level format. They therefore face the practical problem of how to achieve coherence among the programs and norms of the multiple organizations that they will spawn.

Even if all our hypotheses were shown to be correct, and if all the typologies found universal acceptance, we would not be able to predict which regime would be chosen. But we *are* able to advise the policy maker which regime he ought *not* to select, by excluding possibilities and limiting choice. . . .

The best service to be expected from an ideal-typical discussion of regimes is to make people pause and think.

NOTES

1. But, it is said, experts always disagree with each other; how can we speak of a consensus? In the early stages of any shift in paradigm, they certainly do disagree, and there is no consensus. Even later, experts will continue to disagree on certain aspects of their field, but not on all. In the early stages of discussion regarding the creation of regimes, the use of knowledge will be no more consensual than is the current U.S. debate among the experts on the future of nuclear energy. Experts disagree with each other on the facts *and* on the social goals to be realized. Moreover, they do tailor the factual discussion to whatever goal they espouse. But that is not the case during the entire life-cycle of a technology or a theory. At times there is consensus (as there was with respect to nuclear energy in the 1950s and 1960s because the dissidents were few in number and outside the policy-making process); it is permanent consensus that is inconsistent with the process of scientific investigation itself. See Howard Margolis, *Technical Advice on Policy Issues*, Sage Professional Paper No. 03-009 (Beverly Hills, CA.: Sage, 1973).

2. I rely greatly on Robert L. Rothstein *Global Bargaining* (Princeton: Princeton University Press, 1979), in this section, even though he considers the inter-issue linkage in the Integrated Commodity Program to be essentially tactical, used solely to hold the heterogeneous Group of 77 together. Rothstein also shows that, while the parties agreed on many specific economic arguments and demonstrations, they continued to disagree on whether to act in accordance with them in the creation of the UNCTAD-designed Common Fund. What mattered was whether they thought in terms of "best-case" or "worst-case" scenarios. The issue that divided them was whether, in the process of commodity price stabilization, equity (the goal of the G-77) or efficiency (the goal of

Group B) should be maximized. The Common Fund that they eventually agreed to differs from the proposal UNCTAD had used to link the issues.

3. The typology and the rationale on which it is based are adapted from John Gerard Ruggie, "International Responses to Technology: Concepts and Trends," *International Organization,* xxix (Summer 1975), 570–74. For various ways of matching the typology with cognitive modes in explaining institutional variation, see Ernest B. Haas, Mary Pat Williams, and Don Babai, *Scientists and World Order* (Berkeley: University of California Press, 1977), chap. 6.

Politics, Norms, and Peaceful Change: Two Moves to Institutions

FRIEDRICH KRATOCHWIL

INTRODUCTION: THE ORIGINS OF INTERNATIONAL ORGANIZATIONS

Whatever differences might exist among realists, idealists, peace-advocates or secu-rity specialists, there is a near universal consensus that World War I and the subse-quent settlement represented a sharp break with the past. The new beginnings came in response to the changing external and internal conditions, as the Toquevillian vision of the USA and Russia determining the course of events loomed large on the horizon. Internally, the bankruptcy of the old political elites had been demonstrated not only in the case of the losers but also of the victors. The revolutionary stirrings, evidenced by the October Revolution and some uprisings in Germany (only to be ruthlessly suppressed by the proto-fascist 'free cops'), indicated the end of complacency and of the confidence in the inevitabil-ity and nearly automatic progress of civilization. All these events also suggested that a return to business as usual was not possible and that fundamentally new ways of organizing international and domestic politics would have to be considered.

There were, of course, some innovations attempting to address these changing conditions. The new concept of a "collective security system," the idea of self-determination, and the recognition that the conditions of the working class were no longer simply only a matter of benign neglect or 'domestic politics' all belong here. Although of minor practical import, the founding of the ILO and the admis-sion for the first time of non-state representatives into the inner sanctum of an intergovernmental organization indicated a fundamental change in thinking. While the "new" and largely Wilsonian ideas were hotly contested among the European establishments and the various social movements who mobilized public opinion, there seemed to have been a sweeping feeling that the problems had to be addressed by new forms of organization. Somehow most of the official and social actors agreed that formal institutions were necessary in order to deal effec-tively with the contemporary challenges. To that extent the "move to institutions" which David Kennedy has so painstakingly documented, appears to have tran-scended liberal, syndicalist and even radical feminist lines.

The belief in the effectiveness of formal organization seems to have been but-tressed by two converging notions, i.e. that political problems could be solved by bringing to bear some technical know-how—an idea that had been gaining cur-rency since St. Simon—and that formal organizations represented, because of their greater efficiency, the 'solution'. Bureaucracies would, as Weber suggested, sooner or later crowd out other forms of organizing. But the "move to institutions" might actually have been much more subtle than the wholesale adoption of the techni-cal-bureaucratic perspective attaining its full expression in functionalism. Liberal

106

statesmen, even the "idealist" Woodrow Wilson, like Kant before him, seem to have been less than enamoured with the prospects of some inchoate world governmental structure. Rather they hoped that the spread of democracy and the preponderance of the economic and military potential of democratic states in the aftermath of the war would make peace possible.[1]

It is, of course, the peace movements contesting the monopoly of the decision-making elites in negotiating the peace settlement and the belief in the efficacy of formal structures that Carr, one of the founders of "realism," castigates as utopianism. In identifying these movements with the liberal tenets of the "harmony of interest" and the bureaucratic mode of problem-solving, Carr not only suggested the inappropriateness of these efforts—quite puzzling in view of his socialist leanings and that ideology's privileging of the "masses"—he also misconstrued the actual events, an error that prevents us from critically appraising the changing nature of organization in the international arena and from drawing the appropriate lessons.[2] As a matter of fact, some of the gravest shortcomings of the post-war settlement were not those identified by realists, but had to do with the insufficient attention given at Versailles to the management of the international economy.

It was only on their second try, after World War II at Bretton Woods, that the designers of institutions hit upon the felicitous solution of 'multilateralism'[3] as an organizational form. Only multilateralism was able to accommodate the new responsibility of states for full-employment while taking care of the externalities which the beggar-thy-neighbour policies had created when states had attempted to pursue full-employment policies. Similarly, today new externalities arise for states from "liberalization," when point-of-entry barriers to trade have been virtually eliminated, when production has been globalized, and financial markets have been integrated. A new balance between positive and negative effects, creating new winners and losers, has to be struck. Otherwise the political consensus that sustained the "first move to institutions," and which is essential for the functioning of new institutions, is in danger. True, a return to classical protectionism and the conflicts of yesteryear seem unlikely—not least because many of the protectionist measures which governments could formerly use have lost their bite[4]—but there is the possibility that conflicts might arise out of the growing disenchantment with some of the illiberal consequences of globalization. In a way, the increased liberalization of the economy might result in a serious incompatibility with another tenet of liberalism: democratic theory and the notion of positive rights. To that extent, the second move to institutions could not only undo much of the achievements of the first, but fundamentally alter once more the social bases on which domestic and international legal and political orders rest. . . . A further discussion of the "first" and the "second" move to institutions seems in order.

THE FIRST MOVE: THE LEAGUE AND THE UNITED NATIONS

Let us begin again with the first move. At the outset, we notice that the first move was reformist and perhaps far less radical than some of the contemporary movements and, with hindsight, also its realist critics had thought. Indeed, as David

Kennedy suggests,[5] the ambiguous "history" of the founders of the League and the inconsistencies in the narratives are important indicators for appraising the actual transformation. While originally the American peace movement was characterized by establishment figures such as Elihu Root, William Howard Taft, Andrew Carnegie and Theodore Marburg, the decade following the outbreak of the war saw a decisive shift towards radical feminist and progressive movements. These movements pushed the project from the institutionalization of legal settlement to international and social reform. However, as the war drew to a close, the initiative passed again to the more statist lawyers and officials who were engaged in post-war planning. Thus, the plans produced by Wilson's aids hardly mentioned judicial settlement. Instead they envisaged a political assembly for the resolution of international disputes and attempted to bring war into the framework of institutional sanctions and collective security. In other words, the institutionalization of the international *political* process, rather than radical social reform or pacifism, provided the main source of inspiration.

While it might be understandable that the actors in 1919 could have felt that they were riding the wave of the future, the many exclusions that occurred as well as the shifts in the positions of the participants themselves make such accounts highly problematic. A closer look reveals that many of the pre-war pragmatists became utopians at Versailles or after. For instance, the realist Smuts had, at times during the negotiations, utopian moments, as evidenced by his optimism when he saw the League as the heir to "Europe's great estate." Thus, most of the historical accounts maintain a narrative structure implying some system transforming progress within a continuity. While emphasizing reform, they were as distant from radical and allegedly irresponsible demands of social reform as they were from the calls for a return to the old order. As Kennedy points out:

> By mobilizing the rhetoric of war and peace, law and politics, or utopianism and realism, participants and historians have characterized the establishment of the international institutional regime as the crest of a progressive wave breaking forward from extremes which an institutionalized and redeemed international process must continually exclude. The architects of the new order both situated themselves at the cutting edge of a tradition and sought to continue and displace the work of earlier peace advocates. By contrast to wartime resisters and agitators, the institution builders styled their work a return to order from chaos and to reason from religious ideological passion. Sane hands were again at the helm. At the same time, these men represented the worldly embodiment of a human ideal. The torch of idealism had been passed to an institutionalized generation, inheriting, as it excluded the vision of women and wartime radicals.[6]

Nowhere does the ambiguity of the narrative that emphasizes the transformative character of the move become more visible than in the case of war. War, one of the traditional and accepted institutions of the state system, was now seen as a radical "rupture" to be exorcised from inter-state relations. By identifying war with chaos, and peace with systematic organization, the "move to institutions" created the topos that peace was synonymous with organization. Violence and disintegration were now thoroughly externalized from international relations and projected upon actors beyond the pale, such as terrorists or aggressors. The transformative effect of this narrative was that it not only imparted coherence to efforts at insti-tutionalization in the past, but it sometimes suggested that the main achievement of this move was not so much the victory of law over politics, but rather that both violence and radical demands for systemic transformation had been cast aside in favour of crisis management. At the same time this move suggests that the repeti-tion of history and its cycles of war and peace-making recognized by realists as the only means for ordering the international system[7] had been transcended.

To that extent the new understanding established a coherence between past and present. It legitimized an understanding in which different organizational forms were shown to be the "forerunners" of the present organizational system, while not challenging the state system and its operation. Thus, the Concert is the forerunner of the Council, the former river commissions become antecedents to the functional agencies, and efforts at arbitration are the "roots" for the Permanent (or International) Court of Justice. To that extent the establishment of the UN can be viewed just as the second part of this first move which attempted to incorpo-rate the lessons learned from the failure of the League [of Nations]. These lessons made it necessary to have an organization "with teeth" instead of relying on the good will of its members. It placed universal responsibility for peace and security on the Great Powers thereby attempting to solve the collective action problem that is bound to arise when enforcement becomes an issue.

The story of the failure of the collective security arrangement, the emergence of alliances and blocs, and the substitution of peace-keeping for classical enforcement measures envisaged by Chapter 7 of the Charter have all been told many times. So has the story of human rights and the mandate system that facilitated decolonization by basing the justification of colonial rule increasingly on notions of "trust" and a right to self-determination. The realization that the governmental authority of the colonial powers could no longer be justified by the classical international law prin-ciple of conquest or unequal treaties served, in turn, as a crystallization point for the local opposition and led finally to the rather smooth emancipation of the colonial world. It is in this context that political problems of legitimization and delegitimiza-tion rather than those of the management of force became one of the main contri-butions of the UN to peaceful change. In a way, though, the success of the world organization was also its bane. In the increasingly heated debates of the seventies where automatic majorities passed condemnation after condemnation, the instru-ment of censoring lost much of its bite. First the Great Powers and then increasingly also other industrial states refused to participate in these "politicized" spectacles.

But the narrative of continuity and change on the basis of lessons learned hides some of the discontinuities and innovations that characterized this second episode of the first move. It also concerns the story of one "lesson" whose organi-zational implementation had no forerunner or precedent, namely, "multilateral-ism" as a new organizational form. These multilateral institutions proved surprisingly resilient in the post-war era, even though fundamental changes had undermined many of its foundations and the various *ad hoc* adjustments for meet-ing the emergencies seemed hardly promising. In short, this second episode of the first move concerns the institutionalization of the world economic system on the basis of shared understandings. John Ruggie has called this compromise between liberalism's laissez-faire prescriptions and the policy commitment to full employment, "embedded liberalism."

The multilateral institutions based on this compromise provided a solution for several problems which deep-seated changes in the nature politics, of economics and society, had thrust upon decision-makers in the inter-war period and for which the conventional wisdoms and ideologies had no answers. Accustomed to separating neatly politics and the economy and defining the role of the state as a guarantor for functioning markets, liberalism had in the Great Transformation[8] of the nineteenth century succeeded in dismantling most of the laws and privileges that stood in the way of an efficient allocation of resources. The establishment of a labour market, of arms-length free trade and of the "private" gold standard set the parameters for economic activity. Even if not fully realized, the fundamental social and economic changes of this Great Transformation affected the architecture of both internal and external politics. Internally, social dislocations together with the slow but increasing emancipation of the working class created incentives to organize in to order counteract the deleterious effects of unrestrained laissez-faire. Externally, imperialism could be seen as a response to both economic crises and fears that the existing economic arrangements of free trade might be too fragile to ensure access (quite aside from the empirically dubious arguments of the higher returns on investment that Hilferding and Lenin invoked).

One point, however, was pretty clear to all decision-makers who were engaged in World War I. Because of the impossibility of adjusting the classical European balance by traditional means, the classical nostrums for reviving the European balance were no longer available. Territorial concessions were, if not directly unavailable, nevertheless costly. Because of nationalism no self-respecting government could conceive of the "treason" of transferring part of its territory in the same way as the sovereigns of the *ancien regime* had done without many qualms. Furthermore, the fact that power increasingly depended more on industrial capacity than territory made the task of balancing even harder, since one had to control the *economic growth* and *innovative capacity* of one's competitors. Only under the condition that key economic areas were adjacent to one's own territory could one even consider territorial incorporation. Furthermore, it became clear to all chancelleries that a dynamic economy required far greater territorial units than even the largest European nation states provided. Finally, the tremendous costs of the war made the vision of a return to normalcy afterwards all the more unlikely the longer the hostilities continued. Consequently, when the war was not over as expected within a few weeks or months, most Foreign offices engaged in speculations on how this quandary could be resolved in a post-war settlement.

In Germany, the Chancellor, Bethman Hollweg, had already written on September 9, 1914, a memorandum addressing this issue. The document has been quoted by Fritz Fischer[9] as proof of the imperialist design of the German government and has been dubbed the "*Septemberprogramm.*" According to Fischer, Germany adhered to these war goals until the end of the war. Although the programme considered some territorial annexations in France and Belgium, newer historical research[10] has cast doubt on Fischer's main theses, i.e. that this programme represented a masterplan. . . .

In France, Etienne Clementel, the minister for industry and commerce, engaged in similar planning exercises in 1915. His proposal provided, aside from the return of Alsace-Lorraine to France, a regime of control over the Saar area and Luxembourg and a Customs Union with Belgium and Italy in order to cement France's economic hold on Western Europe. Encouraged by the Czar, who predicted the collapse and disintegration of the Reich,[11] the French position became increasingly punitive as the war went on.

In Britain, discussions about economic security took longer to shape up,[12] as here the conflicts between the goal of economic security through control and discrimination of Germany, and the aim of re-establishing British commercial and financial preponderance, became painfully obvious. After all, the latter goal depended on the revival of intra-European trade and the maintenance of a liberal economic order. Only the Inter-allied Conference on economic relations of June 1916 resolved this conflict in favour of economic security, since close economic cooperation among the Entente was linked to the continuation of discriminatory measures against Germany after the war. In April of 1917 the Imperial War Committee "having due regard to the interest of our Allies" pleaded for the introduction of an imperial preference system and thus laid the foundation for transforming the Empire into an economic bloc.

When in 1918 London finally accepted that a revival of the British economy should be financed by reparations from Germany, the idea of a European economic reconstruction and the return to a liberal trading order were doomed. The rest of the story is well known. For a while, the informal recycling scheme let Germany pay its reparations with U.S. loans, so that Great Britain and France could pay their debts to the United States. But failure to pay reparations led to the occupation of the Rhineland, thereby creating new scores, as the pursuit of security had entirely subverted the liberal idea that the economy was a self-regulating system of private exchanges. Besides, the structural issue of how a general recovery could be achieved was never faced up to. On the one hand much depended on reparations extracted from the vanquished, but economic security also made discrimination against that very country necessary, jeopardizing Germany's capacity to earn the sums necessary to meet the bill. The crash of 1929 ended all illusions. The radical delinking from the world economy and the erection of economic blocs were the result. The Schachtian system of bilateral economic relations based on barter and non-convertible currencies was one (exploitative) answer to the economic crisis, as was the Imperial Preference tariff. Beggar-thy-neighbour policies were designed to place the burdens of unemployment on others, as states scrambled to find solutions for the realization of the new state goal: full employment.

Only during the post-Second World War planning phase did the U.S. decisionmakers hit upon a solution that allowed for both the welfare state and a liberal international economic order. Through the organizational implements of "multilateralism," structures were created that established not only the compatibility between international and domestic political structures,[13] but could also solve the problem of externalities which otherwise result from unilateral actions. International supervisory institutions like the IMF and GATT (after the demise of the plans for an international trade organization) were charged with providing and maintaining the non-discriminatory liberal regimes. Instead of blocs, convertible currencies and non-discrimination provided for the integration of losers and winners alike. Economies flowing from complementary endowments in resources were also utilized through the encouragement of the integration (rather than unilateral control) of entire sectors of the economy for which, e.g., the High Authority of the European Coal and Steel Community was given special powers. Loans and grants rather than reparations provided the initial capital for putting Europe back on the track of recovery. In an ironic twist "security" was again identified with economic prosperity (until Korea, when notions of security again became militarized), although the measures adopted here were not those of control by a victor. In Kennan's original analysis and in the rationale of the Marshal Plan the threat to a peaceful world emanated less from the military threat of a Soviet invasion than from the likelihood of internal political disorder caused by the inability to initiate a rapid recovery. Consequently, economic rather than military means were considered the appropriate measure for meeting this threat.[14]

It is not possible to provide a comprehensive historical account of the "peaceful change" that these organizations allowed and that led rather quickly to unprecedented prosperity. For our purposes it is sufficient to point out that the system functioned perhaps as much by fortuitous circumstance as by design. There was above all a structural problem in the world monetary system that could not be resolved. As the economist Triffin had already demonstrated in the 1950s, the dilemma consisted in the fact that sufficient liquidity was only provided when the United States consistently ran deficits and engaged in expansionary monetary policies. But such a strategy eventually had to transmit inflationary pressures to the entire system thereby upsetting the balance of rights and duties among the members for structural adjustment. The inability of creating a new consensus for this problem came to a head with the closing of the "gold window." The failure to reestablish a viable new regulatory regime ushered in not only the era of floating exchange rates, it also prepared the way for the integration of the world's financial markets. Capital controls—seen by Keynes as an absolute must in order to preserve free trade on the one hand but shelter the governments from the dangers of speculative flows on the other hand—no longer worked and were successively abandoned by virtually all states. To that extent the eroding consensus on the respective rights and duties of states for adjustment, the lack of effectiveness of the old policy prescriptions, the increasing disembeddedness of the world economy have engendered a crisis in our understanding and in designing new institutions that would facilitate peaceful change.

THE "SECOND MOVE" TO INSTITUTIONS: LIBERALIZATION AND GLOBAL GOVERNANCE

On the surface the dominant theme of the narrative of the demise of the Cold War is that of the success of liberalism in its philosophical, economic, and political dimensions. Not only has liberalism succeeded in making human rights a matter of universal concern, the United States has "won" the Cold War, and even the former opponents are busy designing constitutions modelled on those of the Western liberal states. Internationally, the UN is no longer blocked from taking actions, and the defeat of aggressors as well as various peace-keeping operations promise, if not a new world order, at least a new vigour in the attempts by international institutions to prevent conflicts from escalating. Finally, the call for a New International Economic Order has ceased, and many of its former advocates are following the advice of monetarists by dismantling the structures credited with having inhibited economic growth in the past.

True, a few years after the "end of history"[15] many of these claims seem somewhat hollow. The ugliness of civil war in Bosnia, the horrors of genocidal massacres in Rwanda, and the abject misery and poverty that have engulfed many states of the former Soviet empire provide sufficient doubt about the appropriateness of such a narrative. Nevertheless, doubts can be assuaged. Is the American economy not booming, contrary to all expectations? Is the expansion of NATO not a step in the direction of giving the notion of democratic peace some institutional under-pinnings? And could not the growth of human rights movements and the expansion of non-governmental organizational networks be ushering in a new, and for the first time, truly global civil society?

These are indeed important developments, but I have serious doubts whether all, or even most, of the conclusions follow. After all, an equally plausible counter narrative would draw attention to the following questions. What happened to the hopes for a new world order and future Great Power cooperation? Have the experiences of Rwanda and Bosnia not shown the limits of the old recipes of peacekeeping? Are the operations of peacemaking that require different techniques and potentially open-ended commitments politically and financially feasible, especially if such commitments further proliferate? Is the speculation of the emergence of a global civil society based on human rights committing a similar mistake to that of legalism after World War I, in that one is led to believe that laws and norms can create new structures by simply following the logic of the law? Is the success of the American economy bringing benefits to all, or will the impact of declining real wages and the increasing income gap ruin the middle class and thus one of the foundations for a liberal democratic order?

These are indeed troubling questions, and the fact that we cannot answer them in a straightforward fashion does not augur well for our grasp of the problems involved. There is indeed ample reason to move away from the original triumphalism and to focus first of all on the development of better analytical tools for assessing our predicament. Indeed, similar to the situation eighty years ago, we are again facing a crisis of momentous proportions. While I cannot, of course, provide ready-made solutions, I want to cast some doubts upon the generative themes of the narrative of "liberalization." It seems to misinterpret the events and provide faulty guidance for the design of the institutions in this second move. In particular, I want to call into question the proposition that the changes brought about by globalization are either insignificant and thus do not challenge our institutional structures, or of a "liberal" nature and thus are necessarily compatible with, or even enhancing, our liberal *democratic* institutions. Furthermore, while I do not believe that these changes can be interpreted as the ascendancy of the "market" over the state, the increasing disembeddedness of economic processes from its political and social moorings creates distinct dangers for our domestic and international order. Finally, I am also skeptical that these problems are properly addressed by the discourse of "global governance." A brief discussion is in order.

That increasing interdependencies can have significant impact on the state and its capacity to govern has been grist to the mill of international relations scholars, economists and futurologist alike. Thus one of the first questions concerns whether or not interdependence has increased. To that extent the view, whether propagated by Kenneth Waltz[16] or by Milton Friedman,[17] that levels of interdependence characteristic of today's economy were not unknown in previous eras, seems to suggest that there is nothing new under the sun; and that both the political system and the market can continue to work in the same way as before, only perhaps a bit more efficiently. The usual empirical support for such a proposition relies on comparing the size of the external sector of the economy as measured by the percentage of GNP. But such an analysis fails to take into account the changing structure of trade. While it was formerly arms-length trade in products, most of today's trade is intra-firm trade. The fundamental change in the structure of production makes it difficult to decide what an "American" automobile is nowadays, as its component parts come from all corners of the world. But this observation also implies that trade occurs now in the form of exchanges among *administrative hierarchies* rather than external markets.

. . . The above discussion should have driven home the fact that the reality of modern trade is no longer that of arms-length exchange or that of an exchange between countries with different factor endowments. The international division of labour and the benefits of trade that accrued originally to "countries" are now internalized at the level of the firm. This observation has several corollaries. First, it suggests that purely national firms will experience a decrease in the margins of classical comparative advantage when compared to multinationally organized firms. Second, multinational firms, because of their organizational form, can move either through the actual transfer of production, or through bookkeeping operations, the location where value is added and taxes are assessed. Third, since the gains from trade no longer accrue to the country as such, especially not to the immobile factors of production such as labour (with the exception of highly skilled and mobile managers), firms become serious contenders in the international arena. Furthermore, these considerations explain: the boom of the stock market (as profits rise), the increasing concentration of industries and the formation of strategic alliances; the decline of real wages in most industrial countries; the growing wage differentials particularly in the upper brackets since there no meaningful market exists; finally it explains the lack of significant "trickle-down effects" of the boom, and the increasing difficulties of states to act as redistributive agencies and provide for social welfare.

From that it should also be clear that such a trend cannot be described as "liberalization" in any meaningful way, since it leads inevitably to concentration (a situation which classical economic analysis considered detrimental to welfare). Even if newer models suggest that, contrary to classical analyses, competition might not cease even in oligopolistic markets and thus prices might actually decline when firms collaborate on research and product development, there remains a certain uneasiness with such arguments. It does not take much reflection to see that these developments are potentially dangerous, as fewer and fewer people benefit from both the boom and the lower prices. Therefore, visceral reactions from the great majority who feel that they are the losers of this globalization trend are rather likely. The disembedding of the economy puts economic market liberalism squarely at odds with another part of liberalism: democratic theory and its notions of distributive justice.

The predicament is not helped by the fact that this fundamental transformation cannot be understood simply as the ascendancy of the economy over the state and that the realization of the anarchist ideal of the possibilities of private ordering is around the corner. Consequently, one has to question the implication that politics will become less important, as networks will become the dominant organizational form in the future. It is certainly true that changes in production increasingly depend on access to capital and "know-how," embodied in transnational networks. But the conclusion therefore that states as territorial organizations have ceased to be important does not follow for two interdependent reasons, one legal, the other political. The legal argument turns on the issue of property rights, which makes the image of a purely "private ordering" rather problematic *ab initio*. As Peter Evans recently remarked:

> If an economically stateless world could deliver in practice a global equilibrium that met the needs of TNCs, then eclipse (of the state) might indeed be in the offing. In fact, transnational investors trying to integrate operations across a shifting variety of national context need competent predictable public sector counterparts even more than do old-fashioned domestic investors who can concentrate their time and energy on building relations with a particular individual apparatus.[18]

Thus oddly enough the process of globalization requires the state, and a "strong" state at that, and, by extension, also international regulatory regimes and dispute-settling mechanisms of considerable bite. The importance of secure property rights is even further enhanced by the emergence of a service economy where increasingly ideas and skills, not tangible products, are traded. Since the cost of production of ideas is practically zero, the "franchising" of ideas is not subject to decreasing returns (other than fashions, or changes of taste) so that profits increase continuously with the size of the market. To that extent the limits result not from marginal costs in production but in the duration and scope of the patents, or the generally recognized intellectual property rights. Thus, the role of the state as guarantor of rights is more important than ever before. It is not the state *per se* that has not lost its rationale, rather its *functions* have been dramatically changed by the developments that we lump together under the heading of globalization.[19]

The picture of globalization as a process of homogenization, leading towards technocratic forms of rule in the economic as well as the political realm is rather superficial. First, as several studies have indicated, politics still matters and domestic institutions channel liberalization in quite different ways.[20] Even global firms differ significantly in their make-up,[21] as there does not seem to exist only one way of tackling problems. Thus, organizational structures which have been sedimented by past decisions continue to exert considerable influence. Second, quite different from the philosophical argument that we are part of just another episode of the relentless historical process leading to ever more inclusive forms of political organization, the spread of "universalism" is strongly counteracted by the equally strong assertion of particularities. Precisely because the "packed imagery of the visionary global culture is either trivial or shallow, a matter of mass commodity advertisement,"[22] the norm of self-determination has served as a powerful tool for groups which seek to assert their independence in order to preserve their identity. To that extent we had better remember that the state as a political community is also a *membership organization* and the issue of belonging addresses more than some irrational needs.

Conceiving of a community as something which "unites" all its citizens is important precisely because it provides the means of ascribing responsibilities and of indicating the levers for political action. Thus, persons who are excluded from influence, because they cannot participate in networks or markets owing to their lack of resources, are still part of the "public" to which decision makers and bureaucrats have to answer. In other words, the point is not so much that functioning markets and networks need regulators, although this is certainly a problem when national regulations can be avoided and equivalent international institutions are not in place, as the debt crisis showed. The point is rather to whom do these regulators have to answer? Is it only shareholders, inventors, and marketing agencies which have acquired intellectual property, or is it the public at large? But which public, since networks are characterized by the disappearance of publics?

In short, what is missing in debates about strong vs. weak states, the ascendancy of the market over the state, and so on is *politics* plain and simple. By identifying it—different from realists who saw politics as potential violence—with government and governmental structures, the advocates of the strong state submit to the illusion of a neo-Weberian vision of bureaucratic efficiency and rationality. But, as we all know, politics is different: it is not only about dilemmas (rather than about simple administrative measures); it is also about representative choices and their legitimization; in modern times it is about gaining the consent of the governed. Precisely because the present transformations deeply affect our accustomed ways of dealing with problems, rules that affect our way of life need to be buttressed by a broad-based consensus. Administrative rationality is insufficient to deal with those problems, as has been demonstrated by Ulrich Beck.[23] Starting from the traditional notion of risk, Beck shows that such notions cannot guide us in dealing with modern risks. The uninsurability of an increasing number of problems suggests this much. Years ago, Habermas pointed to the legitimization crisis of the modern state[24] in which administrative procedures . . . overwhelm efforts at building political consensus. These pressures have increased and it is cold comfort to know that networks and strong bureaucracies will continue to be part of our social reality as we face the "second move."

This argument certainly does not imply that nothing has changed or that the states with which we have been familiar will persist in the same form. Notions of multilevel governance have not only been used in analyzing such phenomena as the EU which neither fits the classical notions of federal state or a confederation nor the template that the complex processes of negotiations among "stakeholders" at various levels is "on the way" to a classical "sovereign" (super)state. Similar notions have also entered our debates in international politics. The focus on "global governance" was not only designed to call attention to the regulatory issues that globalization had raised and often had left unattended in the overly optimistic hope that unseen hands and "private orderings" could serve as substitutes. It also was attempting to capture the complexity of interactions between public and private actors, between formal organizations and elements of "civil society" that are involved in providing the "public goods" which were formerly the exclusive domains of states. Here, as we have seen, very often the new emerging spaces opening up for political action through the empowerment of movements and organizations of global civil society have been emphasized in the discussions.

The more technocratic version of the global governance discourse is more interventionist and aims at the "reform" of state institutions through some forms of tutelary regimes supervised or implemented by international organizations. Thus benchmarks for "democratization," the "rule of law" (Haiti, Croatia), supervision of elections, even the administration of states in "transition" (Cambodia, East Timor) are examples of these undertakings. They are supposed to make out of rogue states or failed states "members" of the international community by subjecting them to some disciplinary control of their social and political structures. Thus different from the former tasks of "enforcement" and peace keeping, which presupposed functioning state structures as addresses for the coercive power or the assurance provided by the blue helmets that supervised a truce, the modern "governance" problem is far more interventionist and reformist.

In assessing these changes several observations are in order. One concerns the new mode of "governmentality" which moves from "enforcement" and occasional but unsystematic punishment to a more continuous "disciplinary" control, as has been pointed out by Foucault. This trend then reinforces a second important factor that has been part of the "move" to institutions: the idea of expertise and the substitutions of administration and technical advise for "old-style" politics. This element has not only engendered notions of "functionalism" and "neofunctionalism." It also discounts "local knowledge" and stresses the universal applicability of the prescriptions and programs imposed or administered by the "experts." Whether we are dealing here with issues of policing, human rights, or "conditionality" attached to financial aid packages, the reigning orthodoxy seems to be—as critics outside and inside of international institutions have often pointed out—that "one size fits all." This might not only result in inefficiencies but actual "mistakes" as problems are misdiagnosed (see the criticism of Stiglitz in regard to the IMF's handling of financial crises), or important trade-offs between competing values are papered over (see for example the criticism below of the WTO and ecological concerns).

Third, given the enormity of the task implied by such a reformist strategy and given the meager resources available for meeting the needs it is not surprising that many interventions fail and that and that "help" provided by international organizations is rather episodic rather than transforming depending more on transitory interest of donors (public and private) that are evoked by the media or publicity stunts rather than by a viable, coherent, and sustained strategy of reform or transformation. The first problem is exemplified by such humanitarian interventions as Somalia, the second by the publicity stunts of Greenpeace as in the Brent Spar case that not only prevented a critical and even handed assessment of the alternatives available for an ecologically sound solution, it also calls attention to the fact that despite self-serving claims of organizations of civil society being a "non governmental" organization and part of "global civil society" does not necessarily imply that its actions serve the "global interest."

Fourth, in view of the often-technocratic nature of the advice based on some alleged universally valid knowledge, the interventions fail because they do not involve the "local" political forces which—after the peace makers have gone—have to run their societies. As important as the "civilizing mission" of INGO and NGO interventions might be, ultimately they have to be evaluated in terms of their contribution to the building of viable local political structures. To that extent we should perhaps take more seriously Benedict Anderson's observation that there is in nearly all states a tomb of the unknown soldier but none of the unknown Marxist, or, we might add, of the international "professional."

There is apparently some force to nationalist ideology that other ideologies have difficulty in matching, even though it might have nothing to do with primordialism; but might be a response to the changes of modernity. After the death of God—the traditional guarantor of order—"the people" remain the only source of legitimacy. By joining pre-modern ties and sentiments, characteristic of traditional ethnic communities, with modern ideas of popular sovereignty, nationalism provided a partial answer to the crisis of meaning engendered by modernity.

To that extent, notions of a world society and of the victory of universalism against the assertions of more particular identities seem rather anaemic, as are the strangely technocratic visions of "private ordering," or of networks that displace the common space that a political order is able to create. . . . Since politics is about *projects* which are never complete and which constantly move between the *is* and the *ought*, its analysis cannot be reduced to the logic of law, to the structural constraints of the international system, to the economy of force, or to a historical trend. Those who had contributed to the institution-building of the "first move" failed in a way because of their inadequate understanding. Their failure was costly, even though it made the success of the second episode of the "first move" possible. But even those lessons seem of limited use to us who are now faced by the problems of a "second move" to "global" institutions.

NOTES

1. For a good discussion of these points see Andrew Moravcsik, "A Liberal Theory of International Politics," *International Organization,* 51 (Autumn 1997), pp. 513–54.
2. For a further discussion of the role of the various peace movements in the pre- and post-WWI era, see Cecelia Lynch, *Beyond Appeasement: Reinterpreting Interwar British and US Peace Movements* (Ithaca, NY: Cornell University Press, 1999).

3. For a definition of this institutional form and its role in post WWII policy, see John Ruggie (ed.), *Multilateralism Matters: The Theory and Praxis of an Institutional Form* (New York: Columbia University Press, 1993); see also John Ruggie, *Winning the Peace: America and World Order in the New Era* (New York: Twentieth Century Fund, 1996).

4. For a fundamental discussion of these points, see Richard Cooper, *Economic Policy in an Interdependent World* (Cambridge, MA: MIT Press, 1986).

5. David Kennedy, "The Move to Institutions," *Cardozo Law Review*, 8 (April 1987), pp. 841–988.

6. Ibid., pp. 897f.

7. See, for example, Robert Gilpin, *War and Change in World Politics* (Cambridge: Cambridge University Press, 1981).

8. For a comprehensive treatment of this issue, see Karl Polanyi, *The Great Transformation* (Boston: Beacon Press, 1957).

9. Fritz Fischer, *Griff nach der Weltmacht: Die Kriegszielpolitik des Kaiserlichen Deutschlands* 1914–1918 (Düsseldorf: Droste, 1961).

10. See, for example, Georges Henri Soutou, *L'Or et le Sang, Les Buts de Guerre Economiques et la Permiere Guerre Mondiale* (Paris: Fayard, 1989).

11. Horst Günther Linke, 'Rußlands Weg in den Ersten Weltkrieg' und seine Kriegsziele 1914–18', in Wolfgang Michalka (ed.), *Der Erste Weltkrieg*, pp. 54–94.

12. See Matthias Peter, "Britische Kriegsziele und Friedensvorstellungen," ibid., pp. 95–124.

13. On the link between the regulatory state structures emerging from the 'New Deal' and the organizations of the Bretton Woods system, see Ann Marie Burley, "Regulating the World: Multilateralism, International Law and the Projection of the New Deal Regulatory State," in John Ruggie (ed.), *Multilateralism Matters*, ch. 4.

14. On this point, see my "The Embarrassment of Changes: Realism as the "science" of *Reapolitik* without Politics," *Review of International Studies*, 19 (1993), pp. 1–18.

15. See, for example, Francis Fukuyama, *The End of History and the Last Man* (London: Penguin, 1992).

16. See Kenneth Waltz, "The Myth of National Interdependence," in Charles Kindleberger (ed.), *The International Corporation* (Cambridge, MA: MIT Press, 1970).

17. Milton Friedman, "The world is less internationalized in any immediate, relevant pertinent sense today than it was in 1913, or in 1929," in Milton Friedman, "Internationalization of the US Economy," *Fraser Forum*, Feb. 1989, p. 8, as quoted in John Ruggie, *Winning the Peace*, p. 145.

18. Peter Evans, "The Eclipse of the State? Reflections on Stateness in an Era of Globalization," *World Politics*, 50 (Oct. 1997), pp. 62–87.

19. For a good discussion of this point, see Philip Cerny, "Globalization and the Changing Logic of Collective Action," *International Organization*, 49 (Autumn 1995), pp. 595–626. See also his *The Changing Architecture of Politics* (London: Sage 1990).

20. See, for example, Louis Pauly, *Opening Financial Markets: Banking Politics on the Pacific Rim* (Ithaca, NY: Cornell University Press, 1988).

21. Louis Pauly and Simon Reich, "Enduring MNC Differences Despite Globalization," *International Organization*, 51 (Winter 1997), pp. 1–30.

22. Anthony Smith, *Nations and Nationalism in a Global Era* (Cambridge: Polity Press, 1995), p. 23.

23. Ulrich Beck, *Risikogesellschaft: Auf dem Weg in eine andere Moderne* (Frankfurt: Suhrkamp, 1986).

24. See Jürger Habermas, *Legitimationsprobleme im Spütkapitalismus* (Frankfurt: Suhrkamp 1973).

CHAPTER 3

Regimes and Organizational Forms

This chapter focuses on how variations in organizational form affect international cooperation and regimes. Throughout the 1960s and 1970s, "functionalists" and various students of bureaucracy argued that the efficiencies stemming from formal bureaucratic structures would lead other forms of organizing international affairs to fall by the wayside. The rapid proliferation of formal international organizations that were marked by such structures—including both multipurpose organizations, such as the United Nations (UN), organizations structured along functional lines, such as the World Health Organization and the International Labor Organization, and organizations vested with the competence to craft policy, such as the High Authority of the European Coal and Steel Community—seemed to support such a reading of the historical record.

Over the past three decades, however, various scholars of international organization have challenged this reading and have advanced a number of arguments about the links between the organizational form of international institutions and the effectiveness of cooperation among the participating states. In contrast to realist theories, all of these scholars maintain that states do not exist in an anarchic environment characterized by only sporadic episodes of collaboration and cooperation. This research has prompted a reassessment of the extent of bureaucratic efficiency, it has contributed to a more fine-grained evaluation of different forms of international organization, and it has stimulated an interesting debate on whether modern states can be understood as simple, hierarchically structured organizations. Not only is the global system populated by a dense network of different kinds of formal institutions, these researchers also point to different functions that various organizational forms serve. Thus, we encounter periodic conferences where member-states review an international organization's progress on a given issue, cross-national governmental networks of departments and bureaus, as well as more traditional, formal organizations that can promote cooperation (such as the World Postal Union, the International Monetary Fund [IMF], and the UN).

Similarly, in light of the wide variety of institutional forms that exist in the global system, many scholars of international organization have argued that the very distinction between anarchy and hierarchy that is often drawn in international relations theory (see Chapter 1) is too blunt and no longer useful as an analytical tool. Even within states, in the view of these scholars, complex networks spanning the divide between the public and the private realm have reduced the usefulness of viewing states as formal hierarchies. Further, the existence of multiple negotiating arenas for a given issue-area (for example, the "Group of 10," the World Trade Organization, the IMF, etc. in the case of the international economy) means that global governance of an area is often complex and is carried out by various different institutions simultaneously.

Finally, various scholars of international organization have challenged the claim that hierarchies are the organizational form that best ensures efficient and successful outcomes. Some of this research draws on recent work outside of political science showing that organizations in rapidly changing environments are more likely to achieve their goals if they are decentralized rather than hierarchical. Similarly, bureaucratic organizations can become susceptible to certain pathologies, as centrally planned economies illustrate in the extreme.

One problem is that formal organizations and bureaucracies frequently lack good instruments for evaluating their performance. Further, the instruments that are chosen can sometimes be manipulated by individuals who have a stake in these institutions. Another problem is that "customers" of a bureaucracy have no direct means of voicing their displeasure when the bureaucracy's outputs are not satisfactorily delivered. The organization theory developed by the "new institutionalism" provides an interesting perspective on this problem. Rather than focusing on the organization and its internal structure, the new institutionalism analyzes exchanges between organizations and the environment. From the standpoint of this approach, the way in which revenue is acquired and used and how information is handled become crucial variables. Consequently, the solution to the aforementioned problems is either to introduce more features of a "market" in the arena where an organization operates, or to strengthen the "voice" of the recipients of an institution's services.

For example, new institutionalist researchers argue that both donor countries and international organizations have "contracted out" much of the delivery of their foreign aid to nongovernmental organizations (NGOs) in the hope that NGOs would be especially effective in outflanking corrupt state institutions in the host countries (thereby enhancing the effectiveness of aid), while introducing competition in the delivery of aid that would increase efficiency. In the same vein, NGOs and transnational activist networks often work with international organizations to organize local stakeholders and ensure that they have a voice in the objectives and policies being undertaken. In various cases, these efforts have led to a change in the agenda of international organizations. Poverty reduction, for example, has become explicitly identified as a chief objective for both the IMF and World Bank, instead of assuming that promoting economic development and the creation of market-based institutions were sufficient to combat poverty. These efforts also allowed the World Bank to avoid costly fights with local groups that had opposed some of its projects because the World Bank had not adequately assessed the environmental and demographic impacts of these programs.

The articles in this chapter address these points. Anne-Marie Slaughter's contribution focuses on the expansion of global networks among governmental agencies. While networks usually have been thought of as links among members of a global civil society (particularly among NGOs and activists engaging in "principled politics"), Slaughter shows how the operations of governments are deeply embedded in such networks. She demonstrates that the traditional image of states interacting through exchanges mediated by their foreign office is misleading. Tax authorities track income earned at home and also abroad, aided by the collaboration of internal revenue services worldwide. Courts increasingly refer to each other's decisions, creating a new form of transnational law.

Ronald Mitchell addresses the efficiency and effectiveness of international regimes. His primary emphasis is on the factors that promote compliance with regimes and thereby enhance their effectiveness. Central in this regard is the design of international regimes, their rules and their procedures. In the environmental area, which is Mitchell's empirical focus, the antipollution regime for the high seas comprises a discharge subregime and an equipment subregime. While it is usually assumed that a regime will be successful when sanctions deter potential violations, Mitchell shows that the equipment regime, which relies on indirect sanctions (such as denial of insurance or operating certificates that prevents tankers from doing business), is more effective than the discharge regime, which relies on direct sanctions. The latter is much less successful in fostering compliance due to both the difficulty of establishing and tracing violations and the relatively small fines imposed on violators that are caught compared to the benefits that firms obtained from violating the regime.

Margaret Keck and Kathryn Sikkink analyze the impact that activist networks have on politics, particularly in the area of human rights. Keck and Sikkink argue that although these transnational coalitions seldom possess the traditional resources needed to influence policy, they gain leverage by exercising "symbolic" power. Transnational coalitions use "framing" (of an issue) and "shaming" (exposing clear cut violations of standards) as the main vehicles to influence policy and enhance the effectiveness of the human rights regime. By linking groups across national boundaries and establishing links with international organizations, human rights networks help to break down the traditional walls that shielded norm violations by providing a "domestic jurisdiction" defense. They also strategically employ the "boomerang" effects of human rights norms by holding states accountable to the standards they have officially agreed to.

A more critical evaluation of international organizations is provided by Michael Barnett and Martha Finnemore, who address the issue of organizational pathologies. Their sociological approach exposes why organizations are not necessarily efficient and effective solutions to international problems. Barnett and Finnemore point out that organizations can attain a great deal of autonomy from their member-states and exercise power that is legitimated by their expertise.

International organizations have power because they give meaning to situations and problems. But in contrast to the more optimistic views espoused by functionalism, neoliberal institutionalism, and various other perspectives, Barnett and Finnemore stress that these organizations can abuse that power, contributing to inefficient outcomes in the global system.

Governing the Global Economy Through Government Networks

ANNE-MARIE SLAUGHTER

...The litany of threats to State sovereignty is familiar: global financial flows, global corporations, global television, global computing, and global transportation networks. The generally accepted account of how such threats render State borders increasingly permeable and thus State power increasingly feeble conceives of sovereignty itself as a curiously static attribute, as if State power depended on maintaining territory as a hermetically sealed sphere. However, as Abram and Antonia Chayes point out, sovereignty in the post-Cold War and even the post-Second World War world is increasingly defined not by the power to insulate but by the power to participate—in international institutions of all kinds.[1] As globalization literally turns the world inside-out, nationalizing international law and internationalizing national law, the opportunities for such participation expand exponentially. What is new is that the resulting institutions are as likely to be transgovernmental as they are international or supranational. The result is indeed a "power shift," but more within the State than away from it.[2]

Traditional conceptions of international law and international relations assume that States are the primary actors on the international stage and that States themselves are unitary, opaque, and capable of rational calculation. ....

Furthermore, it follows from this conception of the international system and of States as the primary actors within it that the rules governing international life must be a product of either State practice or negotiation. The resulting rules and institutions are described as being by States, for States, and of States. ....

The conventional debate over globalization and the attendant decline of State power is handicapped by this traditional conception of States and State institutions. In fact, the State is not disappearing; it is disaggregating into its component institutions. The primary State actors in the international realm are no longer foreign ministries and heads of state, but the same government institutions that dominate domestic politics: administrative agencies, courts, and legislatures. The traditional actors continue to play a role, but they are joined by fellow government officials pursuing quasi-autonomous policy agendas. The disaggregated State, as opposed to the mythical unitary State, is thus hydra-headed, represented and governed by multiple institutions in complex interaction with one another abroad as well as at home.

The corollary of the disaggregation of the State in foreign relations is the rise of government networks. Courts, administrative agencies, legislators, and heads of State are all networking with their foreign counterparts. Each of these institutions has the capacity not only to represent "the national interest" in interactions with its foreign counterparts, but also to act on a subset of interests arising from its particular domestic function that are likely to be shared by its foreign counterparts. ....

More broadly still, they define transgovernmentalism as a distinctive mode of global governance: horizontal rather than vertical, composed of national government officials rather than international bureaucrats, decentralized and informal rather than organized and rigid.

. . . This [essay] will focus on two particular types of government networks among financial regulators: central bankers, securities regulators, insurance commissioners, and antitrust officials. The first type are the relatively more formal transgovernmental regulatory organizations (TROs). The members of these organizations are domestic agencies, or even subnational agencies such as provincial or State regulators, in contrast to conventional international organizations, which are comprised primarily, or solely, of nation-States. These transgovernmental organizations tend to operate with a minimum of physical and legal infrastructure. Most lack a foundational treaty, and operate under only a few agreed objectives or by-laws. Nothing they do purports to be legally binding on their members and mechanisms for formal enforcement or implementation are rare. Instead, these functions are left to the members themselves. But despite this informal structure and loose organization, these organizations have had an important influence on international financial regulatory co-operation.

The second type of government network consists of agreements between the domestic regulatory agencies of two or more States. The last few decades have witnessed the emergence of a vast network of such agreements, which effectively institutionalize channels of regulatory co-operation between specific countries. These agreements embrace principles that can be implemented by the regulators themselves. Widespread use of Memoranda of Understanding (MOUs) and even less formal initiatives has sped the growth of governmental networks. Further, while these agreements are most commonly bilateral arrangements, they may also evolve into plurilateral arrangements, offering greater flexibility with less formality than traditional international organizations.

Government networks have many advantages. They are fast, flexible, cheap, and potentially more effective, accountable, and inclusive than existing international institutions. They can spring up virtually overnight, address a host of issues, and form "mega-networks" that link existing networks. As international actors from non-governmental organizations (NGOs) to corporations have already recognized, globalization and the information technology revolution make networking the organizational form of choice for a rapidly changing and varied environment. . . .

In addition, government networks are comprised of national government officials rather than international officials, which avoids any need for two-level adoption or implementation of international rules. The actors who make the rules or formulate the principles guiding government networks are the same actors who have the power to enforce them. This attribute of government networks can work to enhance both effectiveness and accountability. . . .

As domestic political resistance to globalization in many countries triggers a backlash against both existing international institutions and the prospect of new ones, transgovernmental activity by elected or even appointed national officials will seem less threatening than a burgeoning supranational bureaucracy. . . .

Government networks tend to be functionally oriented and easy to expand, meaning that they can include any actors who perform similar functions, whether private or public, national or supranational, regional or local. The result is a vast array of opportunities for participation in rule-making by an eclectic mix of actors.

These are rosy scenarios. Government networks also have disadvantages and worrisome features. Most of these fall under the heading of accountability, both domestic and international. First is the concern that government networks reflect technocracy more than democracy, that their purported effectiveness rests on shared functional values rather than on responsiveness to underlying social and political issues. Such concerns spawn a need to build mechanisms for accountability to domestic constituencies in countries participating in government networks. Second, however, is a set of concerns about global accountability: concerns about the politics of insulation and the politics of imposition. . . .

In addition to concerns about accountability, critics of government networks have also charged them with reflecting if not encouraging a minimalist global agenda and displacing traditional international organizations. Both of these claims are overblown. . . . The agenda pursued by government networks is generally a transnational regulatory agenda rather than a more traditional agenda devoted to providing global public goods, but they are hardly a *cause* of the asserted decline in resources allocated to combating global poverty, to human rights, and health care. . . .

Section 1 [below] describes the evolution of a number of the most important transgovernmental regulatory organizations in the global economic and financial arena. Section 2 explores the development of less formal bilateral and plurilateral ties, largely between the United States and other countries. Section 3 canvasses problems with existing government networks and sketches their implications for the larger project of global governance.

1. AGENCIES ACROSS BORDERS: TRANSGOVERNMENTAL REGULATORY ORGANIZATIONS

The key identifying feature of government networks is the interaction across borders of government institutions with similar functions and facing similar problems. This interaction is more highly developed in the financial regulatory area than in any other, leading one scholar to coin the term "international financial regulatory organizations" (IFROs).[3] . . . From this perspective, international financial regulatory organizations are more accurately described as a category of transgovernmental regulatory organizations.

1.1. The Basle Committee on Banking Supervision

Established in 1975 under the Bank for International Settlements (BIS), the Basle Committee is a standing group of the Central Bank Governors of the G-10 countries, Switzerland, and Luxembourg.[4] The Basle Committee exists without a formal constitution or by-laws, and operates without its own staff or facilities. Its founding mandate was a press communiqué, issued by the Bank Governors through the BIS. The BIS itself is a private bank, located in Basle, Switzerland, that is mostly owned by the central banks of twenty-nine countries.[5] It was founded in the interwar period to "promote the co-operation of central banks and provide additional facilities for international financial operations."[6] Although the charter membership of the BIS and the Basle Committee overlaps, the BIS does not formally participate in the Committee. None the less, the small staff of the BIS serves as the Basle Committee's secretariat, and the Committee meets four times a year in Basle at the BIS.

The Basle Committee is not an open organization. Membership is strictly limited to the world's most powerful banking States and will likely remain so.[7] Conducting its business in secret, the Committee makes every effort to maintain a low profile. . . .

The stated objectives of the Basle Committee are very broad. It describes itself as a "forum for ongoing cooperation among member countries on banking supervisory matters" that aims to "strengthen international cooperation, improve the overall quality of banking supervision worldwide, and ensure that no foreign banking establishment escapes supervision."[8] In practice, the Committee only makes consensus-based "recommendations," which are then left for the Governors to implement within their own national systems. Even though the Committee derives its formal authority solely from the support of the Central Bank Governors, its recommendations have been implemented by member and non-member countries alike.[9]

The Basle Committee's recommendation-making process exemplifies the distinctive nature of transgovernmental regulatory co-operation. The Committee's 1988 Capital Accord, setting minimum capitalization standards for international banks under the regulatory power of the Central Bank Governors, provides an instructive example. Following several secret meetings, the Basle Committee announced that agreement on a proposal had been reached. A six-month period followed, during which time the Committee accepted comments from private bankers and other interested parties. The final version of the Accord appeared in the summer of 1988, after which time the Governors of the member banks implemented the agreed standards.

The drafters of the Accord used simple language in writing the agreement, deliberately avoiding legalese. The use of more informal language is not unusual; the products of Committee agreements are usually short, generally worded documents which, as Peter Cooke has stated, "do not have, and were never intended to have, legal force."[10] Furthermore, unlike most treaties or other legal agreements, the 1988 Accord has been subject to frequent amendments since its promulgation and is intended to evolve over time.

Despite their informality and professed lack of authority, Basle Committee members consider the agreements binding, even if they do not "approach the legal status of treaty."[11] Given the lack of an independent mechanism for monitoring non-compliance, enforcement is left to the members of the Committee themselves, with pressure from their colleagues. Specific meetings review the implementation and consistency of the agreements. As all member countries have implemented the 1988 Accord's capital adequacy requirements, and countries not party to the original agreement continue to join,[12] the Basle Committee's system of enforcement, however informal, appears to be quite effective. In fact, the adoption of the capital adequacy standards has been so effective that governments did not withdraw their support of the Accord even when many scholars argued that the resulting deceleration in bank lending intensified the recession of the early 1990s in the United States and other industrialized countries.[13] Some members of the United States Congress proposed that the Accord should be scrapped or amended, since it was obviously "harming" the domestic economy.[14] However, no action was taken on these proposals, demonstrating the degree of autonomy and influence over domestic government that the Basle Committee has achieved.

Why does this system function as effectively as it does? The primary reason for success seems to be the Basle Committee's facilitation of close personal contacts among the Central Bank Governors. . . . The Basle Committee also seeks to organize and facilitate networking among the rest of the world's central bankers and other financial regulators. . . .

The Basle Committee is recognized as a significant player in international financial regulation. It has effectively promulgated binding international standards, even though such standards have at times proved expensive and burdensome for member States. Moreover, it has proved itself competent in developing new principles of banking supervision, such as the "consolidated supervision" standard adopted in the Basle Concordat, which expands the regulatory responsibilities of member governors beyond territorial borders as a matter of first principle. Most recently, after close consultation with bank supervisors from sixteen developing countries, it has developed and promulgated a set of principles designed to codify the basic "elements of a sound supervisory system."[19]

1.2. The International Organisation of Securities Commissioners

The International Organisation of Securities Commissioners (IOSCO) is a global network of securities regulators.[16] It has over 150 members, divided among "ordinary members" comprised of national securities commissions or self-regulatory organizations such as stock exchanges from countries with no official government regulatory agency; "associate members" comprised of provincial or regional securities regulators when the national regulatory agency is already a member; and "affiliate members" comprised of international or regional organizations charged with the regulation or development of capital or other organizations recommended by the Executive Committee.[17] Unlike the Basle Committee, membership in IOSCO has not been limited to regulators from prosperous countries, and even includes non-governmental regulators such as private stock exchanges. IOSCO has no charter or founding treaty. It maintains an evolving set of by-laws and has established a permanent secretariat in Montreal.[18] . . . IOSCO monitors members' compliance with agreed standards through informal methods of self-reporting. Like the Basle Committee, membership in IOSCO leads to an element of moral suasion in implementing common standards.[19]

IOSCO has made some notable contributions in the areas of information sharing and enforcement agreements. The "ancestor" of all reciprocal information-sharing MOUs was issued by IOSCO in 1986 as a "Resolution on Reciprocal Assistance,"[20] and has been signed by forty agencies.[21] The Organisation also created widely used "Principles for Memoranda of Understanding," which lay down basic guidelines for creating enforcement MOUs for securities law violations.[22] . . . As discussed below, this groundwork, along with a combination of other factors, has led to a whole network of bilateral MOUs that regulate insider trading and information exchange.

However, IOSCO has not achieved the success of the Basle Committee in implementing global standards for securities regulators. Indeed, IOSCO's attempt to develop capital adequacy standards for securities firms failed in 1992, and its efforts in this regard have been abandoned. In addition, many resolutions passed by IOSCO are not implemented at the domestic level. These failures highlight the inability of government networks to exercise any coercive power over their members. . . .

1.3. Networked Networks

At least in the financial arena, government networks proliferate by joining together in networks of networks. This organizational form is so flexible, cheap, and easy to establish that "mega-networks" are a natural development. Two prominent examples are the Joint Forum on Financial Conglomerates and the Year 2000 Network.

The Joint Forum was established in 1996 under the auspices of the Basle Committee, IOSCO, and IAIS. It is comprised of senior bank, insurance, and securities supervisors from thirteen countries, with the EU Commission attending in an observer capacity.[23] In a prior, even less formal, incarnation as the "Tripartite Group," it issued a discussion paper in 1995 on the supervision of financial conglomerates, which urges the development of uniform standards and information exchange, and underscores the need for "intensive cooperation between supervisors" and their "right to exchange prudential information."[24] It has subsequently prepared a number of papers for consideration by its three parent organizations on subjects such as capital adequacy principles and a framework and principles for supervisory information sharing.[25]

Another more specialized example is the creation of the Joint Year 2000 Council by the Basle Committee, the BIS Committee on Payment and Settlement Systems (CPSS), IOSCO, and IAIS. The formation of the Council was welcomed by the G-7 Finance Ministers; its Secretariat is provided by the BIS. Its mission is to encourage the development of co-ordinated national strategies to address the Year 2000 problem, including the development of a global databank of contacts in individual countries covering a wide range of actors in both the private and public sectors. . . .

1.4. Common Features of Transgovernmental Regulatory Organizations

The transgovernmental regulatory organizations described above share a number of common features. Zaring emphasizes their informal charters and by-laws, flexible internal organization, relative secrecy, and status as "substate actors," meaning that they are composed of State institutions rather than of "member States."[26] Their creation is generally *ad hoc,* and they tend to have only minimal structural components such as founding treaties, by-laws, and staff. The extremely limited budgets of these organizations inhibit the development of a strong central or supranational character,[27] and ensure that each retains a highly flexible internal organization.[28]

Members of TROs emphasize the voluntary nature of participation; the agreements reached are generally phrased in non-legal (although sometimes technical) language and are largely the product of consensus. Importantly, the members insist that the agreements reached by these kinds of transgovernmental organizations are non-binding.[29] The resolutions, MOUs, or communiqués agreed on by these organizations are rarely, if ever, elevated to treaty status by the members of the organization. More often the domestic actors themselves implement agreements, avoiding the need for domestic legislation or ratification. A final, complementary, feature is a general lack of formal mechanisms to monitor compliance—at best the members themselves tend to exercise informal oversight. . . .

An important dimension of TRO effectiveness is the "nationalization of international law." TROs do not aspire to exercise power in the international system independent of their members. Indeed, the main purpose of TROs is to help national regulators to apprehend those who would harm the interests of their citizens, or otherwise to enhance the enforcement of national laws by co-ordinating efforts across borders or promulgating common solutions to problems which each State already faces within its own borders. The result is an international rule-making process that directly engages national officials and national promulgation and enforcement mechanisms, without formal translation and implementation mechanisms from the international to the national.

2. AGENCIES ACROSS BORDERS: BILATERAL AND PLURILATERAL REGULATORY CO-OPERATION

National regulatory agencies also reach out to their counterparts across borders and co-operate in developing joint, harmonized, or co-ordinated policies and agendas outside TROs. These bilateral and plurilateral agreements between domestic agencies, ranging from highly formalized treaties to completely informal initiatives, comprise a second type of government network dedicated to transnational regulatory co-operation. The impulse to engage in *ad hoc* negotiations or discussions on policy has occurred primarily between bilateral partners, although the success of bilateral agreements encourages bilateral partners to consult additional parties, resulting in plurilateral co-operation. As with TROs, bilateral and plurilateral regulatory co-operation is particularly strong in the financial arena.

2.1 MOUs and MLATs

At the centre of the spectrum of agreements lies the standard building block of the informal international order, the MOU. Transnational regulators sign MOUs as non-binding statements of their intent to co-operate in order to address specific regulatory problems. Should concrete ideas or policies result from the negotiations, the regulatory authorities themselves are charged with implementing the decisions in their respective countries. MOUs have proliferated in recent decades, steadily gaining in popularity as a mode of conducting transgovernmental regulatory business.

The comparison between the process of creating MOUs and more formal agreements such as Mutual Legal Assistance Treaties (MLATs) is instructive.[30] Both MOUs and MLATs are, in essence, agreements between regulators in specific and discrete subject areas. The formal distinction is that MLATs are actual treaties; they create legally binding obligations whereas MOUs do not create legal burdens. As a result, creating a MLAT typically involves all the traditional organs of the unitary State model: diplomatic negotiation among State officials, precise and contested drafting of a treaty, and a formal domestic implementation process, such as Senate ratification in the United States, or passage of implementing legislation elsewhere. . . .

Thus, where possible, domestic agencies have sought to avoid the delay and burden of treaty negotiations in favour of quick, less formal, and purportedly non-binding MOUs. Unlike MLATs or other treaties, MOUs are agreed by the regulators themselves, if possible without the involvement of traditional diplomatic actors. MOU agreements are often brief, and drafted in non-legal language. And, perhaps most importantly, MOUs are fast—both in the negotiation process, and in the implementation process, which typically is performed directly by the agency itself, without any involvement of the domestic legislature or other domestic actors. . . .

Examples of areas in which regulators have taken the MOU route include securities regulation,[31] commodities regulation,[32] antitrust,[33] environmental regulation,[34] and health policy.[35] In some cases the development of MOU-networks has been explicitly supported by national legislation. For example, in the 1980s, the SEC proposed legislation authorizing it to investigate suspected violations of United States securities laws in foreign countries, while permitting foreign securities officials to do the same in the United States.[36] One purpose of this legislation was to promote the exchange of information through MOUs.

Of course, use of one or the other type of bilateral agreement is not limited to particular subject-matters; MOUs and MLATs may be used interchangeably and are also often used together. For example, after the Swiss MLAT was signed in 1977, the United States and Swiss securities agencies negotiated a separate MOU to share information regarding insider trading investigations. The additional agreement was necessary because insider trading was not a criminal violation under the Swiss Penal Code, even after conclusion of the formal treaty, and thus insider trading fell outside the scope of the MLAT.

2.2. Informal Initiatives

Informal initiatives lie at the opposite end of the bilateral agreement spectrum from MLATs. The joint survey of the internal management and financial controls of several international securities firms undertaken jointly by the SEC and the British Securities and Investments Board in July 1995 provides one example of such an initiative. The two regulatory agencies sought to co-operate to improve the supervision of securities firms' foreign affiliates in the light of problems recently experienced by Baring's Bank. . . .

In another informal initiative, the SEC has created an international institute for securities market development. The institute "is part of [the SEC's] continuing effort to assist foreign countries with developing capital markets that are critical to a dynamic free enterprise system. The SEC has been particularly generous in supplying technical help to many Eastern European countries."[37] . . .

3. REGULATING THE GLOBAL ECONOMY THROUGH GOVERNMENT NETWORKS: IMPLICATIONS AND PROBLEMS

What are the implications of government networks? At the most general level, they offer a new vision of global governance: horizontal rather than vertical, decentralized rather than centralized, and composed of national government officials rather than a supranational bureaucracy. They are *potentially* both more effective and more accountable than traditional international institutions, at least for some purposes. They simultaneously strengthen the power of the State and equip State actors to interact meaningfully and innovatively with a host of other actors. These include public actors at the supranational, subnational, and regional levels, private actors such as corporations and NGOs, and "mixed" actors that are privately organized but increasingly perform public functions. Further, government networks are optimally adapted to the technology of the Information Age, existing more in virtual than real space. Finally, as the form of governance changes, function is likely to follow suit, enabling government networks to deploy resources away from command and control regulation and towards a variety of catalysing and supporting roles.[38]

Yet government networks trigger both suspicion and anxiety. The suspicion is of a burgeoning global technocracy, insensitive to political choices driven by more than functional considerations and unresponsive to existing mechanisms of democratic governance at the national or international levels. The anxiety is a function of many of the same network attributes that are positively evaluated above. As any feminist who has battled "the old boy network" will quickly recognize, the informality, flexibility, and decentralization of networks means that it is very difficult to establish precisely who is acting and when. Influence is subtle and hard to track; important decisions may be made in very informal settings. As Martti Koskenniemi argues . . . giving up form and validity is ceding fundamental constraints on power.[39] . . .

At this stage of the analysis, a review of some of the principal criticisms of government networks that have been advanced in print and in public audiences, together with some tentative responses, may help guide future research agendas. This section distils three such criticisms: lack of accountability; promotion of a minimalist and exclusionary policy agenda; and marginalization and displacement of traditional international organizations. After reviewing each critique, I set forth some initial responses, many of which will also pose questions for further study.

3.1. A New Technocratic Élite

The sharpest criticisms of government networks emphasize their lack of accountability. According to Philip Alston, if [Slaughter's] analysis "is correct . . . , [i]t implies the marginalisation of governments as such and their replacement by special interest groups . . . It suggests a move away from arenas of relative transparency into the back rooms . . . and the bypassing of the national political arenas to which the United States and other proponents of the importance of healthy democratic institutions attach so much importance."[40] Antonio Perez, identifying a related argument about networks among national and international bureaucrats in Abram and Antonia Chayes's *The New Sovereignty,* accuses them of adopting "Platonic Guardianship as a mode of transnational governance," an open "move toward technocratic elitism."[41] And Sol Picciotto, who also chronicles the rise of government networks but from a more explicitly critical perspective, argues: "A chronic lack of legitimacy plagues direct international contacts at the sub-State level among national officials and administrators."[42] He attributes this lack of legitimacy to their informality and confidentiality, precisely the attributes that make them so attractive to the participants.[43]

Such charges are much easier to make than to prove. To begin with, concerns about accountability assume that government networks are developing and implementing substantive policies in ways that differ significantly from outcomes that would be reached as the result of purely national processes or of negotiations within traditional international institutions. Although reasons exist to accept this premise with regard to policy initiatives such as the 1988 Capital Accord adopted by the Basle Committee,[44] it is less clear regarding other networks, even within the financial arena. Network initiatives are theoretically subject to the normal political constraints on domestic policy-making processes once they have been introduced at the domestic level. Arguments that they circumvent these constraints rest on the presumed ability of national officials in the same issue area to collude with one another in ways that strengthen their respective positions *vis-à-vis* bureaucratic rivals or legislative overseers back home. This presumption is often contested by experts in the different fields of financial regulation and requires further research on a case by case basis.

More generally, many government networks remain primarily talking shops, dedicated to the sharing of information, the cross-fertilization of new ideas, and the development of common principles based on the respective experiences of participating members. The power of information is soft power, persuasive rather than coercive.[45] It is "the ability to get desired outcomes because others want what you want."[46] Specific government institutions may still enjoy a substantial advantage over others due to the quality, quantity, and credibility of the information they have to exchange.[47] But in giving and receiving this information, even in ways that may significantly affect their thinking, government officials are not exercising power in the traditional ways which polities find it necessary to hold them accountable for. We may need to develop new metrics or even new conceptions of accountability geared towards the distinctive features of power in the Information Age.

A second and related response raises the question whether and when direct accountability is necessary for legitimate government. Some domestic institutions, such as courts and central banks, are deemed to act legitimately without direct accountability. Legitimacy may be conferred or attained independent of mechanisms of direct accountability—performance may be measured by outcomes as much as by process. Insulated institutions are designed to counter the voters' changing will and whim, in order to garner the benefits of expertise and stability and to protect minorities. Many of the policy arenas in which government networks are likely to be most active are those in which domestic polities have agreed that a degree of insulation and expertise is desirable. Thus, it is not automatically clear that the transgovernmental extension of these domestic activities poses legitimacy problems.

A third response is: "accountable compared to what?" The presumed accountability or lack thereof of government networks must be contrasted with the accountability of international organizations on the one hand and NGOs on the other. International organizations are widely perceived as being accountable only to diplomats and international lawyers, which helps explain their relative disrepute in many countries. And accountable to whom? The United Nations suffers from the perennial perception that it is answerable primarily to its own bureaucracy; the International Monetary Fund and, to a lesser extent, the World Bank are widely seen as fronts for the United States; European Union institutions have been in crisis over a purported "democracy deficit" for much of this decade. . . .

NGOs hardly fare better. Although they must routinely sing for their supper and thus depend on their ability to persuade individual and institutional contributors of the worth of their activities, many, if not most, are single issue groups who target a particular demographic and political segment of society and may well wield power quite disproportionate to the number of their supporters. . . .

In this context, government networks have a number of potential advantages. First, they are composed of the same officials who make and implement regulations domestically. To the extent that these networks do actually make policy, and to the extent that the policies made and subsequently adopted at the national level differ significantly from the outcome of a purely domestic regulatory process, it is reasonable to expect that other domestic political institutions—legislators, courts, or other branches of the bureaucracy—will extend their normal oversight functions to transgovernmental as well as domestic activities. Alston rejects this claim as excessively optimistic, arguing that all the organs of the State have been significantly weakened by globalization and the neo-liberal economic agenda that has accompanied it.[48] That, however, is a separate argument, which is considered separately below. It is also an argument with far broader implications: if the State is really so weakened, then the prospects of enhancing the accountability of any of the important actors in international life are slim indeed.

A promising development that suggests that State institutions with a more directly representative mandate are not yet dead is the growth of legislative networks: links among those national officials who are most directly responsible for ensuring bureaucratic accountability. In some areas, national legislation has been used to facilitate the growth of government networks.[49] In others, such as human rights and the environment, national legislators are increasingly recognizing that they have common interests. In the European Union, governments are increasingly having to submit their European policies to special parliamentary committees, who are themselves networking.[50] The result, according to German international relations scholar Karl Kaiser, is the "reparliamentarization" of national policy.[51] . . .

A final response to the accountability critique is that the critics are missing a more significant point about the changing nature of power itself. Government networks are far better suited to exercising "soft power" than "hard power"—that is, the power flowing from an ability to convince others that they want what you want rather than an ability to compel them to forgo their preferences by using either threats or rewards.[52] Soft power rests much more on persuasive than coercive authority, a base that may in turn require a capacity for genuine engagement and dialogue with others. To the extent that government officials seek to persuade but then find that they must in turn allow themselves to be persuaded in their interactions with their foreign counterparts, what should mechanisms of accountability be designed to accomplish? . . .

3.2. A Minimalist Global Agenda

A second major critique of government networks is that they instantiate a radically scaled-back global policy agenda. Alston observes that the formulation of the transgovernmental policy agenda focuses on issues that are essentially spillovers from the domestic policy agendas of the industrialized world, leaving out global poverty, malnutrition, human rights, refugees, the persecution of minority groups, and disease.[53] . . . He is making a more important point, arguing that the transgovernmental regulatory agenda is *displacing* the traditional internationalist agenda of providing public goods to solve international collective action problems. That is a much more serious charge, but it confuses the symptoms with the disease. How can the emergence of transgovernmental regulatory networks addressing domestic policy issues that have become globalized be adduced as a *cause* of declining interest in an older but perennial set of international problems? . . .

3.3. Displacing International Institutions

. . . A final critique of government networks implicates an idea, and perhaps an ideal, of internationalism: a distinction between international and domestic politics that is embodied in and protected by a conception of national sovereignty. However much their agendas now address issues once of purely domestic concern, international organizations still operate in a self-consciously international space. They employ independent international bureaucrats, whose loyalty is supposed to shift away from their national governments. And when they convene meetings of relevant national officials, as they frequently do, those officials are at the very least wearing dual hats, formally representing their governments in external affairs. As a result, the resolutions or even rules adopted can be resisted at the national level as being external and imposed.

One of the major advantages of government networks, at least from the perspective of those who are often frustrated by the difficulty of ensuring compliance with international rules and norms, is that they directly engage the national officials who have the power to implement domestic policy changes. As a result, the policies they adopt, implement, or at least promote are much harder to combat on grounds of national sovereignty. From a theoretical perspective, government networks straddle and ultimately erase the domestic/international divide. But from the perspective of some governments, such as the Mexican environmental officials participating in the North American Free Trade Agreement (NAFTA) "environmental enforcement network," the result is a politics of imposition that is but the latest face of imperialism, or at least hegemony.

This critique must also be contextualized. In many international issue areas, such as human rights or environmental regulation, or even many types of financial regulation, the point is precisely to penetrate national sovereignty. The policy decisions that are the subject of international concern are being made at the domestic level. Conversely, rules and principles being adopted in the international or transgovernmental sphere are supposed to shape governments' relations with their own systems. Further, these goals are often shared by many domestic actors. Thus, to say that government networks are particularly effective at penetrating the face of national sovereignty and defusing opposition based on the "imposition" of foreign or international rules and institutions is as likely to be praise as censure.

3.4. Advantages of Government Networks: Bringing the (Disaggregated) State Back In

The danger in responding to specific criticisms is always that of losing sight of the forest. In this case, much of the critique of transgovernmentalism betrays reflexive hostility and poverty of imagination—a defensive attachment to a liberal internationalist agenda that champions international organizations either as ends in themselves or as the only means to achieve transcendent policy goals. For many, even those who share the underlying policy goals, this agenda is nothing more than yesterday's *status quo*: the welfare State at home, international bureaucracy abroad. Transgovernmentalism may in some cases be associated with other policy agendas, such as neo-liberal economics. But it also reflects the rise of an organizational form as a mode of adaptation to a host of factors, from technology to the decline of inter-State conflict, that cannot be wished or argued away. It is a choice, of course, whether to celebrate or lament this development. But here again, the choice even to frame transgovernmentalism as an issue offers numerous advantages that its critics apparently have not stopped to ponder.

First, and most important, transgovernmentalism is all about bringing the State back in as an important international actor. . . . The point of presenting transgovernmentalism as a "new world order," in contrast to the claims of liberal internationalists who seek to devolve power ever upward to international organizations and "new medievalists" who predict or even call for the demise of the Westphalian system, was to argue that State power was disaggregating rather than disappearing. State actors are exercising their power by different means and through different channels. Alston is quite right to claim that this is a partial image—"one . . . layer out of a much more complex set of strata."[54]

A second major advantage of government networks concerns the ways in which they can be used to strengthen individual State institutions without labelling the State as a whole as "weak," "failed," "illiberal," or anything else. Networks target specific institutions, imposing particular conditions or at least goals regarding the level and quality of their functioning and often providing direct information and even material aid. The SEC, for example, distributes considerable technical assistance through its network of MOUs with other securities regulation agencies.[55] The criteria for participation have little to do with the political system as a whole and a great deal to do with technical or professional competence. . . .

4. CONCLUSION

Many international lawyers will not like the message of this [essay]. It seems an assault on all that internationalists have laboured so painstakingly to build in the twentieth century. It offers a horizontal rather than a vertical model of global governance, an informal and frequently selective set of institutions in place of formal and highly scripted fora in which each State is accorded an equal voice. Alternatively, government networks may appear trendy but inconsequential—talking shops at best and opportunities for foreign junkets at worst. After all, international institutions have proliferated over the past decades and seem sufficiently robust that at least one noted political scientist has posed the question "why do they never die?"[55]

In fact, government networks are here to stay and will assume increasing importance in all areas of international life. They are the optimal form of organization for the Information Age. Note the responses to the East Asian financial crisis; amid calls for a new Bretton Woods agreement to craft and implement a new international architecture, the real forum for policy innovation and implementation is the G22. Governmental networks are less likely to displace international organizations than to infiltrate and complement them; they will also be the ideal fora for pioneering initiatives and pilot projects among smaller groups of States. In economic regulation in particular, they develop easily as they are based on shared technical expertise among regulators and the escalating demands of a globalized economy among both the richest States and the most promising emerging markets. . . .

Every age needs its own idealistic vision: the Information Age will celebrate the exchange of ideas over the imposition of ideology. Networks are the medium for that exchange, a medium that, like others before it, will itself become the message. The result will be the effective adaptation of national governments to the growth of networks among the private and semi-public actors they supposedly govern. The State will thus be able to retain its position as a primary locus of political, economic, and even social power in the international system, but shifts in both the organization and the nature of that power will ultimately transform the State itself.

NOTES

1. Abram and Antonia Chayes, *The New Sovereignty* (Cambridge, Mass.: Harvard University Press, 1996).
2. See Jessica T. Mathews, "Power Shift" (1997) 1 *Foreign Affairs* 76.
3. David Zaring, "International Law by Other Means: The Twilight Existence of International Financial Regulatory Organizations" (1998) 33 *Texas International Law Journal* 281.
4. Peter Cooke, "Bank Capital Adequacy" (1991), excerpted in Hal S. Scott and Philip A. Wellons, *International Finance: Transaction, Policy, and Regulation* (2nd edn., Westbury, NY: Foundation Press, 1995) at 232; Joseph J. Norton, "Trends in International Bank Supervision and the Basle Committee on Banking Supervision" (1994) 48 *Consumer Finance Law Quarterly,* 415, 417.
5. *The Bank for International Settlements: A Profile of an International Institution* (Basle: Bank for International Settlements, 1991), at 2.
6. Statute of the Bank for International Settlements, 20 Jan. 1930, reprinted in *Bank for International Settlements, Basic Texts* (Basle: Bank for International Settlements, 1987), 11.
7. General Accounting Office, Report to Congressional Committees, "International Banking—Strengthening the Framework for Supervising International Banks" (Mar. 1994), at 37.
8. Basle Committee on Banking Supervision, *Annexure C* (1995), para. 3.
9. For example, Brazil's Central Bank adopted the Basle Accord in Aug. 1994. Scott and Wellons, *International Finance,* at 249.
10. Peter Cooke, Chair of the Basle Committee, quoted in Joseph Jude Norton, *Devising International Bank Supervisory Standards* (London: Graham and Trotman, 1995), 177.
11. According to Charles Freeland, a member of the Committee. See Freeland, "The Work of the Basle Committee," in Robert C. Effros (ed.), *Current Legal Issues Affecting Central Banks* (Washington: International Monetary Fund, 1992), 232.
12. See Scott and Wellons, *International Finance* (3rd edn., 1996), at 249.
13. See e.g. Robert Litan, "Nightmare in Basle" (Nov./Dec. 1992) The International Economy 7.
14. Scott and Wellons, *International Finance,* at 251.
15. Press Statement, 22 Sep. 1997, http://www.bis.org/press/p970922.htm. The principles themselves can be found at http://www.bis.ord.
16. See Paul Guy, "Regulatory Harmonization to Achieve Effective International Competition," in F. R. Edwards and H. T. Patrick (eds.), *Regulating International Financial Markets: Issues and Policies* (Boston: Kluwer, 1992), 291. For an in-depth look at the organization and functioning of the IOSCO, see David Zaring, "International Law," at 20–31.
17. For a list of IOSCO members, see http://www.iosco.org/index4.html.
18. See Zaring, "International Law."
19. See Zaring, "International Law," at 27.
20. IOSCO Annual Report 1990.
21. See Michael D. Mann and Lise A. Lustgatten, "Internationalization of Insider Trading Enforcement: A Guide to Regulation and Cooperation" (1993) 7 PLI/Corp 798.
22. See generally Michael D. Mann *et al.,* "The Establishment of International Mechanisms for Enforcing Provisional Orders and Final Judgements Arising From Securities Law Violations" (1992) 55 *Law & Contemporary Problems* 303.
23. See http://www.bis.org/publ/bcbs34.htm. The members of the Joint Forum are Australia, Belgium, Canada, France, Germany, Italy, Japan, The Netherlands, Spain, Sweden, Switzerland, the United Kingdom, and the United States.

24. "US Objections Prompt Limited Global Pact on Financial Services" (21 Aug. 1995) 14 (16) *Banking Policy Reporter* 17.

25. See http://www.bis.org/publ/bcbs34.htm.

26. See Zaring, "International Law," at 39.

27. In fact, IOSCO's annual revenues do not amount to $US 750,000; IAIS did not exceed $US 125,000 in 1994; and while the Basle Committee does not disclose its dues, "since it does not support a secretariat, they are presumably also minimal." See ibid., at 43.

28. See ibid., at 40.

29. See e.g. Interview with Paul Leder, Deputy Director, Office of International Affairs, SEC, 11 Jan. 1996; as quoted ibid., at 43.

30. See generally "Note, International Securities Law Enforcement: Recent Advances in Assistance and Cooperation" (1994) 27 *Vanderbilt Journal of Transnational Law* 635; Charles Vaughn Baltic III, "Note The Next Step in Insider Trading Regulation: Internal Cooperative Efforts in the Global Securities Market" (1991–2) 2 *Law and Policy in International Business* 167.

31. See Brad Begin, "A Proposed Blueprint for Achieving Cooperation in Policing Transborder Securities Fraud" (1986) 27 *Vanderbilt Journal of International Law* 65; Paula Jimenez, "Comment, International Securities Enforcement Cooperation Act and Memoranda of Understanding" (1990) 31 *Harvard International Law Journal* 295. See also Mark S. Klock, "Comment, A Comparative Analysis of Recent Accords Which Facilitate Transnational SEC Investigations of Insider Trading" (1987) 11 *Maryland Journal of International Law and Trade* 243.

32. In June 1995 the US Commodities Future Trading Commission and Italy's Commissione Nazionale per la Società à la Borsa signed a mutual assistance agreement entitled "Memorandum of Understanding on Consultation and Mutual Assistance for the Exchange of Information." The MOU authorizes US and Italian regulators to request and obtain accessed information contained in each other's files, take statements from persons subject to each other's jurisdiction, and obtain documents regarding futures trading (Aug. 1995) 11 *International Enforcement Law Reporter* 318. In May 1995 the Mexican National Banking and Securities Commission and the USCFTC negotiated a MOU to facilitate the exchange of information and improve the enforcement of laws and regulations related to the futures and options markets in the United States and Mexico.

33. See Nina Hachigian, "Essential Mutual Assistance in International Antitrust Enforcement" (1995) 29 *International Lawyer* 117, 138.

34. See James D. Vieregg *et al.*, "Cross-Border Environmental Law Enforcement" (20 Oct. 1994) *ALI-ABA Course of Study: Criminal Enforcement of Environmental Laws*, C964 ALI-ABA 455.

35. For example, in Nov. 1991 the US Food & Drug Administration participated in an International Conference on Harmonisation, which included drug regulators and pharmaceutical manufacturers from the EC, Japan, and USA (the countries which account for the vast majority of drug production, research, and development). The FDA agreed to accept data collected in foreign clinical tests and explored the possibility of developing common standards. David W. Jordan, "Note, International Regulatory Harmonization: A New Era in Prescription Drug Approval" (1992) 25 *Vanderbilt Journal of Transnational Law* 471; see also Rosemarie Kanusky, "Comment, Pharmaceutical Harmonization: Standardizing Regulations Among the United States, the European Economic Community, and Japan" (1994) 16 *Houston Journal of International Law* 665.

36. The International Securities Enforcement Cooperation Act, S. 2544, 100th Cong., 2d Sess. (1988). On 19 Nov. 1988, Congress adopted a less comprehensive version of S. 2544, the Insider Trading and Securities Fraud Enforcement Act of 1988, 15 U.S.C. § 78 (1988).

37. Stewart J. Kaswell, "SEC Chair Breeden Underscores the Importance of the Rule of Law" (Summer 1992) *ABA International Law News* 5.

38. The public management section of the OECD (called PUMA) has launched a major regulatory reform initiative that operates through a "regulatory management and reform network." A major focus of reform efforts is the shift away from "command and control regulations" to a wide range of alternative instruments, many of them market-based or relying on self-regulation incentives. For an overview of this programme, see the PUMA website at http://www.oecd.org/puma/regref/work.htm. In the United States similar work has been done under Vice President Al Gore's "Reinventing Government" initiative.

39. Martti Koskenniemi, "Carl Schmitt, Hans Morgenthau, and the Image of Law in International Relations, *The Role of Law in International Politics*, edited by Michael Byers. Copyright © 2000 Oxford University Press.

40. Philip Alston, "The Myopia of the Handmaidens: International Lawyers and Globalisation" (1997) 8 *European Journal of International Law* 435, 441.

41. Antonio Perez, "Who Killed Sovereignty? Or: Changing Norms Concerning Sovereignty In International Law" (1996) 14 *Wisconsin International Law Journal* 463, 476.

42. Sol Picciotto, "Networks in International Economic Integration: Fragmented States and the Dilemmas of Neo-Liberalism" (1996–7) 17 *Northwestern Journal of International Law and Business* 1014, 1047.

43. Ibid., at 1049.

44. Ethan B. Kapstein, *Supervising International Banks: Origins and Implications of the Basle Accord* (Princeton: Department of Economics, Princeton University, 1991).

45. Robert O. Keohane and Joseph S. Nye Jr., "Power and Interdependence in the Information Age" (1998) 77 *Foreign Affairs* 81, 86.

46. Ibid.

47. See ibid., at 89–92 (discussing "the politics of credibility").

48. Alston, "Myopia of the Handmaidens," at 442.

49. MOUs between the SEC and its foreign counterparts, for example, have been directly encouraged and facilitated by several United States statutes passed expressly for the purpose. Faith T. Teo, "Memoranda of Understanding among Securities Regulators: Frameworks for Cooperation, Implications for Governance" (1998), 29–43 (ms on file with author, Harvard Law School).

50. Shirley Williams, "Sovereignty and Accountability in the European Union," in Robert Keohane and Stanley Hoffman (eds.), *The New European Community* (Boulder, Colo.: Westview Press, 1991).

51. Karl Kaiser, "Globalisierung als Problem der Demokratie" (Apr. 1998) *Internationale Politik* 3.

52. Keohane and Nye, "Power and Interdependence," at 86.

53. Alston, "Myopia of the Handmaidens," at 439.

54. Alston, "Myopia of the Handmaidens," at 444.

55. Teo, "Memoranda," at 23–4.

56. Susan Strange, "Why Do International Organizations Never Die?," in B. Reinalda and V. Verbeek (eds.), *Autonomous Policy Making by International Organizations* (London: Routledge, 1998), 213.

Regime Design Matters: International Oil Pollution and Treaty Compliance

RONALD B. MITCHELL

Regime design matters.[1] International treaties and regimes have value if and only if they cause people to do things they would not otherwise do. Governments spend considerable resources and effort drafting and refining treaty language with the (at least nominal) aim of making treaty compliance and effectiveness more likely. This article demonstrates that whether a treaty elicits compliance or other desired behavioral changes depends upon identifiable characteristics of the regime's compliance systems.[2] As negotiators incorporate certain rules into a regime and exclude others, they are making choices that have crucial implications for whether or not actors will comply.

. . . Interest in issues of compliance and verification has a long history in the field of nuclear arms control.[3] More recently, this interest in empirically evaluating how international institutions, regimes, and treaties induce compliance and influence behavior has broadened to include other security areas as well as international trade and finance.[4] Concern over the fate of the earth's environment recently has prompted a further extension into questions of whether and how environmental treaties can be made more effective at eliciting compliance and achieving their goals.[5]

Researchers in all these issue-areas face two critical questions. First, given that power and interests play important roles in determining behavior at the international level, is any of the compliance we observe with international treaties the result of the treaty's influence? Second, if treaties and regimes can alter behavior, what strategies can those who negotiate and design regimes use to elicit the greatest possible compliance? This article addresses both these questions by empirically evaluating the international regime controlling intentional oil pollution. . . . Since the late 1970s, the treaties have established two quite different compliance systems, or "subregimes," to accomplish this goal. One has prohibited tanker operators from discharging oil in excess of specified limits. The other has required tanker owners to install expensive pollution-reduction equipment by specified dates. Treaty parties viewed both subregimes as equally legitimate and equally binding.[6] The two subregimes regulated similar behavior by the same nations and tankers

The research reported herein was conducted with support from the University of Oregon and the Center for Science and International Affairs of Harvard University. Invaluable data were generously provided by Clarkson Research Studies, Ltd. The article has benefited greatly from discussions with Abram Chayes, Antonia Chayes, William Clark, and Robert Keohane and from collaboration with Moira McConnell and Alexei Roginko as part of a project on regime effectiveness based at Dartmouth College and directed by Oran Young and Marc Levy. John Odell, Miranda Schreurs, David Weil, and two anonymous reviewers provided invaluable comments on earlier drafts of this article.

over the same time period. The absence of differences in power and interests would suggest that compliance levels with the two subregimes would be quite similar.[7] According to collective action theory, these cases are among the least likely to provide support for the hypothesis that regime design matters: subregime provisions required the powerful and concentrated oil industry to incur large pollution control costs to provide diffuse benefits to the public at large.[8] Indeed, the lower cost of complying with discharge limits would suggest that compliance would be higher with those limits than with equipment requirements.

Not surprisingly, violations of the limits on discharges have occurred frequently, attesting to the ongoing incentives to violate the agreement and confirming the characterization of oil pollution as a difficult collaboration problem.[9] A puzzle arises, however, from the fact that contrary to expectation compliance has been all but universal with requirements to install expensive equipment that provided no economic benefits. The following analysis clearly demonstrates that the significant variance across subregimes can only be explained by specific differences in subregime design. . . .

COMPLIANCE THEORY AND DEFINITIONS

Explaining the puzzle of greater compliance with a more expensive and economically inefficient international regulation demands an understanding of existing theories about the sources of compliance in international affairs. Realists have inferred a general inability of international regimes to influence behavior from the fact that the international system is characterized by anarchy and an inability to organize centralized enforcement. . . . Treaties are epiphenomenal: they reflect power and interests but do not shape behavior.

This view does not imply that noncompliance is rare in international affairs. Although nations will violate rules whenever they have both the incentives and ability to do so, as Hans Morgenthau notes, "the great majority of the rules of international law are generally observed by all nations."[10] For the realist, behavior frequently conforms to treaty rules because both the behavior and the rules reflect the interests of powerful states. More specifically, compliance is an artifact of one of three situations: (1) a hegemonic state forces or induces other states to comply; (2) the treaty rules merely codify the parties' existing behavior or expected future behavior; or (3) the treaty resolves a coordination game in which no party has any incentive to violate the rules once a stable equilibrium has been achieved.[11]

Treaty rules correlate with but do not cause compliance. Therefore, efforts to improve treaty rules to increase compliance reflect either the changed interests of powerful states or are misguided exercises in futility. The strength of this view has led to considerable attention being paid to whether rules influence behavior and far less being paid to design features that explain why one rule influences behavior and another does not.

In contrast, international lawyers and institutionalists contend that the anarchic international order need not lead inexorably to nations violating agreements whenever doing so suits them. Other forces—such as transparency, reciprocity, accountability, and regime-mindedness—allow regimes to impose significant constraints on international behavior under the right conditions.[12] Implicit in the institutionalist view is the assumption that power and interests alone cannot explain behavior: a given constellation of power and interests leaves room for nations to choose among treaty rules that will elicit significantly different levels of compliance. High compliance levels can be achieved even in difficult collaboration problems in which incentives to violate are large and ongoing.

In essence, this debate revolves around whether in a realm of behavior covered by an international agreement, that behavior is ever any different than it would have been without the agreement. If we define "treaty-induced compliance" as behavior that conforms to a treaty's rules because of the treaty's compliance system, institutionalists view treaty-induced compliance as possible. In contrast, realists see all compliance as "coincidental compliance," that is, behavior that would have occurred even without the treaty rules.

The debate between these theories highlights the demands placed on research that seeks to identify those design characteristics of a regime, if any, that are responsible for observed levels of compliance. I define compliance, the dependent variable, as an actor's behavior that conforms with an explicit treaty provision. Speaking of compliance with treaty provisions rather than with a treaty captures the fact that parties may well comply with some treaty provisions while violating others. A study of "treaty compliance" would aggregate violation of one provision with compliance with another, losing valuable empirical information.[13] Restricting study to the explicit rules in a treaty-based regime allows the analyst to distinguish compliance from noncompliance in clear and replicable ways. Obviously, a focus on explicit rules ignores other potential mechanisms of regime influence, such as norms, principles, and processes of knowledge creation.[14] However, this restrictive definition has the virtue of bringing the debate to a level at which research on actual treaties and actual compliance can contribute to the intellectual and policy debates.

This article evaluates the features of a regime that may determine compliance by differentiating among three parts of any compliance system: a primary rule system, a compliance information system, and a noncompliance response system. The primary rule system consists of the actors, rules, and processes related to the behavior that is the substantive target of the regime. In the choice of who gets regulated and how, the primary rule system determines the pressures and incentives for compliance and violation. The compliance information system consists of the actors, rules, and processes that collect, analyze, and disseminate information on instances of violations and compliance. Self-reporting, independent monitoring, data analysis, and publishing comprise the compliance information system that determines the amount, quality, and uses made of data on compliance and enforcement. The noncompliance response system consists of the actors, rules, and processes governing the formal and informal responses—the inducements and sanctions—employed to induce those in noncompliance to comply. The noncompliance response system determines the type, likelihood, magnitude, and appropriateness of responses to noncompliance. These categories provide the framework used in the remainder of this article to evaluate the oil pollution regime's sources of success and failure in its attempt to elicit compliance.

TWO SUBREGIMES FOR INTERNATIONAL OIL POLLUTION CONTROL

For most people, oil pollution conjures up images of tanker accidents such as that of the *Exxon Valdez*.[15] While oil from such accidents poses a concentrated but localized hazard to the marine environment, the waste oil traditionally generated during normal oil transport has posed a more diffuse but ubiquitous threat. After a tanker delivers its cargo, a small fraction of oil remains onboard, adhering to cargo tank walls. Ballasting and tank-cleaning procedures mixed this oil—averaging about 300 tons per voyage—with seawater, creating slops. These in turn were most easily and cheaply disposed of by discharging them overboard while at sea.[16] By the 1970s, the intentional discharges made on thousands of tanker voyages were putting an estimated million tons of oil into the oceans annually.[17] While scientific uncertainty remains regarding the extent of damage to marine life caused by such chronic but low-concentration discharges, their impact and that of accidents on seabirds and resort beaches have produced regular international efforts at regulation.[18]

Intentional oil discharges were one of the first pollutants to become the subject of an international regulatory regime.[19] In the International Convention for the Prevention of Pollution of the Seas by Oil (OILPOL) of 1954, nations addressed the coastal oil pollution problem by limiting the oil content of discharges made near shore.[20] By the late 1970s, the regime's major provisions, now contained in the International Convention for the Prevention of Pollution from Ships (MARPOL), consisted of restrictions on both tanker operations and tanker equipment that relied on quite different compliance systems.[21]

The Discharge Subregime

The discharge subregime of the last fifteen years evolved from the initial regulations of 1954. That agreement constituted a compromise between the United Kingdom—which wielded strong power in oil markets but had strong environmental nongovernmental organizations pushing it to reduce coastal pollution—and Germany, the Netherlands, the United States, and other major states that viewed any regulation as either environmentally unnecessary or as harmful to their own shipping interests. Although the United Kingdom had sought to restrict tanker discharges throughout the ocean, the final agreement limited the oil content of discharges made within fifty miles of any coastline to 100 parts oil per million parts water (100 ppm). In 1962, the British pushed through an amendment applying this 100 ppm standard to discharges made by new tankers regardless of their distance from shore.

The principle underlying the 1962 amendment—that crude oil could float far enough that discharge zones would not effectively protect coastlines—had gained sufficient support by 1969 that nations agreed to limit discharges by all tankers throughout the ocean. The pressure to amend the 1954/62 agreement came from two different sources. On one side, the thirty-five million gallons of oil spilled by the grounding of the *Torrey Canyon* off Britain and France on 18 March 1967 and growing environmentalism, especially in the United States, supported a push for stronger regulations.[22] The previously resistant United States replaced the United Kingdom as the leading activist state and especially sought to ensure that amendments would address the growing evidence of enforcement problems with existing regulations.

On the other side, oil companies rightly interpreted the 1962 amendments as a wake-up call that discharge standards would soon be replaced by expensive equipment requirements. In response, Shell Marine International developed and promoted an operational means by which tankers could reduce oil discharges without any new equipment.[23] The load-on-top procedure (LOT) involved consolidating ballast and cleaning slops in a single tank, letting gravity separate out the water so it could be decanted from beneath the oil, and loading the next cargo on top of the remaining slops. . . . The problem was that normal operation of LOT produced discharges that exceeded the 100 ppm standard. If this criterion had remained in effect, tankers would have had to install expensive new equipment to comply with OILPOL, defeating LOT's major economic virtue. With the support of France, the Netherlands, Norway, and the now less-activist United Kingdom, oil and shipping companies therefore also sought to amend the treaty. Oil companies considered LOT so effective that they wanted diplomats to scrap the 1954/62 zonal approach altogether. The pressures for greater environmental protection, however, led them to support the more limited objective of redefining the limits on discharges from the 100 ppm "content" criterion to one that could be monitored using existing on-board equipment.[24]

In a unanimously accepted compromise in 1969, more stringent and enforceable regulations were framed in terms that averted equipment requirements. Within the fifty-mile near-shore zones, discharges could now only involve "clean ballast" that left no visible trace; outside the fifty-mile zones, discharges could not exceed 60 liters of oil per mile (60 l/m). . . . Although compliance with this standard required a tanker to reduce its average discharges by almost 98 percent, Shell's J. H. Kirby claimed that "any responsibly run ship, no matter how big, could operate" within these standards if it used LOT.[25] The low total discharge limit also allowed port authorities to assume that any tanker with completely clean tanks had blatantly violated the agreement.[26] These standards took effect in 1978 and remain in force today through their incorporation into the 1973 MARPOL agreement.

The Equipment Subregime

. . . The United Nations Conference on the Human Environment and negotiation of the London Dumping Convention in 1972 set the stage for a major overhaul of the OILPOL agreement. IMCO hosted a major conference in 1973 to negotiate the MARPOL treaty. Its goal was the replacement of OILPOL's rules with rules that would cover all major types of vessel-source marine pollution.

The U.S. government had become increasingly concerned that the ease with which tanker crews could violate discharge standards and the massive resources and diligence needed to detect violations were preventing effective mitigation of the growing oil pollution problem.[27] By 1972, Congress had adopted legislation that threatened to require all American tankers as well as all tankers entering U.S. ports to install expensive pollution-reducing equipment. The legislation included a proposal to require all large tankers to install double hulls to address accidental spills and segregated ballast tanks (SBT) to address intentional discharges. . . . Discharge requirements clearly were cheaper, more economically efficient, and "in theory . . . a good idea."[28] However, environmental pressures and growing evidence that LOT was neither as widespread nor as effective as had been hoped led the United States and the United Kingdom to support rules that offered easier and more effective enforcement.

The largely U.S.-based oil companies initially opposed SBT requirements but eventually supported them as preferable to threatened U.S. unilateral rules. Many shipping states also reluctantly supported SBT requirements. They believed such requirements would avert an even more costly double bottom requirement. . . .

By 1977, a spate of accidents in the United States and continuing enforcement concerns led President Jimmy Carter to propose that SBT requirements be applied to all tankers, not just large new tankers.[29] Given (1) that the United States was again explicitly threatening unilateral action and (2) that the 1973 MARPOL agreement still had been ratified by only three states, IMCO called a second major conference in 1978.[30] State positions reflected the fact that retrofitting existing tankers with SBT would reduce each tanker's (and the fleet's) cargo capacity by some 15 percent.[31] Greece, Norway, and Sweden saw this as a means to put scores of their laid up independent tankers back to work. However, most states saw SBT retrofitting as extremely expensive.[32] Just as the 1962 amendments had prompted LOT development, the 1973 MARPOL agreement prompted oil companies to perfect a technique known as crude oil washing (COW), which entailed spraying down cargo tanks with the cargo itself rather than with seawater. Operating COW equipment during cargo delivery transformed oil that otherwise would have been discharged as slops into usable delivered cargo, simultaneously reducing oil pollution and increasing cargo owner revenues. The industry proposal for COW as an alternative to SBT produced a compromise in which tankers built after 1982 had to install both SBT and COW, while existing tankers had to be retrofitted with either SBT or COW by 1985. The 1978 Protocol Relating to the International Convention for the Prevention of Pollution from ships was made an integral part of the 1973 MARPOL agreement. While MARPOL and its protocol, known collectively as MARPOL 73/78, did not enter into force until 1983, their standards regulated all new construction after 1979.

OBSERVED COMPLIANCE LEVELS

Available evidence demonstrates a wide divergence in levels of compliance under these two subregimes. During the same time period in which almost every tanker owner was retrofitting existing tankers and buying new tankers to conform with MARPOL's requirements for SBT and COW, large numbers of tanker operators continued to discharge oil well in excess of legal limits. The variance between the observed compliance rates with the two subregimes is quite marked.

Violations of the clean ballast, 60 l/m, and total discharge standards in place since 1978 have been common. Oil company surveys from the 1970s show that neither oil company nor independent tankers reduced average discharge levels to the one fifteen-thousandth limit in any year between 1972 and 1977. Although oil company tankers dramatically reduced average discharges in the early 1970s, discharges remained at three times the legal limit. The two-thirds of the fleet operated by independent oil transporters did far worse, with discharges that were thirty times the legal limit and that were not much below levels that a tanker practicing no pollution control would have produced.[33] The trends in these discharges suggest that few tankers complied with the limit after it took legal effect in 1978.[34]

Other evidence confirms the frequency of discharge violations. A 1981 National Academy of Sciences estimate of oil pollution relied on an assumption that 50 percent of the world's tanker fleet was violating the total discharge limit.[35] A 1989 revision of that study assumed 15–20 percent of tankers were still violating this limit, although it provided no evidence to support the dramatic improvement.[36] . . .

The variety of sources pointing to violation of the discharge standards contrasts sharply with the uniformity of evidence that compliance with the equipment standards has been exceptionally high. By 1981, one shipping research firm already had evidence that new tankers were being built with SBT and existing tankers were being retrofitted with SBT and/or COW.[37] Recent national and international studies as well as industry experts reveal a common assumption that all tankers comply with the equipment standards although none provides empirical support for this assumption.[38] . . .

The variance between the subregimes is more remarkable when one considers that both international politics and private economics would lead us to expect higher compliance with the discharge standards, not the equipment standards. The discharge standards had been adopted unanimously. In contrast, several powerful nations opposed the equipment standards in both 1973 and 1978. Tankers seeking the economic benefits of conserving oil could have done so most cheaply by using the equipment-free option of LOT, not by installing COW or the even more expensive SBT. Indeed, in 1978, one academic analyst, Charles Okidi, predicted that the enormous costs of SBT would make compliance "negligible."[39]

In short, the empirical evidence of higher compliance levels with the equipment subregime runs contrary to predictions based on a simple analysis of exogenous power and interests. How do we explain what appears to be a significant divergence between theory and observed outcomes? Was any of the observed compliance treaty-induced? . . .

WAS COMPLIANCE TREATY-INDUCED?

Before we can explain how one subregime produced such dramatically higher compliance levels than another within the same issue-area, we need to assure ourselves that we can accurately attribute this variance to features of the regime. Taking realist analysis seriously requires that we avoid attributing causation where only spurious correlation exists. Factors other than variation in the compliance systems of the two subregimes may explain the observed behaviors. Did tanker owners and operators act any differently than they would have in the absence of international regulations? The following accounting of incentives to comply with regulations from both within and outside of the regime strongly suggests (1) that increased use of LOT owes more to economics than to international law, (2) that increased installation of COW equipment owes much to economics but also reflects the MARPOL regime's influences, and (3) that increased installation of SBT largely is due to MARPOL influences.

LOT

Several pieces of evidence indicate that the 1969 rules had little to do with the observed increase in the use of LOT by tanker operators. A large share of tankers simply did not use LOT or comply with the discharge standards. The continuing noncompliance with discharge standards did not result from an inability to use LOT—a noncomplex procedure that required no new equipment—but from insufficient incentives to use it.

. . . The subregime's failure effectively to detect, identify, prosecute, and penalize violators left tanker operators' incentives to comply with it largely uninfluenced. . . .

Given the absence of these pathways for regime influence, it is not surprising to find that economic influences readily explain the pattern of LOT usage. A tanker operator's first-order incentives to use LOT depended on the costs of recovering waste oil, the value of that oil, and the ownership of the oil being transported. This last factor meant that oil companies had far greater incentives to adopt LOT than did independent transporters. The latter carry oil on charter to cargo owners and are paid for the amount of oil initially loaded, known as the bill-of-lading weight, not for the amount delivered. Therefore, discharging waste oil at sea costs the independent transporter nothing. Indeed, using LOT reduces the bill-of-lading weight in subsequent cargo by the amount of remaining slops, thereby reducing the payment that the independent transporter receives. . . .

The decrease in average discharges of oil company tankers in the 1970s and the absence of a similar decrease in discharges of independent tankers correlate more with these divergent incentives and with rising oil prices than with any treaty proscription. Oil companies' greater incentives to conserve oil explain why their average discharges were lower than those of independent tankers in 1972 and why they decreased discharges more rapidly after the 1973 oil price hikes. If the regime, rather than economics, were influencing oil company behavior, these decreases should have occurred only after the total discharge limits took legal effect in 1978, not after 1973. The far smaller decrease in average discharge among independents reflects the fact that conserved oil had little value to them.

Nevertheless, the OILPOL regime does appear to have been responsible for the timing of LOT development in the early 1960s and to have at least contributed to some adoption of LOT. Oil company representatives noted at the time that they had developed LOT in response to the increasing pressures for equipment requirements that were evident at the 1962 conference. . . .

COW

The almost universal installation of COW equipment initially tempts one to conclude that compliance was treaty-induced. The contrast in rates of use of LOT and COW suggest that differences in the designs of the corresponding subregimes may be responsible, given that both methods allowed a tanker operator to reduce waste oil. However, closer evaluation reveals that here, too, economic factors played an important role, although not an exclusive one.

Like LOT, COW has economic as well as environmental benefits. COW's costs include those for the washing machines and the additional time and labor needed to wash tanks in port during delivery rather than during the ballast voyage.[40] As with LOT, the offsetting benefit of more delivered cargo accrues to the cargo owner. However, the tanker operator also benefits: the decrease in oil left on board increases the tanker's effective cargo capacity and reduces sludge buildup, which can lead to large repair and maintenance costs. Compared with a tanker that was not practicing pollution control, using COW produced a net savings per voyage of $9,000.

These economic incentives to adopt COW are borne out by the evidence of the timing of its adoption. In many instances, tankers adopted COW before required to do so by MARPOL. . . .

The contrast to the SBT requirements also confirms the role of economics. The higher capital costs of SBT and the significant reduction to cargo-carrying capacity that SBT involved imposed a net cost per voyage on a tanker with SBT of $1,500 relative to a tanker with no pollution-control equipment. A new tanker installing both COW and SBT, as required by MARPOL, faced costs of almost $8,000 per voyage. Owners of large tankers built before 1980, who were allowed to choose between SBT and COW, installed COW equipment on 89 percent of their tankers and SBT on only 36 percent. Owners also installed COW equipment on 95 percent of large tankers built between 1980 and 1982, even though MARPOL only required them to install SBT. COW's economic benefits certainly appear to be a major influence on COW installations.

Several details suggest that economics were not the sole influence on behavior, however. If they were, we should expect companies to achieve the economic goal of conserving oil by the cheapest and most cost-effective means possible, that is, by LOT, not COW. We should also expect to see the same divergence between the behavior of independent carriers and oil companies as we observed in the LOT case. Yet the 99 percent compliance rate attests to the fact that all tanker owners were installing COW. The adoption of COW more frequently than SBT does not imply that the subregime was ineffective, only that when the subregime left owners with alternatives, their choices were driven by costs. In contrast to clear flaws in the compliance system supporting discharge standards, as I detail below, the design of the compliance system supporting equipment requirements provided several means of successfully reducing both the incentives and ability of tanker owners to violate COW requirements. Thus, an interplay among economics and subregime characteristics appears to have been the source of widespread COW adoption.

SBT

Adoption of the SBT standard provides an unambiguous example of subregime influence on behavior. Unlike COW or LOT, tanker owners had no economic incentives to install this technology. SBT's additional piping and equipment added several million dollars to the cost of a new tanker, representing almost 5 percent of total cost.[41] Installing SBT also reduced cargo capacity, especially when installed on an existing tanker. Yet these costs provided no offsetting benefits in the form of reduced cargo wastage. Even those governments that had supported the 1978 proposal that all tankers be retrofitted with SBT admitted that SBT would increase the cost of carrying oil by 15 percent; some oil company estimates ran up to 50 percent.[42] As late as 1991, oil and shipping interests opposed mandatory SBT retrofitting as being too expensive.[43]

The pattern of observed SBT installation follows that which one would predict for behavior driven by effective treaty rules rather than economics. Among tankers currently in the fleet, more than 98 percent of those required to install SBT have done so despite the significant costs involved. Figure 1 graphs the percentages of current tankers using SBT and COW by year of construction. The timing of the increase in the number of tankers installing SBT seen in the figure reinforces the conclusion that owners installed SBT only under the regulatory threat posed by the subregime's compliance system. In short, owners have installed SBT only when MARPOL required them to do so. As one analyst noted, "If there were not a regulatory requirement, there would not be SBT."[44] Within several years, the subregime had caused a radical change in tanker owner behavior.

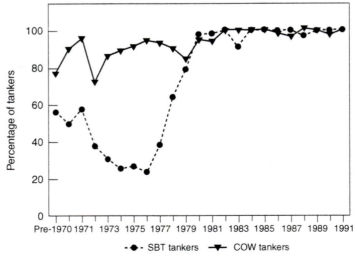

FIGURE 1. PERCENTAGE OF TANKERS WITH SEGREGATED BALLAST TANKS (SBT) AND/OR CRUDE OIL WASHING EQUIPMENT (COW) ON BOARD IN 1991, BY YEAR OF TANKER CONSTRUCTION

Source. Electronic version of Clarkson Research Studies, Ltd., *The Tanker Register* (London: Clarkson Research Studies, Ltd., 1991), provided to the author.

One alternative explanation of SBT adoption deserves special attention. At least one analyst has claimed that hegemonic pressures exerted by the United States explain the success of MARPOL.[45] Certainly the negotiation history demonstrates that the SBT requirements of 1973 and 1978 resulted directly from threats of unilateral U.S. regulation. . . . Admitting that MARPOL's rules resulted from hegemonic pressures, however, does not imply that subsequent behaviors result from that same pressure. As international diplomats are all too well aware, resources adequate to elicit votes for a resolution during a conference may prove inadequate to cause corresponding changes in behavior. The relevant question is, "Could the United States, through unilateral measures, have induced so many tanker owners to install SBT?" Available evidence suggests not.

While the United States wields tremendous diplomatic leverage, it wields nothing near hegemonic power in oil transportation markets. Since the United States became concerned about oil pollution in the late 1960s, it has been responsible for less than 5 percent of new tankers built, less than 7 percent of tanker registrations, and less than 20 percent of world oil imports.[46] Given SBT's high costs, oil transportation companies would have been more likely to respond to unilateral U.S. equipment requirements by installing SBT on a sufficient number of tankers to service the U.S. market than by installing it on all tankers. . . .

MECHANISMS OF INFLUENCE

. . . Which of the many differences between the two subregimes best explain the different levels of observed compliance? In what ways did the equipment subregime "get it right" where the discharge standards failed? In subsequent portions of this article, I shall show how the design of the equipment regime induced compliance by (1) eliciting monitoring and enforcement and (2) reducing opportunities for violation.

Enhancing Transparency

The equipment subregime had one major advantage over the discharge subregime in its significantly higher transparency level. Violations of the SBT and COW requirements simply were far easier to observe than violations of any discharge standard.

Consider the two compliance information systems. Both OILPOL and MARPOL required tanker captains to note discharges in record books and to make those books available to port authorities for inspection. This obvious reliance on self-incrimination made naval and aerial surveillance programs the more common means of detecting illegal discharges. The total discharge standard of one fifteen-thousandth of cargo capacity improved on this system by providing a criterion that could be monitored by tank inspections in port without relying on information supplied by the tanker captain. Practically speaking, these inspections were restricted to ports in oil-exporting states, since discharges occurred after delivery, on a tanker's return to port to load more cargo.

In contrast, the compliance information system for equipment standards relied on the fact that buying or retrofitting a tanker requires the knowledge and consent of at least three other actors: a builder, a classification society, and an insurance company. Agents in each of these industries would know of a violation even before it was committed. MARPOL also required flag state governments, or classification societies nominated by them, to survey all tankers to ensure compliance before issuing the required International Oil Pollution Prevention (IOPP) certificate and to conduct periodic inspections thereafter.[47] As part of the process of evaluating tankers to provide insurers with the information needed to set rates, classification societies regularly monitor compliance with international construction requirements through representatives stationed in shipyards.[48] Finally, MARPOL gave all port states the legal authority to inspect a tanker's IOPP certificate and its equipment to ensure compliance with the equipment requirements.

The equipment standards subregime made violations more transparent than violations in the discharge standards subregime in several ways. To begin with, regulating the tanker builder-tanker buyer transaction yielded a drastically reduced number of events to be monitored. While several thousand tankers ply the world's oceans, they are owned, built, and classified by only a few owners, shipyards, and classification societies. A tanker making ten trips per year could violate the total discharge standard three hundred times in its thirty-year life but could only violate the equipment requirements once.

Equipment standards also required authorities to monitor far fewer locations to detect violations. The discharge process standards—100 ppm, clean ballast, and 60 1/m—required patrols of wide areas of ocean to detect slicks that often could not be linked with the responsible tanker. . . .

. . . Even if a responsible tanker could be identified, determining whether the 100 ppm or 60 1/m criterion had been exceeded generally was difficult. The total discharge standard could have eliminated this problem, but oil-exporting states never established inspection programs. These flaws in the design of the discharge standards compliance system were not necessarily inherent or insurmountable. . . . However, such programs would have involved huge expenditures of resources to produce only a low probability of successful deterrence.

In the first years after OILPOL was signed, evidence quickly demonstrated that only the Federal Republic of Germany and the United Kingdom were making any significant efforts to monitor compliance with discharge standards.[49] By the late 1970s, the Americans, British, Dutch, and French had instituted aerial surveillance programs.[50] Many other countries used aerial surveillance during the 1980s.[51] However, these programs were most often small and nonsystematic. The Dutch program flew more surveillance flights per year in the late 1970s than at any time in the 1980s, and the United States discontinued its program in the 1980s due to budgetary pressures.[52] Reports to IMO from 1983 to 1990 show that only one-quarter of the sixty-seven MARPOL signatories had any programs to detect discharges at sea.[53] British and Dutch data confirm the problems of identifying perpetrators: the British could link detected spills to tankers in only 22 percent of cases and the Dutch, in only 14 percent.[54]

The entry into force of total discharge standards in 1978 allowed inspectors in oil-loading ports to assume that any incoming tanker with all tanks free of slops had violated the very low limit placed on total discharges. However, even those oil-exporting states that were party to MARPOL had strong disincentives to inspect ships in their ports: ports that were conducting inspections were less attractive loading sites than neighboring ports that were not conducting inspections. Not surprisingly, most governments did not alter their enforcement strategies in response to the greater potential for enforcement provided by the promulgation of total discharge standards. In contrast, considerable evidence confirms that the equipment regime significantly changed the ways in which nations and classification societies conducted tanker inspections. Many of the states that originally had opposed the 1973 and 1978 U.S. proposals for equipment regulations subsequently have conducted the in-port inspections needed to detect violations. In 1982, the maritime authorities of fourteen European states signed a Memorandum of Understanding on Port State Control, committing themselves annually to inspect 25 percent of ships entering their ports for violations of maritime treaties, including MARPOL.[55] Notably, until 1992, the memorandum of understanding explicitly excluded inspections for discharge violations from its mandate, limiting cooperation to inspection for equipment violations. . . .

The effectiveness of these governmental inspections depends at least in part on the initial issue of accurate IOPP certificates by flag states or classification societies designated by them. Reports to IMO for 1984 to 1990 show that missing and inaccurate pollution certificates declined steadily from 9 percent to 1 percent; the memorandum of understanding secretariat reports similar declines—from 11 percent to 3 percent.[56] These trends suggest that after an initial period of learning how to issue and inspect certificates, classification societies and governments both now issue thorough and accurate certifications. Like port state governments, flag states and classification societies appear to have altered their behavior to become active participants in the equipment subregime's compliance information system. It would seem unlikely that classification societies and flag states would have responded in the same fashion to U.S.-only legislation.

The greater transparency of violations of equipment requirements served perhaps most importantly to reassure other tanker owners that their own compliance would not place them at a competitive disadvantage in the marketplace. An environmentally concerned tanker operator inclined to comply with the discharge standards could not escape the knowledge that others probably would not comply. The economic incentives to discharge oil at sea, the absence of transparency about who was and who was not complying, and the attendant inability of enforcement efforts to effectively deter discharges charges precluded any assumption other than that many competitors would violate the discharge standards to reduce their costs. The greater transparency of equipment requirements assured a tanker owner installing SBT and COW that all other owners also were doing so. Each company could rest assured that its competitors also would have to incur equipment costs or be sanctioned for not doing so. . . .

Facilitating Potent but Low-cost Sanctions

Greater transparency translated into higher levels of compliance with equipment standards only because the compliance system also induced likely and potent sanctions. The noncompliance response system of the discharge subregime failed to do the same. Even after a violation was detected, tanker operators were unlikely to be successfully prosecuted and equally unlikely to receive a stiff penalty. In contrast, the equipment subregime authorized governments to use the administrative sanction of detention, which made both the likelihood and the cost of being penalized far higher for the equipment standards than for discharge standards. The incentives and abilities of governments to prosecute and to impose large penalties for violation were far lower under the discharge standards than under the equipment standards.

Detected discharge violations frequently remained unprosecuted because the subregime relied on customary international law with its deference to enforcement by flag states. Both OILPOL and MARPOL required a government that detected a discharge violation at sea to forward all evidence to the flag state for prosecution. Only if a tanker discharged illegally within a state's twelve-mile territorial sea and then entered a port of that state could that state prosecute a tanker registered elsewhere. Flag states have generally been less than aggressive in following up on evidence referred to them.[57] Flag states often lack the ability to prosecute, since tankers flying their flag may rarely enter their ports. They also have few incentives to prosecute because vigorous enforcement on their part would induce owners to take their registrations, and the large associated fees, to a less scrupulous state.[58] The fact that pollution occurred off another state's coastline and that many developing flag states lack vocal environmental constituencies only reinforced these disincentives to prosecute. . . .

Under the discharge standards, even states sincerely seeking to prosecute and convict a violator faced major obstacles to success. As already noted, evidence of a violation often failed to produce a violator, and otherwise convincing evidence often failed to meet the legal standards of proof needed for conviction. Evidentiary hurdles should have decreased with the prohibition of discharges that produced visible traces. However, even with aerial photographs of discharges, tankers frequently avoid conviction.[59] Between 1983 and 1990, port and coastal states discarded for lack of evidence an average of 36 percent of cases occurring in territorial seas and successfully convicted and fined less than 33 percent of all detected violators.[60] An additional 20 percent of high-seas cases referred to flag states were not prosecuted for the same reason, and less than 15 percent of all referrals resulted in fines being imposed.[61] Indeed, according to Paul Dempsey, from 1975 through 1982 "ninety-two percent of all fines were imposed through port state enforcement."[62] . . .

When conviction was successful, governments rarely imposed penalties adequate to deter future discharge violations as required by MARPOL.[63] Since 1975, the average fine imposed by states never has exceeded $7,000 and actually has decreased over time.[64] A Friends of the Earth International study concluded that fines have remained "very low in comparison to the price the vessel would have to pay for using port reception facilities."[65] . . . Owen Lomas points out that the problem is further exacerbated by the fact that "shipowners and their insurers routinely indemnify the masters of their ships against fines imposed upon them for oil pollution."[66]

In place of the discharge subregime's legal system of prosecution, conviction, and fines, the equipment subregime relied on quite different responses to noncompliance. The most immediate sanctions involved the ability of classification societies, insurers, and flag state governments to withhold the classification, insurance, and pollution prevention certificates that a tanker needed to conduct international trade. As John Foxwell put it, tankers "cannot get insurance without certification, and can't get certification without compliance."[67] These sanctions amounted to preventing any illegally equipped tanker from doing business. Even if an owner could devise a means to avoid these direct economic effects, a noncompliant tanker that could not trade to all ports would still bring a far lower price in the large tanker resale market.[68]

Besides these market-based sanctions, the equipment subregime obligated port states either to detain tankers with false pollution prevention certificates or inadequate equipment or to bar them from port.[69] As administrative sanctions, these responses skirted both flag state and port state legal systems—and the associated sensitivities regarding legal sovereignty. Paradoxically, this strategy made port states more likely to use detention and flag states more willing to accept it. . . .

Coupling the equipment requirements themselves with these administrative sanctions completely eliminated the legal and evidentiary problems that make even clear violations of discharge standards difficult to prosecute successfully. Detention imposed opportunity costs on a tanker operator of several thousand dollars per day, and forced retrofitting could cost millions of dollars—far exceeding the fines for discharge violations.[70] . . .

While many states inspected tankers for compliance with equipment requirements, most have not detained noncompliant ships frequently. IMO records from 1984 to 1990 reveal that seven of fifteen states, including Japan, have detained ships at least once. Only Germany, the United Kingdom, and the United States have detained ships often. This undoubtedly reflects a reluctance on the parts of some states to detain foreign tankers as well as the fact that most tankers were equipped appropriately in the first place.

Although few states detained ships, available evidence supports the conclusion that the subregime altered enforcement behavior. Not one of the states that detained ships began to do so until after MARPOL took effect in 1983.[71] Even the United States waited until that year—ten years after the detention provision had been accepted. Consider the counterfactual: it is unlikely that the United States would have detained tankers for breaching U.S.-only requirements for SBT, even though it had the practical ability to do so. Without MARPOL, such detentions would have constituted a major infringement of flag state sovereignty. . . .

The equipment subregime operated not by convincing reluctant actors to enforce rules with which they disagreed but by removing the legal barriers that inhibited effective enforcement by those states and nonstate actors willing to enforce them. Classification societies had interests in ensuring that the tankers they classified were able to trade without fear of detention. The incorporation of equipment requirements into their classification criteria provided the foundation for insurers to penalize noncompliant tankers. The willingness of a few environmentally concerned oil-importing states to inhibit tankers that lacked the required equipment from trading freely posed an extremely potent threat to a tanker owner. However, the ability and willingness of these states to threaten this sanction depended on removing international legal barriers to its use. Once these barriers were removed, imposing sanctions involved few costs to those imposing them, whether classification societies, insurers, or port state authorities. It thereby made detention more likely, even though it created no new incentives for states to impose sanctions. In a case of "nothing succeeds like success," the various threats of the equipment subregime's noncompliance system led to initial compliance by almost all tankers, making it rare that sanctions ever needed to be imposed.

Coercing Compliance Rather than Deterring Violation

The compliance systems of the two subregimes differ most strikingly in the fundamental model underlying their regulatory strategies. The equipment standards subregime relied on a "coerced compliance" strategy, which sought to monitor behavior to prevent violations from occurring in the first place. The discharge standards subregime was deterrence-oriented, attempting to detect, prosecute, and sanction violations after they occurred to deter future violations.[72] This basic difference in orientation made the compliance task facing the equipment standards subregime more manageable than that facing the discharge standards subregime. The underlying strategy choice had important consequences for the level of compliance achieved: inhibiting the ability to violate treaty provisions proved far more effective than increasing the disincentives for violating them.

MARPOL's equipment standards created a remarkably effective system for detecting and sanctioning violations. Even if this compliance system had relied exclusively on the threat of oil-importing states detecting and detaining noncompliant tankers, most tankers would have installed COW and SBT. However, the equipment subregime's strength really came from the fact that it rarely had to use the more potent sanctions it made possible. Involving shipbuilders, classification societies, and insurers in the regulatory process could well have produced the same outcome even without the additional threat of detention. The subregime relied on surveying behavior and preventing violations rather than detecting and investigating them afterwards.[73] . . .

NOTES

1. This article summarizes the arguments made in Ronald B. Mitchell, *Intentional Oil Pollution at Sea: Environmental Policy and Treaty Compliance* (Cambridge, Mass.: MIT Press, forthcoming).

2. The term "compliance system" comes from Oran Young, *Compliance and Public Authority: A Theory with International Applications* (Baltimore, Md.: Johns Hopkins University Press, 1979), p. 3.

3. See, for example, Abram Chayes, "An Inquiry into the Workings of Arms Control Agreements," *Harvard Law Review* 85 (March 1972), pp. 905–69; Coit D. Blacker and Gloria Duffy, eds., *International Arms Control: Issues and Agreements,* 2d ed. (Stanford, Calif.: Stanford University Press, 1984); and Antonia Handler Chayes and Paul Doty, *Defending Deterrence: Managing the ABM Treaty into the Twenty-first Century* (Washington, D.C.: Pergamon-Brassey's International Defense Publishers, 1989).

4. See, for example, John S. Duffield, "International Regimes and Alliance Behavior: Explaining NATO Conventional Force Levels," *International Organization* 46 (Autumn 1992), pp. 819–55; Ethan Kapstein, *Governing the Global Economy: International Finance and the State* (Cambridge, Mass.: Harvard University Press, 1994); and Joseph M. Grieco, *Cooperation Among Nations: Europe, America, and Non-tariff Barriers to Trade* (Ithaca, N.Y.: Cornell University Press, 1990).

5. For example, see Peter Haas, Robert Keohane, and Marc Levy, eds., *Institutions for the Earth: Sources of Effective International Environmental Protection* (Cambridge, Mass.: MIT Press, 1993); Peter H. Sand, *Lessons Learned in Global Environmental Governance* (Washington, D.C.: World Resources Institute, 1990); and Peter M. Haas, "Do Regimes Matter? Epistemic Communities and Mediterranean Pollution Control," *International Organization* 43 (Summer 1989), pp. 377–403. Current projects that deal with questions of regime compliance and effectiveness (and their principal investigators) include those being conducted at, or with funding from, Dartmouth College (Oran Young and Marc Levy); the European Science Foundation (Kenneth Hanf and Arild Underdal); the Foundation for International Environmental Law and Diplomacy (James Cameron); the Fridtjof Nansen Institute (Steinar Andresen); Harvard University (Abram Chayes and Antonia Chayes); Harvard University (William Clark, Robert Keohane, and Marc Levy); the International Institute for Applied Systems Analysis (David Victor and Eugene Skolnikoff); and the Social Science Research Council (Edith Brown Weiss and Harold Jacobson).

6. Thomas M. Franck, *The Power of Legitimacy Among Nations* (New York: Oxford University Press, 1990).

7. Case selection that holds these other factors constant avoids the notorious difficulties of measuring power and interests and allows us to "attribute variance in collective outcomes to the impact of institutional arrangements with some degree of confidence"; see Oran Young, *International Cooperation: Building Regimes for Natural Resources and the Environment* (Ithaca, N.Y.: Cornell University Press, 1989), p. 208. On difficulties in measuring power, see David A. Baldwin, "Power Analysis and World Politics: New Trends Versus Old Tendencies," *World Politics* 31 (January 1979), pp. 161–93.

8. Michael McGinnis and Elinor Ostrom, "Design Principles for Local and Global Commons," Workshop in Political Theory and Policy Analysis, Bloomington, Ind., March 1992, p. 21. Olson's argument that small groups supply public goods more often than large groups assumes that group members benefit from providing the good, which is not true in the oil pollution case; see Mancur Olson, *The Logic of Collective Action: Public Goods and the Theory of Groups* (Cambridge, Mass.: Harvard University Press, 1965), p. 34.

9. See Arthur A. Stein, *Why Nations Cooperate: Circumstance and Choice in International Relations* (Ithaca, N.Y.: Cornell University Press, 1990); and Robert Axelrod and Robert O. Keohane, "Achieving Cooperation Under Anarchy: Strategies and Institutions," in

Kenneth Oye, ed., *Cooperation Under Anarchy* (Princeton, N.J.: Princeton University Press, 1986).

10. Hans Joachim Morgenthau, *Politics Among Nations: The Struggle for Power and Peace,* 5th ed. (New York: Alfred A. Knopf, 1978), p. 267.

11. On this distinction, see Stein, *Why Nations Cooperate.*

12. See, for example, Abram Chayes and Antonia Chayes, "Compliance Without Enforcement: State Behavior Under Regulatory Treaties," *Negotiation Journal* 7 (July 1991), pp. 311–30; Young, *International Cooperation;* Robert O. Keohane, "Reciprocity in International Relations," *International Organization* 40 (Winter 1986), pp. 1–27; and Stephen D. Krasner, ed., *International Regimes* (Ithica, N.Y.: Cornell University Press, 1983).

13. At the extreme, if all parties violated treaty provision A and complied with treaty provision B, they could all be classified as in partial compliance, ignoring the important variance in compliance rates.

14. See Haas, Keohane, and Levy, *Institutions for the Earth;* George W. Downs and David M. Rocke, *Tacit Bargaining, Arms Races, and Arms Control* (Ann Arbor: University of Michigan Press, 1990); Charles Lipson, "Why Are Some International Agreements Informal?" *International Organization* 45 (Autumn 1991), pp. 495–538; and Abram Chayes and Antonia Handler Chayes, "On Compliance," *International Organization* 47 (Spring 1993), pp. 188–92.

15. The *Exxon Valdez* wrecked in Prince William Sound, Alaska, on 24 March 1989.

16. For comparison, the *Exxon Valdez* spilled thirty-five thousand tons.

17. National Academy of Sciences, *Petroleum in the Marine Environment* (Washington, D.C.: National Academy of Sciences, 1975). See also National Academy of Sciences and National Research Council, *Oil in the Sea: Inputs, Fates, and Effects* (Washington, D.C.: National Academy Press, 1985).

18. See, for example, National Academy of Sciences and National Research Council, *Oil in the Sea;* and Joint Group of Experts on the Scientific Aspects of Marine Pollution (GESAMP), *The State of the Marine Environment,* Reports and Studies no. 39 (New York: United Nations, 1990).

19. For the history of oil pollution control from the 1920s through the 1970s, see Sonia Zaide Pritchard, *Oil Pollution Control* (London: Croom Helm, 1987); for a history from the 1950s through the 1970s, see R. Michael M'Gonigle and Mark W. Zacher, *Pollution, Politics, and International Law: Tankers at Sea* (Berkeley: University of California Press, 1979).

20. "International Convention for the Prevention of Pollution of the Sea by Oil," 12 May 1954, *Treaties and Other International Agreements Series (TIAS),* no. 4900 (Washington, D.C.: U.S. Department of State, 1954).

21. See *International Convention for the Prevention of Pollution from Ships (MARPOL),* 2 November 1973, reprinted in *International Legal Materials (ILM),* vol. 12 (Washington, D.C.: American Society of International Law, 1973), p. 1319 (hereafter cited by abbreviation, volume, and year); and *Protocol of 1978 Relating to the International Convention for the Prevention of Pollution from Ships,* 17 February 1978, reprinted in *ILM,* vol. 17, 1978, p. 1546 (hereafter cited together as *MARPOL 73/78*).

22. M'Gonigle and Zacher, *Pollution, Politics, and International Law,* p. 100.

23. J. H. Kirby, "The Clean Seas Code: A Practical Cure of Operation Pollution," in *Third International Conference on Oil Pollution of the Sea: Report of Proceedings, Rome 7–9 October 1968* (Winchester, England: Warren and Son, 1968), pp. 201–19.

24. Kirby, "The Clean Seas Code," p. 206.

25. Kirby, "The Clean Seas Code," p. 208.

26. See Kirby, "The Clean Seas Code," pp. 200 and 209; and William T. Burke, Richard Legatski, and William W. Woodhead, *National and International Law Enforcement in the Ocean* (Seattle: University of Washington Press, 1975), p. 129.

27. M'Gonigle and Zacher, *Pollution, Politics, and International Law,* p. 108.
28. See statements submitted by the U.S. delegation to the 13th Preparatory Session for an International Conference on Marine Pollution in 1973: IMCO/IMO doc. MP XIII/2(c)/5, 23 May 1972. (Using note 30 as a guide, this would be the 5th document issued relating to agenda item 2[c]). See also doc. MP XIII/2(a)/5, 1 June 1972; G.Victory, "Avoidance of Accidental and Deliberate Pollution," in *Coastal Water Pollution: Pollution of the Sea by Oil Spills* (Brussels: North Atlantic Treaty Organization [NATO], 2–6 November 1970), p. 2.3.
29. Jacob W. Ulvila, "Decisions with Multiple Objectives in Integrative Bargaining," Ph.D. diss., Harvard University, 1979, appendix A1.1.
30. M'Gonigle and Zacher, *Pollution, Politics, and International Law,* pp. 122 and 130.
31. See Sonia Z. Pritchard, "Load on Top: From the Sublime to the Absurd," *Journal of Maritime Law and Commerce* 9 (April 1978), pp. 185–224 at p. 194.
32. For an excellent discussion of state positions during both the 1973 and 1978 conferences, see M'Gonigle and Zacher, *Pollution, Politics, and International Law,* pp. 107–42.
33. See, for example, the estimate of 0.3 percent in James E. Moss, *Character and Control of Sea Pollution by Oil* (Washington, D.C.: American Petroleum Institute, 1963), p. 47, and the estimate of 0.4 percent in IMCO/IMO doc. OP I/21, 15 January 1965, of the Oil Pollution subcommittee. (Using note 30 as a guide, this indicates the only document issued relating to agenda item 21 at the 1st meeting of the subcommittee.)
34. Unfortunately, oil companies discontinued the surveys after 1977. Personal communication from Arthur McKenzie, Tanker Advisory Center, New York, 1992.
35. Informational document of the Marine Environment Protection Committee: IMCO/IMO doc. MEPC XVI/Inf.2, 4 November 1981.
36. IMCO/IMO doc. MEPC 30/Inf.13, 19 September 1990, p. 15.
37. Drewry Shipping Consultants, Ltd., *The Impact of New Tanker Regulations,* Drewry publication no. 94 (London: Drewry Shipping Consultants, Ltd., 1981), p. 25.
38. See IMCO/IMO doc. MEPC 30/Inf.13, 19 September 1990, p. 8; Second International Conference on the Protection of the North Sea, *Quality Status of the North Sea,* p. 57; Pieter Bergmeijer, "The International Convention for the Prevention of Pollution from Ships," paper presented at the 17th Pacem in Maribus conference, Rotterdam, August 1990, p. 12; and personal interview with E. J. M. Ball, Oil Companies International Marine Forum, London, 26 June 1991.
39. Charles Odidi Okidi, *Regional Control of Ocean Pollution: Legal and Institutional Problems and Prospects* (Alphen aan den Rijn, The Netherlands: Sijthoff and Noordhoff, 1978), p. 34.
40. Drewry Shipping Consultants, Ltd., *Tanker Regulations: Enforcement and Effect,* Drewry publication no. 135 (London: Drewry Shipping Consultants, Ltd., 1985), p. 25.
41. See Philip A. Cummins, Dennis E. Logue, Robert D. Tollison, and Thomas D. Willett, "Oil Tanker Pollution Control: Design Criteria Versus Effective Liability Assessment," *Journal of Maritime Law and Commerce* 7 (October 1975), pp. 181–82; and Charles S. Pearson, *International Marine Environmental Policy: The Economic Dimension* (Baltimore, Md.: The Johns Hopkins University Press, 1975), p. 98.
42. See IMCO/IMO doc. MEPC V/Inf. 4, 8 March 1976, p. A18; and M'Gonigle and Zacher, *Pollution, Politics, and International Law,* p. 134.
43. See IMCO/IMO doc. MEPC 31/8/5, 4 April 1991; and Osborne and Ferguson, "Technology, MARPOL, and Tankers," p. 6-2.
44. Personal interview with Sean Connaughton, marine transportation analyst, American Petroleum Institute, Washington, D.C., 8 April 1992.
45. Jesper Grolin, "Environmental Hegemony, Maritime Community, and the Problem of Oil Tanker Pollution," in Michael A. Morris, ed., *North–South Perspectives on Marine Policy* (Boulder, Colo.: Westview Press, 1988).

46. See Lloyd's Register of Shipping, *Annual Summary of Merchant Ships Completed* (London: Lloyd's Register of Shipping, various years); Lloyd's Register of Shipping, *Statistical Tables* (London: Lloyd's Register of Shipping, various years); and United Nations, *Statistical Yearbook* (New York: United Nations, various years).

47. *MARPOL 73/78,* Annex I, Regulations 4 and 5.

48. Personal interview with John Foxwell, Shell International Marine, London, 27 June 1991.

49. IMCO/IMO doc. OP/CONF/2, 1 September 1961.

50. See James Cowley, "IMO and National Administrations," *IMO News,* no. 4, 1988, pp. 6–11; Smit-Kroes, *Harmonisatie Noordzeebeleid;* and IMCO/IMO doc. MEPC 21/Inf.9, 25 March 1985.

51. James McLoughlin and M. J. Forster, *The Law and Practice Relating to Pollution Control in the Member States of the European Communities: A Comparative Survey* (London: Graham and Trotman, 1982).

52. Personal interview with Daniel Sheehan, U.S. Coast Guard, Washington, D.C., 9 April 1992.

53. Gerard Peet, *Operational Discharges from Ships: An Evaluation of the Application of the Discharge Provisions of the MARPOL Convention by Its Contracting Parties* (Amsterdam: AIDEnvironment, 1992), annexes 5 and 10.

54. See United Kingdom Royal Commission on Environmental Pollution, *Eighth Report: Oil Pollution of the Sea* (London: Her Majesty's Stationery Office, 1981), p. 195; and Smit-Kroes, *Harmonisatie Noordzeebeleid.*

55. "Memorandum of Understanding on Port State Control," reprinted in *ILM,* vol. 21, 1982, p. 1.

56. Secretariat of the Memorandum of Understanding on Port State Control, *Annual Report* (The Hague: The Netherlands Government Printing Office, various years).

57. See Organization for Economic Cooperation and Development (OECD), "OECD Study on Flags of Convenience," *Journal of Maritime Law and Commerce* 4 (January 1973), pp. 231–54.

58. Paul Stephen Dempsey, "Compliance and Enforcement in International Law—Oil Pollution of the Marine Environment by Ocean Vessels," *Northwestern Journal of International Law and Business* 6 (Summer 1984), pp. 459–561 and p. 576 in particular.

59. See ibid., p. 526; and personal interview with Ronald Carly, Ministry of Transportation, Brussels, 10 June 1991.

60. Peet, *Operational Discharges from Ships,* pp. 17–18, Tables 11 and 12; and Marie-Jose Stoop, *Olieverontreiniging door schepen op de noordzee over de periode 1982–1987: opsporing en vervolging* (Oil pollution by ships on the North Sea 1982–1987: Investigations and prosecution) (Amsterdam: Werkgroep Noordzee, July 1989).

61. Ronald Bruce Mitchell, "From Paper to Practice: Improving Environmental Treaty Compliance," Ph.D. diss., Harvard University, Cambridge, Mass., 1992, Table 5-1.

62. Dempsey, "Compliance and Enforcement in International Law," p. 537.

63. *MARPOL 73/78,* Article 4(4).

64. Mitchell, "From Paper to Practice," Table 4–5.

65. IMCO/IMO doc. MEPC 29/10/3, 15 January 1990.

66. Owen Lomas, "The Prosecution of Marine Oil Pollution Offences and the Practice of Insuring Against Fines," *Journal of Environmental Law,* vol. 1, no. 1, 1989, p. 54. See also IMCO/IMO doc. MEPC 32/14/3, 17 January 1992.

67. Personal interview with John Foxwell, Shell International Marine, London, 27 June 1991.

68. Bergmeijer, "The International Convention for the Prevention of Pollution from Ships," p. 12.
69. *MARPOL 73/78*, Articles 5(2) and 5(3).
70. Personal interviews with John Foxwell; and with Richard Schiferli, Memorandum of Understanding Secretariat, Rijswijk, The Netherlands, 17 July 1991.
71. Personal interview with Daniel Sheehan.
72. Neither strategy was incentive-based, as was the funding of compliance under the Montreal Protocol and Framework Convention on Climate Change. For development of the distinction between these three strategies, see Albert J. Reiss, Jr., "Consequences of Compliance and Deterrence Models of Law Enforcement for the Exercise of Police Discretion," *Law and Contemporary Problems* 47 (Fall 1984), pp. 83–122; and Keith Hawkins, *Environment and Enforcement: Regulation and the Social Definition of Pollution* (Oxford: Clarendon Press, 1984).
73. Reiss, "Consequences of Compliance and Deterrence Models of Law Enforcement for the Exercise of Police Discretion."

Transnational Advocacy Networks in International and Regional Politics

MARGARET E. KECK and KATHRYN SIKKINK

World politics at the end of the twentieth century involves, alongside states, many non-state actors who interact with each other, with states, and with international organizations. This article considers how these interactions are structured in networks, which are increasingly visible in international politics. Some involve economic actors and firms. Some are networks of scientists and experts whose professional ties and ideas underpin their efforts to influence policy (Haas, 1992). Others are networks of activists, distinguishable largely by the centrality of principled ideas or values in motivating their formation. We call these *transnational advocacy networks*.

Advocacy networks are significant transnationally, regionally and domestically. They may be key contributors to a convergence of social and cultural norms able to support processes of regional and international integration. By building new links among actors in civil societies, states and international organizations, they multiply the opportunities for dialogue and exchange. In issue areas such as the environment and human rights, they also make international resources available to new actors in domestic political and social struggles. By thus blurring the boundaries between a state's relations with its own nationals and the recourse both citizens and states have to the international system, advocacy networks are helping to transform the practice of national sovereignty.

Scholars have been slow to recognize either the rationality or the significance of activist networks. Motivated by values rather than by material concerns or professional norms, they fall outside our accustomed categories. Yet more than other kinds of transnational networks, advocacy networks often reach beyond policy change to advocate and instigate changes in the institutional and principled bases of international interactions. When they succeed, they are an important part of an explanation for changes in world politics. *A transnational advocacy network includes those actors working internationally on an issue, who are bound together by shared values, a common discourse, and dense exchanges of information and services.*[1] At the core of the relationship is information exchange. What is novel in these networks is the ability of non-traditional international actors to mobilize information strategically to help create new issues and categories, and to persuade, pressurize, and gain leverage over much more powerful organizations and governments. Activists in networks try not only to influence policy outcomes, but to transform the terms and nature of the debate. . . .

---

*This article is based on our book *Activists Beyond Borders: Advocacy Netowrks in International Politics* (Ithaca: Cornell University Press, 1998). The Editor-in-Chief wishes to thank Cornell for permission to publish material drawn from the book.

Simultaneously principled and strategic actors, transnational advocacy networks "frame" issues to make them comprehensible to target audiences, to attract attention and encourage action, and to "fit" with favourable institutional venues. By framing, we mean "conscious strategic efforts by groups of people to fashion shared understandings of the world and of themselves that legitimate and motivate collective action" (McAdam et al., 1996, p. 6). Network actors bring new ideas, norms and discourses into policy debates, and serve as sources of information and testimony. . . .

Shared norms often provide the foundation for more formal institutional processes of regional integration. In so far as networks promote norm convergence or harmonization at the regional and international levels, they are essential to the social and cultural aspects of integration. They also promote norm implementation, by pressuring target actors to adopt new policies, and by monitoring compliance with regional and international standards. As far as is possible, they seek to maximize their influence or leverage over the target of their actions. In doing this they contribute to changing the perceptions that both state and societal actors may have of their identities, interests and preferences, to transforming their discursive positions, and ultimately to changing procedures, policies and behaviour. . . .

Networks are *communicative structures*. To influence discourse, procedures and policy, transnational advocacy networks may become part of larger policy communities that group actors from a variety of institutional and value positions. Transnational advocacy networks may also be understood as political spaces, in which differently situated actors negotiate—formally or informally—the social, cultural and political meanings of their joint enterprises. In both of these ways, transnational networks can be key vehicles for the cultural and social negotiations underpinning processes of regional integration.

We refer to transnational networks (rather than coalitions, movements, or civil society) to evoke the structured and structuring dimension in the actions of these complex agents. By importing the network concept from sociology and applying it transnationally, we bridge the increasingly artificial divide between international relations and comparative politics. Moreover, the term "network" is already used by the actors themselves; over the last two decades, individuals and organizations have consciously formed and named networks, developed and shared networking strategies and techniques. . . .

Our theoretical apparatus draws upon sociological traditions that focus on complex interactions among actors, on the intersubjective construction of frames of meaning, and on the negotiation and malleability of identities and interests. These have been concerns of constructivists in international relations theory and of social movement theorists in comparative politics, and we draw from both traditions. The networks we study participate simultaneously in domestic and international politics, drawing upon a variety of resources, *as if they were part of an international society*. However, they use these resources strategically to affect a world of states and international organizations constructed by states. Both these dimensions are essential. Rationalists will recognize the language of incentives and constraints, strategies, institutions and rules, while constructivists and social constructionists will be more comfortable with our emphasis on norms, social relations and intersubjective understandings. We are convinced that both matter; whilst recognizing that goals and interests are not exogenously given, we can think about the strategic activity of actors in an intersubjectively structured political universe. The key to doing so is remembering that the social and political contexts within which networks operate contain contested understandings as well as stable and shared ones. Network activists can operate strategically within the more stable universe of shared understandings at the same time as they try to reshape certain contested meanings.

Part of what is so elusive about networks is how they seem to embody elements of agent and structure simultaneously. Our approach must therefore be both structural and actor-centred. We address five main questions:

1. What is a transnational advocacy network?
2. Why and how do they emerge?
3. How do they work?
4. Under what conditions can they be effective—that is, when are they most likely to achieve their goals?
5. What are the implications of network activities for the social and cultural processes of regional integration?

Although we had initially expected that transnational networks would function in quite different ways from domestic social movements, we found that many of the characteristic strategies, tactics and patterns of influence resembled those outlined in the literature on social movements. Organizations and individuals within advocacy networks are political entrepreneurs, mobilize resources like information and membership, and show a sophisticated awareness of the political opportunity structures within which they operate (Tarrow, 1994). . . .

WHAT IS A TRANSNATIONAL ADVOCACY NETWORK?

Networks are forms of organization characterized by voluntary, reciprocal and horizontal patterns of communication and exchange. Organizational theorist Walter Powell calls them a third mode of economic organization, distinctly different from markets and hierarchy (the firm). "Networks are "lighter on their feet" than hierarchy" and are "particularly apt for circumstances in which there is a need for efficient, reliable information . . . ," and "for the exchange of commodities whose value is not easily measured" (Powell, 1990, pp. 295–6, 303–4). His insights into economic networks are extraordinarily suggestive for an understanding of political networks. Policy networks also form around issues where information plays a key role, and around issues where the value of the "commodity" is not easily measured.

In spite of differences between the domestic and international realms, the network concept travels well because it stresses the fluid and open relations among committed and knowledgeable actors working in specialized issue areas. We call them advocacy networks because advocates plead the causes of others or defend a cause or proposition; they are stand-ins for persons or ideas. . . .

Some issue areas reproduce transnationally the webs of personal relationships that are crucial in the formation of domestic networks. Advocacy networks have been particularly important in value-laden debates over human rights, the environment, women, infant health, and indigenous peoples. These are all areas where through personal, professional and organizational contexts, large numbers of differently situated individuals became acquainted with each other over a considerable period, and developed similar world views. When the more visionary among them proposed strategies for political action around apparently intractable problems, the potential was transformed into an action network.

Major actors in advocacy networks may include the following:

1. international and domestic NGOs, research and advocacy organizations;
2. local social movements;
3. foundations;
4. the media;
5. churches, trade unions, consumer organizations, intellectuals;
6. parts of regional and international intergovernmental organizations;
7. parts of the executive and/or parliamentary branches of governments.

Not all these will be present in each advocacy network. Initial research suggests, however, that international and domestic non-governmental organizations (NGOs) play a central role in most advocacy networks, usually initiating actions and pressuring more powerful actors to take positions. NGOs introduce new ideas, provide information, and lobby for policy changes.

Social scientists have barely addressed the political role of activist NGOs as *simultaneously* domestic and international actors. There is a literature on NGOs and networks in specific countries (Frühling, 1991; Scherer-Warren, 1993). Much of the existing literature on NGOs comes from development studies, and either ignores interactions with states or spends little time on political analysis (see, for example, Korten, 1990). Examining their role in advocacy networks helps both to distinguish NGOs from, and to see their connections with, social movements, state agencies and international organizations.

Groups in a network share values and frequently exchange information and services. The flow of information among actors in the network reveals a dense web of connections among these groups, both formal and informal. The movement of funds and services is especially notable between foundations and NGOs, but some NGOs provide services such as training for other NGOs in the same, and sometimes other, advocacy networks. Personnel also circulate within and among networks.

Relationships *among* networks within and between issue areas are similar to those that scholars of social movements have found in the case of domestic activism. Individuals and foundation funding have moved back and forth among them. Environmentalists and women's groups have looked at the history of human rights campaigns for models of effective international institution-building. Because of these interactions, refugee resettlement and indigenous peoples' rights are increasingly central components of international environmental activity, and vice versa; mainstream human rights organizations have joined the campaign for women's rights. Some activists consider themselves part of an "NGO community." This convergence highlights important dimensions that these networks share: the centrality of values or principled ideas, the belief that individuals can make a difference, creative use of information, and the employment by non-governmental actors of sophisticated political strategies in targeting their campaigns. Besides sharing information, groups in networks create categories or frames within which to organize and *generate* information on which to base their campaigns. The ability to generate information quickly and accurately, and deploy it effectively, is their most valuable currency; it is also central to their identity.

WHY AND HOW TRANSNATIONAL ADVOCACY NETWORKS HAVE EMERGED

The kinds of groups characteristic of advocacy networks are not new; some have existed since the nineteenth century campaign for the abolition of slavery. Nevertheless, their number, size, professionalism, and the density and complexity of their international linkages have grown dramatically in the last three decades, so that only recently can we speak of *transnational* advocacy networks (Keck and Sikkink, 1998).

International networking is costly. Geographical distance, nationalism, the multiplicity of languages and cultures, and the costs of fax, telephone, mail, or air travel make the proliferation of international networks a puzzle that needs explanation. Under what conditions are networks possible and likely, and what triggers their emergence?

Transnational advocacy networks appear most likely to emerge around those issues where:

1. channels between domestic groups and their governments are hampered or severed where such channels are ineffective for resolving a conflict, setting into motion the "boomerang" pattern of influence characteristic of these networks;
2. activists or "political entrepreneurs" believe that networking will further their missions and campaigns, and actively promote them;
3. international conferences and other forms of international contacts create arenas for forming and strengthening networks.

THE BOOMERANG PATTERN

It is no accident that "rights" claims may be the prototypical language of advocacy networks. Governments are the primary "guarantors" of rights, but also among their primary violators. When a government violates or refuses to recognize rights, individuals and domestic groups often have no recourse within domestic political or judicial arenas. They may seek international connections to express their concerns and even to protect their lives.

Many transnational advocacy networks link activists in developed countries with others in or from less developed countries. These kinds of linkages are most commonly intended to affect the behaviour of *states*. When the links between state and domestic actors are severed, domestic NGOs may directly seek international allies to try to bring pressure on their states from outside. This is the "boomerang" pattern of influence characteristic of transnational networks where the target of their activity is to change a state's behaviour. This is most common in human rights campaigns. Similarly, indigenous rights campaigns, and environmental campaigns supporting the demands of local peoples for participation in development projects that would affect them, frequently involve this kind of triangulation. Where governments are unresponsive to groups whose claims may none the less resonate elsewhere, international contacts can "amplify" the demands of domestic groups, pry open space for new issues, and then echo these demands back into the domestic arena. . . .

Linkages are important for both sides. For the less powerful Third World actors, networks provide access, leverage and information (and often money) they could not expect to have on their own. For northern groups, they make credible the assertion that they are struggling with, and not only "for," their southern partners. Not surprisingly, such relationships can produce considerable tensions. It is not uncommon to see reproduced internally the power relations that the networks are trying to overcome. Increasingly, network members are forced to address this problem.

Just as injustice and oppression may not produce movements or revolutions by themselves, claims around issues amenable to international action need not produce transnational networks. Activists are "people who care enough about some issue that they are prepared to incur significant costs and act to achieve their goals" (Oliver and Marwell, 1992, p. 252). . . .

Networks are normally formed around particular campaigns or claims. Networks breed networks; as networking becomes a repertoire of action that is diffused transnationally, each effort to network internationally is less difficult than the one before. Over time, in these issue areas, participation in transnational networks has become an essential component of the collective identities of the activists involved. The political entrepreneurs who become the core networkers for a new campaign have often gained experience in earlier ones.

Opportunities for network activities have increased over the last two decades, in part through the efforts of the pioneers among them. Network activists have been creative in finding new venues in which to pursue claims—a process we discuss in the next section. The proliferation of international organizations and conferences has provided foci for the contacts. Cheaper air travel and new electronic and communication technologies speed information flows and simplify personal contact among them.

Underlying the trends discussed here, however, is a broader cultural shift. The new networks depended on creating a new kind of global public (or civil society), which grew as a cultural legacy of the 1960s. . . .

Obviously, internationalism was not invented in the 1960s. Several longstanding ethical traditions have justified actions by individuals or groups outside the borders of their own state. Broadly speaking, we could designate these as religious beliefs, the solidarity traditions of labour and the left, and liberal internationalism. While many activists working in advocacy networks are from one of these traditions, they no longer tend to define themselves in terms of these traditions or the organizations that carried them. This is most true for activists on the left, for whom the decline of socialist organizations capped a growing disillusionment with much of the left's refusal to address seriously the concerns of women, the environment, and human rights violations in eastern bloc countries.

Advocacy networks in the north often function in a cultural milieu of internationalism that is generally optimistic about the promise and possibilities of international networking. For network members in developing countries, however, justifying external intervention or pressure in domestic affairs is a much trickier business, except when lives are at stake. Linkages with northern networks require high levels of trust, because arguments justifying intervention on ethical grounds often sound too much like the "civilizing" discourse of colonial powers, and can work against the goals they espouse by producing a nationalist backlash.

HOW DO TRANSNATIONAL ADVOCACY NETWORKS WORK?

Transnational networks seek influence in many of the same ways that other political groups or social movements do, but because they are not powerful in the traditional sense of the word, they must use the power of their information, ideas and strategies to alter the information and value context within which states make policies. . . . We have developed a nuanced typology of the kinds of tactics that networks use. These include:

   a. *information politics,* or the ability to move politically usable information quickly and credibly to where it will have the most impact;
   b. *symbolic politics,* or the ability to call upon symbols, actions or stories that make sense of a situation or claim for an audience that is frequently far away (see also Brysk, 1994, 1995);
   c. *leverage politics,* or the ability to call upon powerful actors to affect a situation where weaker members of a network are unlikely to have influence; and
   d. *accountability politics,* or the effort to oblige more powerful actors to act on vaguer policies or principles they formally endorsed.

The construction of cognitive frames is an essential component of transnational networks" political strategies. David Snow has called this strategic activity *frame alignment*—"by rendering events or occurrences meaningful, frames function to organize experience and guide action, whether individual or collective" (Snow et al., 1986). *Frame resonance* concerns the relationship between an organization's interpretive work and its ability to influence broader public understandings. The latter involves both the frame's internal coherence and its fit with a broader political culture (Snow and Benford, 1988). In recent work, Snow and Benford (1992) and Tarrow (1992), in turn, have given frame resonance a historical dimension by joining it to Tarrow's notion of protest cycles. Struggles over meaning and the cre-ation of new frames of meaning occur early in a protest cycle, but over time, "a given collective action frame becomes part of the political culture—which is to say, part of the reservoir of symbols from which future movement entrepreneurs can choose" (Tarrow, 1992, p. 197).

Network members actively seek ways to bring issues to the public agenda, both by framing them in innovative ways and by seeking hospitable venues. Some-times they create issues by framing old problems in new ways; occasionally they help to transform other actors' understandings of their identities and their inter-ests. Land-use rights in the Amazon, for example, took on an entirely different character and gained quite different allies when viewed in a deforestation frame than in either social justice or regional development frames.

Transnational networks normally involve a small number of activists in a given campaign or advocacy role. The kinds of pressure and agenda politics in which they engage rarely involve mass mobilization, except at key moments, although the peoples whose cause they espouse may engage in mass protest (for example, the expelled population in the Narmada Dam case). Boycott strategies are a partial exception. Instead, network activists engage in what Baumgartner and Jones (1991), borrowing from law, call *venue shopping*: "This strategy relies less on mass mobilisation and more on the dual strategy of the presentation of an image and the search for a more receptive political venue" (p. 1050). The recent coupling of indigenous rights and environmental struggles is a good example of a strategic venue shift by *indigenista* activists, who found the environmental arena more recep-tive to their claims than had been human rights venues.

Information Politics

Information binds network members together and is essential for network effec-tiveness. Many information exchanges are informal—through telephone calls, e-mail and fax communications, and the circulation of small newsletters, pamphlets and bulletins. They provide information that would not otherwise be available, from sources that might not otherwise be heard, and make it comprehensible and useful to activists and publics who may be geographically and/or socially distant.

Non-state actors gain influence by serving as alternative sources of information. Information flows in advocacy networks provide not only facts, but also *testimonies*—stories told by people whose lives have been affected. Moreover, they interpret facts and testimony; activist groups frame issues simply, in terms of right and wrong, because their purpose is to *persuade* people and stimulate them to take action.

How does this process of persuasion occur? An effective frame must show that a given state of affairs is neither natural nor accidental, identify the responsible party or parties, and propose credible solutions. This requires clear, powerful mes-sages that appeal to shared principles, and which often have more impact on state policy than the advice of technical experts. An important part of the political struggle over information is whether an issue is defined primarily as technical, subject to consideration by "qualified" experts, or as something that concerns a much broader global constituency.

Even as we highlight the importance of testimony, however, we have to recognize the mediations involved. The process by which testimony is discovered and presented normally involves several layers of prior translation. Transnational actors may identify what kinds of testimony would be valuable, then ask an NGO in the area to seek out people who could tell those stories. They may filter through expatriates, through travelling scholars, through the media. There is frequently a huge gap between the story's telling and its retelling. . . . Local people, in other words, sometimes lose control over their stories in a transnational campaign.

Non-governmental networks have helped to legitimize the use of testimonial information along with technical and statistical information. Linkage of the two is crucial: without the individual cases, activists cannot motivate people to seek to change policies. Increasingly, international campaigns by networks take this two-level approach to information. In the 1980s even Greenpeace, which initially had eschewed rigorous research in favour of splashy media events, began to pay more attention to getting the facts right. . . .

A dense web of north–south exchange, aided by computer and fax communication, means that governments can no longer monopolize information flows as they could a mere half-decade ago. These technologies have had an enormous impact on moving information to and from Third World countries, where mail services are often both slow and precarious. We should note, however, that this gives special advantages to organizations that have access to such technologies.

The central role of information in all these issues helps to explain the drive to create networks. Information in these issue areas is both essential and dispersed. Non-governmental actors depend upon their access to information to help make them legitimate players. Contact with like-minded groups at home and abroad provides access to information necessary to their work, broadens their legitimacy, and helps to mobilize information around particular policy targets. Most NGOs cannot afford to maintain staff in a variety of countries. In exceptional cases, they send staff members on investigation missions, but this is not practical for keeping informed on routine developments. Forging links with local organizations allows groups to receive and monitor information from many countries at low cost. Local groups, in turn, depend on international contacts to get their information out, and to help to protect them in their work.

The media are essential partners in network information politics. To reach a broader audience, networks strive to attract press attention. Sympathetic journalists may become part of the network, but more often network activists cultivate a reputation for credibility with the press, and package their information in a timely and dramatic way to draw press attention.

Symbolic Politics

Activists frame issues by identifying and providing convincing explanations for powerful symbolic events, which in turn become catalysts for the growth of networks. Symbolic interpretation is part of the process of persuasion by which networks create awareness and expand the constituency. Awarding the Nobel Peace Prize to Rigoberta Menchu, during the International Year of Indigenous People, heightened public awareness of the situation of indigenous peoples in the Americas. The ability of the indigenous people's movement to use 1992, the 500th anniversary of the voyage of Columbus to the Americas, to raise a host of indigenous issues revealed the ability of networks to use symbolic events to reshape understandings (Brysk, 1994).

The coup in Chile played this kind of catalytic role for the human rights community. Often it is not one event, but the juxtaposition of disparate events that makes people change their minds and take action. For many people in the US, it was the juxtaposition of the coup in Chile, the war in Vietnam, Watergate, and civil rights that gave birth to the human rights movement. Likewise, the juxtaposition of the hot summer of 1988 in the US with dramatic footage of the Brazilian rainforest burning may have convinced many people that global warming and tropical deforestation were serious and linked issues. . . .

Leverage Politics

Activists in advocacy networks are concerned with political effectiveness. Their definition of effectiveness often involves some policy change by "target actors" which might be governments, but might also be international financial institutions like the World Bank, or private actors like transnational corporations. In order to bring about policy change, networks need to both persuade and pressurize more powerful actors. To gain influence the networks seek *leverage*—a word that appears often in the discourse of advocacy organizations—over more powerful actors. . . . Identifying points of leverage is a crucial strategic step in network campaigns. We discuss two kinds of leverage: material leverage and moral leverage.

Material leverage usually takes the form of some kind of issue-linkage, normally involving money or goods (but potentially also including votes in international organizations, prestigious offices, or other benefits). The human rights issue became negotiable because other governments or financial institutions connected human rights practices to the cut-off of military and economic aid, or to worsening bilateral diplomatic relations. Human rights groups obtained leverage by providing US and European policy-makers with information that persuaded them to cut off military and economic aid. . . .

Moral leverage involves what some commentators have called the "mobilisation of shame," where the behaviour of target actors is held up to the bright light of international scrutiny. Where states place a high value on international prestige, this can be effective. In the baby-food campaign, network activists used moral leverage to convince states to vote in favour of the WHO/UNICEF Codes of Conduct. As a result, even the Netherlands and Switzerland, both major exporters of infant formula, voted in favour of the code.

Although NGO influence often depends on securing powerful allies, making those links still depends on their ability to mobilize the solidarity of their members, or of public opinion via the media. In democracies, the potential to influence votes gives large membership organizations an advantage in lobbying for policy change; environmental organizations, several of whose memberships number in the millions, are more likely to have this added clout than are human rights organizations.

Accountability Politics

Networks devote considerable energy to convincing governments and other actors to change their positions on issues. This is often dismissed as inconsequential change, since talk is cheap—governments change discursive positions hoping to divert network and public attention. Network activists, however, try to make such statements into opportunities for accountability politics. Once a government has publicly committed itself to a principle—for example, in favour of human rights or democracy—networks can use those positions, and their command of information, to expose the distance between discourse and practice. This is embarrassing to many governments, who may try to save face by closing the distance.

UNDER WHAT CONDITIONS DO ADVOCACY NETWORKS HAVE INFLUENCE?

To assess the influence of advocacy networks we must look at goal achievement at several different levels. We identify the following types or stages of network influence:

1. issue creation and attention/agenda setting;
2. influence on discursive positions of states and regional and international organizations;
3. influence on institutional procedures;
4. influence on policy change in "target actors" which may be states, international or regional organizations, or private actors like the Nestlé corporation;
5. influence on state behaviour.

Networks generate attention to new issues and help to set agendas when they provoke media attention, debates, hearings and meetings on issues that previously had not been a matter of public debate. Because values are the essence of advocacy networks, this stage of influence may require a modification of the "value context" in which policy debates take place. The theme years and decades of the United Nations, such as International Women's Decade and the Year of Indigenous People, were international events promoted by networks that heightened awareness of issues.

Networks influence discursive positions when they help to persuade states and international organizations to support international declarations or change stated domestic policy positions. The role that environmental networks played in shaping state positions and conference declarations at the 1992 Earth Summit in Rio de Janeiro is an example of this kind of impact. They may also pressurize states to make more binding commitments by signing conventions and codes of conduct.

At a more concrete level, the network has influence if it leads to changes in policies, not only of the target states, but also of other states and/or international institutions. These changes are easier to see, but their causes can be elusive. We can speak of network impact on policy change where human rights networks have pressured successfully for cut-offs of military aid to repressive regimes, where repressive practices diminish because of pressure, or even where human rights activity affects regime change or stability. We must take care to distinguish between policy change and change in behaviour; official policies may predict nothing about how actors behave in reality.

We speak of stages of impact, and not merely types of impact, because we believe that increased attention and changes in discursive positions make governments more vulnerable to the claims these networks raise. . . . Meaningful policy and behavioural change is thus more likely when the first three types or stages of impact have occurred.

Both *issue characteristics* and *actor characteristics* are important parts of our explanation of how networks affect political outcomes and the conditions under which networks can be effective. Issue characteristics like salience and resonance within existing national or institutional agendas can tell us something about where networks are likely to be able to insert new ideas and discourse into policy debates. Success in influencing policy depends on the strength and density of the network, and its ability to achieve leverage.

As we look at the issues around which transnational advocacy networks have organized most effectively, we find two characteristic issues that appear most frequently:

1. those involving bodily harm to vulnerable individuals, especially when there is a short and clear causal chain (or story) about who bears responsibility;
2. issues involving *legal* equality of opportunity.

The first responds to a normative logic, and the second to a judicial and institutional one. Issues involving physical harm to vulnerable or innocent individuals appear more likely to resonate transnationally. . . . Both issues of "harm" and "innocence" or vulnerability are highly interpretive and contested. [However,] we argue that issues involving bodily harm to populations perceived as vulnerable or innocent are more likely to lead to effective transnational campaigns than other kinds of issues. This helps to explain why it has been easier to work on torture or disappearance than some other human rights issues, and why it has been easier to protest against torture of political prisoners than against torture of common criminals or to abolish capital punishment. It is also useful for understanding that those environmental campaigns that have had the greatest transnational effect have been those that stress the connection between protecting environments *and* the (often vulnerable) people who live in those environments. . . .

The second issue around which transnational campaigns appear to have greater effectiveness is that of greater legal equality of opportunity. Notice that we stress *legal* equality of *opportunity*, not of outcome. One of the most successful international campaigns was the anti-apartheid campaign. What made apartheid such a clear target was the legal denial of the most basic aspects of equality of opportunity.

TRANSNATIONAL NETWORKS AND REGIONAL INTEGRATION

Many scholars now recognize that the state no longer has a monopoly over public affairs and are seeking ways to describe the sphere of international interactions under a variety of names: transnational relations, international civil society, and global civil society (Lipschutz, 1992; Peterson, 1992). In their views, states no longer look unitary from the outside. Increasingly dense interactions among individuals, groups, actors from states and regional and international institutions appear to involve much more than re-presenting interests on a world stage.

Recent empirical work in sociology has gone a long way towards demonstrating the extent of changes "above" and "below" the state. The world polity theory associated with John Meyer, John Boli, George Thomas and their colleagues, conceives of an international society in a radically different way. For these scholars, it is the area of diffusion of world culture—a process that itself constitutes the characteristics of states (Thomas et al., 1987; Boli and Thomas, 1999). The vehicles for its diffusion become global intergovernmental and non-governmental organizations, but neither the sources of norms nor the processes through which global cultural norms evolve are adequately specified (Finnemore, 1996). Proponents of world polity theory present international organizations and NGOs as "enactors" of some basic cultural principles of the world culture: universalism, individualism, rational voluntaristic authority, human purposes, and world citizenship. There is thus no meaningful distinction between those espousing norms that reinforce existing institutional power relationships, and those that challenge them.

We argue that different transnational actors have profoundly divergent purposes and goals. To understand how change occurs in the world polity we have to unpack the different categories of transnational actors, and understand the quite different logic and process in these different categories. The logic of transnational advocacy networks, which are often in conflict with states over basic principles, is quite different from the logic of other transnational actors who provide symbols or services or models for states. In essence, world polity theorists eliminate the struggles over power and meaning that for us are central to normative change.

Our research suggests that many transnational networks have been sites of cultural and political negotiation rather than mere enactors of dominant Western norms. Western human rights norms have indeed been the defining framework for many networks, but how these norms are articulated is transformed in the process of network activity. For example, issues of indigenous rights and cultural survival have been at the forefront of modern network activity, and yet they run counter to the cultural model put forward by the world polity theorists.

In other words, as modern anthropologists realize, culture is not a totalizing influence, but a field that is constantly changing. Certain discourses—like that of human rights—provide a language for negotiation. Within this language certain moves are privileged over others; human rights is a very disciplining discourse. But it is also a permissive discourse that allows different groups within the network to renegotiate meanings. . . .

Network theory can thus provide an explanation for transnational change, a model that is not just one of "diffusion" of liberal institutions and practices, but one through which the preferences and identities of actors engaged in transnational society are sometimes mutually transformed through their interactions with each other. . . .

NOTE

1. We developed this definition based on a discussion in Mitchell (1973, p. 23).

REFERENCES

Baumgartner, F.; Jones, B., 1991. Agenda dynamics and policy subsystems, *Journal of Politics* 53, pp. 1044–74.

Boli, J.; Thomas. G., (eds), 1999. *Constructing World Culture: International Non-Governmental Organization Since 1875.* Stanford.

Brysk, A., 1994. Acting globally: Indian rights and international politics in Latin America. In D. Van Cott (ed.), *Indigenous Peoples and Democracy in Latin America,* New York: St Martins/ Inter-American Dialogue, pp. 29–51.

Brysk, A., 1995. Hearts and minds: bringing symbolic politics back in, *Polity* 27 (Summer), pp. 559–85.

Dalton, R., Kuechler, M.; Burklin, W., 1990. The challenge of new movements. In R. Dalton, M. Kuechler (eds), *Challenging the Political Order: New Social and Political Movements in Western Democracies,* Cambridge: Polity.

Finnemore, M., 1996. *National Interests in International Society.* Ithaca: Cornell.

Frühling, H., 1991. *Derechos Humanos y Democracia: La contribución de las Organizaciones Nogubernamentales.* Santiago: IIDH.

Haas, P. (ed.), 1992. *Knowledge, Power and International Policy Coordination. International Organization,* vol. 6.

Katzenstein, P. (ed.), 1996. *The Culture of National Security: Norms and Identity in World Politics.* New York: Columbia.

Keck, M.; Sikkink, K., 1998. *Activists beyond Borders: Advocacy Networks in International Politics.* Ithaca: Cornell.

Klotz, A., 1995. *Norms in International Relations: The Struggle against Apartheid.* Ithaca: Cornell.

Korten, D., 1990. *Getting to the 21st Century: Voluntary Action and the Global Agenda.* Hartford, CT: Kumarian.

Lipschutz, R., 1992. Reconstructing world politics: the emergence of global civil society, *Millennium* 21, pp. 389–420.

McAdam, D., McCarthy, J.; Zald, M. (eds), 1996. *Comparative Perspectives on Social Movements: Political Opportunities, Mobilizing Structures, and Cultural Framings.* New York: Cambridge.

Mitchell, J., 1973. Networks, norms, and institutions. In J. Boissevian, J. Mitchell (eds), *Network Analysis,* The Hague: Mouton.

Oliver, P.; Marwell, G., 1992. Mobilizing technologies for collective action. In A. Morris, C. Mueller (eds), *Frontiers in Social Movement Theory,* New Haven, CT: Yale University Press.

Peterson, M. J., 1992. Transnational activity, international society, and world politics, *Millennium* 21.

Powell, W., 1990. Neither market nor hierarchy: network forms of organization, *Research in Organizational Behaviour* 12, pp. 295–336.

Scherer-Warren, I., 1993. *Redes de Movimentos Sociais.* São Paulo: Loyola.

Snow, D.; Benford, R., 1988. Ideology, frame resonance, and participant mobilisation. In B. Klandermans, H. Kriesi, S. Tarrow (eds), *From Structure to Action: Comparing Social Movement Research across Cultures,* Greenwich, CT: JAI, pp. 197–217.

Snow, D.; Benford, R., 1992. Master frames and cycles of protest. In A. Morris, C. Mueller (eds), *Frontiers in Social Movement Theory,* New Haven, CT: Yale University Press, pp. 133–55.

Snow, D., et al., 1986. Frame alignment processes, micromobilisation, and movement participation, *American Sociological Review* 51.

Stone, D., 1989. Causal stories and the formation of policy agendas, *Political Science Quarterly* 104, pp. 281–300.

Tarrow, S., 1992. Mentalities, political cultures, and collective action frames: constructing meanings through action. In A. Morris, C. Mueller (eds), *Frontiers in Social Movement Theory,* New Haven, CT: Yale University Press.

Tarrow, S., 1994. *Power in Movement.* New York: Cambridge University Press.

Thomas, G.; Meyer, J.; Ramirez, F.; Boli, J. (eds), 1987. *Institutional Structure: Constituting State, Society, and Individual.* Newbury Park, CA: Sage.

The Politics, Power, and Pathologies of International Organizations

MICHAEL N. BARNETT and MARTHA FINNEMORE

Do international organizations really do what their creators intend them to do? In the past century the number of international organizations (IOs) has increased exponentially, and we have a variety of vigorous theories to explain why they have been created. Most of these theories explain IO creation as a response to problems of incomplete information, transaction costs, and other barriers to Pareto efficiency and welfare improvement for their members. Research flowing from these theories, however, has paid little attention to how IOs actually behave after they are created. Closer scrutiny would reveal that many IOs stray from the efficiency goals these theories impute and that many IOs exercise power autonomously in ways unintended and unanticipated by states at their creation. Understanding how this is so requires a reconsideration of IOs and what they do.

In this article we . . . explain both the power of IOs and their propensity for dysfunctional, even pathological, behavior. Drawing on long-standing Weberian arguments about bureaucracy and sociological institutionalist approaches to organizational behavior, we argue that the rational-legal authority that IOs embody gives them power independent of the states that created them and channels that power in particular directions. Bureaucracies, by definition, make rules, but in so doing they also create social knowledge. They define shared international tasks (like "development"), create and define new categories of actors (like "refugee"), create new interests for actors (like "promoting human rights"), and transfer models of political organization around the world (like markets and democracy). However, the same normative valuation on impersonal, generalized rules that defines bureaucracies and makes them powerful in modern life can also make them unresponsive to their environments, obsessed with their own rules at the expense of primary missions, and ultimately lead to inefficient, self-defeating behavior. . . .

Developing an alternative approach to thinking about IOs is only worthwhile if it produces significant insights and new opportunities for research on major debates in the field. Our approach allows us to weigh in with new perspectives on at least three such debates. First, it offers a different view of the power of IOs and whether or how they matter in world politics. . . . Global organizations do more

*We are grateful to John Boli, Raymond Duvall, Ernst Haas, Peter Haas, Robert Keohane, Keith Krause, Jeffrey Legro, John Malley, Craig Murphy, M. J. Peterson, Mark Pollack, Andrew Moravcsik, Thomas Risse, Duncan Snidal, Steve Weber, Thomas Weiss, and two anonymous referees for their comments. We are especially grateful for the careful attention of the editors of *International Organization*. Earlier versions of this article were presented at the 1997 APSA meeting, the 1997 ISA meeting, and at various fora. We also acknowledge financial assistance from the Smith Richardson Foundation and the United States Institute of Peace.

than just facilitate cooperation by helping states to overcome market failures, collective action dilemmas, and problems associated with interdependent social choice. They also create actors, specify responsibilities and authority among them, and define the work these actors should do, giving it meaning and normative value. Even when they lack material resources, IOs exercise power as they constitute and construct the social world.[1]

Second and related, our perspective provides a theoretical basis for treating IOs as autonomous actors in world politics and thus presents a challenge to the statist ontology prevailing in international relations theories. Despite all their attention to international institutions, one result of the theoretical orientation of neoliberal institutionalists and regimes theorists is that they treat IOs the way pluralists treat the state. IOs are mechanisms through which others (usually states) act: they are not purposive actors. . . . Weber's insights about the normative power of the rational-legal authority that bureaucracies embody and its implications for the ways bureaucracies produce and control social knowledge provide a basis for challenging this view and treating IOs as agents, not just as structure.

Third, our perspective offers a different vantage point from which to assess the desirability of IOs. While realists and some policymakers have taken up this issue, surprisingly few other students of IOs have been critical of their performance or desirability.[2] Part of this optimism stems from central tenets of classical liberalism, which has long viewed IOs as a peaceful way to manage rapid technological change and globalization, far preferable to the obvious alternative—war.[3] Also contributing to this uncritical stance is the normative judgment about IOs that is built into the theoretical assumptions of most neoliberal and regimes scholars and the economic organization theories on which they draw. IOs exist, in this view, only because they are Pareto improving and solve problems for states. Consequently, if an IO exists, it must be because it is more useful than other alternatives since, by theoretical axiom, states will pull the plug on any IO that does not perform. We find this assumption unsatisfying. IOs often produce undesirable and even self-defeating outcomes repeatedly, without punishment much less dismantlement, and we, as theorists, want to understand why. . . . Drawing from research in sociology and anthropology, we show how the very features that make bureaucracies powerful can also be their weakness.

We begin by examining the assumptions underlying different branches of organization theory and exploring their implications for the study of IOs. We argue that assumptions drawn from economics that undergird neoliberal and neorealist treatments of IOs do not always reflect the empirical situation of most IOs commonly studied by political scientists. Further, they provide research hypotheses about only some aspects of IOs (like why they are created) and not others (like what they do). We then introduce sociological arguments that help remedy these problems.

In the second section we develop a constructivist approach from these sociological arguments to examine the power wielded by IOs and the sources of their influence. Liberal and realist theories only make predictions about, and consequently only look for, a very limited range of welfare-improving effects caused by IOs. Sociological theories, however, expect and explain a much broader range of impacts organizations can have and specifically highlight their role in constructing actors, interests, and social purpose. We provide illustrations from the UN system to show how IOs do, in fact, have such powerful effects in contemporary world politics. In the third section we explore the dysfunctional behavior of IOs. . . . We construct a typology, mapping these theories according to the source of dysfunction they emphasize, and show that the same internally generated cultural forces that give IOs their power and autonomy can also be a source of dysfunctional behavior. We use the term *pathologies* to describe such instances when IO dysfunction can be traced to bureaucratic culture. . . .

THEORETICAL APPROACHES TO ORGANIZATIONS

Within social science there are two broad strands of theorizing about organizations. One is economistic and rooted in assumptions of instrumental rationality and efficiency concerns; the other is sociological and focused on issues of legitimacy and power.[4] The different assumptions embedded within each type of theory focus attention on different kinds of questions about organizations and provide insights on different kinds of problems.

The economistic approach comes, not surprisingly, out of economics departments and business schools for whom the fundamental theoretical problem, laid out first by Ronald Coase and more recently by Oliver Williamson, is why we have business firms. Within standard microeconomic logic, it should be much more efficient to conduct all transactions through markets rather than "hierarchies" or organizations. Consequently, the fact that economic life is dominated by huge organizations (business firms) is an anomaly. The body of theory developed to explain the existence and power of firms focuses on organizations as efficient solutions to contracting problems, incomplete information, and other market imperfections.[5]

This body of organization theory informs neoliberal and neorealist debates over international institutions. . . . After all, why else would states set up these organizations and continue to support them if they did not serve state interests?

Approaches from sociology provide one set of answers to this question. They provide reasons why, in fact, organizations that are not efficient or effective servants of member interests might exist. In so doing, they lead us to look for kinds of power and sources of autonomy in organizations that economists overlook. Different approaches within sociology treat organizations in different ways, but as a group they stand in sharp contrast to the economists' approaches in at least two important respects: they offer a different conception of the relationship between organizations and their environments, and they provide a basis for understanding organizational autonomy.

IOs and Their Environment

The environment assumed by economic approaches to organizations is socially very thin and devoid of social rules, cultural content, or even other actors beyond those constructing the organization. Competition, exchange, and consequent pressures for efficiency are the dominant environmental characteristics driving the formation and behavior of organizations. Sociologists, by contrast, study organizations in a wider world of nonmarket situations, and, consequently, they begin with no such assumptions. Organizations are treated as "social facts" to be investigated; whether they do what they claim or do it efficiently is an empirical question, not a theoretical assumption of these approaches. Organizations respond not only to other actors pursuing material interests in the environment but also to normative and cultural forces that shape how organizations see the world and conceptualize their own missions. Environments can "select" or favor organizations for reasons other than efficient or responsive behavior. For example, organizations may be created and supported for reasons of legitimacy and normative fit rather than efficient output; they may be created not for what they do but for what they are—for what they represent symbolically and the values they embody.[6]

Empirically, organizational environments can take many forms. Some organizations exist in competitive environments that create strong pressures for efficient or responsive behavior, but many do not. Some organizations operate with clear criteria for "success" (like firms that have balance sheets), whereas others (like political science departments) operate with much vaguer missions, with few clear criteria for success or failure and no serious threat of elimination. Our point is simply that when we choose a theoretical framework, we should choose one whose assumptions approximate the empirical conditions of the IO we are analyzing. . . .

IO Autonomy

Following economistic logic, regime theory and the broad range of scholars working within it generally treat IOs as creations of states designed to further state interests.[7] Analysis of subsequent IO behavior focuses on processes of aggregating member state preferences through strategic interaction within the structure of the IO. IOs, then, are simply epiphenomena of state interaction. . . .

These theories thus treat IOs as empty shells or impersonal policy machinery to be manipulated by other actors. Political bargains shape the machinery at its creation, states may politick hard within the machinery in pursuit of their policy goals, and the machinery's norms and rules may constrain what states can do, but the machinery itself is passive. IOs are not purposive political actors in their own right and have no ontological independence. . . .

The relevant question to ask about this conceptualization is whether it is a reasonable approximation of the empirical condition of most IOs. Our reading of detailed empirical case studies of IO activity suggests not. Yes, IOs are constrained by states, but the notion that they are passive mechanisms with no independent agendas of their own is not borne out by any detailed empirical study of an IO that we have found. Field studies of the European Union provide evidence of independent roles for "eurocrats."[8] Studies of the World Bank consistently identify an independent culture and agendas for action.[9] Studies of recent UN peacekeeping and reconstruction efforts similarly document a UN agenda that frequently leads to conflict with member states.[10] . . .

Principal-agent analysis, which has been increasingly employed by students of international relations to examine organizational dynamics, could potentially provide a sophisticated approach to understanding IO autonomy.[11] Building on theories of rational choice and of representation, these analysts understand IOs as "agents" of states ("principals"). The analysis is concerned with whether agents are responsible delegates of their principals, whether agents smuggle in and pursue their own preferences, and how principals can construct various mechanisms to keep their agents honest.[12] This framework provides a means of treating IOs as actors in their own right with independent interests and capabilities. . . .

. . . There are good reasons to assume that organizations care about their resource base and turf, but there is no reason to presume that such matters exhaust or even dominate their interests. Indeed, ethnographic studies of IOs describe a world in which organizational goals are strongly shaped by norms of the profession that dominate the bureaucracy and in which interests themselves are varied, often in flux, debated, and worked out through interactions between the staff of the bureaucracy and the world in which they are embedded.[13]

Various strands of sociological theory can help us investigate the goals and behavior of IOs by offering a very different analytical orientation than the one used by economists. Beginning with Weber, sociologists have explored the notion that bureaucracy is a peculiarly modern cultural form that embodies certain values and can have its own distinct agenda and behavioral dispositions. Rather than treating organizations as mere arenas or mechanisms through which other actors pursue interests, many sociological approaches explore the social content of the organization—its culture, its legitimacy concerns, dominant norms that govern behavior and shape interests, and the relationship of these to a larger normative and cultural environment. Rather than assuming behavior that corresponds to efficiency criteria alone, these approaches recognize that organizations also are bound up with power and social control in ways that can eclipse efficiency concerns.

THE POWER OF IOs

IOs can become autonomous sites of authority, independent from the state "principals" who may have created them, because of power flowing from at least two sources: (1) the legitimacy of the rational-legal authority they embody, and (2) control over technical expertise and information. The first of these is almost entirely neglected by the political science literature, and the second, we argue, has been conceived of very narrowly, leading scholars to overlook some of the most basic and consequential forms of IO influence. Taken together, these two features provide a theoretical basis for treating IOs as autonomous actors in contemporary world politics by identifying sources of support for them, independent of states, in the larger social environment. . . .

Sources of IO Autonomy and Authority

To understand how IOs can become autonomous sites of authority we turn to Weber and his classic study of bureaucratization. Weber was deeply ambivalent about the increasingly bureaucratic world in which he lived and was well-attuned to the vices as well as the virtues of this new social form of authority.[14] Bureaucracies are rightly considered a grand achievement, he thought. . . . But such technical and rational achievements, according to Weber, come at a steep price. Bureaucracies are political creatures that can be autonomous from their creators and can come to dominate the societies they were created to serve, because of both the normative appeal of rational-legal authority in modern life and the bureaucracy's control over technical expertise and information. We consider each in turn.

Bureaucracies embody a form of authority, rational-legal authority, that modernity views as particularly legitimate and good. In contrast to earlier forms of authority that were invested in a leader, legitimate modern authority is invested in legalities, procedures, and rules and thus rendered impersonal. This authority is "rational" in that it deploys socially recognized relevant knowledge to create rules that determine how goals will be pursued. The very fact that they embody rationality is what makes bureaucracies powerful and makes people willing to submit to this kind of authority. . . .

When bureaucrats do something contrary to your interests or that you do not like, they defend themselves by saying "Sorry, those are the rules" or "just doing my job." "The rules" and "the job" are the source of great power in modern society. It is because bureaucrats in IOs are performing "duties of office" and implementing "rationally established norms" that they are powerful.

A second basis of autonomy and authority, intimately connected to the first, is bureaucratic control over information and expertise. A bureaucracy's autonomy derives from specialized technical knowledge, training, and experience that is not immediately available to other actors. While such knowledge might help the bureaucracy carry out the directives of politicians more efficiently, Weber stressed that it also gives bureaucracies power over politicians (and other actors). It invites and at times requires bureaucracies to shape policy, not just implement it.[15]

The irony in both of these features of authority is that they make bureaucracies powerful precisely by creating the appearance of depoliticization. The power of IOs, and bureaucracies generally, is that they present themselves as impersonal, technocratic, and neutral—as not exercising power but instead as serving others; the presentation and acceptance of these claims is critical to their legitimacy and authority.[16] Weber, however, saw through these claims. According to him, the depoliticized character of bureaucracy that legitimates it could be a myth: "Behind the functional purposes [of bureaucracy], of course, 'ideas of culture-values' usually stand."[17] . . .

In addition to embodying cultural values from the larger environment that might be desirable or not, bureaucracies also carry with them behavioral dispositions and values flowing from the rationality that legitimates them as a cultural form. Some of these, like the celebration of knowledge and expertise, Weber admired. Others concerned him greatly, and his descriptions of bureaucracy as an "iron cage" and bureaucrats as "specialists without spirit" are hardly an endorsement of the bureaucratic form.[18] . . .

Examples of the ways in which IOs have become autonomous because of their embodiment of technical rationality and control over information are not hard to find. The UN's peacekeepers derive part of their authority from the claim that they are independent, objective, neutral actors who simply implement Security Council resolutions. UN officials routinely use this language to describe their role and are explicit that they understand this to be the basis of their influence. As a consequence, UN officials spend considerable time and energy attempting to maintain the image that they are not the instrument of any great power and must be seen as representatives of "the international community" as embodied in the rules and resolutions of the UN.[19] The World Bank is widely recognized to have exercised power over development policies far greater than its budget, as a percentage of North/South aid flows, would suggest because of the expertise it houses. While competing sites of expertise in development have proliferated in recent years, for decades after its founding the World Bank was a magnet for the "best and brightest" among "development experts." Its staff had and continues to have impressive credentials from the most prestigious universities and the elaborate models, reports, and research groups it has sponsored over the years were widely influential among the "development experts" in the field. This expertise, coupled with its claim to "neutrality" and its "apolitical" technocratic decision-making style, have given the World Bank an authoritative voice with which it has successfully dictated the content, direction, and scope of global development over the past fifty years.[20] Similarly, official standing and long experience with relief efforts have endowed the UNHCR with "expert" status and consequent authority in refugee matters. This expertise, coupled with its role in implementing international refugee conventions and law ("the rules" regarding refugees), has allowed the UNHCR to make life and death decisions about refugees without consulting the refugees, themselves, and to compromise the authority of states in various ways in setting up refugee camps.[21] Note that, as these examples show, technical knowledge and expertise need not be "scientific" in nature to create autonomy and power for IOs.

The Power of IOs

If IOs have autonomy and authority in the world, what do they do with it? A growing body of research in sociology and anthropology has examined ways in which IOs exercise power by virtue of their culturally constructed status as sites of authority; we distill from this research three broad types of IO power. We examine how IOs (1) classify the world, creating categories of actors and action; (2) fix meanings in the social world; and (3) articulate and diffuse new norms, principles, and actors around the globe. All of these sources of power flow from the ability of IOs to structure knowledge.[22]

Classification

An elementary feature of bureaucracies is that they classify and organize information and knowledge. This classification process is bound up with power. "Bureaucracies," writes Don Handelman, "are ways of making, ordering, and knowing social worlds." They do this by "moving persons among social categories or by inventing and applying such categories."[23] The ability to classify objects, to shift their very definition and identity, is one of bureaucracy's greatest sources of power. . . . Consequences of this bureaucratic exercise of power may be identity defining, or even life threatening.

Consider the evolving definition of "refugee." The category "refugee" is not at all straightforward and must be distinguished from other categories of individuals who are "temporarily" and "involuntarily" living outside their country of origin—displaced persons, exiles, economic migrants, guest workers, diaspora communities, and those seeking political asylum. The debate over the meaning of "refugee" has been waged in and around the UNHCR. The UNHCR's legal and operational definition of the category strongly influences decisions about who is a refugee and shapes UNHCR staff decisions in the field.[24]. . . Guy Gran similarly describes how the World Bank sets up criteria to define someone as a peasant in order to distinguish them from a farmer, day laborer, and other categories. The classification matters because only certain classes of people are recognized by the World Bank's development machinery as having knowledge that is relevant in solving development problems.[25] Categorization and classification are a ubiquitous feature of bureaucratization. . . . To classify is to engage in an act of power.

The Fixing of Meanings

IOs exercise power by virtue of their ability to fix meanings, which is related to classification.[26] Naming or labeling the social context establishes the parameters, the very boundaries, of acceptable action. Because actors are oriented toward objects and objectives on the basis of the meaning that they have for them, being able to invest situations with a particular meaning constitutes an important source of power.[27] IOs do not act alone in this regard, but their organizational resources contribute mightily to this end.

There is strong evidence of this power from development studies. Arturo Escobar explores how the institutionalization of the concept of "development" after World War II spawned a huge international apparatus and how this apparatus has now spread its tentacles in domestic and international politics through the discourse of development. The discourse of development, created and arbitrated in large part by IOs, determines not only what constitutes the activity (what development is) but also who (or what) is considered powerful and privileged, that is, who gets to do the developing (usually the state or IOs) and who is the object of development (local groups).[28]

Similarly, the end of the Cold War encouraged a reexamination of the definition of security.[29] IOs have been at the forefront of this debate, arguing that security pertains not only to states but also to individuals and that the threats to security may be economic, environmental, and political as well as military. . . .[30]

One consequence of these redefined meanings of development and security is that they legitimate, and even require, increased levels of IO intervention in the domestic affairs of states—particularly Third World states. This is fairly obvious in the realm of development. The World Bank, the International Monetary Fund (IMF), and other development institutions have established a web of interventions that affect nearly every phase of the economy and polity in many Third World states. As "rural development," "basic human needs," and "structural adjustment" became incorporated into the meaning of development, IOs were permitted, even required, to become intimately involved in the domestic workings of developing polities by posting inhouse "advisors" to run monetary policy, reorganizing the political economy of entire rural regions, regulating family and reproductive practices, and mediating between governments and their citizens in a variety of ways.[31] . . .

The consequences of redefining security may be similar. Democratization, human rights, and the environment have all now become tied to international peace and security, and IOs justify their interventions in member states on these grounds, particularly in developing states. For example, during the anti-apartheid struggle in South Africa, human rights abuses came to be classified as security threats by the UN Security Council and provided grounds for UN involvement there. Now, that linkage between human rights and security has become a staple of the post–Cold War environment. Widespread human rights abuses anywhere are now cause for UN intervention, and, conversely, the UN cannot carry out peacekeeping missions without promoting human rights.[32] . . .

Diffusion of Norms

Having established rules and norms, IOs are eager to spread the benefits of their expertise and often act as conveyor belts for the transmission of norms and models of "good" political behavior.[33] There is nothing accidental or unintended about this role. Officials in IOs often insist that part of their mission is to spread, inculcate, and enforce global values and norms. They are the "missionaries" of our time. Armed with a notion of progress, an idea of how to create the better life, and some understanding of the conversion process, many IO elites have as their stated purpose a desire to shape state practices by establishing, articulating, and transmitting norms that define what constitutes acceptable and legitimate state behavior. . . .

Consider decolonization as an example. The UN Charter announced an intent to universalize sovereignty as a constitutive principle of the society of states at a time when over half the globe was under some kind of colonial rule; it also established an institutional apparatus to achieve that end (most prominently the Trusteeship Council and the Special Committee on Colonialism). These actions had several consequences. One was to eliminate certain categories of acceptable action for powerful states. Those states that attempted to retain their colonial privileges were increasingly viewed as illegitimate by other states. Another consequence was to empower international bureaucrats (at the Trusteeship Council) to set norms and standards for "stateness." Finally, the UN helped to ensure that throughout decolonization the sovereignty of these new states was coupled with territorial inviolability. . . . The UN encouraged the acceptance of the norm of sovereignty-as-territorial-integrity through resolutions, monitoring devices, commissions, and one famous peacekeeping episode in Congo in the 1960s.[34]

Note that, as with other IO powers, norm diffusion, too, has an expansionary dynamic. Developing states continue to be popular targets for norm diffusion by IOs, even after they are independent. The UN and the European Union are now actively involved in police training in non-Western states because they believe Western policing practices will be more conducive to democratization processes and the establishment of civil society. But having a professional police establishment assumes that there is a professional judiciary and penal system where criminals can be tried and jailed; and a professional judiciary, in turn, presupposes that there are lawyers that can come before the court. Trained lawyers presuppose a code of law. The result is a package of reforms sponsored by IOs aimed at transforming non-Western societies into Western societies.[35] Again, while Western states are involved in these activities and therefore their values and interests are part of the reasons for this process, international bureaucrats involved in these activities may not see themselves as doing the bidding for these states but rather as expressing the interests and values of the bureaucracy.

Other examples of this kind of norm diffusion are not hard to find. The IMF and the World Bank are explicit about their role as transmitters of norms and principles from advanced market economies to less-developed economies.[36] . . . . The European Bank for Reconstruction and Development has, as part of its mandate, the job of spreading democracy and private enterprise. The OSCE is striving to create a community based on shared values, among these respect for democracy and human rights. This linkage is also strong at the UN as evident in *The Agenda for Democratization* and *The Agenda for Peace*.[37] Once democratization and human rights are tied to international peace and security, the distinctions between international and domestic governance become effectively erased and IOs have license to intervene almost anywhere in an authoritative and legitimate manner.[38]

Realists and neoliberals may well look at these effects and argue that the classificatory schemes, meanings, and norms associated with IOs are mostly favored by strong states. Consequently, they would argue, the power we attribute to IOs is simply epiphenomenal of state power. This argument is certainly one theoretical possibility, but it is not the only one and must be tested against others. Our concern is that because these theories provide no ontological independence for IOs, they have no way to test for autonomy nor have they any theoretical cause or inclination to test for it since, by theoretical axiom, autonomy cannot exist. . . .

THE PATHOLOGIES OF IOs

Bureaucracies are created, propagated, and valued in modern society because of their supposed rationality and effectiveness in carrying out social tasks. These same considerations presumably also apply to IOs. Ironically, though, the folk wisdom about bureaucracies is that they are inefficient and unresponsive. Bureaucracies are infamous for creating and implementing policies that defy rational logic, for acting in ways that are at odds with their stated mission, and for refusing requests of and turning their backs on those to whom they are officially responsible.[39]

IOs, too, are prone to dysfunctional behaviors, but international relations scholars have rarely investigated this, in part, we suspect, because the theoretical apparatus they use provides few grounds for expecting undesirable IO behavior.[40] The state-centric utility-maximizing frameworks most international relations scholars have borrowed from economics simply assume that IOs are reasonably responsive to state interests (or, at least, more responsive than alternatives), otherwise states would withdraw from them. This assumption, however, is a necessary theoretical axiom of these frameworks; it is rarely treated as a hypothesis subject to empirical investigation.[41] With little theoretical reason to expect suboptimal or self-defeating behavior in IOs, these scholars do not look for it and have had little to say about it. Policymakers, however, have been quicker to perceive and address these problems and are putting them on the political agenda. It is time for scholars, too, to begin to explore these issues more fully.

In this section we present several bodies of theorizing that might explain dysfunctional IO behavior, which we define as behavior that undermines the IO's stated objectives. Thus our vantage point for judging dysfunction (and later pathology) is the publicly proclaimed mission of the organization. There may be occasions when overall organizational dysfunction is, in fact, functional for certain members or others involved in the IO's work, but given our analysis of the way claims of efficiency and effectiveness act to legitimate rational-legal authority in our culture, whether organizations actually do what they claim and accomplish their missions is a particularly important issue to examine. Several bodies of theory provide some basis for understanding dysfunctional behavior by IOs, each of which emphasizes a different locus of causality for such behavior. Analyzing these causes, we construct a typology of these explanations that locates them in relation to one another. Then, drawing on the work of James March and Johan Olsen, Paul DiMaggio and Walter Powell, and other sociological institutionalists, we elaborate how the same sources of bureaucratic power, sketched earlier, can cause dysfunctional behavior. We term this particular type of dysfunction *pathology*.[42] We identify five features of bureaucracy that might produce pathology, and using examples from the UN system we illustrate the way these might work in IOs.

Extant theories about dysfunction can be categorized in two dimensions: (1) whether they locate the cause of IO dysfunction inside or outside the organization, and (2) whether they trace the causes to material or cultural forces. Mapping theories on these dimensions creates the typology shown in Figure 1.

Within each cell we have identified a representative body of theory familiar to most international relations scholars. Explanations of IO dysfunction that emphasize the pursuit of material interests within an organization typically examine how competition among subunits over material resources leads the organization to make decisions and engage in behaviors that are inefficient or undesirable as judged against some ideal policy that would better allow the IO to achieve its stated goals. Bureaucratic politics is the best-known theory here. . . . In this view, decisions are not made after a rational decision process but rather through a competitive bargaining process over turf, budgets, and staff that may benefit parts of the organization at the expense of overall goals.[43]

Another body of literature traces IO dysfunctional behavior to the material forces located outside the organization. Realist and neoliberal theories might posit that state preferences and constraints are responsible for understanding IO dysfunctional behavior. In this view IOs are not to blame for bad outcomes, states are. IOs do not have the luxury of choosing the optimal policy but rather are frequently

	Internal	External
Material	Bureaucratic politics	Realism/ neoliberal institutionalism
Cultural	Bureaucratic culture	World polity model

FIGURE 1. THEORIES OF INTERNATIONAL ORGANIZATION DYSFUNCTION

forced to chose between the bad and the awful because more desirable policies are denied to them by states who do not agree among themselves and/or do not wish to see the IO fulfill its mandate in some particular instance. . . . The important point of these theories is that they trace IO dysfunctional behavior back to the environmental conditions established by, or the explicit preferences of, states.

Cultural theories also have internal and external variants. . . . The world polity model exemplifies theories that look to external culture to understand an IO's dysfunctional behavior. There are two reasons to expect dysfunctional behavior here. First, because IO practices reflect a search for symbolic legitimacy rather than efficiency, IO behavior might be only remotely connected to the efficient implementation of its goals and more closely coupled to legitimacy criteria that come from the cultural environment.[44] For instance, many arms–export control regimes now have a multilateral character not because of any evidence that this architecture is the most efficient way to monitor and prevent arms exports but rather because multilateralism has attained a degree of legitimacy that is not empirically connected to any efficiency criteria.[45] Second, the world polity is full of contradictions; for instance, a liberal world polity has several defining principles, including market economics and human equality, that might conflict at any one moment. Thus, environments are often ambiguous about missions and contain varied, often conflicting, functional, normative, and legitimacy imperatives.[46] Because they are embedded in that cultural environment, IOs can mirror and reproduce those contradictions, which, in turn, can lead to contradictory and ultimately dysfunctional behavior.

Finally, organizations frequently develop distinctive internal cultures that can promote dysfunctional behavior, behavior that we call "pathological." The basic logic of this argument flows directly from our previous observations about the nature of bureaucracy as a social form. Bureaucracies are established as rationalized means to accomplish collective goals and to spread particular values. To do this, bureaucracies create social knowledge and develop expertise as they act upon the world (and thus exercise power). But the way bureaucracies are constituted to accomplish these ends can, ironically, create a cultural disposition toward undesirable and ultimately self-defeating behavior.[47] Two features of the modern bureaucratic form are particularly important in this regard. The first is the simple fact that bureaucracies are organized around rules, routines, and standard operating procedures designed to trigger a standard and predictable response to environmental stimuli. These rules can be formal or informal, but in either case they tell actors which action is appropriate in response to a specific stimuli, request, or demand. This kind of routinization is, after all, precisely what bureaucracies are supposed to exhibit—it is what makes them effective and competent in performing complex social tasks. However, the presence of such rules also compromises the extent to which means-ends rationality drives organizational behavior. Rules and routines may come to obscure overall missions and larger social goals. They may create "ritualized behavior" in bureaucrats and construct a very parochial normative environment within the organization whose connection to the larger social environment is tenuous at best.[48]

Second, bureaucracies specialize and compartmentalize. They create a division of labor on the logic that because individuals have only so much time, knowledge, and expertise, specialization will allow the organization to emulate a rational decision-making process.[49] Again, this is one of the virtues of bureaucracy in that it provides a way of overcoming the limitations of individual rationality and knowledge by embedding those individuals in a structure that takes advantage of their competencies without having to rely on their weaknesses. However, it, too, has some negative consequences. Just as rules can eclipse goals, concentrated expertise and specialization can (and perhaps must) limit bureaucrats' field of vision and create subcultures within bureaucracy that are distinct from those of the larger environment. . . .

Once in place, an organization's culture, understood as the rules, rituals, and beliefs that are embedded in the organization (and its subunits), has important consequences for the way individuals who inhabit that organization make sense of the world. It provides interpretive frames that individuals use to generate meaning.[50] This is more than just bounded rationality; in this view, actors' rationality itself, the very means and ends that they value, are shaped by the organizational culture.[51] Divisions and subunits within the organization may develop their own cognitive frameworks that are consistent with but still distinct from the larger organization, further complicating this process.

All organizations have their own culture (or cultures) that shape their behavior. The effects of bureaucratic culture, however, need not be dysfunctional. Indeed, specific organizational cultures may be valued and actively promoted as a source of "good" behavior, as students of business culture know very well. Organizational culture is tied to "good" and "bad" behavior, alike, and the effects of organizational culture on behavior are an empirical question to be researched.

To further such research, we draw from studies in sociology and anthropology to explore five mechanisms by which bureaucratic culture can breed pathologies in IOs: the irrationality of rationalization, universalism, normalization of deviance, organizational insulation, and cultural contestation. . . .

Irrationality of Rationalization

Weber recognized that the "rationalization" processes at which bureaucracies excelled could be taken to extremes and ultimately become irrational if the rules and procedures that enabled bureaucracies to do their jobs became ends in themselves. Rather than designing the most appropriate and efficient rules and procedures to accomplish their missions, bureaucracies often tailor their missions to fit the existing, well-known, and comfortable rulebook.[52] Thus, means (rules and procedures) may become so embedded and powerful that they determine ends and the way the organization defines its goals. One observer of the World Bank noted how, at an operational level, the bank did not decide on development goals and collect data necessary to pursue them. Rather, it continued to use existing data-collection procedures and formulated goals and development plans from those data alone.[53] UN-mandated elections may be another instance where means become ends in themselves. The "end" pursued in the many troubled states where the UN has been involved in reconstruction is presumably some kind of peaceful, stable, just government. Toward that end, the UN has developed a repertoire of instruments and responses that are largely intended to promote something akin to a democratic government. Among those various repertoires, elections have become privileged as a measure of "success" and a signal of an operation's successful conclusion. Consequently, UN (and other IO) officials have conducted elections even when evidence suggests that such elections are either premature or perhaps even counterproductive (frequently acknowledged as much by state and UN officials).[54] In places like Bosnia elections have ratified precisely the outcome the UN and outside powers had intervened to prevent—ethnic cleansing—and in places like Africa elections are criticized as exacerbating the very ethnic tensions they were ostensibly designed to quell. . . .

Bureaucratic Universalism

A second source of pathology in IOs derives from the fact that bureaucracies "orchestrate numerous local contexts at once."[55] Bureaucrats necessarily flatten diversity because they are supposed to generate universal rules and categories that are, by design, inattentive to contextual and particularistic concerns. Part of the justification for this, of course, is the bureaucratic view that technical knowledge is transferable across circumstances. Sometimes this is a good assumption, but not always; when particular circumstances are not appropriate to the generalized knowledge being applied, the results can be disastrous.[56]

Many critics of the IMF's handling of the Asian financial crises have argued that the IMF inappropriately applied a standardized formula of budget cuts plus high interest rates to combat rapid currency depreciation without appreciating the unique and local causes of this depreciation. These governments were not profligate spenders, and austerity policies did little to reassure investors, yet the IMF prescribed roughly the same remedy that it had in Latin America. The result, by the IMF's later admission, was to make matters worse.[57]

Similarly, many of those who worked in peacekeeping operations in Cambodia were transferred to peacekeeping operations in Bosnia or Somalia on the assumption that the knowledge gained in one location would be applicable to others. Although some technical skills can be transferred across contexts, not all knowledge and organizational lessons derived from one context are appropriate elsewhere. The UN has a longstanding commitment to neutrality, which operationally translates into the view that the UN should avoid the use of force and the appearance of partiality. This knowledge was employed with some success by UN envoy Yasushi Akashi in Cambodia. After his stint in Cambodia, he became the UN Special Representative in Yugoslavia. As many critics of Akashi have argued, however, his commitment to these rules, combined with his failure to recognize that Bosnia was substantially different from Cambodia, led him to fail to use force to defend the safe havens when it was appropriate and likely to be effective.[58]

Normalization of Deviance

. . . Bureaucracies establish rules to provide a predictable response to environmental stimuli in ways that safeguard against decisions that might lead to accidents and faulty decisions. At times, however, bureaucracies make small, calculated deviations from established rules because of new environmental or institutional developments, explicitly calculating that bending the rules in this instance does not create excessive risk of policy failure. Over time, these exceptions can become the rule—they become normal, not exceptions at all: they can become institutionalized to the point where deviance is "normalized." The result of this process is that what at time t_1 might be weighed seriously and debated as a potentially unacceptable risk or dangerous procedure comes to be treated as normal at time t_n. Indeed, because of staff turnover, those making decisions at a later point in time might be unaware that the now-routine behavior was ever viewed as risky or dangerous.

We are unaware of any studies that have examined this normalization of deviance in IO decision making, though one example of deviance normalization comes to mind. Before 1980 the UNHCR viewed repatriation as only one of three durable solutions to refugee crises (the others being third-country asylum and host-country integration). In its view, repatriation had to be both safe and voluntary because forced repatriation violates the international legal principle of nonrefoulement, which is the cornerstone of international refugee law and codified in the UNHCR's convention. Prior to 1980, UNHCR's discussions of repatriation emphasized that the principles of safety and voluntariness must be safeguarded at all costs. According to many commentators, however, the UNHCR has steadily lowered the barriers to repatriation over the years. Evidence for this can be found in international protection manuals, the UNHCR Executive Committee resolutions, and discourse that now weighs repatriation and the principle of nonrefoulement against other goals such a peace building. . . .

Insulation

Organizations vary greatly in the degree to which they receive and process feedback from their environment about performance. Those insulated from such feedback often develop internal cultures and worldviews that do not promote the goals and expectations of those outside the organization who created it and whom it serves. These distinctive worldviews can create the conditions for pathological behavior when parochial classification and categorization schemes come to define reality—how bureaucrats understand the world—such that they routinely ignore information that is essential to the accomplishment of their goals.[59]

Two causes of insulation seem particularly applicable to IOs. The first is professionalism. Professional training does more than impart technical knowledge. It actively seeks to shape the normative orientation and worldviews of those who are trained. Doctors are trained to value life above all else, soldiers are trained to sacrifice life for certain strategic objectives, and economists are trained to value efficiency. Bureaucracies, by their nature, concentrate professionals inside organizations, and concentrations of people with the same expertise or professional training can create an organizational worldview distinct from the larger environment. Second, organizations for whom "successful performance" is difficult to measure—that is, they are valued for what they represent rather than for what they do and do not "compete" with other organizations on the basis of output—are protected from selection and performance pressures that economistic models simply assume will operate. The absence of a competitive environment that selects out inefficient practices coupled with already existing tendencies toward institutionalization of rules and procedures insulates the organization from feedback and increases the likelihood of pathologies.

IOs vary greatly in the degree to which the professionals they recruit have distinctive worldviews and the degree to which they face competitive pressures, but it is clearly the case that these factors insulate some IOs to some degree and in so doing create a tendency toward pathology. The World Bank, for example, has been dominated for much of its history by economists, which, at least in part, has contributed to many critiques of the bank's policies. In one such critique James Ferguson opens his study of the World Bank's activity in Lesotho by comparing the bank's introductory description of Lesotho in its report on that country to facts on the ground; he shows how the bank "creates" a world that has little resemblance to what historians, geographers, or demographers see on the ground in Lesotho but is uniquely suited to the bank's organizational abilities and presents precisely the problems the bank knows how to solve. This is not simply "staggeringly bad scholarship," Ferguson argues, but a way of making the world intelligible and meaningful from a particular perspective—the World Bank's.[60] The problem, however, is that this different worldview translates into a record of development failures, which Ferguson explores in detail.

Insulation contributes to and is caused by another well-known feature of organizations—the absence of effective feedback loops that allow the organization to evaluate its efforts and use new information to correct established routines. . . . Thus Jarat Chopra observes that the lessons-learned conferences that were established after Somalia were structurally arranged so that no information could come out that would blemish the UN's record. Such attempts at face saving, Chopra cautions, make it more likely that these maladies will go uncorrected.[61] Sometimes new evaluative criteria are hoisted in order to demonstrate that the failures were not really failures but successes.

Cultural Contestation

Organizational coherence is an accomplishment rather than a given. Organizational control within a putative hierarchy is always incomplete, creating pockets of autonomy and political battles within the bureaucracy.[62] . . . Consequently, different constituencies representing different normative views will suggest different tasks and goals for the organization, resulting in a clash of competing perspectives that generates pathological tendencies.

The existence of cultural contestation might be particularly true of high-profile and expansive IOs like the UN that have vague missions, broad and politicized constituencies, and lots of divisions that are developed over time and in response to new environmental demands. Arguably a number of the more spectacular debacles in recent UN peacekeeping operations might be interpreted as the product of these contradictions.

Consider the conflict between the UN's humanitarian missions and the value it places on impartiality and neutrality. Within the organization there are many who view impartiality as a core constitutive principle of UN action. On the one hand, the UN's moral standing, its authority, and its ability to persuade all rest on this principle. On the other hand, the principles of humanitarianism require the UN to give aid to those in need—values that are particularly strong in a number of UN relief and humanitarian agencies. These two norms of neutrality and humanitarian assistance, and the parts of the bureaucracy most devoted to them, come into direct conflict in those situations where providing humanitarian relief might jeopardize the UN's vaunted principle of neutrality. Bosnia is the classic case in point. On the one hand, the "all necessary means" provision of Security Council resolutions gave the UN authority to deliver humanitarian aid and protect civilians in the safe havens. On the other hand, the UN abstained from "taking sides" because of the fear that such actions would compromise its neutrality and future effectiveness. The result of these conflicts was a string of contradictory policies that failed to provide adequately for the UN's expanding humanitarian charges.[63] According to Shashi Tharoor, a UN official intimately involved in these decisions, "It is extremely difficult to make war and peace with the same people on the same territory at the same time."[64] . . .

. . . Cultural contestation within an organization frequently originates from and remains linked to normative contradictions in the larger environment. Demands from states can be extremely important determinants of IO behavior and may override internal cultural dynamics, but they can also set them in place if conflicting state demands result in the creation of organizational structures or missions that are prone to pathology. As we begin to explore dysfunctional and pathological behavior, we must bear in mind the complex relationship between different causal pathways, remaining closely attentive to both the internal organizational dynamics and the IO's environment. . . .

NOTES

1. See Finnemore 1993 and 1996b; and McNeely 1995.
2. See Mearsheimer 1994; and Helms 1996.
3. See Commission on Global Governance 1995; Jacobson 1979, 1; and Doyle 1997.
4. See Powell and DiMaggio 1991, chap. 1; and Grandori 1993.
5. See Williamson 1975 and 1985; and Coase 1937.

6. See DiMaggio and Powell 1983; Scott 1992; Meyer and Scott 1992, 1–5; Powell and DiMaggio 1991; Weber 1994; and Finnemore 1996a.

7. Note that empirically this is not the case; most IOs now are created by other IOs. See Shanks, Jacobson, and Kaplan 1996.

8. See Pollack 1997; Ross 1995; and Zabusky 1995; but see Moravcsik 1999.

9. See Ascher 1983; Ayres 1983; Ferguson 1990; Escobar 1995; Wade 1996; Nelson 1995; and Finnemore 1996a.

10. Joint Evaluation of Emergency Assistance to Rwanda 1996.

11. See Pollack 1997; Lake 1996; Vaubel 1991; and Dillon, Ilgen, and Willett 1991.

12. See Pratt and Zeckhauser 1985; and Kiewit and McCubbins 1991.

13. See Ascher 1983; Zabusky 1995; Barnett 1997b; and Wade 1996.

14. See Weber 1978, 196–97; Weber 1947; Mouzelis 1967; and Beetham 1985 and 1996.

15. See Gerth and Mills 1978, 233; Beetham 1985, 74–75; and Schaar 1984, 120.

16. We thank John Boli for this insight. Also see Fisher 1997; Ferguson 1990; Shore and Wright 1997; and Burley and Mattli 1993.

17. Gerth and Mills 1978, 199.

18. See Weber [1930] 1978, 181–83; and Clegg 1994a, 152–55.

19. See David Rieff, "The Institution that Saw No Evil," *The New Republic,* 12 February 1996, 19–24; and Barnett 1997b.

20. See Wade 1996; Ayres 1983; Ascher 1983; Finnemore 1996b; and Nelson 1995.

21. See Malkki 1996; Hartigan 1992; and Harrell-Bond 1989.

22. See Foucault 1977, 27; and Clegg 1994b, 156–59. International relations theory typically disregards the negative side of the knowledge and power equation. For an example, see Haas 1992.

23. Handelman 1995, 280. See also Starr 1992; and Wright 1994, 22.

24. See Weiss and Pasic 1997; Goodwin-Gill 1996; and Anonymous 1997.

25. Gran 1986.

26. See Williams 1996; Clegg 1994b; Bourdieu 1994; Carr [1939] 1964; and Keeley 1990.

27. Blumer 1969.

28. See Gupta 1998; Escobar 1995; Cooper and Packard 1998; Gran 1986; Ferguson 1990; and Wade 1996.

29. See Matthews 1989; and Krause and Williams 1996.

30. See UN Development Program 1994; and Boutros-Ghali 1995.

31. See Escobar 1995; Ferguson 1990; and Feldstein 1998.

32. World Conference on Human Rights 1993.

33. See Katzenstein 1996; Finnemore 1996b; and Legro 1997.

34. See McNeely 1995; and Jackson 1993.

35. Call and Barnett forthcoming.

36. Wade 1996.

37. Boutros-Ghali 1995 and 1996a,b.

38. Keen and Hendrie, however, suggest that nongovernmental organizations and IOs can be the long-term beneficiaries of intervention. See Keen 1994; and Hendrie 1997.

39. March and Olsen 1989, chap. 5.

40. Two exceptions are Gaflaroti 1991; and Snidal 1996.

41. Snidal 1996.

42. Karl Deutsch used the concept of pathology in a way similar to our usage. We thank Hayward Alker for this point. Deutsch 1963, 170.

43. See Allison 1971, 144; and Bendor and Hammond 1992.

44. See Meyer and Rowan 1977; Meyer and Zucker 1989; Weber 1994; and Finnemore 1996a.

45. Lipson 1999.

46. McNeely 1995.
47. See Vaughan 1996; and Lipartito 1995.
48. See March and Olsen 1989, 21–27; and Meyer and Rowan 1977.
49. See March and Olsen 1989, 26–27; and March 1997.
50. See Starr 1992, 160; Douglas 1986; and Berger and Luckman 1966, chap. 1.
51. See Campbell 1998, 378; Alvesson 1996; Burrell and Morgan 1979; Dobbin 1994; and Immergut 1998, 14–19.
52. Beetham 1985, 76.
53. See Ferguson 1990; and Nelson 1995.
54. Paris 1997.
55. Heyman 1995, 262.
56. Haas 1990, chap. 3.
57. See Feldstein 1998; Radelet and Sachs 1999; and Kapur 1998.
58. Rieff 1996.
59. See Berger and Luckman 1967, chap. 1; Douglas 1986; Bruner 1990; March and Olsen 1989; and Starr 1992.
60. Ferguson 1990, 25–73.
61. Chopra 1996.
62. See Clegg 1994a, 30; Vaughan 1996, 64; and Martin 1992.
63. See Barnett 1997a; David Rieff, "We Hate You," *New Yorker,* 4 September 1995, 41–48; David Rieff, "The Institution That Saw No Evil," *The New Republic,* 12 February 1996, 19–24; and Rieff 1996.
64. Quoted in Weiss 1996, 85; also see Rieff 1996, 166, 170, 193.

REFERENCES

Alger, Chadwick. 1963. United Nations Participation as a Learning Process. *Public Opinion Quarterly* 27 (3):411–26.

Allison, Graham. 1971. *Essence of Decision.* Boston: Little, Brown.

Alvesson, Mats. 1996. *Cultural Perspectives on Organizations.* New York: Cambridge University Press.

Amnesty International. 1997a. In Search of Safety: The Forcibly Displaced and Human Rights in Africa. AI Index, 20 June, AFR 01/05/97. Available from <www.amnesty.org/ailib/aipub/1997/10100597.htm>.

———. 1997b. Rwanda: Human Rights Overlooked in Mass Repatriation. Available from <www.amnesty.org/ailib/aipub/1997/AFR/147002797.htm>.

Anonymous. 1997. The UNHCR Note on International Protection You Won't See. *International Journal of Refugee Law* 9 (2):267–73.

Arendt, Hannah. 1977. *Eichmann in Jerusalem: A Report on the Banality of Evil.* New York: Penguin.

Ascher, William. 1983. New Development Approaches and the Adaptability of International Agencies: The Case of the World Bank. *International Organization* 37 (3):415–39.

Ayres, Robert L. 1983. *Banking on the Poor: The World Bank and World Poverty.* Cambridge, Mass.: MIT Press.

Baldwin, David, ed. 1993. *Neorealism and Neoliberalism.* New York: Columbia University Press.

Barnett, Michael. 1997a. The Politics of Indifference at the United Nations and Genocide in Rwanda and Bosnia. In *This Time We Knew: Western Responses to Genocide in Bosnia,* edited by Thomas Cushman and Stjepan Mestrovic, 128–62. New York: New York University Press.

————. 1997b. The UN Security Council, Indifference, and Genocide in Rwanda. *Cultural Anthropology* 12 (4):551–78.

Beetham, David. 1985. *Max Weber and the Theory of Modern Politics.* New York: Polity.

————. 1996. *Bureaucracy.* 2d ed. Minneapolis: University of Minnesota Press.

Bendor, Jonathan, and Thomas Hammond. 1992. Rethinking Allison's Models. *American Political Science Review* 82 (2):301–22.

Berger, Peter, and Thomas Luckmann. 1966. *The Social Construction of Reality.* New York: Doubleday.

Blumer, Herbert. 1969. *Symbolic Interactionism: Perspective and Method.* Englewood Cliffs, N.J. Prentice-Hall.

Bourdieu, Pierre. 1994. On Symbolic Power. In *Language and Symbolic Power,* edited by Pierre Bourdieu, 163–70. Chicago: University of Chicago Press.

Boutros-Ghali, Boutros. 1995. *Agenda for Peace.* 2d ed. New York: UN Press.

————. 1996a. Global Leadership After the Cold War. *Foreign Affairs* 75:86–98.

————. 1996b. *Agenda for Democratization.* New York: UN Press.

Bruner, Jerome. 1990. *Acts of Meaning.* Cambridge, Mass.: Harvard University Press.

Burley, Anne-Marie, and Walter Mattli. 1993. Europe Before the Court: A Political Theory of Integration. *International Organization* 47 (1):41–76.

Burrell, Gibson, and Gareth Morgan. 1979. *Sociological Paradigms and Organizational Analysis.* London: Heinemman.

Call, Chuck, and Michael Barnett. Forthcoming. Looking for a Few Good Cops: Peacekeeping, Peace-building, and U.N. Civilian Police. *International Peacekeeping.*

Campbell, John. 1998. Institutional Analysis and the Role of Ideas in Political Economy. *Theory and Society* 27:377–409.

Carr, Edward H. [1939] 1964. *The Twenty Year's Crisis.* New York: Harper Torchbooks.

Chimni, B. 1993. The Meaning of Words and the Role of UNHCR in Voluntary Repatriation. *International Journal of Refugee Law* 5 (3):442–60.

Chopra, Jarat. 1996. Fighting for Truth at the UN. *Crosslines Global Report,* 26 November, 7–9.

Chopra, Jarat, Age Eknes, and Toralv Nordbo. 1995. *Fighting for Hope in Somalia.* Oslo: NUPI.

Claude, Inis L., Jr. 1966. Collective Legitimization as a Political Function of the United Nations. *International Organization* 20 (3):337–67.

Clegg, Stewart, 1994a. Power and Institutions in the Theory of Organizations. In *Toward a New Theory of Organizations,* edited by John Hassard and Martin Parker, 24–49. New York: Routledge.

————. 1994b. Weber and Foucault: Social Theory for the Study of Organizations. *Organization* 1 (1): 149–78.

Coase, Ronald. 1937. The Nature of the Firm. *Economica* 4 (November):386–405.

Commission on Global Governance. 1995. *Our Global Neighborhood.* New York: Oxford University Press.

Cooper, Frederick, and Randy Packard, eds. 1998. *International Development and the Social Sciences.* Berkeley: University of California Press.

Cox, Robert. 1980. The Crisis of World Order and the Problem of International Organization in the 1980s. *International Journal* 35 (2):370–95.

————. 1992. Multilateralism and World Order. *Review of International Studies* 18 (2):161–80.

————. 1996. The Executive Head: An Essay on Leadership in International Organization. In *Approaches to World Order,* edited by Robert Cox, 317–48. New York: Cambridge University Press.

Cox, Robert, and Harold Jacobson. 1977. Decision Making. *International Social Science Journal* 29 (1):115–33.

Cox, Robert, Harold Jacobson, Gerard Curzon. Victoria Curzon, Joseph Nye, Lawrence Scheinman, James Sewell, and Susan Strange. 1974. *The Anatomy of Influence: Decision Making in International Organization.* New Haven, Conn.: Yale University Press.

Deutsch, Karl. 1963. *The Nerves of Government: Models of Political Communication and Control.* Glencoe, Ill.: Free Press.

Dillon, Patricia, Thomas Ilgen, and Thomas Willett. 1991. Approaches to the Study of International Organizations: Major Paradigms in Economics and Political Science. In *The Political Economy of International Organizations: A Public Choice Approach,* edited by Ronald Vaubel and Thomas Willett, 79–99. Boulder, Colo.: Westview Press.

DiMaggio, Paul J., and Walter W. Powell. 1983. The Iron Cage Revisited: Institutional Isomorphism and Collective Rationality in Organizational Fields. *American Sociological Review* 48:147–60.

Dobbin, Frank. 1994. Cultural Models of Organization: The Social Construction of Rational Organizing Principles. In *The Sociology of Culture,* edited by Diana Crane, 117–42. Boston: Basil Blackwell.

Douglas, Mary. 1986. *How Institutions Think.* Syracuse, N.Y.: Syracuse University Press.

Doyle, Michael. 1997. *Ways of War and Peace.* New York: Norton.

Escobar, Arturo. 1995. *Encountering Development: The Making and Unmaking of the Third World.* Princeton, N.J.: Princeton University Press.

Featherston, A. B. 1995. Habitus in Cooperating for Peace: A Critique of Peacekeeping. In *The New Agenda for Global Security: Cooperating for Peace and Beyond,* edited by Stephanie Lawson, 101–18. St. Leonards, Australia: Unwin and Hyman.

Feld, Werner J., and Robert S. Jordan, with Leon Hurwitz. 1988. *International Organizations: A Comparative Approach.* 2d ed. New York: Praeger.

Feldstein, Martin. 1998. Refocusing the IMF. *Foreign Affairs* 77 (2):20–33.

Ferguson, James. 1990. *The Anti-Politics Machine: "Development," Depoliticization, and Bureaucratic Domination in Lesotho.* New York: Cambridge University Press.

Finnemore, Martha. 1993. International Organizations as Teachers of Norms: The United Nations Educational, Scientific, and Cultural Organization and Science Policy. *International Organization* 47:565–97.

———. 1996a. Norms, Culture, and World Politics: Insights from Sociology's Institutionalism. *International Organization* 50 (2):325–47.

———. 1996b. *National Interests in International Society.* Ithaca, N.Y.: Cornell University Press.

Fisher, William. 1997. Doing Good? The Politics and Antipolitics of NGO Practices. *Annual Review of Anthropology* 26:439–64.

Foucault, Michel. 1977. *Discipline and Punish.* New York: Vintage Press.

Gallaroti, Guilio. 1991. The Limits of International Organization. *International Organization* 45 (2):183–220.

Gerth, H. H., and C. Wright Mills. 1978. *From Max Weber: Essays in Sociology.* New York: Oxford University Press.

Goodwin-Gill, Guy. 1996. *Refugee in International Law.* New York: Oxford Clarendon.

Gran, Guy. 1986. Beyond African Famines: Whose Knowledge Matters? *Alternatives* 11:275–96.

Grandori, Anna. 1993. Notes on the Use of Power and Efficiency Constructs in the Economics and Sociology of Organizations. In *Interdisciplinary Perspectives on Organizational Studies,* edited by S. Lindenberg and H. Schreuder, 61–78. New York: Pergamon.

Gupta, Akhil. 1998. *Postcolonial Developments: Agriculture in the Making of Modern India.* Durham, N.C.: Duke University Press.

Haas, Ernst. 1990. *When Knowledge Is Power.* Berkeley: University of California Press.

Haas, Ernst, and Peter Haas. 1995. Learning to Learn: Improving International Governance. *Global Governance* 1 (3):255–85.

Haas, Peter, ed. 1992. Epistemic Communities. *International Organization* 46 (1). Special issue.

Handelman, Don. 1995. Comment. *Current Anthropology* 36 (2):280–81.

Harrell-Bond, Barbara. 1989. Repatriation: Under What Conditions Is It the Most Desirable Solution for Refugees? *African Studies Review* 32 (1):41–69.

Hartigan, Kevin. 1992. Matching Humanitarian Norms with Cold, Hard Interests: The Making of Refugee Policies in Mexico and Honduras, 1980–89. *International Organization* 46:709–30.

Helms, Jesse. 1996. Saving the UN. *Foreign Affairs* 75 (5):2–7.

Hendrie, Barbara. 1997. Knowledge and Power: A Critique of an International Relief Operation. *Disasters* 21 (1):57–76.

Heyman, Josiah McC. 1995. Putting Power in the Anthropology of Bureaucracy. *Current Anthropology* 36 (2):261–77.

Hirsch, John, and Robert Oakley. 1995. *Somalia and Operation Restore Hope: Reflections on Peacemaking and Peacekeeping.* Washington, D.C.: USIP Press.

Human Rights Watch. 1997. Uncertain Refuge: International Failures to Protect Refugees. Vol. 1, no. 9 (April).

Hurrell, Andrew, and Ngaire Woods. 1995. Globalisation and Inequality. *Millennium* 24 (3):447–70.

Immergut, Ellen. 1998. The Theoretical Core of the New Institutionalism. *Politics and Society* 26 (1): 5–34.

Jackson, Robert. 1993. The Weight of Ideas in Decolonization: Normative Change in International Relations. In *Ideas and Foreign Policy,* edited by Judith Goldstein and Robert O. Keohane, 111–38. Ithaca, N.Y.: Cornell University Press.

Jacobson, Harold. 1979. *Networks of Interdependence.* New York: Alfred A. Knopf.

Joint Evaluation of Emergency Assistance to Rwanda. 1996. *The International Response to Conflict and Genocide: Lessons from the Rwanda Experience.* 5 vols. Copenhagen: Steering Committee of the Joint Evaluation of Emergency Assistance to Rwanda.

Kapur, Devesh. 1998. The IMF: A Cure or a Curse? *Foreign Policy* 111:114–29.

Katzenstein, Peter J., ed. 1996. *The Culture of National Security: Identity and Norms in World Politics.* New York: Columbia University Press.

Keck, Margaret, and Kathryn Sikkink. 1998. *Activists Beyond Borders.* Ithaca, N.Y.: Cornell University Press.

Keeley, James. 1990. Toward a Foucauldian Analysis of International Regimes. *International Organization* 44 (1):83–105.

Keen, David. 1994. *The Benefits of Famine: A Political Economy of Famine and Relief in Southwestern Sudan, 1983–89.* Princeton, N.J.: Princeton University Press

Kennedy, David. 1986. International Refugee Protection. *Human Rights Quarterly* 8:1–9.

Keohane, Robert O. 1984. *After Hegemony.* Princeton, N.J.: Princeton University Press.

Kiewiet, D. Roderick, and Matthew McCubbins. 1991. *The Logic of Delegation.* Chicago: University of Chicago Press.

Krasner, Stephen D. 1991. Global Communications and National Power: Life on the Pareto Frontier. *World Politics* 43 (3):336–66.

———. 1983a. Regimes and the Limits of Realism: Regimes as Autonomous Variables. In *International Regimes,* edited by Stephen Krasner, 355–68. Ithaca, N.Y.: Cornell University Press.

Krasner, Stephen D., ed. 1983b. *International Regimes.* Ithaca, N.Y.: Cornell University Press.

Krause, Keith, and Michael Williams. 1996. Broadening the Agenda of Security Studies: Politics and Methods. *Mershon International Studies Review* 40 (2):229–54.

Lake, David. 1996. Anarchy, Hierarchy, and the Variety of International Relations. *International Organization* 50 (1):1–34.

Lawyers Committee for Human Rights. 1991. *General Principles Relating to the Promotion of Refugee Repatriation.* New York: Lawyers Committee for Human Rights.

Legro, Jeffrey. 1997. Which Norms Matter? Revisiting the "Failure" of Internationalism. *International Organization* 51 (1):31–64.

Lipartito, Kenneth. 1995. Culture and the Practice of Business History. *Business and Economic History* 24 (2):1–41.

Lipson, Michael. 1999. International Cooperation on Export Controls: Nonproliferation, Globalization, and Multilateralism. Ph.D. diss., University of Wisconsin, Madison.

Malkki, Liisa. 1996. Speechless Emissaries: Refugees, Humanitarianism, and Dehistoricization. *Cultural Anthropology* 11 (3):377–404.

March, James. 1988. *Decisions and Organizations.* Boston: Basil Blackwell.

———. 1997. Understanding How Decisions Happen in Organizations. In *Organizational Decision Making,* edited by Z. Shapira, 9–33. New York: Cambridge University Press.

March, James, and Johan P. Olsen. 1989. *Rediscovering Institutions: The Organizational Basis of Politics.* New York: Free Press.

Martin, Joan. 1992. *Cultures in Organizations: Three Perspectives.* New York: Oxford University Press.

Matthews, Jessica Tuchman. 1989. Redefining Security. *Foreign Affairs* 68 (2):162–77.

McNeely, Connie. 1995. *Constructing the Nation-State: International Organization and Prescriptive Action.* Westport, Conn.: Greenwood Press.

Mearsheimer, John. 1994. The False Promise of International Institutions. *International Security* 19 (3):5–49.

Meyer, John W., and Brian Rowan. 1977. Institutionalized Organizations: Formal Structure as Myth and Ceremony. *American Journal of Sociology* 83:340–63.

Meyer, John W., and W. Richard Scott. 1992. *Organizational Environments: Ritual and Rationality.* Newbury Park, Calif.: Sage.

Meyer, Marshall, and Lynne Zucker. 1989. *Permanently Failing Organizations.* Newbury Park: Sage Press.

Miller, Gary, and Terry M. Moe. 1983. Bureaucrats, Legislators, and the Size of Government. *American Political Science Review* 77 (June):297–322.

Moe, Terry M. 1984. The New Economics of Organization. *American Journal of Political Science* 28:739–77.

Moravcsik, Andrew. 1997. Taking Preferences Seriously: Liberal Theory and International Politics. *International Organization* 51 (4):513–54.

———. 1999. A New Statecraft? Supranational Entrepreneurs and International Cooperation. *International Organization* 53 (2):267–306.

Mouzelis, Nicos. 1967. *Organization and Bureaucracy.* Chicago: Aldine.

Murphy, Craig. 1994. *International Organizations and Industrial Change.* New York: Oxford University Press.

Nelson, Paul. 1995. *The World Bank and Non-Governmental Organizations.* New York: St. Martin's Press.

Ness, Gayl, and Steven Brechin. 1988. Bridging the Gap: International Organizations as Organizations. *International Organization* 42 (2):245–73.

Niskanen, William A. 1971. *Bureaucracy and Representative Government.* Chicago: Aldine.

Paris, Roland. 1997. Peacebuilding and the Limits of Liberal Internationalism. *International Security* 22 (2):54–89.

Perry, William. 1996. Defense in an Age of Hope. *Foreign Affairs* 75 (6):64–79.

Pollack, Mark. 1997. Delegation, Agency, and Agenda-Setting in the European Community. *International Organization* 51 (1):99–134.

Powell, Walter W., and Paul J. DiMaggio, eds. 1991. *The New Institutionalism in Organizational Analysis*. Chicago: University of Chicago Press.

Pratt, John, and Richard J. Zeckhauser. 1985. *Principals and Agents: The Structure of Business*. Boston: Harvard Business School Press.

Price, Richard. 1997. *The Chemical Weapons Taboo*. Ithaca, N.Y.: Cornell University Press.

Radelet, Steven, and Jeffrey Sach. 1999. What Have We Learned, So Far, From the Asian Financial Crisis? Harvard Institute for International Development, 4 January. Available from <www.hiid.harvard.edu/pub/other/aea122.pdf>.

Rieff, David. 1996. *Slaughterhouse*. New York: Simon and Schuster.

Rittberger, Volker, ed. 1993. *Regime Theory and International Relations*. Oxford: Clarendon Press.

Ross, George. 1995. *Jacques Delors and European Integration*. New York: Oxford University Press.

Ruggie, John. 1996. *Winning the Peace*. New York: Columbia University Press.

———. 1998. What Makes the World Hang Together. *International Organization* 52 (3):855–86.

Sandholtz, Wayne. 1993. Choosing Union: Monetary Politics and Maastricht. *International Organization* 47:1–40.

Sagan, Scott. 1993. *The Limits of Safety: Organizations, Accidents, and Nuclear Weapons*. Princeton, N.J.: Princeton University Press.

Schaar, John. 1984. Legitimacy in the Modern State. In *Legitimacy and the State*, edited by William Connolly, 104–33. Oxford: Basil Blackwell.

Schien, Edgar. 1996. Culture: The Missing Concept in Organization Studies. *Administrative Studies Quarterly* 41:229–40.

Scott, W. Richard. 1992. *Organizations: Rational, Natural, and Open Systems*. 3d ed. Englewood Cliffs, N.J.: Prentice-Hall.

Shanks, Cheryl, Harold K. Jacobson, and Jeffrey H. Kaplan. 1996. Inertia and Change in the Constellation of Intergovernmental Organizations, 1981–1992. *International Organization* 50 (4):593–627.

Shapira, Zur, ed. 1997. *Organizational Decision*. New York: Cambridge University Press.

Shore, Cris, and Susan Wright. 1997. Policy: A New Field of Anthropology. In *Anthropology of Policy: Critical Perspectives on Governance and Power*, edited by Cris Shore and Susan Wright, 3–41. New York: Routledge Press.

Sigelman, Lee. 1986. The Bureaucratic Budget Maximizer: An Assumption Examined. *Public Budgeting and Finance* (spring):50–59.

Snidal, Duncan. 1996. Political Economy and International Institutions. *International Review of Law and Economics* 16:121–37.

Starr, Paul. 1992. Social Categories and Claims in the Liberal State. In *How Classification Works: Nelson Goodman Among the Social Sciences*, edited by Mary Douglas and David Hull, 154–79. Edinburgh: Edinburgh University Press.

Strange, Susan. 1997. *The Retreat of the State*. New York: Cambridge University Press.

Thomas, Daniel C. Forthcoming. *The Helsinki Effect: International Norms, Human Rights, and Demise of Communism*. Princeton, N.J.: Princeton University Press.

UN Development Program. 1994. *Human Development Report 1994*. New York: Oxford University Press.

UN Peacekeeping Missions. 1994. The Lessons from Cambodia. Asia Pacific Issues, Analysis from the East-West Center, No. 11, March.

Vaubel, Roland. 1991. A Public Choice View of International Organization. In *The Political Economy of International Organizations,* edited by Roland Vaubel and Thomas Willett, 27–45. Boulder, Colo.: Westview Press.

Vaughan, Diane. 1996. *The Challenger Launch Decision. Chicago:* University of Chicago Press.

Wade, Robert. 1996. Japan, the World Bank, and the Art of Paradigm Maintenance: The East Asian Miracle in Political Perspective. *New Left Review* 217:3–36.

Walkup, Mark. 1997. Policy Dysfunction in Humanitarian Organizations: The Role of Coping Strategies, Institutions, and Organizational Culture. *Journal of Refugee Studies* 10 (1):37–60.

Waltz, Kenneth. 1979. *Theory of International Politics.* Reading, Mass.: Addison-Wesley.

Wapner, Paul. 1996. *Environmental Activism and World Civic Politics.* Albany: State University of New York Press.

Weber, Max. 1947. *Theory of Social and Economic Organization.* New York: Oxford University Press.

———. [1930] 1968. *The Protestant Ethic and the Spirit of Capitalism.* New York: Routledge.

———. 1978. Bureaucracy. In *From Max Weber: Essays in Sociology,* edited by H. H. Gerth and C. Wright Mills, 196–44. New York: Oxford.

Weber, Steven. Origins of the European Bank for Reconstruction and *Development. International Organization* 48(1):1–38.

Weingast, Barry R., and Mark Moran. 1983. Bureaucratic Discretion or Congressional Control: Regulatory *Policymaking* by the Federal Trade Commission. *Journal of Political Economy* 91 (October):765–800.

Weiss, Thomas. 1996. Collective Spinelessness: U.N. Actions in the Former Yugoslavia. In *The World and Yugoslavia's Wars,* edited by Richard Ullman, 59–96. New York: Council on Foreign Relations Press.

Weiss, Tom, and Amir Pasic, 1997. Reinventing UNHCR: Enterprising Humanitarians in the Former Yugoslavia, 1991–95. *Global Governance* 3 (1):41–58.

Wendt, Alexander. 1995. Constructing International Politics. *International Security* 20 (1):71–81.

———. 1998. Constitution and Causation in International Relations. *Review of International Studies* 24 (4):101–17. Special issue.

Williams, Michael. 1996. Hobbes and International Relations: A Reconsideration. *International Organization* 50 (2):213–37.

Williamson, Oliver. 1975. *Markets and Hierarchies, Analysis and Antitrust Implications: A Study in the Economics of Internal Organization.* New York: Free Press.

———. 1985. *The Economic Institutions of Capitalism: Firms, Markets, Relational Contracting.* New York: Free Press.

World Conference on Human Rights. 1993. Vienna Declaration on Human Rights, adopted 14–25 June. UN Document A/CONF.157/24 (Part 1), 20; A/CONF.157/23 DPI/1394/Rev.1 DPI/1676 (95.1.21), 448; DPI/1707 ST/HR/2/Rev.4, 383.

Wright, Susan. 1994. "Culture" in Anthropology and Organizational Studies. In *Anthropology of Organizations,* edited by Susan Wright, 1–31. New York: Routledge.

Zabusky, Stacia. 1995. *Launching Europe.* Princeton, N.J.: Princeton University Press.

Zieck, Marjoleine. 1997. *UNHCR and Voluntary Repatriation of Refugees: A Legal Analysis.* The Hague: Martinus Nijhoff.

CHAPTER 4

Functions of IOs: Legitimization, Norm Creation, and Sanctions

In Chapter 2, we discussed two perspectives on international organizations, one emphasizing instrumental rationality and another that is "reflective" in orientation. The first perspective views organizations as solutions to problems. The second views them as having transformative capacities as well, influencing the preferences of actors and the nature of the problem for which a solution is sought. In addition, the first approach focuses more on the "executive" element of international organizations—that is, on actions by the organization that are authorized by its charter, on the agreed-upon goals of the organization, and on issues of supervision. The second perspective, in contrast, stresses their legitimizing and "legislative" element. The latter approach stresses that organizations are less enforcers of rules and regulations than teachers and developers of practices that are deemed legitimate.

In fact, various researchers have argued that international organizations often play both an executive and a legislative role. Many institutions certify, based on submitted reports or inspections, that a state is in compliance with their rules. But it is also common for an international organization to develop solutions to problems that enhance its legitimacy. For example, the International Monetary Fund (IMF) requires borrowers to make their economic activities and records transparent. They can borrow additional funds only by agreeing to carry out the policy recommendations drawn up by the IMF. Determining whether countries have used funds in the way that the IMF intended is an executive function. But the policy recommendations that must be agreed to in order to obtain additional funds can have a legislative function. These policies can involve far reaching interventions into society that are legitimized and presented as quasi-technical choices based on an accepted economic theory.

This combination of executive and legislative roles is also apparent in cases where civil violence has erupted and UN "peacekeepers" are called in to calm the unrest and deliver emergency aid. Clearly, the peacekeepers are charged with ending (or at least containing) the violence and the UN often attempts to craft ways to better monitor the government's behavior. However, the UN's activities in these cases usually extend well beyond executive action, such as separating the contending parties and restoring order. In places like Cambodia and Kosovo, achieving these goals required the creation of viable and legitimate social and political structures—activities that have a legislative quality. As such, while the executive actions of international organizations tend to be more visible and attract more attention than legislative actions, various scholars have emphasized that both of them need to be considered.

The articles in this chapter address these issues. Inis Claude's contribution stresses the "collective legitimization" that occurs in universal international organizations, particularly the UN. For example, in the aftermath of World War II, various independence movements challenged colonial powers. Claude argues that the UN provided a forum for debate over decolonization and, later, a place where former colonies were included as new members of the international system. Furthermore, Claude maintains that the principle of self-determination was central to the collective legitimization of decolonization and independence movements in colonies. Because even most colonial powers accepted this principle, it was difficult for them to argue that those norms did not apply when independence from their rule was sought.

John Pace examines the human rights regime and the machinery that exists for influencing and monitoring the actions of governments. He traces how human rights protections have become increasingly institutionalized at the UN and indicates how monitoring created impulses for further legal developments. Both the abolition of apartheid and the expansion of the human rights agenda can be traced to discussion within the UN committees charged with monitoring the implementation of human rights instruments.

Daniel Drezner analyzes the link between interstate cooperation and the success of economic sanctions. Various observers have pointed out that economic sanctions are most effective when a wide variety of states impose them on a given target. To promote such cooperation, international organizations might be crucial. Drezner distinguishes two distinct problems associated with sanctions: (1) a bargaining problem, in which a primary sanctioner attempts to garner multilateral support for the imposition of sanctions; and (2) an enforcement problem, in which sanctioners have to be convinced not to stop imposing sanctions. Drezner's analysis shows that the relationship between interstate cooperation and the success of sanctions is more complicated than is generally recognized. For example, great powers run a significant risk during the bargaining stage of failing to marshal support for the imposition of effective sanctions. On the other hand, multilateral support does not seem to be a precondition for the imposition of effective sanctions. Nonetheless, international organizations do play a crucial role in buttressing cooperation among sanctioning states in the enforcement stage, by reducing the likelihood that sanctioners with only a weak preference for sanctions will cease imposing them. Deviations by such states often jeopardize the sanctioning coalition and can lead other sanctioners to weaken their efforts, undermining the effectiveness of sanctions.

Jarat Chopra's article addresses the complicated nature of peacekeeping and peacemaking missions. Central to his analysis is the strength of institutions within the country where these operations take place. Sometimes the problem is the combination of stable institutions and a powerful, oppressive regime (for example, the case of El Salvador). In other cases, however, state institutions are extremely weak (for example, Cambodia) or extragovernmental actors like warlords set the terms under which international organizations and nongovernmental organizations can operate (for example, Somalia). This raises various dilemmas, including how much to cooperate with the existing government or extragovernmental authorities and whether the experiences and the recipes developed in dealing with the last emergency are really applicable to the next one. The worst dilemmas, Chopra argues, arise when the peacekeepers become hostages. For example, during the Bosnian War, the creation of safe zones in Srebrenica could not be maintained and the "protectors" became onlookers and co-perpetrators of the actrocities committed there.

Collective Legitimization as a Political Function of the United Nations

INIS L. CLAUDE, JR.

As the United Nations has developed and as its role in world affairs has been adapted to the necessities and possibilities created and the limitations established by the changing realities of international politics, collective legitimization has emerged as one of its major political functions. By this I mean to suggest that the world organization has come to be regarded, and used, as a dispenser of politically significant approval and disapproval of the claims, policies, and actions of states, including, but going far beyond, their claims to status as independent members of the international system. In this essay I shall undertake to refine and elaborate this rough definition of collective legitimization and to discuss the performance of this role by the United Nations. It is essential in the beginning, however, to provide a foundation by offering some observations about the general problem of political legitimacy.

THE PROBLEM OF POLITICAL LEGITIMACY

. . . The urge for formally declared and generally acknowledged legitimacy approaches the status of a constant feature of political life. This urge requires that power be converted into authority, competence be supported by jurisdiction, and possession be validated as ownership. Conversely, if we look at it from the viewpoint of those who attack the status quo, it demands that the *de facto* be denied or deprived of *de jure* status, that the might of their antagonists not be sanctified as right. The principle is the same whether we are dealing with those who want the *is* to be recognized as the *ought* or with those who are setting out to convert their *ought* into a newly established *is*. Politics is not merely a struggle for power but also a contest over legitimacy, a competition in which the conferment or denial, the confirmation or revocation, of legitimacy is an important stake.

. . . Political realism is always easier to entertain in the abstract than in the particular instance. The American "realist" who likes the ring of the generalization is not likely to insist that it rings true in the case of a national hero like Abraham Lincoln or of a contemporary whose human characteristics are readily visible— Dwight D. Eisenhower or Lyndon B. Johnson, for instance. When one turns from generalization about rulers to consideration of individual cases, one is struck by the observation that the urge to possess and exercise power is usually qualified by concern about the justification of such possession and exercise. . . .

In part, this reflects the fact that power holders are burdened, like other human beings, by the necessity of satisfying their own consciences. By and large, they cannot comfortably regard themselves as usurpers or tyrants but require some basis for convincing themselves of the rightness of their position.

In a larger sense, however, this argument confirms rather than denies the power-oriented character of politics. Power and legitimacy are not antithetical, but complementary. The obverse of the legitimacy of power is the power of legitimacy; rulers seek legitimization not only to satisfy their consciences but also to buttress their positions. Legitimacy, in short, not only makes most rulers more comfortable but makes all rulers more effective—more secure in the possession of power and more successful in its exercise. Considerations of political morality combine with more hardheaded power considerations to explain the persistence of concern about legitimacy in the political sphere.

Two fundamental concepts figure prominently and persistently in the history of the problem of political legitimacy: law and morality. Lawyers tend simply to translate legitimacy as *legality,* capitalizing upon the derivation and literal meaning of the word. Similarly, moralists are inclined to claim a monopoly, treating political legitimacy as a problem of moral justification. Law and morality are both well-established and important legitimizing principles, but neither singly nor in combination do they exhaust the field. Each of them requires its own legitimization; the legitimacy of the positive law, or of the prevailing moral code, is sometimes the precise issue at stake in a political controversy. Moreover, relations between law and morality are variable. They sometimes reinforce each other, as when morality enjoins obedience to law or law codifies and sanctions the demands of morality. However, they may also come into conflict, as when morality condones disobedience to an unjust law or the law commands citizens to fulfill their public duty rather than follow the dictates of their private moral convictions. In the final analysis, the problem of legitimacy has a political dimension that goes beyond its legal and moral aspects. Judges and priests and philosophers usually make themselves heard, but they do not necessarily have the last word; the process of legitimization is ultimately a political phenomenon, a crystallization of judgment that may be influenced but is unlikely to be wholly determined by legal norms and moral principles.

While different principles of legitimacy and agents of legitimization may be simultaneously operative within a given political unit and among the constituent units of the global political system, there is nevertheless a tendency for a single concept of legitimacy to become generally dominant in a particular era, to achieve widespread acceptance as the decisive standard. Indeed, the existence of such a consensus may be regarded as the essential characteristic of a cohesive and stable political system at either the national or the international level. Like most fashions, fashions in legitimization change from time to time, and the crucial periods in political history are those transitional years of conflict between old and new concepts of legitimacy, the historical interstices between the initial challenge to the established concept and the general acceptance of its replacement. Thus, the era of modern European politics was ushered in by the substitution of the Voice of the People for the Voice of God (a change thinly concealed by the myth that the Voice of the People *is* the Voice of God) as the determinant of political legitimacy. The democratic principle has achieved widespread acceptance as the criterion of legitimate government within the state, however far short of general applicability it may have fallen as an operative political principle; the democratic pretensions of undemocratic regimes do not detract from, but lend support to, the proposition that popular consent is broadly acknowledged as the legitimizing principle in contemporary political life. The modern era has also seen the establishment of national self-determination as the basis of legitimate statehood, and the global extension of the reach of this legitimizing principle has been one of the most significant developments of recent decades.

At any given time the operative significance of the dominant principle of legitimacy tends to be less than that of the agency of legitimization. This means that the crucial question is not *what* principle is acknowledged but *who* is accepted as the authoritative interpreter of the principle or, to put it in institutional terms, *how* the process of legitimization works. There is, of course, a correlation between the nature of the legitimizing principle and the identity of its applicator. For instance, the principle of divine right tends to call for an ecclesiastical spokesman, and the consent theory implies reliance upon a democratic electoral process. In the long run, perhaps, the principle may be decisive; a secular change in the ideology of legitimacy can be expected ultimately to bring about the repudiation of the old and the recognition of a new agency or process of legitimization. Thus, over time, papal decrees have lost, and plebiscite results and public opinion surveys have gained, influence in the legitimizing process. Nevertheless, in the short run, a paraphrase of the maxim that "the Constitution means what the judges say it means" can be generalized. Principles of legitimacy are necessarily rather vague and uncertain in their applicability, and the nature of the process by which their application is decided or the means by which legitimacy is dispensed can be of the greatest importance.

LEGITIMIZATION IN INTERNATIONAL RELATIONS

Against this background I should like to discuss these two propositions: (1) that the function of legitimization in the international realm has tended in recent years to be increasingly conferred upon international political institutions; and (2) that the exercise of this function is, and probably will continue to be, a highly significant part of the political role of the United Nations.

The first proposition implies that the current fashion of legitimization of the status and behavior of states in the international arena emphasizes the *collective* and the *political* aspects of the process. While statesmen have their own ways of justifying their foreign policies to themselves and their peoples, independently of external judgments, they are well aware that such unilateral determinations do not suffice. They are keenly conscious of the need for approval by as large and impressive a body of other states as may be possible, for multilateral endorsement of their positions—in short, for collective legitimization. Moreover, it is a political judgment by their fellow practitioners of international politics that they primarily seek, not a legal judgment rendered by an international judicial organ.

This is not to say that international law has no place in the contemporary procedures of legitimization. States do occasionally resort, and even more frequently propose to resort, to the International Court of Justice (ICJ) or to *ad hoc* arbitral tribunals, and still more often they invoke legal arguments in justification of their positions or denunciation of those of their opponents. One might argue that states should rely predominantly or exclusively upon judicial interpretation of international law for the handling of issues concerning legitimacy, and one might expect that in a more settled period of international relations a heavier reliance upon adjudication might develop. But my present concern is with what *is,* not with what should be or might be, and it is a fact of present-day international life that, for whatever reasons of whatever validity, statesmen exhibit a definite preference for a political rather than a legal process of legitimization.

. . . Collective legitimization has developed, for better or for worse, as essentially a political function, sought for political reasons, exercised by political organs through the operation of a political process, and productive of political results.

Even when states resort to the International Court of Justice, they often appear to seek a judicial contribution to the success of their cause in the political forum rather than to express a preference for the legal over the political process of legitimization. Thus, the request for an advisory opinion concerning certain aspects of the United Nations financial crisis, addressed to the International Court in 1961, was designed to strengthen the case for a reassertion by the General Assembly of its competence to assess Members for support of peacekeeping operations. Somewhat similarly, the South West Africa case, brought before the Court in 1960, was undoubtedly initiated by Ethiopia and Liberia with the hope of obtaining judicial support for an intensified prosecution of South Africa in the General Assembly. The use of the Court in these instances clearly reflects the intention to pursue the issue of legitimacy in the political forum, not to transfer it to the judicial forum. . . .

The function of collective legitimization is not, in principle, reserved exclusively to the United Nations. The United States has placed considerable reliance upon the Organization of American States (OAS) as an instrument for justifying its policy in various cases involving Latin American states, and the anticolonial bloc has used special conferences, beginning with the Asian-African Conference at Bandung in 1955, to proclaim the illegitimacy of continued colonial rule. However, the prominence of the United Nations in the pattern of international organization and its status as an institution approximating universality give it obvious advantages for playing the role of custodian of the seals of international approval and disapproval. While the voice of the United Nations may not be the authentic voice of mankind, it is clearly the best available facsimile thereof, and statesmen have by general consent treated the United Nations as the most impressive and authoritative instrument for the expression of a global version of the general will. The notion that the United Nations gives expression to "world public opinion" is largely a myth, propagated by the winners of diplomatic battles in the Organization in order to enhance the significance of their victories. It would be more accurate to say that the judgments of the Organization represent the preponderant opinion of the foreign offices and other participants in the management of the foreign affairs of the governments of Member States. However, the issue of what the United Nations actually represents is less important than the fact that statesmen have conferred the function of collective legitimization primarily upon that Organization.

This function has been given relatively little attention in analyses of the political role of the United Nations. Most studies have tended to focus upon the operational functions of the Organization—its programs, interventions, and peacekeeping ventures. Our action-oriented generation has concentrated on the question of what the United Nations can and cannot *do,* on the issue of its executive capacity, rather than on its verbal performance. When forced to pessimistic conclusions regarding the possibilities of United Nations action, the typical analyst or editorialist falls back upon the dismal assertion that the Organization is in danger of being reduced to a mere debating chamber, a contemptible talk-shop. Given this negative attitude toward the verbal function, it is small wonder that serious efforts to analyze its significance have been rare. . . .

Collective legitimization is an aspect of the verbal rather than the executive functioning of the United Nations, and in some sense it is a result of the Organization's incapacity for decisive intervention in and control of international relations. One might argue that the United Nations has resorted to saying "thou should" because it is in no position to say "thou shalt" and to saying "thou may" because it cannot say "thou must." It authorizes and endorses in compensation for its inability to effectuate commands, and it condemns and deplores in compensation for its inability to prohibit and prevent. However, the mood expressed in a *New York Times* editorial which, noting the danger that financial difficulties would prevent the United Nations from undertaking further peacekeeping operations, warned that "the end result would be abandonment of its Charter obligation to enforce peace and suppress aggression and a consequent slump into the status of a debating society"[1] is neither realistic nor conducive to a perceptive appraisal of the actual and potential capabilities of the Organization. It reflects an exaggerated conception of what the United Nations might have been; surely, no one who had consulted the Charter and the expectations of its framers in preference to his own hopes and ideals could ever have believed that the United Nations promised to be a dependable agency for enforcing peace and suppressing aggression in an era of great-power division. Even more, it reflects an exaggerated contempt for international debating societies and a disinclination to examine the question of what it is possible for the United Nations to do when it cannot do the impossible.

If we can learn to judge the United Nations less in terms of its failure to attain the ideals that we postulate and more in terms of its success in responding to the realities that the world presents, we shall be in a better position to analyze its development. Approaching the Organization in this spirit, we find that its debating-society aspect is not to be deplored and dismissed as evidence of a "slump" but that it deserves to be examined for evidence of the functional adaptation and innovation that it may represent. My thesis is that the function of collective legitimization is one of the most significant elements in the pattern of political activity that the United Nations has evolved in response to the set of limitations and possibilities posed by the political realities of our time.

The development of this function has not been, in any meaningful sense, *undertaken* by the United Nations, conceived as an independent institutional actor upon the global stage. Rather, it has been thrust upon the Organization by Member States. Collective legitimization is an answer not to the question of what the United Nations can *do* but to the question of how it can be *used*.

Statesmen have been more perceptive than scholars in recognizing and appreciating the significance of this potentiality for utilization of the Organization. They have persistently, and increasingly, regarded the United Nations as an agency capable of bestowing politically weighty approval and disapproval upon their projects and policies. As will be illustrated in the following section of this article, the General Assembly and, to a lesser degree, the Security Council have been used for this purpose. The debates within and negotiations around these political organs have largely concerned the adoption or rejection of resolutions designed to proclaim the legitimacy or the illegitimacy of positions or actions taken by states. Governments have exerted themselves strenuously to promote the passage of resolutions favorable to their cause and the defeat of unfavorable resolutions. In reverse, they have attempted to block resolutions giving approval and to advance those asserting disapproval of their opponents' positions.

The scale of values developed by Members of the United Nations may be represented schematically by the following device in which states A and B are assumed to be engaged in a dispute:

> Approval of A's position
> Disapproval of B's position
> Acquiescence in A's position
> Acquiescence in B's position
> Disapproval of A's position
> Approval of B's position

In this scheme A's preferences would run in descending order from the top of the list, and B's from the bottom of the list. Parliamentary battles over the endorsement, the acceptance, and the condemnation of positions taken by states are a standard feature of the proceedings of the United Nations.

One may question whether proclamations of approval or disapproval by organs of the United Nations, deficient as they typically are in both formal legal significance and effective supportive power, are really important. The answer is that statesmen, by so obviously attaching importance to them, have made them important. Artificial or not, the value of acts of legitimization by the United Nations has been established by the intense demand for them. . . .

I do not mean to suggest that states are willing to accept in principle or to follow in consistent practice the proposition that the collective judgment of the General Assembly or any other international body is decisive. While states vary in the degree to which they display respect for the function of collective legitimization, this variation appears to reflect differences in experience and expectation rather than in commitment to the principle of the validity of collective evaluation. Any state can be expected to assert the validity of acts of legitimization that support its interests and to deny that acts contrary to its interests are worthy of respect. However, the vigorous effort that states customarily make to prevent the passage of formal denunciations of their positions or policies indicates that they have respect for the significance, if not for the validity, of adverse judgments by international organs. While states may act in violation of General Assembly resolutions, they evidently prefer not to do so, or to appear not to do so, on the ground that collective approbation is an important asset and collective disapprobation a significant liability in international relations. A state may hesitate to pursue a policy that has engendered the formal disapproval of the Assembly not because it is prepared to give the will of that organ priority over its national interest but because it believes that the adverse judgment of the Assembly makes the pursuit of that policy disadvantageous to the national interest. . . .

Clearly, statesmen do not attach identical importance to all judgments of legitimacy pronounced by political organs of the United Nations but weight the significance of resolutions according to the size and composition of the majorities supporting them and the forcefulness of the language in which they are couched. This variation in the impressiveness of formal resolutions was anticipated in the Charter provisions requiring a two-thirds majority for decisions on important questions in the General Assembly (Article 18, paragraph 2), and unanimity of the permanent members of the Security Council in decisions on nonprocedural matters in that body (Article 27, paragraph 3). In practice, it is evident that a Security Council resolution supported by all the permanent members is taken more seriously than one on which three of them abstain, that the support or opposition of India is treated as more significant than that of Iceland in evaluating a resolution of the General Assembly, and that a unanimous decision of the latter body deserves and receives more attention than a narrowly passed resolution. Moreover, a clear and firm act of approval or disapproval carries more weight than a vague and ambiguous pronouncement, and a series of resolutions, pointing consistently in the same direction, is more impressive than an isolated case. While states value even narrow parliamentary victories, achieved by garnering votes wherever they may be found and diluting the language of resolutions as much as may be necessary, they obviously recognize that the most convincing legitimization is provided by the cumulative impact of repeated and unambiguous endorsements of their positions, supported by massive majorities that include the bulk of the most important and most influential states.

SOME INSTANCES OF COLLECTIVE LEGITIMIZATION

The United Nations has been heavily involved in matters relating to the question of the ratification and solidification of the status claimed, as distinguished from the policies followed, by political entities. Generally, this can be subsumed under the heading of membership business; admission to or seating in the Organization has tended to take on the political meaning, if not the legal implication, of collective recognition. New states have been inclined to regard the grant of membership as the definitive acknowledgment of their independence. . . . The prompt admission of Israel to the United Nations was clearly regarded, by both friends and foes of the new state, as a major contribution to its capacity to survive in a hostile neighborhood. The issue of conferment of status arose in a different way when Malaysia was elected to a Security Council seat by the General Assembly. Indonesia's subsequent withdrawal from the Organization, ostensibly in protest against that action, can be interpreted as a tribute to the potency of collective legitimization, for Indonesia evidently felt that the United Nations had given an intolerably valuable boost to Malaysia's international stock.

A major campaign has been waged in the United Nations to delegitimize colonialism, to invalidate the claim of colonial powers to legitimate possession of overseas territories—in short, to revoke their sovereignty over colonies. This movement culminated in the overwhelming adoption by the General Assembly of sweeping anticolonial declarations in 1960 and subsequently. The implication of this anticolonial triumph became clear in late 1961 when India was cited before the Security Council for its invasion of Goa. India's defense was, in essence, the assertion that the process of collective legitimization had operated to deprive Portugal of any claim to sovereignty over Goa and thus of any right to protest the invasion—which, by virtue of the same process, had become an act of liberation, terminating Portugal's illegal occupation of Goa.

This case illustrates the proximity of the political and the legal aspects which is frequently implicit and occasionally explicit in the operation of the process of collective legitimization. India was accused in legal terms, and it responded in similar vein. The rejoinder by and on behalf of India proclaimed, in effect, that an accumulation of multilateral denunciations of colonialism had effectively abrogated the legal right of European states to rule non-European territories; these acts had created a new law under which colonialism was invalid. Despite this exchange of legal arguments, it appears that India's real concern was not so much to clear itself legally as to vindicate itself politically. It regarded the political approval or acquiescence of the United Nations as a more important consideration than any legal judgment. In a basic sense, India won the case. Although it obtained no formal endorsement of its position, it carried through its conquest of Goa without incurring formal condemnation, and its Western critics, by declining to take the issue to the Assembly, conceded that they could not expect to win, in that organ, a political verdict unfavorable to India. . . . Thus, in one of its aspects, collective legitimacy represents a political revolt against international law.

It should be noted that ex-colonial states have not confined themselves to using the United Nations for legitimization of the campaign for definitive liquidation of the colonial system. In the economic sphere they have undertaken, in concert with other underdeveloped countries, to use the Organization to secure the establishment and general acceptance of the doctrine that they have a right to receive, and advanced states have a duty to provide, assistance in promoting economic development. Toward the same end they have invoked the support of the Organization for policies designed to free themselves from obligations and arrangements that they regard as exploitative and inimical to economic progress, including foreign ownership or control of their basic natural resources. In an era of rising economic expectations, intensive effort on the part of many new states to establish solid economic foundations for their national structures, and extreme sensitivity to vestiges of the old system of colonial domination, the legitimizing function of the United Nations has had particular significance for the realm of economic policy. . . .

The United States, like India in the Goa case, has in some instances profited from collective legitimization in its minimal form: United Nations acquiescence or avoidance of United Nations condemnation. In some of these cases the United States has pioneered in the development of the strategy of involving a regional organization in the process. When the United States became involved in the overthrow of the Guatemalan government in 1954, it vigorously asserted the claim that the United Nations should disqualify itself from considering the case in favor of the Organization of American States. This tactic, which clearly reflected American respect for the potency of United Nations disapprobation, was practically, though not technically, successful. In the Cuban crisis of late 1962 the United States altered its strategy, opting to combine the functioning of the OAS and the United Nations rather than to set them off against each other. On this occasion the American scheme, successfully executed, was to secure the legitimizing support of the regional organization and then to use this asset in the effort to obtain the approval, or avoid the disapproval, of the Security Council with respect to the measures taken against Soviet involvement in Cuba.

[Later] the United States has been conspicuously reluctant to press the United Nations for formal consideration of the situation in South Vietnam in which American forces have become heavily engaged. This restraint has no doubt derived from lack of confidence that a United Nations organ would endorse the claim of the United States that its military commitment constitutes a legitimate counterintervention against illegitimate intrusions by Communist states. . . .

CONCLUSION

This account of selected instances in which the United Nations has been involved in the process of collective legitimization suggests that there is great variation in the effectiveness of the positions taken by the Organization. It is seldom possible to make confident estimates of the degree of influence upon state behavior exerted by United Nations resolutions, although the intensity of the concern exhibited by states about the outcome of votes in the Organization indicates that the seal of approval and the stigma of disapproval are taken seriously.

There is also room for disagreement and uncertainty concerning the merits and demerits of collective legitimization. The entrusting of this function to such an organization as the United Nations is pregnant with both valuable and dangerous possibilities, as the cases discussed may suggest. The endorsement of a United Nations organ can strengthen a good cause, but it can also give aid and comfort to a bad cause—and we can have no guarantee that international political institutions, any more than national ones, will distribute their largess of legitimacy in accordance with the dictates of justice or wisdom. Habitual utilization of the

United Nations as an agency for pronouncing on the international acceptability of national policies and positions may inspire statesmen to behave with moderation and circumspection; their concern regarding the outcome of deliberations by the Organization may stimulate them to make compromises designed to improve their chances of securing collective approval or avoiding collective disapproval. On the other hand, this use of the United Nations may promote its exploitation as an arena within which propaganda victories are sought, to the detriment of its role in promoting diplomatic settlements. Collective legitimization may stimulate legal changes that will make international law more worthy of respect and more likely to be respected, but it may also encourage behavior based upon calculation of what the political situation will permit rather than consideration of what the principles of order require. In short, the exercise of the function of collective legitimization may be for better or for worse, whether evaluated in terms of its effect upon the interests of a particular state or upon the prospects for a stable and orderly world. The crucial point is that, for better or for worse, the development of the United Nations as custodian of collective legitimacy is an important political phenomenon of our time.

NOTE

1. *The New York Times.* September 16, 1963.

The Development of Human Rights Law in the United Nations, Its Control and Monitoring Machinery

JOHN P. PACE

INTRODUCTION

In preparing this article, we have endeavoured to represent the action of the United Nations in the field of human rights in its historical perspective. This is in order to demonstrate that the present situation is the result of an evolution in international relations, and in the common denominators of human rights as they emerged in the United Nations, and more particularly, in the Commission on Human Rights. We are therefore applying the term "human rights law" in its immediate context of the International Bill of Human Rights, and more particularly the two International Covenants, and only peripherally is reference made to the other four international human rights instruments which are actively monitored by their respective treaty bodies.

Moreover, the "control" machinery should be understood in its international political context and not in a "judicial" or "quasi-judicial" sense. The "monitoring" machinery is applied here in its wider human rights context as embracing those *ad hoc* procedures that developed over the years, and especially since the late seventies. Thus the paper dwells in some detail on the landmark decision of the Commission on Human Rights in 1967 to establish an Ad Hoc Working Group of Experts for the purposes of investigating a particular situation.

Similarly, the article attempts to demonstrate that the successive development of other tools, such as awareness–building approaches launched at the end of the eighties, and the new face of advisory services and technical cooperation that followed, lead to a focus on the right to development and the role of the United Nations system in supporting Governments to create conditions that would enable them to fulfil their international legal obligations.

EARLY EVOLUTION

The origin of United Nations human rights law as we know it today, may be found in the Charter of the United Nations which contains references to human rights in Articles 1, 13, 55, 62, 68, and 76. . . .

On 16 February 1946, the Economic and Social Council established the Commission on Human Rights and on 21 June 1946, the Council requested the Commission for "suggestions regarding ways and means for the effective implementation of human rights and fundamental freedoms" (ECOSOC resolutions 9(II)).

On 10 December 1948, the General Assembly adopted the Universal Declaration of Human Rights setting down in the very first paragraph of its preamble the recognition, "of the inherent dignity and of the equal and inalienable rights of all members of the human family as the foundation of freedom, justice and peace in the world."

As of 10 December 1948, therefore, the Charter and the Declaration, constituted the first two (complementary) documents, one an emanation of the other, sharing the common goals of freedom, justice and peace. At the time of the adoption of the Universal Declaration, the international community still had to define the content and implications of these norms and, more difficult still, had to work out the way in which they were to be put into effect.

History has shown that the first of the tasks, i.e. the definition of the content and implications of these norms, took much longer than it was ever thought that it might take, and the second task, i.e. their implementation proved virtually insurmountable.

These two factors, together with the international political situation emerging in the fifties, put human rights on a very theoretic level indeed. Priority was taken up by maintaining international peace and security for the sake of preventing a third world war; so the time was not yet ripe for the international community to dedicate the necessary attention to realizing human rights to the level that it had undertaken in the Charter.

Whilst the international community in its first thirty years concentrated on avoiding another world conflagration, it was also completing its ranks through the process of decolonization and the emergence of the States that were to give it the profile that it has today. The polarization of the Cold War and the influence that the relations between the Big Powers had on the smaller nations led to the emergence of the non-aligned movement, a phenomenon that was to influence the evolution of human rights law in the United Nations.

This was the time within the United Nations when the right to self-determination was the priority right for some, civil and political rights were the priority rights for others, whilst a third school of thought gave priority to "collective" as distinct from "individual" rights. The search for the definition of these rights which, in 1948, it was assumed, would take but a few months—as evidenced by the establishment of three Working Groups with the aim of completing the "package" more or less at the same time—in fact took nearly four decades.

After the early and somewhat understandable optimism of the late forties it soon became evident that whereas the Declaration itself would not run into serious difficulties, the drafting of a Covenant would take much longer. The first attempt at drafting such a covenant took place between 1947 and 1952. With the adoption of the Declaration, the General Assembly requested the preparation "as a matter of priority" of a Draft Covenant of Human Rights and of draft measures of implementation. Soon enough, in the drafting of this Covenant "the big divide" became evident between the treatment to be accorded to Civil and Political Rights on one hand and to Economic Social and Cultural Rights on the other. Thus, in spite of repeated statements between 1950 and 1952 reaffirming the interdependence of these rights, reality was going in the opposite direction. In 1950 the General Assembly declared that these rights were "interconnected and interdependent" and that "when deprived of economic, social and cultural rights, man does not represent the human person whom the Universal Declaration regards as the ideal of the free man."

At that time, the Commission on Human Rights was still considering a unitary Draft Covenant. By 1951, the Commission on Human Rights had considered drafts on 14 articles covering economic, social and cultural rights and an additional ten articles on the implementation of such rights, essentially consisting of what was later to become a system of periodic reports by States. It was clear by that time, however, that the notion of having one Covenant to cover the five groups of rights had run into serious problems. That same year, the Economic and Social Council, after debating the question of the implementation mechanism for Civil and Political Rights and for Economic, Social and Cultural Rights, invited the General Assembly to reconsider having one Covenant. In 1952, the General Assembly, after a long debate agreed to authorize the drafting of *two* Covenants, albeit reaffirming the universality of human rights. This *de facto* breach in the integral or homogeneous approach to human rights was to characterize the work of the Commission on Human Rights for the next 25 years.

On 16 December 1966, the General Assembly adopted and opened for signature, ratification of and accession to the two International Covenants. It took another ten years for the entry into force for these two instruments.[1] Thus the first opportunity to give formal implementation to the provisions of the International Covenant on Civil and Political Rights only materialized in the late seventies.[2]

Parallel to this slow but steady work on drafting the International Covenants during the late sixties and early seventies, we see two additional tools emerging in the search for implementation of these norms. These are:

- the procedure regulating the handling of individual complaints, by which the Commission, with ECOSOC resolution 1503 (XL VIII), was enabled to act—diametrically opposed to the statement adopted by the Commission at its first session according to which, 'the Commission recognizes that it has no power to take any action in regard to any complaints concerning human rights'[3]
- the emergence of the *ad hoc* or extra-conventional protection of human rights.

By the beginning of the eighties these implementation tools, conventional, individual and extra-conventional, had evolved to an extent that gave the Commission a truly meaningful potential of scrutiny into human rights situations. . . .

THE SHIFT TO *AD HOC* PROCEDURES OF IMPLEMENTATION

The Commission on Human Rights in March 1967 adopted the key decision. During its twenty-third session (the drafting of the Covenants having been completed), the Commission had before it a letter from the Chairman of the Special Committee on Policies of Apartheid of the Government of the Republic of South Africa, addressed to the Chairman of the Commission on Human Rights, requesting him "to draw the attention of the Commission on Human Rights to the continuing ill-treatment of prisoners, detainees, and persons in police custody in the Republic of South Africa, particularly the numerous opponents of apartheid who have been imprisoned under arbitrary laws." The letter concluded, "The Special Committee therefore hopes that the Commission on Human Rights will consider the matter urgently and take steps to secure an international investigation with a view to ameliorating the conditions of these victims.". . .

The debate in the Commission[4] was not an easy one, reflecting the divide between those who felt that the Commission on Human Rights did not have the power to investigate, and those who considered that the Commission could, and should, be able to address situations of human rights on an *ad hoc* basis.

A resolution (2 (XXIII)) was adopted on 6 March 1967, after much procedural debate—the Commission actually went through no less than thirty-two voting and adoption processes—by which the Commission, among other things, decided ". . . to establish, in accordance with resolution 9 (II) of 21 June 1946 of the Economic and Social Council, an *Ad Hoc* Working Group of Experts composed of eminent jurists and prison officials to be appointed by the Chairman of the Commission to:

a. Investigate the charges of torture and ill-treatment of prisoners, detainees or persons in police custody in South Africa;
b. Receive communications and hear witnesses and use such modalities of procedure as it may deem appropriate;
c. Recommend action to be taken in concrete cases;
d. Report to the Commission on Human Rights at the earliest possible time."[5]

This was followed by similar resolutions in 1969 (on the protection of the civilian population of the Arab territories occupied by Israel) and 1975 (on the situation of human rights in Chile). Since then, virtually without interruption, the Commission has established such *ad hoc* procedures, that the focus of implementation of human rights law shifted away from the conventional implementation of international human rights norms. Thus by the late eighties, the momentum gathered by these procedures was such that the Commission on Human Rights dedicated most of its attention to these *ad hoc* or special procedures.

Although they focused on investigating and seeking to redress negative human rights situations, the extra-conventional procedures were, of course, imperfect solutions since they resulted from a focus on a single (and therefore selective) issue or concern rather than a standard-setting process. By this period, therefore, the United Nations agenda on human rights needed to be revised to take into account these developments and the consequent need, identified by several of these *ad hoc* procedures, to assist governments to create conditions that would permit them to adhere to their international human rights legal obligations.

It was at this point that the right to development, as a human rights issue, emerged as the ultimate tool in the efforts of the United Nations to secure conditions that would make human rights law a viable proposition. As of the mid-eighties four significant decisions of the General Assembly and the Commission on Human Rights were to provide these approaches and finally launch the process of the re-integration of human rights norms. These new approaches took the form of activities for promotion of and education on these norms.

In 1986, the General Assembly proclaimed the Declaration on the Right to Development. Article 1 of the Declaration states: "The right to development is an inalienable right by virtue of which every human person and all peoples are entitled to participate in, contribute to, and enjoy economic, social, cultural and political development, in which all human rights and fundamental freedoms can be fully realized. . . ." Article 2 states: "The human person is the central subject of development and should be the active participant and beneficiary of the right to development. . . ." The Declaration thus reaffirmed the integral, inter-dependent nature of the established international human rights norms, and their focus on the individual as the subject of these international human rights norms.

In 1987 the United Nations Voluntary Fund for Technical Co-operation for Human Rights was set up, making it possible to provide additional resources for the process of strengthening of infrastructures and awareness-building at the national and regional levels. In 1988 (the commemoration of the fortieth anniversary of the adoption of the Universal Declaration) the General Assembly launched a World Campaign for Human Rights. In 1990, the General Assembly decided to convene a World Conference on Human Rights to take place in 1993. This Conference, the second of its kind in the history of the United Nations (the first one took place in Tehran in 1968), was to fix the priorities for the future, in its own words, "the spirit of our age and the realities of our time."

These four decisions constitute a significant phase in the development of international human rights law. They re-affirm international commitment, focus on the right to development (as defined above), emphasize the need to adopt measures for education and promotion, and provide international support to the efforts of States to create conditions that would enable them to carry out their international legal obligations under the Covenants.

To achieve this, the aim is to harness the potential of the international system, governmental and non-governmental, and to use these channels to gain access to specific sectors of society. So far, such efforts have focused principally on the classical areas where human rights have traditionally been situated, viz. within the general context of constitutional law and particularly, in the area of administration of justice. With new momentum, the focus may radiate to other areas of the international system, thus strengthening support for the respect for economic and social rights.

The adoption of the Declaration on the Right to Development by the General Assembly of the United Nations on 4 December 1986 constitutes a milestone in the evolution of the promotion and protection of human rights by the United Nations. . . .

THE CONVENTIONAL PROCEDURES

As a result of this evolution, and during these years, the conventional procedures continued to gain momentum, albeit slowly. The procedures set out at Part IV of each of the two Covenants set out the terms for their implementation. They require States Parties to submit reports "on the measures they have adopted which give effect to the rights recognized herein and on the progress made in the enjoyment of those rights . . ." (Article 40, ICCPR) and "on the measure which they have adopted and the progress made in achieving the observance of the rights recognized herein" (Article 16, ICESCR).

The International Covenant on Civil and Political Rights has 140 States parties, and the International Covenant on Economic, Social and Cultural Rights, 137 (as at 5 February 1998).[6] The other four human rights conventions all have over one hundred States Parties (Convention against Torture and Other Cruel, Inhuman or Degrading Treatment or Punishment, 104, the Convention on the Elimination of All Forms of Racial Discrimination, 150, the Convention on the Elimination of All Forms of Discrimination against Women, 161, and the Convention on the Rights of the Child, 191).

The treaty bodies established to monitor the implementation of these human rights instruments have developed their procedures and among them, present an ongoing machinery in the form of regular meetings of the Committees and their working groups.

The Human Rights Committee monitors the International Covenant on Civil and Political Rights. It is composed of eighteen members elected by the States Parties to the Covenant for a four-year term, half the membership being elected every two years. It meets three times a year, for three weeks; two working groups of not more than five members meet for one week before each session. Under the Covenant, the first report of a State Party is due within one year of the entry into force of the Covenant for the State Party, and subsequent reports are due every five years. The Committee invites representatives of the State Party to introduce the report of the State Party concerned. Immediately prior to the session, a working group reviews the State Party's report to be taken up in Committee, identifies the issues to be raised with representatives, and prepares them with a list of questions so that they may prepare responses for the meeting in which the report is taken up. The Committee's examination of the reports takes place in public, and it makes recommendations on ways to give better effect to the Covenant at national level. In addition to making recommendations, the Committee also makes General Comments, which are designed to assist in the interpretation of the scope and meaning of the various articles of the Covenant.

The Committee on Economic, Social and Cultural Rights monitors the implementation of the ICESCR. It is made up of eighteen members, elected for a four-year term by the Economic and Social Council from a list of nominees proposed by States Parties to the Covenant (as distinct from the Human Rights Committee, which is elected directly by the States Parties). The Committee meets twice a year for three weeks. States Parties undertake to submit a first report within two years of the entry into force of the Covenant for that State Party, and there-after, once every five years. Reports are initially reviewed by a pre-session working group of the Committee, and after a preliminary review, the working group appoints one member to give particular consideration to each report, and prepares written questions which are submitted to the State party concerned, who are required to reply in writing prior to their appearance before the Committee. The pre-sessional working group meets immediately upon the conclusion of a session of the Committee, thus giving States Parties the time leading up to the following session, when their reports are due to be examined by the Committee. The Committee gives it findings on the status of the Covenant in the State Party, in its "Concluding Observations" which it issues upon completion of its consideration of a report. The Committee adopts these observations in private sessions and makes them public on the last day of each of its sessions. The Committee also makes "General Comments" with a view to assisting States Parties in fulfilling their reporting obligations and, more important, in giving an authoritative interpretation by the Committee of certain provisions of the Covenant. Another characteristic in the working methods of the Committee is its "General Discussions," whereby, at each of its sessions, during one day, it focuses on a topic considered of direct relevance to the Committee in its work. Such general discussions have been held on substantive aspects of certain provisions of the Covenant, as well as on institutional aspects.

The scope of this article does not allow for a detailed description of the working methods of the treaty bodies, neither does it permit an in-depth assessment of their performance record. Our purpose here is to highlight the fact that these procedures are indeed the core mechanism in the control and monitoring machinery of the United Nations system of human rights law and that they have also developed in response to challenges arising from the overall evolution of human rights implementation.

RECENT EVOLUTION

We have endeavoured to show that the process of formulation and implementation of human rights law has, as its foundation, the Charter and the Universal Declaration of Human Rights. In spite of the acknowledged desire for a homogeneous approach, expressed from the very outset, and since reiterated consistently, it is a historical fact that substantive human rights law developed in separate sectors, principally civil and political rights on one hand and economic, social and cultural rights on the other. It is also a historical fact that tools for implementation developed in distinct layers, consisting of formal or conventional treaty monitoring mechanisms, followed by *ad hoc* or special procedures, and later promotional and technical cooperation activities, which today have further developed into field operations in certain cases.

The World Conference on Human Rights, Vienna, 1993, with its emphasis on the universality of human rights, whilst acknowledging the significance of "national and regional particularities, and various historical, cultural and religious backgrounds," and the inter-dependence of democracy, development and respect for human rights, set out formula for reintegrating human rights law. The establishment of a High Commissioner for Human Rights in 1993 provided the institution that would apply this reintegration. The Reform of the United Nations proposed by Secretary-General Kofi Annan and endorsed by the General Assembly in 1997 makes it a programmatic reality. . . .

But perhaps the most important level of adjustment is at the level of the United Nations system itself, where the experience of agencies and programmes, both inter- and non-governmental, will be applied to create conditions for States Members of the United Nations to enter international human rights treaty obligations. This process has started, with the setting up of the institution known as the Office of the High Commissioner for Rights, and the participation of this OHCHR in all four executive committees set up by the Secretary-General to enhance coordination and focus of activities for the benefit of Member States.

Never in the history of the development of human rights law, has the United Nations been, so close to realization of the spirit and letter of the Charter of the United Nations. On the other hand, the effort that needs to be put into this process, cannot be under-estimated and serious obstacles, both known and yet to emerge, will have to be addressed and surmounted.

NOTES

1. On 3 February 1976, the International Covenant on Economic, Social and Cultural Rights entered into force upon the thirty-fifth ratification and a few weeks later, on 23 March 1976, the International Covenant on Civil and Political Rights and its Optional Protocol entered into force. By 20 September 1976, the first Human Rights Committee was elected launching the implementation mechanism of the Covenant on Civil and Political Rights. On 28 March 1979, Article 41 of the International Covenant on Civil and Political Rights came into effect, ten States Parties having made the declaration under paragraph 1 of this article recognizing the competence of the Human Rights Committee to receive and consider communications to the effect that a State Party "claims that another State Party is not fulfilling its obligations under the present Covenant."

2. The International Covenant on Economic, Social and Cultural Rights had to wait for another seven years before its implementation mechanism was to be put on the same level as that of its twin Covenant, with the establishment of the Committee on Economic, Social and Cultural Rights.

3. E/259, Report to the Economic and Social Council on the First session of the Commission, 27 January to 10 February 1947, Chapter V, §22.

4. According to the report of the Commission (E/CN.4/940 - E/4322):

   "219. Several representatives raised the question whether, and to what extent, the Commission on Human Rights was competent to consider specific instances of the violation of human rights such as that present under item 24, and to take action in the matter. It was generally agreed that Article 2, §7, of the Chapter was not applicable to the case under consideration. Some members held that the protection of fundamental human rights, at least following the entry into force of the Charter and in view of the numerous measures adopted by the United Nations, had ceased to be a question essentially within the domestic jurisdiction of States. It was pointed out that under the provisions of the Charter, and particularly Articles 55 and 56, the Republic of South Africa had an obligation to cooperate with the United Nations in the field of human rights and that, in pursuance of these provisions, the other Member States had a duty to continue their efforts to remedy such situations. Other representatives expressed the view that Article 2 §7, was not applicable in the present instance because the situation as a whole came under Chapter VII of the Charter.

   "220. Some representatives expressed the view that when the Economic and Social Council had laid down the Commission's terms of reference in 1946, it has intended that the Commission should concern itself mainly, if not exclusively, with the preparation of studies and international instruments of a general nature. They expressed doubts regarding the steps which, in view of the terms of reference, the Commission could take under agenda item 24. They believed that at most, it could submit recommendations to the Council and to the General Assembly for approval. In particular, the Commission should, they maintained, urge ratification of the international covenants on human rights and of the International Convention on the Elimination of All Forms of Racial Discrimination. Other representatives took the view that Economic and Social Council resolution 9(II) had empowered the Commission to set up ad hoc groups of experts.

"221. Several other representatives considered that, although the Commission's terms of reference might originally have been limited, they had been considerably broadened by General Assembly resolution 2144 (XXI), §12 of which invited the Commission to "give urgent consideration to ways and means of improving the capacity of the United Nations to put a stop to violation of human rights wherever they may occur." Although some were inclined to believe that that resolution merely empowered the Commission to recommend measures to other bodies, several representatives were of the opinion that the text gave the Commission the necessary authority to adopt specific measures itself in the event of human rights violations. A recommendation limited to the problem of ratifying the covenants and the International Convention on the Elimination of All Forms of Racial Discrimination would in the circumstances, serve no useful purpose, since the Republic of South Africa could not be expected to become party to any of those instruments in the near future.

"222. Questions concerning the Commission's competence were raised more particularly with regard to an important element of the twelve-Power resolution: the proposed establishment of a body to investigate charges with which item 24 was concerned and to submit a report and recommendations to the Commission. Some representatives doubted whether the Commission could itself set up an "international commission of experts" to carry out such investigations, as the twelve-Powers had proposed. In their view, the Commission could only recommend such action to the Economic and Social Council; in any event, the Council's approval was necessary. In that connexion, they cited Economic and Social Council resolution 5(I) concerning the establishment of subcommissions. . . .

"223. Most representatives considered, however, that the Commission had the necessary powers to deal with the matter and that at least there could be no doubt of its competence to set up an 'ad hoc group of experts,' as proposed in the revised twelve-Power draft resolution. In that connexion, they pointed out that under Economic and Social Council resolution 9(II) of 21 June 1946, the Commission had been authorized to 'call in ad hoc working groups of non-governmental experts in specialized fields or individual experts, without further reference to the Council, but with the approval of the President of the Council and the Secretary-General. . . .'"

5. The draft resolution had been submitted by the Democratic Republic of the Congo, Dahomey, India, Iran, Iraq, Jamaica, Morocco, Nigeria, Pakistan, Philippines, Senegal and the UAR. Amendments had been submitted by Austria, by Tanzania and by the USA. The result of the roll-call vote on the draft resolution as a whole, i.e. after the amendments, separate votes on the various parts of the draft, etc., was as follows: *In favour:* Argentina, Austria, Chile, Congo (Democratic Republic of), Costa Rica, Dahomey, Greece, Guatemala, India, Iran, Iraq, Israel, Jamaica, Morocco, Nigeria, Pakistan, Philippines, Poland, Senegal, Sweden, Ukrainian SSR, USSR, UAR, Tanzania, Yugoslavia. *Abstaining:* France, Italy, New Zealand, UK, USA. (E/CN.4/940-E/4322, §267)

6. Haiti, Mozambique, Thailand and the United States have ratified the ICCPR but not the ICESCR.

Bargaining, Enforcement, and Multilateral Sanctions: When Is Cooperation Counterproductive?

DANIEL W. DREZNER

INTRODUCTION

A common thread in the economic sanctions literature is the assumption that multilateral cooperation among the potential sanctioning states is a necessary and/or sufficient condition for generating a successful outcome.[1] . . .

Intuitively, the link between international cooperation and sanctions success seems obvious. Empirically, however, the results are rather surprising. Repeated statistical tests show either no link or a negative correlation between cooperation and sanctions success. At least four studies conclude that successful episodes of economic coercion exhibit the least levels of cooperation among the sanctioning states.[2] No statistical test has shown a significant positive correlation between policy success and international cooperation among the sanctioning states.

This empirical puzzle presents vexing problems for the policy and scholarly communities. If international cooperation is not correlated with sanctions success, then U.S. foreign policy has been badly misguided in this area.

This puzzle also goes to the heart of the debate about the role of multilateral cooperation, and by extension international organizations, in the international system. A central tenet of cooperation theory is that if a sufficient number of powerful states collaborate, they can manage the international system and punish defections from the rules of the game.[3] . . . The sanctions evidence, however, suggests that cooperation is overvalued. If repeated tests of a theory reveal contradictory or inconclusive findings, that theory needs to be reformulated. Is there a theory of cooperation that can explain why multilateral support has no apparent effect on the outcome of economic coercion?

I address these larger theoretical issues by examining possible explanations for why cooperation and sanctions success are not correlated. I do so by breaking down the issue of cooperation into its component problems. As James Fearon has

Previous versions of this article were presented at the 1997 Annual Meeting of the International Studies Association in Toronto, Canada, and at Columbia University's International Political Economy Workshop. I am grateful to David Baldwin, Christian Davenport, Page Fortna, Kurt Taylor Gaubatz, James McAllister, Helen Milner, Jim Morrow, Roland Paris, Eric Reinhardt, Bruce Russett, Richard Tucker, the editors of *IO*, and two anonymous referees for their comments and suggestions.

observed,[4] cooperation problems can be parsed into bargaining and enforcement phases. Cooperation could be sabotaged by bargaining difficulties and/or a lack of enforcement. Furthermore, sanctions involving multilateral cooperation involve two separate cooperation dilemmas: one between the sanctioning states and the target, and one between the primary sanctioner and other sanctioners. These two dimensions create a typology of explanations for successful and unsuccessful sanctions efforts involving multilateral cooperation:

- Cooperation fails because it is associated with tough bargaining strategies between the sanctioning states and the target.
- Cooperation fails because successful bargaining between the primary and secondary sanctioners makes it impossible to compromise with the target country.
- Cooperation fails because the primary sanctioner is unable to enforce the application of sanctions, due to defections by private rent-seeking actors (sanctions busting) or by nation-states (backsliding).

The results presented here suggest strongly that multilateral economic sanctions are sabotaged not by bargaining problems, but rather by enforcement difficulties. Without the support of an international organization, ad hoc coalitions of sanctioners are inherently fragile. In particular, states are prone to backsliding, initially agreeing to cooperate but facing incentives to defect over time. This fragility gives the sanctioned state an incentive to wait out the coalition rather than acquiesce to the sanctioning countries' demands. Uninstitutionalized cooperation is therefore counterproductive in generating concessions from the targeted country. International organizations can turn fragile agreements to cooperate into a robust coalition by enforcing a previously agreed-on equilibrium. International organizations do this by acting as a coordinating mechanism for reassurance and information, enabling governments to resist domestic pressures, and providing side payments to increase the value of continued cooperation. Thus, in matters of economic statecraft, cooperation has a knife-edge property. With the support of international organizations, cooperation is advantageous for the primary sanctioner; without this support, cooperation leads to a significantly worse outcome than unilateral efforts.

These results have some intriguing implications for both policy and theory. They suggest that sanctioning states incur significant risks when they lobby for international support. Multilateral cooperation is neither necessary nor sufficient for a great power to effectively use economic coercion. Unilateral sanctions can be more effective than multilateral effort; a small and sturdy stick is better than a large and brittle one. Theoretically, the results suggest that cooperation is not as robust an outcome as some theorists suggest. Even after a cooperative equilibrium is achieved, backsliding can disrupt it. However, the results show that international organizations play a decisive role in sustaining cooperation over time; they also suggest the mechanism through which this is accomplished. International organizations maintain cooperation not through the *ex post* punishment of defectors but through the *ex ante* reassurance of actors by developing common conjectures and blunting domestic pressures to defect.

I first briefly examine why it is assumed that international cooperation is a prerequisite for sanctions success and address the lack of empirical support for this assumption. I next outline the possible explanations for this anomaly and develop testable hypotheses for each explanation. I then describe and explain the data used to test the hypotheses, test the possible explanations, and evaluate the results. I conclude by offering implications for policy and theory that follow from the findings in this article as well as some suggestions for future research.

THEORIES AND FACTS ABOUT MULTILATERAL ECONOMIC SANCTIONS

Consistent with the terminology used in the literature, I refer to the sanctioning countries as senders and sanctioned countries as targets. Lisa Martin observes that although sanctions are often mandated by international organizations, one country is usually the instigator.[5] I refer to this country as the primary sender and the other cooperating states as secondary senders.

For most analysts of economic sanctions, international cooperation seems so transparently useful that it is assumed to be a necessary condition for sanctions to extract any political concessions. Robert Gilpin writes, "Whereas positive leverage is usually a unilateral action, negative leverage in almost all cases must be multilateral. To be effective, other states must give it their support."[6] . . .

There are economic and normative reasons for the importance of multilateral cooperation. The economic argument runs as follows: Sanctions must impose costs in order for the target to prefer conceding. However, cutting off bilateral economic exchange does not automatically affect the target country's terms of trade. It can be very easy for countries to redirect their economic exchange to other suppliers and markets. For sanctions to work, the primary sender must have the ability to alter the target country's terms of trade regardless of the targeted regime's efforts to substitute. Trade theory suggests that in a world of homogeneous goods and commodities with high substitution elasticities, only a sender with more than half the productive capability of a certain good has the ability to influence the terms of trade.[7] Few individual countries have this capability, and it is always ephemeral. However, sanctions with reasonably high levels of international cooperation should impose greater costs on the targeted country because of the inability to locate alternative markets.

The normative motivation for international cooperation is that the greater the number of countries and institutions supporting a sanctions effort, the greater the moral suasion. International relations theorists usually mention this argument in passing, but it carries greater weight with policy activists. As David Hendrickson observes, "The broader the scope of concerted action, the more it seems the action has the sponsorship of international society as a whole."[8] Abram Chayes and Antonia Handler Chayes concur, noting that "Broad support is a safeguard to ensure that the action is not simply the imposition of the will of the stronger. It establishes the legitimacy of the enterprise."[9] . . . According to this argument, broad-based cooperation drains realpolitik from the dispute. If only one country threatens sanctions, the targeted state might view it as a threat to their security and sovereignty. If the international community agrees to employ sanctions, the target has more difficulty framing the issue as narrowly distributive.

U.S. policymakers have placed a high premium on multilateral cooperation and devoted significant resources to attracting international support. The Clinton administration spent more than a year trying to convince the UN Security Council to sanction North Korea prior to the Agreed Framework between the two countries in 1994.[10] The Bush administration devoted extensive diplomatic resources, and forgave large economic debts, in order to obtain and enforce the UN sanctions against Iraq. . . .

The logic for securing multilateral cooperation appears self-evident; it increases the costs to the target and lends greater moral credence to the sanctioning effort. But it does not jibe with the statistical evidence. Previous tests of the sanctions data compiled by Gary Hufbauer, Jeffrey Schott, and Kimberly Elliott show international cooperation to have no effect on sanctions success.[11] The results are the same regardless of whether the testing procedure is bivariate or multivariate.[12] The result is also robust to different codings of the dependent variable. Using Hufbauer, Schott, and Elliott's original measure of success,[13] a more methodologically sound variant,[14] or a measure controlling for the absolute magnitude of concessions,[15] does not change the result.

One possible explanation is that Hufbauer, Schott, and Elliott's measure of cooperation has been miscoded. Their data set has come under considerable criticism for its case selection and coding.[16] It is possible that their cooperation measure is either biased or simply too error prone. The data, however, supports their coding. Table 1 compares Hufbauer, Schott, and Elliott's ordinal coding of the extent of cooperation with the affected volume of the target country's trade, according to the International Monetary Fund's *Direction of Trade Annual*.[17] As the degree of cooperation increases, there is a significant increase in the target country's affected volume of trade, even though the primary sender's share holds roughly constant. Table 1 reveals three facts. First, Hufbauer, Schott, and Elliott's ordinal measure accurately reflects the extent of international cooperation.

TABLE 1. THE PATTERN OF INTERNATIONAL COOPERATION IN SANCTIONS EVENTS

Category	Number of observations	Percentage of target's trade with primary sender	Percentage of target's trade with all senders	Percentage of observations
No cooperation	61	18.0	18.0	55.5
Minor cooperation	24	18.3	20.3	21.8
Modest cooperation	15	14.4	38.2	13.6
Significant cooperation	10	21.1	56.2	9.1
Total	110	17.7	25.0	100.0

Sources: Hufbauer, Schott, and Elliott 1990; International Monetary Fund, *Direction of Trade Annual*, 1950–1990.

Second, states do not actively seek cooperation only when their unilateral ability to apply economic pressure is reduced. Third, the predominant outcome is no cooperation with the primary sender, with less than 10 percent of the observations leading to significant cooperation. This observation corrects the popular perception that sanctions usually attract significant multilateral cooperation.

With no apparent methodological explanation to account for this, I now turn to possible theoretical explanations for the ineffectiveness of cooperation. Either multilateral cooperation is truly irrelevant or the straightforward prediction of increased cooperation leading to increased success is overly simplistic and further analysis is required.

PARSING THE PROBLEM OF SANCTIONS COOPERATION

Why does the extent of multilateral sanctions support have no appreciable effect on the outcome? The question dovetails into current debates about the utility of international cooperation and the role that international organizations play in fostering cooperation. The answer to the sanctions puzzle depends on one's model of cooperative behavior. In this section I outline three different explanations of multilateral cooperation that could explain the empirical puzzle and present testable hypotheses for each approach. . . .

Bargaining Between the Primary Sender and the Target

For most issues requiring cooperation, international actors first bargain among an infinite array of cooperative solutions, with each outcome resulting in a different distribution of benefits. The bargaining phase resembles a coordination game along the Pareto frontier.[18] All players are better off if they can reach a bargain and receive a positive flow of benefits. In order to avoid the costs of continued deadlock, everyone is better off negotiating a quick bargain. However, if the actors expect the bargain to have long-lasting implications, they will have more of an incentive to hold out for a more favorable distribution of payoffs, even if it means a sustained deadlock. In that situation, each actor also has a greater incentive to increase the opportunity costs of deadlock for the other player.[19] Other things being equal, an increase in the costs of no agreement for one actor will make that actor's bargaining position less tenable, improving the distributional position of the other actors. Economic sanctions can be one way of increasing the costs of deadlock for other actors.

Looked at in this way, a sanctions dispute represents a bargaining tactic between the primary sender and the target. The outcome of the dispute depends on both states' expectations of the long-run implications of any bargain. The more significant the bargain is for future payoffs, the more resistant both sides will be to conceding, and the more incentive each actor will have for increasing the costs of deadlock for the other side. For the sender, this situation translates into a search for multilateral cooperation. More cooperation worsens the target country's terms of trade, increasing the target's costs of no agreement. However, it also means that the target is willing to incur greater costs in order to secure a better settlement. In bargaining situations where both sides place a large value on the long-run implications of any bargain, one would expect the sender to make efforts to obtain international cooperation and the target to refuse to make any concessions. Thus multilateral cooperation could fail because it is strongly associated with issues and/or dyads that the target is most reluctant to concede.

U.S. sanctions against Iran represent an example of this dynamic at work. The United States has been concerned with the overall orientation of Iran's foreign and domestic policies under the theocracy established in the wake of the 1979 revolution. In January 1984 the United States imposed trade sanctions because of Iran's promotion of terrorism against Israel and attempts to acquire weapons of mass destruction.[20] This sanctions dispute involved important issues between actors that anticipated long-lasting effects from any bargaining concessions. Not surprisingly, over the past fifteen years the United States has invested heavily in securing multilateral support for sanctions. It succeeded in obtaining support from Japan and its NATO allies for denying Iran access to sophisticated military and nuclear technology. In 1996 President Clinton signed the Iran and Libya Sanctions Act to apply pressure on Japan, Russia, and the European Union to cooperate with the sanctions. This act targeted non-American firms that invested in Iran's energy sector. Although protested by the European Union and Japan, the act helped to deny Iran access to any appreciable amount of foreign capital.[21] Although the sanctions have imposed significant costs on Iran, they have failed to alter Iran's foreign policies because Iran was unwilling to concede on such a core issue of sovereignty.

Multilateral cooperation failed because it was associated with a bargaining dispute that both sides saw as important. According to this hypothesis, multilateral cooperation does not lead to successful sanctions because cooperation is correlated with high degrees of sender and target resolve. Unfortunately, resolve is an unobservable variable, making testing difficult.[22] However, we can test to see if cooperation is associated with situational factors that increase the likelihood that the issue at stake is significant for both the target and sender, leading to tougher bargaining strategies. If this bargaining hypothesis is true, then the extent of multilateral cooperation should be correlated with three factors. First, cooperation should be positively correlated with the occurrence of a territorial dispute. It is a truism in international relations that territorial issues have a high degree of salience for all nation-states.[23] Senders and targets that have a territorial dispute should have intense preferences on the subject and bargain accordingly. Second, cooperation should be positively correlated with expectations of future conflict between the target and sender. States that are enduring rivals tend to view their bilateral relations as a zero-sum game.[24] They will be concerned that any concession made in the present will weaken their bargaining position in the future, either because of a material shift in cumulative power resources or a softening of their reputation.[25] In this environment, any issue will have an increased salience. Third, cooperation should also be positively correlated with the length of the sanctions episode. If the sender and target place a high value on the issue at stake, they should be more willing to tolerate a sustained deadlock, which implies a longer period of imposed sanctions.

Bargaining Between the Primary Sender and Secondary Senders

Multilateral sanctions involve two separate bargaining problems: one involving the primary sender and the target and one involving the primary sender and other potential senders. It is possible that the bargain to secure international cooperation undercuts the ability of the primary sender to strike a bargain with the target country. For states to agree to multilateral sanctions, they must coordinate among a morass of equilibrium strategies. What exactly should be demanded? How extensive should the sanctions be? How can target compliance be determined? Unless the actors can agree on which outcome to aim at, there is no cooperation. One way to navigate the coordination dilemma is to look for shared norms and principles as focal points, that is, strategies or beliefs common to most of the actors.[26] The primary sender can socially construct the dispute so as to activate a legitimate norm, providing a focal point for the sender coalition. For example, the United States was clearly concerned about the distribution of energy resources following the Iraqi invasion of Kuwait. To appeal for UN support, however, the Bush administration framed the issue as one of violated sovereignty. The Security Council members were able to agree to sanction once they reached a focal point of punishing the sovereignty violation.[27] Through this rhetorical appeal to a violated principle, the primary sender might be better able to procure support from multilateral institutions.

Although activating resonant norms might make it easier to reach a bargain among senders, these norms could make it difficult to extract any concessions from the target.[28] . . . Johan Galtung observed precisely this sort of behavior in Rhodesia after it was sanctioned.[29] Target states can use their defiance of global norms as a way of counteracting the enhanced resolve of the sanctions coalition.

Second, in appealing to a consensual norm, the sender also endows the demand with an all-or-nothing quality, increasing the likelihood of the target country standing firm. Any attempt to compromise with the target would lead to a breakdown of cooperation among the senders as the sanctioning coalition moves away from the focal point. Negotiation would be difficult, since the sender coalition needs to hold fast to its demand of a reversion to the stated norm. In finding a norm that all sender states can support, the primary sender can raise the stakes in the dispute with the target country; there are few insignificant norms in the international system.[30] Most studies of economic sanctions agree that raising the value of the demanded concession makes success more difficult.[31] The target country may prefer making some concessions to continuing a deadlock. However, if faced with the stark choice of total acquiescence or the continuation of sanctions, the target may decide that the costs of sanctions are less than those of conceding.

The UN sanctions against South Africa represent an example of this type of normative appeal. After sanctions were imposed, there were no negotiations between the Afrikaner government and the coalition of sender countries. Rather, Audie Klotz shows that the sanctioning states were more concerned with adhering to the agreed norm of a complete abolition of apartheid.[32] The sanctioning states did not particularly care how the South African state reacted; their hope was to prevail through the socialization of South African elites and their eventual acceptance of the antiapartheid norm. In the end, despite concessions that began in 1989 from the white South African government, most sanctions were not lifted until all aspects of apartheid were dismantled.[33] Although this rigid appeal to norms led to a successful outcome in South Africa, it can also backfire. In the process of resolving the wars in the former Yugoslavia, the appeal to norms made it almost impossible to reach a compromise; as Susan Woodward observes, "The 'law of the instrument' was particularly detrimental because it set up a major conflict among the sanctions' purposes: protecting the instrument and international norms became more important over time than the actual outcome in Yugoslavia."[34]

This problem of inflexible demands and prolonged stalemates should be particularly acute when the primary sender uses an international organization as a mechanism for gaining cooperation. Although norms and principles may exist without an institutional reference, they are more likely to be embedded within international organizations; indeed, international organizations are often created with the expressed purpose of promoting specific norms.[35] A norm powerful enough to attract the support of an international organization should also be more difficult to compromise. It would call into question the integrity of the international organization and its founding ideas. Thus all of the bargaining problems associated with using norms are likely to be exacerbated when an international organization is enlisted to promote multilateral cooperation.

If bargaining between the primary sender and secondary senders undercuts the effect of multilateral cooperation, two hypotheses follow. First, there should be a positive correlation between sanctions involving a sender claim that the target is violating another state's territorial sovereignty and the active response by an international organization.[36] . . . Sovereignty violations go to the core of Westphalian society.[37] Second, other things being equal, sanctions involving claims of sovereignty violations should last longer than other sanctions episodes. States that cooperate because of a set of common beliefs will be reluctant to alter their position, causing the target country to prefer a sustained deadlock. This response can lead to an indefinite stalemate.

The Enforcement of Multilateral Cooperation

The preceding two hypotheses argue that multilateral cooperation is sabotaged by roadblocks at the bargaining stage. The other possibility is that cooperation fails because of problems at the enforcement stage. Unlike bargaining problems, which closely resemble coordination games, enforcement problems resemble the prisoners' dilemma. Once a multilateral coalition forms to sanction, it is presumed that all cooperating states benefit politically from the act of sanctioning. However, sanctioning states incur the costs of disrupting economic exchange, whereas sanction busters reap the benefits of rent seeking. . . .

These pressures to defect from the agreed-upon sanctions should be more acute as the size of the sanctions coalition increases. As the number of cooperating states increases, so do the economic rents that could be accrued for defecting. Monitoring also becomes more difficult as the number of states increases.[38] The importance of each secondary sender decreases as the number of senders increases. Therefore, the temptation to defect would be particularly acute at high levels of international cooperation.

Defection from a cooperation equilibrium can come in two forms. Either private agents engage in illicit trading in order to seek greater than normal profits, or secondary senders could announce an official change in policy and overtly trade with the target country. Although in game-theoretic terms these actions look similar (defection from a game of cooperation), the requirements for prevention are somewhat different.

Covert sanction busting is carried out by private agents with the goal of extracting economic rents. Defections by private actors abound in recent multilateral efforts at economic coercion. In May 1992 the UN Security Council imposed universal trade sanctions against Yugoslavia in response to Serbia's role in promoting ethnic conflict in the region. Six months later, however, the Security Council acknowledged that the sanctions were ineffective. Along the borders of Serbia and Montenegro, trade was brisk. A stronger enforcement regime was instituted, including the placement of customs inspectors in Macedonia, establishing a maritime exclusion zone, and freezing Serbia's financial assets. These additional measures tightened the sanctions, but they still failed to prevent oil and other strategic goods from arriving in the country. According to one report, more than one thousand trucks laden with goods passed between Macedonia and Serbia during a typical week. Even Albania, hardly an ally of the Serbs, was unable to prevent significant cross-border traffic.[39]

This type of enforcement problem is endemic to multilateral sanctions. The enforcement costs of regulating the thousands of private agents with an incentive to defect is extremely high. . . .

The second type of defection is for secondary senders to explicitly reverse course and lift their sanctions on the target country. States have the same economic incentives to lift sanctions as private actors: to extract improved terms of trade. However, sender countries will face political as well as economic pressure to defect. Domestic pressure within sender countries to reverse the sanctions will first arise from sectors that rely on trade with the target. This pressure will increase over time. Opposition groups will have the added argument that the sanctions should be lifted because they fail to alter the target country's behavior. These groups can logroll with other export sectors leery of any trade restrictions[40] as well as interests that oppose strategic co-operation with the primary sender. Secondary senders incapable of preventing illicit trade with the target will have an additional incentive to formally lift the sanctions. Private sanctions busting increases the size of a country's informal economy, strengthening actors outside the zone of state control. The distorting effects of these activities on the sender's political economy can destabilize the government in power. The greater the degree of illicit activity, the greater the political pressure on the sender government to legalize such activities.

This type of breakdown in cooperation is potentially more serious than the activities of private agents. If secondary senders decide to reverse their sanction decision, a backsliding phenomenon may result. . . . If other countries choose not to cooperate, the incentive of other states to participate in sanctioning decreases. The contagion effect means that an initial burst of cooperation can lead to an imposing sanctions coalition even if each state's support for a coercion strategy is wafer-thin. Such a coalition can still fall apart due to the fragility of the equilibrium. If the target state refuses to back down immediately, one country's change of mind could trigger a cascade effect across the entire coalition as uncertainty increases. Backsliding can cause the cooperation to erode and eventually dissolve, leading even the initial sender to back down.

The 1979 U.S. grain embargo of the Soviet Union illustrates the dilemma of backsliding. Eight days after President Carter announced the grain embargo, representatives from the world's primary grain exporters—Canada, the European Community, Australia, and Argentina—met and issued a statement pledging to limit their sales to the Soviet Union and not exploit the U.S. embargo. None of the countries endorsed the Soviet invasion, and all considered themselves better off if the Soviet Union was punished. Furthermore, the belief that all of the other countries preferred to sanction compelled even the most reluctant state, Argentina, to a cooperative strategy. Only a few days after this pronouncement, however, the Soviets offered Argentina a 25 percent markup from market prices in order to ensure a steady inflow of grain. The Argentine minister of agriculture then declared that it would not participate in the embargo. In April 1980 it signed a long-term grain deal with the Soviet Union, guaranteeing exports for five years. . . .

In formal game-theoretic terms the defection by private actors and nation-states would appear to be the same. In practice, they are quite different and lead to different enforcement strategies. The number of private actors is considerably greater, and it can be presumed that the profit motive will be enough of an incentive for some firms and individuals to try and circumvent the sanctions. With this kind of defection, sanctions can be maintained only through monitoring and enforcement of any trade with the target state. Although monitoring cannot eliminate sanctions busting, it can raise the costs of illicit trade to such a level that the magnitude of sanctions busting is manageable.

Preventing nation-states from officially defecting is another matter entirely. The problem is not just to prevent states from defecting but also to lower expectations of future defections. If secondary senders do not expect other members of the coalition to hold fast, the temptation to defect first increases. In order for the coalition to hold together, each member must share the common conjecture that other members are still committed to cooperation. Furthermore, it is difficult to enforce a sanctioning equilibrium by punishing defectors with additional sanctions. Theoretically, such an enforcement mechanism suffers from a time inconsistency problem; although the sender coalition has an incentive to say it will punish defectors from the coalition, the incentives change after the defection occurs.[41] Only through inducements can a sender coalition reduce the incentive of some states to defect.

The presence and support of an international organization can ameliorate both kinds of defection problems. International organizations can possess enforcement powers that punish private agents who carry on illicit trade with the target state. Even if international organizations lack enforcement powers, they increase the flow of information, reducing monitoring costs and making free riding easier to detect. Analysts have shown elsewhere that institutions can enforce agreements just through monitoring and information exchange.[42]

In the case of overt defection, international organizations can transform a fragile cooperation equilibrium into a more robust one. International organizations possess three attributes that prevent backsliding. First, they can channel side payments to wavering states in order to increase the value of continued cooperation. The side payments made to Jordan, Turkey, and other frontier states sanctioning Iraq are an example of this mechanism. Second, through routinized and repeated interactions, they can provide a forum for reassurance to all of the members of the sanctioning coalition.[43] . . . If each sender is reassured that other senders are standing firm, the incentive to violate an IO mandate decreases. Finally, they give sender elites a way to blunt domestic pressures to change policy. Through the fashioning of binding agreements and the moral suasion of sender elites, international organizations can prevent senders from switching their preferences during the imposition of sanctions.[44] For example, in the 1993–94 dispute with North Korea over its nuclear weapons program, Japan was reluctant to impose economic sanctions against North Korea without UN backing. . . .

The two variants of the enforcement problem lead to a common prediction: there should be marked differences in the success rate of multilateral sanctions with institutional support compared to other sanctions. Once an international institution supports the sanctions, the negative effects of sanctions busting and backsliding are controlled, whereas the positive effects of cooperation still operate. Institutionalized cooperation (the interaction term between the institutional support and cooperation measures) should generate greater concessions by preventing free riding and reducing the probability of backsliding.

The free-riding variant of the enforcement thesis provides an additional hypothesis. There should be no correlation between the target's costs and the extent of cooperation if there is no institutional support. Without institutional support, it is easier for secondary senders to claim they are cooperating and still free ride.[45] This would sever the connection between multilateral cooperation and increased economic costs to the target. Therefore, if the observed level of international cooperation increases, the actual costs of the sanctions to the target country should remain constant.

The backsliding variant of the enforcement thesis also provides an additional hypothesis. Multilateral cooperation without the backing of an international organization should be significantly less effective than unilateral efforts. Target states are more likely to stand firm and wait out an ad hoc sender coalition, because the expected probability of secondary senders backsliding outweighs the terms of trade effect of any additional cooperation. . . .

DATA DESCRIPTION

I use events data from Hufbauer, Schott, and Elliott to test the hypotheses.[46] Their data set covers sanctions cases from 1914 to 1990. Consistent with the literature,[47] for some of the tests I have removed the cases where regular military force was used to end the dispute, because these cases do not measure the success or failure of economic sanctions. . . . Unless otherwise noted, the data come from Hufbauer, Schott, and Elliott. What follows is a brief explanation of the data and any changes made to the Hufbauer, Schott, and Elliott data set.

Sanctions success measures the extent to which the target country met the sender's publicly stated demand. Success is narrowly defined as "the extent to which the policy outcome sought by the sender country was in fact achieved."[48] This variable is coded on a four-point scale.

Concession size is also used to account for the size of the original demand. One of the problems with the sanctions success measure is that it is only a partial measure of concession magnitude because it omits the relative significance of the original demand. A partial concession to a large demand (halting an invasion) might be more beneficial to the sender than a complete concession to a smaller demand (a diplomatic note of apology). It is necessary to create a measure for the size of the concession eventually made by the target. Combining the success measure with the demand size, it is possible to develop a measure of concession size that gauges the absolute size of the concession.[49] Concession size is coded from zero (no concession) to 4 (major concession).

The proxy variable for a sustained deadlock will be the duration of the sanctions episode. Duration measures the number of years sanctions were maintained. The figures come originally from Hufbauer, Schott, and Elliott but have been updated to 1995. The modal outcome was an episode of less than a year, and the mean was roughly five years. Seventy percent of the episodes lasted less than five years, indicating that sustained deadlock was not a common occurrence.

International cooperation is an ordinal variable, described earlier in Table 1. Institutional support is a dummy variable equal to 1 if an international organization called for or enforced sanctions against the target country. . . .

The target's opportunity costs of sanctions measures the economic costs suffered by the target regime as a percentage of its gross national product. One of the admirable qualities of the Hufbauer, Schott, and Elliott research effort is the care taken to estimate the cost to the target of sanctions. Rather than use gross trade figures, they estimate the price elasticities of demand and supply of the disrupted trade in order to determine the true economic cost. This measure represents a good approximation of the cost of asset-specific investment to the target.[50] Previous tests have shown this variable to be significant and positively correlated with a successful outcome.

The control variables used in the various statistical tests are consistent with those used in other econometric studies of economic coercion.[51] Hufbauer, Schott, and Elliott do not provide comparable cost figures for the sender country and use an ordinal measurement instead. However, it is possible, using the information in their cases, to develop a cardinal measure of the sender's opportunity costs of sanctions. This measure is expected to be negatively correlated with sanctions success.

The alignment and realignment measures are proxies for conflict expectations. Hufbauer, Schott, and Elliott use an ordinal coding of the prior relationship; it ranges from 1 (hostile) to 3 (amicable). This measure is useful because it incorporates intangible elements of the bilateral relationship that other possible measures lack. However, Hufbauer, Schott, and Elliott fail to code when the target country chooses to respond to the sanctions by balancing away from the primary sender, a response with significant implications for the outcome. Balancing behavior should raise expectations of future conflict, increasing the concern for relative gains and reputation and thus lead to a reduced number of concessions. If the target realigns, the prior relationship does not affect the outcome; the post-balancing alignment is the important term. The realignment term will take a larger value if the target was previously a close ally. For example, if the target realigns from a neutral to an antagonistic relationship, the realignment term takes a value of 1; if the target realigns from a cordial to an antagonistic relationship, the realignment term takes a value of 2. This way, the balancing term accounts for the extent of the realignment. The alignment term is expected to be positively correlated with sanctions success, whereas the realignment term should take a negative coefficient.

Territorial dispute is a dummy variable that takes on a value of 1 if the sanctions event corresponds to a territorial dispute as coded by Paul Huth.[52] Claims of territorial sovereignty is a dummy variable equal to 1 when either the primary sender or the target claims that its territorial sovereignty is violated. It is calculated by adding to Huth's data set any colonial dispute as well as disputes where the sender objects to the target's use of force in another country.

It is logical to assume that third-party assistance to the target country would reduce the likelihood of sanctions success. A dummy variable equals 1 if the target received material assistance from a third-party government. Hufbauer, Schott, and Elliott develop a trichotomous measure of the target regime's domestic stability. The higher the value, the more stable the target country. Finally, to control for the fact that the United States has been the primary sender in over half of the sanctions episodes, hegemon is a dummy variable that takes on a value of 1 if the United States was the primary sender after 1945.

COOPERATION AND SANCTIONS

The first explanation for the failure of multilateral cooperation is that cooperation is merely a symptom of tough bargaining between the primary sender and the target. As posited earlier, if this is the case, international cooperation should be positively correlated with three variables associated with tough bargaining strategies:

the presence of a territorial dispute, an antagonistic relationship between the target and sender, and the duration of the sanctions episode.

Table 2 shows an ordered probit regression that includes the bargaining measures as independent variables.[53] The results show that none of the bargaining measures is significantly correlated with cooperation. The strongest of the measures is alignment, which is negatively correlated with cooperation but does not even meet the 20 percent significance level. Territoriality is insignificant and trends in the contrary direction. To control for multicollinearity, bivariate tabular comparisons of multilateral cooperation with the bargaining variables were run. Again, no statistically significant correlations emerged. Taken together, the evidence suggests that multilateral cooperation is not correlated with tough bargaining between the target and primary sender. This finding is consistent with previous multivariate tests that show cooperation not to be associated with significant demands or conflict expectations.[54]

If bargaining between the sender and target does not undercut the effect of multilateral cooperation, perhaps the bargaining among senders does have that effect. According to this explanation, the use of potent norms and principles by the primary leads to more multilateral support. At the same time, it produces inflexible demands that make both sides prefer deadlock to a negotiated solution, leading to longer sanctions disputes. This approach also predicts that the effect of norms would be heightened when multilateral institutions are involved.

Table 3 shows the results of a probit regression with institutional support as the dependent variable. If the norms argument holds, the sovereignty claim should be positively correlated and statistically significant. There is no support for this explanation, as shown in Table 3. The sovereignty measure is positively correlated but does not approach statistical significance. A bivariate test yields somewhat stronger results: a positive correlation that just misses statistical significance ($p = .066$).

Although the use of norms may be only weakly correlated with institutional support, such an appeal may still produce a sustained deadlock. As a final test of the bargaining theses, I use the Weibull estimation of the determinants of the length of a sanctions episode; the results are shown in Table 4.[55] If bargaining among senders

TABLE 2. CAUSES OF COOPERATION

Variable	Coefficient	t-statistic
Territorial dispute	−0.083	−0.215
Alignment	−0.214	−1.242
Realignment	0.691	1.925
Cost to primary sender	−0.288	−0.769
Political stability of target regime	−0.018	−0.115
Third-party assistance to target	0.720	2.622**
Threat or use of military force	0.144	0.692
Log likelihood	−121.131	
Number of observations	115	

** $p < .01$.
* $p < .05$.

TABLE 3. CAUSES OF INSTITUTIONAL SUPPORT

Variable	Coefficient	t-statistic
Constant	−1.347	−1.852
Appeal to sovereignty norms	0.232	0.710
Alignment	−0.087	−0.425
Realignment	0.443	1.097
Cost to primary sender	−0.166	−0.429
Third-party assistance to target	0.685	2.216**
Political stability of target regime	0.195	0.985
Threat or use of military force	0.081	0.353
Log likelihood	−60.301	
Number of observations	124	

**$p < .01$.
*$p < .05$.

leads to a reification of demands, which in turn leads to a sustained deadlock, one would expect to see the use of sovereignty norms having a positive and significant effect on the duration of the sanctions episode. If the bargaining resolve of the sender and the target explains the failure of cooperation, then that measure should be positively correlated with the length of the sanctions episode. Table 4 shows that the sovereignty measure is negative and insignificantly correlated with the length of the sanctions episode. Although the institutional support and cooperation measures take a positive sign, neither variable approaches statistical significance.[56] The insignificance of these measures casts further doubt on the bargaining theses. The results suggest that using norms does have much success in attracting institutional support, and it does not translate into a sustained deadlock between the sender coalition and the target.

TABLE 4. DEPENDENT VARIABLE: SANCTIONS LENGTH

Variable	Coefficient	t-statistic
Constant	3.049	4.659**
Appeal to sovereignty norms	−0.128	−0.496
Institutional support	0.479	1.052
International cooperation	0.007	0.035
Alignment	−0.526	−3.176**
Realignment	0.727	1.856
Target assistance	0.287	0.908
Target regime's domestic stability	−0.211	−1.347
Number of observations	112	
Sigma	1.015	
Log likelihood	−163.23	

**$p < .01$.
*$p < .05$.

Finally, I consider the enforcement thesis. If the interaction term of institutionalized cooperation is positive, the enforcement thesis would acquire more credibility. Institutions would succeed in preventing sender coalitions from covertly defecting or overtly disintegrating, and they would communicate this fact to the target country, leading to more sizable concessions. If the cooperation measure is negative, the backsliding variant is supported; ad hoc sanctions coalitions are so fragile that they generate fewer concessions than unilateral sanctions.

Table 5 shows the effect of institutional support on sanctions outcomes; it provides the statistical results using both sanctions success and concession size as dependent variables. The results strongly support the enforcement thesis. The interaction term of institutionalized cooperation is positive in both regressions. Using sanctions success, the measure just misses statistical significance ($p = .065$); when concession size is the dependent variable, the measure is significant at the 5 percent level. If an international organization supports the sanctions, cooperation from other countries has a positive and significant effect on the magnitude of the target's concessions. The cooperation measure, by contrast, takes on a negative sign and is significant at the 1 percent level in both regressions. Without organizational support, increased levels of cooperation lead to significantly fewer concessions than any unilateral action. These results are consistent with the enforcement argument, particularly the backsliding variant.

There are two variations of the enforcement thesis: international organizations prevent private agents from sanctions busting, and international organizations prevent states from backsliding from promises to cooperate. If international cooperation failed because of free-rider problems, one would expect to see no correlation

TABLE 5. THE EFFECT OF INSTITUTIONAL SUPPORT ON SANCTIONS OUTCOMES

Independent variable	Dependent variable: Sanctions success		Dependent variable: Concession size	
	Estimated coefficient	t-statistic	Estimated coefficient	t-statistic
Support from international institutions	−1.280	−1.053	−1.396	−1.165
International cooperation	−0.557	−2.619**	−0.594	−2.784**
Institutionalized cooperation	0.779	1.848	0.915	2.180*
Target's opportunity costs	0.185	3.127**	0.206	3.585**
Sender's opportunity costs	−7.713	−2.004*	−7.810	−2.091*
Alignment	0.381	2.160*	0.370	2.136*
Realignment	−1.411	−3.361**	−1.496	−3.637**
Third party assistance to target	−.289	−0.898	−0.343	−1.077
Hegemon	0.001	0.010	0.019	0.182
Log likelihood	−131.841		−151.829	
Number of observations	110		110	

**$p < .01$.
*$p < .05$.

between the levels of international cooperation and the target's costs of sanctions, unless there is institutional support to monitor private attempts to illicitly trade with the target country. Table 6 displays the cost figures at different levels of international cooperation. The data call into question the free-riding variant of the enforcement thesis. There is a clear increase in the target's costs with an ordinal increase in the level of international cooperation. At the higher levels of cooperation, the presence of institutional support leads to a further increase in costs, but the difference is not particularly great.[57] If there is a free-rider problem, it does not appear to have a significant effect on the costs incurred by the target country.

As a further test, an ordinary least squares regression was run with the target's costs as the dependent variable. If the free-riding variant were true, then cooperation with institutional support should lead to an increase in the target's costs, but cooperation without such support should have a negative effect on the dependent variable. Therefore, this approach predicts that the interaction term of institutionalized cooperation should be positive and significant, but the cooperation measure should be negatively correlated with the target's costs.

Table 7 shows the opposite to be true. International cooperation is positively correlated with the damage inflicted on the sanctioned country. The effect is statistical[ly] significan[t] at the 5 percent level. In contrast, the interaction term between institutional support and cooperation has a negative and insignificant effect. The institution measure is positive but statistically insignificant. All of the control variables trend in the expected directions. These results lead to two conclusions. First, even if private agents circumvent sanctioning efforts, those problems are not significant. Second, institutional support does not guarantee that the target country will suffer significantly more economic damage.[58]

The findings in this section provide strong empirical support for the enforcement argument, particularly the backsliding variant. In sanctions disputes, an initial burst of cooperative behavior may rest on wafer-thin support. Without organizational support and reassurance, cooperation is fragile. This fragility gives the target state the incentive to wait out multilateral sanctions to see if the sender coalition collapses. Theory and evidence suggest that international organizations can enforce the sanctions bargain, preventing wavering states from switching preferences and defecting.

TABLE 6. COOPERATION, INSTITUTIONS, AND THE TARGET'S COSTS OF SANCTIONS

Level of international cooperation	Costs imposed on target as a percentage of GNP	Costs imposed on target (no institutional support)	Costs imposed on target (institutional support)
No cooperation	1.03	1.04	0.10
Minor cooperation	1.94	2.19	0.18
Modest cooperation	2.08	1.00	2.35
Significant cooperation	3.59	3.27	3.73

TABLE 7. DEPENDENT VARIABLE: TARGET'S COSTS

Variable	Coefficient	t-statistic
Constant	−2.481	−1.657
International cooperation	0.735	1.967*
Institutional support	−1.146	−0.502
Institutionalized cooperation (interaction term)	0.139	0.176
Cost to primary sender	4.516	1.189
Target regime's domestic stability	−0.625	−1.864
Alignment	1.181	3.324**
Significance of sender's demand	1.140	2.218*
Number of observations	110	
R^2	.279	
Adjusted R^2	.229	
Durbin-Watson statistic	1.990	
Standard error of the regression	2.483	

** $p < .01.$
* $p < .05.$

IMPLICATIONS FOR THEORY AND POLICY

Based on the findings in this article, I suggest some preliminary answers to the empirical puzzle of cooperation and economic sanctions. At first glance, there would seem to be no significant correlation between the extent of cooperation among sanctioning states and the extent of the target's concessions. This view actually masks two significant yet contradictory dynamics of international cooperation. On the one hand, multilateral sanctions that lack the support of an international organization are significantly less effective than unilateral measures. This outcome is the result of enforcement difficulties. Although sender states might be able to fashion a cooperative bargain to sanction, the equilibrium is not robust. Over time, domestic incentives might change such that secondary senders prefer ending their sanctions. Even if only one state changes its mind, the cooperative equilibrium can collapse. Even the original sender will often prefer to back down rather than remain isolated in a futile strategy of maintaining sanctions.

On the other hand, multilateral sanctions that have the support of an international organization are significantly more effective than unilateral efforts. Organizational support can convert a fragile cooperation equilibrium into a more robust one. International organizations prevent backsliding by giving wavering states the means to resist domestic pressures and by reassuring states that a cooperative equilibrium will be maintained. Members of the sanctions coalition are forced to add the costs and benefits of supporting the organization to the payoffs involved in sanctioning. States that value the existence and maintenance of international organizations will be less willing to violate a previous commitment. So long as wavering states are held in line, the contagion effect will prevent backsliding. Target states will offer concessions to institutionalized sanctions, whereas they are more tempted to wait out ad hoc coalitions. With the support of an international organization, the normative and material effects of multilateral cooperation are plainly observed.

The backsliding phenomenon also suggests a partial answer to the question of why primary senders would invest significant resources in obtaining international cooperation if it can backfire. The ideal for a primary sender is to secure institutionalized cooperation—both increased cooperation and institutional support for that coalition. However, given the principle of multilateralism that defines the decision-making structure in most international organizations,[59] obtaining the support of an international organization entails lobbying not only individual foreign governments but also their representatives within these organizations.[60] The effect of this lobbying has a knife-edge property. With institutional support, the odds of success are improved; without it, the odds are reduced. . . .

For policymakers, there are several implications. First, these results generate optimism about the ability of policymakers to use international organizations as a way of regulating international affairs. If cooperation had failed due to the bargaining problem, it would have suggested that multilateral economic sanctions have little use in managing the international system. Resolving the enforcement problem is a less onerous task for international organizations than resolving the bargaining problem, since there are fewer distributional concerns at the enforcement stage. However, I am not implying that multilateral cooperation is a cure-all. International cooperation without organizational support is worse than useless, it is counterproductive. The efforts to fashion an ad hoc coalition entail significant costs and distract from the larger dispute with the target country. The lack of organizational support gives the target regime an incentive to wait out the coalition because the probability of backsliding is high. Unilateral sanctions, even if less costly, are more likely to succeed because they imply a more credible commitment on the part of the primary sender.

The empirical results about bargaining and enforcement have additional theoretical implications. First, the results call into doubt some well-known theories of multilateral cooperation. The claims of John Mearsheimer and other neorealists that international institutions have little impact on international affairs must be categorically rejected.[61] International institutions clearly play an independent and significant role in the dynamics of multilateral sanctions. The results also call into doubt neoliberal claims about the ability of states to cooperate under anarchy.[62] Cooperation appears to be a far more fragile equilibrium than neoliberals have predicted. . . .

Most important, this research moves beyond the rather stale debate about whether international organizations matter to a discussion of how they matter. I suggest that international organizations are useful in reassuring states about each others' intentions through the development of common conjectures and the mitigation of domestic political pressures on heads of state. International organizations enforce cooperation, but not through the development of norms, or through traditional enforcement activities. Rather, they reduce the concern that states have about the likelihood of other states defecting, strengthening the common conjecture of continued cooperation. . . .

NOTES

1. See Doxey 1980 and 1987; Gilpin 1984; and Mayall 1984.
2. See van Bergeijk 1994; Bonetti 1997, 329–30; Drezner 1999a, chap. 4; and Hufbauer, Schott, and Elliott 1990, 95–96.
3. Snidal 1985.
4. Fearon 1998.
5. Martin 1992, chap. 1.
6. Gilpin 1984, 639.
7. Gardner and Kimbrough 1990.
8. Hendrickson 1994, 21.
9. Chayes and Chayes 1995, 64.
10. In fact, the chief criticism of the Clinton administration's decision to halt the sanctions machinery against North Korea was that the sunk costs of constructing the international coalition were very high and that the price of reconstructing such a coalition in the future would be prohibitive. See Charles Krauthammer, "Peace in Our Time," *The Washington Post*, 24 June 1994, A27.
11. Hufbauer, Schott, and Elliott 1990.
12. For bivariate testing, see Bonetti 1997; and Hufbauer, Schott, and Elliott 1990. For multivariate testing, see Lam 1990.
13. van Bergeijk 1994.
14. Lam 1990.
15. Drezner 1998.
16. See Morgan and Schwebach 1997; and Pape 1997.
17. IMF. One could argue that since many cases of economic sanctions involve only aid, trade figures are unimportant. Empirically, however, analysts have shown that even aid sanctions have a deleterious affect on trade between the senders and the target. See Hufbauer et al. 1997.
18. See Fearon 1998; and Krasner 1991.
19. See Drezner 1999a; and Fearon 1998.
20. These sanctions are distinct from the multilateral sanctions that were also imposed from 1979 to 1981 because of Iran's seizure of the U.S. embassy and its personnel.
21. Clawson 1998, 92–95.
22. Bueno de Mesquita, Morrow, and Zorick 1997.
23. See Huth 1996; and Vasquez 1993.
24. See Goertz and Diehl 1993; and Vasquez 1993.
25. Drezner 1999a.
26. See Garrett and Weingast 1993; Kreps 1990; Martin and Simmons 1998; and Schelling 1960.
27. Not coincidentally, the only unanimous Security Council action regarding the Iraqi invasion was Resolution 664, which rejected Iraq's legal annexation of Kuwait.
28. This is consistent with the arguments made by Kreps that the most effective norm does not necessarily lead to the most efficient outcome. Kreps 1990.
29. Galtung 1967.

30. For example, in the Iraqi case, the sovereignty demand required Iraq to forfeit all of Kuwait. Iraq's offer in late 1990 to abandon the country except for two strategic islands had to be rejected by the allied coalition, regardless of its merits. Such an agreement would have violated the sovereignty norm on which multilateral action was based.
31. See Baldwin 1985; and Morgan and Schwebach 1997.
32. Klotz 1995 and 1996.
33. There was some variation across the sanctioning states. See Klotz 1995, chap. 9.
34. Woodward 1995, 145.
35. See Finnemore 1996; Keohane 1989; Krasner 1983; and Ruggie 1993.
36. This includes, but is not limited to, claims that the sender's own sovereignty is being violated.
37. Bull 1977.
38. See Axelrod and Keohane 1986; and Kaempfer and Lowenberg 1999.
39. "How Sanctions Bit Serbia's Neighbors," New York Times, 19 November 1995, D3. See also Woodward 1995.
40. One can see this in the United States with the April 1997 formation of USA*Engage (http://www.usaengage.org), a business coalition that opposes most economic sanctions.
41. For more on the time inconsistency problem, see Simmons 1995.
42. Milgrom, North, and Weingast 1991. Furthermore, international organizations can engage in intrusive monitoring activities that would be more problematic for a single nation-state or concert of great powers. Weak states will permit international organizations to take actions that, if performed by another state, would appear to violate national sovereignty.

    Of course, the Serbian example suggests that formal international organizations also have difficulty in monitoring and enforcement. Indeed, the United Nations Association has commissioned a series of studies to examine how to strengthen its enforcement mechanism. Martin and Laurenti 1997. However, if international organizations have the same degree of failure as ad hoc coalitions with collective action problems, the liberal argument that international organizations can overcome collective action problems would be falsified.
43. On this reassurance function, see Martin 1993.
44. See Drezner 1999b; and Goldstein 1996.
45. Hufbauer, Schott, and Elliott's measure of international cooperation, discussed in the subsequent section, is particularly well suited to testing this hypothesis, because as coded it measures the initial commitment of states to cooperate.
46. Hufbauer, Schott, and Elliott 1990.
47. See Lam 1990; Morgan and Schwebach 1997; and Pape 1997.
48. Hufbauer, Schott, and Elliott 1990, 41.
49. For more on this coding schema, see Drezner 1999, chap. 4.
50. One modification is made to this measurement. Hufbauer, Schott, and Elliott incorporated third-country assistance into their cost calculation. For example, if Yugoslavia suffers costs of $100 million from the Soviet Union's coercion effort, but receives $75 million in U.S. aid as a substitute, Hufbauer, Schott, and Elliott set target costs at $25 million. This calculation combines two effects that often occur at different points in the coercion process. To better distinguish between the two effects, the cost variables are calculated excluding third-country assistance.
51. See Drezner 1998; Elliott and Uimonen 1993; and Lam 1990.
52. Huth 1996.

53. All regressions were run using Stata 5.0.
54. Martin 1992, chap. 4. The duration measure was not included in this regression because that measure is temporally preceded by the cooperation measure. This hypotheses is dealt with in Table 4.
55. The Weibull technique is used because it can factor in those cases that are still ongoing and also take into account whether the duration of the episode is time invariant.
56. Including only one of these measures does not affect the results.
57. Part of this difference is explained by the fact that the international organization, in addition to calling on member states to sanction, cuts off multilateral aid to the target country.
58. One possible explanation for this outcome would be that Hufbauer, Schott, and Elliott are only measuring the declared costs of sanctions to the target, and this figure does not take into account the covert sanctions busting explained by this hypothesis. If this is true, the Hufbauer, Schott, and Elliott measure would have overstated the target's costs in cases where an ad hoc sanctions coalition was present more than in cases of unilateral sanctions or institutionalized sanctions. As a check for this, the data were divided into two groups (ad hoc cooperation and all other cases) and separate multivariate ordered probit regressions were run on concession size. If for the ad hoc cases the coefficient for the target's costs either takes a lower value or loses its statistical significance, then the criticism of Hufbauer, Schott, and Elliott would be correct. The tests, however, showed that in both regressions, the target's costs were statistically significant, and the coefficient was actually greater in the ad hoc cases.
59. Ruggie 1993.
60. This description differs from Martin's assumption that institutional support temporally precedes the decision to cooperate. See Martin 1992.
61. Mearsheimer 1994.
62. See Axelrod 1984; Axelrod and Keohane 1986; and Snidal 1985.

REFERENCES

Abbott, Kenneth W., and Duncan Snidal. 1998. Why States Act Through Formal International Organizations. *Journal of Conflict Resolution* 42 (1):3–32.

Axelrod, Robert. 1984. *The Evolution of Cooperation*. New York: Basic Books.

Axelrod, Robert, and Robert O. Keohane. 1986. Achieving Cooperation Under Anarchy: Strategies and Institutions. In *Cooperation Under Anarchy,* edited by Kenneth A. Oye, 226–54. Princeton, N.J.: Princeton University Press.

Baldwin, David A. 1985. *Economic Statecraft*. Princeton, N.J.: Princeton University Press.

Barber, James. 1979. Economic Sanctions as a Policy Instrument. *International Affairs* 55 (3):367–84.

Bayard, Thomas O., Joseph Pelzman, and Jorge Perez-Lopez. 1983. Stakes and Risks in Economic Sanctions. *World Economy* 6 (1):73–87.

Bonetti, Shane. 1997. The Analysis and Interpretation of Economic Sanctions. *Journal of Economic Studies* 24 (5):324–48.

Bueno de Mesquita, Bruce, James D. Morrow, and Ethan Zorick. 1997. Capabilities, Perception, and Escalation. *American Political Science Review* 91 (1):15–28.

Bull, Hedley. 1977. *The Anarchical Society: A Study of Order in World Politics*. New York: Columbia University Press.

Chayes, Abram, and Antonia Handler Chayes. 1995. *The New Sovereignty: Compliance with International Regulatory Agreements.* Cambridge, Mass.: Harvard University Press.

Clawson, Patrick. 1998. Iran. In *Economic Sanctions and American Diplomacy,* edited by Richard N. Haass, 85–106. New York: Council on Foreign Relations.

Cortright, David, and George A. Lopez, eds. 1995. *Economic Sanctions: Panacea or Peacebuilding in a Post–Cold War World?* Boulder, Colo.: Westview Press.

Doxey, Margaret P. 1980. *Economic Sanctions and International Enforcement.* 2d ed. London: MacMillan.

———. 1987. *International Sanctions in Contemporary Perspective.* New York: St. Martin's Press.

Drezner, Daniel. 1998. Conflict Expectations and the Paradox of Economic Coercion. *International Studies Quarterly* 42 (4):709–31.

———. 1999a. *The Sanctions Paradox: Economic Statecraft and International Relations.* Cambridge: Cambridge University Press.

———. 1999b. The Interaction of International and Domestic Institutions. Paper presented at the Conference on International Institutions, Domestic Politics, and Transnational Bargaining, University of Colorado, Boulder, June.

Elliott, Kimberly Ann, and Peter P. Uimonen. 1993. The Effectiveness of Economic Sanctions with Application to the Case of Iraq. *Japan and the World Economy* 5 (4):403–409.

Fearon, James D. 1998. Bargaining, Enforcement, and International Cooperation. *International Organization* 52 (2):269–305.

Finnemore, Martha. 1996. *National Interests in International Society.* Ithaca, N.Y.: Cornell University Press.

Galtung, Johan. 1967. On The Effects of International Economic Sanctions: Examples from the Case of Rhodesia. *World Politics* 19 (3):378–416.

Gardner, Grant W., and Kent P. Kimbrough. 1990. The Economics of Country-specific Tariffs. *International Economic Review* 31 (3):575–88.

Garrett, Geoffrey, and Barry R. Weingast. 1993. Ideas, Interests, and Institutions: Constructing the European Community's Internal Market. In *Ideas and Foreign Policy,* edited by Judith Goldstein and Robert O. Keohane, 173–206. Ithaca, N.Y.: Cornell University Press.

Gilpin, Robert. 1984. Structural Constraints on Economic Leverage: Market-Type Systems. In *Strategic Dimensions of Economic Behavior,* edited by Gordon H. McCormick and Richard E. Bissell, 105–28. New York: Praeger.

Goertz, Gary, and Paul F. Diehl. 1993. Enduring Rivalries: Theoretical Constructs and Empirical Patterns. *International Studies Quarterly* 37 (2):147–71.

Goldstein, Judith. 1996. International Law and Domestic Institutions: Reconciling North American "Unfair" Trade Laws. *International Organization* 50 (4):541–64.

Haass, Richard, ed. 1998. *Economic Sanctions and American Diplomacy.* New York: Council on Foreign Relations.

Hendrickson, David C. 1994. The Democratist Crusade: Intervention, Economic Sanctions, and Engagement. *World Policy Journal* 11 (4):18–30.

Hufbauer, Gary Clyde, Jeffrey J. Schott, and Kimberly Ann Elliott. 1990. *Economic Sanctions Reconsidered: History and Current Policy.* 2d ed. Washington, D.C.: Institute for International Economics.

Hufbauer, Gary Clyde, Kimberly Ann Elliott, Tess Cyrus, and Elizabeth Winston. 1997. U.S. Economic Sanctions: Their Impact on Trade, Jobs, and Wages. Working paper. Washington, D.C: Institute for International Economics.

Huth, Paul K. 1996. *Standing Your Ground: Territorial Disputes and International Conflict.* Ann Arbor: University of Michigan Press.

International Monetary Fund. Various years. *Direction of Trade Annual*. Washington, D.C.: IMF.

Jentleson, Bruce W. 1986. *Pipeline Politics: The Complex Political Economy of East-West Energy Trade*. Ithaca, N.Y.: Cornell University Press.

Kaempfer, William, and Anton Lowenberg. 1999. Unilateral Versus Multilateral International Sanctions: A Public Choice Perspective. *International Studies Quarterly* 43 (1):37–58.

Keohane, Robert O. 1989. *International Institutions and State Power*. Boulder, Colo.: Westview Press.

Keohane, Robert O., and Lisa L. Martin. 1995. The Promise of Institutionalist Theory. *International Security* 20 (1):39–51.

Klotz, Audie. 1995. *Norms in International Relations: The Struggle Against Apartheid*. Ithaca, N.Y.: Cornell University Press.

———. 1996. Norms and Sanctions: Lessons from the Socialization of South Africa. *Review of International Studies* 22 (2):173–90.

Krasner, Stephen D. 1983. Regimes and the Limits of Realism: Regimes as Autonomous Variables. In *International Regimes*, edited by Stephen D. Krasner, 355–68. Ithaca, N.Y.: Cornell University Press.

———. 1991. Global Communications and National Power: Life on the Pareto Frontier. *World Politics* 43 (3):336–66.

Kreps, David M. 1990. Corporate Culture and Economic Theory. In *Perspectives on Positive Political Economy*, edited by James E. Alt and Kenneth A. Shepsle, 90–143. New York: Cambridge University Press.

Lam, San Ling. 1990. Economic Sanctions and the Success of Foreign Policy Goals: A Critical Evaluation. *Japan and the World Economy* 2 (3):239–48.

Lind, Jennifer M. 1997. Gambling with Globalism: Japanese Financial Flows to North Korea and the Sanctions Policy Option. *The Pacific Review* 10 (3):391–406.

Mansfield, Edward D. 1994. Alliances, Preferential Trading Arrangements, and Sanctions. *Journal of International Affairs* 48 (1):119–39.

———. 1995. International Institutions and Economic Sanctions. *World Politics* 47 (4):575–605.

Martin, Lisa L. 1992. *Coercive Cooperation: Explaining Multilateral Economic Sanctions*. Princeton, N.J.: Princeton University Press.

———. 1993. The Rational State Choice of Multilateralism. In *Multilateralism Matters*, edited by John Gerard Ruggie, 91–121. New York: Columbia University Press.

Martin, Lisa L., and Jeffrey Laurenti, 1997. *The United Nations and Economic Sanctions*. New York: UNA-USA.

Martin, Lisa L., and Beth A. Simmons. 1998. Theories and Empirical Studies of International Institutions. *International Organization* 52 (4):729–57.

Mastanduno, Michael. 1992. *Economic Containment: COCOM and the Politics of East-West Trade*. Ithaca, N.Y.: Cornell University Press.

Mayall, James. 1984. The Sanctions Problem in International Economic Relations: Reflections in the Light of Recent Experience. *International Affairs* 60 (4):631–42.

Mearsheimer, John. 1994. The False Promise of International Institutions. *International Security* 19 (3):5–49.

Milgrom, Paul R., Douglass C. North, and Barry R. Weingast. 1991. The Role of Institutions in the Revival of Trade: The Law Merchant, Private Judges, and the Champagne Fairs. *Economics and Politics* 2 (1):1–23.

Morgan, T. Clifton, and Valerie L. Schwebach. 1997. Fools Suffer Gladly: The Use of Economic Sanctions in International Crises. *International Studies Quarterly* 41 (1):27–50.

Morrow, James. 1994. Modeling the Forms of International Cooperation: Distribution Versus Information. *International Organization* 48 (3):387–423.

Olson, Mancur. 1965. *The Logic of Collective Action.* Cambridge, Mass.: Harvard University Press.

Paarlberg, Robert L. 1987. The 1980–81 U.S. Grain Embargo: Consequences for the Participants. In *The Utility of International Economic Sanctions,* edited by David Leyton-Brown, 185–206. London: Croon Helm.

Pape, Robert. 1997. Why Economic Sanctions Do Not Work. *International Security* 22 (2):90–136.

Ruggie, John Gerard. 1993. Multilateralism: The Anatomy of an Institution. In *Multilateralism Matters,* edited by John Gerard Ruggie, 3–48. New York: Columbia University Press.

Schelling, Thomas. 1960. *The Strategy of Conflict.* Cambridge, Mass.: Harvard University Press.

Schweller, Randall, and David Priess. 1997. A Tale of Two Realisms: Expanding the Institutions Debate. *Mershon International Studies Review* 41 (1):1–32.

Simmons, Beth. 1995. *Who Adjusts?* Princeton, N.J.: Princeton University Press.

Snidal, Duncan. 1985. The Limits of Hegemonic Stability Theory. *International Organization* 39 (4): 579–614.

van Bergeijk, Peter A. G. 1994. *Economic Diplomacy, Trade, and Commercial Policy.* Brookfield, Vt.: Edward Elgar.

Vasquez, John A. 1993. *The War Puzzle.* Cambridge: Cambridge University Press.

Woodward, Susan L. 1995. The Use of Sanctions in Former Yugoslavia: Misunderstanding Political Realities. In *Economic Sanctions: Panacea or Peacebuilding in a Post–Cold War World?,* edited by David Cortright and George A. Lopez, 141–51. Boulder, Colo.: Westview Press.

The Space of Peace-Maintenance

JARAT CHOPRA

July 1994 marked another shift in the evolution of United Nations military and civilian operations deployed to end conflicts. Widespread fatigue at the UN Secretariat and the slow pace of reform in the organization as a whole led to some permanent members of the Security Council deploying military forces independently and largely unaccountably, but with nominal approval in the form of vague Security Council resolutions. The UN seemed to have become the broker for a new round of great-power politics, which it had been designed to end. Under blue umbrellas France had already deployed forces in Rwanda, the USA subsequently invaded Haiti and Russia consolidated its forces in Abkhazia. . . .

On the ground, the UN had had to contend with the contradictory phenomena of too much order and authority by a powerful and oppressive government, as in El Salvador or Namibia, and fragmented or entirely anarchical conditions, as in Cambodia and Somalia. Reconstituting legitimate authority either from a recalcitrant centre of power or from disparate ashes in the wake of conflict was approached either diplomatically or militarily. Both proved inadequate in the context of intensely social and political conditions. . . .

In the incoherent malaise of factionalism, a kind of "warlord syndrome" emerged in which the appetites of power could mobilize religion in Lebanon, ethnicity in the former Yugoslavia, and relatively homogenous clan lineages in Somalia. Unchecked by a weakened population below and the diluted resolve of the international community above, factional leaders proliferated and inherited the areas of ineffective UN deployments. . . .

Unfortunately, particularly in the wake of the watershed experience in Somalia, the wrong lessons seem to have been learnt about what is needed and what is possible (see Chopra *et al.*, 1995). Rejecting the damaging consequences of military force, many officials at the UN prefer approaching conflicts diplomatically; in the USA, the principle of decisive force against a clearly defined foe is to be adhered to if force is to be used at all. However, missing from each equation is the apparent necessity to fulfill a political, executive function locally if social conditions are to be transformed from violent conflict to a rule of law that can be maintained, and the territorial implications of this.

If accountable and effective peace missions are to continue to be deployed, then a mechanism for operational political direction and on-going decision-making in the field needs to be devised. Collective mandates from the international community as a whole, as authorized by the Security Council or General Assembly, will be necessary for legality and legitimacy. However, to connect genuine collective accountability and effectiveness in the field, given the limitations of the UN which are now legion, a political directorate may include the UN as *primus inter pares,* but would also include regional organizations, interested and disinterested member states. . . . Recognizing the need for a locally effective international political authority reflects that the evolution of "peace-creating" or "establishing" doctrine has entered a third, and perhaps final, phase of territorial administration.

PEACE-MAINTENANCE

The first phase, the era of traditional "peacekeeping," lasted from 1945 to 1989, during which some 15 operations were deployed (see James, 1990; UN, 1990; Weiss and Chopra, 1992). This Cold War phase was characterized by diplomatic frameworks, the result of what conventional UN parlance referred to as "peace-making." As a consequence of diplomacy, limited military forces and civilian personnel were deployed symbolically to guarantee negotiated settlements, invariably between two sovereign states. For instance, observers in blue berets or peacekeepers in blue helmets supervised a blue line, separating belligerents, in places as diverse as the Golan Heights between Israel and Syria, Kashmir between India and Pakistan, and between Greek and Turkish communities in Cyprus. The UN's deployment to Lebanon in 1978, the last peacekeeping operation for nearly a decade, in the midst of factional militia manipulated by neighbouring governments in Syria and Israel, foreshadowed the future landscape of the UN's Dien Bien Phus.

A turning point occurred in 1989 when a decolonization mission was deployed in Namibia, with a wider range of tasks than the mandates of previous verification observers or interposition forces. In this next phase, between 1989 and 1994, a second generation of UN operations beyond symbolic peacekeeping evolved. During a five-year period, 18 operations were undertaken, more than had been dispatched in the UN's first 45 years. This represented a mood swing from Cold War pessimism to a new unrealistic optimism with nostalgia for the system envisioned in 1945. But it was a brave new world.

In the more challenging environment of internal conflicts, where the conventional necessity of consent of belligerent forces was not always forthcoming, the focus shifted from mere diplomacy to the development of a limited and gradually intensifying use of armed force concept for multinational missions, most dramatically in Somalia. This period also witnessed the emergence of complex, multifunctional operations designed to supervise transitions from conditions of conflict to minimal order, with limited impact in Cambodia and Mozambique. Transitional arrangements required but did not achieve better coordination between military forces, humanitarian assistance and civilian components organizing elections, protecting human rights, or conducting administrative and executive political tasks.

The second era redefined "peace" terms and spawned new ideas that did not develop into operational concepts before they were attempted in the field. In June 1992, UN Secretary-General Boutros Boutros-Ghali presented his plans for a strengthened UN security system, entitled *An Agenda for Peace*. He included under the broad rubric of "peace-making" not only the diplomatic settlement of disputes, but also an entirely different activity: coercive economic sanctions and the use of military force as envisioned in high-intensity enforcement under Article 42 of the UN Charter. . . .

Also under the heading "peace-making," as something more than peace-keeping but less than enforcement against an aggressor, the Secretary-General referred to the notion of "peace-enforcement." This reflected a discussion amongst scholars and practitioners that had crystallized by early 1992 calling for a limited use of force concept,[1] which unfortunately was not adequately developed before large US forces were deployed in Somalia, eventually claiming this label as their mandate. . . .

The term "peacekeeping" was expanded, but it was unclear how far. . . . Traditional peacekeeping nations, such as Canada and Austria, preferred to keep the term and apply it to nearly all UN peace activities—either to ensure the place of their historical experience or due to constitutional restrictions prohibiting them from engaging in enforcement actions. A misnomer emerged: "second generation peacekeeping"; in fact, peacekeeping was a narrowly defined concept and second generation operations were conceived to be no longer reliant on the consent of belligerents or on the use of force only in self-defence. The application of a diplomatic peacekeeping approach in challenging environments proved fatal in the former Yugoslavia, Cambodia, Angola, and in most other operations as well.

An Agenda for Peace further conceived of action before the outbreak and after the conclusion of hostilities. It referred to "preventive diplomacy," which included early identification of crises and troop deployments to avoid their escalation. However, there has been a tendency for international political will not to be mobilized until a pitch of violence manages to shock public opinion, invariably through press imagery—which is not available prior to the outbreak of hostilities. "Post-conflict peace-building" referred to longer-term development, strengthening institutions and fostering conditions that could vitiate violence as a means of social interaction. But this kind of "assistance" is incapable of ensuring the accountability of an oppressive regime or reconstituting fragmented authority.

The current third phase needs to elaborate operational dimensions of a political framework. . . . Despite the danger of adding yet another debased "peace" term to "bluespeak," and not as the result of the desire to coin a new phrase but naturally as a reconsideration of the essential basis of the UN Charter, the goal of "peace-maintenance" can be associated with this phase. It is used here to mean specifically the overall political framework, as part of which the political objectives of diplomatic activities, humanitarian assistance and military and civilian components are not only coordinated but harmonized. It provides a link between the operational and the strategic levels of command and control, and constitutes the exercise by the international community as a whole of political authority within nations.

The UN tends to confuse the terms "diplomatic" and "political." It refers to the "political process" as the attempt to reach a degree of reconciliation between factions or states. This is considered "political" not just because the process addresses the conclusion of a long-term settlement between states, or the establishment of a unified executive authority internally, but also to distinguish it from the other dimensions of an operation—military security, humanitarian assistance, or electoral organization, for instance. However, in such "political processes," the UN behaves as a diplomat and interlocutor, a representative of an authority far away, but fails to exercise political authority itself.

This may be logical between two states, since in each there is a government exercising political authority. In the no-man's-land in between, it is not imperative for the UN to come to terms with its jurisdiction over an area, and with its relationship to the territory, the local population or executive authority. It need be concerned only with the limited locations of its deployments and the placement of troops and armaments of the belligerents, since the government of each state is still juridically responsible for a portion of the buffer zone up to the international boundary, even if the exact position of that boundary is in dispute.

Within a state, this diplomatic approach is not tenable. The UN cannot remain aloof from its relationship to territory and local population, over which it may have claimed jurisdiction, and therefore must recognize its role in the exercise of executive political authority. It may have to fulfil this role independently in anarchical conditions, or jointly with an existing regime. Even in the latter case, if the UN is to ensure accountability effectively, it needs an independent political decision-making capability, as well as law and order institutions at its disposal. . . .

[This] draws the mission into the existing conditions of local authority, as the UN gravitates towards what it is permitted to do by a regime or warlords. It becomes beholden to the will of a government and it fragments in the face of factionalism or in anarchical conditions. In the Western Sahara and El Salvador, the UN strengthened the hand of the stronger, of Morocco and the government in San Salvador, respectively. In Cambodia, the UN joined the Cambodians" competition for control of Phnom Penh, which for centuries never implied control of the rest of the country. In Somalia, the irresistible forces of anarchy fragmented a loosely arranged coalition when the UN proved incapable of replacing US leadership.

To avoid this, the UN must establish a centre of gravity, following a decisive deployment, around which local individuals and institutions can coalesce until a new authority structure is established and transferred to a local, legitimately determined leadership. In the interim period, the UN needs to counterbalance or even displace the oppressor or warlords. This implies that the UN claims jurisdiction over the entire territory, and ought to deploy throughout if it can. It establishes a direct relationship with the local population that will eventually participate in the reconstitution of authority, and which will inherit the newly established institutions.

This is the meaning of a political framework, an overall blue umbrella, under which law and order maintained once a UN centre and periphery are delineated. This is distinct from the notion of intervention as part of interstate relations, in which entry into an area is only partial and territory is incidental to limited objectives. Authority cannot be exercised based on a perceptual axis of inside, outside and between, as is the essence of diplomacy. A political framework is all-pervasive and is connected to the total social process locally. It links that population with an international mandate as the basis of authority, in defiance of malevolent institutions of belligerents. Like the purpose of a rule of law, peace-maintenance must be a means of transforming the position of the weak as against the strong; it is an outside guarantor of a kind of internal self-determination.

Could the UN possibly do this? In the manner that it commands and controls fully integrated operations, the answer is likely to be no. During the second phase, at times the UN had to assume executive political powers on paper, but in the field, with a peacekeeping mandate, it exercised its authority diplomatically, through negotiation rather than independently. Consequently, the UN failed to control political institutions in Cambodia, was manipulated by Morocco in Western Sahara, and in Somalia broke apart into the separate agendas of contributing contingents.

In the last five years the UN as an essentially diplomatic organization has generally failed to meet a historic moment of change that required a political and not diplomatic mindset. This highlights the need for a political international organization for which peace-maintenance operations can provide the germ. Peace-maintenance is a kind of test: if the UN cannot or if member states are unwilling to meet this challenge . . . then the range of peacekeeping operations and beyond will continue to be dysfunctional. . . .

In the meantime, on the ground, the limitations of the UN and the need to address social conditions politically may be bridged by the notion of the interim executive body as a "joint authority," combining legitimacy and effectiveness. Not only would the entire effort be mandated collectively, but the active role of the UN, as a representative of the will of the international community as a whole, would ensure that the authority behaved accountably on behalf of the organization and in accordance with international legal standards, particularly with regard to human rights. Although this accountability may be enhanced by the participation of representatives of regional organizations, giving effect to decisions made will rest with individual states participating with military, policing and other civilian assets. Headquarters of specialized agencies of the UN and non-governmental organizations concerned with humanitarian assistance will have to begin to accept harmonization of objectives if they are to have an optimum impact on victim populations.

Through this unification of international efforts the kind of resources already deployed to the field in the past can be rearranged for effective peace-maintenance. By far the greater difficulty is shifting away from a diplomatic mindset and fostering the willingness to exercise effectively the political powers already assumed by the international community. There is the capability and the need, but is there a genuine depth of sincerity amongst "good samaritan" organizations, agencies and nations to respond successfully?

Ultimately, the critical factor for success or failure of peace-maintenance rests with the role of the local community, whom the effort is intended to help. Reliance on prejudicial local structures has proved mistaken, since the UN serves to affirm and not challenge the status quo. At the same time, warlords and factions are well-armed facts and the power of existing regimes is self-evident. Therefore, they must be part of any equation, but they cannot be permitted to dominate an international authority. No authority, malevolent or benign, can survive without the balance of popular consent in its favour. Successful peace-maintenance is premised on this fact. Therefore, the role local representatives play in a joint authority will have to be determined according to the specifics of the case.

Peace-maintenance is not some colonial enterprise. While there are generic principles that can be learnt regarding the administration of territory and population from any model of governance, the purpose and behaviour of peace-maintenance is the opposite of colonialism. Colonial domination is a unilateral enterprise; a joint interim authority is a collectively accountable body. While a colonial power draws resources from a colony, an international authority directs resources into a nation. A colonial power plays the role of master and the colonized that of servant. But in peace-maintenance, the international authority is the servant of both an international and locally supported rule of law and order. The goal of peace-maintenance is not imposition of an alien system, or a preconceived style of operation functioning in a social vacuum. The intention of a local international authority is precisely to create a flexible decision-making capability that can respond to local needs with political, anthropological and sociological sensitivity. While generic facets of peace-maintenance can be identified, their implementation needs to be locally responsive and directed on an on-going basis. . . .

FROM PLACE TO SPACE

In September 1991, in his final report to the General Assembly on the work of the organization, UN Secretary-General Javier Pérez de Cuéllar warned before his retirement that "the last thing the United Nations needs is a new ideological controversy."[2] The Cold War was over and the cessation of an ideological confrontation that had stunted the institutional development of international organization for 40 years was welcomed. However, by ending the proxy competition of superpowers in their spheres of influence new conflicts and injustices proliferated as nationalist adventurers sought to fill resulting vacuums in the former Yugoslavia, Somalia, Afghanistan and elsewhere. With intensified micro-competition were spawned several questions. What is the UN to do? When should it do something? Why? On the basis of whose authority and which legal provisions? . . .

During the Cold War most of the activities of the UN served in one way or another to protect the territorial integrity or political independence of states. The absolute source of authority for this was either the sovereign consent of the host government or the obligations incumbent upon UN members which had been voluntarily accepted by them as sovereign states. In its second generation, however, the UN was having to protect human rights or deliver humanitarian assistance, which challenged the territorial integrity and political independence of host nations in the absence of their consent. There had to be greater reliance on the legal construct of the collective authority of the Security Council as a representative of the international community as a whole.

This may have been a legitimate source of authority for a mandate not underwritten by host government consent. But it also meant that the Security Council was engineering extra-Charter activity without any architectural design. It was authorizing and deploying operations which did not fit neatly within the existing provisions of Chapters VI and VII and did not have the luxury of host state consent that underwrote traditional peacekeeping missions. It was charged with exceeding its powers, acting in bad faith and failing to be accountable to the larger community it represented (see Caron, 1993; Alvarez, 1995). The notion of international judicial review of the Security Council by the ICJ was raised, but the Court has refused to challenge the authority of the Council, such as in the Lockerbie bombing case, for fear of causing a constitutional crisis within the UN system (see Gowlland-Debbas, 1994).

The powers of the Council are circumscribed under Article 24(2) of the Charter by the purposes and principles of the organization, as well as by customary international law. The wide powers authorized for complex operations in internal conflicts did not contradict the purposes of the UN outlined in Article 1, and in this the Security Council did not necessarily exceed its powers. Problematic, though, was the excessive use of force by powerful nations nominally acting on behalf of the UN, such as the US violation in the Gulf of the customary limitation of proportionality (Gardam, 1993), or the contravention by several contingents in Somalia of the humanitarian laws of war (Amnesty International, 1994: 18–21, 32–34).

More fundamental was an incompatibility between a new set of purposes and an old set of principles: a wider interpretation of Article 1 of the Charter challenged Article 2. Article 2 amounts to the world view of the international system, which locates identity in the connection nationally between population, government and territory, and finality in the sacrosanctity of this linkage. A new operational landscape could not respect the exclusivity of this logic. But there was no meaningful alternative to the familiarity of sovereign statehood, no guidance or clarification of an overall framework in what was unavoidably becoming an ideological and jurisprudential crisis. The Security Council became the *de facto* ultimate source of authority not just for international action, but for responding to a changing worldview paradigm. At the same time, neither did it appreciate its role in this nor would it have been willing or able to tackle such an essential, conceptual issue.

Instead, it reconciled the contradiction between the need for its actions and restrictive principles by an elastic interpretation of the exception to Article 2: enforcement action under Chapter VII. Intrusive missions were justified as responses to threats to international peace and security, regardless of any factual basis for the claim. Did Somali anarchy directly threaten international order? As the principal Charter provisions pertaining to threats to and breaches of the peace, Chapter VII articles had to be manipulated and applied to cases which they were not designed to cover. Chapter VII had been conceived as a set of responses to interstate aggression, escalating in intensity of pressure against a delinquent state. Therefore, the language of Article 42 authorizing the necessary use of force was used, but express reference was made only to Chapter VII as a whole. It was mistakenly believed that Article 42 action could be conducted by forces established solely under Article 43 agreements, which had never been concluded as a result of the Cold War. In fact, nowhere is this stated.

The net result was a skewed exercise of power. An old paradigm was relied on to justify responses to new imperatives, and it dictated the character of those responses. Restoration of specific state institutions and the preservation of order in neighbouring nations was invariably the goal, yet it was the breakdown of such structures generally, the erosion of their reliability and loss of exclusivity that permitted and required operations to challenge the logic of the state. Permanent members of the Security Council cooperated more than ever before in the life of the organization. The General Assembly was forgotten as a mandating authority for peace forces and the Security Council encroached on the Assembly's sphere of competence as it assumed jurisdiction in economic and social affairs. Essentially, the Security Council intervened in a new paradigm without accounting for the implications of operating in that space. Powers assumed on paper or military force used in the field were at times excessive and at others insufficient since operational designs were not aligned with ideological implications.

This in turn was reflected in the field in the gap between goals set for an operation and the ideological baggage of Article 2. . . . Preconceived operational models imposed on local conditions without independent and genuine engagement in the social and political process tended to be either irrelevant, or to tear the social fabric without having any means to mend it: indigenous high hopes for a UN saviour led to alienation by the "God that failed;" large, wealthy and at times corrupt missions altered the local economic balance without any long-term assistance; and contrary to its intentions, the UN usually tipped the balance of power away from the local population towards the most powerful warlord or an oppressive regime because operations were not grounded in a local social process to the extent that even the abusive, but indigenous, bullies were. The struggle to establish a centre of gravity of authority to check, balance or displace self-proclaimed, mini-potentates had to be conducted amongst the local population on local territory, and not through alien, diplomatic institutions. . . .

ADMINISTRATIVE AUTHORITY

Throughout the first and second eras of UN missions, the development of civilian administrative capabilities increasingly shifted in focus from the internal organization of operations to governance over territory. The UN practice in observation of ceasefire lines and armistice agreements, and eventually the deployment of armed forces for the purpose as international referees, gradually emerged during the Cold War. The restrictive political atmosphere meant these activities were limited in scope, had few military, policing or other resources and could be deployed in only rare instances. . . . UN civilian administration developed as part of the evolution of military forces in observation and peacekeeping tasks, which themselves had been subordinated to the diplomatic culture of the UN system. . . .

The first operation deployed for the purpose of transition administration was the UN Temporary Executive Authority (UNTEA), which supervised the decolonization of Dutch West New Guinea and transferred the territory to Indonesia between 1962 and 1963. For seven months a UN Administrator had exclusive and full authority under the direction of the Secretary-General to administer the territory. The Administrator had the power: to appoint governmental officials and members of the representative councils; to legislate for the territory; to issue travel documents to Papuans for travel abroad; and to fulfil UNTEA's commitments and guarantees regarding civil liberties and property rights. UNTEA was to adapt the Dutch institutions in the territory to an Indonesian pattern. Above all, having secured the reins of power, it was to transfer this to a new authority.

It was also envisioned that the UN would conduct a plebiscite in 1969 as a genuine exercise of self-determination to establish whether or not the inhabitants wished to be part of Indonesia. A Representative of the Secretary-General with a staff would advise, assist and participate in the arrangements, which were primarily the responsibility of Indonesia. However, once the territory had been transferred, the matter was effectively closed.

To underwrite UNTEA's authority, a UN Security Force (UNSF) was deployed. It comprised 1500 Pakistani troops and 110 naval personnel to man Dutch patrol vessels transferred to the UN. Its primary task was the maintenance of law and order and to do this it would cooperate with local Papuan police, the Papuan Volunteer Corps, whose links to the Dutch army would be severed, and at the discretion of the Administrator Indonesian armed forces could be used. The UNSF also had an observation role to implement ceasefire terms and supervise the repatriation of prisoners. The force was exclusively responsible to the civilian Administrator.

Despite these extensive powers, UNTEA turned out to be an anomaly. The UN experience in the Congo, occurring simultaneously between 1960 and 1964, effectively halted the development of multifunctional operations and returned the international community to the conventional tasks of peacekeeping (see Rikhye, 1993). The Operation des Nations Unies au Congo (ONUC) was considerably larger, with 20,000 troops at its height, but it was juridically less authoritative than UNTEA. While UNTEA was an exclusive authority that secured power before transferring it, ONUC assisted an authority once power had already been transferred. ONUC's most difficult task was assisting the central government in the restoration and maintenance of law and order as the local authority fragmented and ultimately collapsed with the emergence of a secession. This left ONUC at one point in the position of being the effective authority in the area, which necessitated the Security Council's expansion of its powers to use force.

ONUC did not deploy under the terms of a comprehensive agreement and a mandate addressing the overall problems in the Congo. It operated under limited but vague Security Council resolutions which had to be updated several times. The operation formed its character through trial and error and by reacting to ground conditions as they developed. By the end of the operation, ONUC would have carried out a number of complex tasks. To maintain the territorial integrity and political independence of the Congo, ONUC contemplated using force to compel a Belgian withdrawal and had to prevent the secession of Katanga. To assist the central government in the restoration of law and order, ONUC was to protect life and property from unlawful violence, disarm elements threatening internal law and order, and help reorganize the national security forces. To prevent the occurrence of civil war in the territory and to secure the withdrawal of foreign military forces and mercenaries, ONUC used force to apprehend and deport.

ONUC, therefore, exercised extensive policing powers, but often it did so in the absence of a local central authority, and the UN was not in a position to behave as a replacement. The effective exercise of authority outside a coherent framework, without a comprehensive strategy, meant ONUC could only react to events and could not bridge the gap between the vacuum of authority centrally and the challenge of anarchical nodes of authority around this on the one hand, and the UN's capabilities and mandate on the other. . . .

Many of these issues, however, would not be addressed for nearly three decades. The international community was psychologically unprepared for the UN to assume such extensive powers; Cold War interests confronted third-party impartiality and possibly undesirable outcomes of the UN's role in internal conflicts; and the public perception that ONUC in particular, but also the use of force and the exercise of UN authority generally, had been a failed experiment led to the view that these should not be tried again. Instead, the conventional tasks and practice of peacekeeping crystallized in the Sinai, Cyprus, the Lebanon and elsewhere. Civilian functions reverted from exercising authority to administering peacekeeping operations.

The role of the Special Representative of the Secretary-General (SRSG) developed as a negotiator or at most as a guarantor of settlements, rather than as an instrument of UN authority or as a governor. This kind of civilian authority, of conventional peacekeeping missions, reached its height in 1988 with the UN Good Offices Mission in Afghanistan and Pakistan (UNGOMAP), which did not address the Afghan conflict as such, but verified the Soviet withdrawal from the area. This occurred as the end of the Cold War began to alter the whole landscape of UN operations.

The UN Transition Assistance Group (UNTAG) in 1989 was effectively a joint administrator of Namibia with South Africa, a powerful occupying force about to withdraw (see Crocker, 1990, 1992). The original plan in the 1970s envisioned the UN assuming executive powers and exclusive control over the territory. This proved impossible politically, and given the capabilities of the UN Secretariat and available resources, it would have been unsuccessful operationally. Nevertheless, this partnership approach enabled the UN to develop its own multifunctional approach to problems. The civilian–military interface became an acute issue for the first time, given the unprecedented scope of civilian activities. Although the military Force Commander was subordinated to the civilian Special Representative, this relationship was not well integrated and military assistance to civilian tasks was not as forthcoming as was needed. In the end, due to inertia from previous operations and an inability to predict the results of the Namibia experiment, it turned out that the size of the military component was over-estimated and the civilian resources under-estimated. . . .

. . . The main feature of the Namibian operation was the experience the UN gained in holding elections and verifying them as "free and fair." While the SRSG did not have exclusive responsibility to organize and conduct the election, UNTAG was nevertheless instrumental in drafting an electoral law and ensuring the South African administration's compliance with it. Electoral components would become one of the best developed arms of civilian administration in the future as the UN came to rely more and more on elections as a final point of transitional arrangements and as a means of justifying withdrawal.

However, although not an acute problem in the relatively benign environment of Namibia, a fragmented model of UN administration was developing. UN military units in the countryside were responsible not to the local political officer but to the Force Commander in Windhoek. Similarly, UN civilian police (CIVPOL) units were responsible to their Commissioner in the capital. The police were not responsible for conducting law and order tasks independently. Of conventional policing powers to report incidents, investigate violations, search premises, seize evidence, and arrest and detain individuals, UNTAG CIVPOL had only the first of these. . . .

While Namibia proved to be a comparatively calm environment, in which the occupying power was ultimately cooperative, Cambodia afforded the UN neither, yet it relied too heavily on the Namibia "success." The UN Transitional Authority in Cambodia (UNTAC) in 1992 and 1993 was the most extensive administrative operation to date and tested the UN's ability to exercise authority not just independently but in spite of intransigent local authorities (see Chopra et al., 1993; Chopra, 1994c; Doyle, 1995; Human Rights Watch/Asia, 1995). Although local authority in Cambodia was divided amongst factions, and in fact was traditionally fragmented and disconnected between Phnom Penh and the provinces in the countryside, the UN model of administration was itself fragmented and unable to fulfil its mandate of direct control of local power.

The SRSG could no longer afford to be a diplomat, whose subculture was to maintain a status quo as smoothly as possible or negotiate any change. Now it was a political job and executive powers had to be exercised and not negotiated. But the man in the position was a diplomat and refused to be what the mandate effectively required, a "MacArthur of Cambodia" as he put it.[3] Powers that existed on paper, but that were negotiated rather than exercised, meant that UN authority would be necessarily weak and UNTAC would be unable to transfer power since it had not secured it in the first place.

Even if the SRSG had exercised more of his powers, the operation was limited in its ability to implement executive decisions. UNTAC's authority to "control" Cambodia's administration included the power to politically neutralize ministries through the removal of personnel, but there was no means to enforce this independently and local intransigence meant it could not be done. The concept of UNTAC's CIVPOL was very much a traditional one of assistance in the maintenance of law and order by local forces, and so its powers were restricted to reporting and investigation. But rather like the reactive experience in the Congo, these had to be expanded to include the full powers of search, seizure, arrest and detention. Arrests were made, but detention required a UN jail. For the first time this was established, but it was never used and prisoners were detained by military contingents. The powers of arrest had been necessitated partly by the establishment of a Special Prosecutor as a means for the UN to be seen to be responding to growing political violence as the elections approached. However, the executive core of UNTAC effectively prevented prosecutions for political purposes, contradicting UNTAC's human rights education in the legal system regarding independence of the judiciary. . . .

In the meantime, operations deployed to Western Sahara and El Salvador provided lessons of their own. An operation mandated to hold a referendum in the exercise of Western Sahara's self-determination failed to reach its goal. It was the best example of an operation with the widest powers mandated and the least means available to underwrite these powers. The UN claimed the authority to be an exclusive administrative governor of the area, with powers of repealling local legislation and with military and security units able to exercise full law and order functions independently. Instead, it failed to deploy more than a few hundred observers due to the occupying power's intransigence.[4]

In El Salvador, the first human rights operation outside a larger framework with military and police units was deployed in 1991. Although the process was underwritten by an extensive negotiating capability, linked with the direct involvement of the Secretary-General, the ability of the UN to investigate, report on and sometimes protect human rights rested with the support of the Farabundo Martí National Liberation Front (FMLN). This acted as an enforcement mechanism for the UN by challenging government forces, and its eventual neutralization meant also that the authority of the UN was curtailed as well (see Johnstone, 1995).

Finally, the Somalia experience did not represent the culmination of all these experiments. . . . It evolved almost by itself through four phases: conventional ceasefire observation between July and November 1992; forcible delivery of humanitarian assistance between December 1992 and March 1993; combat operations between June and October 1993; and nation-building properly after October 1993. Although the UN had a mandate to assist Somalis, in the absence of a centralized authority, when restructuring government institutions, it was forced to behave as a *de facto* authority. In effect, the UN did in Somalia what it was supposed to do in Cambodia and it did in Cambodia what it was supposed to do in Somalia.

Even considering the special role of the USA, it can be said that UN authority was exercised more forcefully and independently than before, albeit at times to excess and unaccountably. The Security Council issued its first arrest warrant, detention facilities were established and held overall some 1000 arrested prisoners, but there was no system of prosecution or law in place to regulate this activity. This is the reverse of the former Yugoslav tribunal, which is a system of prosecution without any means of apprehension. The UN's ultimate goal was to hold an election, but this would not have altered the political landscape. More significant was the UN's attempt to establish a Somali police force, judiciary and transitional government from the bottom up, in defiance of the attempt by factions to establish a government controlled by them from the top down.

Somalia was the first place since Dutch West New Guinea where the UN could have secured power and been in a position to transfer it to a legitimate authority. But the UN proved incapable of doing so. How could it successfully administer territory in the future?

TERRITORIAL ADMINISTRATION

There is a fracture between the political legitimacy of decisions made by the international community as a whole and the effectiveness of operations implementing these decisions. On the one hand, this has led to the questionable legitimacy of states implementing UN decisions unaccountably, such as the widely criticized, disproportionate response of the US to Iraqi aggression in Kuwait (see Clark,

1992; Kaikobad, 1993). On the other, it has led to accountable but ineffective UN operations. Peace agreements brokered by UN diplomats could not be translated into action because operational considerations had not been adequately assessed, and either the Secretariat did not have the means or the capability to implement increasingly challenging mandates issued by the Security Council or it was practically not possible to fulfil in the field the military and civilian tasks assumed diplomatically in New York.

While the missing link between diplomatic agreements and the conduct of forces in the field was not critical during the Cold War era of traditional peacekeeping, in the more complex transitional arrangements this led to failures of large parts or the whole of operations. Peacekeeping forces sometimes did not manage to settle conflicts but served only to guarantee the conditions of military or political stalemate, such as in Cyprus and Lebanon. This was because the consent of belligerents to a UN peace process and to the presence of a UN force was enough to enable the operation to fulfil broadly its vague mandate, but there was no mechanism to harness consent initially given to actually resolve the conflict.

After the Cold War, insurgent belligerents were less easily identified than state armies on delimited territory and the distinction between no-man's land and someone's territory blurred. Consent of parties to agreements reached was withdrawn once the UN deployed to the field or new factions and splinter parties emerged after agreements had been concluded. To achieve negotiated settlement initially in any case, peace terms tended to be vague and capable of multiple interpretation, by the UN and each of the parties. The UN did not have the means to militarily enforce its will, relying as it was on the consent-based formula of traditional peacekeeping, and tended to be held hostage to warlords and adventurers. . . .

A UN political directorate may be deployed in one of several transitional scenarios. The UN may assume exclusive responsibility in an area and administer as a governor-in-trust, or it may participate in some joint arrangement in which it assumes responsibilities of a transition phase but does not physically conduct all the tasks of governance. In this case it would exercise varying degrees of authority and either control local authority, enter into a partnership with it or render it assistance.

1. *Governorship*. The UN assumes full responsibilities for conducting the affairs of government. This may occur when there is a total collapse of local state structures or where the state structures were imposed by a colonial or occupying power that has withdrawn. The UN may assume the tasks of governance itself and deploy a specific operation for the purpose or it may assume these responsibilities in name and appoint a single power or group of powers as agents to perform tasks on its behalf. This would require some mechanism of effective accountability that would ensure continued direction by the UN of the powers conducting the operation.

2. *Control*. An operation deployed to the area in question may have been authorized under a mandate to exercise the powers of "direct control." In this event, the UN authority in the field would deploy throughout the instruments of the state or administering authority—including ministries, the judicial system, and police and armed forces. Once deployed, UN officials would observe the local authority conducting the affairs of state

and in the event that it commits an infraction according to the terms of the overall mandate of the transition process, the UN has the overriding authority to "take corrective action" by dismissing personnel or redirecting a local policy decision.

3. *Partnership.* It may be that the local authority is powerful and has adequate resources, either because it is a colonial power decolonizing or another kind of occupying force withdrawing, or it may be a totalitarian regime submitting itself to a democratizing process. In this case, the UN authority-in-trust may behave more as a partner of the local authority, given the coherent structures of governance in place, although it would still be first among equals and as the transition authority have the final say in the transition period.

4. *Assistance.* It may be that the local administration is in general though not complete disarray and the trust authority provides an overall coherence and international standard for the development of government structures. Local structures in place may have been mishandled or abused and spawned an opposition or fragmented into several factions and constituted a source of conflict. The trust authority behaves as a director of administration, selectively correcting flaws in the local system.

In each case, the UN may intend to organize and conduct or supervise an election in order to transfer power from one authority to another. In the interim period, the UN may have assumed juridical authority over the area on paper, even if it has not managed to do this physically. To be an authority in the area, a mission must accept the juridical implications of being in possession of power if it is to be in a position to transfer that power to a new authority. To do so, it must manage to physically wrest authority from an unaccountable regime or assume it and establish a centre of gravity in the midst of anarchical conditions.

Furthermore, a joint authority may have to decide whether, anthropologically, an election is the correct means of establishing or transferring authority. In Cambodia and Somalia, for instance, there were factions that did not share the UN perception that an election implied a winner, a loser and a transfer of power; in both countries it was perceived as just one bargaining chip in a self-developing balance of power. The UN has treated elections more as an exit strategy for itself rather than as a means to sustainable results. As such, they have been short-term responses to conditions requiring longer-term attention. Therefore, joint authority cannot be exclusively reliant on elections as an end by themselves; they can be only one of a number of institutions, all of which require each other as part of a single framework if order is to be sustainable.

In joint forms of administration, the powers of direct control or corrective action will have to be underwritten by an independent capacity to exercise the UN's will. While this will be selectively applied in instances where a flaw exists or an infraction has been committed, the operation will nevertheless need to have available effective means of governance at its disposal. These include UN civilian police forces, an independent means of criminal prosecution and a criminal law developed for UN operations generally that takes account of human rights issues. These activities may be possible only in the context of a secure environment provided by UN military forces. . . .

CONCLUSIONS

"Multifunctional" must be understood to mean the integration of diplomatic, military and humanitarian activities in an overall political strategy for UN operations. The umbrella framework that coordinates these elements will need to be the UN administrator as politician if complex transition arrangements in internal conflicts are to be successful. The tasks of political administration are ultimately the glue that maintains the coherence of a comprehensive strategy. If any of the diplomatic, military or humanitarian aspects of operations dominates the others, an imbalance results from the vacuum of subordinated elements.

The UN to date has not adequately developed political strategies commensurate with diplomatic, military and humanitarian activities. This has led to limited success in the field, and at times to failure. The specifics of military operations and humanitarian assistance are being identified. A similar political process is required. But can the UN do the job? The assumption of enormous administrative tasks seems unlikely given the results of the last five years. At the same time, the evolution of civil administration and the UN's political role in internal conflicts builds on the organization's experience and in joint form it will be more cost-effective than reliance on military enforcement. At the same time, it provides a vehicle for the development of military capabilities in a palatable manner and for humanitarian activities in a better coordinated manner.

If peace-maintenance is to be successfully developed, then it must be collectively underwritten by the international community as a whole. Sovereignty and the barriers that the concept has raised cannot withstand international intervention in issues that are deemed international, and the scope of "international" is widening to the point that UN political authority becomes a necessity rather than an infringement. . . .

NOTES

1. See Mackinlay and Chopra (1992), Brian Urquhart interviewed by Helga Graham (1992). Urquhart (1992) and also Urquhart's (1993) development of this, as well as the commentary on the idea in *New York Review of Books* (24 June and 15 July 1993).
2. This and subsequent quotes are from UN Doc. A/46/1 of 6 September 1991, p. 10.
3. Interview with UNTAC's SRSG Yasushi Akashi, Phnom Penh, November 1992.
4. Compare the application of "peace-maintenance" in this context: Chopra (1994a,d).

REFERENCES

Allott, P. (1990) *Eunomia: New Order for a New World*. Oxford: Oxford, University Press.
Amnesty International (1994) *Peace-keeping and human rights*. AI Doc. IOR 40/01/94 of January 1994.
Alvarez, J. E. (1995) The once and future Security Council. *Washington Quarterly* 18(2), 5–20.
Betts, R. K. (1994) The delusion of impartial intervention. *Foreign Affairs* 73(6), 20–33.

Boutros-Ghali, B. (1992) *An Agenda for Peace.* New York: United Nations Department of Public Information.

Boutros-Ghali, B. (1992–3) Empowering the United Nations. *Foreign Affairs* 17(5), 98–99.

British Army (1994) *Wider peacekeeping,* 3rd draft. British Army Field Manual, January 1994. London: Ministry of Defence.

Caron, D. D. (1993) The legitimacy of the collective authority of the Security Council. *American Journal of International Law* 87(4), 552–588.

Chopra, J. (1994a) Breaking the stalemate in Western Sahara. *International Peacekeeping* 1(3), 303–319.

Chopra, J. (1994b) The obsolescence of intervention under international law. In *Subduing Sovereignty, Sovereignty and the Right to Intervene* (M. Heiberg, ed.) pp. 33–61. London: Pinter Publishers.

Chopra, J. (1994c) *United Nations Authority in Cambodia.* Providence, RI: Thomas J. Watson Jr. Institute for International Studies.

Chopra, J. (1994d) *United Nations Determination of the Western Saharan Self.* Oslo: Norwegian Institute of International Affairs.

Chopra, J. and Weiss T. G. (1992) Sovereignty is no longer sacrosanct: codifying humanitarian intervention. *Ethics and International Affairs* 6, 95–117.

Chopra, J. and Weiss, T. G. (1995) Prospects for containing conflict in the former Second World. *Security Studies* 4(3), 552–583.

Chopra, J., Minear, L. and Mackinlay, J. (1993) *Report on the Cambodian Peace Process.* Oslo: Norwegian Institute of International Affairs.

Chopra, J., Eknes, Å. and Nordsø, T. (1995) *Fighting for Hope in Somalia.* Oslo: Norwegian Institute of International Affairs.

Clarx, R. (1992) *The Fire this Time: U.S. War Crimes in the Gulf.* New York: Thunder's Mouth Press.

Crocker, C. A. (1990) Southern African peace-making. *Survival* 32(3), 221–232.

Crocker, C. A. (1992) *High Noon in Southern Africa: Making Peace in a Rough Neighborhood.* New York: W. W. Norton.

Doyle, M. W. (1995) *UN Peacekeeping in Cambodia: UNTAC's Civil Mandate,* Boulder, CO: International Peace Academy and Lynne Rienner Publishers.

Gardam, J. G. (1993) Proportionality and force in international law. *American Journal of International Law* 87(3), 391–413.

Gowlland-Debbas, V. (1994) The relationship between the International Court of Justice and the Security Council in the light of the *Locherbie* case. *American Journal of International Law* 88(4), 643–677.

Graham, H. (1992) UN can be a real peacemaker in the brave new world. *Observer (London),* 26 January.

Halderman, J. W. (1962) Legal basis for United Nations armed forces. *American Journal of International Law* 56, 972.

Hinsley, F. H. (1963) *Power and the Pursuit of Peace.* Cambridge: Cambridge University Press.

Human Rights Watch/Asia (1995) *Cambodia at War.* New York: Human Rights Watch.

James, A. (1990) *Peacekeeping in International Politics.* London: Macmillan and the International Institute for Strategic Studies.

Johnstone, I. (1995) *Rights and Reconciliation: UN Strategies in El Salvador.* Boulder, CO: International Peace Academy and Lynne Rienner Publishers.

Kaikobad, K. H. (1993) Self-defence, enforcement action and the Gulf Wars, 1980–88 and 1990–91. *British Yearbook of International Law* 1992, 333–335.

Mackinlay, J. and Chopra, J. (1992) Second generation multinational operations. *Washington Quarterly* 15(3), 113–131.

Mackinlay, J. and Chopra, J. (1993) *A Draft Concept of Second Generation Multinational Operations,* 1993. Providence, RI: Thomas J. Watson Jr. Institute for International Studies.

NATO(1994) *NATO Doctrine for Peace Support Operations,* 28 February 1994. Brussels: NATO.

Onuf, N. G. (1994) *Civitas Maxima:* Wolff, Vattel and the fate of republicanism. *American Journal of International Law* 88(2), 280–303.

Rikhye, I. J. (1993) *Military Adviser to the Secretary-General: U.N. Peacekeeping and the Congo Crisis.* London: Hurst & Co. and St. Martin's Press.

Smith, R. (1994) *The Requirement for the United Nations to Develop an Internationally Recognized Doctrine for the Use of Force in Intra-State Conflict.* Camberley: Strategic and Combat Studies Institute.

Terry, J. P. (1994) The evolving US policy for peace operations. *Southern Illinois University Law Journal* 19 (Fall), 119–129.

Touval S. (1994) Why the UN fails. *Foreign Affairs* 73(5), 44–57.

Toynbee, A. J. (1946) *A Study of History.* Oxford: Oxford University Press.

Untied Nations (1990) *The Blue Helmets: A Review of United Nations Peacekeeping.* New York: UN Department of Public Information.

United States Army (1994) *Peace Operations,* Version 6, January 1994, Unpublished draft of US Army FM 100–23. Fort McNair, VA: Training and Doctrine Command, US Army.

Urquhart, B. (1992) A way to stop civil wars. *Providence Journal,* 2 January.

Urquhart, B. (1993) For a UN volunteer military force. *New York Review of Books,* 10 June.

Weiss, T. G. and Chopra, J. (1992) *United Nations Peacekeeping: an ACUNS Teaching Text.* Hanover, NH: Academic Council on the United Nations System.

CHAPTER 5

International Institutions and the Politics of Expertise

This chapter addresses the politics of knowledge and expertise. Functionalism has been crucial to research on the links between knowledge and international organization. Functionalist theories emphasize that international institutions are established to perform specific functions that individuals and governments need to have fulfilled. Furthermore, the form of these institutions follows their function. Even more fundamental to functionalism, however, is the view that political problems can be depoliticized by expertise, both technical and administrative.

Functionalism had its heyday in the aftermath of World War II, when extensive collaboration among the Western powers suggested that governments could interact easily to solve collective problems, even if their respective ministers were not always in agreement. Much of the literature on this topic centered on Western Europe, an area where the rise of regional institutions seemed to fit functionalist models quite well. That functionalism provided answers to formerly intractable political problems seemed to be indicated by the development of the European Coal and Steel Community and later the European Community as vehicles to (1) deepen economic and political integration, (2) take advantage of economic complementarities among member-states (especially Germany and France), (3) help these states to expand their market access and revive their war-torn economies, and (4) prevent another war in Europe and a possible revanchist fallback by Germany as soon as its economic position improved. However, the process of European integration turned out to be far more halting and episodic than functionalist theories would have predicted. Furthermore, in contrast to these theories, it became clear that Europeans were not shifting their loyalties from nation-states to European supranational institutions.

These limitations of functionalism gave rise to neofunctionalism, which stressed that the integration process required regular infusions of energy and that technical administration would not be enough to foster integration. Neofunctionalists believed that scientific and technical experts (or Eurocrats) would be able to develop integrative solutions by enhancing the scope of integration, expanding the scope of what Europeans viewed as their common interests, and averting policy conflicts between European governments. This expertise established a new form of legitimacy that was relatively apolitical and objective, and that contributed to a more consensual style of decision making. Underlying this neofunctionalist logic was the assumption that scientific expertise would be accepted—an assumption that overlooked the fact that scientific controversies are common and frequently quite bitter.

The articles in this chapter develop these points. (The following chapter on regional integration addresses some of these issues in more detail.) Rolf Lidskog and Göran Sundqvist show that the scientific knowledge on which environmental regimes are based is often controversial and thus cannot serve as a neutral ground on which to base political decisions. Rather, science and policy influence each other and both of them require a considerable amount of negotiation in order to produce expert (or epistemic) consensus. By examining the development of the Long Range Transboundary Pollution regime, they show that the creation of an epistemic community emerged as international collaboration in scientific areas became a *political project* involving both government officials and scientists.

Thomas Risse-Kappen's contribution makes a similar point. He argues that the ideas of and communications among epistemic elites are related to two variables: (1) the nature of the domestic structures that regulate the access to decision makers and set the framework for establishing governing coalitions, and (2) the international institutionalization of the norms and values contained in the policies that are advocated by the epistemic community. Focusing on the transformation of conceptions of Soviet security, Risse-Kappen shows that Mikhail Gorbachev's initiatives had their origins in Western Europe. They travelled from Western Europe through an epistemic network to the Soviet academies. Although these ideas had little impact on Soviet policy for some time, opening up the domestic political process created an opportunity to change the thinking of the new political elite. Furthermore, the differential reaction to new Soviet policies in the United States and Germany suggests the importance of domestic structures and the changing notions of legitimacy as embodied in international agreements and instruments.

The final two articles in this chapter critically examine the performance of international organizations, raising questions about the appropriateness of their policies. One problem raised in these articles is professional blindness—that is, framing a problem much too narrowly and thus proposing solutions to it that fail to address the larger issues at stake. Michel Damian and Jean-Christophe Graz argue that the World Trade Organization's (WTO's) focus on trade has systematically subordinated issues of sustainable development and ecological concerns. Furthermore, this organization is dominated by the most economically powerful countries—as well as by key interest groups within these countries. These actors have the ability to prioritize issues areas within the WTO and have established a norm of deferring to "expertise" based on epistemic authority, which invests national and transnational elites with power. While these experts have championed the case for an open trading regime, Damian and Graz maintain that this case is based on a set of assumptions that are highly questionable.

Another problem raised in these articles is that international institutions that propose unsuccessful programs and fail to meet their stated goals can lose any legitimate claim to expertise, especially if the institutions do not learn from these experiences and adjust policy accordingly. Joseph Stiglitz criticizes the policies of the International Monetary Fund (IMF), particularly during the Asian Financial Crisis, and the World Bank on these grounds. Stiglitz not only raises the political issue of *cui bono,* but also addresses the issue of who these institutions are accountable to. These issues are especially pressing when developing countries suffer due to speculation and unwise investments in allegedly "crony capitalist" economies that protect foreign capital from market disciplines. Stiglitz argues that the IMF has refused to take responsibility for mistaken policies that probably exacerbated the Asian crisis, and he discusses various alternative policies that could have eased the crisis. His article indicates that one of the most important yardsticks for the legitimate exercise of the power of expertise is contained in the Hippocratic oath: above all, do no harm.

The Role of Science in Environmental Regimes: The Case of LRTAP

ROLF LIDSKOG and GÖRAN SUNDQVIST

INTRODUCTION

Environmental problems are not new for humankind. They have been around for a long time, and maybe they even have been a permanent companion to humanity's whole existence. However, earlier environmental threats have been considered local, scattered and in many cases relatively simple to manage because they were quite easily defined spatially and temporally. This situation has changed and it is argued that one of the features of today's threats to the environment is that they are increasingly diffuse (difficult to delimit in space and time) and thereby beyond the lay person's range of normal experience. . . .

In science, as well as in the political community, there is a widespread idea that expertise has a pivotal role in our effort to create a sustainable society. It is through science that the scale of the problems, the ground for conflicts and the scope of solutions are defined. . . . This development implies a scientization of environmental policy—no valid action is possible without making science a partner. Also, in political debates all participants often state that their standpoint is scientifically grounded, and experts and counter-experts are mobilized.

However, a scientization of policy also means a politicization of science. When science becomes a partner in environmental policy-making, scientific debates and political ones often overlap. This has led actors to call in question the importance of science in environmental policy-making, instead emphasizing the importance of constellations of interests and power relations when explaining international environmental cooperation.[1]

The aim of this article is to analyse the role of science in international environmental policy-making. The focus is on a theoretical question: How and through which conceptual lenses should social scientists judge the role of science in this area? In answering this question we develop an approach which takes its departure from the sociology of scientific knowledge (SSK). The usefulness of this approach is illustrated by a case study of the Convention on Long-Range Transboundary Air Pollution (LRTAP).

The article is divided into five parts, this introduction being the first of them. The second part is devoted to regime theory and how it conceptualizes the role of science in international environmental policy-making. The third part introduces the perspective elaborated within SSK. On the basis of three key findings from this tradition a framework to analyse the relationship between science and policy is proposed. The fourth part consists of a case study of the LRTAP Convention, which serves to illustrate the relevance and explanatory power of SSK. In the fifth, and concluding part, some general conclusions are drawn as to the relevance of an SSK perspective on science and international regimes, not least when it comes to the role of science in the LRTAP regime.

GLOBAL ENVIRONMENTAL GOVERNANCE

During the last two decades the global environment has developed into the third major issue in world politics, comparable to international security and international economy (Porter and Brown, 1996: 1). The 1972 Stockholm Conference on the Human Environment, the third UN Conference on the Law of the Sea in 1973 (UNCLOS III) and the instigation of the UN Environment Programme (UNEP) in 1973 mark the beginning of a new era of global environmental governance (Keohane and Nye, 1977: 35). Around the beginning of the 1980s, long-range transboundary air pollutants, the depletion of the ozone layer, global warming and worries over the depletion of the world fisheries were issues to be negotiated on a global level. Whereas the 1985 Protocol of the LRTAP Convention and the 1987 Montreal Protocol of the Vienna Convention on the Depletion of the Ozone Layer developed from toothless regimes to more efficient ones, negotiations in other areas enjoyed little success (French, 1997). . . .

International Environmental Regimes

International regimes have been a way to politically manage problems that exceed national boundaries. In most cases they are issue-specific, and doubts have therefore been raised as to whether they have the capability to successfully address fundamental problems.[2] Regimes are mostly weak institutions, normative orders agreed upon by their parties but with low capacity for sanction in the case of someone infringing the rules (Mayer et al., 1993: 393). . . .

Because of the limit on using sanctions and the fact that many regimes seem not to be successfully implemented, the question of regime effectiveness has been raised by a number of scholars (see e.g. Bernauer, 1995; Hisschemöller and Gupta, 1999; Victor et al., 1998; Wettestad and Andresen, 1991; Young, 1999a). A growing concern has been to find out under what circumstances regimes are successful tools for international cooperation on environmental issues.

A number of factors seem to have an impact on regime effectiveness[3]—appropriate institutional and organizational forums; institutional capacity; the development of regimes in neighbouring fields; the development of transnational coalitions; the connection to broader social orders (the economic and political world order). Other, more immediate, factors are the occurrence of landmark meetings and structural changes in power relations, issue linkages and the availability of monitoring mechanisms (Hisschemöller and Gupta, 1999, see also Jacobson and Weiss, 1995; Rittberger and Zörn, 1991; Wettestad, 1999; Young, 1989, 1994).

Some researchers assert that regime effectiveness increases if the issue is limited in scope, and therefore offer the general recommendation to create regimes which focus on single issues (Young, 1989). Another proposed prerequisite for effective regimes is the existence of consensual scientific knowledge (Haas, 1992b; Hisschemöller and Gupta, 1999). Transboundary environmental problems, such as climate change and air pollution, may be good examples of issues where lack of scientific consensus may be an obstacle not only to regime development but also to efficient implementation.

The Importance of Consensual Knowledge

Peter Haas (1989, 1992a, 1993) has strongly emphasized the importance of knowledge, and most of all consensual knowledge, in the construction of regimes. According to him, a knowledge-based approach to regimes must be distinguished from the traditional approach, which he calls institutionalism (Haas, 1997: 195).

Haas argues that institutionalists—for example Robert Keohane and Oran Young—focus on actors, their interests and objectives, and how regimes should be organized in order to support cooperation among actors, i.e., institutional factors that promote cooperation (Haas, 1993: 183). In this approach, nation–states are seen as rational actors involved in international bargaining trying to satisfy their own interests. In those cases where knowledge is emphasized by institutionalists, it is viewed as an input to the process of bargaining with limited opportunity to modify the usually stable interests of the actors.

In contrast to institutionalism, Haas offers an approach which focuses on the importance of policy-relevant and consensual knowledge for the formation of a regime and the shaping of its patterns (Haas, 1993: 187). From the perspective of such an approach, it is not the interests of the actors (states) which shape the regimes, but consensual knowledge. Consensual knowledge has the power to mould the interests of the actors.

Through different empirical studies, Haas stresses the usefulness of this approach. Environmental regimes are not only driven "by state power, but by the application of scientific understanding about ecological systems to the management of environmental policy issues with which decision makers are unfamiliar" (Haas, 1997: 200). Therefore, knowledge—consensual and trusted knowledge—is a necessity for successful environmental cooperation.

Haas introduces the concept "epistemic community" as an analytic tool for investigating the role of science in regime formation and development. An epistemic community is a knowledge-based transnational network of professionals holding political power by cognitive authority (Haas, 1992b: 3). Members of an epistemic community could come from different disciplines but share a common body of knowledge which they interpret in a similar way. They also share values and policy, i.e., a conviction concerning how to enhance human welfare.

According to Haas (1989: 377), a large involvement of experts has contributed to the notion that regimes serve as important vehicles for institutional learning that, in turn, produces convergent state policies. In Haas's analysis, institutional learning is almost exclusively attributed to scientific involvement.

Haas considers his approach to be superior to the institutional approach, both in an explanatory and in a prescriptive way. The strength of the epistemic community model, compared to institutionalism, is that it provides a better understanding of how environmental regimes are shaped and work. Also it has important normative consequences, while it provides

> better environmental policy than institutional models . . . [T]he policy advice of the epistemic community is likely to be better because it is not a direct expression of underlying material interests and because it is more likely to be true than advice from other sources . . . [T]he knowledge claims are relatively non-biased and have passed a consensus test for truth. (Haas, 1997: 205–6)

The main difference, according to Haas, between the institutional model and the epistemic community model is that in the latter, knowledge is able to shape the attitudes of the actors involved in a regime, while in the former a regime is basically made up of the bargaining over interests between involved actors.[4] From the perspective of the epistemic community model, consensual knowledge could be applied directly in the policy process, while from the perspective of the institutional model it has first to be negotiated by political parties in order to reach needed compromises (Haas, 1997: 206).

Beyond an Uncritical View of Science

However, the approach of institutionalists seems not to be essentially different from that of Haas. In his latest book, Young (1999a) emphasizes that besides the utilitarian way of studying international regimes—where states operate according to the cost-benefit model and knowledge has a role only as an input in their calculations—there exists another perspective where regimes stimulate processes of social learning, affect social identities and change discourses. This means that regimes not only change the external environment for a state, but also work as learning facilitators and role definers. The LRTAP regime illustrates this well, where the regime fostered new ways to perceive the problem of acid rain, its effects and how to successfully cope with it (Young, 1999b: 262).

However, even if Haas's criticism of Young seems a bit obsolete, he does make certain points concerning the role different regime theorists attribute to science. There exist a number of studies which restrict science's role as an input to the negotiation process, seeing it as providing only factual evidence. This factual evidence does not affect the preferences of the unitary states, only their evaluation of the environmental issue at stake. From this point of view, Haas's distinction between his approach and that of institutionalism seems relevant and fruitful.

Thus the role of science in the formation, maintenance and implementation of environmental regimes is contested. The issue is whether scientific knowledge is able to shape regimes or is only one factor among a number of others that provide input to the work of regimes.

However both approaches—that of institutionalism and that of epistemic community—seem to share an uncritical view of science. Neither of them has put any effort into critically discussing the contingency and plurality of scientific knowledge (Jasanoff, 1996a: 186). Furthermore they do not explain what it is in scientific knowledge that makes its prescribed role possible. Institutionalists consider science an unproblematic input, coming from the outside to the actors involved in negotiations, while the epistemic community approach postulates a strong power of science in shaping environmental policy. Whereas institutionalists underemphasize the role of science, Haas overemphasizes it by claiming that science is the main source of institutional learning and that this learning is a main producer of convergent state policies (Haas, 1989: 377).

Both approaches misunderstand and simplify the role of science within international environmental regimes, leaning on an unproblematized, almost positivistic, view of science.[5] For the purpose of attaining a deeper understanding of the role of science in international environmental regimes, attention will now be turned to the sociology of scientific knowledge (SSK). SSK, which is based on a constructivist understanding of science, has since the early 1970s been devoted to gaining knowledge concerning science's role in society.[6]

THE CONTRIBUTION OF SSK

Three key findings of SSK are central to understanding the role of science in environmental governance, namely that knowledge never moves freely, that the value of science is the result of negotiations and that science and policy are co-produced (interdependent).

First, scientific knowledge, and indeed knowledge generally, has to be carried by social arrangements in order to be distributed in society. To move, knowledge needs support from actors and the social order. Bruno Latour has vigorously put forward the idea of knowledge as embedded in a social and material context (Latour, 1987, 1988). Knowledge never exists outside of a context. In order to produce, distribute and maintain scientific knowledge in society, material and social networks, as well as prepared (educated) humans, are required. "Facts and machines have no inertia of their own . . . [L]ike kings or armies they cannot travel without their retinues or impedimenta" (Latour, 1987: 250). However, when the networks have been arranged in a supportive way, knowledge appears as moving freely. An important task for the sociologist of science is to make visible and explain the social and material contexts which have been created in order to move science in society.[7]

Second, the value of scientific knowledge, for instance the value of such knowledge for policy, is not given by the content of science, but is negotiated by scientists in social processes where other actors are also involved. The concept of boundary work has been developed and used in order to enhance understanding of how the value of knowledge is to be decided (Gieryn, 1983, 1999; Jasanoff, 1987, 1990). Thomas Gieryn argues that "The boundaries of science are ambiguous, flexible, historically changing, contextually variable, internally inconsistent, and sometimes disputed" (Gieryn, 1983: 792). This gives room for negotiations and, according to Gieryn, all scientists are doing boundary work. When scientists define their own domain as scientific, the work of those outside of this domain is defined as unscientific and/or irrelevant. It is the actors involved who (consciously or unconsciously) do boundary work by judging which knowledge should be considered as valuable and usable for policy work. Sheila Jasanoff, who has studied scientists involved in policy-relevant research, found two main types of boundary work in relation to the questions concerning the usefulness of science for policy work—one trying to narrow the scientific domain and another trying to expand it (Jasanoff, 1987). Which is the more successful strategy has more to do with the political context than with the content of the knowledge concerned.

Third, scientific knowledge and the political order are shaping each other through an interdependent process of evolution. Sheila Jasanoff and Brian Wynne have called this the co-production of science and policy (Jasanoff, 1996b; Jasanoff and Wynne, 1998; Wynne, 1996). Such co-production means a dialectic (or homological) explanation of science and policy which claims that policy influences the production and stabilization of knowledge, while the knowledge simultaneously supports and justifies that policy. People accept some specific knowledge-claim because it supports their policy strategies. In this way causes and effects become functionally interrelated; production of knowledge is also production of policy. Co-production means that uncertain or contested science can grow stronger if the policy context is "right," while on the other hand, a weak policy context can become stronger through the support of science. What usually can explain the co-production of science and policy is that they are part of the same culture, in which a common and supported social project is strengthening the legitimacy of both science and policy (Jasanoff and Wynne, 1998: 16).

From this SSK perspective an alternative understanding of the role of scientific knowledge in environmental governance can be formulated. From the approach of institutionalism, scientific knowledge is viewed as an input reaching the regime from the outside. The negotiations within the regimes are understood as power games where nation-states act in accordance with their interests. Peter Haas has reacted against this approach and criticizes institutionalists for overemphasizing the role of political interests, thereby neglecting the role of science in shaping regimes. Haas, on the other hand, argues that consensual knowledge, carried forward by epistemic communities, has the power to change policy agendas and mould the interests of involved political parties.

The epistemic community approach can be criticized for prescribing rather than explaining the decisive role consensual knowledge has in environmental regimes. SSK emphasizes the necessary role social conditions have for science to acquire the power to influence and shape policy. This means that institutionalists are partly right in their focus on interests. However, to explain science by social factors (or political interests) does not necessarily imply that its power has to be reduced to them. By means of a dual focus on the importance on both scientific knowledge and political interests—concentrating, in fact, on the interdependence between them—it becomes possible to form an alternative to both the institutional model and the epistemic community model.

When it comes to trying to understand environmental regimes, the SSK perspective means that science can play an important role, even the crucial one prescribed by Haas, driving the regime and shaping the interests of the participants. However, this cannot be satisfactorily explained by the internal qualities of scientific knowledge or by the epistemic community alone. It is not science itself that decides what knowledge is counted as valid and usable for the formulation and implementation of the regime. Instead, the decision is made by different institutions and actors, and this has to be explained by social scientists.

Judged from an SSK perspective, institutionalism gives science a too limited role while the epistemic community approach gives it a too important one. Science and policy are always interdependent, which implies that science has a possibility of shaping regimes *if* social conditions are sufficient. Thus, to become relevant for policy-making, science has to be supported by social conditions. In her studies of environmental policy Sheila Jasanoff has proposed four mechanisms by which science may become policy-relevant (Jasanoff, 1996a: 191–4, 1997: 232).

According to her, scientific knowledge can be influential, (1) if it supports politically accepted forms of discourse and reasoning; (2) if communities that have a privileged right to formulate policy ratify it; (3) if convergent economic interests of business and government support it, allowing science to play the role of a visible consensus builder; and (4) if it is part of a general technological culture, where technocratic solutions of political problems are supported. Science and politics are in such a culture expressions of the same underlying social order, which is characterized by the promotion of a technological fix.

These four mechanisms illustrate the three SSK findings described above. In short they tell us that scientific knowledge needs to be adapted to the social and political order to be influential and to acquire the social authority for being policy-relevant. This implies a criticism of the epistemic community approach. However, the mechanisms do not conflict with Haas's thesis. On the contrary, when science has established itself, on the basis of a supportive political order, scientific knowledge and epistemic communities can play the important roles Haas has argued for. Arguing that policy contexts are important for understanding science does not mean that scientific knowledge should be reduced to political interests. This conclusion constitutes a criticism of the institutional model.

THE ROLE OF SCIENCE IN THE LRTAP REGIME

One of the most science-based regimes that exists today is the regime for Long-Range Transboundary Air Pollution (LRTAP), which aims to reduce the emissions of airborne cross-border pollutants within the UNECE region.[8] Scientific effect criteria, embodying the critical loads concept, are today the basic norms within LRTAP, and offer a mechanism for creating a science-based environmental policy (Wettestad, 2000: 116).

An institutional approach, focusing only on the political interests of the states involved, seems not to be satisfactory for explaining the LRTAP regime. On the contrary, there seems to exist a strong epistemic community within the field of long-range transboundary air pollution and therefore Haas's approach could be a more suitable tool to analyse this regime. However, taking the SSK response seriously means that there is a need to explain why an epistemic community is established, and why the actors involved accept a scientization of the issue.[9] In the following, attention will be given to the development of the LRTAP Convention and we use this case to illustrate the relevance of an SSK perspective in analysing the role of science in international environmental governance.

The Establishing of the LRTAP Regime

The start of the LRTAP Convention was not much about science, but more about world politics, first and foremost the relationship between East and West. At the 1975 Helsinki Conference on Security and Cooperation in Europe, the President of the Soviet Union, Leonid Brezhnev, took an initiative to create an international convention on some (unspecified) environmental topic (Björkbom, 1997: 1; Park, 1987: 167). Three years earlier, in 1972, the Eastern bloc had boycotted the UN Conference on the Human Environment in Stockholm, where long-range transport of air pollution and acidification was a main issue. This boycott was based on a conflict concerning diplomatic recognition of the German Democratic Republic (VanDeveer, 1998: 4). In a time characterized by deep-frozen relations between East and West, later amplified by the internationally condemned invasion of Afghanistan, the Soviet Union proposed cooperation. The LRTAP Convention was actually one of very few East–West cooperations in the late 1970s and early 1980s and the first environmental treaty between East and West (Björkbom, 1997: 2; Fraenkel, 1989). It could be argued that the Soviet Union was in urgent need of a foreign policy success (Lundgren, 1998: 289), and cooperation on environmental and scientific issues was considered a possible area.

In November 1979 the Convention on Long-Range Transboundary Air Pollution (LRTAP) was signed by 33 parties—32 nation-states and the European Community Commission (Wettestad, 1999: 85). It has been called the first multilateral treaty explicitly addressing atmospheric environmental matters (Munton et al., 1999: 167). This Convention, which up to now (December 2001) has been ratified by 48 parties, has been in force since 1983 and is the most important public regulator for reduction of the damage to human health and the environment caused by transboundary air pollution in Europe and North America.

However, even if the creation of the Convention must be seen in the context of world politics, science had already had an important role in creating knowledge concerning this problem. As early as October 1967 the Swedish soil scientist Svante Odén presented the hypothesis of acidification of precipitation. Odén argued that acidification should not be seen as a local problem, but as a large-scale regional problem in that "enormous quantities of various forms of sulphur were constantly being pumped into the atmosphere" (Odén quoted in Lundgren, 1998: 76). He argued that there existed a long-distance transport of sulphur dioxide, i.e. that there was a connection between sulphur emissions in Britain and continental Europe and the acidification of Scandinavian lakes, causing harm to valuable fish stocks (Lundgren, 1998: 77). Odén first presented his hypothesis in a Swedish daily, and right from the beginning the discussion on acidification spread outside the scientific community.

At the UN Conference on the Human Environment in Stockholm in 1972 a Swedish case study on transboundary air pollution was presented. The OECD responded the same year by launching a Co-operative Technical Programme to Measure the Long-Range Transport of Air Pollutants (Persson, 1993: 107). Eleven countries participated in this programme, several monitoring stations were set up in most of these countries and emission data exchanged. In 1978 the programme was made independent of the OECD and was thereafter called EMEP, the full name of which is the Co-operative Programme for Monitoring and Evaluation of the Long-Range Transmission of Air Pollutants in Europe. This was the first inter-governmental effort in this field and forms an important background to the Convention established a year later.

The conclusion to be drawn from this first phase is that policy and science should not be viewed as separate entities. At the start of the work on environmental cooperation there were a lot of uncertainties, observed by the actors in the field of international politics as well as in the field of acid rain research. Neither policy nor science—both were weak at this stage—could on its own determine the outcome and create the LRTAP regime. The East–West relation was frozen and in the late 1970s it was only Norway and Sweden which considered acid rain a serious environmental problem (Levy, 1993: 84).

The East–West diplomacy was, however, important for the establishment of the LRTAP Convention and it also accounts for the important role given to science within the regime. A policy context was produced which protected the importance of scientific work and exchange of data between the states involved. The first thing on the agenda for the new Convention was therefore to guarantee the continuation and development of the already established monitoring programme concerning emissions and effects, started by the OECD in 1972 and implemented all around Europe. A protocol on the financing of EMEP was signed in 1984. This programme was viewed as essential to the possibility of there being agreements on emission reductions (Wettestad, 1997: 237). A network of research was established within the regime. This was of great importance for the shaping of continuation, consensual knowledge and integration between the states. Of course this also encouraged the scientization of the work, and the power of the scientists grew (see Levy, 1993: 80–1; Wettestad, 1997: 245–6).

To summarize the establishing of the LRTAP regime in relation to the three SSK themes singled out in the former section, we are able to make the following remarks:

1. The initiatives concerning scientific cooperation—the OECD and EMEP programmes—that preceded the LRTAP Convention created mechanisms for collecting and disseminating information on pollution flows, effects and mitigation options. A "road" for exchange of scientific information and empirical data was thus established, and this made possible the growth and spread of a common knowledge base, concerning both the seriousness of the acid rain issue and the mechanisms of the ecosystems. A research community bound to a particular regime—an epistemic community—developed in Europe, sharing a perspective and producing a common pool of scientific research, not least emission data from the European countries.

2. Politicians carried out boundary work when they tried to neutralize the East–West conflict by suggesting cooperation in the field of environmental protection. Moreover, this was followed up when emphasis was laid on the importance of scientific cooperation, which meant a scientization of the air pollution problem in Europe. The policy-makers demanded scientific cooperation and saw it as playing a key role in the LRTAP regime. The scientists accepted an expanded role for science in environmental governance, and a scientization of the issue gave the scientists room for manoeuvre.

3. The LRTAP regime was created in a situation when scientific results were contested and international environmental policy was weak, as was the political cooperation between East and West in Europe. However, the LRTAP Convention became an important common social project to cooperate on for the states in Europe, acknowledging long-range air pollutants as a serious environmental problem. Therefore the regime quite soon became robust. The politicians' search for neutral—politically uncontroversial—issues to cooperate on was an important explanatory factor with regard to the scientific character of the regime. Science was assessed as a tool for political cooperation and the response to this was a well-developed monitoring programme around Europe. This is a good example of the interdependency between science and policy, i.e. a co-production of knowledge and policy.

The first two of Jasanoff's four mechanisms explaining the policy-relevance of science fit well into the first phase of the LRTAP development. A small group of politicians was given the right to formulate policy and agreed to support scientific cooperation. Scientific reasoning became thereby the politically supported way to handle transboundary air pollution in Europe. From the very beginning science was developed inside the LRTAP regime as a part of a common social project, which was reflected both in science and in policy.

The Critical Loads Concept

Neither in its early formulation nor in its present state does the LRTAP Convention include any specified reductions in relation to compounds. At the basis of the LRTAP Convention is the recognition that airborne pollutants are a major problem and that ratifying states are obliged to "endeavor to limit and, as far as possible, gradually reduce and prevent air pollution including long-range transboundary air pollution" (UNECE, 1979).

It was not until 1985 that the Convention was given teeth, when a protocol on the reduction of sulphur emissions was signed (UNECE, 1985; see Lundgren, 1998: 19; Sprinz and Vaahtoranta, 1994) which called for a reduction of emissions of sulphur dioxide by at least 30 percent, from 1980 to, at the latest, 1993. A similar "emission cut" protocol on nitrogen oxides was signed in 1988, involving the obligation to reduce "annual emissions of nitrogen oxides or their transboundary fluxes so that these, at the latest by 31 December 1994, do not exceed national annual emissions of nitrogen oxides or transboundary fluxes of such emissions for the calender year 1987" (UNECE, 1988). These "big emission cuts" have been explained by reference to the actions of "big players" and "big science" (VanDeveer, 1998: 19). The big players, according to VanDeveer, include Sweden, Norway, Germany, the Netherlands and the UK, and the big science the EMEP programme and the modelling work carried out by the International Institute for Applied Systems Analysis (IIASA).

There is a general finding in the studies of international regimes that consensus, both on policy issues and on scientific findings, is reached more easily if participation is initially limited (Jasanoff, 1996a: 196). The history of LRTAP is a good example of this. A limited number of states, from the beginning only Norway and Sweden, acted strongly on behalf of the larger community of signatories of the Convention. Like public opinion within SSK states, consensual knowledge (or policy) is shaped and carried forward by social actors.

A new era in the work of the LRTAP regime started in 1994, when the *Protocol on Further Reduction of Sulphur Emissions* was signed. This protocol is based on the critical loads approach where effects, and not emissions, are focused upon. It is a question of "[a] quantitative estimate of an exposure to one or more pollutants below which significant harmful effects on specified sensitive elements of the environment do not occur according to present knowledge" (Nilsson and Grennfelt, 1988: 9). To assess effects, rather than cut emissions, is considered delicate and puts great demands on scientific knowledge. Cost-effectiveness in the solutions has from the beginning accompanied the use of the concept of critical loads, which also has increased complexity.

This complexity and the scientific approach are even more apparent in the latest LRTAP protocol—the *Protocol to Abate Acidification, Eutrophication and Ground-level Ozone*—which was signed in Göteborg in November 1999. This is a multipollutant/multieffect protocol, which regulates four types of compound (sulphur dioxide, nitrogen oxides, ammonia and volatile organic compounds) which affect human health, natural ecosystems, materials and crops, due to acidification, eutrophication and ground-level ozone (UNECE, 1999: Article 2).

The signatories have called this "a smart protocol," one of the most sophisticated and most scientifically based protocols ever signed (Thompson, 1999). Obviously, during the 20 years of the LRTAP Convention the regime created by policy-makers and scientists has become more complicated, from one pollutant and flat rate reductions for all, to several compounds, many effects and varying national reductions based on the critical loads approach and also on cost-effectiveness.

Regime analysts agree on this characterization of the latest protocols, claiming that the critical loads approach implies a revolution in the relationship between science and policy in the regulation of international cross-border air pollutants (Levy, 1993: 100; Wettestad, 2000: 103). "For the first time the basis of negotiations of reduction targets was formed by scientifically founded environment standards rather than arbitrarily chosen proposals" (Gehring, 1994: 192). This entails that the regime is in need of continuous scientific support.

To return to the three themes of SSK, some tentative conclusions may be drawn from the second phase of the development of the LRTAP regime.

1. The policy of critical loads needs new "roads" to be built. According to Latour (1987: 232 ff.) there are always *centres of calculation* to be found, which connect the roads and which use them for both collecting and sending information. "[I]nside these centres, specimens, maps, diagrams, logs, questionnaires and paper forms of all sorts are accumulated and are used by scientists and engineers to escalate the proof race" (Latour, 1987: 232). By the use of scientific instruments the world is forced to come to the centre and at the same time it is transformed—condensed, abstracted, universalized—in order to make it easier to manage and control. Cadres of calculators inside these centres produce and distribute trusted knowledge along the roads.

In order to carry forward and implement the critical loads approach, detailed knowledge about the sensitivities of different ecosystems (soils, lakes, crops, human health, etc.) is needed (Grennfelt et al., 1994: 425). In 1990 the first efforts to map relevant parameters in the ecosystems in different parts of Europe were undertaken (Patt, 1998: 7). Maps were constructed which divided Europe into grid cells of 150 km^2. From these maps the most important centre of calculation within the LRTAP regime, IIASA's use of the RAINS model,[10] "used critical loads as a constraint to the optimisation of finding the least-cost emissions reduction pattern throughout Europe" (Patt, 1998: 9).

In the preceding section, it was argued that the EMEP Programme was part of a road-building project among the different parties. The use of the critical loads approach transformed this road into a highway, where new and needed scientific results could travel. Wettestad (1997: 245–6) describes this road in the following way—"[B]y far the most important mechanism within the LRTAP regime has been the provision of information . . . [T]he diverse scientific-political complex, with the well-functioning EMEP monitoring system as a solid core, provided information crucial to the progress of the process."

When the roads are constructed and the centres of calculation are producing trusted knowledge, which is distributed along the roads, they have made themselves indispensable. Therefore it could be argued, as far as the LRTAP regime is based on the critical loads approach, that IIASA's work on the RAINS model and the EMEP programme together form an *obligatory point of passage* for the whole regime (see Latour, 1988: 44).

2. Obviously, the concept of critical loads has been an important point of reference for both scientists and policy-makers. In this respect it works as an instrument of integration between science and policy. The boundary work carried out by scientists and policy-makers seems in the LRTAP case to have been directed towards inclusion and integration rather than towards demarcation and exclusion. The concept of critical loads serves here as an important meeting place, a *boundary object*, which shapes legitimacy within science and politics as well as among citizens. Susan Leigh Star (1989: 21) defines boundary objects as "objects which are both plastic enough to adapt to local needs and constraints of the several parties employing them, yet robust enough to maintain a common identity across sites." Boundary objects are tools for integrating different groups, for example scientists and policy-makers. Such objects create science and policy, while at the same time helping to create consensual attitudes and knowledge.

On the other hand, the establishing of quite a successful consensual LRTAP regime, highly dependent on science, has been made possible by the boundary work designed to exclude many actors. The work of a few "big players," as previously argued, has made this regime possible, and they are also heavily responsible for the research carried out. A regime strongly based on science also excludes many potential participants that do not qualify on scientific merit. Many states in Europe are not able to match the big players and are therefore in practice excluded from substantial participation.[11] In addition, it has been argued that the laggard states, by their cooperation together with the leader countries and through contacts with foreign scientists, have learned a lot about measuring, assessing and solving acid rains problems (Munton et al., 1999: 220 f.)

Furthermore, many nations in the former Eastern Europe are currently working towards being economically and politically integrated into the wider Europe, which implies that they have to adapt their environmental policy to EU standards. The result of this will be converging domestic policy agendas. This is a good example of Jasanoff's third mechanism explaining epistemic consensus by converging interests of business and government.

3. The boundary object of critical loads could also be viewed as an object which is *co-producing* science and policy, making them more dependent on and close to each other, and thereby strengthening the regime. This means a production of mutual understanding, as well as mutual interests, between scientists and policy-makers. Jan Thompson (1999), chairman of the LRTAP Executive Body, put it this way:

> The secret behind the Convention's achievements lies in its flexible framework for joint initiatives, in the political backing it has enjoyed, but first and foremost, in the close interplay between science and policy. The development of new instruments builds on a serial scientific foundation generated by an international network of experts and on interaction between policy makers and scientists with a shared perception of where to go and how to get there.

On the other hand, a situation of broad, but vague, consensus, supported by boundary objects, offers room for manoeuvering, for example for making policy under the cover of unbiased and credible science. The work based on the critical loads approach possesses many uncertainties, of course. The approach of critical loads regulation is basically a choice of policy and should be scrutinized as such. Critical questions could be asked in order to unmask such situations. This is what Jasanoff's fourth mechanism encourages us to do, by asking questions about the connections between the power of science and epistemic communities on the one hand and a technological culture and a technocratic society on the other.

The perspective provided by SSK tells us that scientific work always rests on a bed of values and policy. Therefore it is not appropriate to assume that a science-based regime implies an exclusion of political calculations and choices based on values. The fact is, indeed, that science-based issues and science-based environmental regimes are always the result of a social order, political negotiations and scientific practices.

CONCLUSIONS

. . . Most analysts agree that LRTAP is one of the most research-dependent environmental regimes that exist today, but they offer different understandings of the important role played by science. In our empirical analysis we have argued that science does not only work as an input to the policy process which the regime actors have to evaluate. Neither does science itself have the power to change the representatives' views on transboundary air pollution and the means of solving the problems involved. As shown in the case study, science and policy are co-produced in the development of the regime. The co-production of science and policy is a prerequisite for the creating of effective regimes.

From an SSK perspective it is wrong to see the development of the LRTAP regime as going from a political phase (East–West relationship) to a scientific phase (a new scientific understanding: the concept of critical loads). Instead, it is necessary to consider the interdependency between scientific knowledge and political order. Scientific findings have been important from the early beginnings of the LRTAP work just as the political dimension has always been important, in the 1990s most visibly in the former Eastern Europe, where countries have calculated that supporting the LRTAP process is a good way to show that they are worthy candidates for becoming member states in the EU. This means that science—the use of science as well as the production of scientific data—is always contingent in relation to the social order.

The perspective provided by SSK tells us that scientific work always rest on a bed of values and policy. Therefore it is not appropriate to assume that a science-based regime implies an exclusion of political calculations and choices based on values. On the contrary, science-based environmental regimes are the result of a social order, political negotiations and scientific practices. Scientific knowledge, whether it is considered of importance for policy or not, has always to be explained.

SSK can be an important tool to investigate the role of science in international regimes, both in their formulation and in their implementation. The next step is to develop detailed studies of different environmental regimes, analysing why some are more research-dependent than others as well as investigating the explanatory power of the SSK approach. This research will result in a more sophisticated understanding of science, thereby hopefully making more effective regimes possible.

NOTES

This article has been prepared within the research programme International and National Abatement Strategies for Transboundary Air Pollution (ASTA) (http://asta.ivl.se). The programme is financed by MISTRA, the Swedish Foundation for Strategic Environmental Research. The authors would like to thank Peringe Grennfelt (IVL Swedish Environmental Research Institute) and Martin Letell (Göteborg University) as well as two anonymous referees for helpful comments on an earlier version, and to Malcolm Forbes for generous help with the language.

1. Hasenclever et al. (1997: 1–2) distinguish between three different approaches in the social studies of international cooperation—neoliberal (interest-based), realist (power-based) and cognitive (knowledge-based); cf. Corell (1999: 20–2).
2. According to Young and Demko (1996: 238) international regimes "do not make good vehicles for addressing the basic problems of the overarching world order."
3. Regime effectiveness can be defined in a number of ways. Hisschemöller and Gupta (1999) define it as the capacity of the regime to solve the environmental problems it is meant to solve. Young (1999b; see also Young and Levy, 1999) points to the importance of the behavioural impact of a regime—activities that work in the right direction, even if they fall short of full compliance with a specific regulatory rule, protocols, etc.—when evaluating its effectiveness.
4. Thus the epistemic community model shares the view of discursive democracy, whereas knowledge and a communicative rationality is seen as a way to discover general interests and thereby influence the preferences of citizens (Dryzek, 1990, 1994).
5. See Hovden's (1999) critical examination of regime theory's view of environment, where he claims that it relies on positivistic epistemological assumptions which to a significant degree explain its lack of critical analysis of environmental issues.
6. SSK is most flourishing in the United Kingdom. For two seminal works see Bloor (1976) and Collins (1985).
7. Well-known SSK studies of the tools needed to move science in society are Callon (1986), Latour (1988) and Shapin and Shaffer (1985).
8. The United Nations Economic Commissions of Europe is based in Geneva. The USA and Canada have a bilateral agreement—Memorandum of Intent (1980)—to the LRTAP Convention which is similar in structure and content (Munton et al., 1999).
9. The LRTAP regime has been given much research attention (for references see Wettestad, 1997: 238–9; VanDeveer, 1998: 8). One reason is that it is one of the first environmental regimes, established as early as the 1970s. Another reason is that it is judged, by researchers as well as politicians, as successful. A third reason, which is of the greatest importance for this article, is the close relationship between science and policy, and that this is claimed to be a reason for its success. This is most visible in the conceptualization of the critical loads approach, which makes the regime heavily dependent on science. Most of the research on the LRTAP Convention has been carried out from an institutionalist approach (for two important examples see Levy, 1993 and Wettestad, 1999), but there are also a few studies based on an SSK approach (Patt, 1998 and VanDeveer, 1998).
10. The Regional Acidification Information System (RAINS), an interactive computer model developed at IIASA. See Alcamo, Shaw and Hordijk (1990) for a description of the model.
11. See VanDeveer (1998) for a study of the "excluded" parties in the European periphery.

REFERENCES

Alcamo, J., R. Shaw and L. Hordijk (eds) (1990) *The RAINS Model of Acidification: Science and Strategies for Europe.* Dordrecht: Kluwer Academic Publishers.

Archibugi, D., D. Held and M. Köhler (1998) *Re-imagining Political Community: Studies in Cosmopolitan Democracy.* Cambridge: Polity Press.

Bernauer, T. (1995) "The Effect of International Environmental Institutions: How We Might Learn More," *International Organization* 49(2): 351–77.

Björkbom, L. (1997) "Protection of Natural Ecosystems from Transboundary Air Pollution in Europe," paper presented at the SCOPE UK meeting Effective Use of the Sciences in Sustainable Land Management at the Royal Society, 21 February 1997.

Bloor, D. (1976) *Knowledge and Social Imagery*, 2nd edn, 1991. Chicago: The University of Chicago Press.

Brecher, J. (1993) "The Hierarch's New World Order—and Ours," in J. Brecher, J. Brown Childs and J. Cutler (eds) *Global Visions: Beyond the New World Order*, pp. 3–12. Boston: South End Press.

Callon, M. (1986) "Some Elements of a Sociology of Translation: Domestication of the Scallops and the Fishermen of St Brieuc's Bay," in J. Law (ed.) *Power, Action and Belief: A New Sociology of Knowledge?*, pp. 196–229. London: Routledge & Kegan Paul.

Collins, H.M. (1985) *Changing Order: Replication and Induction in Scientific Practice*, 2nd edn, 1992. Chicago: The University of Chicago Press.

Corell, E. (1999) *The Negotiable Desert: Expert Knowledge in the Negotiations of the Convention to Combat Desertification*. Linköping Studies in Arts and Science 191. Linköping University.

Dryzek, J.R. (1990) *Discursive Democracy: Politics, Policy, and Political Science*. Cambridge: Cambridge University Press.

Dryzek, J.R. (1994) "Ecology and Discursive Democracy: Beyond Liberal Capitalism and the Administrative State," in M. O'Connor (ed.) *Is Capitalism Sustainable? Political Economy and the Politics of Ecology*, pp. 176–95. London: The Guilford Press.

Fraenkel, A.A. (1989) "The Convention on Long-Range Transboundary Air Pollution," *Harvard International Law Journal* 30(2): 447–76.

French, H. (1997) "Learning from the Ozone Experience," in L.R. Brown et al. *State of the World 1997. A Worldwatch Institute Report on Progress Toward a Sustainable Society*, pp. 151–72. New York/London: Norton.

Gehring, T. (1994) *Dynamic International Regimes: Institutions for International Environmental Governance*. Berlin: Peter Lang.

Gieryn, T.F. (1983) "Boundary Work and the Demarcation of Science from Non-Science: Strains and Interests in Professional Ideologies of Scientists," *American Sociological Review* 48: 781–95.

Gieryn, T.F. (1999) *Cultural Boundaries of Science: Credibility on the Line*. Chicago: The University of Chicago Press.

Grennfelt, P., Ø. How and D. Derwent (1994) "Second Generation Abatement Strategies for NO_x, NH_3, SO_2 and VOCs," *Ambio* 23: 425–33.

Haas, P.M. (1989) "Do Regimes Matter? Epistemic Communities and Mediterranean Pollution Control," *International Organization* 43(3): 377–403.

Haas, P.M. (ed.) (1992a) *Knowledge, Power, and International Policy Coordination*. Columbia, SC: University of South Carolina Press.

Haas, P.M. (1992b) "Introduction: Epistemic Communities and International Policy Coordination," *International Organization* 46(1): 1–35.

Haas, P.M. (1993) "Epistemic Communities and the Dynamics of International Environmental Cooperation," in V. Rittberger (ed.) *Regime Theory and International Relations*, pp. 168–201. Oxford: Oxford University Press.

Haas, P.M. (1997) "Scientific Communities and Multiple Paths to Environmental Management," in L.A. Brooks and S.D. VanDeveer (eds) *Saving the Seas: Values, Scientists, and International Governance*, pp. 193–228. Maryland Sea Grant College.

Habermas, J. (1987) *The Theory of Communicative Action. Vol. II: Lifeworld and System*. Boston: Beacon Press.

Hasenclever, A., P. Mayer and V. Rittberger (1997) *Theories of International Regimes*. Cambridge: Cambridge University Press.

Hempel, L.C. (1996) *Environmental Governance: The Global Challenge*. Washington, DC: Island Press.

Hisschemöller, M. and J. Gupta (1999) "Problem-solving through International Environmental Agreements: The Issue of Regime Effectiveness," *International Political Science Review* 20(2): 151–74.

Hovden, E. (1999) "As if Nature Doesn't Matter: Ecology, Regime Theory and International Relations," *Environmental Politics* 8(2): 50–74.

Jacobson, H.K. and E.B. Weiss (1995) "Strengthening Compliance with International Environmental Accords: Preliminary Observations from a Collaborative Project," *Global Governance* 1(2): 119–48.

Jasanoff, S. (1987) "Contested Boundaries in Policy-Relevant Science," *Social Studies of Science* 17: 195–230.

Jasanoff, S. (1990) *The Fifth Branch: Science Advisers as Policymakers*. Cambridge, MA: Harvard University Press.

Jasanoff, S. (1996a) "Science and Norms in Global Environmental Regimes," in F.O. Hampson and J. Reppy (eds) *Earthly Goods: Environmental Change and Social Justice*, pp. 173–197. Ithaca, NY: Cornell University Press.

Jasanoff, S. (1996b) "Beyond Epistemology: Relativism and Engagement in the Politics of Science," *Social Studies of Science* 26: 393–418.

Jasanoff, S. (1997) "Compelling Knowledge in Public Decisions," in L.A. Brooks and S.D. VanDeveer (eds) *Saving the Seas: Values, Scientists, and International Governance*, pp. 229–52. Maryland Sea Grant College.

Jasanoff, S. and B. Wynne (1998) "Science and Decisionmaking," in S. Rayner and E.L. Malone (eds) *Human Choice and Climate Change vol. 1, The Societal Framework*, pp. 1–87. Columbus: Battelle Press.

Keohane, R. and J. Nye (1977) *Power and Interdependence: World Politics in Transition*. Boston/Toronto: Little, Brown.

Latour, B. (1987) *Science in Action: How to Follow Scientists and Engineers through Society*. Cambridge, MA: Harvard University Press.

Latour, B. (1988) *The Pasteurization of France*. Cambridge, MA: Harvard University Press.

Levy, M.A. (1993) "European Acid Rain: The Power of Tote-Board Diplomacy," in P.M. Haas, R.O. Keohane and M.A. Levy (eds) *Institutions for the Earth: Sources of Effective International Environmental Protection*, pp. 75–132. Cambridge, MA: MIT Press.

Low, N., B. Gleeson, I. Elander and R. Lidskog (2000) "After Rio. Urban Environmental Governance?," in theirs (eds) *Consuming Cities: The Urban Environment in the Global Economy after the Rio Declaration*, pp. 281–307. London: Routledge.

Luke, T.W. (2000) "A Rough Road out of Rio. The Right-wing Reaction in the United States against Global Environmentalism," in N. Low, B. Gleeson, I. Elander and R. Lidskog (eds) *Consuming Cities: The Urban Environment in the Global Economy after the Rio Declaration*, pp. 54–69. London: Routledge.

Lundgren, L.J. (1998) *Acid Rain on the Agenda: A Picture of a Chain of Events in Sweden, 1966–1968*. Lund: Lund University Press.

Mayer, P., V. Rittberger and M. Zürn (1993) "Regime Theory: State of the Art and Perspectives," in V. Rittberger (ed.) *Regime Theory and International Relations*, pp. 391–430. Oxford: Oxford University Press.

Munton, D., M. Soroos, E. Nikitina and M.A. Levy (1999) "Acid Rain in Europe and North America," in O.R. Young (ed.) *The Effectiveness of International Environmental Regimes: Causal Connections and Behavioral Mechanisms*, pp. 155–248. Cambridge, MA: MIT Press.

Nilsson, J. and P. Grennfelt (eds) (1988) "Critical Loads for Sulphur and Nitrogen," Report from a UN-ECE and Nordic Council of Ministers workshop held at Skokloster, Sweden, 19–24 March 1988.

Park, C.C. (1987) *Acid Rain: Rhetoric and Reality.* London and New York: Methuen.

Patt, A. (1998) *Analytic Frameworks and Politics: The Case of Acid Rain in Europe.* ENRP Discussion Paper E-98-20, Kennedy School of Government, Harvard University.

Persson, G.A. (1993) "The Acid Rain Story," in G. Sjöstedt, U. Svedin and B. Hägerhäll Aniansson (eds) *International Environmental Negotiations: Process, Issues and Contexts,* pp. 105–116. Stockholm: Utrikespolitiska Institutet and Forskningsrådsnämnden

Porter, G. and J.W. Brown (1996) *Global Environmental Politics.* Boulder, CO: Westview Press.

Rittberger, V. and M. Zürn (1991) "Regime Theory: Findings from the Study of East–West Relations," *Cooperation and Conflict* 26: 165–83.

Shapin, S. and S. Schaffer (1985) *Leviathan and the Air-Pump: Hobbes, Boyle and the Experimental Life.* Princeton, NJ: Princeton University Press.

Sprinz, D. and T. Vaahtoranta (1994) "The Interest-based Explanation of International Environmental Policy," *International Organization* 48(1): 77–105.

Star, S.L. (1989) *Regions of Mind: Brain Research and the Quest for Scientific Certainty.* Stanford, CA: Stanford University Press.

Stoltenberg, T. (1989) "Foreword: Foreign Policy and Science," pp. xiii–xvi in S. Andresen, and W. Østreng (eds) *International Resource Management.* London: Belhaven Press.

Thompson, J. (1999) *Introduction to the Ministerial Declaration on Long-Range Transboundary Air Pollution,* Gothenburg, 30 November 1999.

UNECE (1979) *The Convention on Long-Range Transboundary Air Pollution.*

UNECE (1985) *Protocol to the 1979 Convention on Long-Range Transboundary Air Pollution on the Reduction of Sulphur Emissions or their Transboundary Fluxes by at Least 30 per cent.*

UNECE (1988) *Protocol to the 1979 Convention on Long-Range Transboundary Air Pollution Concerning the Control of Emissions of Nitrogen Oxides or Their Transboundary Fluxes.*

UNECE (1999) *Protocol to the 1979 Convention on Long-Range Transboundary Air Pollution to Abate Acidification, Eutrophication and Ground-level Ozone.*

VanDeveer, S.D. (1998) *European Politics with a Scientific Face: Transition Countries, International Environmental Assessment, and Long-Range Transboundary Air Pollution.* ENRP Discussion Paper E-98-9, Kennedy School of Government, Harvard University.

Victor, D.G., K. Raustiala and E.B. Skolnikof (eds) (1998) *The Implementation and Effectiveness of International Environmental Commitments.* Cambridge, MA: MIT Press.

Vogler, J. (1995) *The Global Commons: A Regime Analysis.* Chichester: John Wiley.

Wettestad, J. (1997) "Acid Lessons? LRTAP Implementation and Effectiveness," *Global Environmental Change* 7(3): 235–49.

Wettestad, J. (1999) *Designing Effective Environmental Regimes: The Key Conditions.* Cheltenham: Edward Elgar.

Wettestad, J. (2000) "The ECE Convention on Long-Range Transboundary Air Pollution: From Common Cuts to Critical Loads," in S. Andresen, T. Skodvin, A. Underdal and J. Wettestad, *Science in International Environmental Regimes: Between Integrity and Involvement,* pp. 95–121. Manchester: Manchester University Press.

Wettestad, J. and S. Andresen (1991) *The Effectiveness of International Resource Coooperation: Some Preliminary Findings.* Oslo: Fridtjof Nansen Institute.

Wynne, B. (1996) "SSK's Identity Parade: Signing Up, Off-and-On," *Social Studies of Science* 26: 357–91.

Young, O.R. (1989) *International Cooperation: Building Regimes for Natural Resources and the Environment.* Ithaca, NY: Cornell University Press.

Young, O.R. (1994) *International Governance: Protecting the Environment in a Stateless Society.* Ithaca, NY: Cornell University Press.

Young, O.R. (ed.) (1999a) *The Effectiveness of International Environmental Regimes: Causal Connections and Behavioral Mechanisms.* Cambridge, MA: MIT Press.

Young, O.R. (1999b) "Regime Effectiveness: Taking Stock," in O.R. Young (ed.) *The Effectiveness of International Environmental Regimes: Causal Connections and Behavioral Mechanisms,* pp. 249–280. Cambridge, MA: MIT Press.

Young, O.R. and G.J. Demko (1996) "Improving the Effectiveness of International Environmental Governance Systems," in O.R. Young, G.J. Demko and K. Ramakrishna (eds) *Global Environmental Change and International Governance.* Hannover and London: University Press of New England.

Young, O.R. and M.A. Levy (1999) "The Effectiveness of International Environmental Regimes," in O.R. Young (ed.) *The Effectiveness of International Environmental Regimes: Causal Connections and Behavioral Mechanisms,* pp. 1–32. Cambridge, MA: The MIT Press.

Zolo, D. (1997) *Cosmopolis: Prospects for World Government.* Cambridge: Polity Press.

Ideas Do Not Float Freely: Transnational Coalitions, Domestic Structures, and the End of the Cold War

THOMAS RISSE-KAPPEN

Efforts to explain the "end of the cold war," that is, the systemic transformation of world politics that started with the turnaround in Soviet foreign policy in the late 1980s, have to find answers to at least two sets of questions. First, why did Soviet foreign policy change as it did rather than in other conceivable ways, thereby setting in motion a process leading to the cold war's end? . . .

Second, how can it be explained that Western powers, that is, the alleged winners of the cold war, never attempted to exploit the situation, thereby accelerating their opponent's collapse? . . .

In response to the first set of questions, I argue that some of the ideas that informed the reconceptualization of Soviet security interests and centered around notions of "common security" and "reasonable sufficiency" originated in the Western liberal internationalist community comprising arms control supporters in the United States as well as peace researchers and left-of-center political parties in Western Europe.[1] This community formed transnational networks with "new thinkers" in the foreign policy institutes and elsewhere in the former Soviet Union. Mikhail Gorbachev, as a domestic reformer and uncommitted thinker in foreign policy, was open to these ideas because they satisfied his needs for coherent and consistent policy concepts. As a result, the new ideas became causally consequential for the turnaround in Soviet foreign policy.

In response to the second set, I claim that these very ideas also had an impact on the Western reactions to the new Soviet policies, albeit to different degrees. I illustrate this point with regard to the cautious American and the enthusiastic (West) German responses to the revolution in Soviet foreign policy.

This and the other articles in this Symposium were prepared for *International Organization* and for Richard N. Lebow and Thomas Risse-Kappen, eds., *International Relations Theory and the End of the Cold War*, forthcoming. The article draws on insights from two collaborative projects: the above-referenced project; and Thomas Risse-Kappen, ed., *Bringing Transnational Relations Back In: Non-state Actors, Domestic Structures, and International Institutions*, forthcoming. I thank the contributors to both projects for helping to clarify my thoughts on the subject. I am also very grateful to Richard Ned Lebow, John Odell, Steve Ropp, Jack Snyder, and several anonymous reviewers for helpful comments on the draft of this article. Moreover, since I cannot claim to be an expert on the former Soviet Union, I owe a lot to the work of Matthew Evangelista and that of Robert Herman. Finally, I thank Janice Stein, who originated this article's title. I would also like to acknowledge the support of Cornell University's Peace Studies Program, Yale University's International Security Program, and the International Studies Program at the University of Wyoming.

Ideas, however, do not float freely. Decision makers are always exposed to several and often contradictory policy concepts. Research on transnational relations and, most recently, on "epistemic communities" of knowledge-based transnational networks has failed so far to specify the conditions under which specific ideas are selected and influence policies while others fall by the wayside.[2] The transnational promoters of foreign policy change must align with domestic coalitions supporting their cause in the "target state" to make an impact. I argue that access to the political system as well as the ability to build winning coalitions are determined by the *domestic structure* of the target state, that is, the nature of its political institutions, state–society relations, and the values and norms embedded in its political culture.

In the former Soviet Union with its state-controlled structure, the transnational actors needed to gain access to the very top of the decision-making hierarchy to have an impact. Their specific ideas and concepts also had to be compatible with the beliefs and goals of the top decision makers.

Access to the U.S. political system, with its society-dominated structure, is comparatively easy, while the requirements for building winning coalitions are profound. Moreover, concepts such as common security were rather alien to a political culture emphasizing pluralist individualism at home and sharp zero-sum conflicts with ideological opponents abroad. As a result, the liberal arms controllers and their societal supporters together with their European allies succeeded in moving the Reagan and Bush administrations toward cautious support for Gorbachev's policies, but not much further.

As to the German "democratic corporatist" structure, access to political institutions is more difficult than in the U.S. case, but strong policy networks such as the party system ensure profound influence once access is achieved. Common security resonated well with a political culture emphasizing consensus-building and compromise among competing interests at home and abroad. The concept was embedded in the German foreign policy consensus even before Gorbachev embraced it. This explains the enthusiastic German response to the new Soviet foreign policy years before the Berlin Wall came down.

In sum, I argue that the transnational networks of liberal internationalists promoting common security, vigorous arms control efforts, and a restructuring of defense postures were active in all three countries but succeeded to very different degrees. The difference in impact can largely be explained by the variation in domestic structures of the three countries.

TRANSNATIONAL RELATIONS AND THE END OF THE COLD WAR

In the following section I first identify the actors who developed the new strategic prescriptions about security and the transnational networks through which these concepts were promoted. I then look at the differential impact of these ideas on the security policies of the three countries discussed here: the Gorbachev revolution in foreign policy and the American and German responses to it.

Transnational Actors and Their Ideas: The Liberal Internationalist Community

Four intellectual communities can be identified that together form a "liberal internationalist community" sharing political values and policy concepts. First, the liberal arms control community in the United States has to be mentioned. Its origins date back to the late 1950s when it was among the first to promote the idea of arms control to stabilize the deterrence system.[3] This community comprises an alliance of (1) natural scientists organized in such groups as the Union of Concerned Scientists (UCS) and the Federation of American Scientists (FAS); (2) policy analysts at various think tanks such as the Brookings Institution; (3) scholars at academic institutions; (4) public interest groups such as the Natural Resources Defense Council (NRDC); and (5) policymakers in the U.S. Congress, mostly liberal Democrats.

The contribution of this group to the broader liberal internationalist agenda during the late 1970s and early 1980s consisted primarily of specific proposals in the nuclear arms control area. The main focus during that time was to oppose the Reagan administration's efforts to do away with nuclear arms control. In particular, the community concentrated on promoting a comprehensive nuclear test ban and on preserving the 1972 Anti-Ballistic Missile (ABM) Treaty threatened by Reagan's Strategic Defense Initiative (SDI).[4]

The second subgroup of the liberal internationalist community consisted of mostly Western European peace researchers based at various institutes such as the Stockholm International Peace Research Institute, the Peace Research Institute in Oslo, the Institute for Peace Research and Security Policy in Hamburg, the Peace Research Institute in Frankfurt, and various universities.

The third group includes European policymakers in Social Democratic and Labour parties and their transnational organization, the Socialist International. Security specialists in the German Social Democratic Party (SPD) as well as the British and Dutch Labour parties were particularly important for the liberal internationalist debate during the period under consideration.[5]

The two European components of the liberal internationalist community shared the concerns of their U.S. counterparts about the future of arms control. But their main contribution to the transnational liberal agenda consisted of developing the concepts of common security and nonoffensive defense (or, to use the German misnomer, *strukturelle Angriffsunfähigkeit,* that is, "structural inability for offensive operations"). . . .

Common security was widely discussed among peace researchers as well as mainstream and center-left parties in the Benelux countries, Great Britain, Scandinavia, and West Germany during the late 1970s and early 1980s. . . . By the time Gorbachev came into power, common sense security was one of the mainstream foreign policy concepts in Europe.

The European peace research community also developed proposals to restructure the Western conventional force posture in such a way that offensive operations would become virtually impossible—nonoffensive defense—and, thus, to overcome the security dilemma by reconciling peaceful intentions with purely defensive capabilities.[6] . . .

The fourth component of the transnational community provided the link with the former Soviet Union. It consists of natural scientists and policy analysts in various institutes, primarily at the Academy of Science (for example, the Kurchatov Institute of Atomic Energy headed by Velikhov, the Space Research Institute headed by Sagdeev, and the foreign policy institutes IMEMO and ISKAN). The Soviet "new thinkers" were mainly on the receiving end of ideas promoted by their European and American counterparts.

These four groups not only shared values and policy concepts but also exchanged frequently their views. Since the connections between the U.S. and the European arms control communities are well-documented, I concentrate on the East–West exchanges.

First, specific nuclear arms control proposals were the subject of increasingly institutionalized contacts between the U.S. arms control community, particularly natural scientists working for the UCS, the FAS, and the NRDC, and Soviet experts such as Velikhov and Sagdeev. Evangelista has documented these exchanges and shown in detail how these interactions influenced Soviet arms control decisions. His analysis provides further empirical evidence for the argument developed in this article.[7]

Second, the concept of common security was introduced to Soviet institutchiks and foreign policy experts through the Palme commission (the Independent Commission for Disarmament and Security, named after former Swedish Prime Minister and Social Democrat Olof Palme).[8] It was founded in September 1980 and brought together mostly elder statesmen and women from around the world to study East–West security issues. Academician Georgii Arbatov, the head of ISKAN, served as the Soviet member, while retired General Mikhail Milstein of the same institute was one of the principal advisers.[9] . . .

Third, there were regular exchanges between various West European Social Democratic and Labour parties—particularly the German SPD—and Communist parties in Eastern Europe and the Soviet Union. These relations had been established during the détente period of the 1970s and were continued throughout the 1980s. . . .

Fourth, the concept of nonoffensive defense reached the Soviet institutchiks primarily through transnational exchanges with Western European peace researchers and military experts. Some of these contacts were initiated through well-known frameworks such as the Pugwash conferences.[10] In 1984, for example, Pugwash established a working group on conventional forces that became a major East–West forum on these issues; it included most of the European peace researchers, such as Anders Boserup, Horst Afheldt, and Albrecht von Müller, specializing in "alternative defense" models. Andrei Kokoshin, deputy director of ISKAN and one of the most prominent "new thinkers" in Soviet foreign policy, participated regularly. He became a leading proponent of a defensive restructuring of the Soviet armed forces. Moreover, the annual Pugwash conferences regularly dealt with issues of defensive restructuring, particularly the 1988 meeting in the Soviet Union. Western experts of the nonoffensive defense community were frequently consulted by the institutchiks and even Soviet military academies.[11] . . .

In sum, liberal internationalist ideas about common security and nonoffensive defense reached "new thinkers" in several Soviet institutes through a variety of transnational exchanges with like-minded groups in the West. But what are the indications that these transnational exchanges were politically consequential, that is, had an impact on the Gorbachev revolution in Soviet foreign policy?[12]

Transnational Exchanges and the Turnaround in Soviet Security Policy

In February 1986 Gorbachev made the following remarks about his vision of security:

> Security cannot be built endlessly on fear of retaliation, in other words, on the doctrines of "containment" or "deterrence." . . . In the context of the relations between the USSR and the USA, security can only be mutual, and if we take international relations as a whole it can only be universal. The highest wisdom is not in caring exclusively for oneself, especially to the detriment of the other side. It is vital that all should feel equally secure. . . . In the military sphere we intend to act in such a way as to give nobody grounds for fear, even imagined ones, about their security.[13]

These remarks excerpted from Gorbachev's report to the Twenty-seventh Party Congress . . . represent the first instance in which the Soviet leader identified himself with a new concept of security alien to traditional Soviet thinking. But was there also a causal link beyond a mere correlation? . . .

One could argue, of course, that these references to Western thinking by Gorbachev were self-serving and meant to legitimize his own views. Even if true, the similarities between his arguments and those of European analysts and policymakers are still striking; and the Soviet leader knew about these affinities. Moreover, as mentioned above, Gorbachev did not hold firm convictions on foreign policy before he entered office. Finally, he matched words with deeds; his policy proposals and actions on nuclear and conventional weapons in Europe directly followed from the newly developed strategic prescriptions on enhancing international security.

The transnational links mentioned above between European institutes and policymakers on the one hand and institutchiks at ISKAN and other Soviet institutes on the other became increasingly important for the reconceptualization of the Soviet approach to security. ISKAN's head, Arbatov—a member of the Palme commission—while certainly not among the most radical "new thinkers," belonged to the inner circle of Gorbachev's foreign policy advisers during the early years of perestroika. . . .

It is thus quite plausible to assume that European ideas about common security reached Gorbachev both directly, through European Social Democrats, and indirectly, through ISKAN and other institutchiks, as well as through his closest advisers such as Yakovlev or Shevardnadze.

Proposals to restructure the Soviet conventional posture toward nonoffensive defense seem to have influenced the leadership in a similar way. The above-cited report to the Twenty-seventh Party Congress already mentioned the defensive orientation of the Soviet military doctrine and the concept of reasonable sufficiency without being specific. One year later, Gorbachev referred to doctrines of defense

"connected with such new or comparatively new notions as the reasonable sufficiency of armaments, non-aggressive defense, elimination of disbalance and asymmetries in various types of armed forces, separation of the offensive forces of the
two blocs, and so on and so forth."[14]

An intensive debate about the implications for the conventional force posture
followed among civilian and military analysts in the Soviet Union. The military in
particular claimed that "defensive defense" referred to the overall goals of Soviet
military doctrine rather than its implementation. The institutchiks argued that reasonable sufficiency should lead to a restructuring of Soviet military forces in such
a way as to preclude the ability to conduct (counter-) offensive operations.[15]
ISKAN analysts such as Vitalii Zhurkin, Sergei Karaganov, and Andrei Kortunov as
well as its deputy head Kokoshin became leading advocates of the concept. The
latter embraced Western ideas of nonoffensive defense and translated them into the
Soviet context. He published various articles on the subject, together with Major
General Valentin Larionov of the General Staff Academy.[16] As mentioned above,
Kokoshin was involved in transnational exchanges at Pugwash and had frequent
contacts with European peace researchers such as Boserup and Lutz Unterseher,
who were also in touch with the junior Arbatov, Karganov, and the bureaucracy of
the Soviet foreign ministry.[17]

In December 1988 Gorbachev showed that he sided with the institutchiks
and the "new thinkers" in Shevardnadze's Foreign Ministry when he announced
large-scale unilateral troop reductions. Shortly afterward, the Soviet Union
accepted the core of Western proposals at the Conventional Forces in Europe
negotiations to establish conventional parity in Central Europe. Two years later, the
Soviet Defense Ministry published a draft statement on military doctrine that
explicitly defined sufficiency as the inability "for conducting large-scale offensive
operations."[18] "New thinking" had reached the defense bureaucracy.

These are just two examples suggesting that important parts of the reorientation
of Soviet security policy were indeed influenced by strategic prescriptions transmitted to the leadership through transnational interactions.[19] Once the foreign policy
experts and their transnational contacts had aligned with the domestic reform coalition in the Soviet Union, the transnational exchanges influenced the very content of
the new Soviet security policy and, thus, the scope of the change. The new leadership needed independent expertise outside the military, which opened a window of
opportunity for civilians.[20] As a result, the institutchiks influenced the attitudes of
policymakers such as Gorbachev and Shevardnadze. The new ideas about common
security and reasonable sufficiency transformed a general uneasiness with the state of
Soviet international affairs into a coherent foreign policy concept. . . .

THE LIMITS OF TRANSNATIONALISM: DOMESTIC STRUCTURES AS INTERVENING VARIABLES

I have tried to document above that a liberal internationalist and transnational
community of scholars, policy analysts, and center-left political parties promoted
new strategic prescriptions such as common security, nonoffensive defense, and
far-reaching arms control agreements during the late 1970s and early 1980s. "New

thinkers" in the Soviet Union picked up these ideas and influenced the views of the Soviet leadership. The particular content of Gorbachev's foreign policy revolution cannot be understood without the input of this transnational community. The transnational community also influenced Western policies in response to Gorbachev, albeit to different degrees. It was less successful in the United States but very effective in West Germany by contributing to create a new foreign policy consensus around common security. In sum, I suggest that the end of the cold war—both in the East and the West—cannot be adequately understood without taking the role of these transnationally transmitted ideas into account.

But the argument has limits. There is considerable variation in the impact of these ideas. Only the Soviet Union under Gorbachev reconceptualized its security policy toward both common security and nonoffensive defense. The German polity achieved a domestic consensus on the former but remained reluctant on the latter, while the American public and elite opinion failed to agree on either of the two concepts. Moreover, the interval between the initial promotion of these ideas in the target countries and their acceptance by the political leaderships varies considerably. If we take the Palme commission report as the first instance in which Soviet institutchiks became exposed to common security, it took less than four years for the ideas to have a policy impact. It took about ten years in Germany to accomplish the same result—from the mid-1970s, when peace researchers and Social Democrats started promoting the strategic prescriptions, to the mid-1980s. In Washington, common security never became as relevant politically as in Moscow and Bonn.

How is this considerable variation in policy impact to be explained? To influence policies, transnational actors need, first, channels into the political system of the target state and, second, domestic partners with the ability to form winning coalitions. Ideas promoted by transnational alliances or epistemic communities do not matter much unless those two conditions are met. In other words, we have to look at intervening variables between transnational alliances and policy change. I suggest that it is differences in domestic structures among the three countries that account for a large extent of the variation in policy impact of the transnationally circulated ideas.

Originally developed in the field of comparative foreign economic policy, domestic structure approaches have generated empirical research across issue-areas to explain variation in state responses to international pressures, constraints, and opportunities.[21] The concept refers to the structure of the political system, society, and the policy networks linking the two. Domestic structures encompass the organizational apparatus of political and societal institutions, their routines, the decision-making rules and procedures as incorporated in law and custom, as well as the values and norms prescribing appropriate behavior embedded in the political culture.

This last point marks a departure from earlier conceptualizations of domestic structures, which emphasized organizational characteristics of state and society but neglected the political culture and thus insights from the "new institutionalism," particularly the focus on communicative action, duties, social obligations, and norms.[22] Political culture, then, refers to those worldviews and principled ideas—values and norms—that are stable over long periods of time and are taken for granted by the vast majority of the population. Thus, the political culture as part of the domestic structure contains only those ideas that do not change often and about which there is societal consensus.[23]

Until about 1988–89, the former Soviet Union represented an extremely state-controlled domestic structure with a highly centralized decision-making apparatus.[24] Such structures lead to top-down policy-making processes, leaving less room for policy innovations unless they are promoted by the top leadership. It follows that leadership beliefs are expected to matter more than attitudes of the wider population.[25]

Centralized and state-dominated domestic structures provide transnational coalitions with comparatively few access points into the political system. They have to reach the top echelon of the decision-making structure directly rather than building winning coalitions in civil society. Prior to Gorbachev's gaining power, the transnational exchanges between Western liberal internationalists and Soviet institutchiks had almost no impact on Soviet foreign policy. Since the top leadership in the former Soviet Union controlled to which voices it wanted to listen, a reform-oriented leadership had to gain power first. It needed to be open-minded, and its worldviews needed to be predisposed toward the strategic prescriptions promoted by the transnational actors. The negligible policy impact of the transnational coalition during the Brezhnev period as compared with the Gorbachev era can thus be explained.

Beyond a general proclivity toward foreign policy change, there also seems to be a more specific reason why Gorbachev was attracted to common security.[26] His domestic reform ideas closely resembled policy concepts promoted by democratic socialism and the Socialist International, which emphasized political democracy and a market economy with a heavy dose of state interventionism. Common security, however, formed the core of the foreign policy beliefs of the European Social Democratic and Labour parties. Gorbachev—who made a strong and, needless to say, successful effort to gain the support of the European Social Democrats—might have been attracted to their foreign policy ideas because they were promoted by groups that also held similar beliefs with regard to domestic politics.

In sum, the combination of a centralized decision-making structure with a reform-oriented leadership explains why the strategic prescriptions promoted by the transnational coalition had such a strong impact on Gorbachev's foreign policy revolution in a comparatively short period of time. Once a channel into the top decision-making circle was open, the transnational coalition profoundly influenced policies. Given the absence of a strong civil society backing the ideas, the impact depended almost entirely on the leadership's willingness to listen.

In contrast to the Soviet Union, the United States represents, of course, a comparatively society-dominated domestic structure with a strong organization of interest groups in which societal demands can be mobilized rather easily. At the same time, it lacks effective intermediate organizations such as a strong party system; and its political system is comparatively fragmented and decentralized without a powerful center (Congress versus Executive, Pentagon versus State Department, etc.).[27] Moreover and throughout the cold war, the American national security culture incorporated rather strong and consensual enemy images of the Soviet Union and defined national security mainly in military terms.[28]

Society-dominated structures are expected to mediate the impact of transnational coalitions in almost the opposite way as state-controlled structures. Transnational actors should have few problems in finding access into the decentralized political system. While this initial hurdle is comparatively low, the task of building a winning coalition is expected to be more complex than in state-dominated systems. Since society-dominated structures are characterized by frequently shifting coalitions, transnational alliances may successfully influence policies in the short run, but their long-term impact is probably rather limited.

Indeed, the liberal arms control community had virtually no problems finding channels into the political system but failed to form stable winning coalitions with a lasting policy impact. The group was successful only to the extent that its demands were compatible with either a public opinion consensus—as in the case of Reagan's return to the arms control table—or the views of powerful players in Congress—as in the case of the preservation of the ABM treaty. The more far-reaching goals of the community, however, required a change in basic attitudes toward the Soviet Union and a mellowing of the U.S. cold war consensus as a precondition of forming a domestic winning coalition. This was possible only after the cold war was over.

Germany represents a third type of domestic structure, the democratic corporatist model.[29] It is characterized by comparatively centralized societal organizations, strong and effective political parties, and a federal government that normally depends on a coalition between at least two parties. As a result and supported by cultural norms emphasizing social partnership between ideological and class opponents, the system is geared toward compromise-oriented consensus-building in its policy networks.

Democratic corporatist structures tend to provide societal and transnational forces with fewer access points to political institutions than do society-dominated systems. Their policy impact should also be more incremental because of the slow and compromise-oriented nature of the decision-making processes. But any impact made is expected to last longer because corporatist structures are geared toward institutionalizing consensus on policies.

As argued above, ideas about common security were gradually picked up, first, by the SPD as one of the two leading mass integration parties and, second, by societal organizations; they thereby reached the constituency of the conservative Christian Democrats. In the end, the polarized debate about détente during the 1970s and about nuclear weapons during the early 1980s evolved into a new consensus centered around common security, which explains the German enthusiasm for the Gorbachev revolution. The structure of German political institutions and policy networks explains why it took much longer for the new ideas to influence policies than in the Soviet case. The German political culture was geared toward class and ideological compromise, and past experiences with *Ostpolitik* explain why common security or security partnership became a consensual belief as the foreign policy equivalent of the domestic social partnership.

In sum, a domestic structure approach that incorporates political culture can account for the differential foreign policy impact of ideas promoted by transnational communities. The channels by which these ideas enter the policymaking process and become incorporated into national foreign policies seem to be determined by the nature of the political institutions. At the same time, the strategic prescriptions need to be compatible with the worldviews embedded in the political culture or held by those powerful enough to build winning coalitions. In the case of the former Soviet Union and its centralized decision-making structure, the transnational coalition's policy ideas required both incorporation into Gorbachev's basic beliefs and his determination to implement reforms in order to have an impact. In the German case, a political culture geared toward compromise and consensus represented a functional equivalent in that it enabled elite and public opinion to accept the strategic prescription of common security. . . .

NOTES

1. I use the term "common security" (in Russian, *vseobshaia bezopasnost'*) throughout the article, even though Soviet/Russian and American authors frequently speak of "mutual security" (*vzaimnaia bezopasnost'*) or "equal security" (*bezopasnos' dlia vsekh*). I do this for two reasons. First, each term refers to the same concept. Second, common security is the generic term for the concept as it was originally used in the German security debate (*gemeinsame Sicherheit*) and later in the Palme commission's report. See Independent Commission on Disarmament and Security Issues, *Common Security: A Blueprint for Survival* (New York: Simon and Schuster, 1982). On the various Russian terms, see Georgii Arbatov, *Zatianuvsheesia vysdorovienie (1953–1988 gg.), Svidetel'stvo sovremennika* (Moscow: Mezhdunarodnye otnosheniia, 1991), pp. 240–41 (This appeared in English as: *The System: An Insider's Life in Soviet Politics* [New York: Random House, 1992].). I thank Matt Evangelista for clarifying the Russian terms for me and for alerting me to Arbatov's book.

2. On epistemic communities, see Peter Haas, ed., *Knowledge, Power, and International Policy Coordination*, a special issue, *International Organization* 46 (winter 1992); and Ernst Haas, *When Knowledge Is Power* (Berkeley: University of California Press, 1990). On transnational relations, see Robert Keohane and Joseph Nye, eds., *Transnational Relations and World Politics* (Cambridge, Mass.: Harvard University Press, 1971).

3. For overviews see Emanuel Adler, "The Emergence of Cooperation: National Epistemic Communities and the International Evolution of the Idea of Nuclear Arms Control," in P. Haas, *Knowledge, Power, and International Policy Coordination*, pp. 101–45; Gert Krell, "The Problems and Achievements of Arms Control," *Arms Control* (December 1981), pp. 247–86.

4. On the domestic arms control debate during the Reagan administration see Dan Caldwell, *The Dynamics of Domestic Politics and Arms Control: The SALT II Treaty Debate* (Columbia: University of South Carolina Press, 1991); Michael Krepon, *Arms Control in the Reagan Administration* (Washington, D.C.: University Press of America, 1989); Bernd W. Kubbig, *Amerikanische Rüstungskontrollpolitik: Die innergesellschaftlichen Auseinandersetzungen in der ersten Amtszeit Ronald Reagans* (U.S. arms control policy: The domestic debates during Reagan's first term) (Frankfurt M.: Campus, 1988); David Meyer, *A Winter of Discontent: The Freeze and American Politics* (New York: Praeger, 1990);

and Philip G. Schrag, *Listening for the Bomb: A Study in Nuclear Arms Control Verification* (Boulder, Colo.: Westview, 1989).

5. On the German debate see Jeffrey Boutwell, *The German Nuclear Dilemma* (Ithaca, N.Y.: Cornell University Press, 1990); and Thomas Risse-Kappen, *Die Krise der Sicherheitspolitik: Neuorientierungen und Entscheidungsprozesse im politischen System der Bundesrepublik Deutschland 1977–1984* (The crisis of security policy: New orientations and decision-making processes in the political system of the Federal Republic of Germany, 1977–1984) (Mainz, Germany: Grünewald-Kaiser, 1988).

6. See, for example, Horst Afheldt, *Defensive Verteidigung* (Defensive defense) (Reinbek, Germany: Rowohlt, 1983); Anders Boserup and Andrew Mack, *Krieg ohne Waffen* (War without weapons) (Reinbek, Germany: Rowohlt, 1974); Anders Boserup, *Foundations of Defensive Defense* (New York: Macmillan, 1990); Bjorn Muller, *Non-offensive Defense: A Bibliography* (Copenhagen: Center for Peace and Conflict Research, 1987); Bjorn Muller, *Common Security and Non-offensive Defense: A Neorealist Perspective* (Boulder, Colo.: Lynne Rienner Publishing, 1992); Studiengruppe Alternative Sicherheitspolitik (Study Group on Alternative Security Policy) *Strukturwandel der Verteidigung* (Structural change of defense) (Opladen, Germany: Westdeutscher Verlag, 1984); Albrecht A.C. von Müller, "Integrated Forward Defense," manuscript, Starnberg, Germany, 1985. On the security dilemma see Robert Jervis, "Cooperation Under the Security Dilemma," *World Politics* 30 (January 1978), pp. 186–214.

7. Matthew Evangelista, *Unarmed Forces: The Transnational Movement to End the Cold War* (Ithaca, N.Y.: Cornell University Press, 1999), and Matthew Evangelista, "Transnational Relations, Domestic Structures, and Security Policy in the U.S.S.R. and Russia," in Risse-Kappen, *Bringing Transnational Relations Back In*.

8. See Independent Commission on Disarmament and Security Issues, *Common Security*.

9. Arbatov, *The System*, pp. 311–12. Milstein frequently published in Western journals. See, for example, Mikhail Milstein, "Problems of the Inadmissability of Nuclear Conflict," *International Studies Quarterly* 20 (March 1976), pp. 87–103.

10. On the history of Pugwash, see Joseph Rotblat, *Scientists in the Quest for Peace: A History of the Pugwash Conference* (Cambridge, Mass.: MIT Press, 1972).

11. For details, see Stephen Kux, "Western Peace Research and Soviet Military Thought"; manuscript, Columbia University, New York, 20 April 1989; and Matthew Evangelista, "Transnational Alliances and Soviet Demilitarization," paper prepared for the Council on Economic Priorities, October 1990, manuscript pp. 33–41. See also Anders Boserup, "A Way to Undermine Hostility," *Bulletin of the Atomic Scientists* 44 (September 1988), pp. 16–19. On the various Pugwash meetings, see Joseph Rotblat and Laszlo Valki, eds., *Coexistence, Cooperation, and Common Security: Annals of Pugwash 1986* (New York: St. Martin's Press, 1988); and Joseph Rotblat and V.I. Goldanskii, eds., *Global Problems and Common Security: Annals of Pugwash 1988* (Berlin: Springer-Verlag, 1989).

12. Tracing the policy impact of transnational coalitions requires extensive data on decision-making processes in order to allow for causal inferences. Compared with these requirements, the evidence presented below still is not satisfactory. For further and more detailed studies see Evangelista, *Unarmed Forces;* Evangelista, "Transnational Relations, Domestic Structures, and Security Policy in the U.S.S.R. and Russia"; and Robert Herman, "Soviet New Thinking: Ideas, Interests, and the Redefinition of Security," Ph.D. diss., Cornell University.

13. M.S. Gorbachev, "Report to the Twenty-Seventh Congress of the Communist Party of the Soviet Union," in M.S. Gorbachev, *Speeches and Writings* (Oxford: Paragon Press, 1986), pp. 71 and 74. For a more coherent and less ambiguous argument about common security see Mikhail Gorbachev, *Perestroika: New Thinking for Our Country and the*

World (New York: Harper and Row, 1987), pp. 140–44. For comprehensive analyses of the new Soviet thinking about security, see Kull, *Burying Lenin;* Raymond Garthoff, *Deterrence and the Revolution in Soviet Military Doctrine* (Washington, D.C.: Brookings Institution, 1990); and Klaus Segbers, *Der sowjetische Systemwandel* (The Soviet system change) (Frankfurt M.: Subrkamp, 1989), pp. 299–330.

14. Gorbachev, *Perestroika*, pp. 142–43. See also his "Report to the Twenty-seventh Congress of the Communist Party of the Soviet Union," p. 74.

15. For details of these arguments, see Garthoff, *Deterrence and the Revolution in Soviet Military Doctrine*, pp. 149–85; Stephen M. Meyer, "The Sources and Prospects of Gorbachev's New Political Thinking on Security," *International Security* 13 (Fall 1988), pp. 124–63; R. Hyland Phillips and Jeffrey I. Sands, "Reasonable Sufficiency and Soviet Conventional Defense," *International Security* 13 (Fall 1988), pp. 164–78; and Willard C. Frank and Philip S. Gillette, eds., *Soviet Military Doctrine from Lenin to Gorbachev, 1915–1991* (Westport, Conn.: Greenwood, 1992).

16. See, for example, Andrei Kokoshin and Valentin Larionov, "Confrontation of Conventional Forces in the Context of Ensuring Strategic Stability," in Hans Günter Brauch and Robert Kennedy, eds., *Alternative Conventional Defense Postures in the European Theater*, vol. 2 (New York: Crane Russak, 1992), pp. 71–82. The Russian original of this article first appeared in 1988. See also Andrei Kokoshin, "Restructure Forces, Enhance Security," *Bulletin of the Atomic Scientists* 44 (September 1988), pp. 35–38; Andrei Kokoshin and Valentin Larionov, *Prevention of War: Doctrines, Concepts, Prospects* (Moscow: Progress, 1991); and Valentin Larionov, "Soviet Military Doctrine: Past and Present," in Frank and Gillette, *Soviet Military Doctrine from Lenin to Gorbachev*, pp. 301–19.

17. For details of these exchanges, see Evangelista, "Transnational Alliances and Soviet Demilitarization," pp. 31–37.

18. Frank and Gillette, *Soviet Military Doctrine from Lenin to Gorbachev*, p. 397.

19. Other examples include arms control proposals on test ban negotiations and the ABM treaty (as indicated by Evangelista, "Transnational Relations, Domestic Structures, and Security Policy in the U.S.S.R. and Russia") and ideas about the "common European home" and the Conference for Security and Cooperation in Europe. See Gorbachev, *Perestroika*, pp. 194–98. I thank one of the anonymous reviewers for alerting me to this.

20. See Pat Litherland, "Gorbachev and Arms Control: Civilian Experts and Soviet Policy," Peace Research Report no. 12 University of Bradford, November 1986; Allan Lynch, *Gorbachev's International Outlook: Intellectual Origins and Political Consequences*, Institute for East–West Security Studies Occasional Paper no. 9 (Boulder, Colo.: Westview, 1989); and Kimberley Martin Zisk, "Soviet Academic Theories on International Conflict and Negotiation: A Research Note," *Journal of Conflict Resolution* 34 (December 1990), pp. 678–93.

21. See, for example, Peter Katzenstein, ed., *Between Power and Plenty* (Madison: University of Wisconsin Press, 1978); Peter Katzenstein, *Small States in World Markets* (Ithaca, N.Y.: Cornell University Press, 1984); Peter Gourevitch, *Politics in Hard Times* (Ithaca, N.Y.: Cornell University Press, 1986); G. John Ikenberry, *Reasons of State: Oil Politics and the Capacities of the American Government* (Ithaca, N.Y.: Cornell University Press, 1988); and G. John Ikenberry, David Lake, and Michael Mastanduno, eds., *The State and American Foreign Economic Policy* (Ithaca, N.Y.: Cornell University Press, 1988). For examples of attempts to apply the approach to other issue-areas, see Michael Barnett, "High Politics is Low Politics: The Domestic and Systemic Sources of Israeli Security Policy, 1967–1977," *World Politics* 42 (July 1990), pp. 529–62; Matthew Evangelista, *Innovation and the Arms Race* (Ithaca, N.Y.: Cornell University Press, 1988); Matthew Evangelista,

"Domestic Structures and International Change," in Michael Doyle and G. John Ikenberry, eds., *New Thinking in International Relations Theory,* forthcoming; and Thomas Risse-Kappen, "Public Opinion, Domestic Structure, and Foreign Policy in Liberal Democracies," *World Politics* 43 (July 1991), pp. 479–512. For the following see also my "Introduction," in Risse-Kappen, *Bringing Transnational Relations Back In.*

22. See, for example, James G. March and Johan P. Olsen, *Rediscovering Institutions: The Organizational Basis of Politics* (New York: Free Press, 1989); G. John Ikenberry, "Conclusion: An Institutional Approach to American Foreign Economic Policy," in G. John Ikenberry et al., *State and American Foreign Economic Policy,* pp. 219–43; and Friedrich Kratochwil, *Rules, Norms, and Decisions* (Cambridge: Cambridge University Press, 1989). For various applications, see Peter Katzenstein and Nobuo Okawara, "Japan's National Security: Structures, Norms, and Politics," *International Security* 17 (Spring 1993), pp. 84–118; Peter Katzenstein and Nobuo Okawara, *Japan's National Security: Structures, Norms, and Policy Responses in a Changing World* (Ithaca, N.Y.: Cornell University Press, 1993); and Thomas Berger, "From Sword to Chrysanthemum: Japan's Culture of Antimilitarism," *International Security* 17 (Spring 1993), pp. 119–50.

23. It is thus important to distinguish between consensual ideas that are stable over time and those that are altered frequently and are promoted by specific groups. The strategic prescriptions discussed in this article are examples of the latter type of ideas. I thank John Odell and an anonymous reviewer for alerting me to this point.

24. See Evangelista, *Innovation and the Arms Race;* and Evangelista, "Transnational Relations, Domestic Structures, and Security Policy in the U.S.S.R. and Russia."

25. A domestic structure approach explains why cognitive and learning theories are so widely used to explain the Gorbachev revolution. See George Breslauer and Philip Tetlock, eds., *Learning in U.S. and Soviet Foreign Policy* (Boulder, Colo.: Westview, 1991); and Janice G. Stein, "Political Learning by Doing: Gorbachev as Uncommitted Thinker and Motivational Learner," *International Organization* 48 (Spring 1994), pp. 155–83. For a similar point see Sue Peterson, "Strategy and State Structure: The Domestic Politics of Crisis Bargaining," Ph.D. diss., Columbia University, New York, 1993.

26. I owe the following argument to Steve Ropp.

27. Of course, U.S. autonomy is greater in national security affairs than in other issue-areas. But compared with the former Soviet state, the difference is still striking.

28. On the "cold war consensus" in the United States and its limits see Bruce Russett, *Controlling the Sword* (Cambridge, Mass.: Harvard University Press, 1990), chap. 3; and Eugene Wittkopf, *Faces of Internationalism: Public Opinion and American Foreign Policy* (Durham, N.C.: Duke University Press, 1990).

29. See Peter Katzenstein, *Corporatism and Change* (Ithaca, N.Y.: Cornell University Press, 1984); and Peter Katzenstein, *Policy and Politics in West Germany* (Philadelphia: Temple University Press, 1989).

The World Trade Organization, the Environment, and the Ecological Critique

MICHEL DAMIAN AND JEAN-CHRISTOPHE GRAZ

In 1986, when the Uruguay Round of the General Agreement on Tariffs and Trade (GATT) began at Punta del Este, the environment did not appear on the agenda at all; today, however, there are no two ways about it: the World Trade Organization (WTO) can no longer operate without regard for environmental considerations. Not only does sustainable development feature in its Preamble as one of its fundamental objectives, but there is also an increasing number of trade disputes which refer to the environment, more or less directly.[1] The environment is now a basic issue for the WTO because it sets trade policy in a comprehensive relationship with the State's role in economic, social, and environmental matters. The relationship between trade, the environment, and sustainable development must therefore take into account the impact on the conditions of exchange of the differentiated responses of human societies towards one another, nature, and the future. . . .

THE HANDLING OF THE ENVIRONMENT AT THE WTO

The international commercial order that emerged after the Second World War did, to a modest extent, anticipate conservation and environmental issues and their implications for the conduct of international trade. It sought to reconcile, on the largest scale, the liberal tradition of international free trade with some major safeguards to protect the newly established role of the state in production, employment, and general social and economic welfare (Graz 1999). It also allowed trade restrictions which would nowadays be described as environmental. The GATT framework (Article XX b and g) allows states to use trade barriers to shelter domestic policies aimed at the defence of certain values associated with conservation of natural resources and the preservation of life.[2]

These values were initially defended at national level, with no repercussions on the conduct of international trade. From the 1960s onwards, however, environmental issues began to leave the sidelines and occupy a growing space within the political agenda. This was most evident, at the domestic level, in the creation of the first environment ministries, national agencies, and ad hoc programmes. The 1972 Stockholm Conference shifted the environmental issue towards the international arena. Within GATT as well as at Stockholm, the environment was at that time essentially regarded as a hindrance to be removed so as to avoid further trade restrictions.

THE INITIAL AGENDA: THE ENVIRONMENT OUTSIDE GATT

The Stockholm Conference was, however, a crucial stage in the emergence of a global approach to social and ecological questions: above all, it fixed in the popular consciousness the idea of "Spaceship Earth," coined a few years earlier by Kenneth Boulding. The very title of the preparatory report, *Only One Earth*, puts the essence of its message in a nutshell. One of its co-authors, René Dubos (who also coined the watchword *Think Globally, Act Locally*), declared "We are now moving into the stage of global social evolution." The problems of Spaceship Earth, he added, affect humanity worldwide and could only be handled from a worldwide perspective (Nations Unies 1972, 22).

Against this background, GATT was invited to make a contribution to the preparatory work for the conference. Business groups in the rich countries were worried that the adoption of strict anti-pollution standards might lessen their competitiveness on world markets and lead to novel protectionist measures. The Trade and Environment Working Group was set up within GATT in 1971 and published its first report in that year. The Report reveals one certainty, one objective, and one misgiving. The certainty was illustrative of the technocratic mindset that was applied in those days to the treatment of environmental problems: "Any conflicts of trade interests arising from variations in national standards . . . may be resolved through existing and evolving arrangements and procedures" (GATT 1971, 25). The objective, in accordance with GATT's own calling, was "to avoid situations in which the institution of national pollution control systems would interfere with the continued expansion of international trade" (ibid. 26). And the worry was that the problem would merely be shifted to "pollution havens": "One possible result of national responses to the environment problem could be an accelerated transfer of industries or processes causing the most pollution to countries facing a less urgent pollution problem" (ibid. 26). The guiding principle at GATT was above all to prevent distortions and hindrances to trade, and to keep the environment on the margins of trade. The only recommendation (No. 103) of the Stockholm Conference pertaining to the relationship between trade and the environment echoed this guiding principle: "all States should . . . agree to not invoke environmental concerns as a pretext for discriminatory trade policies or for reduced access to market."

From Environment to Sustainable Development

Two factors helped to bring the environment more fully within the institutional framework of GATT and subsequently of the WTO. The first change came through the proliferation of Multilateral Environmental Agreements (MEAs) and the strengthening of some of them in response to truly global problems like the hole in the ozone layer and the greenhouse effect. There are now approximately 200 MEAs, nearly 20 of them containing trade-restrictive provisions. The most constraining are the Convention on International Trade in Endangered Species (CITES 1973), the Montreal Protocol on Substances that Deplete the Ozone Layer (1987), the Basel Convention on the Control of Transboundary Movements of Hazardous Wastes and their Disposal (1989), the Cartagena Protocol on Biosafety (2000) and, hypothetically, the Kyoto Protocol on Reduction of Greenhouse Gas Emissions (1997). The crucial issues in these agreements always involve the strengthening of arrangements made for including trade restrictive measures.

The second major change concerns the concealed topic of Stockholm: development. During the 1970s, criticism of the international economic order from many developing countries included radical proposals founded on calls for "inward-looking development" and "ecodevelopment."[3] As the many ventures that stemmed from these debates appeared to be leading nowhere, the United Nations General Assembly set up a new commission, this time with an explicit mandate to consider the link between development and the environment. This was the origin of the Brundtland Report, published in 1987 by the World Commission on the Environment and Development under the title *Our Common Future*. This report stirred up the environment/development debate with an approach tending more towards consensus and leading to a considerable impact on public discussion.

This publication first set up and gave wide currency to the notion of "sustainable development," with the following classic definition: "Environmental protection is . . . inherent in the concept of sustainable development . . . Sustainable development is development that meets the needs of the present without compromising the ability of the future generations to meet their own needs. . . . Even the narrow notion of physical sustainability implies a concern for social equity between generations, a concern that must logically be extended to equity within each generation" (WCED 1987, 40 and 43). The Brundtland Report also drew attention to the relationship between income level and environmental protection: "the reduction of poverty itself is a precondition for environmentally sound development" (ibid. 69). And, lastly, the report called on intergovernmental organisations, especially GATT and UNCTAD (the United Nations Conference on Trade and Development), to tackle more directly the relationship between international trade and the environment (ibid. 101).

The New Approach: The WTO and the Challenge of Sustainable Development

The agenda, to make trade compatible with the environment and sustainable development, became by degrees that of GATT, then of the Rio Conference, and finally of the WTO (Damian, Chaudhuri & Berthaud 1997). However, the definitions of the environment and sustainable development both lack any very readily located boundaries. . . .

The WTO faces difficulties in becoming the appropriate institutional framework for resolving the new field of contestability opened up by these questions of definition of environment and sustainable development. Since the Marrakesh Agreements of 1994, however, it has had to make the environment a matter of priority when it was decided to set up a Committee on Trade and Environment (at the particular insistence of the United States). In terms drawn directly from the Brundtland Report, its mandate is "to identify the relationship between trade measures and environmental measures, in order to promote sustainable development." Yet the positions within the Committee remain so contradictory that it has not been able to reach any noteworthy conclusions. The term environment itself is still considered too controversial to be added to paragraph (b) of Article XX, which is the current statutory basis for trade restrictions on environmental grounds. Moreover the word is taboo both in the "built-in agenda" (the programme of work settled at the Marrakesh Ministerial, mainly concerning agriculture and services) and in the "new subjects" (added by the Singapore Ministerial Declaration in 1996, in particular investment and competition policy). The environment remains one of those "other subjects" (such as labour standards, or e-commerce), which may become the object of negotiations, but only if a consensus emerges to make them so.

Nevertheless, despite this apparently inextricable maelstrom, the WTO manages to settle disputes. How? By self-restraint. It does not give rulings on the "environment," but leaves that to other institutions whose standards it uses, in particular under the Agreement on Technical Barriers to Trade (TBT) and the Sanitary and Phytosanitary Agreement (SPS), both of which came into effect in 1995.[4] Some of these institutions are public ones. For instance, the United Nations Food and Agriculture Organization (FAO) and the World Health Organization (WHO) have drawn up food standards in the Codex Alimentarius, created in 1962, which applies to food hygiene and safety, labelling, and methods of analysis, inspection and certification. The Codex is one of the main sources of standards for the SPS Agreement.[5] Whenever the WTO has to give a ruling on trade conflicts arising out of food issues, it forms its opinion on the basis not of its own corpus of standards (for it has none), but of the Codex. There are other institutions to whose standards it refers, which have a more hybrid status. For example, the International Standards Organization (ISO), whose members are governmental standards institutions in some countries, but often include trade associations. Under the TBT Agreement, international voluntary standards set by a body like the ISO are regarded as an authoritative source for the purposes of the WTO mechanism for settlement of disputes. Mandatory standards set by government agencies, by contrast, are defined as "technical regulations" which, if they are not to be regarded as trade-restrictive must be "legitimate" (TBT Agreement, Articles 2, 9 and Annex 3). The Multilateral Environmental Agreements (MEAs) also constitute standards to which the WTO can refer. Since 2000, the Committee on Trade and Environment has been making greater efforts to clarify the status of the MEAs in relation to the WTO.

It is in this tracery of exogenous institutions and standards that the WTO settles trade disputes connected with the environment and sustainable development. The only jurisdiction of the WTO lies in giving a ruling on whether trade restrictions notified by states are scientifically based and consistent with the WTO's own regulatory framework (above all in terms of non-discrimination and national treatment). This accounts for the WTO's refusal, so far, to recognise the precautionary principle as valid grounds for a restriction, even though that principle is the very basis of the European Union's environmental policy (Article 174.2, formerly 130R, of the consolidated Treaty of Rome). All recent disputes have in fact been decided in the light of "sufficient scientific proof": the risk must be scientifically established, its assessment must have scientific underpinning, and there must be a real probability of these risks becoming fact.

The WTO, then, grants an extensive role to science and expertise. This mode of governance, far from reflecting the widely publicised principle of "best practice," in fact encourages domination by the most powerful. The French representative's testimony to the Executive Committee of the Codex Alimentarius is illuminating here: "the best prepared, the best advised—those who are best armed will have mastery over the others. And the weapon most essential for this mastery goes by the name of *expertise*; the countries with the best network of expertise will, in general, win the day" (Doussin 1998, 17—original emphasis). This major role accorded to science and expertise is typical of a kind of epistemic authority which seeks to invest national and transnational elites with sole rights to the professional expertise regarded as legitimate, as if by so doing it was possible to keep the stuff of politics—conflicts of value, issues of distributive justice—at arm's length (Hewson & Sinclair 1999). And yet, most of the time, science only offers provisional knowledge. It offers interpretations and methods for refining interpretations without necessarily reducing the margin of uncertainty. It cannot then be the sole legitimate voice that sanctions one course rather than another. When it comes to the making of choices by a society, it becomes apparent that what matters, essentially, is not what facts are available but rather what ethical values are applied.

THE ECOLOGICAL CRITIQUE

The liberal paradigm starts from its own ontology as to the nature of the causal relations between the economic sphere and the biosphere. The biosphere is subservient to the economic sphere, which in turn rests upon an anthropocentric, utilitarian and instrumental view of the relationship of humankind to the environment. From growth in all economic variables, we may expect better satisfaction of needs (including that of environmental conservation). "To do with more" is one way it could be put.

The ecological critique marks an ontological shift. The motto is "to do with less," following the famous catchphrase of Georgescu-Roegen. The economic sphere must now find its place within the biosphere, which is finite and with grand regulating laws which economics has to comply with.[6] The realm of ethics and politics governs the relationship of inclusion between the economic sphere and the biosphere. In the academic world, the ecological critique institutionalised during the 1980s, notably through the activities of a learned society, the International Society for Ecological Economics, and its journal, *Ecological Economics*. . . .

In the world of politics, the ecological critique of the liberal world view has found standard-bearers to be reckoned with in the environmentalist movements (Greenpeace 2000; WWF 1999). The international politics of the environment, in emphasising scientific knowledge and the search for global solutions, offers non-governmental players a special means of access to the global political scene (Princen & Finger 1994). The WTO cannot carry out its remit any longer without paying special attention to environmental groups. Radical or pragmatic in approach, they have their part to play both in the suggested reform of the WTO and in some of the environment-related trade disputes. In the United States, especially, groups of environmentalists intervene before the courts and in this way manage to redirect national legislation; and this poses a challenge for the WTO's regulatory framework. They are also to be found in the front ranks of the counter-summits held on the occasion of the ministerial conferences. And, lastly, the more pragmatic ones take part in the various institutional platforms set up in order to give substance to the WTO Secretariat's new approach, one that is to be "balanced and equitable" as between trade liberalisation and sustainable development....

The Critique of Free Trade

The perception of the economy as a subsystem of the biosphere, operating in a finite environment, utterly transforms the relationship that is assumed between free trade and growth. Before the theoretical debate about the two concepts can even get going, free trade gets a number of black marks—on physical grounds—because of the pressures it creates on the environment and on people....

The theoretical objection of ecological economists is based on the restrictive set of assumptions required by the Ricardian theory of comparative advantage: no externalities, stable prices, comparative advantages constant over time, no power relations, and no international factor mobility. This last assumption is the most contested of all: "the empirical cornerstone of the whole classical free trade argument, capital immobility, has crumbled into loose gravel" (Daly & Cobb 1989, 216).

This critique of free trade and the theory of comparative advantage may seem elementary. Debates about the modern theory of international trade have modified the arguments for free trade: it is now said to be suboptimal in theory, yet optimal in practice. Krugman observes that the question is not, in the end, a "scientific," but an "essentially political" one (1993, 364), since to move away from free trade would in all likelihood cause more harm than good. The master-stroke of the ecological critique consists of the way it exchanges conclusions of political economy for recommendations of economic policy. Once free trade no longer stands up as a theory, the "default position" (Daly 1995, 313) might just as well be the protection of national economies against eco-dumping, and the fostering of self-sufficiency.

Under free trade, countries that internalise environmental costs in their prices would be at a disadvantage compared with those which do not. Taking into account ecological cost, even in a small degree, is regarded as unfair, in that it would disallow the implementation of ecological policies even though they may in fact have a quite legitimate price tag. The ecological critique claims that the internalising of environmental costs must be done on a domestic and multilateral basis—though opinions differ as to just how complementary these two avenues are.

The Case for Restricted Trade and Unilateral Rules

Regarding the internalising of environmental costs at domestic level, the first proposal is the erection of ecological tariffs to protect domestic policies against foreign eco-dumping. Daly is one of the stoutest advocates of this approach and maintains that the way such decisions work means they cannot be dismissed as protectionism (Daly & Goodland 1994, 76). The second proposal recognises that more than half of world trade is intra-industry trade: the proposal is that trade should be restricted by turning the "default position" (unlimited specialisation) around, to "strive towards greater self-sufficiency nationally, regionally and locally" (Røpke 1994, 21). An initial corollary of this would be to establish a "new protectionism," that would maximise local commerce and relocate economic activity on the basis of local democracy (Hines & Lang 1993; Prugh, Costanza, & Daly 2000). "Balanced trade" is the second corollary: by limiting trade to what was strictly necessary, countries would not import on credit (which feeds the international mobility of capital) but mainly on the basis of their export revenues, which would likewise be reduced (Daly & Goodland 1994, 90). The recurring call for "self-sufficiency of national communities" is a logical extension of these requirements, since it is thought that they tend to be implemented against such a policy backdrop (Daly & Cobb 1989, 209–235). All these suggestions have in view a negative growth of the economies of the North so as to enable those of the South to grow.

The internalising of environmental costs at the domestic level raises several points. First, Daly adduces in support of his arguments for self-sufficiency (in 10 or more publications) a highly contentious application of Keynes's famous text, *National Self-Sufficiency*, written in 1933. Keynes took the view that, in the quite particular context of the Great Depression, national self-sufficiency had the principal merit of allowing experimentation: "We wish—for the time at least and so long as the present transitional, experimental phase endures—to be our own masters, and to be as free as we can make ourselves from the interferences of the outside world" (Moggridge 1980, Vol. XXI, 240). Here, Keynes is thinking out loud; moreover, the whole latter part of his text is devoted to caveats (he explicitly mentions Mussolini, Germany, and Stalin): "In those countries where the advocates of national self-sufficiency have attained power, it appears to my judgement that, without exception, many foolish things are being done" (243). Daly also pays only slight attention to the three great dangers Keynes complains of in economic nationalism—Silliness, Haste, and Intolerance.

Furthermore, a national policy of self-sufficiency gives no automatic guarantee of domestic sustainability; at least, this is the conclusion we draw from the historical study of Gowdy (1995, 507). Lastly, ecological tariffs could only become a favoured tool for the more powerful national economies. Quite apart from the question of what to do with the proceeds, such tariffs pose at least two problems. The developing countries have just as much right and reason to erect such tariffs on the goods they export, but not the market power to do so. If the developed countries are to tax the negative externalities incorporated in goods from developing countries, then they should likewise reward the positive ones, such as the sustainability imported along with low-cost primary commodities, or the benefits of having the skilled immigrant workers who come from those countries. Once more, the developing countries have not the bargaining power to implement this kind of solution at world level. So far only a few of the wealthiest countries, the United States in particular, have considered tariffs against eco-dumping.

The Case for Fair Trade and Multilateral Rules

Multilateral internalising of environmental costs is the issue which is nowadays generating both the most significant proposals and the heaviest opposition. First among the points at issue is the status of the Multilateral Environmental Agreements and their extension to new fields. They raise a considerable problem, since their negotiation is constantly coming up against the question whether it is possible to have physical controls on a particular trade. Restrictions and prohibitions (for instance, of chlorofluoro-carbons (CFCs) under the Montreal Protocol) represent, at bottom, a break with the price mechanism. This problem goes beyond trade activities themselves, to the prior question of the incidence of production processes and methods on the terms of trade. Now the WTO makes a complete distinction between restrictions on products—which are acceptable under certain conditions—and restrictions involving production processes and methods, which are not permitted, with the sole exception of goods made in prisons (GATT, Article XX, § e). This exception is a crucial one, since it makes explicit the immense gulf between production methods which are ethical, responsible, fair and safe—in short, sustainable—and those which are immoral, irresponsible, unfair, dangerous, or, in other words, unsustainable (Arden-Clarke 1998). The tuna/dolphin dispute between the United States and Mexico which has made such a stir in the press since the early 1980s is surely the clearest illustration of the issues raised by trade restrictions on the basis of production processes and methods.[7]

Indeed, in such conditions, to what sustainability criteria, what technological capacities, and what access to credit for investment in their own technologies can poor countries have recourse in order to avoid new restrictions on their trade? The difficulty of physical restrictions on quantities or processes is that they mingle protection of the environment with protectionism. Whether it is dolphin conservation in the United States/Mexico dispute or safe-guarding the ozone layer, the initial impetus came from scientific studies, followed by campaigns and court action from environmental groups (in these cases, American ones). But it has happened that the economic agents involved have taken the original ecological claims and reformulated them to suit their own interests (in the one case, by accepting that tuna imports from Mexico should be banned; in the other, by pressure on the world chemicals industry to desist from CFC production). To use the terms coined by DeSombre (1995), there is often an alliance between *Baptists* (the environmentalists) and *Bootleggers* (strictly, illicit purveyors of alcohol; more loosely, capitalists). The assessment of physical restrictions can also be twofold: preservation of the biosphere and its resources on the one hand; on the other, high-handed protectionism operated by the powerful against the weak. For this reason, the bundle of clauses which will, in all the Multilateral Environmental Agreements, prove most crucial in persuading the rest of the world to accept the shared preferences of the developed countries, increasingly be those dealing with financial compensation and technology transfer.

The second issue in the multilateral internalisation of costs involves non-physical, monetary measures. Here the ecological economists, along with the environmentalists, advocate incorporating environmental and social costs within international prices (Costanza et al. 1995; Daly & Goodland 1994; WWF 1999). This suggestion takes neoclassical economics at its word; it takes its favourite instrument and makes it a multilateral one, making tariffs, and the resulting price signals, the means of incorporating negative externalities. A practical example which such internalising could well follow is the International Tropical Timber Agreement negotiated under the auspices of UNCTAD in the early 1980s. This agreement (together with some others on tropical products: cocoa, coffee, jute, and rubber) refers explicitly to bringing environmental costs into international pricing. It requires account to be taken of "prices which reflect the costs of sustainable forest management and which are remunerative and equitable."[8] Not one of these agreements, however, has come into force. The oldest attempt at an integrated raw materials programme, dating from the 1970s and 1980s, has also run into the ground; and there is every indication that the internalising in international raw materials agreements is going to take a very long time.

There are in any case many problems with multilateral internalising of externalities by means of prices; these include the redistribution conflicts inherent in the compensation mechanisms, and the ecological and political limitations on giving a monetary value to environmental costs, not to mention the purely monetary constraints on the manipulation of the resulting prices (inflation, exchange rate effects). Here again the heart of the problem is the weak market power, or, more generally, bargaining power, of the developing countries. If the environmentalist movements and ecological economists managed to establish a place for multilateral price internalising of externalities in the corpus of trade and environmental standards and regulations, this would indeed represent a considerable change.[9] . . .

CONCLUSION

From the foregoing, we may summarise the position of environmental issues in the WTO under three basic headings. (1) The international trade agenda has been transformed: the environment and sustainable development have become a component of trade and, consequently, of WTO policy. Its Secretariat has now acknowledged this shift. (2) The WTO's decision-making bodies nevertheless keep trade and the environment in watertight compartments. The jurisdiction of the WTO relates to the negotiation and management of conditions for trade between States. For the settlement of environment-related trade disputes, it confines itself to applying exogenous standards coming from multilateral agreements of various configurations and international institutions, whose status is often hybrid (public, private, intergovernmental, non-governmental, groups of experts, etc.). (3) This twofold issue—the WTO is under pressure to include the environment in its agenda, while it declines to internalise in its own jurisdiction a proper corpus of standards and regulations—is the consequence of the recent ecological and social critique within the international community. This has opened up an unbounded field of contestability of trade policies, especially on the status of free trade and the role of managed, safe, and fair trade. This is the greatest long-term issue at stake in the whole handling of the environment at the WTO.

A long-term issue, then; but also one of history in the making. Those in power who appeal to the liberal paradigm are also those who are obliged to adjust it with the progressive inclusion of some—only some—of their opponents' claims. Recent evolution in the scientific and normative corpus of the major multilateral economic institutions is significant here. While still maintaining the principle that trade and the environment are two distinct domains, the latest important WTO study on the subject is symptomatic of this shift: "In short, trade is not the issue, nor is economic growth. The issue is how to reinvent environmental policies in an ever more integrated world economy so as to ensure that we live within ecological limits" (Nordström & Vaughan 1999, 7). While we wait, we may expect the ecological footprint of the rich world upon the biosphere to remain a matter of acute interest.

NOTES

1. In the period 1980–1990, notifications on environmental grounds represented 7.8% of all notifications of technical barriers to trade; in 1998 the figure was 15%, in 1999 it was 12.5%, and in 2000 it was 15.6% (WTO 2001, 2).

2. Restrictions on trade are permitted for reasons "necessary to protect human, animal or plant life or health" (paragraph b) or for reasons "relating to the conservation of exhaustible natural resources if such measures are made effective in conjunction with restrictions on domestic production or consumption" (paragraph g). These exceptions are not to contravene the principle of non-discrimination, or to be a disguised restriction on international trade.

3. UNEP (the United Nations Environment Programme) did originally refer to eco-development, but subsequently dropped the term under American pressure, the contents of the notion, as promoted, being too radical.

4. The TBT and SPS Agreements both deal with "technical barriers to trade," and in particular with trade discrimination that can be the result of domestic regulations. The TBT Agreement, originally negotiated during the 1960s and extensively revised during the Uruguay Round, has a comprehensive scope applying to all goods. The SPS Agreement is a product of the Uruguay Round. It deals specifically with measures to protect human, animal or plant life or health.

5. For food safety, the WTO uses the Codex; for other sources of standards, such as those for animal health or plant protection, it has recourse to the World Animal Health Organization and the International Plant Protection Convention (based at FAO).

6. Whether the biosphere is in actual fact "finite" presupposes a prior question as to the scale of economic activity in relation to that of the environment; or, alternatively, of the load capacity of the biosphere. It is one on which opinions vary greatly. The more alarmist authorities, especially Daly (who harps constantly on this point), claim that humanity is already taking up 40% of the capacity for photosynthesis implicit in the amount of incident sunlight. Others, including Le Bras (1994, 118–144), consider this figure to be 2.5% at most.

7. The tuna/dolphin affair erupted in 1991, when Mexico complained to GATT about the United States embargo on its tuna exports. The United States replied that the embargo was justified in view of Mexican fishing methods: the nets used were causing the death of dolphins of a species protected under the Marine Mammal Protection Act which the United States Congress had passed in 1972. On two occasions, in 1991 and 1994, GATT upheld the Mexican complaint, on the specific grounds that processes

and production methods were disallowed as reasons for restraint of trade, even when the reason appeared to be such a legitimate one as the protection of an endangered species. GATT's appeal body never in fact came to a formal decision, because of the opposition of the United States; and the embargo remained until April 2000, when the Government came to the conclusion that Mexico was now in compliance with the 1998 principles worked out as part of the International Dolphin Protection Programme. This MEA also resolved the problems raised by "dolphin safe" labelling that had been operating since 1990. In April 2000, however, the controversy reappeared when environmental pressure groups won a case in a California District Court. On this occasion, the Department of Commerce was obliged to return to the former labelling regime, which amounted to a *de facto* embargo on tuna imports from Mexico. After further fruitless consultations, the Government of Mexico was contemplating a complaint on the matter to the WTO (October 2000). This controversy might seem to be just one more story, but it raises some fundamental issues: the protection of dolphins (or even, for some, their "totemisation"); covert protectionism (the United States is the world's largest tuna producer); unilateral imposition of a particular production process (the US-standard tuna net); multilateral extension of environmental standards (International Dolphin Protection Programme); and then, on another view, the all-powerful regulatory framework of the WTO in the face of environmental regulations of sovereign countries which, in the environmentalists" opinion, were quite justified.

8. UNCTAD, *International Tropical Timber Agreement, 1994.* TD/TIMBER.2/16, New York and Geneva: United Nations, Article 1, §e.

9. This proposal takes us back to the old debate over remunerative prices. Starting with the pioneering proposals of the Havana Charter just after the Second World War, projects for institutionalising remunerative prices have for the most part come to nothing. In 1943, working to develop post-war plans on this point, Keynes was well aware that the "reasonable international economic price [would always be] the crux of all such schemes" (Moggridge 1980, Vol. XXVII, 187).

REFERENCES

Arden-Clarke, C. (1998), "Process and Production Methods." In D. Brack (ed.), *Trade and Environment: Conflict or Compatibility?* London, Royal Institute of International Affairs: 72–78.

Bhagwati, J. and Srinivasan, T. N. (1996), "Trade and the Environment: Does Environmental Diversity Detract from the Case for Free Trade?" In J. Bhagwati and R. Hudec (eds.), *Fair Trade and Harmonization. Prerequisites for Free Trade?* Vol. 1, *Economic Analysis.* Cambridge, MA, MIT Press: 159–224.

Costanza, R., Audley, J., Borden, R., Ekins, P., Folke, C., Funtowicz, S. O. and Haris, J. (1995), "Sustainable Trade: A New Paradigm for World Welfare," *Environment* 37 (5): 19–20, 39–44.

Daly, H. E. (1995), "Against Free Trade: Neoclassical and Steady-State Perspectives," *Journal of Evolutionary Economics* 5 (3): 313–326.

Daly, H. (1996), *Beyond Growth. The Economics of Sustainable Development.* Boston, Beacon Press.

Daly, H. E. and Cobb, J. B. (1989), *For the Common Good. Redirecting the Economy toward Community, the Environment, and a Sustainable Future.* Boston, Beacon Press.

Daly, H. and Goodland, R. (1994), "An Ecological-Economic Assessment of Deregulation of International Commerce Under GATT," *Ecological Economics,* 9 (1): 73–92.

Damian M., Chaudhuri, B. and Berthaud, P. (1997), "La libéralisation des échanges est-elle une chance pour le développement durable?" *Revue Tiers-Monde* 38 (150): 427–446.

Desombre, E. R. (1995), "Baptists and Bootleggers for the Environment: The Origins of United States Unilateral Sanctions," *Journal of Environment and Development* 4 (1): 53–75.

Doussin, J.-P. (1998), "Codex alimentarius et Organisation mondiale du commerce, un nouveau role pour les experts?" *Comptes rendus de l'Académie d'agriculture de France* 84 (3): 15–22.

Ebbin, S. and Kasper, R. (1974), *Citizen Groups and the Nuclear Power Controversy: Uses of Scientific and Technological Information*. Cambridge, MA, MIT Press.

Gatt (1971), *Industrial Pollution Control and International Trade*. International Trade Study No. 1, Geneva, GATT, July 1971.

Gowdy, J. M. (1995), "Trade and Environmental Sustainability: An Evolutionary Perspective," *Review of Social Economy* 4: 493–510.

Graz, J.-C. (1999), *Aux Sources de l'OMC. La Charte de La Havane, 1941–1950/Precursor of the WTO. The Stillborn Havana Charter, 1941–1950*. Genève, Droz.

Greenpeace (2000), *The Greenpeace International Seminars on Safe Trade*. Amsterdam: Greenpeace International, July.

Hewson, M. and Sinclair, T. (1999), "The Emergence of Global Governance Theory," In M. Hewson and T. Sinclair (eds.), *Approaches to Global Governance Theory*. Albany, State University of New York Press: 3–22.

Hines, C. and Lang, J. (1993), *The New Protectionism: Protecting the Future Against Free Trade*. London, Earthscan.

Krugman, P. (1993), "The Narrow and Broad Arguments for Free Trade," *The American Economic Review, Papers and Proceedings* 83 (2): 362–366.

Le Bras, H. (1994) *Les limites de la planète. Mythes de la nature et de la population*. Paris, Flammarion.

May, C. (2000), *A Global Political Economy of Intellectual Property Rights. The New Enclosures?* London, Routledge.

Moggridge, D. E. (ed.) (1980), *The Collected Writings of John Maynard Keynes,* Vol. XXI and XXVII, London, Macmillan and Cambridge University Press for the Royal Economic Society.

Nations Unies (1972), *Conférence des Nations Unies sur l'environnement, Stockholm 5–16 juin 1972. Déclaration, plan d'action, recommandations, résolution*, Genève, Centre de l'information économique et sociale à l'office européen des Nations Unies.

Nordström, H. and Vaughan, S. (1999), "Trade and Environment," *Special Studies* 4. Geneva, World Trade Organization.

Princen, T. and Finger, M. (1994), *Environmental NGOs in World Politics*. London, Routledge.

Prugh, T., Costanza, R. and Daly, H. E. (2000), *The Local Politics of Global Sustainability*. Washington, DC, Island Press.

Ropke, I. (1994), "Trade, Development and Sustainability—a Critical Assessment of the "Free Trade Dogma," *Ecological Economics* 9 (1): 13–22.

Rosewarne, S. and Damian, M. (1997), "Towards a Managed International Trade for Sustainable Development: A Critique of Ecological Arguments," in P. Smith and A. Tenner (ed.), *Dimensions of Sustainability*. Baden-Baden, Nomos: 209–215.

WCED (1987), *Our Common Future. Report of the World Commission on the Environment and Development*. Oxford, Oxford University Press.

WTO (2001), *Environmental Database for 2000*. Note by the Secretariat, Committee on Trade and Environment. Geneva, World Trade Organization, 20 June (WT/CTE/W/195).

WWF (1999), *Initiating an Environmental Assessment of Trade Liberalization in the WTO*. Gland, World Wide Fund for Nature.

Democratizing the International Monetary Fund and the World Bank: Governance and Accountability

JOSEPH E. STIGLITZ

Economists typically begin an analysis of the behavior of an organization or an individual by looking at the *incentives* they face—what is the nature and magnitude of their rewards and punishments, and who metes them out? Political discussions more commonly begin with a discussion of *accountability*. Before I discuss the specific problems of the IMF and the World Bank, it will be fruitful to first lay out what I mean by "accountability," relate this notion to incentives, and identify the key problems in designing accountability systems for international financial organizations.

ACCOUNTABILITY: A DEFINITION AND ILLUSTRATION

Accountability requires that: (1) people are given certain objectives; (2) there is a reliable way of assessing whether they have met those objectives; and (3) consequences exist for both the case in which they have done what they were supposed to do and the case in which they have not done so. In a sense, the political notion of accountability corresponds closely to the economists' concept of *incentives*.

Several key problems face a multilateral organization, such as the World Bank or IMF, in establishing a system of accountability. A first problem is created by the existence of a multiplicity of objectives. If organizations fail on one objective, they can always claim that they were trying to accomplish another objective. Whenever there is murkiness about an organization's real objectives, it will be difficult to assess whether the organization has been successful or not, and hence, it will be hard to hold the organization accountable. . . .

Second, it is often quite difficult to ascertain the reasons why an organization may not have met its objectives. This may have occurred because an intervening event took place that the organization or person responsible could not do anything about. In that case, the failure could not, of course, be attributed to the organization or person involved.

Finally, it is often difficult in large organizations to design incentives that lead to individual accountability, even when organizational accountability exists. If widespread consultation and diffuse responsibility exist within an organization, then everyone is "to blame" when things go wrong. But if everyone is to blame, then no one is. . . .

Let me illustrate the issues discussed so far with reference to the IMF. The organization was founded in the aftermath of the Great Depression and World War

II. The Great Depression represented the most significant downturn in the global economy since the beginning of capitalism. The war expenditures brought the global economy out of the Great Depression. At the end of the war, a worry existed that the world would sink back into a slump. In particular, John Maynard Keynes was concerned that countries would reintroduce the kinds of policies that they had pursued at the beginning of the depression. In pursuing "beggar-thy-neighbor" policies, countries had tried to protect their own aggregate demand by cutting back on imports, as a result of which their problems had spread to other countries. Keynes helped establish the IMF to address these concerns. He successfully argued that the cure for recessions was fiscal expansion. The IMF was to have two functions: (1) to provide money to countries in an economic downturn, so as to enable them to pursue more expansionary fiscal policies; and (2) to put pressure on countries to choose expansionary, rather than beggar-thy-neighbor, policies. He believed that an international organization was needed, because a global collective interest would be served by expansionary policies. Thus, the IMF seemed to have a clear set of objectives.

If we look at what happened in the financial crisis in East Asia, however, the IMF actually set forth conditions forcing countries to adopt more contractionary, rather than more expansionary, policies. To be sure, the countries did not engage in beggar-thy-neighbor policies. Rather, they followed what I call "beggar-thyself" policies that were even more detrimental. Both kinds of policies exacerbated the downward spiral within the region. But, unlike beggar-thy-neighbor policies, beggar-thyself policies did not even have the saving grace of benefiting the people of the country that engaged in them. . . .

The question is, why was the IMF advocating and imposing these beggar-thyself policies? Was it a mistake, or was the IMF pursuing other objectives? If it was pursuing *other* objectives, then perhaps the failure in stabilizing East Asia was not a failure in the eyes of the organization. And indeed, the IMF claimed that there were other objectives. One of the *stated* objectives was to preserve global stability—that is, to prevent contagion, even if doing so meant that the countries in East Asia might have to suffer more than they would have with less contractionary policies.[1] Another was to make it more likely that creditors would be repaid. Senior IMF officials were very explicit in not wanting debtors to default on their loans. They viewed that as an abrogation of the sanctity of contracts.[2]

Consider another example. In October 1997, just as the East Asia crisis began, the IMF tried to change its charter in order to make capital market liberalization part of its mandate. Today, even the IMF recognizes that capital market liberalization presents considerable risks for many, if not most, developing countries, and it is now widely recognized that capital market liberalization has contributed to global economic instability. It played a central role in the East Asia crisis, and it helps explain why crises have been more frequent and deeper over the past quarter-century. The pursuit of capital market liberalization thus seems inconsistent with the mandate given to the IMF at its creation: to enhance global economic stability. . . .

The problems posed by the multiplicity of objectives are compounded by a tendency to confuse means and ends. Means that are supposed to be closely connected to well-accepted ends become goals in themselves, and little attention is paid to whether they do, in fact, advance the ultimate end. Privatization was supposed to contribute to economic growth; therefore, it was presumed that the countries in transition that privatized the fastest would grow the fastest. Accordingly, it was not surprising that the IMF put a host of privatization conditions on its loans to those countries and kept track of the number and value of state assets privatized. Those countries that privatized the fastest got the IMF's seal of approval, the teacher's gold stars for good performance. Yet it is now apparent that speed of privatization mattered little: the countries that seemed to be privatizing slowly—Hungary, Poland, and Slovenia—are the countries that have had the most successful transitions. Statistical studies suggest that privatization without restructuring and corporate governance does not contribute to economic growth. But these results are perfectly consistent with what was known *even at the beginning of the transition.* How privatization is conducted (i.e., the institutional infrastructure and macroeconomic policy framework that accompanied it) is every bit as important as privatization itself. . . .

The multiplicity of objectives—including the confusion of means with ends—thwarts the possibility of assessing success. Not long after the East Asian crisis began, the IMF claimed success for its interventions. To me, and to most of those in the affected countries, this seemed peculiar. Unemployment rates had soared and were still three to five times higher than they had been before the crisis. Real wages were down, and incomes remained below 1997 levels. Gross domestic product (GDP) in countries like Indonesia was more than fifteen percent lower than it had been before the crisis, and the countries were still in recession. In what sense, therefore, could the IMF's policies be called a success?

That depends crucially on the definition of the intended goals. The IMF said its interventions were successful, because exchange rates had stabilized. If that was the objective, then the IMF had indeed succeeded, as exchange rates had stabilized. But if the IMF's objectives had been the ones about which Keynes had talked—namely, stabilizing GDP and preventing workers from facing mass unemployment—then the programs had been outright failures. If the objective had been ensuring repayment of creditors, the picture was mixed: the IMF had succeeded in avoiding a unilateral declaration of suspension of payments, a debt moratorium or standstill. . . .

The second problem in assessing the successes and failures of the IMF concerns the extent to which the organization was able to influence events. This is related to another question: what would have happened in the absence of the IMF action—what is the appropriate counterfactual? I have watched the IMF closely over the years, and there is a certain consistency in its responses. When things go well, the IMF claims the credit. When things go badly, it is because others did not do what the IMF told them to do in the manner that they were supposed to, they did not show adequate resolve, and, in any case, matters would have been even worse but for the IMF's intervention. Any seeming failure is not because of mistaken policies but arises from faulty implementation, governments not doing enough, and lack of commitment. At least in its public stance, the IMF seldom moves away from this position of organizational infallibility. Indeed, it often seems to take the position as part of its credo: only if the markets believe that the IMF is infallible will it be able to affect market psychology and to restore confidence. Thus, the IMF has consistently discouraged public discussion of alternative strategies. For example, during and after the East Asia crisis, even after that situation had calmed down, the IMF refused to engage in processes of public evaluation. . . .

One has to be careful in assessing the excuses for the failures. For instance, it is often argued that while the IMF's advice was good, implementation was bad. If only the country had done what it was told to do, recovery would have come sooner. Still, an increasing number of governments are governed by democracies, and democracies do not necessarily obey instantaneously the dictates of international organizations. Their decision-making processes often take time. In the United States, for example, we have been talking about problems in our Medicare system and our social security system for years. Nonetheless, much weaker and younger democracies are somehow expected to change basic institutions within their society—including their basic social safety nets—in a matter of weeks, rather than years or decades. This seems simply unreasonable to me. In any case, whether the IMF likes it or not, there will always be public discussions and criticisms of policies in democracies, especially of policies that are as problematic as the ones the IMF pushes. To argue that policies would have been successful if only they had not been undermined by public discussions is to claim that the policies would have been successful if only the countries involved had not been democratic.

It is similarly indefensible to argue that policies would have worked if they had been implemented better. This argument is only plausible if a record exists of countries in similar situations that have been able to implement these policies successfully. Policies have to be designed so that they can be implemented by the kinds of institutions and individuals existing in the developing world. Otherwise, the IMF is simply saying that its policies might have worked in a world different than the one in which we live. In fact, an awareness of the implementation problems should be a central part of the program design.

By the same token, it is beside the point to state that policies would have worked if not for political problems or social instability. The riots that occurred in Indonesia as a result of the policies imposed by the IMF were predictable, especially given the society's ethnic fragmentation. The IMF might have preferred working in a different environment, but it had a responsibility to take the situation as it stood. . . .

Currently, the multiplicity of objectives, the difficulties of assessing the extent to which objectives have been met, and the problems of ascertaining who is responsible for a failure all contribute to a situation in which the word "accountability" is more a matter of rhetoric than of reality. But this need not be the case. Two of the reforms discussed in the final section of this article could improve the IMF's accountability: clearly identifying its *objectives,* as well as creating a framework *ex ante* for assessing the ex post performance of the IMF.

GOVERNANCE: ACCOUNTABLE TO WHOM?

Before turning to the reform agenda, I want to argue that the IMF's basic problems derive from its governance structure. The IMF was established to pursue a far different set of objectives than the ones it subsequently pursued. This switch took place because the IMF was captured by financial interests, and the capture was the inevitable consequence of the IMF's original governance structure.

Both the IMF and the World Bank deny that they are not accountable. In one sense, they are right. When the organizations were created, they were made accountable to an executive board, which maintains closer oversight than the board of directors of virtually any company. While boards of directors usually meet quarterly, the IMF and the World Bank are overseen by full-time boards. These boards, in turn, are accountable to governments.

Still, one has to recognize how frail these links are. The executive directors are accountable not so much to the governments themselves as to particular agencies within those governments. To be sure, these agencies are accountable to the government, and the government—at least in democracies—is accountable to the people. Yet, because of the length of the chain of accountability and the weaknesses in each link of that chain, an attenuation of accountability occurs. From this perspective, the view that there is a lack of meaningful accountability has some validity. The IMF responds more to those to whom it is directly accountable than to whom it ultimately ought to be responsible. Its governors are finance ministers and central-bank governors, and they represent a particular segment of society. Their interests are very different from those of labor ministers. The whole culture of the IMF would be markedly different if it was accountable to different agencies within the government. Anybody who has worked, as I have, within a democratic government recognizes the vast differences in the interests and cultures of the various government agencies. Even though the Department of State, the Treasury, the Council of Economic Advisers, the Trade Representative, and the Department of Labor are all part of the U.S. government, they report to different constituencies and end up being accountable to those constituencies.

In democratic societies, it is recognized that public decisions are affected by who has a seat at the table. That is why, when the U.S. government makes a decision about economic policy, it does not delegate that decision to the Treasury. Rather, the National Economic Council brings together all the relevant parties. Of course, the Treasury takes the lead on issues on which it is supposed to have expertise. But it always remains only one voice, albeit a powerful one. . . .

All of this might be of little importance if the IMF were merely entrusted with technical decisions, such as arrangements for interbank check clearing. But the IMF's decisions have enormous effects on economies throughout the world. The IMF is not accountable to those who are significantly affected by its policies. The people in East Asia who were thrown out of jobs as a result of the excessively contractionary monetary and fiscal polices, or whose firms were thrown into bankruptcy, have no recourse. They have no way of expressing their dissatisfaction with the policies that were pursued other than to throw out of office the governments responsible for implementing them. But the IMF—the organization that puts the policies into place—and its officials, remain relatively immune and, in that sense, unaccountable. Only when broader global outrage occurs—or when the interests of those to whom the IMF and its officials are directly accountable are adversely affected—will there be consequences.

The problem of accountability is even deeper than the above analysis suggests. I mentioned earlier that the IMF is overseen by finance ministers and central-bank governors. One of the IMF's missions in recent years has been to make central banks more independent—that is, to make them less directly accountable to democratic processes. Whether this is required for ensuring good economic performance is an issue that need not detain us here.[3] The point is that as a result of these efforts, the IMF is becoming more accountable to people who are increasingly less accountable themselves.

Moreover, macroissues are far from merely technical matters; they involve trade-offs requiring political judgments. Even if there are arguments for depoliticalization, this does not mean that decision-making should be unrepresentative. Yet, in most countries, financial interests have a much larger say than do other stakeholders. Indeed, in many countries, key stakeholders have no say at all. Thus, the board of the IMF not only lacks an adequate degree of *direct* political accountability, but also fails the test of representativeness. Not all affected parties have a seat at the table.

The IMF board lacks representativeness in another manner as well. Voting shares in the IMF are in proportion to an outdated and imperfectly measured economic weight of a country. For more than a century, in other democratic processes, wealth has not been a qualification for voting. Richer individuals do not have more votes, even when it comes to issues of economic import. The justification for a system of "one-dollar-one-vote," rather than "one-man-one-vote," is that the IMF is ostensibly a commercial enterprise with shareholders. Larger shareholders (i.e., the richer countries) have more votes, just as they would in a private corporation. This analogy is far from persuasive. In the case of a private firm, a shareholder displeased with the actions of the company can sell his shares. Those who approve of the company's actions may thus wind up holding a larger share. In the case of the IMF, voting shares were determined half a century ago. Since then, economic weights have changed dramatically, but the adjustment of voting rights to reflect these changes has been far from adequate. The IMF is an international public organization, but the lack of legitimacy in its allocation of voting rights undermines its political validity. . . .

REFORMING THE WORLD BANK

New Thinking about Development

. . . In reassessing its course, the World Bank examined how successful development had occurred.[4] Most examples of successful development—for example, China and Botswana—were countries without IMF programs. The lessons that emerged from this reassessment included ones that the World Bank had long recognized: the importance of living within one's budget constraints; the importance of education (including education of females); and macroeconomic stability. However, some new themes emerged: Success comes not only from promoting primary education, but also from establishing a strong technological basis that includes support for advanced training. It is possible to promote equality and rapid growth at the same time. In fact, more egalitarian policies seem to help growth. Support for trade and openness is important,[5] but it is most effective when it encourages exports rather than merely reduces trade barriers on imports. Government plays a pivotal role in successful development by encouraging particular sectors and helping create institutions that promote savings and efficient investment allocation. Successful countries also emphasize competition and the creation of enterprise over privatization and the restructuring of existing enterprises.

Other factors were also studied. While no economy can succeed under hyperinflation, there is no evidence that pushing inflation to ever lower levels yields gains commensurate with the costs.[6] Privatization without the necessary institutional infrastructure in transition countries led to asset-stripping rather than wealth creation. In other countries, privatized firms showed themselves more capable of exploiting consumers than did state monopolies. By contrast, privatization accompanied by regulation and corporate restructuring leads to higher growth. Social capital and cohesion are important to maintain output, spur growth, and ensure that reforms can withstand the vicissitudes of the political process. Predation from the Mafia turns out to be even worse than predation from government bureaucrats. Government makes a difference. Good public institutions—from an independent, qualified judiciary to effective regulation of monopolies and the financial sector—are required. As many countries suffer from too weak a government as from a too-intrusive one. The Asian financial crisis had been brought on by a lack of adequate regulation of the financial sector. Mafia capitalism in Russia was caused by a failure to enforce the basics of law and order. Overall, successful countries pursued a comprehensive development approach that went well beyond technical issues.

Thirty years ago, economists of the left and right agreed that the improvement in the efficiency of resource allocation and the increase in the supply of capital were at the heart of development. They differed only as to whether those changes should be realized through government-led planning or through unfettered markets. In the end neither worked. Today, we recognize that what separates developed countries from less developed ones not only concerns the amount of capital, but also involves knowledge and organization. This includes knowledge of how to produce more efficiently and how to live healthier lives. It also involves the organizational capacity to use the limited resources in the most efficient way possible. Gaps in knowledge and organization, both between more and less developed countries and within developed countries, account for much of the differences in incomes. Closing those gaps has thus become one of the main foci of development strategies. More broadly, development today is considered a transformation of society, which requires more than a solution to technical problems. Projects—such as dams, new schools, or health clinics—alone cannot make a dent in pervasive poverty. Only broad-based policies and institutions can wage a serious war on poverty, the kind of war that might lift up the lives of billions of individuals. . . .

Redefining the Mandate

The World Bank's honest reassessment of development has put it into a difficult position. The Bank recognizes the central importance of matters that are not within its core competence. It emphasizes the importance of "governance"—the rules by which public and private institutions are governed—yet it has on its staff few people that know much about the subject beyond the ability to recite the latest mantra. It could help build good water projects, but could it really help build a good judicial system? And was this what the Bank was supposed to do? If the core mission of the Bank is not lending money, then its own governance structure makes little sense. Why should finance ministers, who know little about poverty, play such a pivotal role? Why should developing countries not be in the driver's seat on the board of the Bank, or at least have a far larger vote there?

The Bank has made enormous strides in its reform. Its rhetoric has changed enormously. It now voices the need to go beyond projects—beyond even policies—to change institutions. It talks not just about limiting the role of the state, but about creating a more effective state. It discusses the impact of corruption on development, when only a few years ago this would have been viewed as crossing the dividing line between economics and politics. It articulates the need to take a comprehensive approach to development that sees development as a transformation of society (see, e.g., Stiglitz 1998b; Wolfsensohn). And it talks about putting the country in the driver's seat, about participation and ownership, and about the salience of poverty. This change in rhetoric has had an impact on thinking about development both in developing countries and inside the Bank itself.

If the Bank has not fully changed, then no one should be surprised. It is not easy for those who entered the Bank in the days when the Washington consensus reigned supreme to buy into the new Bank. They see all the new rhetoric as soft fluff, distracting the Bank from its *core* mission involving tough and often painful decisions. Many in the finance ministries in the more developed countries, and some in academia, say amen to these concerns (see, e.g., Bhagwati; Srinivasan). The risk that soft talk could replace hard analysis certainly exists. However, the Bank is far from that place today. It has changed, both in what it does and how it does it. Earlier I described the changes in the Bank's loan portfolio. Safeguards have been put into place to make it less likely that there will be large adverse effects on the environment, or on minorities within countries. The dialogue between the Bank and governments is now on a far more equal footing—there is less of the colonial overtone left. The Bank is a far more open and transparent organization than it was a decade ago.

But the reforms are fragile and could be reversed easily. Evidence of their precariousness abounds. The Bank refuses to openly discuss economic policies when those policies conflict with the views of its "sister" organization, the IMF. As a result, it is rightly seen as a "partner in crime" in the often-misguided structural adjustment policies—such as those in East Asia and the economies in transition—in which the IMF sets the overall framework. As a result, its reputation in much of the developing world does not stand much higher than that of the IMF. The Bank's reputation gets tarnished when policies of financial-market liberalization lead to soaring interest rates, as they did in Kenya, regardless of whether the Bank or the IMF was responsible. In recent controversies, as we have seen, the Bank's management and board have equivocated on a commitment to openness and transparency. This backfired in the case of a recent report over the Bank's handling of a resettlement project in Western China. In the report, an independent assessment concluded that the Bank had failed to follow its own procedures. The Bank voted not to release the report, but the report was leaked to the press nonetheless and thus became fully available.[7]

Changing a large organization entails redefining both its mission and culture and is not easy to achieve. From this perspective, the World Bank reforms, as incomplete as they may be, are impressive. The contrast between the limited successes of the Bank and the broader failures of the IMF may be instructive.

NOTES

1. My purpose here is not to assess the reasonableness of this objective (i.e., whether contagion was a real threat) or the consistency of the objective with the theories of well-functioning markets that seem to be at the center of much of the IMF's economic models, or to evaluate whether it succeeded in that objective (crises spread from country to country, arguably partly because of the policies that they pursued). Rather, I simply wish to illustrate the difficulties of designing systems of accountability. This example illustrates the difficulty of ascertaining what it was that the organization was supposed to do.

2. To be sure, they argued that the abrogation of contracts would be bad for the economies involved. But there is little reason to believe that it would be worse than contractionary monetary and fiscal policies. Indeed, the standard argument they put forward was that if the countries defaulted, then they would not be able to get capital. Yet the facts, especially in East Asia, suggested that this was hardly a cogent argument: (1) the countries were unlikely to get additional funds in any case until their economies recovered, whether they defaulted or not; (2) given the high savings rate, the countries hardly needed an influx of foreign capital; (3) capital markets are forward looking—once the debt overhang was reduced by restructuring through bankruptcy and once the economy was growing again, capital would flow in (while capital markets might like to punish those who behave badly, there are large numbers of participants in the market, and even if those who have been hurt refuse to lend, new suppliers of capital will enter if they see a profitable opportunity); and (4) history suggests that capital flows do return rather quickly once the economic circumstances warrant it.

3. The IMF believes that having macroeconomic policy determined by independent central banks is somehow better. While there is some evidence that an independent central bank with an exclusive focus on inflation does lead to lower inflation, little evidence exists that it leads to higher economic growth or even greater stability in terms of unemployment and real variables. Interestingly, though one of the arguments for an independent central bank is to bring in *expertise,* the boards of many, if not most, central banks are not dominated by those who have the greatest expertise in macroeconomics.

4. The reassessment actually began earlier, under pressure from the Japanese, and was reflected in the Bank's publication in 1993 of the landmark study *The East Asian Miracle.* The changes in thinking were reflected in the annual reports on development, called the World Development Report. For instance, the 1997 report re-examined the role of the state, the 1998 report focused on knowledge (including the importance of technology) and information (including the imperfections of markets associated with imperfect information), the 1999 and 2001 reports emphasized the role of organizations (not just policies), and the 2000 report took a much broader perspective on poverty (World Bank 1998c, 1999c, 2000, 2001).

5. Not surprisingly, the Bank has still not taken seriously the theoretical and empirical critiques of trade liberalization, such as those provided by Rodrik solo and Rodriguez and Rodrik together. Whatever the intellectual merits of that view, it runs counter to the "official" position of the United States and other G7 governments that trade is good. Given the emphasis on trade expansion in both the Clinton and Bush administrations, the Bank's official position is no surprise.

6. World Bank studies, including those coauthored by my predecessor as Chief Economist at the World Bank, Michael Bruno (formerly head of Israel's central bank), helped provide the empirical validation of this perspective. See Bruno and Easterly.

7. See also the discussion in the *Financial Times* of the handling of the U.S. Treasury Secretary's highly unusual intervention in the World Bank's 2000 World Development Report on Poverty.

REFERENCES

Beattie, Alan. 2000. "Strains" in Bank's Inclusive Model. *Financial Times* 16 June.

Bhagwati, Jagdish. 2000. Letter: Growth Is Not a Passive "Trickle-Down" Strategy. *Financial Times* 27 September.

Bruno, Michael, and William Easterly. 1998. Inflation Crises and Long-Run Growth. *Journal of Monetary Economics* 41:3–26.

Feldstein, Martin. 1998. Refocusing the IMF. *Foreign Affairs* 77:20–33.

Fischer, Stanley. 1999. On the Need for an International Lender of Last Resort. *Journal of Economic Perspectives* 13:85–104.

Furman, Jason, and Joseph E. Stiglitz. 1998. Economic Crises: Evidence and Insights from East Asia. *Brookings Papers on Economic Activity* 2:1–114.

International Monetary Fund. 1997. *The ESAF at 10 Years: Economic Adjustment and Reform in Low-Income Countries*. Occasional paper 156. Washington, DC: International Monetary Fund.

Lederman, Daniel, Ana M. Menendez, Guillermo Perry, and Joseph E. Stiglitz. 2000. Mexico: Five Years after the Crisis. In Boris Plezkovic and Nickolas Stern, eds., *Annual World Bank Conference on Development Economics 2000*. Washington, DC: World Bank.

Meltzer Commission (International Financial Institution Advisory Commission). 2000. *International Financial Institutions Reform*. Washington, DC: United States Congress.

Rodriguez, Francisco, and Dani Rodrik. 2001. Trade Policy and Economic Growth: A Skeptic's Guide to the Cross-National Evidence. In B. Bernanke and K. Rogoff, eds., *NBER Macroeonomics Annual 2000*. Cambridge, MA: MIT Press, 2000, forthcoming.

Rodrik, Dani. 1997. *Has Globalization Gone Too Far?* Washington, DC: Institute for International Economics.

Srinivasan, T. N. 2000. Letter: Variety of Routes to Development Already Known. *Financial Times* 28 September.

Stiglitz, Joseph E. 1997. Dumping on Free Trade: The U.S. Import Trade Laws. *Southern Economic Journal* 64:402–424.

———.1998a. Knowledge for Development, Economic Science, Economic Policy, and Economic Advice. In *Proceedings of the Annual World Bank Conference on Development Economics 1998*. Washington, DC: World Bank.

———.1998b. "Towards a New Paradigm for Development: Strategies, Policies and Processes." 9th Raul Prebisch Lecture delivered at the Palais des Nations, Geneva, 19 October 1998, United Nations Conference on Trade and Development. Reprinted

2001 as chapter 2 in Ha-Joon Chang, ed., *The Rebel Within*. London: Wimbledon Publishing Company.

———.1999. Quis Custodiet Ipsos Custodes? [Who is to Guard the Guards Themselves?] Corporate Governance Failures in the Transition. *Challenge* 42:26–67.

———.2000. Whither Reform? Ten Years of the Transition. In Boris Pleskovic and Joseph E. Stiglitz, eds., *Annual World Bank Conference on Development Economics 1999*. Washington, DC: World Bank.

Wolfensohn, James D. 1998. The Other Crisis. Address to the Board of Governors. Washington, DC: World Bank.

World Bank. 1993. *The East Asian Miracle: Economic Growth and Public Policy*. New York: Oxford University Press.

———. 1997. *World Development Report 1997: The State in a Changing World*. New York: Oxford University Press.

———. 1998a. *Assessing Aid: What Works, What Doesn't, and Why*. New York: Oxford University Press.

———. 1998b. *Global Economic Prospects and the Developing Countries 1998/99: Beyond Financial Crisis*. Washington, DC: World Bank.

———. 1998c. *World Development Report: Knowledge for Development*. New York: Oxford University Press.

———. 1999a. *Education Sector Strategy*. Washington, DC: World Bank.

———. 1999b. *World Development Report 1998/99: Knowledge for Development*. New York: Oxford University Press.

———. 1999c. *World Development Report: Entering the 21st Century*. New York: Oxford University Press.

———. 2000. *World Development Report: Attacking Poverty*. New York: Oxford University Press.

———. 2001. *World Development Report: Building Institutions for Markets*. New York: Oxford University Press.

CHAPTER 6

The Challenge of Regionalism

This chapter addresses the politics of regional economic integration. Since the conclusion of World War II, economic flows have risen dramatically within many geographical regions, and a wide variety of regional institutions have been established to coordinate the economic policies of members. These developments have led many observers to conclude that economic regionalism is on the rise.

Much of the initial interest in regional integration was sparked by the formation of the European Coal and Steel Community (ECSC). As we mentioned in Chapter 5, early research on this institution and on the European Community (EC) was guided by functionalist theories. These theories argued that international institutions are created to perform specific functions that individuals and governments need fulfilled and that the form of these institutions follows their function. European integration, however, was a much rockier process than functionalist theories predicted, leading to the emergence of neofunctionalist theories. This perspective focused on how rising transactions and contacts between states alter attitudes and transnational coalitions, and on how institutions can help to foster this process. Relying on a neofunctionalist approach, various recent studies have concluded that increased economic flows among members of the European Union (EU) over the past decade or so have changed the preferences of domestic actors, prompting them to press for policies and institutions that promote deeper integration.

At the same time, various other theoretical perspectives on integration have emerged as well. Many of them are addressed in the following articles. Central to economic regionalism are what are sometimes referred to as regional integration arrangements (RIAs) or preferential trading arrangements (PTAs). These arrangements include customs unions, which eliminate internal trade barriers and impose a common external tariff; free trade areas, which eliminate internal trade barriers, but do not establish a common external tariff; and common markets, which allow the free movement of factors of production and finished products across national borders. Various recent studies indicate that whether states choose to enter these arrangements, and the economic effects of these arrangements, depend on the preferences of national policy makers and interest groups, as well as on the nature and strength of domestic institutions. Other studies focus on international politics, emphasizing how power relations and multilateral institutions affect the formation of regional institutions, the particular states composing them, and their welfare implications. Still other studies argue that RIAs/PTAs tend to form as strategic reactions to one another.

The articles in this chapter present many of these theoretical perspectives on regional integration. They also address a series of related questions that are central to the study of regionalism. For example, what constitutes a region and exactly what do we mean by regionalism? Why has the extent of regionalism varied over time and across regions? Why do countries pursue regionalism rather than relying on unilateral or multilateral economic strategies? What determines their choice of partners in RIAs/PTAs and what are the political and economic consequences of these arrangements?

Edward D. Mansfield and Helen V. Milner point out that the contemporary spread of RIAs and PTAs is not without historical precedent. As they document, these arrangements fostered an open trading system in the nineteenth century and contributed to economic instability in the period between World War I and World War II. Many debates about regionalism center on whether the recent spate of RIAs/PTAs will foster greater openness or closure in the international trade system. Mansfield and Milner argue that, in light of existing political conditions, the current "wave" of regionalism will be relatively benign. Furthermore, they argue that the decision to join a RIA/PTA is likely to be shaped by the preferences and political influence of different societal groups, the preferences of government officials and the nature of domestic institutions, and international political conditions, particularly power and security relations.

Bob Jessop analyzes how changes within the EU have influenced contemporary statehood. Jessop argues that the territorial organization of power no longer corresponds to the boundaries of nation-states; that governments are becoming less important and that global governance is increasingly supported by alliances of governments, "paragovernments," and nongovernmental organizations; and that domestic policy regimes are increasingly internationalized. The development of the EU, he maintains, represents a broader shift in statehood throughout the world and in global governance. For Jessop, governance has become a multilevel process. The EU helps to promote governance through a set of complex interactions with national, sub-national, multilateral, and other regional institutions.

Finally, Joseph S. Nye examines functionalist and neofunctionalist explanations of integration. Based on a comparative assessment of regional integration in Europe, Latin America, and East Africa, he offers a number of fundamental insights into why RIAs/PTAs are formed, the dynamics of the integration process, and the factors influencing whether this process succeeds. Nye argues that conventional neofunctionalist models need to be amended to account for the many forces that stimulate the integration process, the various actors that are involved in this process, and the broad set of conditions affecting a region's integrative potential.

The New Wave of Regionalism

EDWARD D. MANSFIELD and HELEN V. MILNER

INTRODUCTION

Economic regionalism appears to be growing rapidly. Why this has occurred and what bearing it will have on the global economy are issues that have generated considerable interest and disagreement. Some observers fear that regional economic institutions—such as the European Union (EU), the North American Free Trade Agreement (NAFTA), Mercosur, and the organization of Asia-Pacific Economic Cooperation (APEC)—will erode the multilateral system that has guided economic relations since the end of World War II, promoting protectionism and conflict. Others argue that regional institutions will foster economic openness and bolster the multilateral system. This debate has stimulated a large and influential body of research by economists on regionalism's welfare implications.

Economic studies, however, generally place little emphasis on the political conditions that shape regionalism. Lately, many scholars have acknowledged the drawbacks of such approaches and have contributed to a burgeoning literature that sheds new light on how political factors guide the formation of regional institutions and their economic effects. Our purpose is to evaluate this recent literature.

Much of the existing research on regionalism centers on international trade (although efforts have also been made to analyze currency markets, capital flows, and other facets of international economic relations).[1] . . . At the same time, however, recent research leaves various important theoretical and empirical issues unresolved, including which political factors bear most heavily on regionalism and the nature of their effects.

The resolution of these issues is likely to help clarify whether the new "wave" of regionalism will be benign or malign.[2] . . . Here, we argue that the political conditions surrounding the contemporary episode augur well for avoiding many of regionalism's more pernicious effects, although additional research on this topic is sorely needed.

We structure our analysis around four central questions. First, what constitutes a region and how should regionalism be defined? Second, why has the pervasiveness of regional trade arrangements waxed and waned over time? Third, why do countries pursue regional trade strategies, instead of relying solely on unilateral or multilateral ones; and what determines their choice of partners in regional arrangements? Fourth, what are the political and economic consequences of commercial regionalism?

For helpful comments on earlier drafts of this article, we are grateful to David Baldwin, Peter Gourevitch, Stephen Haggard, Peter J. Katzenstein, David A. Lake, Randall L. Schweller, Beth V. Yarbrough, and three anonymous reviewers. In conducting this research, Mansfield was assisted by a grant from the Ohio State University Office of Research and by the Hoover Institution at Stanford University, where he was a National Fellow during 1998–99.

REGIONALISM: AN ELUSIVE CONCEPT

. . . Disputes over the definition of an economic region and regionalism hinge on the importance of geographic proximity and on the relationship between economic flows and policy choices. A region is often defined as a group of countries located in the same geographically specified area. Exactly which areas constitute regions, however, remains controversial. Some observers, for example, consider Asia-Pacific a single region, others consider it an amalgamation of two regions, and still others consider it a combination of more than two regions. . . .

Various studies, however, define regions largely in terms of . . . nongeographic criteria and place relatively little emphasis on physical location. For example, France and the Francophone countries of Northwest Africa are often referred to as a regional grouping because of their linguistic similarities. . . .

Setting aside the issue of how a region should be defined, questions remain about whether regionalism pertains to the concentration of economic flows or to foreign policy coordination. Some analyses define regionalism as an *economic* process whereby economic *flows* grow more rapidly among a given group of states (in the same region) than between these states and those located elsewhere. . . .

In a recent study, Albert Fishlow and Stephan Haggard sharply distinguish between regionalization, which refers to the regional concentration of economic flows, and regionalism, which they define as a *political* process characterized by economic *policy* cooperation and coordination among countries.[3] Defined in this way, commercial regionalism has been driven largely by the formation and spread of preferential trading arrangements (PTAs). These arrangements furnish states with preferential access to members' markets (for example, the European Economic Community [EEC]/European Community [EC]/ European Union [EU], the European Free Trade Association [EFTA], NAFTA, and the Council for Mutual Economic Assistance [CMEA]); many of them also coordinate members' trade policies vis-à-vis third parties.[4] Among the various types of PTAs are customs unions, which eliminate internal trade barriers and impose a common external tariff (CET); free trade areas (FTAs), which eliminate internal trade barriers, but do not establish a CET; and common markets, which allow the free movement of factors of production and finished products across national borders.[5] . . .

ECONOMIC ANALYSES OF REGIONALISM

Much of the literature on regionalism focuses on the welfare implications of PTAs, both for members and the world as a whole. . . . Preferential trading arrangements have a two-sided quality, liberalizing commerce among members while discriminating against third parties.[6] Since such arrangements rarely eliminate external trade barriers, economists consider them inferior to arrangements that liberalize trade worldwide. Just how inferior PTAs are hinges largely on whether they are trade creating or trade diverting, a distinction originally drawn by Viner. As he explained:

There will be commodities ... for which one of the members of the customs union will now newly import from the other but which it formerly did not import at all because the price of the protected domestic product was lower than the price at any foreign source plus the duty. This shift in the locus of production as between the two countries is a shift from a high-cost to a low-cost point.... There will be other commodities which one of the members of the customs union will now newly import from the other whereas before the customs union it imported them from a third country, because that was the cheapest possible source of supply even after payment of the duty. The shift in the locus of production is now not as between the two member countries but as between a low-cost third country and the other, high-cost, member country.[7]

... Over the past fifty years, a wide variety of empirical efforts have been made to determine whether PTAs are trade creating or trade diverting. As we discuss later, there is widespread consensus that the preferential arrangements forged during the nineteenth century tended to be trade creating and that those established between World Wars I and II tended to be trade diverting; however, there is a striking lack of consensus on this score about the PTAs developed since World War II.[8]

Even if a PTA is trade diverting, it can nonetheless enhance the welfare of members by affecting their terms of trade and their capacity to realize economies of scale. Forming a PTA typically improves members' terms of trade vis-à-vis the rest of the world, since the arrangement almost always has more market power than any constituent party. At the same time, however, Paul Krugman points out that attempts by a PTA to exploit its market power may backfire if other such arrangements exist, since "the blocs may beggar each other. That is, formation of blocs can, in effect, set off a beggar-all trade war that leaves everyone worse off."[9] He argues that these beggar-thy-neighbor effects are minimized when the number of trade blocs is either very large or very small.[10] ...

Consistent with this proposition, a series of simulations by Jeffrey A. Frankel, Ernesto Stein, and Shang-Jin Wei reveal that world welfare is reduced when two or three PTAs exist, depending on the height of the external tariffs of each arrangement.[11] T. N. Srinivasan and Eric Bond and Constantinos Syropoulos, however, have criticized the assumptions underlying Krugman's analysis.[12] In addition, various observers have argued that the static nature of his model limits its ability to explain how PTAs expand and the welfare implications of this process.[13]

A regional trade arrangement can also influence the welfare of members by allowing firms to realize economies of scale. Over three decades ago, Jagdish Bhagwati, Charles A. Cooper and Benton F. Massell, and Harry Johnson found that states could reduce the costs of achieving any given level of import-competing industrialization by forming a PTA within which scale economies could be exploited and then discriminating against goods emanating from outside sources.[14] Indeed, this motivation contributed to the spate of PTAs established by less developed countries (LDCs) throughout the 1960s.[15] More recent studies have examined how scale economies within regional arrangements can foster greater specialization and competition and can shift the location of production among members.[16] Although these analyses indicate that PTAs could yield economic

gains for members and adversely affect third parties, they also underscore regionalism's uncertain welfare implications.[17]

Besides its static welfare effects, economists have devoted considerable attention to whether regionalism will accelerate or inhibit multilateral trade liberalization, an issue that Bhagwati refers to as "the dynamic time-path question."[18]
Several strands of research suggest that regional economic arrangements might
bolster multilateral openness. First, Murray C. Kemp and Henry Wan have demonstrated that it is possible for any group of countries to establish a PTA that does not
degrade the welfare of either members or third parties, and that incentives exist for
the union to expand until it includes all states (that is, until global free trade
exists).[19] Second, Krugman and Lawrence H. Summers note that regional institutions reduce the number of actors engaged in multilateral negotiations, thereby
muting problems of bargaining and collective action that can hamper such negotiations.[20] Third, there is a widespread belief that regional trade arrangements can
induce members to undertake and consolidate economic reforms and that these
reforms are likely to promote multilateral openness.[21]

However, clear limits also exist on the ability of regional agreements to bolster multilateralism. Bhagwati, for example, maintains that although the Kemp-
Wan theorem demonstrates that PTAs could expand until free trade exists, this
result does not specify the likelihood of such expansion or that it will occur in a
welfare-enhancing way.[22] In addition, Bond and Syropoulos argue that the formation of customs unions may render multilateral trade liberalization more difficult
by undercutting multilateral enforcement.[23]

Economic analyses indicate that regionalism's welfare implications have varied starkly over time and across PTAs. As Frankel and Wei conclude, "regionalism
can, depending on the circumstances, be associated with either more or less general liberalization."[24] In what follows, we argue that these circumstances involve
political conditions that economic studies often neglect. Regionalism can also
have important political consequences, and they, too, have been given short shrift
in many economic studies.

REGIONALISM IN HISTORICAL PERSPECTIVE

Considerable interest has been expressed in how the preferential economic
arrangements formed after World War II have affected and will subsequently influence the global economy. We focus primarily on this era as well; however, it is
widely recognized that regionalism is not just a recent phenomenon. Analyses of
the current spate of PTAs often draw on historical analogies to prior episodes of
regionalism. Such analogies can be misleading because the political settings in
which these episodes arose are quite different from the current setting. To develop
this point, it is useful to begin by describing each of the four waves of regionalism
that have arisen over the past two centuries.

The initial episode occurred during the second half of the nineteenth century
and was largely a European phenomenon.[25] Throughout this period, intra-
European trade both rose dramatically and constituted a vast portion of global

commerce.[26] Moreover, economic integration became sufficiently extensive that, by the turn of the twentieth century, Europe had begun to function as a single market in many respects.[27] The industrial revolution and technological advances attendant to it that facilitated interstate commerce clearly had pronounced effects on European integration; but so did the creation of various customs unions and bilateral trade agreements. Besides the well-known German Zollverein, the Austrian states established a customs union in 1850, as did Switzerland in 1848, Denmark in 1853, and Italy in the 1860s. The latter coincided with Italian statehood, not an atypical impetus to the initiation of a PTA in the nineteenth century. In addition, various groups of nationstates forged customs unions, including Sweden and Norway and Moldavia and Wallachia.[28]

The development of a broad network of bilateral commercial agreements also contributed to the growth of regionalism in Europe. Precipitated by the Anglo-French commercial treaty of 1860, they were linked by unconditional most-favored-nation (MFN) clauses and created the bedrock of the international economic system until the depression in the late nineteenth century.[29] Furthermore, the desire by states outside this commercial network to gain greater access to the markets of participants stimulated its rapid spread. As of the first decade of the twentieth century, Great Britain had concluded bilateral arrangements with forty-six states, Germany had done so with thirty countries, and France had done so with more than twenty states.[30] These arrangements contributed heavily to the unprecedented growth of European integration and to the relatively open international commercial system that characterized the latter half of the nineteenth century, underpinning what Douglas A. Irwin refers to as an era of "progressive bilateralism."[31]

World War I disrupted the growth of regional trade arrangements. But a second wave of regionalism, which had a decidedly more discriminatory cast than its predecessor, began soon after the war ended. The regional arrangements formed between World Wars I and II tended to be highly preferential. Some were created to consolidate the empires of major powers, including the customs union France formed with members of its empire in 1928 and the Commonwealth system of preferences established by Great Britain in 1932.[32] Most, however, were formed among sovereign states. For example, Hungary, Romania, Yugoslavia, and Bulgaria each negotiated tariff preferences on their agricultural trade with various European countries. The Rome Agreement of 1934 led to the establishment of a PTA involving Italy, Austria, and Hungary. Belgium, Denmark, Finland, Luxembourg, the Netherlands, Norway, and Sweden concluded a series of economic agreements throughout the 1930s. Germany also initiated various bilateral trade blocs during this era. Outside of Europe, the United States forged almost two dozen bilateral commercial agreements during the mid-1930s, many of which involved Latin American countries.[33]

Longstanding and unresolved debates exist about whether regionalism deepened the economic depression of the interwar period and contributed to political tensions culminating in World War II.[34] Contrasting this era with that prior to World War I, Irwin presents the conventional view: "In the nineteenth century, a network of treaties containing the most favored nation (MFN) clause spurred major tariff reductions in Europe and around the world, [ushering] in a harmonious period of multilateral free trade that compares favorably with . . . the recent GATT era. In the interwar period, by contrast, discriminatory trade blocs and protectionist bilateral arrangements contributed to the severe contraction of world trade that accompanied the Great Depression."[35] The latter wave of regionalism is often associated with the pursuit of beggar-thy-neighbor policies and substantial trade diversion, as well as heightened political conflict.

Scholars frequently attribute the rise of regionalism during the interwar period to states' inability to arrive at multilateral solutions to economic problems. . . . In part, this failure can be traced to political rivalries among the major powers and the use of regional trade strategies by these countries for mercantilist purposes.[36] Hence, although regionalism was not new, both the political context in which it arose and its consequences were quite different than before World War I.

Regionalism Since World War II

Since World War II, states have continued to organize commerce on a regional basis, despite the existence of a multilateral economic framework. To analyze regionalism's contemporary growth, some studies have assessed whether trade flows are becoming increasingly concentrated within geographically specified areas. Others have addressed the extent to which PTAs shape trade flows and whether their influence is rising. Still others have examined whether the rates at which PTAs form and states join them have increased over time. In combination, these studies indicate that commercial regionalism has grown considerably over the past fifty years.

As shown in Table 1—which presents data used in three influential studies of regionalism—the regional concentration of trade flows generally has increased since the end of World War II.[37] Much of this overall tendency is attributable to rising trade within Western Europe—especially among parties to the EC—and within East Asia. . . .

One central reason why trade is so highly concentrated within many regions is that states located in close proximity often participate in the same PTA.[38] That the effects of various PTAs on commerce have risen over time constitutes further evidence of regionalism's growth.[39] As the data in Table 1 indicate, the influence of PTAs on trade flows has been far from uniform. Some PTAs, like the EC, seem to have had a profound effect, whereas others have had little impact.[40] But the data also indicate that, in general, trade flows have tended to increase over time among states that are members of a PTA and not merely located in the same geographic region, suggesting that policy choices are at least partly responsible for the rise of regionalism since World War II.

East Asia, however, is an interesting exception. Virtually no commercial agreements existed among East Asian countries prior to the mid-1990s, but rapid economic growth throughout the region contributed to a dramatic increase in intraregional trade flows.[41] In light of Asia's recent financial crisis, it will be inter-

TABLE 1. INTRAREGIONAL TRADE FLOWS DURING THE POST-WORLD WAR II ERA

A. Intraregional trade divided by total trade of each region

Region	1965	1970	1975	1980	1985	1990
East Asia	0.199	0.198	0.213	0.229	0.256	0.293
Western Hemisphere	0.315	0.311	0.309	0.272	0.310	0.285
European Community	0.358	0.397	0.402	0.416	0.423	0.471
European Free Trade Area	0.080	0.099	0.104	0.080	0.080	0.076
Mercosur	0.061	0.050	0.040	0.056	0.043	0.061
Andean Pact	0.008	0.012	0.020	0.023	0.034	0.026
North American Free Trade Agreement	0.237	0.258	0.246	0.214	0.274	0.246

B. Intraregional merchandise exports divided by total merchandise exports of each region

Region	1948	1958	1968	1979	1990
Western Europe	0.430	0.530	0.630	0.660	0.720
Eastern Europe	0.470	0.610	0.640	0.540	0.460
North America	0.290	0.320	0.370	0.300	0.310
South America	0.200	0.170	0.190	0.200	0.140
Asia	0.390	0.410	0.370	0.410	0.480
Africa	0.080	0.080	0.090	0.060	0.060
Middle East	0.210	0.120	0.080	0.070	0.060
World	0.330	0.400	0.470	0.460	0.520

C. Intraregional exports divided by total exports of each region

Region	1960	1970	1975	1980	1985	1990
European Community	0.345	0.510	0.500	0.540	0.545	0.604
European Free Trade Area	0.211	0.280	0.352	0.326	0.312	0.282
Association of Southeast Asian Nations	0.044	0.207	0.159	0.169	0.184	0.186
Andean Pact	0.007	0.020	0.037	0.038	0.034	0.046
Canada–United States Free Trade Area	0.265	0.328	0.306	0.265	0.380	0.340
Central American Common Market	0.070	0.257	0.233	0.241	0.147	0.148
Latin American Free Trade Association/ Latin American Integration Association	0.079	0.099	0.136	0.137	0.083	0.106
Economic Community of West African States	N/A	0.030	0.042	0.035	0.053	0.060
Preferential Trading Area for Eastern and Southern Africa	N/A	0.084	0.094	0.089	0.070	0.085
Australia-New Zealand Closer Economic Relations Trade Agreement	0.057	0.061	0.062	0.064	0.070	0.076

Source: Data in part A are taken from Frankel, Stein, and Wei 1995; part B, from Anderson and Norheim 1993; and part C, from de Melo and Panagariya 1993.

Note: N/A indicates data unavailable.

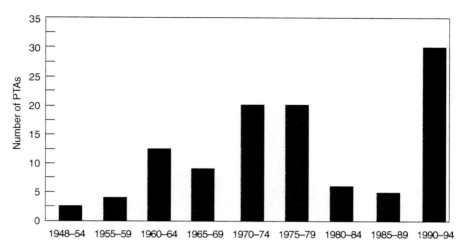

FIGURE 1.   THE NUMBER OF PREFERENTIAL TRADING ARRANGEMENTS NOTIFIED TO THE
GATT, 1948–94.

Source: World Trade Organization 1995.

Note: Each preferential trading arrangement is listed in the year it was signed.

esting to see whether the process of regionalization continues. Severe economic recession within Asia concurrent with robust growth in North America and Western Europe may redirect trade flows across regions. This case illustrates the need we described earlier to distinguish between policy-induced regionalism and that stemming primarily from economic forces. How important the Association of Southeast Asian Nations (ASEAN) and other policy initiatives are in directing commerce should become clearer as the economic crisis in Asia unfolds.

Also indicative of regionalism's growth are the increasing rates at which PTAs formed and states joined them throughout the post–World War II period.[42] Figure 1 reports the number of regional trading arrangements notified to the General Agreement on Tariffs and Trade (GATT) from 1948 to 1994. Clearly, the frequency of PTA formation has fluctuated. Few were established during the 1940s and 1950s, a surge in preferential agreements occurred in the 1960s and 1970s, and the incidence of PTA creation again trailed off in the 1980s.[43] But there has been a significant rise in such agreements during the 1990s; and more than 50 percent of all world commerce is currently conducted within PTAs.[44] Indeed, they have become so pervasive that all but a few parties to the World Trade Organization (WTO) now belong to at least one.[45]

Regionalism, then, seems to have occurred in two waves during the post–World War II era. The first took place from the late 1950s through the 1970s and was marked by the establishment of the EEC, EFTA, the CMEA, and a plethora of regional trade blocs formed by developing countries. These arrangements were initiated against the backdrop of the Cold War, the rash of decolonization following World War II, and a multilateral commercial framework, all of which colored their economic and political effects. . . .

The most recent wave of regionalism has arisen in a different context than earlier episodes. It emerged in the wake of the Cold War's conclusion and the attendant changes in interstate power and security relations. Furthermore, the leading actor in the international system (the United States) is actively promoting and participating in the process. PTAs also have been used with increasing regularity to help prompt and consolidate economic and political reforms in prospective members, a rarity during prior eras. And unlike the interwar period, the most recent wave of regionalism has been accompanied by high levels of economic interdependence, a willingness by the major economic actors to mediate trade disputes, and a multilateral (that is, the GATT/WTO) framework that assists them in doing so and that helps to organize trade relation.[46] . . .

DOMESTIC POLITICS AND REGIONALISM

Although it is frequently acknowledged that political factors shape regionalism, surprisingly few systematic attempts have been made to address which factors most fully determine why states choose to pursue regional trade strategies and the precise nature of their effects. Early efforts to analyze the political underpinnings of regionalism were heavily influenced by "neofunctionalism."[47] Joseph S. Nye points out that "what these studies had in common was a focus on the ways in which increased transactions and contacts changed attitudes and transnational coalition opportunities, and the ways in which institutions helped to foster such interaction."[48] . . .

Societal Factors

As neofunctional studies indicate, the preferences and political influence of domestic groups can affect why regional strategies are selected and their likely economic consequences. Regional trade agreements discriminate against third parties, yielding rents for certain domestic actors who may constitute a potent source of support for a PTA's formation and maintenance.[49] Industries that could ward off competitors located in third parties or expand their share of international markets if they were covered by a PTA have obvious reasons to press for its establishment.[50] So do export-oriented industries that stand to benefit from the preferential access to foreign markets afforded by a PTA. In addition, though it is all but impossible to construct a PTA that would not adversely affect at least some politically potent sectors, it is often possible to exclude them from the arrangement, a tack, for example, that led to "the European Economic Community's exclusion of agriculture (and, in practice, steel and many other goods), the Caribbean Basin Initiative's exclusion of sugar, and ASEAN's exclusion of just about everything of interest."[51]

Regional trade strategies, therefore, hold some appeal for public officials who need to attract the support of both import-competing and export-oriented sectors. The domestic political viability of a prospective PTA, the extent to which it will create or divert trade, and the range of products it will cover hinge partly on the preferences of and the influence wielded by key sectors in each country as well as the particular set of countries that can be assembled to participate in it. . . .

Public officials must strike a balance between promoting a country's aggregate economic welfare and accommodating interest groups whose support is needed to retain office. Gene M. Grossman and Elhanan Helpman argue that whether a country chooses to enter a regional trade agreement is determined by how much influence different interest groups exert and how much the government is concerned about voters' welfare.[52] They demonstrate that the political viability of a PTA often depends on the amount of discrimination it yields. Agreements that divert trade will benefit certain interest groups while creating costs borne by the populace at large. If these groups have more political clout than other segments of society, then a PTA that is trade diverting stands a better chance of being established than one that is trade creating.[53] . . . If so, using preferential arrangements as building blocks to support multilateral liberalization will require surmounting substantial domestic impediments.

Opinion is divided over the ease with which this can be accomplished. Kenneth A. Oye argues that discriminatory PTAs can actually lay the basis for promoting multilateral openness, especially if the international trading system is relatively closed.[54] In his view, discrimination stemming from a preferential arrangement can mobilize and strengthen the political hand of export-oriented (and other antiprotectionist) interests located in third parties, thereby generating domestic pressure in these states for agreements that expand their access to PTA members' markets. Such agreements, in turn, are likely to contribute to international openness. However, Anne O. Krueger maintains that the formation and expansion of PTAs may dampen the support of exporters for broader liberalization. As she puts it, "For those exporters who would support free trade, the value of further multilateral trade liberalization is diminished with every new entrant into a preferential trade arrangement, so that exporters' support for multilateral liberalization is likely to diminish as vested interests profiting from trade diversion increase."[55] Hence, it is not clear whether exporters will support regionalism instead of or in addition to multilateral liberalization.

Equally unclear is why exporters would prefer to liberalize trade on a regional rather than a multilateral basis in the first place. One possibility is that exporters will be more likely to support regional strategies if they operate in industries characterized by economies of scale, since, by protecting these sectors from foreign competition and broadening their market access, the formation of a PTA can bolster their competitiveness. . . .

Though research stressing the effects of societal factors on regionalism offers various useful insights, it also suffers from at least two drawbacks. First, there is a lack of empirical evidence indicating which domestic groups support regional trade agreements, whose interests these agreements serve, and why particular groups prefer regional to multilateral liberalization. . . . Second, we know little about whether, once in place, regional arrangements foster domestic support for broader, multilateral trade liberalization or whether they undermine such support. These issues offer promising avenues for future research.

Domestic Institutions

In the final analysis, the decision to enter a PTA is made by policymakers. Both their preferences and the nature of domestic institutions condition the influence of societal actors on trade policy as well as independently affecting whether states elect to embark on regional trade initiatives. Of course, policymakers and politically potent societal groups sometimes share an interest in forming a PTA. Many regional trade arrangements that LDCs established during the 1960s and 1970s, for instance, grew out of import-substitution policies that were actively promoted by policymakers and strongly supported by various segments of society.[56]

However, PTAs also have been created by policymakers who preferred to liberalize trade but faced domestic obstacles to doing so unilaterally. In this vein, Barry Eichengreen and Jeffrey A. Frankel point out that "Columbia and Venezuela decided in November 1991 to turn the previously moribund Andean Pact into what is now one of the world's most successful FTAs. Policymakers in these countries explain their decision as a politically easy way to dismantle protectionist barriers to an extent that their domestic legislatures would never have allowed had the policy not been pursued in a regional context."[57] Even if influential domestic actors oppose commercial liberalization altogether, institutional factors sometimes create opportunities for policymakers to sidestep such opposition by relying on regional or bilateral trade strategies. Consider the situation Napoleon III faced on the eve of the Anglo-French commercial arrangement. Anxious to liberalize trade with Great Britain, he encountered a French legislature and various salient domestic groups that were highly protectionist. But although the legislature had considerable control over unilateral trade policy, the constitution of 1851 permitted the emperor to sign international treaties without this body's approval. Napoleon, therefore, was able to skirt well-organized protectionist interests much more easily by concluding a bilateral commercial agreement that would have been impossible had he relied solely on unilateral instruments.[58] . . .

Although governments may choose to join regional agreements to promote domestic reforms, they may also do so if they resist reforms but are anxious to reap the benefits stemming from preferential access to other members' markets. Existing members of a preferential grouping may be able to influence the domestic economic policies and the political institutions of prospective members by demanding that they institute domestic reforms prior to accession. Along these lines, there are various cases where PTAs have made the establishment of democracy a necessary condition for membership. Both Spain and Portugal were required to complete democratic transitions before being admitted to the EC. . . . Similarly, Argentina and Brazil insisted that a democratic system of government would have to be established in Paraguay before it could enter Mercosur.[59] More recently, the EU has indicated that various Eastern European countries must consolidate democratic reforms as one precondition for membership. . . .

Using PTA membership to stimulate liberal economic and political reforms is a distinctive feature of the latest wave of regionalism. That these reforms have been designed to open markets and promote democracy may help to account for the relatively benign character of the current wave. Underlying demands for democratic reform are fears that admitting nondemocratic countries might undermine existing PTAs composed of democracies and the belief that regions composed of stable democracies are unlikely to experience hostilities. Both views remain open to question. But if entering a preferential arrangement actually promotes the consolidation of liberal economic and political reforms and mutes the economic and political instability that often accompanies such reforms, then the contemporary rise of regionalism may contribute to both commercial openness and political . . . cooperation.[60] . . .

Furthermore, the extent to which PTAs have been used as instruments for stimulating economic and political liberalization during the current wave of regionalism is quite unusual by historical standards. Chile, for example, withdrew from the Andean Pact in 1976 because it wanted to complete a series of economic reforms that this arrangement prohibited.[61] Moreover, attempts to spur democratization in prospective PTA members are largely unique to the contemporary wave. . . .

A related line of research suggests that the similarity of states' political institutions influences whether they will form a preferential arrangement and its efficacy once established. Many scholars view a region as implying substantial institutional homogeneity among the constituent states. Likewise, some observers maintain that the feasibility of creating a regional agreement depends on prospective members having relatively similar economic or political institutions.[62] If trade liberalization requires harmonization in a broad sense, such as in the Single European Act, then the more homogeneous are members' national institutions, the easier it may be for them to agree on common regional policies and institutions. Others point out that countries in close geographic proximity have much less impetus to establish regional arrangements if their political institutions differ significantly. In Asia, for example, the scarcity of regional trade arrangements is partly attributable to the wide variation in the constituent states' political regimes, which range from democracies like Japan to autocracies like Vietnam and China.[63]

As the initial differences in states' institutions become more pronounced, so do both the potential gains from and the impediments to concluding a regional agreement. Consequently, the degree of institutional similarity among states and the prospect that membership in a regional arrangement will precipitate institutional change in these states may bear heavily on whether they form a PTA.[64] The extant literature, however, provides little guidance about how large institutional differences can be before regional integration becomes politically infeasible.

INTERNATIONAL POLITICS AND REGIONALISM

The decision to form a PTA rests partly on the preferences and political power of various segments of society, the interests of state leaders, and the nature of domestic institutions. . . . [But] interstate power and security relations as well as multilateral institutions have also played key roles in shaping regionalism. Equally important is how regionalism affects patterns of conflict and cooperation among states. We now turn to these issues.

Political Power, Interstate Conflict, and Regionalism

Studies addressing the links between structural power and regionalism have placed primary stress on the effects of hegemony. Various scholars argue that international economic stability is a collective good, suboptimal amounts of which will be provided without a stable hegemon.[65] Discriminatory trade arrangements, in turn, may be outgrowths of the economic instability fostered by the lack of decline of such a country.[66] Offering one explanation for the trade-diverting character of PTAs during the interwar period, this argument is also invoked by many economists who maintain that the current wave of regionalism was triggered or accelerated by the U.S. decision to pursue regional arrangements in the early 1980s, once its economic power waned and multilateral trade negotiations stalled.[67] In fact, there is evidence that over the past fifty years the erosion of U.S. hegemony has stimulated a rise in the number of PTAs and states entering them.[68] But why waning hegemony has been associated with the growth of regionalism since World War II, what effects PTAs formed in response to declining hegemony will have on the multilateral trading system, and whether variations in hegemony contributed to earlier episodes of regionalism are issues that remain unresolved.[69]

Some observers argue that as a hegemon's power recedes, it has reason to behave in an increasingly predatory manner.[70] To buffer the effects of such behavior, other states might form a series of preferential trading blocs, thereby setting off a wave of regionalism. Robert Gilpin suggests that this sort of process began to unfold during the 1980s, giving rise to a system of loose regional economic blocs that is coalescing around Western Europe, the United States, and Japan. . . . The extent to which U.S. hegemony has actually declined and whether such a system is actually emerging, however, remain the subjects of fierce disagreement.

Furthermore, even if such a system is emerging, there are at least two reasons why the situation may be less dire than the preceding account would indicate. First, despite the potential problems of pluralist leadership, it is widely argued that global openness can be maintained in the face of declining (or the absence of) hegemony if a small group of leading countries collaborates to support the trading system.[71] The erosion of U.S. hegemony may have stimulated the creation and expansion of PTAs by a set of leading economic powers that felt these arrangements would assist them in managing the international economy.[72] Drawing smaller states into preferential groupings with a relatively liberal cast toward third parties might reduce the capacity of these states to establish a series of more protectionist blocs and bind them to decisions about the system made by the leading powers. Especially if there is a multilateral framework (like the GATT/WTO) to which each leading power (including the declining hegemon) is committed and that can help to facilitate economic cooperation, the growth of regionalism during periods of hegemonic decline could contribute to the maintenance of an open trading system.

Second, Krugman argues that the dangers posed by a system of three trade blocs are muted if each bloc is composed of countries in close proximity that conduct a high volume of commerce prior to its establishment. Both he and Summers conclude that these "natural" trading blocs reduce the risk of trade diversion and that they make up a large portion of the existing PTAs.[73] . . . [But this] begs an important set of questions: Why do some "natural" trade partners form PTAs while others do not? And why do some "unnatural" partners do so as well? There is ample reason to expect that the answers to these questions hinge largely on domestic political factors and the nature of political relations between states.

Central to the links between international political relations and the formation of PTAs are the effects of trade on states' political-military power.[74] Joanne Gowa points out that the efficiency gains from open trade promote the growth of national income, which can be used to enhance states' political-military capacity.[75] Countries cannot ignore the security externalities stemming from commerce without jeopardizing their political well-being. She maintains that countries can attend to these externalities by trading more freely with their political-military allies than with other states. . . .

Returning to the claims advanced by Krugman and Summers, certain blocs (for example, those in North America and Western Europe), therefore, may appear natural partly because they are composed of allies, which tend to be located in close proximity and to trade heavily with each other.[76] Furthermore, allies may be quite willing to form PTAs that divert trade from adversaries lying outside the arrangement, if they anticipate that doing so will impose greater economic damage on their foes than on themselves. In the same vein, adversaries have few political reasons to form a PTA, and allies that establish one are unlikely to permit their adversaries to join, thus limiting the scope for the expansion of preferential arrangements. . . . It is no coincidence, for instance, that preferential agreements between the EC/EU and EFTA, on the one hand, and various states formerly in the Soviet orbit, on the other, were concluded only after the end of the Cold War and the collapse of the Warsaw Pact.[77] . . .

Another way that regional arrangements can affect power relations is by influencing the economic dependence of members. If states that derive the greatest economic gains from a PTA are more vulnerable to disruptions of commercial relations within the arrangement than other participants, the political leverage of the latter is likely to grow. This point has not been lost on state leaders.

Prussia, for example, established the Zollverein largely to increase its political influence over the weaker German states and to minimize Austrian influence in the region.[78] As a result, it repeatedly opposed Austria's entry into the Zollverein. Similarly, both Great Britain and Prussia objected to the formation of a proposed customs union between France and Belgium during the 1840s on the grounds that it would promote French power and undermine Belgian independence. . . . Furthermore, Albert O. Hirschman and others have described how various major powers used regional arrangements to bolster their political influence during the interwar period and how certain arrangements that seemed likely to bear heavily on the European balance of power (like the proposed Austro-German customs union) were actively opposed.[79]

Since World War II, stronger states have continued to use PTAs as a means to consolidate their political influence over weaker counterparts. The CMEA and the many arrangements that the EC established with former colonies of its members are cases in point. The Caribbean Basin Initiative launched by the United States in

1982 has been described in similar terms.[80] A related issue is raised by Joseph M. Grieco, who argues that, over the past fifty years, the extent of institutionalization in regional arrangements has been influenced by power relations among members.[81] In areas where the local distribution of capabilities has shifted or states have expected such a shift to occur, weaker states have opposed establishing a formal regional institution, fearing that it would reflect the interests of more powerful members and undermine their security. Another view, however, is that regional institutions foster stability and constrain the ability of members to exercise power. A recent study of the EU, for example, concludes that although Germany's power has enabled it to shape European institutions, Germany's entanglement within these institutions has taken the hard edge off its interstate bargaining and eroded its hegemony in Europe.[82]

The links between power relations and PTAs remain important in the contemporary era, although they have not been studied in sufficient depth. But in contrast to the interwar period, there is relatively little indication that regionalism has been the product of active attempts by states to promote their political-military power since World War II. Barry Buzan attributes this change to the emergence of bipolarity, the decline of empires, and the advent of nuclear weapons.[83] The latest wave of regionalism has been marked by especially few instances of states using PTAs to bolster their political-military capacity. That is probably one reason why regionalism has done less to divert trade over the past fifty years than during the interwar period.[84] . . .

Multilateral Institutions, Strategic Interaction, and Regionalism

One of the most distinctive features of the two waves of regionalism occurring since World War II is the multilateral framework in which they arose. Most contemporary PTAs have been established under the auspices of the GATT/WTO, which has attempted to dampen trade diversion by limiting members' ability to discriminate against third parties.[85] But the GATT's success in fostering trade-creating PTAs has been qualified. Many arrangements formed by its economically less-developed members have been highly protectionist, and even the extent to which those preferential groupings established among its developed members have been welfare enhancing is the subject of considerable dispute.

Furthermore, the absence of multilateral management has not always led to the formation of discriminatory regional arrangements. The liberal trading order of the nineteenth century was constructed on a bilateral and regional basis lacking any multilateral foundation. Also, Irwin points out that the economic and political damage caused by trade blocs formed in the 1930s might have been ameliorated if the League of Nations had not insisted on trying to promote the multilateral organization of commerce.[86] In the same vein, Oye argues that regionalism "preserved zones of openness" early in that decade and that decentralized and "discriminatory bargaining was an important force for liberalization" during its middle and end.[87]

Article XXIV of the GATT outlines the conditions under which states are permitted to establish regional integration arrangements. Its stipulation that PTAs eliminate internal trade barriers and its prohibition on increases in the average level of members' external tariffs do not preclude the possibility of trade diversion.[88] But Eichengreen and Frankel note that the latter prohibition "explicitly rules out Krugman's concern" about a beggar-thy-neighbor trade war arising in systems composed of a few large PTAs.[89] To the extent that such a system has been emerging, the GATT/WTO, therefore, may have an important role to play in averting what could otherwise be a destructive wave of regionalism. . . .

Besides attempting to regulate the formation of PTAs, the GATT has made efforts to manage strategic interdependence among them. Preferential arrangements have formed in reaction to one another throughout each wave of regionalism. During the nineteenth century, this tendency was prompted by states' desire to obtain access to MFN treatment. Doing so required them to enter the network of bilateral commercial arrangements undergirding the trading system, which generated increases in the number of these arrangements and countries that were party to one.[90] Throughout the interwar period, PTAs formed in reaction to each other due largely to mercantilist policies and political rivalries among the major powers.[91]

Strategic interaction has continued to guide the development of PTAs since World War II.[92] It has been argued, for example, that EFTA was created in response to the EEC; the latter also spurred various groups of LCDs to form regional arrangements.[93] Furthermore, NAFTA has stimulated the establishment of bilateral economic arrangements in the Western Hemisphere and in the Asia-Pacific region as well as agreements to conclude others.[94] Yet contemporary PTAs have formed in reaction to each other for different reasons than before: GATT members have not established them to obtain MFN treatment, and they are not the products of mercantilist policies. . . .

Although the growth of regional arrangements has been marked by a "contagion" effect throughout each wave we have analyzed, far less damage has accrued to the international trading system as a result during the post–World War II era than during the 1930s. Besides certain factors discussed earlier, the GATT helped to limit such damage by restricting (albeit with varying degrees of success) the ability of participants to form highly discriminatory trade blocs. Moreover, because there is little chance of creating a system composed of "open" bilateral agreements, like that which existed during the nineteenth century, the WTO's capacity to manage the recent cascade of PTAs will continue to be an important determinant of regionalism's cast. . . .

VARIATIONS AMONG REGIONAL INSTITUTIONS

Thus far, we have analyzed PTAs as a whole, without focusing on the differences among them. Yet it is clear that all regional trade institutions are neither created equal nor equally successful in meeting their stated objectives. Significant variations exist in both the institutional design of PTAs and the depth of integration they foster. A number of recent efforts have been made to assess the political causes and consequences of these differences.

The depth of integration within a PTA depends on economic factors, including members' levels of economic development and the extent to which their economies are complementary.[95] It also hinges on many of the political factors that influence the formation of PTAs, as we have suggested throughout this article. But in addition, the institutional design of a regional arrangement affects the degree of integration among participants. For example, some observers argue that an inverse relationship exists between the number of parties to a PTA and the depth of economic integration within it. Deeper integration is more easily attained if states share an interest in economic liberalization; all else equal, the heterogeneity of members' preferences is likely to increase as the number of members grows.[96] For this reason and because of collective action problems, forming a small PTA is easier than forming a large one, regardless of the level of integration eventually attained.[97] Large, highly integrated PTAs can be established. However, rather than trying to do so from scratch, George W. Downs, David M. Rocke, and Peter N. Barsoom suggest that it is more effective to create a smaller PTA composed of states with a preference for liberalizing economic relations and then take on additional members incrementally—precisely the strategy the EC/EU has followed.[98]

Another set of design features that differs across PTAs is the extent of the commercial preferences granted to members, whether they impose a CET, and whether the arrangement explicitly covers issue areas other than trade (for example, monetary relations and immigration and environmental policy). Economists have highlighted the welfare consequences of these institutional variations.[99] . . . Customs unions set a CET, and it may be easier for protectionist groups to ally across states to raise it than to forge an alliance to raise tariffs independently set by each member. In addition, parties to an FTA have an incentive to engage in competitive trade barrier reductions, since doing so will promote foreign investment and exports. Thus, many analysts argue that dynamic processes propel reductions in external tariffs under an FTA, whereas a customs union is likely to set its CET just high enough to protect its least-efficient members.[100]

On the other hand, political factors may render customs unions preferable to FTAs and other preferential arrangements that do not impose a CET. Countries setting trade barriers collectively can dilute the political influence of protectionist interest groups in any given member. Both administrative costs and the level of protection may be higher in an FTA than in a customs union, since elaborate rules of origin and content requirements are necessary to enforce the former type of agreement.[101] Like the formation of PTAs, more generally, both the domestic and the international political environment are likely to shape which type of arrangement states choose to form. How they do so has hardly been explored and is a fruitful avenue for further research.

A final design feature that varies among PTAs is their institutional density. Grieco maintains that the institutionalization of economic relations can be compared across three dimensions: (1) the locus of institutionalization, (2) the scope of activity, and (3) the level of institutional authority.[102] Recently, scholars have expressed particular interest in why certain regions display a high degree of institutionalization (for example, Western Europe) but others do not (for example, Asia). One possibility stressed by economists and political scientists for decades—

and widely criticized of late—is that more highly institutionalized arrangements arise as functional responses to intensified integration among the constituent states.[103] Another possibility, suggested by Miles Kahler, is that the extent of institutionalization depends on the preferences of policymakers and interest groups as well as bargaining among PTA members.[104] Grieco advances a third possibility. As noted earlier, he argues that institutionalization will be forestalled when "less powerful countries in a region have experienced or are experiencing a significant deterioration in their relative capabilities" because of their concerns "that the enhancement of regional economic ties brought about by institutionalization [will] accentuate regional imbalances in capabilities even further in favor of the relatively stronger partners."[105] In his view, for example, the weaker countries of Southeast Asia are likely to oppose the establishment of formal economic institutions, whereas the stronger powers, especially Japan, are likely to press for their development.

In contrast to Grieco's argument, however, Katzenstein points out that "today it is China and Japan who oppose rapid moves toward a formal institutionalization of regional integration," whereas weaker powers like the members of ASEAN seek stronger institutions.[106] Moreover, a wide variety of scholars attribute the lack of formal institutions in East Asia to factors other than local power relations. . . .

Katzenstein proposes some additional reasons for the weak institutionalization of Asian economic relations.[107] First, after World War II the United States promoted the principles of bilateralism in Asia and multilateralism in Europe. Second, the construction of a collective identity facilitates the establishment of formal regional integration, and political actors in Asia have not subscribed to the idea of creating a distinct community. Finally, the distinctive character of Asian states hinders the creation of regional institutions. He maintains that the "network character" of these states, their emphasis on consensus building, and the convergence between public and private spheres in domestic politics differentiate them from European countries and render them less likely to develop formal regional institutions. . . .

CONCLUSIONS

. . .What are some of the key findings arising from research on the causes and consequences of regionalism and what are the key questions that remain unresolved? First, existing work indicates that the preferences and political influence of different societal groups are likely to affect whether a state enters a PTA as well as which sectors are covered by the arrangement and whether it creates or diverts trade. Protectionist groups have an incentive to press for the establishment of PTAs that discriminate in their favor, and government officials that depend on protectionist interests for political support have an incentive to respond to such pressures. Export-oriented interests may also support entering a PTA, if doing so grants them expanded access to vital foreign markets within the bloc or reduces the prospect that their access to these markets will be disrupted in the future.

In practice, however, it may be difficult to construct PTAs that meet the demands of both import-competing and export-oriented interests in prospective members, thereby limiting the scope for their formation. Furthermore, though recent studies of regionalism emphasizing societal factors suggest that the economic cast of PTAs will depend heavily on the interests and political influence of groups in member states, the theoretical and empirical tools needed to make these assessments require refinement. More generally, this body of research has not yet resolved exactly which segments of society are most likely to support regional trade initiatives as opposed to unilateral or multilateral ones, whose interests these initiatives serve, and whether commercial regionalism heightens or undermines the support of various groups for multilateral liberalization.

Second, the preferences of government officials and the nature of domestic institutions influence the establishment and economic effects of PTAs. Of late, certain governments have opted to enter a PTA because doing so seemed likely to facilitate more extensive commercial liberalization than unilateral or multilateral strategies would permit, given the nature of domestic institutions and the interests of potent segments of society. In the same vein, the latest wave of regionalism has been marked by cases where accession to a PTA was used to facilitate liberal economic and political reforms and to dilute the political efficacy of societal groups that opposed such changes. But though the preferences of government officials and the nature of domestic institutions clearly have affected efforts at regional integration, precisely which institutional conditions promote regionalism has not been established. Nor have existing studies identified the conditions under which PTA membership is most likely to stimulate domestic reform. . . .

Third, both the formation of regional trade arrangements and their consequences hinge on international political conditions. Much recent interest has been expressed in whether declining U.S. hegemony has contributed to the latest wave of regionalism. Although the available evidence suggests that PTAs did become more pervasive as hegemony eroded, what underlies this relationship, how it bears on regionalism's welfare consequences, and whether receding hegemony affected prior episodes of regionalism remain matters of dispute. Less widely analyzed of late, but central to various earlier studies, are the links between PTAs and interstate power relations. Due to these effects, for example, states have greater incentives to enter PTAs with their allies than with their foes, which may help to explain why the Cold War's end and the attendant changes in international security relations have coincided with regionalism's growth during the past decade. . . .

Fourth, the period since World War II is the first to experience the growth of regionalism within the context of a multilateral trade system. All but a few members of the WTO currently belong to a PTA and it is centrally important to determine why its members often choose to pursue regional trade initiatives rather than relying solely on multilateral initiatives. One possibility is that they view PTAs as a complement to multilateral liberalization; another is that they view regional and multilateral liberalization as substitutes. This issue lies at the heart of contemporary debates about whether PTAs will be building blocks or stumbling blocks to greater multilateral openness, and existing research on the political economy of regionalism has done little to resolve it. Equally important are questions pertaining to what role the GATT/WTO has played in managing the spread of regionalism. . . .

Fifth, important institutional differences exist among PTAs, including the number of members involved, the extent of the preferential treatment they grant members, whether they impose a CET, and their institutional density. Some analyses of these variations center on domestic factors, such as the prevailing character of policy networks at home and the preferences of interest groups and national policymakers. Others focus on international factors, including power relations, strategic interaction among members, and their political and economic relations with third parties. However, existing research on the political conditions shaping the design of regional institutions is largely suggestive. Moreover, the political consequences of different institutional forms are surrounded more by debate than by theory or evidence. The political sources and effects of institutional variations across PTAs represent an understudied and especially fertile ground for future research.

In this article, we have outlined some of the ways that political factors have influenced the formation and effects of PTAs. The recent literature surveyed here offers some key insights into these relationships. The political underpinnings of regionalism, however, remain murky, and the need for additional research on this topic is glaring. Not only will such research produce a better understanding of regionalism, it is also likely to contribute to broader issues in the field of international relations, including the political economy of national security, the domestic and international sources of foreign economic policy, and the factors influencing the design and strength of international institutions. . . .

NOTES

1. On this issue, see Cohen 1997; Lawrence 1996; and Padoan 1997.
2. Bhagwati distinguishes two waves of regionalism since World War II. The first began in the late 1950s and lasted until the 1970s; the second began in the mid-1980s. These waves are discussed at greater length later in this article. See Bhagwati 1993.
3. Fishlow and Haggard 1992. See also Haggard 1997, 48 fn. 1; and Yarbrough and Yarbrough 1997, 160 fn. 1.
4. See, for example, Bhagwati 1993; Bhagwati and Panagariya 1996, 4–5; de Melo and Panagariya 1993; and Pomfret 1988.
5. See Anderson and Blackhurst 1993; and the sources in footnote 4, above.
6. As de Melo and Panagariya point out, "because under regionalism preferences are extended only to partners, it is discriminatory. At the same time it represents a move towards freer trade among partners." de Melo and Panagariya 1993, 4.
7. Viner 1950, 43. For comprehensive overviews of the issues addressed in this section, see Baldwin and Venables 1995; Bhagwati 1991, chap. 5; Bhagwati and Panagariya 1996; Gunter 1989; Hine 1994; and Pomfret 1988.
8. One reason for the lack of consensus on this issue is the dearth of reliable information about the degree to which price changes induce substitution across imports from different suppliers. Another reason is the difficulty associated with constructing counterfactuals (or "antimondes") that adequately gauge the effects of PTAs. On these issues, see Hine 1994; and Pomfret 1988, chap. 8.
9. Krugman 1991a, 16.

10. See ibid.; and Krugman 1993, 61.
11. Frankel, Stein, and Wei 1995.
12. See Bond and Syropoulos 1996a; and Srinivasan 1993.
13. See Bhagwati and Panagariya 1996, 47; and Srinivasan 1993.
14. See Bhagwati 1968; Cooper and Massell 1965a, b; and Johnson 1965.
15. Bhagwati 1993, 28.
16. See, for example, Krugman 1991b; and Padoan 1997, 108–109.
17. See Baldwin and Venables 1995, 1605–13; and Gunter 1989, 16–21.
18. See Bhagwati 1993; and Bhagwati and Panagariya 1996.
19. Kemp and Wan 1976.
20. See Krugman 1993; and Summers 1991.
21. See, for example, Lawrence 1996; and Summers 1991.
22. Bhagwati 1991, 60–61; and 1993.
23. Bond and Syropoulos 1996b.
24. Frankel and Wei 1998, 216.
25. See, for example, Kindleberger 1975; and Pollard 1974. However, regionalism was not confined solely to Europe during this era. Prior to 1880, for example, India, China, and Great Britain comprised a "tightly-knit trading bloc" in Asia. Afterward, Japan's economic development and its increasing political power led to key changes in intra-Asian trade patterns. Kenwood and Lougheed report that "Asia replaced Europe and the United States as the main source of Japanese imports, supplying almost one-half of these needs by 1913. By that date Asia had also become Japan's leading regional export market." Kenwood and Lougheed 1971, 94–95.
26. Pollard 1974, 42–51, 62–66.
27. Kindleberger 1975; and Pollard 1974. Of course, trade grew rapidly worldwide during this era, but the extent of its growth and of economic integration was especially marked in Europe.
28. See Irwin 1993, 92; and Pollard 1974, 118.
29. See, for example, Irwin 1993; Kenwood and Lougheed 1971; and Pollard 1974.
30. Irwin 1993, 97.
31. Ibid., 114. See also Pollard 1974, 35.
32. Pollard 1974, 145.
33. On the commercial arrangements discussed in this paragraph, see Condliffe 1940, chaps. 8–9; Hirschman [1945] 1980; Kenwood and Lougheed 1971, 211–19; and Pollard 1974, 49. Although our focus is on commercial regionalism, it should be noted that the interwar era was also marked by the existence of at least five currency regions. For an analysis of the political economy of currency regions, see, for example, Cohen 1997.
34. See, for example, Condliffe 1940, especially chaps. 8–9; Hirschman [1945] 1980; Kindleberger 1973; and Oye 1992.
35. Irwin 1993, 91. He notes that these generalizations are somewhat inaccurate, as do Eichengreen and Frankel 1995. But both studies confirm that regionalism had different effects during the nineteenth century, the interwar period, and the present; and both view regionalism in the interwar period as most malign.
36. See Condliffe 1940; Eichengreen and Frankel 1995, 97; and Hirschman [1945] 1980.
37. These define regionalism in somewhat different ways. Anderson and Norheim examine broad geographic areas, de Melo and Panagariya analyze PTAs, and Frankel, Stein, and Wei consider a combination of geographic zones and PTAs. See Anderson and Norheim 1993; de Melo and Panagariya 1993; and Frankel, Stein, and Wei 1995.

38. On the effects of PTAs on trade flows, see, for example, Aitken 1973; Frankel 1993; Frankel, Stein, and Wei 1995; Linnemann 1966; Mansfield and Bronson 1997; Tinbergen 1962; and Winters and Wang 1994.

39. See, for example, Aitken 1973; Frankel 1993; and Frankel, Stein, and Wei 1995.

40. Note, however, that some PTAs—especially Mercosur—have had a large effect on trade since 1990. Their effects are not captured in Table 1. We are grateful to Stephen Haggard for bringing this point to our attention.

41. See Anderson and Blackhurst 1993, 8; Frankel 1993; Frankel, Stein, and Wei 1995; and Saxonhouse 1993.

42. Mansfield 1998.

43. See also de Melo and Panagariya 1993, 3.

44. Serra et al. 1997, 8, fig. 2.

45. World Trade Organization 1996, 38, and 1995.

46. Perroni and Whalley 1996.

47. See, for example, Deutsch et al. 1957; Haas 1958; and Nye 1971.

48. Nye 1988, 239.

49. See Gunter 1989, 9; and Hirschman 1981.

50. For example, Haggard 1997.

51. Eichengreen and Frankel 1995, 101.

52. Grossman and Helpman 1995, 668; and 1994.

53. Grossman and Helpman 1995, 681. See also Pomfret 1988, 190.

54. Oye 1992, 6–7, 143–44.

55. Krueger 1997, 19 fn. 27.

56. See, for example, Krueger 1993, 77, 87; and Nogués and Quintanilla 1993, 280–88.

57. Eichengreen and Frankel 1995, 101.

58. See Irwin 1993, 96; and Kindleberger 1975, 39–40. Moreover, this is not an isolated case. Irwin notes that "Commercial agreements in the form of foreign treaties proved useful in circumventing protectionist interests in the legislature throughout Europe." Irwin 1993, 116 fn. 7.

59. Birch 1996, 186.

60. On these issues, see Haggard and Kaufman 1995; Haggard and Webb 1994; Lawrence 1996; Mansfield and Snyder 1995; and Remmer 1998.

61. Nogués and Quintanilla 1993, 285.

62. For example, ibid.

63. Katzenstein 1997a.

64. For example, Hurrell 1995, 68–71.

65. See Gilpin 1975; Kindleberger 1973; and Lake 1988.

66. See, for example, Gilpin 1975 and 1987; Kindleberger 1973; and Krasner 1976.

67. See, for example, Baldwin 1993; Bhagwati 1993; Bhagwati and Panagariya 1996; Krugman 1993; and Pomfret 1988.

68. Mansfield 1998.

69. See, for example, McKeown 1991; Oye 1992; and Yarbrough and Yarbrough 1992.

70. For example, Gilpin 1987, 88–90, and chap. 10.

71. See, for example, Keohane 1984; and Snidal 1985.

72. On this issue, see Yarbrough and Yarbrough 1992.

73. Krugman 1991a and 1993; and Summers 1991. Of course, these factors may be related, since an inverse relationship tends to exist between transportation costs and trade flows. However, some strands of this argument focus on high levels of trade, which may be a product of geographical proximity, whereas others focus on transportation costs,

which are expected to be lower for states in the same region than for other states. See Bhagwati and Panagariya 1996, 7 fn. 7. Wonnacott and Lutz, who first coined the term "natural trading partners," argue that the economic development of states, the extent to which their economies are complementary, and the degree to which they compete in international markets also influence whether trading partners are natural. These factors, however, have received relatively little attention and we therefore do not examine them here. See Wonnacott and Lutz 1989.

74. On the relationship between trade and political power, see Baldwin 1985; Gowa 1994; Hirschman [1945] 1980; and Keohane and Nye 1977.

75. Gowa 1994.

76. On the relationship between alliances and proximity, see Farber and Gowa 1997, 411. On the relationship between alliances and trade, see Gowa 1994; and Mansfield and Bronson 1997.

77. For a list of these arrangements, see World Trade Organization 1995, 85–87.

78. Viner 1950, 98.

79. See, for example, Condliffe 1940; Hirschman [1945] 1980; Viner 1950, 87–91; and Eichengreen and Frankel 1995, 97.

80. For example, Pomfret 1988, 163.

81. Grieco 1997.

82. Katzenstein 1997b.

83. Buzan 1984.

84. For an empirical analysis of trade creation and trade diversion covering these periods, see Eichengreen and Frankel 1995.

85. See Bhagwati 1991, chap. 5, and 1993; Eichengreen and Frankel 1995; and Finger 1993.

86. Irwin 1993.

87. Oye 1992, 9.

88. Bhagwati 1993, 35–36.

89. Eichengreen and Frankel 1995, 100.

90. Irwin 1993, 97.

91. See, for example, Buzan 1984; Condliffe 1940; and Eichengreen and Frankel 1995.

92. See de Melo and Panagariya 1993, 5–6; Fernández 1997; Mansfield 1998; Oye 1992; Pomfret 1988; and Yarbrough and Yarbrough 1992.

93. Pomfret 1988, 161, 178.

94. For example, Serra et al. 1997, 8–9. Also consistent with these views is evidence linking the depth of integration within PTAs to the establishment of competing economic blocs. For example, Bhagwati and Fernández suggest that heightened European integration contributed to the creation of NAFTA: and Oye and Sandholtz and Zysman point out that NAFTA's formation prompted additional integration within the EU. See Bhagwati 1991, 72; Fernández 1997, 16–19; Oye 1992, 164–65; and Sandholtz and Zysman 1989.

95. See Balassa 1961; Fischer 1993; Foroutan 1993; and Nogués and Quintanilla 1993.

96. On this point, see de Melo, Panagariya, and Rodrik 1993; Downs, Rocke, and Barsoom 1998; and Haggard 1997.

97. See de Melo, Panagariya, and Rodrik 1993; and Olson 1993.

98. Downs, Rocke, and Barsoom 1998.

99. See, for example, de Melo, Panagariya, and Rodrik 1993, 171–75; and Frankel, Stein, and Wei 1995. One especially interesting finding is that, although eliminating trade barriers among members is likely to promote economic integration, less dramatic reductions of these barriers often are preferable on economic grounds.

100. See de Melo, Panagariya, and Rodrik 1993, 171–74; and Wonnacott 1996, 92–95.

101. As Wonnacott explains, "because an FTA allows each member to set its own tariff on
    outside countries, it requires rules of origin (ROOs). Otherwise, there would be an
    incentive for trade deflection—that is, imports would come into the FTA through
    the low-tariff country and be transshipped duty-free into the high-tariff country." For
    discussions of why customs unions are more desirable than FTAs because ROOs in
    the latter tend to be protectionist, see Wonnacott 1996, 90–91; and Krueger 1995.
102. Grieco 1997.
103. For a discussion of this literature, see Kahler 1995.
104. Ibid.
105. Grieco 1997, 176.
106. Katzenstein 1997a, 23.
107. Katzenstein 1997a.

REFERENCES

Aitken, Norman D. 1973. The Effect of the EEC and EFTA on European Trade: A Tempo-
    ral and Cross-Section Analysis. *American Economic Review* 63 (5):881–92.
Anderson, Kym, and Richard Blackhurst. 1993. Introduction and Summary. In *Regional
    Integration and the Global Trading System,* edited by Kym Anderson and Richard Black-
    hurst, 1–15. London: Harvester Wheatsheaf.
Anderson, Kym, and Hege Norheim. 1993. History, Geography, and Regional Economic
    Integration. In *Regional Integration and the Global Trading System,* edited by Kym Ander-
    son and Richard Blackhurst, 19–51. London: Harvester Wheatsheaf.
Bagwell, Kyle, and Robert W. Staiger. 1997. Regionalism and Multilateral Tariff Coopera-
    tion. NBER Working Paper 5921. Cambridge, Mass.: National Bureau of Economic
    Research.
Balassa, Bela A. 1961. *The Theory of Economic Integration.* Homewood, Ill.: Irwin.
Baldwin, David A. 1985. *Economic Statecraft.* Princeton, N.J.: Princeton University Press.
Baldwin, Richard E., and Anthony J. Venables. 1995. Regional Economic Integration. In
    Handbook of International Economics, Vol. 3, edited by Gene M. Grossman and Kenneth
    Rogoff, 1597–1644. Amsterdam: Elsevier.
Baldwin, Robert E. 1993. Adapting the GATT to a More Regionalized World: A Political
    Economy Perspective. In *Regional Integration and the Global Trading System,* edited by
    Kym Anderson and Richard Blackhurst, 387–407. London: Harvester Wheatsheaf.
Bhagwati, Jagdish. 1968. Trade Liberalization Among LCDs, Trade Theory, and GATT
    Rules. In *Value, Capital, and Growth: Essays in Honour of Sir John Hicks,* edited by J. N.
    Wolfe, 21–43. Edinburgh: University of Edinburgh Press.
———. 1991. *The World Trading System at Risk.* Princeton, N.J.: Princeton University Press.
———. 1993. Regionalism and Multilateralism: An Overview. In *New Dimensions in
    Regional Integration,* edited by Jaime de Melo and Arvind Panagariya, 22–51. New York:
    Cambridge University Press.
Bhagwati, Jagdish, and Arvind Panagariya. 1996. Preferential Trading Areas and Multilater-
    alism—Strangers, Friends, or Foes? In *The Economics of Preferential Trade Agreements,*
    edited by Jagdish Bhagwati and Arvind Panagariya, 1–78. Washington, D.C.: AEI Press
Birch, Melissa H. 1996. Economic Policy and the Transition to Democracy in Paraguay. In
    Economic Policy and the Transition to Democracy: The Latin American Experience, edited by
    Juan Antonio Morales and Gary McMahon, 166–90. New York: St. Martin's Press.
Bond, Eric, and Constantinos Syropoulos. 1996a. Trading Blocs and the Sustainability of
    Interregional Cooperation. In *The New Transatlantic Economy,* edited by Matthew B.

Canzoneri, Wilfred J. Ethier, and Vittorio Grilli, 118–41. Cambridge: Cambridge University Press.

———. 1996b. The Size of Trading Blocs: Market Power and World Welfare Effects. *Journal of International Economics* 40 (3–4):411–37.

Busch, Marc L., and Helen V. Milner. 1994. The Future of the International Trading System: International Firms, Regionalism, and Domestic Politics. In *Political Economy and the Changing Global Order*, edited by Richard Stubbs and Geoffrey R. D. Underhill, 259–76. New York: St. Martin's Press.

Buzan, Barry. 1984. Economic Structure and International Security: The Limits of the Liberal Case. *International Organization* 38 (4):597–624.

Cohen, Benjamin J. 1997. The Political Economy of Currency Regions. In *The Political Economy of Regionalism*, edited by Edward D. Mansfield and Helen V. Milner, 50–76. New York: Columbia University Press.

———. 1998. *The Geography of Money*. Ithaca, N.Y.: Cornell University Press.

Condliffe, J. B. 1940. *The Reconstruction of World Trade*. New York: W. W. Norton.

Cooper, Charles A., and Benton F. Massell. 1965a. A New Look at Customs Union Theory. *The Economic Journal* 75:742–47.

———. 1965b. Toward a General Theory of Customs Unions for Developing Countries. *Journal of Political Economy* 73 (5):461–76.

de Melo, Jaime, and Arvind Panagariya. 1993. Introduction. In *New Dimensions in Regional Integration*, edited by Jaime de Melo and Arvind Panagariya, 3–21. New York: Cambridge University Press.

de Melo, Jaime, Arvind Panagariya, and Dani Rodrik. 1993. The New Regionalism: A Country Perspective. In *New Dimensions in Regional Integration*, edited by Jaime de Melo and Arvind Panagariya, 159–93. New York: Cambridge University Press.

Deutsch, Karl W., Sidney A. Burrell, Robert A. Kann, Maurice Lee, Jr., Martin Lichterman, Raymond E. Lindgren, Francis L. Lowenheim, and Richard W. Van Wagenen. 1957. *Political Community and the North Atlantic Area: International Organization in the Light of Historical Experience*. Princeton, N.J.: Princeton University Press.

Downs, George W., David M. Rocke, and Peter N. Barsoom. 1998. Managing the Evolution of Multilateralism. *International Organization* 52 (2):397–419.

Eichengreen, Barry, and Jeffrey A. Frankel. 1995. Economic Regionalism: Evidence from Two Twentieth-Century Episodes. *North American Journal of Economics and Finance* 6 (2):89–106.

Farber, Henry S., and Joanne Gowa. 1997. Common Interests or Common Polities? Reinterpreting the Democratic Peace. *Journal of Politics* 59 (2):393–417.

Fernández, Raquel. 1997. Returns to Regionalism: An Evaluation of Non-Traditional Gains from RTAs. NBER Working Paper 5970. Cambridge, Mass.: National Bureau of Economic Research.

Finger, J. Michael. 1993. GATT's Influence on Regional Arrangements. In *New Dimensions in Regional Integration*, edited by Jaime de Melo and Arvind Panagariya, 128–48. New York: Cambridge University Press.

Fischer, Stanley. 1993. Prospects for Regional Integration in the Middle East. In *New Dimensions in Regional Integration*, edited by Jaime de Melo and Arvind Panagariya, 423–48. New York: Cambridge University Press.

Fishlow, Albert, and Stephan Haggard. 1992. *The United States and the Regionalization of the World Economy*. Paris: OECD Development Center Research Project on Globalization and Regionalization.

Foroutan, Faezeh. 1993. Regional Integration in Sub-Saharan Africa: Past Experience and Future Prospects. In *New Dimensions in Regional Integration*, edited by Jaime de Melo and Arvind Panagariya, 234–71. New York: Cambridge University Press.

Frankel, Jeffrey A. 1993. Is Japan Creating a Yen Bloc in East Asia and the Pacific? In *Regionalism and Rivalry: Japan and the United States in Pacific Asia,* edited by Jeffrey A. Frankel and Miles Kahler, 53–85. Chicago: University of Chicago Press.

Frankel, Jeffrey A., and Shang-Jin Wei. 1998. Regionalization of World Trade and Currencies: Economics and Politics. In *The Regionalization of the World Economy,* edited by Jeffrey A. Frankel, 189–219. Chicago: University of Chicago Press.

Frankel, Jeffrey, Ernesto Stein, and Shang-Jin Wei. 1995. Trading Blocs and the Americas: The Natural, the Unnatural, and the Super-Natural. *Journal of Development Economics* 47 (1):61–95.

Frieden, Jeffry A. 1991. Invested Interests: The Politics of National Economic Policies in a World of Global Finance. *International Organization* 45 (4):425–51.

Gilpin, Robert. 1975. *U.S. Power and the Multinational Corporation: The Political Economy of Foreign Direct Investment.* New York: Basic Books.

———. 1987. *The Political Economy of International Relations.* Princeton, N.J.: Princeton University Press.

Gowa, Joanne. 1994. *Allies, Adversaries, and International Trade.* Princeton, N.J.: Princeton University Press.

Grieco, Joseph M. 1997. Systemic Sources of Variation in Regional Institutionalization in Western Europe, East Asia, and the Americas. In *The Political Economy of Regionalism,* edited by Edward D. Mansfield and Helen V. Milner, 164–87. New York: Columbia University Press.

Grossman, Gene M., and Elhanan Helpman. 1994. Protection for Sale. *American Economic Review* 84 (4):833–50.

———. 1995. The Politics of Free Trade Agreements. *American Economic Review* 85 (4):667–90.

Gunter, Frank R. 1989. Customs Union Theory: Retrospect and Prospect. In *Economic Aspects of Regional Trading Arrangements,* edited by David Greenaway, Thomas Hyclak, and Robert J. Thornton, 1–30. New York: Harvester Wheatsheaf.

Haas, Ernst B. 1958. *The Uniting of Europe: Political, Social, and Economic Forces, 1950–1957.* Stanford, Calif.: Stanford University Press.

Haggard, Stephan. 1997. Regionalism in Asia and the Americas. In *The Political Economy of Regionalism,* edited by Edward D. Mansfield and Helen V. Milner, 20–49. New York: Columbia University Press.

Haggard, Stephan, and Robert R. Kaufman. 1995. *The Political Economy of Democratic Transitions.* Princeton, N.J.: Princeton University Press.

Haggard, Stephan, and Steven B. Webb, eds. 1994. *Voting for Reform: Democracy, Political Liberalization, and Economic Adjustment.* New York: Oxford University Press.

Hine, Robert C. 1994. International Economic Integration. In *Surveys in International Trade,* edited by David Greenaway and L. Alan Winters, 234–72. Oxford: Basil Blackwell.

Hirschman, Albert O. [1945] 1980. *National Power and the Structure of Foreign Trade.* Berkeley: University of California Press.

———. 1981. *Essays in Trespassing: Economics to Politics and Beyond.* Cambridge: Cambridge University Press.

Hoekman, Bernard, and Michael Leidy. 1993. Holes and Loopholes in Integration Agreements: History and Prospects. In *Regional Integration and the Global Trading System,* edited by Kym Anderson and Richard Blackhurst, 218–45. London: Harvester Wheatsheaf.

Hurrell, Andrew. 1995. Regionalism in Theoretical Perspective. In *Regionalism in World Politics,* edited by Louise Fawcett and Andrew Hurrell, 37–73. Oxford: Oxford University Press.

Irwin, Douglas A. 1993. Multilateral and Bilateral Trade Policies in the World Trading System: An Historical Perspective. In *New Dimensions in Regional Integration,* edited by

Jaime de Melo and Arvind Panagariya, 90–119. New York: Cambridge University Press.

Johnson, Harry G. 1965. *The World Economy at the Crossroads: A Survey of Current Problems of Money, Trade, and Economic Development.* Oxford: Clarendon Press.

Kahler, Miles. 1995. *International Institutions and the Political Economy of Integration.* Washington, D.C.: Brookings Institution.

Katzenstein, Peter J. 1997a. Introduction: Asian Regionalism in Comparative Perspective. In *Network Power: Japan and Asia,* edited by Peter J. Katzenstein and Takashi Shiraishi, 1–44. Ithaca, N.Y.: Cornell University Press.

———, ed. 1997b. *Tamed Power: Germany in Europe.* Ithaca, N.Y.: Cornell University Press.

Kemp, Murray C., and Henry V. Wan, Jr. 1976. An Elementary Proposition Concerning the Formation of Customs Unions. *Journal of International Economics* 6 (1):95–97.

Kenwood, A. G., and A. L. Lougheed. 1971. *The Growth of the International Economy 1820–1960: An Introductory Text.* London: Allen and Unwin.

Keohane, Robert O. 1984. *After Hegemony: Cooperation and Discord in the World Political Economy.* Princeton, N.J.: Princeton University Press.

Keohane, Robert O., and Joseph S. Nye. 1977. *Power and Interdependence: World Politics in Transition.* Boston: Little, Brown.

Kindleberger, Charles P. 1973. *The World in Depression, 1929–1939.* Berkeley: University of California Press.

———. 1975. The Rise of Free Trade in Western Europe, 1820–1875. *Journal of Economic History* 35 (1):20–55.

Krasner, Stephen D. 1976. State Power and the Structure of International Trade. *World Politics* 28 (3):317–47.

Krueger, Anne O. 1993. *Political Economy of Policy Reform in Developing Countries.* Cambridge, Mass.: MIT Press.

———. 1995. Free Trade Agreements Versus Customs Unions. NBER Working Paper 5084. Cambridge, Mass.: National Bureau of Economic Research.

———. 1997. Problems with Overlapping Free Trade Areas. In *Regionalism Versus Multilateral Trade Arrangements,* edited by Takatoshi Ito and Anne O. Krueger, 9–24. Chicago: University of Chicago Press.

Krugman, Paul. 1991a. The Move to Free Trade Zones. In *Policy Implications of Trade and Currency Zones: A Symposium,* sponsored by the Federal Reserve Bank of Kansas City, 7–41. Kansas City, Mo.: Federal Reserve Bank.

———. 1991b. *Economic Geography.* Cambridge, Mass.: MIT Press.

———. 1993. Regionalism Versus Multilateralism: Analytical Notes. In *New Dimensions in Regional Integration,* edited by Jaime de Melo and Arvind Panagariya, 58–79. New York: Cambridge University Press.

Kupchan, Charles A. 1997. Regionalizing Europe's Security: The Case for a New Mitteleuropa. In *The Political Economy of Regionalism,* edited by Edward D. Mansfield and Helen V. Milner, 209–38. New York: Columbia University Press.

Lake, David A. 1988. *Power, Protection, and Free Trade: International Sources of U.S. Commercial Strategy.* Ithaca, N.Y.: Cornell University Press.

Lawrence, Robert Z. 1996. *Regionalism, Multilateralism, and Deeper Integration.* Washington, D.C.: Brookings Institution.

Linnemann, Hans. 1966. *An Econometric Study of International Trade Flows.* Amsterdam: North-Holland.

Mansfield, Edward D. 1998. The Proliferation of Preferential Trading Arrangements. *Journal of Conflict Resolution* 42 (5):523–43.

Mansfield, Edward D., and Rachel Bronson. 1997. Alliances, Preferential Trading Arrangements, and International Trade. *American Political Science Review* 91 (1):94–107.

Mansfield, Edward D., and Jack Snyder. 1995. Democratization and the Danger of War. *International Security* 20 (1):5–38.

Mansfield, Edward D., Jon C. Pevehouse, and David H. Bearce. Forthcoming. Preferential Trading Arrangements and Military Disputes. *Security Studies* 9 (1).

McKeown, Timothy J. 1991. A Liberal Trading Order? The Long-Run Pattern of Imports to the Advanced Capitalist States. *International Studies Quarterly* 35 (2):151–72.

McMillan, Susan M. 1997. Interdependence and Conflict. *Mershon International Studies Review* 41 (1):33–58.

Milner, Helen V. 1997. Industries, Governments, and the Creation of Regional Trade Blocs. In *The Political Economy of Regionalism*, edited by Edward D. Mansfield and Helen V. Milner, 77–106. New York: Columbia University Press.

Moravcsik, Andrew. 1998. *The Choice for Europe: Social Purpose and State Power from Messina to Maastricht* Ithaca, N.Y.: Cornell University Press.

Nogués, Julio J., and Rosalinda Quintanilla. 1993. Latin America's Integration and the Multilateral Trading System. In *New Dimensions in Regional Integration*, edited by Jaime de Melo and Arvind Panagariya, 278–313. New York: Cambridge University Press.

Nye, Joseph S., Jr. 1971. *Peace in Parts: Integration and Conflict in Regional Organization.* Boston: Little, Brown.

———. 1988. Neorealism and Neoliberalism. *World Politics* 40 (2):235–51.

Olson, Mancur. 1993. Discussion. In *New Dimensions in Regional Integration*, edited by Jaime de Melo and Arvind Panagariya, 122–27. New York: Cambridge University Press.

Oneal, John R., and Bruce M. Russett. 1997. The Classical Liberals Were Right: Democracy, Interdependence, and Conflict, 1950–1985. *International Studies Quarterly* 41 (2):267–94.

Oye, Kenneth A. 1992. *Economic Discrimination and Political Exchange: World Political Economy in the 1930s and 1980s.* Princeton, N.J.: Princeton University Press.

Padoan, Pier Carlo. 1997. Regional Agreements as Clubs: The European Case. In *The Political Economy of Regionalism*, edited by Edward D. Mansfield and Helen V. Milner, 107–33. New York: Columbia University Press.

Perroni, Carlo, and John Whalley. 1996. How Severe Is Global Retaliation Risk Under Increasing Regionalism? *American Economic Review (Papers and Proceedings)* 86 (2):57–61.

Petri, Peter A. 1993. The East Asian Trading Bloc: An Analytical History. In *Regionalism and Rivalry: Japan and the United States in Pacific Asia*, edited by Jeffrey A. Frankel and Miles Kahler, 21–48. Chicago: University of Chicago Press.

Pollard, Sidney. 1974. *European Economic Integration 1815–1970.* London: Thames and Hudson.

Pomfret, Richard W. T. 1988. *Unequal Trade: The Economics of Discriminatory International Trade Policies.* Oxford: Basil Blackwell.

Remmer, Karen L. 1998. Does Democracy Promote Interstate Cooperation? Lessons from the Mercosur Region. *International Studies Quarterly* 42 (1):25–52.

Russett, Bruce M. 1967. *International Regions and the International System: A Study in Political Ecology.* Chicago: Rand-McNally.

Sandholtz, Wayne, and John Zysman. 1989. 1992: Recasting the European Bargain. *World Politics* 42 (1):95–128.

Saxonhouse, Gary R. 1993. Pricing Strategies and Trading Blocs in East Asia. In *Regionalism and Rivalry: Japan and the United States in Pacific Asia*, edited by Jeffrey A. Frankel and Miles Kahler, 89–119. Chicago: University of Chicago Press.

Serra, Jaime, Guillermo Aguilar, José Córdoba, Gene Grossman, Carla Hills, John Jackson, Julius Katz, Pedro Noyola, and Michael Wilson. 1997. *Reflections on Regionalism: Report of the Study Group on International Trade.* Washington, D.C.: Brookings Institution.

Snidal, Duncan. 1985. The Limits of Hegemonic Stability Theory. *International Organization* 39 (4):579–614.

Srinivasan, T. N. 1993. Discussion. In *New Dimensions in Regional Integration,* edited by Jaime de Melo and Arvind Panagariya, 84–89. New York: Cambridge University Press.

Summers, Lawrence H. 1991. Regionalism and the World Trading System. In *Policy Implications of Trade and Currency Zones: A Symposium,* sponsored by the Federal Reserve Bank of Kansas City, 295–301. Kansas City, Mo.: Federal Reserve Bank.

Thompson, William R. 1973. The Regional Subsystem: A Conceptual Explication and Propositional Inventory. *International Studies Quarterly* 17 (1):89–117.

Tinbergen, Jan. 1962. *Shaping the World Economy: Suggestions for an International Economic Policy.* New York: The Twentieth Century Fund.

Tornell, Aaron, and Gerardo Esquivel. 1997. The Political Economy of Mexico's Entry into NAFTA. In *Regionalism Versus Multilateral Trade Arrangements,* edited by Takatoshi Ito and Anne O. Krueger, 25–56. Chicago: University of Chicago Press.

Viner, Jacob. 1950. *The Customs Union Issue.* New York: Carnegie Endowment for International Peace.

Whalley, John. 1998. Why Do Countries Seek Regional Trade Agreements? In *The Regionalization of the World Economy,* edited by Jeffrey A. Frankel, 63–83. Chicago: University of Chicago Press.

Winters, L. Alan. 1993. The European Community: A Case of Successful Integration? In *New Dimensions in Regional Integration,* edited by Jaime de Melo and Arvind Panagariya, 202–28. New York: Cambridge University Press.

Winters, L. Alan, and Zhen Kun Wang. 1994. *Eastern Europe's International Trade.* Manchester, England: Manchester University Press.

Wonnacott, Paul. 1996. Beyond NAFTA: The Design of a Free Trade Agreement of the Americas. In *The Economics of Preferential Trade Agreements,* edited by Jagdish Bhagwati and Arvind Panagariya, 79–107. Washington, D.C.: AEI Press.

Wonnacott, Paul, and Mark Lutz. 1989. Is There a Case for Free Trade Areas? In *Free Trade Areas and U.S. Trade Policy,* edited by Jeffrey J. Schott, 59–84. Washington, D.C.: Institute for International Economics.

World Trade Organization. 1995. *Regionalism and the World Trading System.* Geneva: World Trade Organization.

———. 1996. *Annual Report 1996: Trade and Foreign Direct Investment.* Vol. 1. Geneva: World Trade Organization.

Yarbrough, Beth V., and Robert M. Yarbrough. 1992. *Cooperation and Governance in International Trade: The Strategic Organizational Approach.* Princeton, N.J.: Princeton University Press.

———. 1997. Dispute Settlement in International Trade: Regionalism and Procedural Coordination. In *The Political Economy of Regionalism,* edited by Edward D. Mansfield and Helen V. Milner, 134–63. New York: Columbia University Press.

Multi-level Governance and Multi-level Metagovernance

Changes in the European Union as Integral Moments in the Transformation and Reorientation of Contemporary Statehood

BOB JESSOP

... In broad terms, governance refers to mechanisms and strategies of coordination adopted in the face of complex reciprocal interdependence among operationally autonomous actors, organizations, and functional systems. Thus, governance occurs in all social fields and its students have examined a wide range of such mechanisms and strategies, including markets, clans, networks, alliances, partnerships, cartels, associations, and states. But governance is sometimes identified more narrowly with one specific mode of coordination: reflexive self-organization based on continuing dialogue and resource-sharing among independent actors to develop mutually beneficial joint projects and to manage the contradictions and dilemmas inevitably involved in such situations. In these terms, governance can be contrasted with *ex post* coordination based on the formally rational pursuit of self-interest by individual agents, and with various forms of *ex ante* imperative coordination concerned with the pursuit of substantive goals established from above. This definition is the primary one adopted below in my discussion of multi-level governance. Such heterarchic mechanisms (as contrasted to market anarchy or bureaucratic hierarchy) have long been used in coordinating complex organizations and systems. They are especially suited for systems (non-political as well as political) that are resistant to top-down internal management and/or direct external control and that co-evolve with other (complex) sets of social relations with which their various decisions, operations, and aims are reciprocally interdependent.

STATE-CENTRIC PERSPECTIVES

State-centred approaches tend to adopt, albeit implicitly more than explicitly, the ideal-typical late nineteenth-century sovereign national state as their reference point and examine the European Union in one of two ways. Some commentators

The arguments on governance in this chapter have benefited from discussions at various times with Henrik Bang, Ulrich Beck, Frank Deppe, Edgar Grande, Liesbet Hooghe, Beate Kohler-Koch, Gary Marks, Markus Perkmann, Road Rhodes, and Gerry Stoker. I also learnt much form the Sheffield conference. Given the idiosyncrasies of its approach to governance as well as many other matters, it is especially important that the usual disclaimers apply.

note the emergence of an increasingly important *new supranational arena* in which sovereign national states attempt to pursue their own national interests. This new arena is a site of intergovernmental (here, international) relations rather than a site to which important sovereign powers have been transferred and so, however important it has become for the joint pursuit of intergovernmental interests, it does not culminate in a new state form. This approach is often termed liberal intergovernmentalism (see especially Hoffman 1995; Moravcsik 1998). Other commentators identify a tendential, emergent, upward *re-scaling* of the traditional form of the sovereign state from the national to the supranational level. This is expected to culminate sooner or later in a new form of supranational statehood. They suggest that the associated re-allocation of formal decision-making powers is leading to a more or less complex form of multi-level government under the overall authority of a supranational super-state (see Taylor 1975; Weiler 1981; Pinder 1991). Whether the joint decision making that characterizes this emerging super-state is a transitional feature or will remain once the super-state is consolidated is still uncertain.

For liberal intergovernmentalists, on the one hand, national states are, and will necessarily remain, the key players in the emerging European political space. States abandon little or none of their sovereign authority and retain a comprehensive constitutional mandate in contrast to the limited powers of the European Union. Thus interstate interactions overwhelmingly take the form of international relations oriented to the pursuit of national interests, involving at best the provisional pooling of sovereignty for the pursuit of joint interests. For some this provides a new means to enhance the power and authority of the national state (e.g. Moravcsik 1998). More generally, rather than the leading to the transcendence of the national state, intergovernmental cooperation is said at most to produce a set of interlocking international arrangements among a self-selected group of national states. While this may eventually lead to a *Staatenbund* or confederation (e.g. a United Europe of National States), it could be blocked at any stage if one or more national states feel that their respective national interests would be hurt if the process continued.

Supranationalists, on the other hand, must posit a paradoxical transitional process in which national states conspire in their own transcendence (*Aufhebung*) as they promote supranational state formation. This involves a re-territorialization of political power as the three key features of the modern sovereign state are re-scaled upwards and re-differentiated vertically: *Staatsgewalt* (organized coercion), *Staatsgebiet* (a clearly demarcated territorial domain of state authority), and *Staatsvolk* (state subjects). This is linked to the re-scaling (and, perhaps, reorganization) of mechanisms for constitutionalizing and legitimating state authority in the expanded territory. Two factors distinguish the emergence of the supranational state (or super-state) from the simple territorial expansion of a single national state that absorbs all (or some) of the territories occupied by other relevant national states. First, it emerges from an agreement among independent national states to surrender their sovereignty and transfer it to a higher authority. Second, each of the affected national states becomes a subordinate unit of the new state whilst keeping the same territorial boundaries. Thus, the new super-state is a multi-tiered state apparatus.

What do these two approaches imply for the analysis of multi-level political relations? First, in the case of the upward re-scaling (or re-territorialization) of state sovereignty, the development of multi-level government could be seen as a transitional effect of the transition. In other words, it would take the form of relations between an emergent, but still incompletely realized, supranational state and existing, not yet transcended, national states. Moreover, if the emergent, but still incomplete, supranational state were to assume the form of a bi- or multi-tiered federal super-state (*Bundesstaat*), there would also be scope for analysing the relations between the different tiers of government with the tools previously used for analysing the dynamics of other federal states. Second, in the case of international relations, multi-level government could be interpreted in terms of distinctive features of the intergovernmental institutional arrangements established by national states and/or the specific governance strategies that they pursue from time to time. In terms of the language introduced by Collinge (1999) to analyse the relativization of scale, while the EU level becomes an increasingly important *nodal* scale in the overall exercise of state power, national states continue to form the *dominant* scale. Given the complexities of state power in such circumstances, it might be more appropriate, then, to call this *multi-level governance in the shadow of national government(s)*.

While liberal intergovernmentalism appears more persuasive than supranationalism, especially for the earlier stages of European economic and political integration, the statist approach as a whole errs on three main grounds: it adopts a restricted account of the state as a sovereign territorial apparatus, employs an anachronistic reference point, and is marred by its very state-centrism. First, although the essence of the state may well consist in the *territorialization of political power*, political power can nonetheless be territorialized in different ways. Yet, analyses of the European Union as an emerging supranational state tend to focus on three features of the state apparatus: (a) its monopoly of organized coercion; (b) the constitutionalization of state power through the rule of law and a clear allocation of authority; and (c) control over its own money, taxes, and state budget. This implies that the most significant criteria for assessing whether a European super-state has emerged are the development of a European *Kriegs-und Friedensgemeinschaft* (a War- and Peace-Community, complete with a European army subject to supranational control, a European police force for internal security, and a European foreign and security policy oriented to the pursuit of distinctively European interests in the wider world system of states), an explicit European constitution (which locates sovereign power at the apex of a multi-tiered political system), . . . and a European monetary system, fisco-financial system, and a large, centralized budget. Anti-federalists already claim that the European Union has developed these features or, at least, will soon do so. Liberal intergovernmentalists note the absence of all or most of these same features and conclude that the European Union is primarily an arena in which traditional national territorial sovereign states compete to influence European policies, politics, and political regimes. Despite these disagreements, however, both sides fetishize formal constitutional and juridical features and ignore de facto state capacities and the modalities of the exercise of state power. They also focus excessively on territoriality at the expense of extra-territorial and non-territorial features.

Second, state-centred theorists overlook the successive historical transformations of the modern territorial state forms from the mid-to-late nineteenth-
century onwards. This means that they adopt an *anachronistic* model of the national
territorial state as their criterion for judging whether and how far a European
super-state has emerged. This claim can be illustrated from Willke's periodization
of the modern state. He distinguishes four stages: the *Sicherheitsstaat*, which is concerned to defend its territorial integrity at home and abroad; the *Rechtsstaat*,
which provides legal security for its subjects; the *Sozialstaat*, which establishes and
extends welfare rights to its subjects; and the *Risikostaat*, which protects its citizens
from a wide range of unexpected and uncontrollable risks. These stages are associated with the primacy of different state resources, namely, *Gewalt* (organized coercion), *Recht* (law grounded in a constitution), *Geld* (national money and state
budgets), and *Wissen* (organized intelligence) (Willke 1992). Although I do not
accept that the "risk state" is the most useful concept for the contemporary state,
Willke's approach does highlight changes in the relative primacy of state resources.
This suggests that the absence of a European army-police, constitution, and massive budgets may be less important than the presence of the EU's ability to mobilize organized intelligence and other forms of soft intervention that shape how
national and regional states deploy their respective capacities (cf. Sbragia 2000).
Overall, this suggests, first, that the key resources in today's *Staatenwelt* (world
of states) . . . are not so much coercion or money but soft law and intelligence;
and, second, that the appropriate model for analysing EU state building is not an
idealized nineteenth-century liberal state but the actually existing late twentieth-
century state—whether this be a competition state, the regulatory state, or the
Schumpeterian workfare post-national regime.

A related aspect of this second problem is the adoption of anachronistic normative assumptions about European political democracy. We should compare the
still emergent EU polity with actually existing national democracies rather than
earlier democratic systems—whether nineteenth-century liberal nightwatchman
states, interwar interventionist states, or postwar Keynesian welfare national states
with catchall governing parties. Contemporary western states tend towards
authoritarian statism, with strong executives, mass-mediatized plebiscitary democracy, and authoritarian mass parties (cf. Poulantzas 1979). Thus, if there is a democratic deficit in the European Union, it may be linked to the contemporary form
of statehood more generally, with deficits on different scales reinforcing each
other. This, in turn, suggests that attempts to develop more democratic forms of
representation and greater democratic accountability must be oriented to a different understanding of the nature and feasibility of democracy.

The third problem with state-centric analyses is precisely their state-centrism.
In particular, they tend to naturalize the state–society distinction. Yet, the boundary between state and society is socially constructed, internal to the political system, and liable to change. Thus, to adequately interpret changes in the European
Union as moments in the reorganization and reorientation of contemporary statehood, we must consider how the wider political system is organized and how
changes in its territorial boundaries may contribute to the more general reorganization of state power. . . .

GOVERNANCE–CENTRIC APPROACHES

Simple governance-centric approaches hold that the constitutionalized monopoly of violence and top-down modes of intervention associated with modern states are irrelevant or even harmful in an increasingly complex global social order. Thus they focus on the tendential *de-statization of politics (or de-hierarchization of the state)* rather than the *de-nationalization of statehood;* and they emphasize the enhanced role of reflexive self-organization in solving complex coordination problems that involve a wide range of partners or stakeholders beyond as well as within the state. This provides two bases on which to analytically distinguish de-centred forms of governance from the activities of centralized sovereign states. On the one hand, the sovereign state can be seen as the quintessential expression of hierarchy (imperative coordination) because it is, by definition, the political unit that governs but is not itself governed. Hence, beyond the sovereign state, we find the anarchy of interstate relations and/or the heterarchy of a self-organizing international society. And, on the other hand, it is primarily concerned with governing activities in its own territorial domain and defending its territorial integrity against other states. In contrast, governance is based on reflexive self-organization (networks, negotiation, negative coordination, positive concerted action) rather than imperative coordination. And it is concerned in the first instance with managing functional interdependencies, whatever their scope (and perhaps with variable geometries), rather than with activities occurring in a defined and delimited territory.

Adopting this approach leads to the view that the European Union is a major emerging site of governance that involves a plurality of state and non-state actors on different levels who attempt to coordinate activities around a series of functional problems. Without reference to non-state as well as state actors and to functional as well as territorial issues, the multi-level governance approach would be hard to distinguish from intergovernmentalism. Thus, the key question becomes how state and non-state actors manage, if at all, to organize their common interests across several territorial levels and/or across a range of functional domains. In this respect there are two main approaches: the self-described multi-level governance approach with its primary stress on the vertical dimension of multi-level governance and a parallel body of work that puts more emphasis on its horizontal dimension through the notion of the "network polity" (sometimes referred to, less fortunately, as the "network state").

In the present context, multi-level governance involves the institutionalization of reflexive self-organization among multiple stakeholders across several scales of state territorial organization. This has two implications. First, state actors would cooperate as negotiating partners in a complex network, pooling their sovereign authority and other distinctive capacities to help realize collectively agreed aims and objectives on behalf of the network as a whole. They would operate at best as *primus inter pares* in a complex and heterogeneous network rather than as immediate holders of sovereign authority in a single hierarchical command structure. Thus, the formal sovereignty of states is better seen as one symbolic and/or material resource among others rather than as the dominant resource. Indeed, from a multi-level governance perspective, sovereignty is better interpreted as a series of specific state capacities (e.g. legislative, fiscal, coercive, or other state powers) rather than as one overarching and defining feature of the state. Thus, states will supply other resources too that are not directly tied to their sovereign control over a national territory with its monopoly of organized coercion, its control over the national money, and its monopoly over taxation (Krätke 1984; Willke 1992). State involvement would therefore become less hierarchical, less centralized, and less directive in character. Other stakeholders in turn contribute other symbolic and/or material resources (e.g. private money, legitimacy, information, expertise, organizational capacities, or power of numbers) to advance collectively agreed aims and objectives. Second, in contrast to the clear hierarchy of territorial powers associated in theory with the sovereign state, multi-level governance typically involves tangled hierarchies and complex interdependence. Thus the European Union functions less as a re-scaled, supranational sovereign state apparatus than as a nodal point in an extensive and tangled web of governance operations concerned to orchestrate economic and social policy in and across many different scales of action with the participation of a wide range of official, quasi-official, private economic interests, and representatives of civil society.

The network polity (or state) provides a complementary account of the nature of the European state political system. Three variants can be noted: Castells' ambiguous claims about the European network state, a Foucauldian view that interprets recent patterns of European governance as a shift to an advanced (neo-) liberal form of governmentality, and governance-theoretical accounts of the network polity. The third variant is the most widespread [on which] I will comment briefly. . . .

. . . Conventional governance-theoretical analyses of the emerging European network polity start out from the difficulties of relying on rigid hierarchical coordination in contexts characterized by complex reciprocal interdependence among different fields across different scales (Pitschas 1995; Ladeur 1997). Ansell (2000: 311) provides a good overview of this approach and summarizes his (and other) findings as follows:

> the networked polity is a structure of governance in which both state and societal organization is vertically and horizontally disaggregated (as in pluralism) but linked together by cooperative exchange (as in pluralism). Organizational structures in the networked polity are organic rather than mechanistic, which means that both knowledge and initiative are decentralized and widely distributed. Horizontal relationships within and across organizations are at least as important as vertical relationships, and organizational relationships in general follow a pattern of many-to-many (heterarchy) rather than many-to-one (hierarchy). Exchange is diffuse and/or social rather [than] discrete and/or impersonal. The logic of governance emphasizes the bringing together of unique configurations of actors around specific projects oriented toward integrative solutions rather than dedicated programs. These project teams will criss-cross organizational turf and the boundary between public and private. State actors with a high degree of centrality in the web of interorganizational linkages will be in a position to provide facilitative leadership in constructing or steering these project teams.

Three main criticisms can be levelled at the main governance-centred approaches. . . . First, reflecting its different disciplinary roots and wide range of applications, work on governance often remains at a largely pre-theoretical stage: it is much clearer what the notion of governance excludes than what it contains. This is reflected in a proliferation of typologies of governance mechanisms constructed for different purposes and a large measure of (often unspoken) disagreement about what is included and excluded, from the overall concept. Thus, many early analyses served to establish that the EU political system cannot easily be assimilated to, or studied in terms of, a traditional conception of government; but it was unclear exactly how multi-level governance operates to produce the European polity, how objects of governance are defined in this context, and how stakeholders are defined. Later work has begun to address these problems but often does so for specific policy areas or policy networks, leaving open the issue of how different multi-level governance regimes are connected, let alone how, if at all, they may acquire a relative unity. Related to this comparative underdevelopment of the governance concept are marked ambiguities in the referents of multi-level governance. For the term is used to capture several trends in the development of the contemporary state—the de-nationalization of statehood, the de-statization of politics, and the re-articulation of territorial and functional powers. The fact that it is used to describe the interaction of three analytically distinct trends (each with its own counter-trend) or, at least, to characterize their combined impact, suggests that the concept may obscure as much as it clarifies about recent changes.

Second, governance theories tend to be closely connected to concerns about problem-solving and crisis management in a wide range of fields. This has led some governance theorists to focus on specific collective decision making or goal-attainment issues in relation to specific (socially and discursively constituted) problems and to investigate how governance contributes to problem solving (for a belated self-criticism on this score, see Mayntz 2001). But this can easily lead to a neglect of problems of governance failure, that is, the tendency for governance to fail to achieve its declared objectives; and, *a fortiori,* neglect of the various responses of different agents or subjects of governance to such failures as they attempt to engage in different forms of metagovernance (on governance failure and metagovernance, see Jessop 1998, 2002*b*). Two aspects of metagovernance are relevant here. On the one hand, because many studies of governance are concerned with specific problem fields or objects of governance, they tend to ignore questions of the relative compatibility or incompatibility of different governance regimes and their implications for the overall unity of the European project and European statehood. And, on the other hand, many empirical studies have overlooked (or, at least failed to theorize) the existence of meta-steering. This complicated process, which Dunsire (1996) has aptly termed "collibration," involves attempts to modify the relative weight and targets of exchange, hierarchy, and networking in the overall coordination of relations of complex interdependence. Yet, such meta-steering is central to many of the disputes over European integration and/or state formation and has long been a key issue on the agenda of the European Union itself, especially regarding the different steps in integration. This is reflected in the increasing resort to partnerships, comitology, social dialogue, and the mobilization of non-governmental organizations (NGO) and social movements as additional elements in the attempts to guide European integration and to steer EU policy making and implementation (cf. Scott and Trubek 2002). The "Lisbon Strategy," with its advocacy of the extension of the "open method of co-ordination," and the recent White Paper on Governance (COM 2001: 428) are the latest phases in this search for appropriate mechanisms of metagovernance (see below).

Third, work on multi-level governance and the network polity poses fundamental issues about the extent to which a network polity will remain tightly anchored in territorial terms (as opposed to being necessarily territorially embedded) despite its highly pluralistic functional concerns and its equally variable geometries. Schmitter raised just such issues in another context, when he identified four possible, ideal-typical future scenarios for the emerging Europolity. These scenarios were generated in true sociological fashion through the formation of a two-by-two property space based on two dichotomized dimensions of political regime formation: (1) an essentially Westphalian versus "neo-medieval" form of territorial organization; and (2) heterogeneous and flexible versus tightly ordered and highly stable functional representation.[1] The most interesting (and, he suggested, more plausible) scenarios both involved flexibility on the second dimension. They are a *condominio* (a neo-medieval state system with flexible functional representation and policy making) and a *consortio* (a largely intergovernmental *Europe des patries* with polycentric, incongruent flexible functional representation and policy making). A Westphalian state re-scaled to the European level with a well-ordered and congruent European system of functional representation (to produce a *stato*, which could be considered equivalent to a supranational European super-state) was deemed unlikely; and a *confederatio* (a neo-medieval territorial arrangement with tightly organized and stable functional representation) was judged even more implausible (Schmitter 1992).

As an open-ended thought experiment only loosely linked to empirical analysis, Schmitter's typological exercise is not directly relevant to my main objectives in this chapter. But it does serve two purposes in the present context. For it suggests, first, that studies of multi-level governance and/or network forms of political organization should not ignore issues of territorial organization; and, second, once both sets of issues are posed together, issues of multi-level metagovernance become central both in practice and in theory. . . .

. . . In this sense, we may be witnessing a re-scaling of the complexities of government and governance rather than a re-scaling of the sovereign state or the emergence of just one more arena in which national states pursue national interests. It is to these complexities at the national scale that I now turn in order to provide some insights into how we might rethink the emerging EU polity.

CHANGES IN STATEHOOD IN ADVANCED CAPITALIST SOCIETIES

Here, I advance three interrelated propositions about recent trends in national states. . . . These three trends are derived from theoretically informed observation of developments in developed capitalist economies in all triad regions rather than

Europe alone. In this sense, their generality across these regions (and, hence, their occurrence elsewhere) suggests they are not generated by processes peculiar to the European region. For this reason they can help to contextualize and interpret recent trends in the development of European statehood (cf. Ziltener 1999). . . .

First, there is a general trend towards the *de-nationalization* of territorial statehood. This trend should not be mistaken, *pace* Shaw (2000), for the rise of a "global state"—at least if the concept of state is to retain its core meaning of the territorialization of a centralized political authority so that a "global state" amounts to a single "world state." Instead it represents a re-articulation of different levels of the territorial organization of power within the global political system. As such it is reflected empirically in the "hollowing out" of the national state apparatus with old and new state capacities being reorganized territorially on subnational, national, supranational, and translocal levels. State powers are moved upwards, downwards, and sideways as state managers on different scales attempt to enhance their respective operational autonomies and strategic capacities. One aspect of this is the gradual loss of the *de jure* sovereignty of national states in certain respects as rule-and/or decision-making powers are transferred upwards to supranational bodies and the resulting rules and decisions are held to bind national states. Another aspect is the devolution of authority to subordinate levels of territorial organization and the development of transnational but inter-local policy making. The overall result is the proliferation of institutionalized scales of political decision making, the increasing complexity of inter-scalar articulation, and a bewildering variety of transnational relations.

Countering this trend is the enhanced role of national states in managing inter-scalar relations. That is, national states seek to control what powers or competencies go up, down, or sideways and to exercise this control so as to enhance their capacities to realize their current state projects; and they also seek, as far as possible, to retain the competence to revoke such transfers of powers and/or to implement them in ways that do least damage to their capacity to secure institutional integration and social cohesion with their corresponding territories. In this sense, even if state powers and competencies are no longer exercised in the framework of the national state *qua* "power container," the advanced states still retain considerable autonomy in regard to how to organize and re-scale state powers to promote state projects. The key question then becomes how far the movement of competencies or powers away from the national state is irreversible either constitutionally . . . or informally (such that attempts to repatriate powers would be regarded as politically illegitimate and/or economically infeasible). This said, it is generally easier for national states to reclaim powers and competencies devolved downwards or sideways than those that are shifted upwards (but see below).

Second, there is a trend towards the *de-statization* of the political system. This involves a shift from govern*ment* to govern*ance* on various territorial scales and across various functional domains. There is a movement from the central role of the official state apparatus in securing state-sponsored projects and political hegemony towards an emphasis on partnerships between governmental, para-governmental, and NGOs in which the state apparatus is often only first among equals. Governance involves the complex art of steering multiple agencies, institutions, and systems that are both operationally autonomous from one another and structurally coupled through various forms of reciprocal interdependence. . . .

Countering this shift is government's increased role in *metagovernance*. For political authorities (on and across all levels) are becoming more involved in all aspects of metagovernance: they get involved in redesigning markets, in constitutional change and the juridical re-regulation of organizational forms and objectives, in organizing the conditions for self-organization, and, most importantly, in the overall process of collibration. In this last respect, they provide the ground rules for governance and the regulatory order in and through which governance partners can pursue their aims; ensure the compatibility or coherence of different governance mechanisms and regimes; act as the primary organizer of the dialogue among policy communities; deploy a relative monopoly of organizational intelligence and information with which to shape cognitive expectations; serve as a "court of appeal" for disputes arising within and over governance; seek to rebalance power differentials by strengthening weaker forces or systems in the interests of system integration and/or social cohesion; try to modify the self-understanding of identities, strategic capacities, and interests of individual and collective actors in different strategic contexts and hence alter their implications for preferred strategies and tactics; and also assume political responsibility in the event of governance failure. These emerging metagovernance roles mean that different forms of coordination (markets, hierarchies, networks, and solidarities) and the different forms of self-organization characteristic of governance take place "in the shadow of hierarchy" (cf. Scharpf 1994: 40).

Third, there is a complex trend towards the internationalization of policy regimes. The international context of domestic state action has extended to include a widening range of extra-territorial or transnational factors and processes; it has become more significant strategically for domestic policy; the key players in policy regimes have also expanded to include foreign agents and institutions as sources of policy ideas, policy design, and implementation; and there is an increasing number of increasingly influential international regimes across a growing range of policy fields. This trend is reflected in economic and social policies as states become more concerned with "international competitiveness" in the widest sense and with the transnational constraints, consequences, and conditions of state action. It is also reflected in the development of global public policy networks and increasingly ambitious plans for the harmonization (not standardization) of policy regimes across many policy fields. Somewhat ambiguously countering yet reinforcing this trend is a growing "interiorization" of international constraints as the latter become integrated into the policy paradigms and cognitive models of domestic policy makers. . . . .

In short, these three changes do not exclude a continuing and central political role for national states. But it is a role that is necessarily redefined as a result of the more general re-articulation of the local, regional, national, and supranational levels of economic and political organization. . . .

I have introduced these three trends for one major reason. If the national state can no longer be understood in terms of the received notion of the sovereign national state, then perhaps this notion is also inadequate for studying the evolving

European Union as a state form. Indeed, we can go further: if the national state is changing in the ways that I have suggested, then the future position and activities of the European Union within a re-territorialized, de-statized, and international-ized *Staatenwelt* must be very carefully reconsidered. What we are witnessing is the re-scaling of the complexities of government and *governance* rather than the re-scaling of the sovereign state or the emergence of just one more arena in which national states pursue national interests.

Much the same point can be made through changes in the state's form and functions regarding capital accumulation. These can be studied along four key dimensions. The first concerns the state's distinctive roles in securing conditions for profitable private business. This is the broad field of economic policy and mat-ters because market forces alone cannot secure these conditions. The second dimension refers to the state's distinctive roles in reproducing labour power indi-vidually and collectively over various time spans from quotidian routines via indi-vidual lifecycles to intergenerational reproduction. This is the broad field of social policy and matters because market forces and civil society alone cannot fully secure these conditions in contemporary conditions. The third dimension refers to the main scale, if any, on which economic and social policies are decided—even if underpinned or implemented on other scales. This is important as economic and social policies are politically mediated and the scales of political organization may not coincide with those of economic and social life. The fourth concerns the rel-ative weight of the mechanisms deployed in the effort to maintain private prof-itability and reproduce labour-power by compensating for market failures and inadequacies. Top-down state intervention is just one of these mechanisms and, as is well known, states as well as markets can fail. This suggests the need for addi-tional governance mechanisms and, *a fortiori,* for an active collibrating role for the state (see above).

Referring to these four dimensions, the postwar state in northwestern Europe can be described ideal-typically as a Keynesian welfare national state (KWNS). First, the state was distinctively *Keynesian* insofar as it aimed to secure full employ-ment in a relatively closed national economy and did so mainly through demand-side management and national infrastructural provision. Second, social policy had a distinctive *welfare* orientation insofar as it (a) instituted economic and social rights for all citizens so that they could share in growing prosperity (and con-tribute to high levels of demand) even if they were not employed in the high-wage, high-growth economic sectors; and (b) promoted forms of collective consumption favourable to the Fordist growth dynamic based on mass production and mass consumption. Third, the KWNS was *national* insofar as these economic and social policies were pursued within the historically specific (and socially con-structed) matrix of a national economy, a national state, and a society composed of national citizens. Within this matrix, the national territorial state was mainly responsible for developing and guiding Keynesian welfare policies. Local and regional states acted mainly as relays for these policies; and, in addition, the lead-ing international regimes established after the Second World War were mainly intended to restore stability to national economies and national states. And, fourth, the KWNS was *statist* insofar as state institutions (on different levels) were the chief supplement and corrective to market forces in a "mixed economy" concerned with economic growth and social integration.

THE EUROPEAN UNION AND MULTI-LEVEL METAGOVERNANCE

I now apply the preceding arguments on metagovernance to the European Union as part of the more general change in the forms of statehood. . . .

It is in this context that we can best interpret the continuities and discontinuities in the development of the European Union as a moment in the structural transformation and strategic reorientation of statehood in a world of states that is not limited to Europe but extends to the global polity (cf. Hettne 1997; Shaw 2000; Sørensen 2001). For the European Union can be seen as a major and, indeed, increasingly important, supranational instance of *multi-level metagovernance* in relation to a wide range of complex and interrelated problems. While the sources and reach of these problems go well beyond the territorial space occupied by its member states, the EU is an important, if complex, point of intersection (or node) in the emerging, hypercomplex, and chaotic system of global governance (or, better, metagovernance) and is seeking to develop its own long-term "Grand Strategy" for Europe (Telò 2002: 266). But it is still one node among several within this emerging system of global metagovernance and cannot be fully understood without taking account of its complex relations with other nodes located above, below, and transversal to the European Union.

It is clearly premature at a time when the European Union is conducting yet another debate on its future governance to predict the eventual shape of what is bound to be a complex and compromise-based form of multi-level metagovernance in the shadow of a post-national form of statehood. This underlines that the development of multi-level metagovernance is a reflexive process, involving intergovernmental conferences and other modes of metaconstitutional conversation (Walker 2000). But there can be little doubt that the overall movement is towards metagovernance rather than a re-scaling of the traditional form of sovereign statehood or a revamped form of intergovernmentalism inherited from earlier rounds of European integration. As an institutionalized form of metagovernance, emphasis falls on efforts at collibration in an unstable equilibrium of compromise rather than on a systematic, consistent resort to one dominant method of coordination of complex interdependence. Apparent inconsistencies may be part of an overall self-organizing, self-adjusting practice of metagovernance within a complex division of government and governance powers. Seen as a form of metagovernance, the emphasis is on a combination of "super-vision" and "supervision," that is, a relative monopoly of organized intelligence and overall monitoring of adherence to benchmarks. But in this evolving framework, there is also a synergetic division of metagovernance labour between the European Council, the specialized Councils, and the European Commission. The European Council is the political metagovernance network of prime ministers that decides on the overall political dynamic around economic and social objectives, providing a "centripetal orientation of subsidiarity" (Telò 2002: 253), acting by qualified majority, and playing a key intergovernmental and monitoring role. The European Commission plays a key metagovernance role in organizing parallel power networks, providing expertise and recommendations, developing benchmarks, monitoring progress, exchanging best practice, promoting mutual learning, and ensuring continuity and coherence across presidencies. This is associated with increasing networking across old and new policy fields at the European level as well as with a widening range of economic, political, and social forces that are being drawn into multi-level consultation, policy formulation, and policy implementation.

New methods of multi-level metagovernance are being developed and combined in a complex system of metagovernance (cf. Scott and Trubek 2002) that is "being made more precise and applied (with adaptations as for its intensity) to other fundamental policy fields, traditionally under the competence of national and sub-national authorities: education, structural reform and internal market, technological innovation and knowledge-based society, research and social protection" (Telò 2002: 253).[2] From a strategic-relational perspective, this clearly implies a shift in the strategic selectivities of the modes of governance and metagovernance in the European Union. For, while it builds on past patterns of liberal intergovernmentalism and neo-functionalist spillover, it has its own distinctive momentum and will weaken more hierarchical forms of coordination (whether intergovernmental or supranational). It also entails complementary changes in the strategic selectivities of national states and subordinate levels of government and governance, calling for new forms of strategic coordination and new forms of (meta-)governance in and across a wide range of policy fields.

The pattern of multi-level metagovernance in the European Union is still evolving and, given the inherent tendencies towards failure typical of all major forms of governance (market, hierarchy, network, etc.) as well as metagovernance itself (Jessop 2002a,b), continuing experimentation, improvization, and adaptation is only to be expected. Nonetheless:

> the perspective would be that of a new system of democratic legitimacy and governance: multi-level (international, national, supranational, transnational), multifaced (territorial, functional, modern and post-modern) and with a multitude of actors (social, economic, political and cultural; institutional and extra-institutional), rather than that of a classical democratic normative model—federal/constitutional or democrat/republican. (Telò 2002: 266; cf. Schmitter 1992) . . .

NOTES

1. I have simplified and renamed the dichotomies on Schmitter's two axes for the sake of brevity; see his text for the complete version, expressed, as usual, inimitably.
2. Telò is commenting on the open method of coordination but his comment can be generalized to other forms of metagovernance, including partnership, comitology, social dialogue, and so forth.

Comparing Common Markets: A Revised Neo-Functionalist Model

J. S. NYE

. . . One of the pioneering political science efforts at providing a causal model of regional integration was developed under the stimulus of events in Western Europe in the late 1950's and not surprisingly it reflects these origins. . . .

In *The Uniting of Europe: Political, Social, and Economic Forces, 1950–1957* Ernst B. Haas took the partially articulated strategy of the neo-functional statesmen, related it more clearly to party and group interests, and put it in theoretical terms that have been enormously fruitful in generating further studies both in Europe and in other areas.[1] Haas, Leon Lindberg, and others have subsequently refined the original academic neo-functionalist formulations and concepts as applied to Europe; Haas and Philippe Schmitter have elaborated the approach still further in developing what is probably the most widely accepted paradigm for comparative analysis. . . .[2]

The neo-functional approach can be modified so that it is not too Europocentric to be useful as a framework for comparative analysis if the following revisions are made: (1) the dependent variable is stated less ambiguously, (2) the idea of a single path from quasi-technical tasks to political union by means of spillover is dropped and other potential process forces and paths are included; (3) more political actors are added; and (4) the list of integration conditions is reformulated in the light of comparative work that has been done on integration processes in less developed areas.

1. THE DEPENDENT VARIABLE

The ambiguities of the terms used in the study of integration are well known, and "automatic politicization," the dependent variable of the Haas-Schmitter paradigm, is no exception. . . .

Economic "liberals" restrict this operationally to what John Pinder calls "negative economic integration"[3]—the removal of discriminatory obstacles to free trade within a region. Skeptics of the liberal approach (as many economists are on the basis of the structural imperfections of markets in less developed countries) or those interested in a degree of economic interdependence which involves positive action because it costs governments some of their sovereignty or freedom of action will choose positive economic integration or economic union as the dependent variable and will measure it by the amount of shared services and degree of coordination of policies. Our choice of collective decisionmaking in the policies involved in an economic union has the virtue of closeness to the manifest motives and interests of the actors involved in integration schemes in less developed states as well as closeness to what seems to be the "neither fish nor fowl" institutional shape of the current integration process in Europe. . . .

II. ACTORS AND INTENTIONS

In the original neo-functionalist model the important actors are integrationist-technocrats and various interest groups which get governments to create a regional economic integration organization for a variety of convergent aims. Once done and depending on the degree of initial commitment this action unleashes the new forces of sector imbalance or *engrenage,* increased flows of transactions, and involvement of an increasing number of social groups which gradually focus their activities at the regional level.

These process forces or mechanisms in turn lead to two outcomes: (1) National governmental decisionmakers, under the joint pressures of the inconvenience of sector integration and of groups eager to preserve their gains from sector integration, agree to increase the initial grant of power to the regional institutions and (2) group activities and eventually mass loyalties increasingly flow to the regional center as it answers more and more of the interests previously satisfied by the national governments. The net effect is a continuous and automatic process leading to political unions if there are: (1) certain "background" conditions of symmetry between the national units, social pluralism, high transaction flows, and elite complementarity; (2) initiation conditions mentioned above; and (3) process conditions of technocratic decision-making style ("supranationality in practice"), rising transactions, and adaptability on the part of governments. . . .

The impact of Charles de Gaulle on the process of European integration led Haas to revise this theory and add another type of political actor—what he called the actor with "dramatic-political" aims.[4] Even in a setting like post-war Europe in which politics is highly bureaucratized and welfare is a predominant popular concern[5] a dramatic political leader was able to prevail over leaders with incremental economic aims and to divert the integration process from the predicted course. . . .

In the original neo-functionalist model, developed at a time when many observers were noting the bureaucratization of politics, the decline of ideology, and the growing popular concern for welfare and when foreign policies were held more closely in the vise of cold-war bipolarity, the national decisionmakers in the model were assumed to be economic incrementalists and thus be responsive to the economic logic of integration. It was thought that the technocrat-politicians could bypass the electoral or support politicians and forge links to the ever stronger regional organization until *engrenage* had proceeded so far that it was too late for anyone to change the pattern.

In this sense the neo-functionalists relied on "integration by stealth" and the positive role of popular ignorance. To a considerable extent this fit the early days of LAFTA and CACM. This picture is less accurate as a description of the *initiation* of European integration (Robert Schuman, Konrad Adenauer, and Alcide de Gaspari obviously played vital roles), but it is reasonably accurate for the workings of the ECSC. The protective cloak of noncontroversiality quickly wears out, however, as more sensitive interests are touched and as political heat generated by the integration process grows. Indeed there are some political climates in which economic issues are sufficiently highly politicized from the start that the cloak of noncontroversiality cannot be worn in the first place. Thus whatever the value of the simplified neo-functionalist model for explaining the early stages of integration in some settings, it quickly loses its explanatory value. . . .

Once we admit that (except for the early stages of integration in certain settings) important decisions affecting the integration process must be channeled through the political legitimizing leadership, we greatly enrich the model by admitting the possibility of negative as well as positive syndromes of responses resulting from the impact of the process forces upon the national decisionmakers. Actors can pull back from common tasks and institutions as well as increase their scope and authority.

There is also a third possible syndrome of responses to the impact of the process forces—the maintenance of the status quo. If the process forces are not too strong, the political leaders may prefer to tolerate the inconvenience of living with them rather than face what from their view are the political costs of negative or positive feedback. . . .

III. PROCESS MECHANISMS

A wide variety of reasons may be needed to account for the initial creation of a regional economic organization. Among the most important are the rise of a new reformist elite with incremental economic goals that is conscious of the welfare implications of existing market sizes and events in the external environment that impress upon both mass opinion and political legitimizing leaders the political cogency or usefulness of asserting their regional identity in an institutional form. . . .

As we have seen, the early neo-functionalist model gave essentially four process mechanisms that follow the creation of a common market: (1) the inherent functional linkages of tasks; (2) increasing flows or transactions; (3) deliberate linkages and coalitions; and (4) economic pressure groups, including at a later state the formation of groups at the regional level. Subsequent work by other scholars has suggested at least three other process mechanisms that may arise or be enhanced by the creation of a regional economic organization: (5) involvement of external actors; (6) regional ideology and intensification of regional identity; and (7) elite socialization.

These process mechanisms can be divided into those which follow from the liberalization or removal of state barriers to the free flow of goods and factors and those which are created by the establishment of administrative institutions. Whether political decisionmakers can ignore the pressures for decisions that the process mechanisms create or whether they will be forced into integrative or disintegrative decisions will depend upon the strength of the process mechanisms and upon conditions to be outlined below. . . .

A. Functional Linkage of Tasks

The concept of "spillover" has frequently been misapplied to cover any sign of increased cooperation, thus robbing it of its explanatory value. . . . Haas used the term to cover both perceived linkages between problems arising out of their inherent technical characteristics and linkages deliberately created or overstated by political actors (what might be called "cultivated spillover"). Despite these problems and the lesser effectiveness of the force than was originally believed to be the case, the perception that imbalances created by the functional interdependence or inherent linkages of tasks can press political actors to redefine their common tasks remains an important insight. In Walter Hallstein's words, "the material logic of the facts of integration urges us relentlessly on from one step to the next, from one field to another."[6]

For example, after tariff barriers were reduced in the European Economic Community (EEC), profit margins of firms and their competitive positions were more strongly affected by different systems of taxation, and this fact led to the adoption by the EEC countries of a common system of calculating tax on value added. When French costs began to increase relative to those of the Federal Republic of Germany (West Germany) by about 3 percent a year (i.e., inflation was higher in France than in West Germany), the initial result was the monetary crisis of November 1968 and French imposition of measures to restrain trade in order to protect its balance of payments. The longer term impact was to persuade the governments to accept a plan proposed by the Commission of the European Communities for coordination of short- and medium-term economic policies. . . .

The redefinition of tasks need not mean an upgrading of common tasks. The response can also be negative. If the conditions to be spelled out below have not resulted in a positive experience for a major coalition of actors, the inconvenience created by the imbalance may be overcome by undoing the original linkage. . . .

B. Rising Transactions

If the initiation of a regional integration scheme gives rise to an unexpected response by societal forces that result in a large rise in transactions . . . , political actors may (1) be faced with the overburdening of the institutions they have established for dealing with such transactions and with the need to curtail the transactions; (2) try to deal with them through national measures; or (3) increase the capacity of the common institutions that they have established.

. . . In other words, rising transactions need not lead to a significant widening of the scope (range of tasks) of integration but may lead rather to the intensification of central institutional capacity to handle a particular task.

Whether the feedback from rising transactions has a positive or negative effect on further progress toward economic union depends, again, on changes in the conditions below. . . .

C. Deliberate Linkages and Coalition Formation

Coalition formation tends to be based on what we called "cultivated spillover." In contrast to pure spillover in which the main force comes from a common perception of the degree to which problems are inextricably intertwined in a modern economy, problems are deliberately linked together into package deals not on the basis of technological necessity but on a basis of political and ideological projections and political possibilities. . . .

Two contrasting examples come from the EEC. A 1960 package deal hastened internal tariff cuts to satisfy those eager to advance the common market and simultaneously lowered the external tariff to satisfy those concerned about a loss of foreign trade. In contrast, in 1965 the Commission of the European Communities was unsuccessful with its proposed package deal of agricultural prices favorable to France, direct revenues for the EEC commission, and direct elections to the European Parliament.[7] The proposal touched off the 1965 EEC crisis, and there were no more successful large-scale package deals until the summit meeting at the Hague in December 1969. In other words, bureaucratic activism can also lead to bureaucratic slapdown in which packages are untied by politicians. . . .

D. Elite Socialization

The initiation of an integration scheme creates opportunities both for political decisionmakers attending meetings and bureaucrats seconded to regional institutions to develop personal ties and a possible corporate feeling. Leon Lindberg and Lawrence Scheinman have both focused attention on the increased contacts of politicians, national bureaucrats, and commission bureaucrats through the various meetings and institutions of the EEC. . . .[8]

If the conditions listed below are not favorable or change in an unfavorable direction, however, increased personal contact may enhance the potential acrimony (as it did, for example, in East Africa in 1963). Even if the contact results in socialization of political or bureaucratic decisionmakers into a system perspective, if integrative conditions become worse this may merely result in the isolation of the most prointegration actors from political effectiveness. Some accounts of bureaucrats returning from Brussels to Paris and Bonn support this view. . . .

E. Regional Group Formation

Once a regional integration scheme is established, it may serve as the stimulus for private groups to create various types of formal and informal nongovernmental regional organizations to reflect and protect their common interests at the regional level. In addition to representing a shift of political activity toward the regional level and a potential source of regional pressure on national governments these nongovernmental groupings themselves have elite socialization effects. . . .

In general, however, these regional nongovernmental organizations remain a weak force. In many cases the types of interests that are aggregated at the regional level tend to be very general, with more specific interests and structures remaining at the national level. For instance, despite the existence of regional trade union secretariats in Brussels, the idea of collective bargaining at the European level in response to the creation of a European market has not taken hold—in part because of the divisions in the labor movement but also because of the importance of national governmental power in collective bargaining. . . .

F. Ideological-Identitive Appeal

A taste shared by smaller groups to be identified as a larger group is frequently one of the factors that leads to initiation of regional integration schemes. Once established, a regional organization, by the symbol of its existence as well as by its actions (e.g., the efforts of the Hallstein commission, particularly before 1965), may heighten this sense of identitive appeal. . . .

In some cases a sense of permanence and strong identitive appeal can help groups or governments to tolerate short-term losses or sacrifices in the belief that they will be requited later. Finally, the stronger the myth of permanence, the more likely are businessmen to invest on the basis of the larger market and thus to make the myth reality in the concrete form of new industrial investments—as happened in the early days of the EEC. . . .

G. Involvement of External Actors in the Process

The original neo-functionalist formulation paid insufficient attention to the role of external factors in integration processes. . . . We are now beyond the stage of the initial criticism when we can talk of "catalysts" or "external factors" in general terms.[9] Building upon the distinction between passive and active external factors (those of a broad nature not affected by the process contrasted with those that represent deliberate action by external actors affected by the creation of a regional scheme), I include regional actor *perceptions* of the external situation as one of the integrative conditions that we will examine below and consider only *involvement* of external actors in the integration scheme as a process mechanism.

An integration process can involve various actors, including other governments, other international organizations, and nongovernmental actors such as international corporations. For example, the United States Agency for International Development and the United Nations Economic Commission for Latin America have both played important roles in the Central American Common Market. . . .

In summary, the response of political decisionmakers to the pressures generated by these process mechanisms will depend partly on the strength of the pressures— i.e., are they weak enough that the inconvenience they create is easier to tolerate than the political costs that might be incurred by a positive or negative response? . . .

IV. INTEGRATIVE POTENTIAL

The second determinant of the type of response is a set of conditions that we will refer to as the integrative potential of a region. . . . The following list of conditions that constitute the integrative potential of a region is based on the Haas and Schmitter checklist but with certain omissions, additions, and restatements. The first amendment is to drop their categorization by stages (background, initiation, process) and replace it with a distinction between structural conditions which are conceived as relatively stable variables more determined by factors other than the integration process and perceptual conditions which are quite volatile during an integration process and are determined more by the integration process itself. . . .

A. Structural Conditions

The structural conditions that affect the nature of the initial commitment and the later impact of the process forces that follow the initiation of an economic integration scheme are as follows:

I. Symmetry or Economic Equality of Units
This is restatement of Haas's and Schmitter's "size in the specific functional context of the union." At first glance it seems to contradict the proposition that "core areas" and unequal size may be helpful conditions for integration. Citing Karl Deutsch and Amitai Etzioni, Bruce Russett argues that there is no

> very convincing theory or evidence about international integration that indicates that the prospective members of a new unit should be the same size. (On the contrary, the idea of a powerful core area to provide centripetal force is rather more persuasive.)[10]

Yet others argue that economic integration cannot be successful between unequal partners. Given the tendency of industry to cluster to take advantage of the external economies available from the presence of other industries in more developed parts of a region, there is a danger that (in Gunnar Myrdal's terms) the "spread" effects of increased economic activity will be less important to the poorer areas than the "backwash" effect of the attraction of resources from the poorer to the richer areas. A case frequently cited is the deleterious effect of the unification of Italy upon southern Italy in the nineteenth century.

There are several points worth noting about this apparent theoretical dispute over the role of size in integration theory. First, it vanishes in the face of more precise formulation of what we mean by integration. What may be true of one type of integration (for example, trade) may not be of another (for example, political union). Problems of unequal size have plagued the Latin American Free Trade Association, but they did not stop the Sardinian leadership in the creation and maintenance of common institutions in Italy in the face of an elite sense of national identity and within the nineteenth century international system in which an aspect of coercion was acceptable. And it is worth remembering that Deutsch's original hypothesis about "cores" was formulated in relation to a number of historical cases of security community.... [11]

If inequality is interpreted not in simple terms of square miles, or even gross national product (GNP), but rather as a level of development with per capita GNP as the indicator, a simple scattergram quickly indicates a relationship between trade integration and level of development. The number of cases is few, but it seems roughly true that in nonhegemonial regional economic organizations the more equal the level of development (measured by per capita GNP), the higher the regional trade integration (intraregional exports as a percentage of total exports).... Moreover, no economic integration scheme (common market or free trade area) which does over 20 percent of its trade intraregionally has more than a 2:1 ratio of difference in per capita incomes (Portugal, in EFTA, is the exception).

If inequality is interpreted not in terms of level of development but in terms of total size of the economy (measured in GNP), then size seems to have a very different effect in less developed than in developed areas. Relatively high degrees of trade integration have been achieved by integration schemes among developed countries in which the ratio of the largest to smallest economies (in GNP) is more than 5:1. Among less developed countries, however, the only schemes with trade integration over 20 percent have ratios of largest to smallest (in terms of GNP) of less than 2.5:1. It almost looks as if the lower the per capita income of the area, the greater the necessary homogeneity in size of economy.

While one must be cautious about using this evidence when the number of cases is so few, there are also intuitive grounds for believing that where income is lower and welfare is scarcer problems of its distribution are likely to be more strongly contested. In addition, it is more likely that backwash effects and clustering of industry to take advantage of external economies will be more politically apparent and difficult to resolve in smaller and poorer economies with fewer poles of growth. . . .

2. Elite Value Complementarity

Whether corresponding elite groups do or do not think alike makes a difference; witness the effects of the addition of a Gaullist elite to the constellation of Christian-Democratic and Socialist decision-makers in Europe in the mid-1950's. But which elites count and how much complementarity is necessary? . . .

. . . For our purpose it is the elites who control economic policy decisions that matter. These are not the same in all settings and may change over time with the politicization of a process as we shall see below. In general, the greater the complementarity of elites with effective power over economic policy as reflected in similar statements and policies toward the most salient political-economic issues in their region, the better the conditions for positive or integrative response to the pressure for decisions arising from the process mechanism.

3. Pluralism (Modern Associational Groups)

Functionally specific, universalistic, achievement-oriented groups in all member states were important components of the neo-functional path in Europe. The relative absence or weakness of such groups in many less developed countries has been shown to make integration more difficult . . . by depriving regional bureaucrats of potential allies and by depriving governments of channels of information useful in the formation of realistic economic policy.

. . . Our hypothesis is that the greater the pluralism in all member states, the better the conditions for an integrative response to the feedback from the process forces.

4. Capacity of Member States to Adapt and Respond

This is a slight adaptation of the Haas-Schmitter condition to include Deutsch's concept of "internal noise" which inhibits the capacity to respond.[12] Governments in less developed countries are notoriously weak in their capacity to commit their societies. . . .

Moreover, competing demands of internal instability . . . on decisionmakers' attention may hinder the capacity of the more prosperous states to "hear" the messages from their weaker partners or to respond to them. . . .

Our hypothesis for this condition is that the greater the internal instability and other factors that diminish the capacity of the key decisionmakers in economic policy (both public and private) to adapt and respond to problems and crises, the more likely that feedback from the process mechanisms will have a negative effect. . . .

B. Perceptual Conditions

The following three perceptual conditions, on the other hand, are highly affected by the process of integration.

I. Perceived Equity of Distribution of Benefits

All students of comparative regional integration emphasize the importance of this condition. It differs from the structural condition of symmetry because it is based on perception by the actors. There is often a gap between the actual changes in economic symmetry in a region and the perception of equity among decision-makers.

The politics of regional economic integration is not only the "politics of cooperation" but also the "politics of status" between states that have been traditional rivals. The cooperative or welfare aspect is more like a nonzero-sum game, and it is relevant . . . to use aggregate economic data to show that all states are better off or that even if a state like Honduras has not gained as much as El Salvador or Tanzania as much as Kenya, it is better off than it would have been without the common market.

The status aspect, however, is more like a zero-sum game. What matters is how decisionmakers perceive that they have gained or lost status or rank in relation to their neighbors. This is not always predictable from the hard data of economic changes. Rather it will be affected by the sensitivity of the traditional competition (such as the Franco-German rivalry) between the states and the personal predilections of particular decisionmakers. . . . The hypothesis accompanying this condition is of course that the higher the perceived equitable distribution in all countries, the better the conditions for further integration.

2. Perceptions of External Cogency

The way that regional decisionmakers perceive the nature of their external situation and the manner in which they should respond to it is an important condition determining agreement on further integration. There are a variety of relevant perceptions such as a sense of external threat from a giant neighbor, loss of status felt by Europeans and Latin Americans as a result of bipolarity and simple demonstration effects ("everybody's doing it"). . . .

Other aspects of external dependence might be operationalized by looking at economic and military aid and perhaps also at drawings on the International Monetary Fund (IMF), at alliances, and at organizational memberships. Again, however, the important question is the existence of common perceptions of the cogency of such dependence, particularly when different dependences pull in different directions—e.g., differing French and West German perceptions of what to do about dependence on the United States and the way these differences affected their policies toward European integration. . . . [13]

3. Low (or Exportable) Visible Costs

A key tenet of neo-functional strategy is to make integration seem relatively cost-less by carefully choosing the initial steps. Where visible costs are low it is easier to get agreement on the first steps that will start the process of *engrenage*. Over time, of course, costs are likely to become higher and more visible. . . .

Regional integration schemes usually involve a strong protectionist element, whether it be European farmers or Central American manufacturers or national- ized industries in the LAFTA countries. Strictly speaking, this protection repre- sents a real cost to consumers *inside* the region (compensated in the long run perhaps if there are infant industries being protected, though this is hardly the case in European coal and agriculture) as well as to foreigners in terms of their trade that is diverted (which may not be fully compensated by new trade created).[14]

Nonetheless, in accord with Harry Johnson's theory of economic nationalism the widely dispersed and less visible costs of protectionist subsidies are not as polit- ically influential as are the concrete benefits to the specific groups being protected. Thus to the extent that it looks as though only outsiders are being hurt and the vis- ible costs can be "exported," agreement on integration policies may be easier. . . .

V. PHASING AND CONSEQUENCES

. . .What is the likely sequence of interactions between forces, conditions, and actors over time? Do the relationships change during the course of a process? Is the process likely to be continuous, even assuming no major change in exogenous forces? Obvi- ously, the sequences and phasing of integration process will vary with the politics of each region. Nonetheless, we can introduce some order into the study by formulat- ing certain hypotheses about the likely shape of the integration process and try to establish the conditions under which those hypotheses are likely to be true.

We will hypothesize four conditions that are likely to characterize an integra- tion process over time: (1) politicization; (2) redistribution; (3) reduction of alter- natives; and (4) externalization. . . .

A. Politicization

If, over the course of time, positive responses to the process forces lead to higher levels of integration (stronger institutions and greater coordination of economic policy), we would expect the process to become more "political." By political we mean the process by which conflicting visions of a common interest are agitated or settled.[15]

At the other end of the continuum of controversy are technical procedures which involve the choice of "optimal" solutions by reputed experts by apparently "rational" criteria. It is worth noting, however, that a number of subjects that are apparently technical in the sense of depending on expertise may not be amenable to purely technical procedures. For example, European cooperation in the science and technology field has been highly politicized or controversial right from the outset perhaps because of its symbolic content and the difficulties of making precise calcu- lations of benefits in a new field.[16] Similarly, economic issues which fall closer to the technical-administrative end of the continuum of controversialism in the European context are frequently highly politicized from the outset in African settings.

We would expect politicization to increase during the course of an integra- tion process for several reasons. More groups become involved through the effects of rising transactions, inherent linkages, or deliberate coalition formation. The larger the numbers, the more likely the possible divergent interpretations of the common interest in integration. The growth of the powers of the central institutions not only makes them more visible to mass opinion but may also stimulate action by groups opposed to integration, including national bureaucrats jealous of incursion into their powers. . . .

The greater the politicization of subjects, the less amenable they are to the quiet technocratic decisionmaking style that

> stresses the role of uninstructed experts who tend to agree among themselves with respect to the reasoning patterns and antecedent conditions relevant to a decision, *and* with respect to the outcome to be attained.[17]

This does not necessarily mean that further integration is impossible. It does mean, however, that reaching decisions may be more difficult and involve a wider range of forces. . . .

B. Redistribution

As economic integration progresses, it is likely to have an effect on the distribution of welfare, status, and power both among groups within the member states and between the member states themselves. Within states certain groups or areas are more likely than others to benefit from rising transactions, package deals and coalitions, or alliances with external actors. Certain political actors and bureaucrats will benefit more than others from their involvement in integration, particularly if public support for integration increases during the process. . . .

Redistribution is not totally bad for an integration process though it has obviously unfavorable effects in a region. . . . In Europe the prospect of redistribution is a major incentive for actors to push for further progress in integration. Roy Blough and Jack Behrman have argued that one of the causes of stagnation in LAFTA is the existence of so many guarantees against redistribution that there are few incentives for integration.[18] A certain amount of redistribution is necessary whether it be a new technocratic elite increasing its power or an area or two within a market serving as leading points of growth.

A crucial question with redistribution is the phasing of the growth of the process forces flowing from liberalization compared to those coming from the common institutions. If the role of the common institutions is increased and agreement is reached on common approaches, for example, to regional incomes policy or industrial location policy, the most severe effects of redistribution may be controlled. However, such policies involve difficult political coordination (and a more consciously perceived sacrifice of sovereign control). In the short run, governments often find it politically easier to promote integration indirectly ("negative" integration) through liberalization of their respective trade policies than to agree upon common approaches and the consequences of liberalization ("positive" integration). . . .

C. Reduction of Alternatives

An early neo-functionalist hypothesis was that integration was automatic. Once *engrenage* took place, it would become increasingly difficult and costly and thus impossible for political leaders to disentangle their nations. Although the original formulation was oversimplified and therefore misleading, the notion of automaticity was based on a useful insight. The sovereign alternatives open to political decisionmakers are reduced as an integration process goes forward.

As transactions rise and more groups (including external actors) become involved, the pressures on decisionmakers are greater. Similarly, the stronger the ideological-identitive appeal becomes. . . , the stronger the pressure on the political decisionmaker and the fewer his political alternatives. As more tasks become interrelated through inherent links or package deals the costs of disintegrative actions become greater because there is the danger of pulling the whole house of cards down.

While it would at first appear that reduced alternatives would have an unambiguously good effect over the course of the integrative process, higher costs do not necessarily determine the actions of all political decisionmakers. Having fewer alternatives is not the same as having no alternatives.

In some cases decisionmakers may not perceive or may deliberately ignore diminished alternatives and thus precipitate crises. In other cases the knowledge that other countries are equally ensnared by the diminished alternatives may be a positive incentive for the leader more willing to practice brinksmanship to provoke crises deliberately. Finally, the further integration progresses, the larger the crises are likely to become both because a greater degree of interdependence has been created and because the resistance of some political leaders may become more intense as integration approaches the security and identitive areas of greatest concern to them. . . .

D. Externalization

Schmitter has argued that whatever the original intentions, as integration proceeds member states will be increasingly forced to hammer out a collective external position vis-à-vis nonparticipant third parties because the further integration proceeds, the more third parties will react to it, either with support or hostility. . . . [19]

While a sense of external identity is important in the early stages of the process and perhaps again at higher levels of integration, it seems that too great involvement in the problems of external policies in the middle stages of integration may have a braking effect. It diverts attention, raises anticipated problems that make package deals and coalitions based on the existing structure of interests more difficult, and precipitates unnecessary crises. These in turn may stimulate opposition groups and speed up politicization through the involvement of political leaders and mass opinion in sensitive areas at too early a stage.

VI. CONCLUSIONS

What are the likely effects of the outcomes of an integration process over time? . . . First, in most settings the process of politicization means that low-cost integration and technocratic style decisionmaking procedures are unlikely to last very long and certainly not until a widespread popular support or a powerful coalition of intensely concerned interests have developed to the point at which they determine the decisions of political decisionmakers.

Second, the ability to reach difficult political agreement on "positive integration" measures to cope with the problems created by redistribution is likely to lag behind the forces created by more easily agreed upon liberalization measures. Alternatively, in settings in which market forces are weak and liberalization cannot be agreed upon it seems likely that process forces will also be weak.

Third, the sense of reduced alternatives and the precipitation of larger crises will probably fail to have an integrative effect the closer the issues come to the security and identitive areas that are of greatest concern to popular political leaders. These are also the areas in which they are least likely to have the clear overriding common interests that make crises productive rather than destructive. Finally, the pressures both inside and outside the region for a common external policy are likely to develop more rapidly than popular or group support for a high degree of integration develops in these generally more controversial fields.

In brief, unless the structure of incentives offered by the international system is seriously altered, the prospects for common markets or microregional economic organizations leading in the short run (of decades) to federation or some sort of political union capable of an independent defense and foreign policy do not seem very high. . . .

If common markets do not lead to federation, does this mean that they must slip backward or fall apart? Is there no point of equilibrium in between? The belief that common markets must go forward or fall backward is widely accepted. Indeed, it was an essential part of the neo-functional myth. . . .

While this does seem to be the case when one looks at integration from the perspective of a simple neo-functionalist model, it no longer seems necessarily to be the case according to our revised model. Indeed our basic hypothesis is that most political decisionmakers will opt for the status quo at any level as long as the process forces or popular pressures are not strong enough to make this choice unbearable for them. . . .

Moreover, as Lawrence Krause and Leon Lindberg have pointed out and the case of EFTA shows, this type of market integration need not greatly strengthen the regional institutions. In short, it seems most likely that under the current structure of international incentives dramatic-political decisionmakers will find some point of equilibrium at which they would rather tolerate the inconvenience of the existing level of process forces than incur the greater political costs of full integration or disintegration. . . .

Looked at from the perspective of our model, there are several reasons why the success of integration is limited in less developed areas. In the first place the economic structure of underdevelopment is likely to result in weaker process forces. Taking the forces resulting from liberalization—imperfect market mechanisms, lack of entrepreneurial resources, and inadequate infrastructure—all inhibit the rate at which transactions rise. Looser interdependence of economic sectors limits the pressures arising from inherent linkage of tasks. In addition, in many cases ideological biases against capitalist market mechanisms and nationalist reactions against external actors attracted by the prospects of a larger market lead to political inhibitions of the process forces resulting from liberalization.

Turning to the process forces resulting from the creation of new institutions, lack of administrative resources hampers regional bureaucracies. Premature politicization of economic issues greatly reduces the scope for bureaucratic initiative and quietly arranged package deals. . . .

This is not to say that all economic issues are emotionally laden "high politics" in less developed countries and technically soluble "low politics" in developed settings. The salience of an issue area and its susceptibility to a consensual style of decision varies with each particular political context. There is greater monetary coordination in East Africa than in Europe (where it involves questions of Franco-German balance of power).[20] Labor migration is easy for the Nordic countries but not for Central America. On the question of a common external tariff the situation is reversed. The basic point, however, is that in many less developed areas a greater number of economic issue areas tend to become highly politicized than is the case in more developed settings.

Not only is it probable that process forces will be weaker in less developed areas but the integrative potential is likely to be lower. As we saw above, the lower the income and the lower the level of industrialization, the lower the tolerance to differences in symmetry and the more sensitive the problem of equitable distribution of benefits. Not only does the problem of redistribution require more coordination of positive policy and thus involve a greater sense of loss of sovereignty, but the resources available for compensating for redistribution are in shorter supply, and many of the lags result from problems of human resource and infrastructure that cannot be cured in the short run.

Low levels of modern associational pluralism restrict the role of groups in the integration process at the same time that traditional pluralism and other problems of internal malintegration are likely to create a setting of internal noise that restricts the capacity of governments to adapt and respond. Finally, perceived external cogency is possibly higher for less developed countries because of their high dependence on a few commodities which often have sluggish growth rates and because of their vulnerability to penetration by outside actors. But where this vulnerability differs among member states and where dependence of member states is on different outside forces (e.g., British and French Africa and the situation in the Caribbean),[21] external cogency may not be perceived in the same way by all the potential partners.

NOTES

1. Ernst B. Haas, *The Uniting of Europe: Political, Social, and Economic Forces, 1950–1957* (Standford, CA: Stanford University Press, 1958).

2. Leon N. Lindberg, *The Political Dynamics of European Economic Integration* (Stanford, CA: Stanford University Press, 1963); Ernst B. Haas and Philippe C. Schmitter, "Economics and Differential Patterns of Political Integration: Projections about Unity in Latin America," *International Organization,* Autumn 1964 (Vol. 18, No. 4), pp. 705–737.

3. John Pinder, "Problems of Economic Integration," in G. R. Denton (ed.), *Economic Integration in Europe* (London: Weidenfeld and Nicolson, 1969), p. 145.

4. Ernst B. Haas, "The *Uniting of Europe* and the Uniting of Latin America," *Journal of Common Market Studies,* June 1967 (Vol. 5, No. 4), pp. 315–343.

5. See Stephen Graubard (ed.), *A New Europe?* (Boston: Houghton Mifflin Co., 1964).

6. *European Community,* June 1967 (No. 103), p. 11.

7. See John Lambert, "The Constitutional Crisis 1965–66," *Journal of Common Market Studies,* May 1966 (Vol. 4, No. 3), pp. 195–228.

8. See Lawrence Scheinman, "Some Preliminary Notes on Bureaucratic Relationships in the European Economic Community," *International Organization,* Autumn 1966 (Vol. 20, No. 4), pp. 750–773; and Leon Lindberg and Stuart Scheingold, *Europe's Would-Be Polity: Patterns of Change in the European Community* (Englewood Cliffs, NJ: Prentice-Hall, 1970), chapter 4.

9. J. S. Nye, "Patterns and Catalysts in Regional Integration," *International Organization,* Autumn 1965 (Vol. 19, No. 4), pp. 870–884.

10. Bruce M. Russett, *International Regions and the International System: A Study in Political Ecology* (Chicago: Rand McNally & Co., 1967), p. 21.

11. Contrary to the "balance of power" theory, security-communities seem to develop most frequently around cores of strength.... Karl W. Deutsch, and others, *Political Community and the North Atlantic Area: International Organization in the Light of Historical Experience* (Princeton, NJ: Princeton University Press, 1957), p. 10.

12. See Karl Deutsch, "Communication Theory and Political Integration," in Philip Jacob and James Toscano (ed.), *The Integration of Political Communities* (Philadelphia: J. B. Lippincott Co., 1964), pp. 46–74.

13. Stanley Hoffmann, "The European Process at Atlantic Crosspurposes," *Journal of Common Market Studies,* February 1965 (Vol. 3, No. 2), pp. 85–101.

14. Harry G. Johnson, *Economic Nationalism in Old and New States* (London: George Allen and Unwin, 1968), chapter 1.

15. E. C. Banfield, in *A Dictionary of the Social Sciences,* ed. by Julius Gould and William L. Kolb (Glencoe, IL: Free Press [compiled under the auspices of the United Nations Educational, Scientific and Cultural Organization], 1964.

16. See Robert L. Pfaltzgraff and James L. Deghand, "European Technological Collaboration: The Experience of the European Launcher Development Ogranization," *Journal of Common Market Studies,* September 1968 (Vol. 7, No. 1), pp. 22–34; also Robert Gilpin, *France in the Age of the Scientific State* (Princeton, NJ: Princeton University Press, 1968), chapter 12.

17. Haas and Schmitter, *International Organization,* Vol. 18, No. 4, p. 715.

18. Roy Blough and Jack N. Behrman, "Problems of Regional Integration in Latin America," (Committee for Economic Development, Supplementary Paper No. 22), in *Regional Integration and the Trade of Latin America* (New York: Committee for Economic Development, 1968), p. 31.

19. Philippe C. Schmitter, "Three Neo-Functionalist Hypotheses about International Integration," *International Organization,* Winter 1969 (Vol. 23, No. 1), p. 165.

20. Hans O. Schmitt, "Capital Markets and the Unification of Europe," *World Politics,* January 1968 (Vol. 20, No. 2). pp. 228–244.

21. See Aaron Segal, *The Politics of Caribbean Economic Integration* (Puerto Rico: Institution of Caribbean Studies, 1968).

CHAPTER 7

Transformative Change and Global Governance

We began this reader with a discussion of how international politics is organized. By focusing on international organization in the collective singular, we attempted to avoid limiting analysis to either the system of nation-states or the output of particular international organizations. Following much research in the field of international organization, we aimed to cast the net wider by considering a wide array of both formal and informal institutions and regimes. We also emphasized that international organization is an approach to world politics, rather than just a subfield of international relations. Since this approach does not take the existence of international trans-historical structures for granted, it has both a "critical" and a "practical" dimension.

As the articles in this reader indicate, various important questions arise when order is no longer identified exclusively with hierarchy, but rather seen as the product of many different arrangements that cut across the traditional distinctions of hierarchy and anarchy, the inside and the outside of nation-states, and the public and the private spheres. By focusing less on power relations, the resulting approach is likely to become less parsimonious and elegant than many traditional approaches to the study of international relations. In this chapter, however, David Dessler argues that parsimony is highly overrated in theory-building and can become quite debilitating if not applied with extreme caution.

Much of the reader has addressed the complexities of the organization of international affairs. Instead of assuming that there is a best way of organizing the international system, we saw that there are many ways of organizing international affairs. Which way is chosen will depend on the trade-offs among them, the cognitive limitations of decision makers, how the problem in question is framed, and which solutions are viewed as legitimate by the actors involved. One complicating factor is that it is often difficult to agree on what is legitimate. Equally, what is viewed as a legitimate course of action may have unanticipated adverse consequences. For example, many observers now recognize that globalization is not an inevitable process, but rather one that is due to policy choices. While these choices—including an open trade regime and rules that promote capital mobility—are widely viewed as legitimate, some observers argue that they have had a harmful impact on the environment, that they have fostered greater income inequality, and the like. Thus it is not accidental that an emerging theme in the field of international organization is that of "global governance," in which questions of justice and recognition loom large.

But while this literature often implies that governance of the global system is becoming more effective, there is plenty of evidence that fundamental challenges lie ahead. Terrorists have successfully challenged long-held views about who can legitimately claim to be an actor in the international system, and government responses to terrorism have impacted civil liberties and freedoms. Privatizing certain forms of knowledge by assigning property rights has threatened the ability to fight some of the most egregious public health problems of our times, such as AIDS. Environmental problems continue to pose significant problems, and forging appropriate policy responses is hampered by disagreements among governments, collective action problems, contested scientific knowledge, and half-hearted implementation.

The articles in this chapter address some of these problems. Dessler's piece has initiated an important debate about epistemological issues and their implications for theory-building in international politics. He suggests that classical structuralist theories (like neorealism) are unable to analyze transformative change and that they limit the set of interesting puzzles out of a problematic tendency to overemphasize parsimony. Dessler argues that parsimony is only one aspect of good theorizing. The theory's scope and the range of phenomena to which it can be applied must also be considered. Furthermore, a transformative theory of change contains a static structural theory, but the reverse does not hold.

Paul Wapner analyzes the emergence of global "civic politics," a phenomenon that he observes while examining environmental politics and the formation of trans-nationally active nongovernmental organizations. Global civic politics does not follow the traditional notion of civic groups trying to influence governments. Nor does it involve influencing the political space "above" nation-states, particularly international organizations. Instead, Wapner views global civic politics as a situation that involves both domestic and global politics and where both the public and the private sectors are present. These civic groups, he argues, do far more than the "conscious-raising" efforts that many observers link to activist networks.

Saskia Sassen argues that the relationship between the nation-state and the global economy is not well understood. In order for the global economy to function effectively, various standards must be adhered to. In some cases, these standards are coordinated by an international institution. Often, however, standards develop and are maintained through private agents and by national governments, as has occurred increasingly frequently with the rise of globalization. Sassen maintains that the role of private agents and national governments in setting global economic standards is underappreciated, that the interaction between the global economy and the state is more complex than is generally known, and that changes in this interaction have led to the creation of new and alterations in existing institutional forms.

Finally, Richard Higgott addresses issues of global governance from a post-Westphalian perspective. Higgot argues that a more principled debate about the legitimacy and justice of existing international arrangements has become necessary. International organizations and regimes seem to fail in their own mission. Attempts to reform these organizations are quite complex and require different tools than the discourse of "good governance" of global problems suggests. This discourse tends to emphasize criteria such as greater efficiency and the spread of democracy. Both goals are laudable, but they pay insufficient attention to variations in local circumstances, which are often poorly suited to attaining these goals.

What's at Stake in the Agent-Structure Debate?

DAVID DESSLER

. . . In this article, I seek to determine how philosophical insight might yield an empirical payoff and, specifically, to show how the metaphysical victories claimed by scientific realism over its philosophical rivals might be exploited to generate a progressive research program in the structural analysis of international politics. I take as a baseline for this analysis what in current parlance is known as the "agent-structure problem" in social theory. This problem is, strictly speaking, a philosophical one. It emerges from two uncontentious truths about social life: first, that human agency is the only moving force behind the actions, events, and outcomes of the social world; and second, that human agency can be realized only in concrete historical circumstances that condition the possibilities for action and influence its course. . . .

The remainder of this article is divided into five sections. The first section argues that a theory's *ontology* (the substantive entities and configurations the theory postulates) is both the basis of its explanatory power and the ultimate grounding of claims it may have to superiority over rival theories. Imre Lakatos's methodology of theory-choice is consistent with this conception of the link between ontology and theory. The second section assesses Waltz's approach to structural theory, termed here the *positional model*. Unlike other critiques of Waltz, the one developed here firmly differentiates between the ontology of Waltz's structural approach and the theory based on it. The positional ontology is shown to recognize only the unintended features of systemic organization. The third section of the article outlines an alternative ontology of international structure, called the *transformational model,* premised on the philosophy of scientific realism. The transformational model views structure as a means to action rather than as an environment in which action takes place. It gives central ontological position to social rules, both constitutive and regulative, intended and unintended. The fourth section offers a direct comparison of the positional and transformational models and discusses the empirical promise of a transformational research program. It also demonstrates that the positional model recognizes the structural status of unintended rules only, suppressing or ignoring the role of intended rules, and hence is incapable of generating full structural explanations of state action. Here the main thesis of the article is fully articulated: *Because the transformational model of structure provides a more comprehensive ontology than the positional model and is capable of grounding discussion of a wider range of phenomena than any positional theory, it provides a more promising basis for progressive theoretical research.* The fifth section of the article concludes that the stakes in the agent-structure debate are indeed high and that they deserve the attention of all those interested in developing explanatory theories of international politics and, in particular, theories of peaceful change.

THE RELATION BETWEEN THEORY, ONTOLOGY, AND EXPLANATORY POWER

In this section, I consider the distinction between theory and ontology and advance the scientific realist contention that ontology is the basis of a theory's explanatory power. I take "theory" to refer generally to testable explanations of observed behavior. Theory does not merely locate or describe associations between observable phenomena; it explains them. What is tested in testing a theory is not an association but the explanation of it. . . .

"Ontology" refers to the concrete referents of an explanatory discourse.[1] A theory's ontology consists of the real-world structures (things, entities) and processes posited by the theory and invoked in the theory's explanations. The ontology of a discourse constrains but does not determine correct explanations in that discourse.[2] In classical physics, the ontology consists of space, time, and matter, meaning that all the entities or processes to which a classical explanation refers are embodiments of or relations between space, time, and matter. Newton's laws, for example, refer to mass, force, and acceleration. It should be stressed that an ontology is a *structured* set of entities; it consists not only of certain designated kinds of things but also of connections or relations between them. . . . In international relations theory, the statement "A system consists of a structure and interacting units" represents an ontological claim.

According to scientific realism, theories explain by showing how phenomena are products or aspects of an underlying ontology.[3] For example, a fever is explained as a by-product of the biochemical processes induced by a virus in the body. . . . A theory's explanatory power comes from its ability to *reduce* independent phenomena—that is, to show how apparently unconnected phenomena are actually products of a common ontology.[4] Biochemical explanations of disease are powerful because they show how apparently independent symptoms and signs are co-products of a single underlying process. For example, a cough and fever (among other clinical signs) are shown to be common aspects of, say, influenza. In this case, reduction is achieved by showing how independent phenomena—symptoms and signs that could and do appear independently in other circumstances, such as cough, fever, muscular aches, and so on—are features of a given ontological process (the workings of a virus). . . .

In general, the greater the number of independent phenomena a theory reduces, the better that theory is. That is, the richer and more comprehensive the underlying ontology, the better the theory. Newton's physics showed there was a connection between the variables in the law of free fall and Kepler's laws, thus reducing (ontologically uniting) terrestrial and planetary phenomena. The fall of an apple and the orbit of the moon, previously considered entirely unrelated phenomena, became just two examples of how collections of atoms behave when subject to gravity.[5] Einstein's general theory of relativity unified temporal, spatial, gravitational, and dynamical phenomena within a single ontological framework.[6] Indeed, one reason relativity theory earned widespread acceptance even before much experimental support had been collected was its ability to reduce many more independent phenomena than classical mechanics could. This feature of relativity theory was not one simply of correspondence with the facts; what made the theory convincing was not only that it explained well but also that it explained so many different phenomena within one ontological framework. The lesson is that theories which reduce more independent phenomena are, *ceteris paribus,* preferable to those which reduce fewer.[7]

This conclusion converges with important arguments advanced by Lakatos in his studies of the methodology of theory-choice in science. Lakatos is critical of the methodology of "naive falsificationism," which involves simple tests of a given theory against the empirical record at a given point in time. Lakatos argues, first, that a theory is not to be evaluated alone against the evidence, holding it up against arbitrary standards of parsimony, elegance, power, and so on. Instead, it is properly evaluated only in comparison to other theories, in terms of standards not exogenously imposed but generated through the process of comparison itself.[8] Second, Lakatos argues that theories should be assessed not at a single point in time but in dynamic profile as part of an ongoing research program. Research programs are to be evaluated in terms of their ability to generate, in ongoing studies, increasingly powerful explanations from a stable core of standards and assumptions. In sum, according to Lakatos, theory-choice is both *comparative* and *dynamic.* . . .

THE POSITIONAL MODEL OF INTERNATIONAL STRUCTURE

Waltz's ontological model of the international system is based on an explicit analogy with economics. . . . "International-political systems, like economic markets, are individualist in origin, spontaneously generated, and unintended."[9] This statement suggests a fundamental ontological distinction between structure at one level of the international system and interacting units at another.[10] Waltz develops a number of terms to describe these levels and their differences. Structure refers to the "arrangement," "positioning," "organization," or "situation" of the units in the system. The units, which can be characterized and differentiated by their "attributes" or "properties," exhibit "interactions," "interconnections," and "relations" in their actions or behavior. Corresponding to the ontological distinction between the arrangement of units and their interaction is an epistemological distinction between systemic and reductionist theories.[11] A systems-level theory shows how "the organization of units affects their behavior and their interactions," while reductionist theories "explain international outcomes through elements and combinations of elements located at the national or subnational level." . . . [12]

Ontologically, then, structure is viewed as the unintended positioning, standing, or organization of units that emerges spontaneously from their interaction. To describe and understand structure—the initial step in constructing a theory of international politics—we must be careful to distinguish it, Waltz insists, from the underlying behavior of the units. We must separate the *interaction* of units from their *arrangement.* Both features, Waltz notes, might be described by the term "relation," but only the latter is permitted in a definition of structure: " . . . To define a structure requires ignoring how units relate with one another (how they interact) and concentrating on how they stand in relation to one another (how they are arranged or positioned)."[13] The arrangement of units, unlike their attributes and interaction, "is a property of the system," not of the units.[14] Therefore, while the attributes and interactions of states must be confined to the unit-level, Waltz argues, the arrangement of those states is properly considered a systemic feature.

It is important to stress that according to this ontology, structure refers only to the spontaneously formed, unintended conditions of action generated by the coactivity of separable units. Structure is, so to speak, a by-product rather than a product of interaction. Not only is it unintended, but it is essentially impervious to attempts to modify it or control its effects. . . . In sum, the positional model views structure as those conditions of action that are (1) spontaneous and unintended in origin, (2) irreducible to the attributes or actions of individual units, and (3) impervious to attempts to change them or escape their effects.

Having outlined the ontology of his approach, Waltz begins the move from model to theory, from a description of the ontology of structure to a theoretical definition of it. We know what structure *is*—the unintended arrangement, organization, or positioning of units in a system—but we have not yet determined how best to describe it and deploy it in causal explanation. . . .

Waltz directs us to three questions about the configuration of units in the system, the answers to which he offers as a tripartite theoretical definition of structure.[15] (1) What is the principle by which the parts of a system are arranged? In the international system, it is anarchy. (2) What functions are specified for the units? The functions of states are not formally differentiated. (3) What is the distribution of capabilities across the units of the system? In the international system, bipolar and multipolar distributions exhaust recent historical experience. Waltz then argues that because states are functionally similar, "the second part of the definition drops out" in characterizing systems change;[16] hence, international structures are to be defined and compared according to two basic dimensions of state placement: anarchy and the distribution of power.

Waltz's structural theory is meant to explain recurring patterns of actions and outcomes in the interstate system.[17] The persistence of interstate war is attributed to anarchy, and the enduring stability of the postwar international order is attributed to the bipolar distribution of power.[18] Waltz also links structure to specific actions and outcomes. For example, the American-Soviet arms race after World War II, peace within postwar Europe, China's intervention in the Korean War, and Soviet negotiations with Germany in the 1920s and 1930s are all claimed by Waltz to be specific consequences of the workings of structure in international politics.[19] How are we to assess these claims? . . . Lakatos insists that these questions must be answered not through simple appeal to the evidence but, rather, in terms of comparisons with a rival approach. This rival approach, rooted in scientific realism, must first be explicated.

THE TRANSFORMATIONAL MODEL OF INTERNATIONAL STRUCTURE

The Ontology of Society According to Scientific Realism

The scientific realists' agent-structure solution, as described by Roy Bhaskar, starts from a simple premise—namely, that "all [social] activity presupposes the prior existence of social forms."

> Thus consider *saying, making,* and *doing* as characteristic modalities of human agency. People cannot communicate except by utilizing existing media, produce except by applying themselves to materials which are already formed, or act save in some or other context. Speech requires language; making materials; actions conditions; agency resources; activity rules. . . . [S]ociety is a necessary condition for any intentional human act at all.[20]

"Structure" refers, in this ontology, to the social forms that preexist action, these forms being conceived as analogous to language. Social structure stands in relation to social action as language stands in relation to discourse (speech and writing). . . .

According to [this] transformational model, action is to be viewed by the social scientist as speech is viewed by the linguist: as the skilled accomplishment of actors utilizing the available media through which action becomes possible. The primitive entities comprising this ontology are actors, actions, and the materials for action (in contrast to the positional ontology, which consists of actors, actions, and the arrangement of actors). The transformational model suggests two important connections between action and the materials (structure) presumed by it. First, structure both enables action and constrains its possibilities. Second, structure is the outcome as well as the medium of action. Consider the language model. As a set of semantic and syntactic rules, language is the medium making communication possible; at the same time, it constrains the ways in which that communication can be effected. The rules of language make it possible to speak sensibly, and they put limits on what counts as sensible speech. Furthermore, language is not only the medium of discourse—being drawn upon and instantiated in speaking and writing—but it is also the outcome of that discourse, being "carried" through space and time by its usages. Thus, all social action presupposes social structure, and vice versa. An actor can act socially only because there exists a social structure to draw on, and it is only through the actions of agents that structure is reproduced (and, potentially, transformed). . . .

The structural relation between part and whole, which in the positional model reflects the distinction between units and their arrangement, becomes in the transformational view akin to the relation between message and code or between speech and language. Note the particular conception of structural causality the latter approach implies. Again, the language analogy is useful. The English language does not cause or bring about discourse in the way that a spark, stimulus, or vector force causes resultant behavior. Rather, it affects action by enabling certain possibilities of discourse and disabling or excluding others. In Aristotelian terms, structure is a *material cause* rather than an *efficient cause* of behavior. Structure alone explains only the possibilities (and impossibilities) of action.[21] As with the positional approach or any other structural model, a transformational explanation cannot alone explain outcomes. Structure cannot provide a complete explanation of action any more than the English language completely explains a given use of it or any more than the material from which a statue is crafted completely explains the statue itself. A complete explanation must appeal not only to the material but also the efficient causes of action, which can be located only within a theory of the agents.

The starting point of the scientific realist approach to international structural theory is therefore the recognition that state action is possible and conceivable only if there exist the instruments through which that action can in fact be carried out. Two sorts of instruments or media of action are necessary.[22] First, nations must have *resources,* the physical attributes that comprise "capability." A military strategy requires military forces; monetary policy, financial instruments; trade policy, the goods and physical infrastructure of trade; and so on. Second, nations must have available *rules,* the media through which they communicate with one another and coordinate their actions. For policy not only relies upon physical capability, but it also requires a framework of meaning through which use of that capability becomes recognizable as policy (as intended, meaningful behavior) and through which these intended meanings can form the basis for patterned state interaction. The importance of resources is acknowledged in the positional model, which defines "arrangement" in terms of the distribution of capability. But the role of rules in state action remains untheorized in that approach, and therefore some initial remarks toward a theory of rules would be appropriate at this point.

Constitutive and Regulative Rules

The notion of "rule" occupies a central spot in the ontology of the transformational model. . . .

A rule is, in its most basic sense, an understanding about how to proceed or "go on" in given social circumstances. . . . [Rules] are "procedures of actions, aspects of praxis" that "appl[y] over a range of contexts and occasions" and "allow for the methodical continuation of an established sequence."[23] Now this is necessarily a broad definition, not least because it must encompass at least two types of rules, constitutive and regulative.[24] *Regulative rules* prescribe and proscribe behavior in defined circumstances. As John Searle notes, they "regulate antecedently or independently existing forms of behavior; for example, many rules of etiquette regulate interpersonal relationships which exist independently of the rules."[25] Traffic laws, building fire codes, and the requirements set down in an arms control treaty all exemplify the regulative dimension of rules. The penalty for not following such rules typically involves some sort of sanctioning behavior on the part of another. *Constitutive rules,* on the other hand, "create or define new forms of behavior."[26] The rules of chess, for example, define an activity by setting down explanations of what counts as a move of the knight, what constitutes a checkmate, and so on. Not to follow constitutive rules is to make oneself misunderstood or incomprehensible—to perform a social action incorrectly or to fall outside the boundaries of a meaningful "form of life."[27] Constitutive rules take the form, "X counts as Y in context C," while regulative rules fit the form, "Do X in context C."

Although I will continue here with the well-established practice of considering constitution and regulation as products of two different types of rule, it is worth noting that constitutive rules have regulative implications, and vice versa. . . . [28] To be following constitutive rules is to participate in a form of life, to make oneself understood according to the structure of meanings that defines action in that realm. . . .

The constitutive/regulative typology can be applied usefully in the analysis of international structure. Constitutive rules, which I will also term here "conventions," are standardized, relatively unchanging practices that constitute a "vocabulary" (a stock of meaningful actions, or signs) for international communication. Conventions enable signals of support, opposition, hostility, friendship, condemnation, indifference, commitment, resignation, and so on.[29] For example, military exercises can be timed and located either to signal a nation's commitment to supporting a specific policy or outcome or to signal its hostility or opposition to the policies of another nation.[30] Conventions include verbal as well as "physical" practices. . . .

Regulative rules are defined here as public claims, backed by sanctions, that prescribe, proscribe, or permit specified behavior for designated actors in defined circumstances. Such rules take the form, "Actor A should do X in context C." They are backed by sanctions and thus are to be distinguished from mere regularities or routines. The internality of sanctions to rules implies a division between followers (or violators) and enforcers of rules—the "targets" and "sources" of sanctioning behavior. The dynamics of rule-making bind followers and enforcers together in a relationship which, though usually asymmetrical, constrains in both directions.

Rules need not be stated explicitly. Cohen introduces an important distinction between *tacit* and *formal* regulative rules, which he conceives on a continuum: "At one end of the spectrum are found rules arrived at by tacit agreement and which are not directly negotiated either in writing or by word of mouth. At the other end of the spectrum are rules deriving from formal negotiations and expressed in formal, binding agreement. In between are rules of the game contained in the 'spirit' of formal agreements, verbal 'gentlemen's' agreements, and 'non-binding,' though written, understandings." . . . [31]

COMPARING THE POSITIONAL AND TRANSFORMATIONAL MODELS

The Positional Model's Implicit Reliance on Social Rules

The transformational model's focus on rules may suggest that it is best suited to the study of a certain type of conduct—namely, institutional conduct—while the positional model is more appropriate for the study of interaction within anarchy. For is the interstate system not uniquely the political realm in which rules have little, if any, role to play in determining behavior? . . . However, to the scientific realist, this conclusion is misplaced. Scientific realism insists that *all* social action depends on the preexistence of rules, implying that even under anarchy, rules are an essential prerequisite for action.[32] It asserts the impossibility and inconceivability of social behavior without rules; the issue of whether a centralizing authority exists or not is beside the point. Rules are, in the transformational model, both logically and praxiologically necessary for social action. . . . The positional theory is a case in point. Structure is defined there only as anarchy and a distribution of power. But, clearly, anarchy and power distribution cannot alone and in themselves lead to any behavior. Some link between this environment and the realm of action is needed. Here the concept of rationality is introduced. As Keohane points out, "The link between system structure and actor behavior is forged by the rationality assumption, which enables the theorist to predict that leaders will respond to the incentives and constraints imposed by their environments." . . .[33]

The scientific realist would stress that the rationality assumption brings rules into the explanatory framework without acknowledging them as such. According to the transformational model, if it is true that the international imperative is survival, it is also true that knowing how to survive means knowing the rules of the game. For example, a nation in a position of declining power may act rationally by allying itself with other powers. This rational action presumes the existence of the rules of interstate communication and coordination utilized in any treaty-making process. Rationality is thus not merely an assumption about the *manner* in which nations calculate and act; it is also an assumption about the *means* through which those actions are carried out. The rationality assumption in the positional model thus presupposes the existence of rules in international relations. Structure must consist of something more than anarchy and the distribution of power. It must also encompass the media through which rational action is effected.

A brief example from Waltz's work illustrates this important point. Waltz puts great emphasis on the notions of competition and socialization, two "pervasive processes" that "encourage similarities of attributes and of behavior."[34] To show how structure molds behavior through socialization, Waltz gives the example of Soviet behavior just after the Russian Revolution. . . .

. . . [But] what are the units socialized *to*, if not (at a minimum) understandings of conventions? If Waltz's theory did not presume the existence of a set of rules constitutive of "the system" to which nations are socialized, it could not explain how state behavior is constrained by structure. What compelled the Soviets to take action so similar to that of other states, even though it was at odds with their own ideology, was, in Waltz's terms, the rationally directed motive to survive in an anarchic realm. But this is just a shorthand for saying that the Soviets, having recognized the precariousness of their security position, resorted to use of the existing system of conventions through which great powers communicate and negotiate with one another, and they were thus able to bolster their security position by making deals with foreign powers. Waltz sees as evidence of the Soviets' socialization the deals undertaken with "that other pariah power and ideological enemy, Germany."[35] The scientific realist would stress that such deals can be made only between nations who can communicate, who draw on a shared set of constitutive rules with which alliances can be forged and through which they gain meaning. Without at least an implicit presumption of such rules, no sense can be made of rationality in international relations, and no bridge can be forged theoretically between positional structure and action.

Thus, the difference between the transformational and positional ontologies is not that one recognizes the existence of rules and the other does not. Both models recognize the efficacy of rules in international politics, and theories based on either model must appeal to the existence of rules, even if only implicitly. The difference between these ontologies lies in their conception of the *relation* between rules and action. In the positional ontology, rules (conventions and norms) are fixed parameters of action, unintentionally reproduced, which constrain and dispose behavior so as to preserve the rule structure. In the transformational ontology, they are the material conditions of action which agents appropriate and through action reproduce or transform, possibly intentionally. It is worth exploring this difference in some detail.

Recall that in the positional ontology, structure is an unintended by-product of rational, self-interested efforts to survive. Rules, which give shape and meaning to rationality and thereby make survival possible, are a necessary (if theoretically suppressed) component of structure. . . .

In the transformational view, by contrast, structure is a medium of activity that in principle can be altered through that activity. Any given action will reproduce or transform some part of the social structure; the structural product itself may be intended or unintended. In general, social action is both a product (an intended action) and a by-product (the reproduction of rules and resources implicated in the intended action). The linguistic analogy is again useful. When people speak a language, they are typically carrying out an intentional action (such as ordering a meal or supporting a philosophical argument) and at the same time are unintentionally reproducing the conditions which make that intentional action possible (reproducing language itself). . . .

The possibility that rules may become the objects of intentional action and that they may be transformed through action returns us to the issue of how such real-world entities as alliances, trade pacts, and arms control agreements are to be treated by structural theory. The positional ontology limits structure to what is both irreducible to action and unintentional in origin. Thus, entities that are intentionally produced, such as alliances, cannot be part of structure. Waltz is explicit on this point. Alliances are a feature not of the organization of systems, he argues, but of "the accommodations and conflicts that may occur within them or the groupings that may now and then form." . . . [36] This theoretical conclusion is entirely consistent with the underlying positional ontology. Intentional action and the products of intentional action, such as alliances and treaties, must be relegated to the unit-level in this ontology.

However, according to scientific realism, this conclusion is mistaken. While it is true that such things as alliances emerge from state interaction, they are not simply *aspects* of that interaction; they are *products* of it. . . . The rules that make up an alliance or trade agreement may be reproduced or transformed by subsequent activity, but they cannot be reduced to it. NATO, for example, rather than being just an aspect of the (unit-level) interaction among a select number of states is a real (system-level) structure of rules that regulates and gives meaning to a wide range of current and contemplated behavior by those states. NATO cannot be reduced to the activities carried out in its name, such as military exercises and meetings of foreign ministers. It consists also of relatively enduring rules and norms that these actions draw upon, reproduce, and transform. These rules, inscribed in a written treaty that exists independently of the activities it enables and regulates, are a legitimate component of structure, deserving to be treated as such by structural theory.

According to scientific realism, then, the positional model offers a *truncated* ontology of structure. . . . By conflating the unintended with the irreducible, the positional model is incapable of recognizing those features of the system's organization that are both irreducible to interaction and intentially produced (intended products). It thus bars from structural theory an entire class of structural elements in international politics. . . . The transformational ontology, by contrast, shows why all rules deserve structural status and provides a basis for integrating them in structural explanation. Because the ontology it postulates is richer and more comprehensive than its positional rival, the transformational model promises theory that is more powerful than its positional counterpart.

The Empirical Promise of a Transformational Research Program

The problem with Waltz's theory is not the explanatory schema it sets forth but the ontology on which it is based. . . .

Waltz is reluctant to concede that other structural theories, even those based on a positional ontology, might be advisable. . . .

. . . [He] fears that broadening the definition of structure to include other systemic features will introduce a "reasoning [that] makes the criteria of inclusion infinitely expansible," rendering structural theory a mishmash of causal considerations best treated separately. . . . [37]

Waltz is correct to stress the importance of parsimony. The more efficient the means to given explanatory ends, the better the explanation, other things being equal. But Waltz mistakenly defines parsimony only in terms of the number of independent variables in a theory, ignoring the ontology from which those variables are drawn. The number of independent variables one wishes to include in an explanation is generally a matter of subjective choice, dictated by what sort of explanation one wishes and how accurate it must be. To explain the path of a falling object, we may need only the law of gravitation if our requirements are not too severe. But if we wish to know the path of the object's fall in great detail, we will need to include consideration of the wind, rain, air resistance, Coriolis force, and the like. The choice between a single-variable theory that explains a little and a multivariable theory that explains a lot will generally be determined by the requirements of engineering rather than by the standards of science. . . .

Parsimony, in any case, is not gauged simply by the number of variables in a theory. Ontology too can prove more or less efficient in grounding explanatory efforts. After all, if parsimony were simply a matter of minimizing the number of variables in an explanation, Newton's explanation of the planets' orbital paths would be better than Einstein's. The Newtonian calculations require only the universal law of gravitation, and they leave only a small portion of the orbits unexplained. Einstein's calculations introduce complex relativistic corrections to the Newtonian laws, and in so doing explain only slightly more than those laws. If we need to know only the rough paths of the planets, say for purposes of telescopic tracking, the simpler Newtonian theory may be preferable on practical grounds. But Einstein's remains a better theory, and not only because it explains some planetary motion that Newton's cannot. Einstein's theory is better because it is more parsimonious in a basic ontological sense: it grounds explanations not only of planetary orbits but also of a number of unrelated and otherwise unexplainable phenomena. . . .

But why is a transformational model needed to examine the nature of rules and rule-following behavior in the interstate system? Why can we not simply take Waltz's theory as a starting point and then bring rules into the analysis when and where they are warranted? The basic problem was explained earlier in this section: the ontology underlying Waltz's theory makes no room for intentional rules as structural features of the system. If we start with Waltz's theory, we have no way of grounding a consideration of such rules without appealing to an outside ontology and thereby losing the parsimony of that theory. The transformational ontology grounds consideration of intentional rules not only by making their existence explicit but also by providing a useful model of how they exist in relation to action. . . . To appreciate the power of the transformational model, it is worth examining the differences in these configurations more closely.

In the positional model, structure is an *environment* in which action takes place. Structure means the "setting" or "context" in which action unfolds. In a positional approach, international structure stands in relation to state action much as an office building stands in relation to the workday activities that take place within its walls: it is a fixed, enduring set of conditions that constrains and disposes, shapes and shoves behavior. . . .

In the transformational approach, by contrast, structure consists of *materials for action*. Rather than being an environment or "container" in which behavior takes place, it is a medium, a means to social action. An office building, in this view, is not so much a setting for the activities of workers as it is an enabling structure that workers make use of to get their jobs done.[38] Certainly, structure is a constraint on action; the insights of the positional model are not sacrificed in the scientific realist approach. Travel through air-conditioning ducts and out of upper-story windows will be sanctioned, either by the rules of the workplace or by the law of gravitation. But by configuring structure as a means to action, rather than as an environment in which action takes place, a more powerful and comprehensive treatment of the conditions of action becomes possible. Rules are not concrete girders constraining action but, instead, are media through which action becomes possible and which action itself reproduces and transforms. Action is constrained and enabled by rules; the rules are the outcome as well as the medium of that action. . . .

What might be the shape of a research program predicated on the ontology of scientific realism? One established research area in which the advantages of the transformational model can be immediately exploited is that dealing with the creation and maintenance of international institutions. The ontology of the transformational model provides the conceptual tools to describe and explain institutions and to investigate their enabling and constraining qualities. . . . In transformational terms, institutions consist of *formal, regulative* rules. In contrast to the positional approach, the transformational model supplies an ontology that not only is suitable for the study of such rules but also is capable of showing the continuities (as well as the discontinuities) between institutionalized and noninstitutionalized behavior.

Keohane notes that institutions are embedded in enduring "practices" of international politics, the most important of which is sovereignty.[39] The idea of embeddedness suggests a *stratification* of the international rule structure, which can be understood as a hierarchical dependence of both constitutive and regulative rules in which higher-order rules presume the existence of more sedimented (lower-order) ones. That is, some rules underpin not only action but also other rules or rule-structures. For example, when two nations sign an arms control treaty, they not only adopt a set of operative arms control regulations, but they also reproduce the rules associated with the underlying practice of sovereignty (rules that give the nations the very identity required to make treaties possible). Thus, the rules associated with the practice of sovereignty, which regulate a good number of "surface" activities (for example, the activities of diplomatic personnel around the world), also underpin and support a great number of other regulative rules in international politics. This suggests why the violation of any of the deeply sedimented rules that define sovereignty, such as in the seizing of hostages at the American Embassy in Teheran in 1979, will be met with profound resistance within the system. . . .

The immediate challenge to the transformational research program is to provide an initial framework for identifying and classifying rules of various sorts. The integrative power of a transformational program will depend on developing an encompassing schema showing relations and connections between various types of rules. Such a framework cannot be constructed through a priori analysis nor through a purely inductive strategy. Instead, initial ideas must be ventured and then applied in research, and the results used to modify and extend the initial concepts. As this classificatory framework is developed, several empirical questions need to be addressed. How are rules recognized by actors? How are they made, reproduced, and transformed? Why do states sometimes adhere to rules and at other times break or ignore them? Why do states sometimes enforce rules by sanctioning violators and at other times ignore the rule-breaking of others? These basic questions, as well as others, are aimed not at generating a static list of rules associated with behavior in various circumstances but at bringing to light *how* it is that rules, which are both the medium and the outcome of action, affect action the way they do. . . .

CONCLUSION: STAKES IN THE AGENT-STRUCTURE DEBATE

The history of science shows that when a new theory confronts well-established scientific thought, it typically faces two difficulties. First, the scientific community's familiarity with established theory works to obscure the new theory's powers and possibilities.[40] Second, the new theory's initial state of underdevelopment leaves it vulnerable to skeptical attacks from those who correctly perceive the theory's ambiguities and uncertainties. But, as the corpus of Lakatos's work demonstrates, any attempt at single-point "naive falsificationism" would be a mistake. . . .

. . . The transformational model merits our confidence because it is derived from the basic principles of scientific realism. It will take time to develop the model and amass the empirical results necessary to judge its usefulness. In the meantime, we can look forward to at least three advantages of adopting the transformational approach.

First, because many of the research questions entailed by a transformational model can be answered only by looking at the policymaking processes within states, a transformational approach can draw explicit links between structural and unit-level theories. The elaboration and testing of some of the structural theory must take place at the level of foreign policy decision making. Recall that no structural theory can alone predict state behavior, and therefore no such theory can be tested by referring to the outcomes of state action alone. However, a transformational structural theory claims to explain the forces within the decision- and policy-making processes that generate state behavior, and thus the theory can be tested against the record of these processes. . . .

Second, in addition to the "vertical" linkages between unit- and system-level theory, the transformational approach grounds the development of "horizontal" linkages between issue-areas in international politics. The concern for reputation, for example, cuts across processes of both conflict and cooperation. The importance of reputation to the "high" politics of national security is well appreciated. For example, when discord arises, a reputation for being "tough"—for showing a willingness to bear costs in pursuit of goals—may help secure the cooperation or acquiescence of others. But reputation is important in the "low" politics of trade and finance as well. . . . Insofar as reputation derives from rule-enforcing and rule-following reliability, it requires structural exposition and analysis. The transformational model provides a comprehensive ontology for such analysis. While the positional ontology favors the study of "high" over "low" politics, the transformational model integrates the two realms. . . .

Third, and perhaps most significant, the transformational approach to structural theory provides a promising basis for constructing explanations of peaceful change, a task that has been identified as the most pressing contemporary challenge to theorists of international relations. . . . [41] Waltz sees the efforts of theorists concerned with understanding the possibilities for change in the state system ("critical theory") as different in kind from his attempts to explain recurring patterns of action ("problem-solving theory").[42] Critical theorists, he maintains, "would transcend the world as it is; meanwhile we have to live in it."[43] But must

our efforts to explain the world as it is condemn us to giving up hope of changing it? Scientific realism insists not. . . . Therein lies perhaps the most crucial stake
in the agent-structure debate.

NOTES

1. See Stephen Gaukroger, *Explanatory Structures: Concepts of Explanation in Early Physics and Philosophy* (Atlantic Highlands, NJ: Humanities Press, 1978), p. 39; and Roy Bhaskar, *Scientific Realism and Human Emancipation* (London: Verso, 1986), p. 36. In this article, I use "model" interchangeably with "ontology."

2. Gaukroger, *Explanatory Structures,* p. 64.

3. See Jerrold Aronson, *A Realist Philosophy of Science* (New York: St. Martin's Press, 1984); Rom Harre, *The Principles of Scientific Thinking* (Chicago: University of Chicago Press, 1970); Rom Harre, *Varieties of Realism,* part 4 (Oxford: Blackwell, 1986); and S. Korner, *Categorical Frameworks* (Oxford: Blackwell, 1974). The terminology of "common ontol-ogy" is Aronson's. Harre speaks of "source analogues," Korner of "common categorical frameworks."

4. In *A Realist Philosophy of Science,* p. 174, Aronson states that "two phenomena are inde-pendent in that it is (physically) possible for one to occur without the other and vice versa."

5. Ibid., p. 271.

6. Ibid., pp. 182–83.

7. Einstein used this lesson to protect one of his theoretical predictions from countervail-ing empirical evidence. In late 1905, the experimental physicist Walter Kaufmann reported measurements of the mass of the electron at variance with claims Einstein had set forth in earlier research. Einstein rejected Kaufmann's measurements, claiming that the "systematic deviation" reported between those measurements and Einstein's pre-dictions likely indicated an "unnoticed source of error" in Kaufmann's work. Kauf-mann's data were to be dismissed because, in Einstein's professed "opinion," they supported theories that were not convincing alternatives to Einstein's own. And what made Einstein's theory more convincing was its ontological breadth. Einstein thus cited, as an independent criterion of theory-choice, the ontological power of his the-ory, in order to reject as implausible the data that contradicted his theory. Significantly, Einstein proved to be correct (though this was not shown for three decades). See the account in Arthur I. Miller, *Imagery in Scientific Thought* (Cambridge, MA: MIT Press, 1986), chap. 3; quotes are from pp. 118–19.

8. According to Lakatos, "There is no falsification before the emergence of a better the-ory." See Imre Lakatos, *The Methodology of Scientific Research Programmes: Philosophical Papers,* vol. 1 (Cambridge: Cambridge University Press, 1978), p. 35.

9. Kenneth Waltz, *Theory of International Politics* (Reading, MA: Addison-Wesley, 1979), p. 91.

10. Ibid., p. 40.

11. Ibid., p. 18.

12. Ibid., pp. 39 and 60.

13. Ibid., p. 80.

14. Ibid.

15. Ibid., pp. 81–99.

16. Ibid., p. 101.

17. Ibid., p. 69.

18. See the following works of Waltz: *Theory*, p. 66; "The Stability of a Bipolar World," *Daedalus* 93 (Summer 1964), pp. 882–87; and *Man, the State and War* (New York: Columbia University Press, 1959).

19. Waltz, *Theory*, pp. 125 and 127–28; and Waltz, "Reflections on *Theory of International Politics*: A Response to My Critics," in Robert Keohane, ed., *Neorealism and Its Critics* (New York: Columbia University Press, 1986), p. 332.

20. Roy Bhaskar, *The Possibility of Naturalism* (Atlantic Highlands, NJ: Humanities Press, 1979), p. 43.

21. Alexander Wendt, "The Agent-Structure Problem in International Relations Theory," *International Organization* 41 (Summer 1987), p. 362.

22. Anthony Giddens, *Profiles and Critiques in Social Theory* (Berkeley: University of California Press, 1983), chap. 3.

23. Anthony Giddens, *The Constitution of Society* (Berkeley: University of California Press, 1984), pp. 20–21.

24. The seminal article on this subject is that of John Rawls, "Two Concepts of Rules," *Philosophical Review* 64 (January 1955), pp. 3–32. See also W. V. O. Quine, "Methodological Reflections on Current Linguistic Theory," in Donald Davidson and Gilbert Harmon, eds., *Semantics of Natural Language* (Boston: Riedel, 1972), pp. 442–54; and the broader discussion in Friedrich Kratochwil and John Gerard Ruggie, "International Organization: A State of the Art on an Art of the State," *International Organization* 40 (Autumn 1986), pp. 753–75. The present essay draws primarily on the influential work by John R. Searle, *Speech Acts: An Essay in the Philosophy of Language* (Cambridge: Cambridge University Press, 1969).

25. Searle, *Speech Acts*, p. 33.

26. Ibid.

27. Peter Winch, *The Idea of Social Science and Its Relation to Philosophy* (London: Routledge & Kegan Paul, 1958).

28. Anthony Giddens, *Central Problems in Social Theory* (London: Macmillan, 1979), p. 66.

29. See . . . David S. Clarke, Jr., *Principles of Semiotic* (London: Routledge & Kegan Paul, 1987), especially chap. 4, "Communication," pp. 73–103.

30. See Barry M. Blechman and Stephen S. Kaplan, *Force Without War: U.S. Armed Forces as a Political Instrument* (Washington, DC: Brookings Institution, 1973); and Stephen S. Kaplan, *Diplomacy of Power: Soviet Armed Forces as a Political Instrument* (Washington, DC: Brookings Institution, 1981).

31. Raymond Cohen, *International Politics: The Rules of the Game* (London: Longman, 1981), p. 50. See also Paul Keal, *Unspoken Rules and Superpower Dominance* (New York: St. Martin's Press, 1983), chap. 3.

32. The claim that "system" presupposes "rules" is distinct from the argument that the international political system represents a "society" reflecting shared norms. In Bull's version of this latter argument, an international society "exists when a group of states, conscious of certain common interests and common values, form a society in the sense that they conceive themselves to be bound by a common set of rules in their relations with one another, and share in the workings of common institutions." Bull conceptualizes "rules" in the regulative sense only—"general imperative principles which require or authorize prescribed classes of persons or groups to behave in prescribed ways"—and links rules to the achievement and maintenance of "order," implying "a pattern of activity that sustains the elementary or primary goals of . . . international society." Thus, when Bull declares the existence of "a common set of

rules" in international politics, he means a common dedication to the achievement of shared values, interests, or norms. By contrast, when the scientific realist speaks of a common set of rules, all that is necessarily implied is the shared convention of meaning that the very idea of social action in international relations presupposes. Above quotes are from Hedley Bull, *The Anarchical Society* (New York: Columbia University Press, 1977), pp. 13, 54, and 8. . . .

33. Robert Keohane, "Theory of World Politics: Structured Realism and Beyond," in Keohane, *Neorealism and Its Critics*, p. 167.

34. Waltz, *Theory*, pp. 74 and 76.

35. Ibid., p. 128.

36. Ibid., p. 98.

37. Waltz, "Reflections on *Theory*," p. 239.

38. In addition to walls and floors, structure in the transformational model could include typewriters, computers, paper, pencils, telephones, and intercoms—the materials with and through which work is completed. In the positional model, such materials are incorrectly relegated to the unit-level. . . .

39. Robert Keohane, "International Institutions: Two Approaches," *International Studies Quarterly* 32 (December 1988), p. 384.

40. See Norwood Russell Hanson, *Patterns of Discovery: An Inquiry into the Conceptual Foundations of Science* (Cambridge: Cambridge University Press, 1958), chaps. 1, 2, and 4.

41. See Robert Gilpin, *War and Change in World Politics* (New York: Cambridge University Press, 1981); and Robert Keohane, "Theory of World Politics." For an important theoretical and historical analysis of the determinants of peaceful systemic change, see Charles F. Doran, *The Politics of Assimilation: Hegemony and Its Aftermath* (Baltimore, MD: Johns Hopkins University Press, 1971).

42. Waltz, "Reflections on *Theory*," p. 338. The distinction is Robert Cox's, presented in "Social Forces, States, and World Orders: Beyond International Relations Theory," in Keohane, Neorealism and Its Critics, pp. 204–205.

43. Waltz, "Reflections on *Theory*," p. 338.

Politics Beyond the State: Environmental Activism and World Civic Politics

PAUL WAPNER

Interest in transnational activist groups such as Greenpeace, European Nuclear Disarmament (END), and Amnesty International has been surging. Much of this new attention on the part of students of international relations is directed at showing that transnational activists make a difference in world affairs, that they shape conditions which influence how their particular cause is addressed. Recent scholarship demonstrates, for example, that Amnesty International and Human Rights Watch have changed state human rights practices in particular countries.[1] Other studies have shown that environmental groups have influenced negotiations over environmental protection of the oceans, the ozone layer, and Antarctica and that they have helped enforce national compliance with international mandates.[2] Still others have shown that peace groups helped shape nuclear policy regarding deployments in Europe during the cold war and influenced Soviet perceptions in a way that allowed for eventual superpower accommodation.[3] This work is important, especially insofar as it establishes the increasing influence of transnational nongovernmental organizations (NGOs) on states. Nonetheless, for all its insight, it misses a different but related dimension of activist work—the attempt by activists to shape public affairs by working within and across societies themselves.

Recent studies neglect the societal dimension of activists' efforts in part because they subscribe to a narrow understanding of politics. They see politics as a practice associated solely with government and thus understand activist efforts exclusively in terms of their influence upon government. . . .

Such a narrow view of politics in turn limits research because it suggests that the conception and meaning of transnational activist groups is fixed and that scholarship therefore need only measure activist influence on states. This article asserts, by contrast, that the meaning of activist groups in a global context is not settled and will remain problematic as long as the strictly societal dimension of their work is left out of the analysis. Activist efforts within and across societies are a proper object of study and only by including them in transnational activist research can one render an accurate understanding of transnational activist groups and, by extension, of world politics.

The author wishes to thank the John D. and Catherine T. MacArthur Foundation and the School of International Service at the American University for generous financial support for this project. The author also wishes to thank Daniel Deudney, Richard Falk, Nicholas Onuf, Leslie Thiele, and Michael Walzer for helpful comments on earlier drafts.

This article focuses on activist society-oriented activities and demonstrates that activist organizations are not simply transnational pressure groups, but rather are political actors in their own right. The main argument is that the best way to think about transnational activist societal efforts is through the concept of "world civic politics." When activists work to change conditions without directly pressuring states, their activities take place in the civil dimension of world collective life or what is sometimes called global civil society.[4] Civil society is that arena of social engagement which exists above the individual yet below the state.[5] It is a complex network of economic, social, and cultural practices based on friendship, family, the market, and voluntary affiliation.[6] Although the concept arose in the analysis of domestic societies, it is beginning to make sense on a global level. . . . Global civil society as such is that slice of associational life which exists above the individual and below the state, but also across national boundaries. When transnational activists direct their efforts beyond the state, they are politicizing global civil society. . . .

One can appreciate the idea of world civic politics by drawing an analogy between activist efforts at the domestic and international levels. According to Melucci, Habermas, Offe, and others, the host of contemporary domestic peace, human rights, women's, and human potential movements in the developed world both lobby their respective governments and work through their societies to effect change. . . . [T]he early years of Solidarity in Poland and Charter 77 in Czecho-slovakia illustrate the multifaceted character of activist politics. Recognizing the limits of influencing their respective states, Solidarity and Charter 77 created and utilized horizontal societal associations involving churches, savings associations, lit-erary ventures, and so forth to bring about widespread change. As with the other organizations, this does not mean that they ignored the state but rather that they made a strategic decision to explore the political potential of unofficial realms of collective action.[7] In each instance groups target government officials when it seems likely to be efficacious. If this approach fails or proves too dangerous, how-ever, they seek other means of affecting widespread conditions and practices.[8] Analytically, these other means are found in civil society.

Moved up a political notch, this form of politics helps explain the efforts of transnational activist groups. Amnesty International, Friends of the Earth, Oxfam, and Greenpeace target governments and try to change state behavior to further their aims. When this route fails or proves less efficacious, they work through transnational economic, social, and cultural networks to achieve their ends. The emphasis on world civic politics stresses that while these latter efforts may not translate easily into state action, they should not be viewed as simply matters of cultural or social interest. Rather, they involve identifying and manipulating instruments of power for shaping collective life. . . .

In the following I analyze the character of world civic politics by focusing on one relatively new sector of this activity, transnational environmental activist groups (TEAGs). As environmental dangers have become part of the public con-sciousness and a matter of scholarly concern in recent years, much attention has been directed toward the transboundary and global dimensions of environmental degradation. Ozone depletion, global warming, and species extinction, for instance, have consequences that cross state boundaries and in the extreme threaten to change the organic infrastructure of life on earth. Responding in part to increased knowledge about these problems, transnational activist groups have emerged whose members are dedicated to "saving the planet." . . . This article demonstrates that, while TEAGs direct much effort toward state policies, their political activity does not stop there but extends into global civil society. In the following, I describe and analyze this type of activity and, in doing so, make explicit the dynamics and significance of world civic politics.

This article is divided into five sections. The first places my argument within the theoretical literature of international relations to highlight where my thesis is similar to and yet different from earlier efforts to underscore the role of nongovernmental organizations. The second is an empirical presentation of the way TEAGs specifically practice world civic politics. It describes how they foster an ecological sensibility and explicates the significance of this form of politics. The third section outlines how environmental groups pressure corporations and explores the political dimension of this strategy. The fourth section describes how TEAGs empower local communities and considers the ramifications for world politics. In each of these instances activists operate outside the province of state-to-state interaction yet engage in genuine political activity. The final section evaluates the concept of world civic politics from a theoretical perspective. . . .

BEYOND THE TRANSNATIONALIST DEBATE

Throughout the 1960s and early 1970s NGOs were the objects of tremendous scholarly attention. At the time the statecentric model of world politics was undergoing one of its many attacks and NGOs were enlisted in the assault. Many scholars argued that since nonstate actors were growing in number and power, students of world politics would be better served by paying attention to these as well as, if not instead of, nation-states. . . .

The debate over the relative importance of the state in world affairs had an impact in the field insofar as it convinced realists—those who most explicitly privileged the state in the 1960s and 1970s—that NGOs matter.[9] To be sure, this took some effort. Defenders of the strictly statecentric model argued, for example, that the proliferation of NGOs was a function of hegemonic stability and thus derivative of interstate behavior.[10] Others challenged the contention that transnationalism was increasing interdependence between states and hence restricting states' ability to control events, and argued instead that the amount of interdependence had actually been on the decrease.[11] . . .

The debate about NGOs, while important, suffered premature closure, because scholars ultimately saw NGO significance in terms of state power. That is, NGOs assumed prominence in subsequent studies only to the extent that they affected state policies; their influence on world affairs apart from this role was neglected.[12] One of the reasons for this is that the debate itself was framed in a way that could have had only this result. Scholars saw the controversy as a "unit of analysis" problem. They argued over which variable was the proper object of research in world politics. In order to understand world affairs, should one study, for instance, MNCs, the state, revolutionary groups, or transnational political parties? With the problem formulated in this way, transnationalists were associated with a "sovereignty at bay" model of world politics, which claimed that NGOs were eclipsing states as the key independent actors in world affairs.[13] Unfortunately, this set up the debate as an either/or proposition: either the state was the primary mover and shaker of world affairs or it was not. . . .

More recently, a resurgence of interest in NGOs has led to efforts to conceptualize them outside the unit-of-analysis problem. Most of this work is part of a broader set of concerns loosely associated with the so-called third debate, the argument over the proper paradigm for studying international relations. The origins of the third debate lie in the questioning of the statecentric model of the 1970s and 1980s, but it has since expanded to include epistemological, ontological, and axiological concerns.[14] . . .

Throughout the earlier transnationalist debate, scholars never questioned the essential quality of world political activity. Having lost part of the argument, after being forced to acknowledge the centrality of the state, they failed to ask what constitutes relevant political behavior, what power is, and which dimensions of collective life are most significant for bringing about changes in human practices. Students of international relations fell back on the traditional notion that genuine political activity is the interaction of nation-states, that power consists in the means available to states, and that the state system is *the* arena for affecting human behavior throughout the world. Thus, NGOs became important, but only because they influenced state behavior. They did not affect world affairs in their own right.[15] Current research can fall into this same trap if not understood to be part of a more fundamental type of examination.[16]

This article studies NGOs with a particular focus on the meaning of world politics. It eschews an understanding in which the multifarious activities of actors gain relevance only insofar as they affect states, and concentrates instead on identifying NGO activity that orders, directs, and manages widespread behavior throughout the world. . . .

DISSEMINATING AN ECOLOGICAL SENSIBILITY

Few images capture the environmental age as well as the sight of Greenpeace activists positioning themselves between harpoons and whales in an effort to stop the slaughter of endangered sea mammals. Since 1972, with the formal organization of Greenpeace into a transnational environmental activist group, Greenpeace has emblazoned a host of such images onto the minds of people around the world. Greenpeace activists have climbed aboard whaling ships, parachuted from the top of smokestacks, plugged up industrial discharge pipes, and floated a hot air balloon into a nuclear test site. These direct actions are media stunts, exciting images orchestrated to convey a critical perspective toward environmental issues. . . . The overall intent is to use international mass communications to expose antiecological practices and thereby inspire audiences to change their views and behavior vis-à-vis the environment.[17]

Direct action is based on two strategies. The first is simply to bring what are often hidden instances of environmental abuse to the attention of a wide audience: harpooners kill whales on the high seas; researchers abuse Antarctica; significant species extinction takes place in the heart of the rain forest; and nuclear weapons are tested in the most deserted areas of the planet. Through television, radio, newspapers, and magazines transnational activist groups bring these hidden spots of the globe into people's everyday lives, thus enabling vast numbers of people to "bear witness" to environmental abuse.[18] Second, TEAGs engage in dangerous and dramatic actions that underline how serious they consider certain environmental threats to be. . . .

Raising awareness through media stunts is not primarily about changing governmental policies, although this may of course happen as state officials bear witness or are pressured by constituents to codify into law shifts in public opinion or widespread sentiment. But this is only one dimension of TEAG direct action efforts. The new age envisioned by Hunter is more than passing environmental legislation or adopting new environmental policies. Additionally, it involves convincing all actors—from governments to corporations, private organizations, and ordinary citizens—to make decisions and act in deference to environmental awareness. Smitten with such ideas, governments will, activists hope, take measures to protect the environment. When the ideas have more resonance outside government, they will shift the standards of good conduct and persuade people to act differently even though governments are not requiring them to do so. In short, TEAGs work to disseminate an ecological sensibility to shift the governing ideas that animate societies, whether institutionalized within government or not, and count on this to reverberate throughout various institutions and collectivities.

The challenge for students of international relations is to apprehend the effects of these efforts and their political significance . . . When analyzing the peace movement, for instance, a fluid approach recognizes that activists aim not only to convince governments to cease making war but also to create more peaceful societies. This entails propagating expressions of nonviolence, processes of conflict resolution, and, according to some, practices that are more cooperative than competitive. A fluid approach looks throughout society and interprets shifts in such expressions as a measure of the success of the peace movement.[19] Similarly, a fluid approach acknowledges that feminist groups aim at more than simply enacting legislation to protect women against gender discrimination. Additionally, they work to change patriarchal practices and degrading representations of women throughout society. . . .

Applied to the international arena, a fluid approach enables one to appreciate, however imperfectly, changes initiated by transnational activists that occur independently of state policies. With regard to TEAGs, it allows one to observe how an environmental sensibility infiltrates deliberations at the individual, organizational, corporate, governmental, and interstate levels to shape world collective life.

Consider the following. In 1970 one in ten Canadians said the environment was worthy of being on the national agenda; twenty years later one in three felt not only that it should be on the agenda but that it was the most pressing issue facing Canada.[20] In 1981, 45 percent of those polled in a U.S. survey said that protecting the environment was so important that "requirements and standards cannot be too high and continuing environmental improvements must be made regardless of cost"; in 1990, 74 percent supported the statement.[21] This general trend is supported around the world. . . .

These figures suggest a significant shift in awareness and concern about the environment over the past two decades. . . . Two decades ago corporations produced products with little regard for their environmental impact. Today it is incumbent upon corporations to reduce negative environmental impact at the production, packaging, and distribution phases of industry.[22] When multilateral development banks and other aid institutions were established after the Second World War, environmental impact assessments were unheard of; today they are commonplace.[23] Finally, twenty years ago recycling as a concept barely existed. Today recycling is mandatory in many municipalities around the world, and in some areas voluntary recycling is a profit-making industry. . . .

A final, if controversial, example of the dissemination of an ecological sensibility is the now greatly reduced practice of killing harp seal pups in northern Canada. Throughout the 1960s the annual Canadian seal hunt took place without attracting much public attention or concern. In the late 1960s and throughout the 1970s and 1980s the International Fund for Animals, Greenpeace, the Sea Shepherds Conservation Society, and a host of smaller preservation groups saw this—in hindsight inaccurately, according to many—as a threat to the continued existence of harp seals in Canada. They brought the practice to the attention of the world, using, among other means, direct action. As a result, people around the globe, but especially in Europe, changed their buying habits and stopped purchasing products made out of the pelts. . . .

When people change their buying habits, voluntarily recycle garbage, boycott certain products, and work to preserve species, it is not necessarily because governments are breathing down their necks. Rather, they are acting out of a belief that the environmental problems involved are severe, and they wish to contribute to alleviating them. They are being "stung," as it were, by an ecological sensibility. This sting is a type of governance. It represents a mechanism of authority that can shape widespread human behavior.

MULTINATIONAL CORPORATE POLITICS

In 1991 the multinational McDonald's Corporation decided to stop producing its traditional clamshell hamburger box and switch to paper packaging in an attempt to cut back on the use of disposable foam and plastic. In 1990 Uniroyal Chemical Company, the sole manufacturer of the apple-ripening agent Alar, ceased to produce and market the chemical both in the United States and abroad. Alar, the trade name for daminozide, was used on most kinds of red apples and, according to some, found to cause cancer in laboratory animals. Finally, in 1990 Starkist and Chicken of the Sea, the two largest tuna companies, announced that they would cease purchasing tuna caught by setting nets on dolphins or by any use of drift nets; a year later Bumble Bee Tuna followed suit. Such action has contributed to protecting dolphin populations around the world.

In each of these instances environmental activist groups—both domestic and transnational—played an important role in convincing corporations to alter their practices. . . .

. . . [I]n the case of dolphin-free tuna, Earth Island Institute (EII) and other organizations launched an international campaign in 1985 to stop all drift-net and purse seine fishing by tuna fleets. For unknown reasons, tuna in the Eastern Tropical Pacific Ocean swim under schools of dolphins. . . . Its efforts, along with those of Greenpeace, Friends of the Earth, and others, were crucial to promoting dolphin-safe tuna fishing.[24] One result of these efforts is that dolphin kills associated with tuna fishing in 1993 numbered fewer than 5,000. This represents one-third the mortality rate of 1992, when 15,470 dolphins died in nets, and less than one-twentieth of the number in 1989, when over 100,000 dolphins died at the hands of tuna fleets.[25] These numbers represent the effects of activist efforts. Although governments did eventually adopt domestic dolphin conservation policies and negotiated partial international standards to reduce dolphin kills, the first such actions came into force only in late 1992 with the United Nations moratorium on drift nets. Moreover, the first significant actions against purse seine fishing, which more directly affects dolphins, came in June 1994 with the United States International Dolphin Conservation Act.[26]

In each instance, activist groups did not direct their efforts at governments. They did not target politicians; nor did they organize constituent pressuring. Rather, they focused on corporations themselves. Through protest, research, exposés, orchestrating public outcry, and organizing joint consultations, activists won corporate promises to bring their practices in line with environmental concerns. The levers of power in these instances were found in the economic realm of collective life rather than in the strictly governmental realm. Activists understand that the economic realm, while not the center of traditional notions of politics, nevertheless furnishes channels for effecting widespread changes in behavior; they recognize that the economic realm is a form of governance and can be manipulated to alter collective practices.

Perhaps the best example of how activist groups, especially transnational ones, enlist the economic dimensions of governance into their enterprises is the effort to establish environmental oversight of corporations. In September 1989 a coalition of environmental, investor, and church interests, known as the Coalition for Environmentally Responsible Economies (CERES), met in New York City to introduce a ten-point environmental code of conduct for corporations. One month later CERES, along with the Green Alliance, launched a similar effort in the United Kingdom. The aim was to establish criteria for auditing the environmental performance of large domestic and multinational industries. The code called on companies to, among other things, minimize the release of pollutants, conserve nonrenewable resources through efficient use and planning, utilize environmentally safe and sustainable energy sources, and consider demonstrated environmental commitment as a factor in appointing members to the board of directors. Fourteen environmental organizations, including TEAGs such as Friends of the

Earth and the International Alliance for Sustainable Agriculture, publicize the CERES Principles (formerly known as the Valdez Principles, inspired by the Exxon *Valdez* oil spill) and enlist corporations to pledge compliance. What is significant from an international perspective is that signatories include at least one Fortune 500 company and a number of multinational corporations. Sun Company, General Motors, Polaroid, and a host of other MNCs have pledged compliance or are at least seriously considering doing so. Because these companies operate in numerous countries, their actions have transnational effects.

The CERES Principles are valuable for a number of reasons. In the case of pension funds, the code is being used to build shareholder pressure on companies to improve their environmental performance. Investors can use it as a guide to determine which companies practice socially responsible investment. Environmentalists use the code as a measuring device to praise or criticize corporate behavior. Finally, the Principles are used to alert college graduates on the job market about corporate compliance with the code and thus attempt to make environmental issues a factor in one's choice of a career. Taken together, these measures force some degree of corporate accountability by establishing mechanisms of governance to shape corporate behavior. To be sure, they have not turned businesses into champions of environmentalism, nor are they as effectual as mechanisms available to governments. At work, however, is activist discovery and manipulation of economic means of power.[27] . . .

EMPOWERING LOCAL COMMUNITIES

For decades TEAGs have worked to conserve wildlife in the developing world. Typically, this has involved people in the First World working in the Third World to restore and guard the environment. First World TEAGs—ones headquartered in the North—believed that Third World people could not appreciate the value of wildlife or were simply too strapped by economic pressures to conserve nature. Consequently, environmental organizations developed, financed, and operated programs in the field with little local participation or input. . . .

In these kinds of efforts, TEAGs are not trying to galvanize public pressure aimed at changing governmental policy or directly lobbying state officials; indeed, their activity takes place far from the halls of congresses, parliaments, and executive offices. Rather, TEAGs work with ordinary people in diverse regions of the world to try to enhance local capability to carry out sustainable development projects. The guiding logic is that local people must be enlisted in protecting their own environments and that their efforts will then reverberate through wider circles of social interaction to affect broader aspects of world environmental affairs.[28]

Independent of the content of specific projects, the efforts of TEAGs almost always bring local people together.[29] They organize people into new forms of social interaction, and this makes for a more tightly woven web of associational life. To the degree that this is attentive to ecological issues, it partially fashions communities into ecologically sensitive social agents. This enables them more effectively to resist outside forces that press them to exploit their environments, and it helps them assume a more powerful role in determining affairs when inter-acting with outside institutions and processes. To paraphrase Michael Bratton, hands-on eco-development projects stimulate and release popular energies in sup-port of community goals.[30] This strengthens a community's ability to determine its own affairs and influence events outside its immediate domain.

The dynamics of environmental destruction often do not originate at the local or state level. Poor people who wreck their environments are generally dri-ven to do so by multiple external pressures. Embedded within regional, national, and ultimately global markets, living under political regimes riven by rivalries and controlled by leadership that is not popularly based, penetrated by MNCs, and often at the mercy of multilateral development banks, local people respond to the con-sumptive practices and development strategies of those living in distant cities or countries.[31] Once empowered, however, communities can respond to these pres-sures more successfully. For example, since 1985 tens of thousands of peasants, landless laborers, and tribal people have demonstrated against a series of dams in the Narmada Valley that critics believe will cause severe environmental and social damage. The Sardar Sarovar projects are intended to produce hydroelectric energy for the states of Gujarat, Madhya Pradesh, and Maharashtra and have been sup-ported by the governments of these states, the Indian government, and until recently the World Bank. Resistance started locally, but since 1985 it has spread with the formation by local and transnational groups of an activist network that operates both inside India and abroad to thwart the project. . . .

Local empowerment affects wider arenas of social life in a positive, less reac-tive fashion when communities reach out to actors in other regions, countries, and continents. Indeed, the solidification of connections between TEAGs and local communities itself elicits responses from regional, national, and international insti-tutions and actors. This connection is initially facilitated when TEAGs that have offices in the developed world transfer money and resources to Third World com-munities. In 1989, for example, northern NGOs distributed $6.4 billion to devel-oping countries, which is roughly 12 percent of all public and private development aid.[32] Much of this aid went to local NGOs and helped to empower local communities.[33]

This pattern is part of a broader shift in funding from First World govern-ments. As local NGOs become better able to chart the economic and environmen-tal destinies of local communities, First World donors look to them for expertise and capability. For instance, in 1975 donor governments channeled $100 million through local NGOs; in 1985 the figure had risen to $1.1 billion.[34] This represents a shift on the part of Official Development Assistance (ODA) countries. In 1975 they donated only 0.7 percent of their funding through Third World NGOs; in 1985 the figure rose to 3.6 percent.[35] This pattern is further accentuated when First World governments turn to transnational NGOs in the North for similar expertise. According to a 1989 OECD report, by the early 1980s virtually all First World countries adopted a system of cofinancing projects implemented by their national NGOs. "Official contributions to NGOs" activities over the decades have been on an upward trend, amounting to $2.2 billion in 1987 and representing 5 percent of total ODA," according to the report.[36] While much of this was funneled through voluntary relief organizations such as Catholic Relief Services, overall there has been an upgrading in the status of NGOs concerned with development and environmental issues.[37]

Increased aid to local NGOs has obvious effects on local capability. It enhances the ability of communities to take a more active and effectual role in their economic and environmental destinies. The effects are not limited, however, to a more robust civil society. Many of the activities and certainly the funding directly challenge or at least intersect with state policies; thus, governments are concerned about who controls any foreign resources that come into the country. . . . Empowering local communities diminishes state authority by reinforcing local loyalties at the expense of national identity. At a minimum, this threatens government attempts at nation building. Put most broadly, TEAGs pose a challenge to state sovereignty and more generally redefine the realm of the state itself. Thus, while TEAGs may see themselves working outside the domain of the state and focusing on civil society per se, their actions in fact have a broader impact and interfere with state politics.

Nevertheless, it would be misleading to think about TEAGs as traditional interest groups. . . .

The grassroots efforts of transnational environmental activists aim to engage people at the level at which they feel the most immediate effects—their own local environmental and economic conditions. At this level, TEAGs try to use activism itself, rooted in the actual experience of ordinary people, as a form of governance. It can alter the way people interact with each other and their environment, literally to change the way they live their lives. To the degree that such efforts have ramifications for wider arenas of social interaction—including states and other actors—they have world political significance.

WORLD CIVIC POLITICS

The predominant way to think about NGOs in world affairs is as transnational interest groups. They are politically relevant insofar as they affect state policies and interstate behavior. In this article I have argued that TEAGs, a particular type of NGO, have political relevance beyond this. They work to shape the way vast numbers of people throughout the world act toward the environment using modes of governance that are part of global civil society.

Greenpeace, Sea Shepherds Conservation Society, and EarthFirst!, for example, work to disseminate an ecological sensibility. It is a sensibility not restricted to governments nor exclusively within their domain of control. Rather, it circulates throughout all areas of collective life. To the degree this sensibility sways people, it acts as a form of governance. It defines the boundaries of good conduct and thus animates how a host of actors—from governments to voluntary associations and ordinary citizens—think about and act in reference to the environment.

A similar dynamic is at work when TEAGs pressure multinational corporations. These business enterprises interact with states, to be sure, and state governments can restrict their activities to a significant degree. They are not monopolized by

states, however, and thus their realm of operation is considerably beyond state control. Due to the reach of multinational corporations into environmental processes,
encouraging them to become "green" is another instance of using the governing
capacities outside formal government to shape widespread activities.

Finally, when TEAGs empower local communities, they are likewise not
focused primarily on states. Rather, by working to improve people's day-to-day
economic lives in ecologically sustainable ways, they bypass state apparatuses and
activate governance that operates at the community level. As numerous communities procure sustainable development practices, the efforts of TEAGs take effect.
Moreover, as changed practices at this level translate up through processes and
mechanisms that are regional, national, and global in scope, the efforts by TEAGs
influence the activities of larger collectivities, which in turn shape the character of
public life.

I suggested that the best way to think about these activities is through the category of "world civic politics." When TEAGs work through transnational networks
associated with cultural, social, and economic life, they are enlisting forms of governance that are civil as opposed to official or state constituted in character. Civil,
in this regard, refers to the quality of interaction that takes place above the individual and below the state yet across national boundaries. The concept of world
civic politics clarifies how the forms of governance in global civil society are distinct from the instrumentalities of state rule.

At the most foundational level, states govern through legal means that are supported by the threat or use of force. To be sure, all states enjoy a minimum of loyalty from their citizens and administrate through a variety of nonlegal and
noncoercive means. Ultimately, however, the authority to govern per se rests on
the claim to a monopoly over legitimate coercive power. By contrast, civic power
has no legally sanctioned status and cannot be enforced through the legitimate use
of violence. It rests on persuasion and more constitutive employment of power in
which people change their practices because they have come to understand the
world in a way that promotes certain actions over others or because they operate
in an environment that induces them to do so. Put differently, civic power is the
forging of voluntary and customary practices into mechanisms that govern public
affairs. When TEAGs disseminate an ecological sensibility, pressure corporations, or
empower local communities, they are exercising civic power across national
boundaries. They are turning formerly nonpolitical practices into instruments of
governance; they are, that is, politicizing global civil society.

The distinction between state and civic power rests on the more fundamental
differentiation between the state and civil society as spheres of collective life.
According to Hegel, the thinker most associated with contrasting the two, civil
society is a sphere or "moment" of political order in which individuals engage in
free association. Although it is an arena of particular needs, private interests, and
divisiveness, it is also one in which citizens can come together to realize joint
aims.[38] . . .

The same is true at the global level, and the notion of world civic politics is
not meant to obscure this. While global civil society is analytically a distinct sphere
of activity, it is shaped by, and in turn shapes, the state system. States' actions greatly

influence the content and significance of economic, social, and cultural practices throughout the world and vice versa. While not emphasized above, when TEAGs disseminate an ecological sensibility, pressure corporations, or work to empower local communities, their efforts are neither immune from nor wholly independent of state activity. In each instance, activist efforts intersect with the domain of the state even if this is not the initial intention.[39] What is absolutely essential to recognize, however, is that it is not the entanglements and overlaps with states and the state system that make efforts in global civil society "political." Transnational activism does not simply become politically relevant when it intersects with state behavior. Rather, its political character consists in the ability to use diverse mechanisms of governance to alter and shape widespread behavior. That these networks happen to imbricate the domain of states reveals more about the contours and texture of the playing field within which activists and others operate than about the character of politics itself.

At stake in this analysis, then, is the concept of world politics. Implicit is the understanding that politics in its most general sense concerns the interface of power and what Cicero called *res publico,* the public domain.[40] . . .

NOTES

1. See, for example, David Forsythe, *Human Rights and World Politics,* 2d ed. (Lincoln: University of Nebraska Press, 1989); Kathryn Sikkink, "Human Rights Issue-Networks in Latin America," *International Organization* 47 (Summer 1993); Robert Goldman, "International Humanitarian Law: Americas Watch's Experience in Monitoring Internal Armed Conflict," *The American University Journal of International Law and Policy* 9 (Fall 1993).

2. See, for example, Kevin Stairs and Peter Taylor, "Non-Governmental Organizations and the Legal Protection of the Oceans: A Case Study," and Barbara Bramble and Gareth Porter, "Non-Governmental Organizations and the Making of U.S. International Environmental Policy," both in Andrew Hurrell and Benedict Kingsbury, eds., *The International Politics of the Environment* (Oxford: Clarendon Press, 1992); Lee Kimble, "The Role of Non-Governmental Organizations in Antarctic Affairs," in Christopher Joyner and Sudhir Chopra, eds., *The Antarctica Legal Regime* (Dordrecht, Netherlands: Martinus Nijhoff, 1988); Gareth Porter and Janet Brown, *Global Environmental Politics* (Boulder, Colo.: Westview Press, 1991); P. J. Sands, "The Role of Non-Governmental Organizations in Enforcing International Environmental Law," in W. E. Butler, ed., *Control over Compliance with International Law* (Dordrecht, Netherlands: Martinus Nijhoff, 1991).

3. See, for example, Thomas Rochon, *Mobilizing for Peace: The Antinuclear Movements in Western Europe* (Princeton: Princeton University Press, 1988); David Cortright, *Peace Works: The Citizen's Role in Ending the Cold War* (Boulder, Colo.: Westview Press, 1993).

4. On the concept of "global civil society," see Richard Falk, *Explorations at the Edge of Time* (Philadelphia: Temple University Press, 1992); and Ronnie Lipschultz, "Restructuring World Politics: The Emergence of Global Civil Society," *Millennium* 21 (Winter 1992).

5. There is no single, static definition of civil society. The term has a long and continually evolving, if not contestable, conceptual history. For an appreciation of the historical

roots of the term and its usage in various contexts, see Jean Cohen and Andrew Arato, *Civil Society and Political Theory* (Cambridge: MIT Press, 1992); John Keane, "Despotism and Democracy: The Origins and Development of the Distinction between Civil Society and the State, 1750–1850," in Keane, ed., *Civil Society and the State: New European Perspectives* (London: Verso, 1988).

6. I follow a Hegelian understanding of civil society, which includes the economy within its domain. Later formulations, most notably those offered by Gramsci and Parsons, introduce a three-part model that differentiates civil society from both the state and the economy. See Talcott Parsons, *The System of Modern Societies* (Englewood Cliffs, N.J.: Prentice-Hall, 1971); Antonio Gramsci, *Prison Notebooks* (New York: International Publishers, 1971). For an extensive argument to exclude the economy from civil society, see Cohen and Arato (fn. 5).

7. In these cases, groups could not politicize existing civil societies but actually had to create them. See Adam Michnik, *Letters from Prison and Other Essays,* trans. Maya Latynski (Berkeley: University of California Press, 1985); Václav Haval, *Open Letters: Selected Writings, 1965–1990,* ed. Paul Wilson (New York: Alfred Knopf, 1991).

8. The danger of engaging the state in places like Poland provided the impetus to create horizontal associations. This was the central idea behind the Polish "self-limiting revolution," which recognized the power of the state with its Soviet support and hence the improbability of toppling it. See Michnik (fn. 7).

9. For an overview of the debate, see Ray Maghroori and Bennett Ramberg, eds., *Globalism versus Realism: International Relations" Third Debate* (Boulder, Colo.: Westview Press, 1982); and Kalevi J. Holsti, *The Dividing Discipline: Hegemony and Diversity in International Theory* (Boston: Allen and Unwin, 1985).

10. Robert Gilpin, "The Politics of Transnational Economic Relations," in Keohane and Nye, eds., *Transnational Relations and World Politics* (Cambridge: Harvard University Press, 1972).

11. Kenneth N. Waltz, *Theory of International Politics* (New York: Random House, 1979).

12. See, for example, Werner Feld and Robert Jordan, *International Organizations: A Comparative Approach* (New York: Praeger, 1983); and Harold Jacobson, *Networks of Interdependence: International Organizations and the Global Political System* (New York: Alfred Knopf, 1984).

13. The term "sovereignty at bay" comes from the title of the 1971 book by Raymond Vernon (New York: Basic Books). It is important to note that Vernon was not a proponent of the transnationalist challenge, even though the title of his book provided a catchphrase to encapsulate the host of arguments advanced by its proponents. See Raymond Vernon, "*Sovereignty at Bay:* Ten Years After," *International Organization* 35 (Summer 1981).

14. See K. J. Holsti, "Mirror, Mirror on the Wall, Which Are the Fairest Theories of All," *International Studies Quarterly* 37 (September 1987); and Yosef Lapid, "The Third Debate: On the Prospects of International Theory in a Post-Positivist Era," *International Studies Quarterly* 33 (September 1989). For one of the more provocative books to emerge from reflection on the third debate, see R. B. J. Walker, *Inside/Outside: International Relations as Political Theory* (Cambridge: Cambridge University Press, 1993).

15. The very term "nongovernmental organization" betrays a statecentric understanding of politics.

16. This is not to imply that studies of the influence of NGOs on states are unnecessary. There is still much to understand regarding the extent to which NGOs influence governments and the quality of their lobbying efforts. A focus on world civic politics, then, is not meant to supplant a statecentric notion of international politics so much as to augment it.

17. For discussions on the media-directed dimension of ecological political action, see Rik Scarce, *Eco-Warriors: Understanding the Radical Environmental Movement* (Chicago: Noble Press, 1990); David Day, *The Environmental Wars* (New York: Ballantine Books, 1989); Robert Hunter, *Warriors of the Rainbow: A Chronicle of the Greenpeace Movement* (New York: Holt, Rinehart and Winston, 1979); Walter Truett Anderson, *Reality Isn't What It Used to Be* (San Francisco: Harper and Row, 1990), chap. 7.

18. Bearing witness is a type of political action that originated with the Quakers. It requires that one who has observed a morally objectionable act (in this case an ecologically destructive one) must either take action to prevent further injustice or stand by and attest to its occurrence; one may not turn away in ignorance. For bearing witness as used by Greenpeace, see Hunter (fn. 17); Michael Brown and John May, *The Greenpeace Story* (Ontario: Prentice-Hall Canada, 1989); Greenpeace, "Fifteen Years at the Front Lines," *Greenpeace Examiner* 11 (October–December 1986).

19. Paul Joseph, *Peace Politics* (Philadelphia: Temple University Press, 1993), 147–51; Johan Galtung, "The Peace Movement: An Exercise in Micro-Macro Linkages," *International Social Science Journal* 40 (August 1989), 377–82.

20. Linda Starke, *Signs of Hope: Working toward Our Common Future* (New York: Oxford University Press, 1990), 2, 105.

21. Mathew Wald, "Guarding the Environment: A World of Challenges," *New York Times,* April 22, 1990, p. A1.

22. See Council on Economic Priorities, *Shopping for a Better World* (New York: Council on Economic Priorities, 1988); Cynthia Pollock Shea, "Doing Well by Doing Good," *World Watch* 2 (November–December 1989). According to a 1991 Gallup poll, 28 percent of the U.S. public claimed to have "boycotted a company's products because of its record on the environment," and, according to Cambridge Reports, in 1990, 50 percent of respondents said that they were "avoiding the purchase of products by a company that pollutes the environment"—an increase of 18 percent since 1987. Quoted in Riley Dunlap, "Public Opinion in the 1980s: Clear Consensus, Ambiguous Commitment," *Environment* 33 (October 1991), 36. See, more generally, Bruce Smart, *Beyond Compliance: A New Industry View of the Environment* (Washington, D.C.: World Resources Institute, 1992).

23. Jeremy Warford and Zeinab Partow, "Evolution of the World Bank's Environmental Policy," *Finance and Development,* no. 26 (December 1989).

24. Dave Phillips, "Breakthrough for Dolphins: How We Did It," *Earth Island Journal* 5 (Summer 1990); idem, "Taking Off the Gloves with Bumble Bee," *Earth Island Journal* 6 (Winter 1991); "Three Companies to Stop Selling Tuna Netted with Dolphins," *New York Times,* April 13, 1990, pp. A1, A14.

25. "Dolphin Dilemmas," *Environment* 35 (November 1993), 21.

26. "U.S. Law Bans Sale of Dolphin-UnSafe Tuna," *Earth Island Journal* 9 (Summer 1994), 7.

27. See CERES Coalition, *The 1990 Ceres Guide to the Valdez Principles* (Boston: CERES, 1990); Valerie Ann-Zondorak, "A New Face in Corporate Environmental Responsibility: The Valdez Principles," *Boston College Environmental Affairs Law Review* 18 (Spring 1991); Jack Doyle, "Valdez Principles: Corporate Code of Conduct," *Social Policy* 20 (Winter 1990); Joan Bavaria, "Dispatches from the Front Lines of Corporate Social Responsibility," *Business and Society Review,* no. 81 (Spring 1992).

28. See Vandana Shiva, "North-South Conflicts in Global Ecology," *Third World Network Features,* December 11, 1991; John Hough and Mingma Norbu Sherpa, "Bottom Up vs. Basic Needs: Integrating Conservation and Development in the Annapurna and Michiru Mountain Conservation Areas of Nepal and Malawi," *Ambio* 18, no. 8 (1989);

Robin Broad, John Cavanaugh, and Walden Bellow, "Development: The Market Is Not Enough," *Foreign Policy*, no. 81 (Winter 1990); Philip Hurst, *Rainforest Politics: Eclogical Destruction in South East Asia* (Atlantic Highlands, N.J.: Zed Books, 1990).

29. Outside contact may also splinter traditional associations causing economic and social dislocation. See, for example, James Mittelman, *Out from Underdevelopment: Prospects for the Third World* (New York: St. Martin's Press, 1988), 43–44.

30. Bratton, "The Politics of Government-NGO Relations in Africa," *World Development* 17, no. 4 (1989), 574.

31. See "Whose Common Future," *Ecologist* (special issue) 22, no. 4 (July–August 1992); Robert McC. Adams, "Foreword: The Relativity of Time and Transformation," in B. L. Turner et al., eds., *The Earth as Transformed by Human Action* (New York: Columbia University Press with Clark University, 1990). For how these pressures work in one particular area, see Susanna Hecht and Alexander Cockburn, *The Fate of the Forest: Developers, Destroyers and Defenders of the Amazon* (New York: Harper Perennial, 1990).

32. Robert Livernash, "The Growing Influence of NGOs in the Developing World," *Environment* 34 (June 1992), 15.

33. Such funding was evident in the preparatory meetings organized for the United Nations Conference on Environment and Development (UNCED). Organizations such as WWF spent thousands of dollars to bring Third World NGOs to Geneva, New York, and eventually to Brazil to attend the proceedings.

34. Michael Cernea, "Nongovernmental Organizations and Local Development," *Regional Development Dialogue* 10 (Summer 1989), 117. One should note that although the overall trend is to fund local NGOs, the amount of money going to local NGOs decreased in 1987. It increased the following year, however.

35. Cernea (fn. 34), 118, table 1. One should note that the reason for this shift in funding is a combination of the perceived failure of governments to promote development, the proved effectiveness of NGO responses to recent famines throughout Africa, and donor's preference for private sector development. See Anne Drabek, "Editor's Preface," *World Development* 15, supplement (Autumn 1987).

36. Organization for Economic Cooperation and Development (OECD), *Development Cooperation in the 1990s: Efforts and Policies of the Members of the Development Assistance Committee* (Paris: OECD, 1989), 82.

37. Julie Fisher, *The Road from Rio: Sustainable Development and the Nongovernmental Movement in the Third World* (Westport, Conn., Praeger, 1993).

38. As a moment of social organization, civil society sits at an intermediate stage of collective development that finds its apex at the state. The state, however, does not supersede civil society but rather contains and preserves it in order to transform it into a higher level of social expression. The state's job, as it were, is to enable universal interest—in contrast to private interest—to prevail. In Hegelian terminology, it allows for the realization of ethical life in contrast to the abstract morality available in civil society. See *Hegel's "Philosophy of Right,"* trans. T. M. Knox (London: Oxford University Press, 1967).

39. There are, of course, many instances when activists *do* target the state, in which the interface of global civil society and the state system is critical to strategies pursued by TEAGs. For an extended discussion of this type of action, see Paul Wapner, *Environmental Activism and World Civic Politics* (Albany, N.Y.: SUNY Press, 1996).

40. Cited in Sheldon Wolin, *Politics and Vision: Continuity and Innovation in Western Political Thought* (Boston: Little, Brown, 1960), 2.

Making the Global Economy Run: The Role of National States and Private Agents

SASKIA SASSEN

INTRODUCTION

The global economic system requires the implementation of a broad range of standards. This has happened most visibly through supranational institutions, notably the WTO (World Trade Organization) and the IMF (International Monetary Fund). Two less visible and less noted mechanisms that have played a crucial role are, on the one hand, a whole new world of private agents, such as financial firms and credit-rating agencies, and on the other, a variety of legislative and judiciary measures executed inside national states to ensure guarantees and protection of global capital and markets. This participation of national states in the implementation of international economic systems is not new. But it has intensified enormously over the last decade with globalisation.

One of the reasons this has not received more attention and study, is the presence of very powerful assumptions in the general understanding of economic globalisation. One of these is the zero-sum game: whatever the global economy gains, the national state loses, and vice-versa. The other is the assumption that if an event takes place in a national territory it is a national event, whether a business transaction or a judiciary decision. This has left the role of national states under-examined or reduced to the condition of mere victim of the forces of globalisation.

It is not simply the push by global firms and markets that is shaping the dynamics of interaction as is implied in much of the literature on the declining significance of the national state under globalisation. States are also shaping the dynamics of interaction. They are doing so in the form of resistance and of accommodation (Mittelman 1996). In doing so, however, national states themselves are transformed (Jessop 1990, Sassen 1996). While many sectors of the national state lose influence and resources with globalisation, some gain power because of it.

The interaction between the national state and the global economy is, then, more complex than is typically captured in images of the declining significance of the state at one end of the spectrum or the notion that nothing has really changed in the power of the state, at the other end. I conceptualise the line between the national and the global economies as a new frontier zone. It is a zone of politico-economic interactions that produce new institutional forms and alter some of the

This article continues the debate of *ISSJ* No. 160 "Globalisation." It is based on a longer research project on governance in the global economy. A first part of this project was published as *Losing Control? Sovereignty in an Age of Globalisation*. The author thanks the Schoff Memorial Fund for its support.

old ones. Nor is it just a matter of reducing regulations or shrinking the role of government generally. For instance, in many countries, the need for autonomous central banks in the current global economic system has required a thickening of regulations in order to de-link them from the influence of the executive branch of government.

NEGLECTED ELEMENTS IN EXPLANATIONS OF GLOBALISATION

We cannot understand globalisation by focusing merely on international trade and investment and other cross-border flows. This type of focus easily leads to the notion that globalisation comes simply from the outside. Neither is it adequate merely to focus on the often minimal share of foreign inputs in national economies: in most countries the share of foreign in total investment, the share of international in total trade, and the share of foreign in total stock market value, are all very small. However, to infer from this that economic globalisation is not really a significant issue, misses a crucial feature of its current phase: the fact that most global processes materialise in national territories and do so to a large extent through national institutional arrangements, from legislative acts to firms, and thereby are not necessarily counted as "foreign." Conversely, for that same reason we cannot simply assume that because a transaction takes place on national territory and in a national institutional setting it is *ipso facto* national. In my reading, the imbrications of global actors and national institutions are far more ambiguous. We need to decode what is national in the national.

One key implication is that economic globalisation has actually strengthened certain components of national states, notably those linked to international banking functions, such as ministries of finance, even as it has weakened many others. A second important implication is that insofar as certain components of national states are engaged in the implementation and governing of the global economy, there is a bridge for citizens to exercise some of their powers with respect to the global economy.

The internal transformation of the national state is shaped both by trends towards standardisation, as in the growing convergence of the roles of central banks, and by national particularities. The tension between these is well illustrated by some aspects of the current Asian financial crisis. We are seeing different responses by the Asian countries involved in IMF "rescue packages." At the same time, the emerging consensus in the community of states to further globalisation has created a set of specific obligations on participating states, no matter how reluctant some of them might be.

STATE AND NON-STATE CENTRED MECHANISMS FOR GLOBALISATION

Implementing today's global economic system in the context of national territorial sovereignty requires multiple policy negotiations. One of the roles of the state with respect to today's global economy, unlike earlier forms of the world economy, has been to negotiate the intersection of national law and foreign actors—whether firms, markets or supranational organisations. What makes the current phase distinctive is, on the one hand, the existence of an enormously elaborate body of law which secures the exclusive authority of national states over their territory to an extent not seen in the 19th century (Kratochwil 1986, Ruggie 1993), and on the other, the considerable institutionalising of the "rights" of non-national firms, the "legalising" of a growing array of cross-border transactions, and the growing, and increasingly institutionalised, participation by supranational organisations in national matters (Kennedy 1992, Rosen and McFadyen 1995).[1]

We generally use terms such as "deregulation," "financial and trade liberalisation," and "privatisation," to describe the outcome of this negotiation. The problem with such terms is that they only capture the withdrawal of the state from regulating its economy. They do not register all the ways in which the state participates in setting up new frameworks through which globalisation is furthered (Mittelman 1996, Shapiro 1993), nor do they capture the associated transformations inside the state. One way of putting it then, would be to say that certain components of the national state operate as necessary instrumentalities for the implementation of a global economic system.

There is much more going on in these extremely complex negotiations than the concept "deregulation" captures. While the negotiations may preserve the integrity of national territory as a geographic condition, they also transform the exclusive authority of the state over its territory, i.e. the national and international frameworks by which national territory has assumed an institutional form over the last 70 years (Sassen 1998). Even in the case of the privatisation of public sector firms, there is not just a change in ownership status, but also a shift of regulatory functions from the government to the private sector where they re-emerge under other forms, most notably, private corporate legal and accounting services.

The global economy needs to be implemented, reproduced, serviced, financed. There is a vast array of highly specialised functions that need to be executed and infrastructures that need to be secured. Global cities, with their complex networks of highly specialised service firms and labour markets, are strategic sites for these functions.[2] Each such city is located somewhere, so that the global economy to a large extent materialises on national territories.[3]

My argument here, developed more fully in Sassen (1996, 1998), is that because global processes materialise to a large extent in national territories, many national states have had to become involved in implementing the global economic system, although at times peripherally, and in this process have experienced transformations of various aspects of their institutional structure.

We can see the ambiguity of the distinction between "national" and "global" in the normative weight gained by the logic of the global capital market in setting criteria for key national economic policies, imposing itself on important aspects of national economic policy-making. Autonomy of the central bank, anti-inflation policies, parity in exchange rates, and the variety of other items usually included under so-called "IMF conditionality," have all become a set of norms. (This is discussed more fully in Sassen 1996, chapter 2.)

This new normativity can be seen at work in the design of the "solution" to the Mexican economic crisis of December 1994. This crisis was declared to be a consequence of the global financial markets having "lost confidence" in the government's leadership of its economy and the "solution" was aimed at restoring that confidence. The fact that this "solution" brought with it the bankruptcy of middle sectors of the economy and of households, who suddenly confronted interest rates that guaranteed their bankruptcy, was not factored in the equation. The key was to secure the confidence of "investors," that is to guarantee them a profitable return—and today "profitable" has come to mean very high returns.

Today we see the (attempted) imposition of that same set of norms on several countries in Asia, no matter how different the underlying conditions are from those of Mexico and each of the Asian countries involved.[4] The actual architecture of the crisis may well have more to do with the aggressive attempts to globalise these economies from outside than with their governments' leadership of these economies. Corruption, favouritism and weak banking systems were features of these economies long before the current financial crisis and throughout their period of growth, when they were much admired and put up as models for Latin America, the Caribbean and Africa.

In this context I read the financial crisis as a dynamic that has the effect of destabilising national monopoly control of these economies, and IMF conditionality as facilitating a massive transfer to foreign ownership. The outcome is further globalisation and further imposition of the new norms. However the actual materialisation of these conditions will go through specific institutional channels and assume distinct forms in each country, with various levels of resistance, submission and consent—whence my notion of this dynamic as having the features of a frontier zone.

THE ROLE OF PRIVATISATION

There are also more subtle ways in which globalisation operates through national institutions and in national terrain. This can be illustrated with a key feature of globalisation, privatisation. But first a few numbers to illustrate the scope of privatisation.

According to the World Bank, revenues generated by privatisation reached US$21 billion in 1995, compared with $3.5 billion in 1989. Of these, 40% originated from privatisations in Europe/Central Asia; 26% from East Asia/Pacific; 22% from Latin America/Caribbean; 3–4% from sub-Saharan Africa, South Asia, Middle East/North Africa each.[5] Between 1980–91 all industrialised and developing countries saw 6800 firms privatised. In contrast, from 1990–1994, the total for all countries reached 45,300, of which 15 "transition" countries alone saw 30,740 firms privatised. That is more than 6 times the number in the much longer earlier period; and they were sold in half the time. The Mexico peso crisis slowed down privatisations in Latin America, but they have now picked up again. In East Asia privatisations have tended to be few in numbers but huge in size. Indonesia and

Malaysia saw two of the biggest deals with the sale of PT Telekom and Petronas Gas (US$1.1 billion in revenues for the latter).[6]

This enormous transfer of firms from public to private sectors is not simply a change in ownership regime. It is also a privatising of co-ordination and governance functions, which move from the public to the private corporate sectors. In most countries the national capital is also the leading financial and business centre. But in some countries there was also a geographic shift, for example transfer may take place from Washington's government world to New York City's corporate world, from New Delhi to Bombay, from Brasilia to São Paulo. What were regulatory functions embedded in government bureaucracies are transferred to the corporate world, where they re-emerge as corporate management functions or specialised corporate services. Insofar as foreign investors and foreign firms are increasingly part of this privatisation of public sector firms—and indeed, in many cases, are the main investors—we could argue that this represents not only a privatising of economic governance functions but also an incipient de-nationalising of such functions (see Sassen 1996, chapter 1).

THE NEW INTERMEDIARIES

Economic globalisation has also been accompanied by the creation of new legal regimes and practices and the expansion and renovation of some older forms that have the effect of replacing public regulation and law with private mechanisms, sometimes even bypassing national legal systems. The importance of private oversight institutions, such as credit rating agencies, has increased with the deregulation and globalisation of the financial markets. These agencies are now key institutions in the creation of order and transparency in the global capital market and have considerable power over sovereign states through their authority in rating government debt. Also the rise of international commercial arbitration as the main mechanism for resolving cross-border business disputes entails a declining importance of national courts in these matters—a privatising of this kind of justice (Dezalay and Bryant 1995, Salacuse 1991). Further, the new international rules for financial reporting and accounting that are to be implemented in 1998 and 1999 also relocate some national functions to a privatised international system.

All of these begin to amount to a privatised system of governance ensuring order, respect for contracts, transparency, and accountability in the world of cross-border business transactions. To some extent this privatised world of governance has replaced various functions of national states in ensuring the protection of the rights of firms. It contributes to new dynamics in the zone of interaction between national institutions and global actors. The state continues to play a crucial, but no longer exclusive, role in the production of "legality" around new forms of economic activity.

This new intermediary world of strategic agents contributes to the management and co-ordination of the global economy. These agents are largely, though not exclusively, private. And they have absorbed some of the international functions that used to be carried out by states in the recent past, as was the case, for instance, with international trade under predominantly protectionist regimes in the decades following the Second World War. Their role is dramatically illustrated by the case of China. When the Chinese government in 1996 issued a 100-year bond to be sold, not in Shanghai, but mostly in New York, it did not deal with Washington, but with J. P. Morgan.

Private firms in international finance, accounting and law, the new private standards for international accounting and financial reporting, and supra-national organisations such as WTO, all play strategic non-government-centred governance functions. But they do so in good part inside the territory of national states.

Many of these rather abstract issues are well illustrated by the work being done to create new private international standards for accounting and financial reporting. They can also be illustrated by the aggressively innovative deals launched by the major financial service firms in the last few years to sell what had often been considered unsaleable, or at least not gradable debt, and to ensure the continuing expansion of the financial markets.

THE NEW ACCOUNTING STANDARDS

The International Accounting Standards Committee (IASC) is an independent private sector body that has been working intensely to create uniform standards to be used by business and government. It wants to bring these standards on line by 1999. In 1995 the International Organization of Securities Commission agreed to endorse the IASC's standards, and set March 1998 as the target date for completion of a body of international accounting standards. While this is a world of private actors and private standards, national states are crucial presences in the whole operation. It is worth noting that by early 1997, IASC standards had been accepted by all stock exchanges except Japan, Canada and the US—though these eventually also joined.[7]

This evolution was not without incidents that made it clear to what extent national governments and firms resisted or had difficulty accepting the concept of standards acceptable in other countries, let alone uniform international standards as pursued by the IASC. For instance, Japan resisted changing its national accounting system, one lacking the standards of "transparency" that have become the norm in international transactions. It was indeed Japan's reluctance to implement such standards of transparency in a wide range of business activities in conjunction with its reluctance to continue deregulating its financial sector which, it seems to the author, aborted Tokyo's rise as a major international financial centre. Tokyo remained too Japanese. Japan's Ministry of Finance is now gradually implementing a whole set of measures aimed at deregulation and transparency. The sharpest pressure for change is coming from Japan's increasing dependence on international markets and trade. Indeed, the only Japanese financial institution listed on the NY Stock Exchange, The Bank of Tokyo-Mitsubishi Bank, conformed to US accounting standards long before the Japanese government's decision to adopt international standards.

The case of Japan is interesting because it is one of the powerful countries in the world. It has resisted implementing the IASC standards but finally agreed under pressure of its own firms. The US stock exchange, another powerful actor, resisted even longer and insisted on having its own standards (or something approaching them) to be the international norm, but eventually accepted the IAS standards. These are instances that illustrate the degree of contestation in the new frontier zone where the encounter of global actors and national institutions is enacted.

WORKING TO "SOLVE" FINANCIAL CRISES

The role of the new intermediaries is also revealed in the strategic work done by leading financial services firms in the wake of the Mexico financial crisis. It provides us with some interesting insights about these firms' role in changing the conditions for financial operation, about the ways in which national states participated, and the formation of a new institutionalised intermediary space for governing the global economy. J. P. Morgan worked with Goldman Sachs and Chemical Bank to develop several innovative deals that brought back investors to Mexico's markets. Further, in July 1996, an enormous US$6 billion five-year deal that offered investors a Mexican floating rate note or syndicated loan—backed by oil receivables from the state oil monopoly PEMEX—was twice oversubscribed. It became somewhat of a model for asset-backed deals from Latin America, especially oil-rich Venezuela and Ecuador. Key to the high demand was that the structure had been designed to capture investment grade ratings from S&P and Moody's (it got BBB- and Baa3). This was the first Mexican deal with an investment grade. The intermediaries worked with the Mexican government, but on their terms—this was not a government-to-government deal. They secured acceptability in the global financial market, as evidenced by the high level of oversubscription and the high ratings. And it allowed the financial markets to grow on what had been a crisis.

After the Mexico crisis and before the first signs of the Asian one, we see a large number of very innovative deals with debts for sale. Typically these deals involved novel concepts of how to sell debt and what could be a saleable debt. Often the financial services firms structuring them also implemented minor changes in depository systems to bring them more in line with international standards. The aggressive innovating and selling on the world market of what had hitherto been thought to be too illiquid and risky for such a sale further contributed to strengthen this intermediary space for cross-border transactions operating partly outside the inter-state system.

NOTES

1. This institutionalising of the rights of non-national economic actors has a parallel in the implementation of rights for immigrants (see e.g. Heisler 1986, Jacobson 1996, Sassen 1998, chapter 2). Further, there is a parallel with the way that subjects other than the national state, notably non-governmental organisations (NGOs), are emerging as objects of international law and as subjects in international relations. This is explored for the case of immigrants and women in Sassen (1996a).

2. A global city is a node in a network, and in this sense different from the old capitals of empires or the more general concept of the world city (see Sassen 1998, chapters 1 and 10). The network of global cities today cuts across the old North-South divide (it includes São Paulo and Bombay, for instance) and strengthens territorial disparities, both inside developed and less developed countries. For instance, the corporate worlds of São Paulo and of New York gain strength, power and wealth; the worlds of the middle class and of the working class lose in both cities (see also Friedmann 1995 for an overview). I see the cross-border network of global cities as concentrating a significant share of institutional orders that are partially denationalised, and hence see this network as a partially denationalised—rather than internationalised—strategic geography (see Sassen 1998, chapters 1, 9 and 10; Sassen 1999).

3. For concrete applications of these propositions see Knox and Taylor (1995), Peraldi and Perrin (1996), Hitz *et al.* (1995); and *Social Justice* 1993. A key aspect of the spatialisation of global economic processes which I cannot develop here (but see Sassen 1998, chapter 9) is digital space (see also Aspen Institute 1998). One of the interesting features about finance is that although it is one of the most digitalised and dematerialised industries, when it hits the ground it does so in some of the largest and densest concentrations of infrastructure, structures and markets for resources.

4. The data used in this and the next section come from a data set that is part of the author's project "Governance and Accountability in the Global Economy" (Department of Sociology, University of Chicago).

5. Based on a report "The challenge of privatisation" prepared by John Nellis, senior manager of the Enterprise Reform and Privatisation section of the World Bank. In the 1980s almost all investment in privatisation was through foreign direct investment. By 1991 there was an enormous increase, up to 40%, in total volume of investment and in the share of this investment that was portfolio rather than direct investment. By 1994, the portfolio share had reached 60%. Portfolio investment is far more mobile than direct investment; hence it can move in and out of a country with considerable ease, contributing to the financial crisis in several developing countries. In terms of total capital flows to developing countries, portfolio investment was 93% for 1997.

6. According to *The Economist*, privatisation revenues from 1985 to 1995 in Britain were US$85 billion; France, almost US$34 billion; Italy US$17 billion; Netherlands about US$10 billion; Spain about US$9 billion; Germany under US$5 billion. Overall for the European Union, 1994 saw one of the highest revenue years, with US$34 billion in sales through privatisations.

7. One of the issues for the US has been that it considers its own standards more stringent than the new standards being proposed. It is also the case that Anglo-American standards have emerged as *de facto* international standards over the last few years, thereby greatly expanding the market for Anglo-American firms.

REFERENCES

Aspen Institute. 1998. *The Global Advance of Electronic Commerce. Reinventing Markets, Management and National Sovereignty,* A Report of The Sixth Annual Aspen Institute Roundtable on Information Technology (Aspen, Colorado, August 21–23, 1997), David Bollier, Rapporteur, Washington, DC. The Aspen Institute, Communications and Society Program.

Dezalay, Y. and Bryant, G. 1995. "Merchants of Law as Moral Entrepreneurs: Constructing International Justice from the Competition for Transnational Business Disputes," *Law and Society Review,* 29 (1): 27–64.

Friedman, J. 1995. "Where we stand: A decade of world city research." In: *World Cities in a World-System,* P. J. Knox and P.J. Taylor (eds.), pp. 21–47. Cambridge University Press: Cambridge.

Heisler, M. 1986. "Transnational Migration as a Small Window on the Diminished Autonomy of the Modern Democratic State," *Annals (American Academy of Political And Social Science),* 485 (May): 153–166.

Hitz, Keil, Lehrer, Ronneberger, Schmid, Wolff (eds). 1995, *Capitales Fatales.* Rotpunkt Verlag: Zurich.

Jacobson, D. 1996. *Rights Across Borders: Immigration and the Decline of Citizenship.* Johns Hopkins Press: Baltimore.

Jessop, R. 1990. *State Theory: Putting Capitalist States in Their Place.* Pennsylvania State University Press: University Park.

Kennedy, D. 1992. "Some Reflections on 'The Role of Sovereignty in the New International Order.' " In *State Sovereignty: The Challenge of a Changing World: New Approaches and Thinking on International Law,* 237 (Proceedings of the 21st Annual Conference of the Canadian Council on International Law, Ottawa, October 1992).

Knox, P. J. and Taylor, P. J. (eds). 1995. *World Cities in a World-System.* Cambridge University Press: Cambridge.

Kratochwil, F. 1986. "Of Systems, Boundaries and Territoriality," *World Politics,* 34 (October): 27–52.

Mittelman, J. (ed.) 1996. *Globalization: Critical Reflections. International Political Economy Yearbook,* IX. Lynne Rienner Publishers: Boulder, CO.

Peraldi, M. and Perrin E. (eds). 1996. *Réseaux productifs et territoires urbains.* Presses Universitaires du Mirail: Toulouse.

Rosen, F. and McFadyen D. (eds). 1995. *Free Trade and Economic Restructuring in Latin America* (A NACLA Reader), Monthly Review Press: New York.

Ruggie, J. G. 1993. "Territoriality and beyond: problematizing modernity in international relations," *International Organization* 47, 1 (Winter): 139–174.

Salacuse, J. 1991. *Making Global Deals: Negotiating in the International Marketplace.* Houghton Mifflin: Boston.

Sassen, S. 1996. *Losing Control? Sovereignty in an Age of Globalization.* The 1995 Columbia University Leonard Hastings Schoff Memorial Lectures. Columbia University Press: New York.

Sassen, S. 1996a. "Toward a Feminist Analytics of the Global Economy," *Indiana Journal of Global Legal Studies,* IV (Fall): 7–41.

Sassen, S. 1998. *Globalization and its Discontents. Selected Essays 1984 to 1998.* New Press: New York.

Sassen, S. 1999. "Global Financial Centers," *Foreign Affairs* Vol. 78 (1) (January/February).

Shapiro, M. 1993. "The Globalization of Law," *Indiana Journal of Global Legal Studies,* 1 (Fall): 37–64.

Social Justice. 1993. *Global Crisis, Local Struggles.* Special Issue, *Social Justice,* XX: 3–4.

Taylor, P. J. 1995. "World cities and territorial states: the rise and fall of their mutuality." In P. J. Knox and P. J. Taylor (eds), *World Cities in a World-System,* pp. 48–62. Cambridge University Press: Cambridge.

Walker, R. B. J. 1993. *Inside/Outside: International Relations as Political Theory.* Cambridge University Press: Cambridge.

Contested Globalization: The Changing Context and Normative Challenges

RICHARD HIGGOTT

INTRODUCTION

Even leading globalizers—that is, proponents of the continued liberalization of the global economic order occupying positions of influence in either the public or private domain—now concede that in its failure to deliver a more just global economic order, globalization may hold within it the seeds of its own demise. As James Wolfenson, President of the World Bank, noted in an address to the Board of Governors of the Bank in October 1998, " . . . [i]f we do not have greater equity and social justice, there will be no political stability and without political stability no amount of money put together in financial packages will give us financial stability." . . .

Conventional accounts of justice have failed to address the changing nature of the social bond. Rather they have supposed the presence of a stable political society, community or state as the site where justice can be instituted or realized. Indeed, it is often assumed that a stable political order is a condition of justice and justice requires a clear site of authority and a clearly demarcated society. In short, conventional accounts of justice have tended to assume a Westphalian cartography of clear lines and stable identities. . . . In doing so conventional theories of justice—essentially liberal individualist theory (and indeed liberal democratic theory more generally)—have to date limited our ability to think about political action beyond the territorial state. . . .

. . . In this context, therefore, the general aim of this article is to ask a series of questions about the nature of contemporary global governance that assumes a need for greater distributive justice at the global level for the world's poor, but without elaborating the details of what that greater justice (other than advances in poverty alleviation) might look like. The article will examine the current policy debate on global governance issues to see what change, if any, is in train and what impact any such change is likely to have on advancement in the direction of greater global justice. In this regard the article offers a narrative account of some recent changes in the agenda of global governance. In addition, the article tries to capture the flavour of change in intellectual thinking about these issues. Specifically, it argues that we are seeing a "mood swing" in both the theory and the practice of international political economy, indeed international relations in general, at the dawn of a new century.

The outcome of this mood swing is a greater concentration in the international policy community on the "governance" or "management" of globalization than was apparent in the more fundamentalist free-market days of the last two decades of the twentieth century. But it is the specific argument of the article that there is a difference between governance and politics. The principal limitation of the global governance agenda at the beginning of the twenty-first century is shown to be the underdeveloped nature, if indeed not suppressed nature, of its understanding of the salience of politics. Politics . . . needs to be understood as not only the pursuit of effective and efficient government, but also as a normative, indeed explicitly ethical, approach to the advancement of a more just agenda of global economic management. . . .

There are a range of ways to explain this changing climate of opinion in the domain of both practitioner and analyst. They are discussed in the first section. But the central aim of the article is to ask where this mood swing is taking us. . . .

In specific terms the interests of the theorist and practitioner of the market must meet seriously the interests of the normative theorist of international politics in a manner that has not occurred since the heyday of Keynesianism. If we take the signals of growing resistance to globalization of the late 1990s to be salient, markets must start to deliver what citizens want or continue on a fraught road to increasing delegitimation and contest. In the past, interest in the question of legitimation has been largely the domain of the normative political theorist of the bounded sovereign state. This bifurcation cannot be sustained under conditions of globalization. With no utopian teleology implied, it is perhaps time to start thinking about how we conceptualize a "global polity," or at least an international system with "polity-like" characteristics.[1]

If the liberalization of the international economy is to continue, or indeed not be rolled back, then metaphorically, Hayek will have to concede more ground to Polanyi and Keynes than practitioners, indeed scholars too, would have imagined just a few years before the end of the twentieth century. That this must happen is less to do with any substantial ideological rejection of the market rather than a re-recognition by some, and an initial learning by many, that markets are social constructs that need to be governed. . . . Global governance must find a way to take account of the need to legitimize and democratize those policy processes that occur beyond the boundaries of the state.

The article unfolds in three stages. In Part 1 the characteristics of the "mood swing"—from the Washington Consensus to the Post Washington Consensus—are outlined. This change in mood is predicated on a narrow definition of globalization as the process of *economic liberalization* and the emergence of an agenda for global governance as a response to this process. . . . Throughout the twentieth century, notwithstanding failed attempts to build institutions like the League of Nations, the growth of multilateral and regional institutions reflects what one scholar has called an evolving "constitutionalization" of world order.[2]

But enveloped in the language of a Post Washington Consensus, the new global governance agenda is clearly a response to the backlash that followed the financial crises that has hit the emerging markets of Asia, Latin America and Russia since 1997 and other subsequent forms of resistance to globalization. The Consensus–post-Consensus metaphor attempts to capture the flavour of these changes. . . . In Part 2 of the article the limits of the Post Washington Consensus to questions of governance are subjected to scrutiny. The essence of the critique is that the Post Washington Consensus represents an exercise in "governance without politics." Prescriptively, this will not do. We need to bring politics back in to the management of the global economic order, thus Part 3 of the article is a plea for an invigorated normative scholarship of international political economy.

1. IN THE MOOD: THE END OF THE WASHINGTON CONSENSUS AND THE EMERGENCE OF "CONTESTED GLOBALIZATION"

The resistance to globalization . . . can be identified in a number of different ways and in a large body of secondary committed quasi-academic and analytical literature that identifies a range of limitations in, and objections to, globalization as a neoliberal project.[3] Influential in the development of the mood of resistance to globalization has been a range of events in the world of international political economy and international politics as practiced in the closing stages of the twentieth century. Four events are illustrative of this mood swing.

Firstly, the failure of the OECD to establish the Multilateral Agreement on Investment. Rightly or wrongly (and the analysis is contested) this was thought to represent a signal victory for NGO mobilization of opposition to a major neoliberal international initiative *via* the use of the modern technology of the internet.[4] The second factor was the financial crises that hit Asia in the second half of 1997 and then spread to Latin America and Russia in early 1998. The Asian crises were seen initially in some parts of the international policy community, as former IMF President Michel Camdessus described it, as "a window of opportunity" to consolidate the Anglo-American model of economic development at the expense of the Asian developmental state. However, the longer term reading is one that identifies these crises as significant sources of backlash against the unfettered nature of the globalization project and the spur to a rethink about the role of regulation, re-regulation and the capacity of the state in the political economy of globalization.[5]

The third event was what is now commonly known as "the battle of Seattle" that aborted attempts at the third Ministerial Meeting of the WTO to set in train the new multilateral (Millennium) round of trade negotiations. Again the significance that one attaches to this event is contested in a range of quarters. For some, such as Mary Kaldor, it was a victory for political globalization from below.[6] In more restrained fashion, the significance of Seattle was that it brought together that range of non-state actors who, in their many different ways over the previous decade, had commenced the discussion about what the nature of an opposition to the most rapacious aspects of globalization might look like. In contrast to the activities of NGOs throughout the 1990s,[7] the debate at Seattle was not just issue-specific (gender, environment, social exclusion, development) but also more generally it reflected on the wider question of the very nature of the kind of global polity that might/should/could emerge out of the mitigation or reform of globalization. . . .

The fourth factor in bringing a change in mood to wider attitudes towards globalization is less an event and more the development of a perception that global liberalization brings with it increased inequality. There is much empirical data (not always consistent it should be added) on this issue. The best sources do, however, identify a rapid post–World War II growth in global income gaps. The income gap ratio between the 20 per cent of the world's population in the richest countries and the 20 per cent in the poorest grew from 30:1 in 1960 to 60:1 in 1990 and 74:1 in 1995. The poorest 20 per cent of the world's population account for only 1 per cent of total global GDP and 40 per cent of the world's population live in absolute poverty.[8] Whether the relationship between increased inequality and globalization is causally related or merely a correlation is theoretically very important, and there is emerging evidence to suggest that there is indeed a causal relationship.[9] But the correlation alone is sufficient to make it a political issue of the utmost importance. It is the identification of the correlation that causes the dispossessed to believe that globalization is a source of their plight.

While the increase in the relative gap at the top and bottom of the scales is hard to dispute, other data can provide evidence of increased aggregate welfare generation overall from which more people in absolute terms have benefited from globalization. The strongest economic point that can be made is that across the twentieth century a "massive divergence in income levels and growth performance" has been conclusively demonstrated.[10] As important as these data are, they are invariably silent on the politics of these numbers.

The important factor in the politics of globalization is the degree to which it is perceived to exacerbate inequality and the degree to which the existing institutions are thought by those who claim to speak for the dispossessed, to underwrite the *status quo* rather than work for its eradication. . . .

The existing architecture is insufficiently flexible to respond to what we might call the "new politics of contested globalization." It has led to the end of that orthodoxy (the Washington Consensus) that dominated the 1980s and 1990s and the emergence of a Post Washington Consensus.[11] The principal element of this change is the development of an understanding, amongst leading policymakers of the international institutional policy community, of the importance of the need for a stronger "governance dimension" to the international economic order. "Governance" here, as the next section will demonstrate, is to be distinguished from "politics." At the present historical juncture, global economic managers are attempting to develop a global governance system, what others such as Stephen Gill might call a "constitution for global capitalism,"[12] but absent some of the more basic polity-like characteristics that accompany governance systems within the jurisdictions of sovereign states. I characterize this process as the emergence of a "Post Washington Consensus."[13]

The basic argument is not that these events reflect a fundamentally new aspect of the process of "global politicization." Rather, they should be seen as the minimum response from the international policy community to manage the increasing hostility towards the liberalization and deregulation processes that have been at the heart of globalization. But they may well consolidate a growing trend towards the emergence rudimentary "polity-like" qualities to the international system. The Post Washington Consensus is discussed in the next section. Its limitations are addressed in Part 3.

THE POST WASHINGTON CONSENSUS: GLOBAL GOVERNANCE WITHOUT POLITICS

The global market place of the 1980s and the first 6–7 years of the 1990s was an "ethics-free zone." This was the case whether one was observing practice (both public and private sector) in the international political economy or whether one was leading the scholar on the global economy. In the domain of practice, processes of trade liberalization, financial deregulation and asset privatization were increasing the tempo of the globalization of the world economy. Free enterprise and the market culture had triumphed. Proof of this was to be found, as the economists would say, "in the numbers." These numbers reflected massive increases in aggregate welfare overall and not only in the developed world, but also in the rapid processes of industrialization that were taking place in the newly industrializing economies, especially those to be found in East Asia. . . .

. . . Few of those engaged in either the theory or practice of the international political economy in this period seemed to be much interested in the relationship between the stuff of the (international) political theorist; that is, normative questions of justice and fairness. The goddess of growth was on the throne and for all who agreed to worship her such normative issues were simply not relevant. In the academic domain of the economist, liberal economic theory had triumphed; again as in the policy world, the proof of the pudding was in the numbers. The rest of the social sciences were merely the indulgence of rich universities in developed countries. The Cold War was over and the North–South Divide that had led to demands for a New International Economic Order in the 1970s (if the noise that was emanating from the marginalized South, as opposed to the booming South, was any guide) had become a distant memory.

But the end of one century and the beginning of a new one . . . has seen something of a transition in this pattern of practice and thinking. The ethical dimension has found its way into the theory of globalization.[14] In the policy world too, the Post Washington Consensus is not merely driven by the desire to contain the incipient revolt against globalization. There is also in some quarters a genuine recognition of the importance of tackling ethical questions of justice, fairness and inequality.[15] It is in this dual context, and following from the emergence of the new politics of contested globalization, that we can identify the key aspects of the new governance. At this stage there is a disjunction between the new politics and the new governance. The new governance clearly lags the new politics. There are at least three reasons for this.

Firstly, the flagging of the importance of "governance issues" by the international financial institutions emerged in part to help them dig themselves out of the intellectual hole into which their adherence to unfettered free market ideals throughout the 1980s and first half of the 1990s had forced them. The financial crises since 1997 have provided a way out of the "economism" that dominated policymaking throughout the 1980s and 1990s.[16]

Secondly, if governance is about the conditions for ordered rule and collective action it differs little from *government* in terms of output. The crucial differences become those of process, structure, style and actors. In the recent public policy literature, governance refers to " . . . the development of governing styles in which boundaries between and within public and private sectors have become blurred."[17] But this definition neither notes the way globalization has blurred the domestic-international divide as material fact, nor the longer term historical development of systems of emerging international norms and regimes (both public and private) that represent the elements of a framework of "governance without government" under globalization.[18]

Thirdly, given the impact of globalization, "governance" becomes an essential term for understanding not only transnational processes that require institutional responses but also for identifying those non traditional actors (third and voluntary sector non-state actors such as NGOs, GSMs and networks) that participate in the governance of a globalized economy beyond the traditional confines of government. Thus the concept of "global governance" becomes a mobilizing agent for broadening and deepening policy understanding beyond the traditional international activities of states.

It is in this evolving theoretical context that the initial Washington Consensus (WC) which governed international economic thinking throughout the 1980s and 1990s became a moving feast as the major financial institutions, at odds with each other over the appropriate policy responses to the 1997 financial crises, sought a new approach—paradigm even. The original well known buzzwords of the WC were liberalization, deregulation and privatization. To these the Post Washington Consensus (PWC) has added civil society, social capital, capacity building, governance, transparency, a new international economic architecture, institution building and safety nets.

These themes had, of course, been emerging in the World Bank for some time[19] where influential figures such as then chief economist Joseph Stiglitz, and President James Wolfensen, helped to move the Bank beyond the initial consensus.[20] From the time of the Asian crisis even the WTO has begun to take these issues more seriously.[21] The IMF too has responded, albeit somewhat more slowly. Add to the PWC the UNDP initiatives on "governance" and "global public goods"[22] and the UN's "Global Compact"[23] with the private sector to promote human rights and raise labour and environmental standards, and we had, as we entered the new millennium, a new rhetoric of globalism to accompany globalization as process.

Amongst these activities, potentially most interesting for this article is the attempt by the UN to develop the Global Compact. It may become of significance throughout the first decade of the twenty-first century. While it fits firmly within a neoliberal discourse for developing an interaction between the international institutions and the corporate world, it is an important recognition of the need to globalize some important common values. In this regard, it has strong constructivist overtones too. This should perhaps not be a surprise when one considers its intellectual driving force. That the "global compact" reads like an attempt to globalize embedded liberalism is perhaps to be expected. The intellectual architect of this agenda was John Ruggie in his capacity as Chief Adviser for Strategic Planning to UN Secretary General Kofi Annan (1997–2000). . . .

The PWC's understanding of governance is underwritten by: (1) a managerialist ideology of effectiveness and efficiency of governmental institutions and (2) an understanding of civil society based on the mobilization and management of social capital rather than one of representation and accountability. . . . The PWC does not reject the WC emphasis on open markets. Rather, the PWC is an attempt to institutionally embed, and even maybe, as the UNDP would have it, "human-ize," globalization and the earlier technocratic, prescriptive elements of the WC.[24]

Given that the PWC holds a sanitized view of the sociopolitical dimensions of the development process, why is it an important break with the past? Because it is at least a recognition that governance, if not necessarily politics, matters. This is not historically trivial. Such a recognition was noticeably absent from the econo-mistic analyses of the impact of globalization over the last two decades. Along with the works of a few economists (Stiglitz, Rodrik and Krugman) it demonstrates a growing sensitivity to some of the political complexities inherent in the reform processes. . . .

Theorists are still groping for a universally acceptable definition of "social and economic justice." But given the strong perception that globalization, in its unadulterated form, results in unequal treatment for some states and, more impor-tantly, exacerbates poverty for the weakest members of international society, then globalization is seen to deny justice. In the current debate, poverty alleviation seems to have a stronger claim than equality in prevailing definitions of justice.[25] Thus the important normative question is: what is the relevant community or society to which "social justice" pertains and in what domains should the question of justice be addressed?

This question has traditionally been understood in the contexts of the values that actors attach to their behaviour within market structures. But markets are not the only sites of action. The domain issue is at the core of "the global governance" question. And, as is now widely understood in the international relations literature, governments are no longer the only actors. NOGs, global social movements, net-works, epistemic communities and international organizations all play significant roles in the wider global governance agenda; albeit that, in both in theory and practice, the political process invariably trails the integrated and globalizing ten-dencies in the world economy. As a consequence, the prevailing anarchical order of the state system is inadequate to the task of managing most of the agenda of globalization. . . .

Since global governance is an imprecise term, one normative question for stu-dents of international relations over the next few years must be to determine how much authority we should invest in the concept, given the wide-ranging way in which it is used. Currently, understandings of global governance can range along a continuum from basic, informal processes, to enhanced transparency in interstate policy coordination, through to the somewhat grander, although still essentially liberal, visions of a rejuvenated system exhibited in the Commission on Global Governance's *Our Global Neighbourhood*.[26]

But if we accept the argument that the transnationalization of market forces is exacerbating inequality, then the avenue for mitigating this gap lies with a reformist agenda for the global rules and norms that underwrite the current inter-national institutional architecture. Currently driven by "northern" agendas, it is those states most disadvantaged by globalization that are "rule-takers."[27] As a result such rules lack legitimacy even where states actually possess the necessary governmental effectiveness to enforce them should they so wish. Either way, these processes have negative implications for a consensual evolution of global governmental norms.

A starting assumption for the development of a PWC-style global governance is that it, and the continuance of a state system, are not inimical. But to recognize that state power will not go away is not to cling to some Westphalian legend. Rather it is to recognize that states, and interstate relations, remain the principal sites of politics. As a result, the research agenda on global governance is complex. It may therefore help to identify two interconnected understandings of it that are in one way or another coming together in the era of the Post Washington Consensus.

(1) *Global governance as the enhancement of effectiveness and efficiency in the delivery of public goods.* This is a fashionable policy concept, especially in the international institutions which see their role as consolidating or institutionalizing the "gains" made by the processes of global economic integration. But it fails to recognize that the successful internationalization of governance can, at the same time, exacerbate the "democratic deficit." This approach forgets that states are not only problem-solvers, their policy elites are also strategic actors with interests of, and for, themselves. Thus much collective action problem-solving in international relations is couched in terms of effective governance. It is rarely posed as a question of justice, responsible or accountable government, or democracy. . . .

(2) *Global governance as a normative enterprise to enhance democracy.* Paradoxically, the language of democracy and justice takes on a more important rhetorical role in a global context at the same time as globalization attenuates the hold of democratic communities within the confines of the territorial state. Indeed, as the role of the nation state as a vehicle for democratic engagement becomes more problematic, the clamour for democratic engagement at the global level becomes stronger. But these are not stable processes. Understanding of, and attention to, the importance of normative questions of governance and state practice as exercises in accountability and democratic enhancement must catch up with our understanding of governance as exercises in effectiveness and efficiency. The debate is largely divided between theorists and practitioners.

The current theoretical debate over the prospects for transnational democracy mirrors many of the wider debates in contemporary political theory over the nature of democracy in the twenty-first century.[28] Unsurprisingly, the debate within the policy community is narrowly focused. There is still a reluctance in the economic policy community to recognize the manner in which markets are sociopolitical constructions whose functioning (and legitimacy) depends on their possessing wide and deep support within civil society. But one key approach of late has been an increasing effort by the international institutions to identify those agents who can advance the cause of greater accountability and transparency in the management of the international institutions while not undermining the overriding goal of effectiveness and efficiency. In this context the greater incorporation of selected non-state actors into the deliberative process of these organizations is a principal goal of contemporary policy reform. While the incorporation of civil society actors into the policy process is seen as a necessary condition for the legitimation of the liberalizing agenda, most international institutions still see non-state actors as both boon and bane.[29]

The "Post-politics" of the Post Washington Consensus

These two interpretations of global governance (it is hard to call them definitions) stand respectively in relationship to the Washington and Post Washington Consensuses. The initial Consensus was an attempt by an international managerial-*cum*-policy elite to create a set of global *economic* norms to be accepted by entrants to the global economy under the guidance of the existing international institutions. Can the Post Washington Consensus be seen as an attempt to induce support for a new set of *sociopolitical* norms to legitimate globalization by mitigating its worst excesses? If captured by the existing international institutions (claiming that they are the only available sites of global governance) then, reflecting the ideology of globalism in its neoliberal guise, definition (1): effectiveness and efficiency, may well become the dominant mode of understanding global governance. Critical analysts can be forgiven, therefore, for not seeing the growing interest in global governance. . . .

Democratic accountability, definition (2), is currently *at best* a secondary component. Globalization might have rapidly generated a set of technological and economic connections; but it has yet to generate an equivalent set of shared values and sense of community, even amongst those agents actively involved in discussions about greater global participation. Indeed, much of the policy prescriptive work on governance currently being undertaken in or around the international institutions treats governance as a neutral concept in which rational decision-making and efficiency in outcomes, not democratic participation, is privileged.

In this regard, the debate on global governance within the international institutions (UN, World Bank, IMF and WTO) remains firmly within a dominant liberal institutionalist tradition; ethically normative discussions about democracy and justice beyond the borders of the territorial state are still largely technocratic ones about how to enhance transparency and, in limited contexts, accountability. They fail, or in some instances still refuse, to address the assymmetries of power over decision-making that characterize the activities of these organizations. . . .

The liberal institutionalist view is also essentially the reformist view held for the international institutional leaders by senior global decision-makers from US Treasury Secretary Lawrence Summers to UN Secretary-General Kofi Annan. Annan called for better accountability to improve global governance after the abortive MTN Ministerial Meeting in Seattle in November 1999 and Summers called for greater transparency and accountability for the IMF at its Spring 2000 meeting.[30] . . .

The preferred term in international policy circles is "global public policy,"[31] not global governance. The aim is to make provision for the collective delivery of global public goods.[32] "Public policy" has none of the ideological and confrontational baggage present in the notion of "politics." Institutional analysis, with its concerns for understanding the mechanisms of collective choice in situations of strategic interaction, is similarly "de-politicized." This is not to deny that recent rationalist theorizing of cooperation has not been a major advance on earlier realist understandings.[33] But the problem with rationalist and strategic choice approaches is not what they do, but what they omit. They make little attempt to understand governance as issues of *politics* and *power*. This has implications for the operational capability and intellectual standing of the international institutions.

In essence, the governance agenda as constructed by the international institutions in the Post Washington Consensus era has largely stripped questions of power, domination, resistance and accountability from the debate. To the extent that the international institutions recognize that political resistance is a legitimate part of the governance equation, it is a problem to be solved. It is not seen as a *perpetual* part of the process. In this regard, for many key players, global governance is not about politics. There are no problems that cannot be "governed away." Governance, *pace* definition (1) as effectiveness and efficiency, is "post-political." Agendas are set and implementation becomes the name of the game. Notwithstanding the fragmented and dissaggregated nature of political community in a global era, there is no place outside of the rubric of the existing governance structures for non-state political action on global policy issues.

The PWC view of good governance implies the universalization of an understanding of governance based on efficiency and effectiveness, in which democracy is a secondary component. Indeed, much of the prescriptive work on governance currently being undertaken in or around the international institutions treats governance as a neutral concept in which rationality in decision-making and efficiency in outcomes is uppermost. Nowhere is this better illustrated than in the efforts of those around the World Bank and the UNDP to develop public-private partnerships and global public policy networks for the collective provision of public goods. . . .

Moreover, this agenda has only a limited notion of public good, largely consistent with a liberal individualist ideology. Any notion of serious redistribution of wealth in the direction of the world's poorest is not considered a public good. Indeed, such support for the world's poor as there is, understood as development aid, is seen by some to be on the brink of collapsing.[34] The global public goods literature, indeed the global governance agenda more generally, does not address this issue. . . .

Yet as is apparent from activities within the various international institutions—such as the World Bank's "Global Development Network Initiative" (GDNI)[35] and other efforts (and some notable failures to engage civil society in the global policy debates too)—that this blindness to the inevitability of "politics" cannot long prevail. Civil society in this sense is becoming to global governance what international markets are to economic globalization. But, for a range of reasons, closing the "participation gap"[36] by incorporating non-state agencies into this process is not without its own problems. . . .

The first is that, despite their visibility, NGOs and other non-state actors cannot approximate the legitimacy of the national state as the repository of sovereignty and policymaking authority, nor its monopoly over the allegiance of the society(ies) it is supposed to represent. Second and related, despite the appeal of expanding the parameters of participation to include these important actors, it is widely recognized that they are often less democratically accountable than the states and inter-state organizations they act to counter and invariably less democratic in their internal organization than their outward participatory activities would suggest.[37] Third, the implementation of resolutions taken in "global" negotiations, or often by international organizations, remains primarily the function of national states, or at the very least depends on their compliance and complementary activity at the national level for their implementation.

These observations point to significant anomalies in the system. The expansion of participation to non-state actors such as NGOs and GSMs does not solve the problem of the under-representation of developing country states, nor their agendas for greater fairness and redistribution, in the more formalized policy processes. "Global" governance issues are dominated by the powerful states and alliance constructions and interest representations which feature in the structures of international organizations and groupings such as the G7. Various calls for the expansion of the G7 into the G16, G20 or similar, recognize that in order to be effective, global economic leadership needs diversification, and that collaboration in the provision of public goods depends on an extended participation. . . .

As a consequence a case can be made that the PWC is likely to be as challenged in the long run as the WC. It cannot constitute a template for an emerging "global governance" agenda, nor even an emerging policy agenda. It suffers from the same failings as its predecessor. The PWC is no less universalizing, and attempts to be no less homogenizing, than the WC itself. Global policy debates, in this way, remain reliant on a set of "generalizable," but essentially Western liberal, principles and policy prescriptions. Even while they offer a more subtle understanding of market dynamics than in the early years of global neoliberalism, these prescriptions still demonstrate a penchant for universalizing notions of a "one-size-fits-all convergence" on issues of policy reform under conditions of globalization. Such prescriptions may well be resisted in the developing world as but a new form of Western hegemony.[38] . . .

Thus the international institutions may find themselves on some sort of waste-ground between market economics (in which the state is inactive) and a raging debate about the significance and appropriate functions of state institutions. For example, in the "good governance" and the social capital-state debates, the World Bank seeks, on the one hand, to plug the "developmental gaps" and close the "participation gaps" by engaging civil society. On the other hand, it seeks to dictate what states do and how they do it, as it attempts to both downplay the centrality of the state in global bargaining and offset societal opposition to the state's continued pursuit of neoliberal economic coherence. A similar disjuncture can be seen in attempts by the WTO to secure greater NGO input into the deliberations on the continued reform of the trading system while at the same time fearing the potentially disruptive effect that any such widening of the deliberative process might have on the traditional highly structured nature of trade negotiations.

These fears were realized at Seattle where not only American workers, but Asian and Latin American policy elites were not in accord with their counterparts in the developed world as to what are mutually agreed public goods. To give but one example, the widely held view amongst the economic policy and corporate elites of the developed world that the extension of the remit of the WTO is a public good is not equally shared in the developing world at the end of the twentieth century. Many developing countries do not have the technical ability to keep pace with the current WTO "Built-in Agenda" from the Uruguay Round, let alone the desire and political conviction to take on board a range of new agenda items (in the areas of investment, competition policy, labour standards, transparency) currently being pushed by the developed countries in general and the US in particular. . . .

Finally, civil society critics of globalization, with their focus on the inter-state bodies such as the IMF, WTO and the World Bank as the instruments of global governance, miss the influence emanating from networks and institutions of private authority and transnational interests. But recent literature demonstrates the increasing influence of networks and sources of private authority ranging over the semi-private regulation of global environmental and labour standards, the regulation of borrowing *via* bond rating agencies, through *ad hoc* regulatory processes for telecommunications and the internet and even the increasingly integrated nature of syndicated criminal activity.[39]

This mix and match of emerging and increasingly well organized egalitarian social movements, and similarly well organized structures of vested economic interest, prevent us painting a simple picture of how global governance is emerging. It is for this reason that we should think rather of the global system taking on complex, cross cutting, polity-like features not dissimilar to those that developed within states in the eighteenth and nineteenth century. . . .

Despite the seepage of power from states down to local communities and up to supranational organizations, the state remains the principal repository of sovereign authority. Moreover, it is within the most powerful of states and the international institutions they control that a robust methodologically individualist neoliberalism remains the driving ideology. It is here that the polity-like characteristics of the global system break down. The vast majority of the world's population (and the states within which they live) remain rule-takers. The rules that they are forced to take, underwritten by this neoliberal ideology, do not, indeed cannot, address the ethical issues surrounding the task of alleviating the lot of the poor and the dispossessed. Consequently, there is a need to think beyond the Post Washington Consensus.

3. BEYOND THE POST WASHINGTON CONSENSUS—SCHOLARLY, NORMATIVE, POLITICAL AND ETHICAL CHALLENGES

It has been argued that the shift from a Washington Consensus to a Post Washington Consensus represents a "mood swing" in world politics that has raised the salience of the "global governance" dimension of international relations. It is also argued that the principal limitation of an attempt to create a new consensus around the need for governance, seen as effective and efficient management of global problems by the provision of global public goods by global policy networks, is its lack of an understanding of politics and a wider normative commitment to the creation of a global ethic of poverty alleviation *via* a commitment to redistribution. . . .

[The] growing concern with inequality, however, is perceived to occur on at least two planes. Firstly, within states, between those sectors of the economy that are the beneficiaries of current innovation and liberalization (especially in services and information technology) on the one hand and the "losers" in those sectors of the economy that have become less relevant in this historical juncture (especially agriculture and manufacturing) on the other. On a second plane, an increased global inequality between states, and the capacity of states to withstand global economic pressures, is also demonstrable. The conclusion from these perceptions is that a world that sustains major magnitudes of inequality is likely to be unstable. But this is not simply the view of the dispossessed and the "losers" in the globalization race.

It is also a view that is increasingly to be found amongst established and respected mainstream scholars[40] and, most interestingly, within the mainstream of the economics profession where there is now, as was much less so the case until the late 1990s, acknowledgement of the importance of welfare safety nets of the kind developed under the Post-World War II embedded liberal compromise.[41] Most significantly, as indicated at the outset of this article, an increasing number of senior office holders of the major international financial institutions have recognized the destabilizing effects of unfettered liberalization and the growing perception that it exacerbates inequality, and as Paul Krugman intimated, it may be necessary to save liberalism from itself. . . . In order to do so, what is needed is a revitalized multidisciplinary "international political economy."

This new international political economy would go "beyond economics." It would combine the breadth of vision of the classical political economy of the mid-nineteenth century with the analytical advances of twentieth-century social science. Driven by a need to address the complex and often all-embracing nature of the globalizing urge, the methodology of the new international political economy would reject old dichotomies—between agency and structure, and states and markets—which fragmented classical political economy into separate disciplines in the wake of the marginalist revolution in economic thought.[42] Rather, the new international political economy would aspire to a hard-headed materialist (that is, real world) political economy that recognized the limits of methodologically individualist, choice-based economic theory.[43] Instead, it would explain how choice is affected by the social meanings of objects and actions. Indeed, if there is one thing that the emerging processes of globalization teach us, it is that monocausal explanations of economic phenomena lack sufficient explanatory power. Such a view now holds increasing sway at the dawn of a new century. Moreover, it holds sway not just among Third World economic nationalists and radical academic critiques of a global neoliberal agenda but also within sections of the mainstream economics community.

This reformist position also reflects a long overdue resistance to the often overstated virtues of parsimony. In this regard the current era should offer no easy location for specialist parsimonious theorizing.[44] The new international political economy would operate from an assumption that what the marginalist revolution separated, globalization is bringing together. We are in a period of complex contest between the desire for grand totalizing narratives and theories of globalization on the one hand, and the need to produce specific histories of various actors and sites of resistance (be they states, classes, regions, or other localist forms of organization) to the grander projects on the other. The new international political economy must eschew this dichotomy. It should seek to be multi-disciplinary and theoretical in intellectual spirit, and empirically grounded in history, at the same time as it aspires to a normatively progressive research programme.

At the core of these concerns must be the changing institutional patterns which characterize alternative models of capitalism and the mechanisms by which a global economy and a global culture are constructed. Its normative agenda should be underwritten by a strong policy impetus towards the issues of enhancing justice and fairness under conditions of globalization—especially in the developing world's relationship with the developed.[45] Above all the new international political economy would foreground power in its *structural* as well as its *relational* form and recognize the need to ask the important Lasswellian questions about power of the "who gets what, when and how" variety.[46]

The new international political economy has major implications for how we understand the current governance agenda emanating from the international policy community. Largely because it is driven by members of a deterritorialized transnational policy elite, the current policy agenda has no conception of the residual strength of identity politics, the importance of social bonds within communities, the manner in which globalization appears to be picking many traditional social bonds apart without creating new sources of solidarity and, by implicit extension, no ethical agenda for addressing these questions.[47] . . . The development of a Post Washington Consensus represents but one step on the learning curve for the international policy community, but it does not address the justice and poverty questions on the international agenda. The absence of a wide-scale acceptance of the "legitimacy" of any top-down agenda in the developing world remains, for quite appropriate reasons, a major challenge for the international policy community under conditions of globalization. These are issues of ethics and politics, not just governance.

CONCLUSION

The CERES Principles are valuable for a number of reasons. In the case of pension funds, the code is being used to build shareholder pressure on companies to improve their environmental performance. Investors can use it as a guide to determine which companies practice socially responsible investment. Environmentalists use the code as a measuring device to praise or criticize corporate behavior. Finally, the Principles are used to alert college graduates on the job market about corporate compliance with the code and thus attempt to make environmental issues a factor in one's choice of a career. Taken together, these measures force some degree of corporate accountability by establishing mechanisms of governance to shape corporate behavior. To be sure, they have not turned businesses into champions of environmentalism, nor are they as effectual as mechanisms available to governments. At work, however, is activist discovery and manipulation of economic means of power.[48]

NOTES

1. This theme is developed in Morten Ougaard, "Approaching the Global Polity," Working Paper 42/99, (University of Warwick: Centre for the Study of Globalization and Regionalization, October 1999) and in more detail in a collection of forthcoming essays in Morten Ougaard and Richard Higgott (eds.) *The Global Polity* (London: Routledge, 2001).

2. See Daniel Elazar, *Constitutionalizing Globalization* (Boston, MA: Rowman & Littlefield, 1998).

3. Good secondary discussions of debates about the emergence of globalization and the different ways of analysing this phenomenon are now numerous and need not be reviewed here. The literature is now too voluminous to review here. Perhaps the most comprehensive text on the subject is David Held et al., *Global Transformation* (Cambridge: Polity Press, 1998). But the best single authored text is without doubt Jan Aart Scholte, *Globalization: A Critical Introduction* (Basingstoke, UK: Macmillan, 2000). For a flavour of the *range* of literature on offer see the essays in Richard Higgott and Tony Payne (eds.). *The New Political Economy of Globalization,* 2 vols. (Aldershot, UK: Edward Elgar, 2000). For a flavour of the critiques, see Gerry Mander and Edward Goldsmith (eds.), *The Case Against the Global Economy: And For A Turn Toward the Local* (San Francisco: Sierra Club Books, 1997); Richard Falk, *Predatory Globalization* (Cambridge: Polity Press, 1999); and the essays in Don Kalb et al., *The Ends of Globalization* (Oxford: Rowman and Littlefield, 2000).

4. See Stephen J. Kobrin, "The MAI and the Clash of Globalizations," *Foreign Policy,* 112 (Fall, 1998); Elizabeth Smythe, "State Authority and Investment Security: Non State Actors and the Negotiation of a Multilateral Agreement on Investment at the OECD," in Richard Higgott, Geoffrey Underhil and Andreas Bieler (eds.), *Non State Actors and Authority in the Global System* (London, Routledge, 2000).

5. See Martin Rhodes and Richard Higgott, "Asian Crises and the Myth of Capitalist Convergence," *The Pacific Review,* 13:1 (2000), pp. 1–19.

6. See Mary Kaldor's "Civilising Globalization: The Implications of the Battle of Seattle," *Millennium: A Journal of International Studies,* 29:4 (2000), pp. 105–14.

7. For a discussion of the role of NGOs as sites of opposition to the globalization discourse, see Cecilia Lynch, "Social Movements and the Problem of Globalization," *Alternatives,* 23:2 (1998), pp. 149–73.

8. Data from United Nations, *Human Development Report* (New York, Oxford University Press, 1999). For a good discussion of the complexity of the relationship between inequality and globalization, see the essays in Andrew Hurrell and Ngaire Woods (eds.), *Inequality, Globalization and World Politics* (Oxford: Oxford University Press, 1999).

9. The literature is reviewed in Ethan Kapstein, "Winners and Losers in the Global Economy," *International Organization,* 54:2 (2000), pp. 359–84.

10. See the excellent discussion of the available data on these issues in Nicholas Crafts "Globalization and Growth in the Twentieth Century," IMF Working Paper 00/44, Washington DC.

11. This is not the place to develop a full exposition of the Washington Consensus save only to note that the term was originated by John Williamson to reflect shared opinion on the key parameters of global economic managament, and specifically policy

prescriptions for financial adjustment in developing countries, within the Washington international financial community that included not only the US administration, but also the major international financial institutions and "think-tanks" such as the IIE. To be fair to Williamson, he merely called it "the Washington Consensus." He cannot be held accountable for the expansion of its use and the pejorative connotations that have been attached to the epithet by other observers of these processes. See John Williamson, "What Washington Means by Policy Reform," in John Williamson (ed.), *Latin American Adjustment, How Much Has Changed?* (Washington: Institute for International Economics, 1990). For discussions see Paul Krugman, "Dutch Tulips and Emerging Markets," *Foreign Affairs,* 14:1 (1995), pp. 28–9; Robin Broad and John Cavanagh, "The Death of the Washington Consensus," *World Policy Journal,* 16:3 (1999), pp. 79–88 and Moises Naim "Washington Consensus or Washington Confusion, *Foreign Policy,* 118 (Spring 2000), p. 103.

12. Stephen Gill, "*The Constitution of Global Capitalism.*" Paper presented to the British International Studies Association, Manchester, 20–22 December, 1999.

13. For a detailed elaboration of this argument see Richard Higgott, "Economic Globalization and Global Governance: The Emergence of a Post Washington Consensus," in Volker Rittberger and Albrecht Schnabel (eds.), *The UN Global Governance System in the Twenty-First Century* (Tokyo: UNU Press, 2001).

14. Of all the *fin de siècle* literature, amongst the most influential is likely to be Nobel prize winner Amartya Sen's attempts to humanize economics in *Development as Freedom* (New York: Basic Books, 1999).

15. Of the policy literature under written by a recognition of the importance of the normative agenda, see Michael Edwards, *Future Positive: International Cooperation in the 21st Century* (London: Earthscan, 1999).

16. For an elaboration, see Higgott, "Taming Economics, Emboldening International Relations."

17. Gerry Stoker, "Governance as Theory: Five Propositions," *International Social Science Journal,* no. 155 (1999), p. 17.

18. See the pioneering essays in Ernst Otto Czempiel and James N. Rosenau, *Governance without Government: Order and Change in World Politics* (Cambridge: Cambridge University Press, 1992). See also Volker Rittberger (ed.), *Regime Theory and International Relations* (Oxford: Clarendon Press, 1993).

19. See Cynthia Hewit de Alcantara, "Uses and Abuses of the Concept of Governance," *International Social Science Journal,* 155 (1998), pp. 105–113.

20. See Joseph Stiglitz, Towards a New Paradigm for Development: Strategies, Policies and Processes," *The 1998 Prebisch Lecture,* Geneva, UNCTAD, 19 October, 1998. To be found at http://www.worldbank.org/html/etme/jssp101998.htm and "Towards a New Paradigm for Development"; see also his "More Instruments and Broader Goals: Moving Towards a Post-Washington Consensus," *The 1998 WIDER Lecture;* Helsinki, 7 January, 1999.

21. See Jan Aart Scholte, Robert O'Brien and Marc Williams, "The WTO and Civil Society," Working Paper no. 14 (Warwick University: ESRC Centre for the Study of Globalization and Regionalization, July 1998).

22. See UNDP, *Governance for Sustainability and Growth* (New York, July 1997) and Inge Kaul, Isabelle Grunberg and Marc A. Stern (eds.), *Global Public Goods: International Cooperation in the 21st Century* (New York: Oxford University Press for the UNDP, 1999).

23. *The Global Compact: Shared Values for the Global Market* (New York: UN, n.d.); *Business Leaders Advocate Stronger UN and Take Up Secretary General's Global Compact* (New York, UN Press Release, 5 July, 1999) and *The Global Compact: Shared Values for a Global Market* (New York: UN Department of Public Information, DPI/2075, October 1999);

Mark Zacher, *The United Nations and Global Commerce* (New York: UN Department of Public Information, 1999). See also John Ruggie and Georg Kell, "Global Markets and Social Legitimacy: The Case of the "Global Compact"," paper presented to an International Workshop entitled *Governing the Public Domain: Redrawing the Line Between the State and the Market* (York University, Ontario: Robarts Centre for Canadian Studies, November 1999).

24. *Globalization with a Human Face: The UN Human Development Report* (New York: Oxford University Press for the UNDP).

25. See the excellent paper by Ngaire Woods, "Order, Globalization and Inequality," in Hurrell and Woods (eds.), *Inequality, Globalization and World Politics.*

26. London: Oxford University Press, 1995.

27. Hurrell and Woods, *Inequality, Globalization and World Politics,* Introduction.

28. See the excellent review by Antony McGrew, "From Global Governance to Good Governance: Theories and Prospects of Democratising the Global Polity," in Ougaard and Higgott, *The Global Polity,* forthcoming.

29. See P. J. Simmons, "Learning to Live with NGOs," *Foreign Policy,* 111 (1998).

30. See Kofi Annan, *Renewing the UN* (New York: United Nations, 1999) and Lawrence Summers. *Statement to the International Monetary Fund Financial Committee,* Washington, 16 April 2000.

31. See Wolfgang H. Reinecke, *Global Public Policy: Governing without Government* (Washington, DC: Brookings, 1998).

32. See Kaul et al., *Global Public Goods.*

33. See Robert O. Keohane, *After Hegemony: Collaboration and Discord in the World Economy* (Princeton, NJ: Princeton University Press, 1984); Helen V. Milner, *Interests, Institutions and Information: Domestic Politics and International Relations* (Princeton, NJ: Princeton University Press, 1997).

34. See Jean Claude Therien and Carolyn Lloyd, "Development Assistance on the Brink," *Third World Quarterly,* 21:1 (2000), pp. 21–38.

35. On the GDN, see the essays in Diane Stone (ed.), *Banking on Knowledge: The World Bank's Global Development Network* (London: Routledge, 2000).

36. Kaul et al., "Introduction."

37. See Leon Gordenker and Thomas G. Weiss, "NGO Participation in the Global Policy Process," *Third World Quarterly,* 16:3 (1995), pp. 543–55.

38. For an elaboration on this point see Richard Higgott and Nicola Phillips, "After Triumphalism: The Limits of Liberalization in Asia and Latin America," *Review of International Studies,* 26:4 (2000).

39. See John Braithwaite and Peter Drahos, *Global Business Regulation* (Cambridge: Cambridge University Press, 2000); A Claire Cutler, Virginia Haufleur, and Tony Porter (eds.), *Private Authority and International Affairs* (Albany, NY: SUNY Press, 1999) and H. Richard Friman and Peter Andreas (eds.), *The Illicit Global Economy and State Power* (Boulder, CO: Rowman and Littlefield, 2000).

40. See for example, Fouad Ajami, "On the New Faith," *Foreign Policy,* 119 (Summer) 2000, pp. 30–34; and Ethan Kapstein, "Distributive Justice and International Trade," *Ethics and International Affairs,* 13 (1999), pp. 175–204.

41. On the embedded liberal compromise and the challenge presented to it by globalization, see John G. Ruggie, "International Regimes, Transactions and Change: Embedded Liberalism in the Post War Economic Order," *International Organization,* 36:2 (1982) and "At Home Abroad, Abroad at Home: International Liberalization and Domestic Stability in the New World Economy," *Millennium: Journal of International*

Studies, 24:3 (1995), pp. 507–26. Of recent significant supporting statements in favour of the mitigation of the market by the underwriting of this compromise, see Dani Rodrik, *Has Globalization Gone Too Far?* (Washington, DC Institute for International Economics), and Paul Krugman, *The Return of Depression Economics* (London: The Allen Lane Press, 1999); but see also Jagdish Bhagwati, "The Capital Myth: The Difference Between Trade in Widgets and Trade in Dollars," *Foreign Affairs,* 77:3 (June 1988); Joseph Stiglitz, Towards a New Paradigm for Development: Strategies, Policies and Processes," *The 1998 Prebisch Lecture,* Geneva, UNCTAD, 19 October, 1998. To be found at http://www.worldbank.org/ html/etme/jssp 101998.htm; and "More Instruments and Broader Goals: Moving Towards a Post Washington Consensus," *The 1998 WIDER Lecture:* Helsinki, 7 January, 1999.

42. See James Caporaso and David Levine, *Theories of Political Economy* (New York: Cambridge University Press, 1992).

43. For a discussion of these limits see Amartya Sen, "Rational Fools: A Critique of the Behavioral Foundations of Economic Theory," *Philosophy and Public Affairs,* 6:4 (1977), pp. 713–44, and Ben Fine, "The Triumph of Economics: Or, 'Rationality Can be Dangerous to Your Reasoning,' " in James G. Carrier and Daniel Miller (eds.), *Virtualism: A New Political Economy* (New York: Berg, 1998).

44. Albert Hirschmann, "Against Parsimony: Three Easy Ways of Complicating Some Categories of Economic Discourse," in Hirschmann (ed.), *Rival Views of Market Society and Other Recent Essays* (New York: Viking Books).

45. Anthony Payne, "The Political Economy of Area Studies?" *Millennium: A Journal of International Studies,* 1999.

46. See Susan Strange, *States and Markets* (London: Frances Pinter, 1998).

47. See Richard Devetak and Richard Higgott, "Justice Unbound? Globalization, States and the Transformation of the Social Bond," International Affairs, 75:3 (1999), pp. 483–98.

48. See CERES Coalition, *The 1990 Ceres Guide to the Valdez Principles* (Boston: ceres, 1990); Valerie Ann-Zondorak, "A New Face in Corporate Environmental Responsibility: The Valdez Principles," *Boston College Environmental Affairs Law Review* 18 (Spring 1991); Jack Doyle, "Valdez Principles: Corporate Code of Conduct," Social Policy 20 (Winter 1990); Joan Bavaria, "Dispatches from the Front Lines of Corporate Social Responsibility," *Business and Society Review,* no. 81 (Spring 1992).

CREDITS